Corsica

written and researched by

David Abram

with additional contributions by

Theo Taylor, Geoffrey Young and Nia Williams

**ROUGH
GUIDES**

www.roughguides.com

Introduction to

Corsica

'*Kalliste*' – 'the most beautiful' – was what the ancient Greeks called Corsica, and the compliment holds as true today as ever. In few corners of the Mediterranean will you find water as translucent, sand as soft and white, and weather so dependably warm and sunny; and nowhere else has seascapes as dramatic as the red porphyry Calanches of the west coast, and the striated white cliffs in the far south. Crowning it all, a mass of forested valleys herringbone from the island's granite spine, which rises to a mighty 2706m at Monte Cinto, snow-encrusted even at the height of summer.

That these extraordinary landscapes have survived the ferro-concrete revolution of the past few decades unscathed seems miraculous when you consider the fate of comparably beautiful parts of southern Europe. Nearly two million visitors descend on the island annually (two thirds of them in July and August), yet purpose-built resorts are few and far between, while high-rise blocks remain outnumbered by extravagant Baroque churches and old fortified houses built to protect families formerly embroiled in vendettas. Overlooked by Corsica's trademark seventeenth-century watch-towers, long stretches of the shore remain backed by unbroken maquis, while forests of holm oak, chestnut trees and magnificent Laricio pines carpet the interior valleys, dotted with pretty stone villages. "Provence without the Brits" is how rural Corsica is often described in holiday

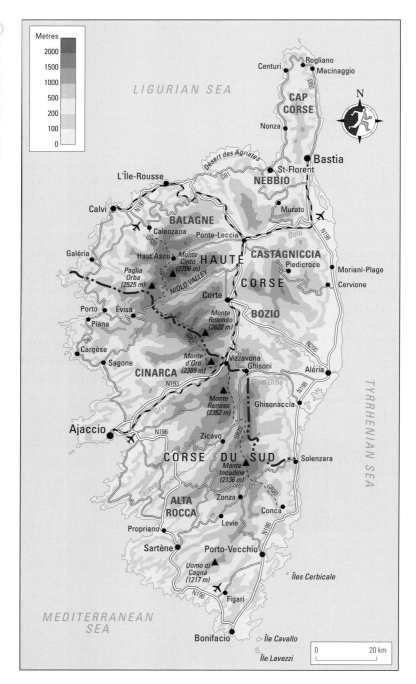

brochures, but the gloss fails to convey the island's distinctive grandeur: the wildness of its uplands, the vivid atmosphere of its remote settlements, and arresting emptiness of its valleys and woodlands, where wild boar are still more numerous than people.

Corsica's pristine state is largely the legacy of economic neglect, compounded by the impact of two world wars and mass out-migration in the twentieth century. Lured by the island's abundant natural resources and strategic position on the Mediterranean seaways, successive invaders – from the Greeks, Carthaginians and Romans, to the Aragonese, Italians, British and French – all came and conquered, but none were able to establish lasting prosperity. Nor were they ever able to subjugate fully the rebellious spirit of the islanders themselves, who at various times in their history have mounted fierce resistance to colonial occupation. In the nineteenth century, an armed uprising established a fully independent government led by one of the most charismatic political figures of the Enlightenment, Pascal Paoli. Before it was ruthlessly crushed by the French, the regime introduced the vote for women and a democratic constitution which would later be used a model for that of the United States.

Violent opposition to French rule flared up once again in the mid-1970s, since when nationalist paramilitary groups have been waging a bloody campaign against the state and its representatives, both on the island and on the Continent. Among ordinary islanders, support for the armed struggle – whose bombings and shootings have claimed hundreds of lives but seldom, if ever, affect tourists – has dwindled to virtually nil over the past decade. Yet the desire for greater autonomy remains as fervent as ever, in spite of the fact that the island imports virtually everything it needs and receives huge financial support from Paris and the EU.

Having had to struggle for centuries to preserve their language and customs, Corsicans have gained a reputation for being suspicious of outsiders. You will, for example, get a very frosty response indeed (or worse) if you attempt to broach the subject of nationalist violence, the Mafia, religious brotherhoods or belief in occult phenomena such as the Evil Eye. But express admiration for those facets of island life which the islanders are overtly proud of – such

Breathtakingly unspoilt scenery and distinctive Mediterranean way of life

Fact file

● Corsica's population hovers around 260,000, just over eight percent of which is made up of immigrant workers from North Africa. An estimated 800,000 islanders live in mainland France, mostly in Marseille, Paris and the Bouches du Rhône region.

● The island is 183km from north to south and 85km wide at its broadest point, with a surface area of 8682 square kilometres – roughly the same as that of Crete, or half of Wales. Its nearest neighbour, Sardinia, is three times larger.

● Corsica has its own regional assembly, answerable to the national parliament in Paris. A recent package of radical devolutionary measures, which would have granted it tax-raising and legislative powers, was dumped after the Gaullist victory in the elections of 2002.

● In 2001, a poll commissioned by *Paris Match* magazine showed that 65 percent of Corsicans opposed full independence, with only 17 percent in favour of a separate state (the majority of them youngsters). By contrast, 43 percent of people polled in mainland France said they supported independence for Corsica.

● Eighty percent of islanders regard Corsican as their mother tongue, but only a tiny number still use it as their first language; French is now the lingua franca.

as their cuisine, fine wines, enigmatic carved menhirs and polyphony singing – and you'll soon feel the warmth of traditional hospitality.

Save for the ubiquitous nationalist graffiti, sprayed-out road signs and odd fire-bombed villa or beach restaurant, Corsica's dark underbelly is barely discernible these days, as its population is drawn ever closer to the European mainstream. Lasting impressions tend instead to be dominated by the things which have beguiled travellers since Boswell first raved about the island in the mid-eighteenth century: the breathtakingly unspoilt scenery and distinctive Mediterranean way of life which, although bearing strong resemblances to the cultures of neighbouring Tuscany and Sardinia, the French Riviera and Sicily – somehow manages to remain quite different from any of them.

Two hundred years of French rule have had limited tangible effect on Corsica, an island where Baroque churches, Genoese fortresses, fervent Catholic rituals and an indigenous language saturated with Tuscan influences show a more profound affinity with neighbouring Italy. During the long era of Italian supremacy the northeast and southwest

of Corsica formed two provinces known as *Diqua dei monti* – "this side of the mountains" – and *Díla dei monti*, the uncontrollable "side beyond". Today the French *départements* of Haute-Corse and Corse du Sud roughly coincide with these territories, and remain quite different in feel.

Where to go

C apital of the north, **Bastia** was the principal Genoese stronghold and its fifteenth-century old town has survived almost intact. Of the island's two large towns, this is the more purely Corsican, and commerce rather than tourism is its main concern. Also relatively undisturbed, the northern **Cap Corse** harbours inviting sandy coves and coastal villages such as Erbalunga and Centuri-Port. Within a short distance of Bastia, the fertile region of the **Nebbio** has a scattering of churches built by Pisan stoneworkers, the prime example being the cathedral of Santa Maria Assunta at the appealingly chic little port of **St–Florent**.

vii

Le maquis

Napoléon Bonaparte, Corsica's most illustrious son, famously claimed he could smell his homeland while exiled on Elba – it was probably the maquis he was talking about. From the minute you set foot on the island, the pervasive fragrance of Corsica's aromatic scrub subtly assails the senses with its peppery blend of rosemary, lavender, cistus, sage, juniper, mastic and myrtle. In spring, the dark green belt, which thrives around the coastal zone below 800m, erupts into a blaze of pink and yellow flowers. Many of the plants are still gathered for their medicinal or cosmetic properties: the ladanum gum exuded by cistus, for example, is picked from the beards of goats to make myrrh.

Although the bane of walkers, the spiny maquis was a boon for Corsican *bandits d'honneurs*, who traditionally used it for cover when they were forced to flee after committing a vendetta murder. During World War II, the local Resistance also exploited its hidden trails to evade detection by the Italian Gestapo. The partisan movement in time became known as Le Maquis, while its activists were dubbed maquisards – monikers that would later be applied to the whole anti-German Resistance network on the continent.

To the west of here, **L'Île Rousse** and **Calvi**, the latter graced with an impressive citadel and a fabulous sandy beach, are the island's major resort towns – and their hilly hinterland, the **Haute-Balagne**, offers plenty of hilltop villages to explore, as well as access to the northern reaches of the vast **Parc Naturel Régional**, an astounding area of forested valleys, gorges and peaks. The spectacular **Scandola** nature reserve, a part of the northwest coast that lies within the boundaries of the park, can be visited by boat from the tiny resort of **Porto**, from where walkers strike into the magnificently wild **Spelunca Gorge** and **Forêt d'Aïtone**.

Sandy beaches and rocky coves punctuate the **west coast** all the way down to **Ajaccio**, Napoléon's birthplace and Bastia's traditional rival. Its pavement cafés and palm-lined boulevards are packed with tourists in summer, but comparatively few of them make it to nearby **Filitosa**, greatest of the many prehistoric sites scattered across this, the most heavily visited, half of the island. The resort of

Propriano lies close to Filitosa and to stern **Sartène**, seat of the wild feudal lords who once ruled this region and still the quintessential Corsican town.

More megalithic sites are to be found south of Sartène on the way to **Bonifacio**, a comb of ancient buildings perched atop furrowed white cliffs at the southern tip of the island. Equally popular **Porto-Vecchio**, the spot that has perhaps suffered most from the tourist boom, provides a springboard for excursions to the dazzling beaches of the south, or alternatively to the pine forest of **Ospédale**, or even to the windswept **Col de Bavella**, whose flattened pines and gigantic cliffs so inspired Edward Lear. The **eastern plain** has less going for it, but the Roman site at **Aléria** is worth a visit for its excellent museum, while to the north of Aléria lies the **Castagniccia**, a swath of chestnut trees and alluring villages.

Corte, standing at the heart of Corsica, is the best base for exploring the stupendous mountains and gorges of the interior, with the remote valleys of the **Niolo** and **Asco** a stone's throw away. Dominating these, **Monte Cinto** marks the northern edge of the island's spine of high peaks, closely tracked by the epic **GR20**, regarded as Europe's toughest and most spectacular hike. The route, and several other of the superb **long-distance** walks on offer in Corsica, are covered in a separate chapter. Accounts of shorter day walks, and of ascents of the island's major peaks – Monte Cinto, Monte Rotondo, Monte d'Oro and Monte Renoso – appear throughout the Guide.

Polyphonies corses

Nothing evokes quite so vividly the essence of Corsica's troubled soul as its **polyphonic singing**. Bearing influences as diverse as Roman-Christian liturgy, Genoese madrigals, Islamic prayer and even, many musicologists have argued, prehistoric chant, the expansive harmonies and passing dissonances that characterize the form evoke a sense of both the island's distant past and the passion with which Corsicans today identify with their homeland. When she first encountered polyphony in a remote mountain village in the late-1940s, Dorothy Carrington claimed "it was like hearing a voice from the depths of the earth; a song from the dawn of time; from a beginning that one never dares believe is accessible."

When to go

Whatever kind of holiday you intend to take, the **best times of year** to visit Corsica are **late spring** and **late summer** or **early autumn**, when you're guaranteed sunshine without the stifling heat or crowds of July and August. The wild flowers carpeting the island in April and May make these delightful months to come, and autumn is just as good for scenic colour – the Castagniccia in particular is a riot of russet tones at this time of year. Beachgoers will be ensured a tan as late as October, and even if you plan a visit in the depths of winter you're unlikely to encounter much rain, though snow on the high mountains can restrict driving through the passes in January, February and March, and visibility is often obscured by mists.

Crowds are likely to be a problem only in the major resorts such as Porto-Vecchio and L'Île Rousse, especially in the summer school holidays – *les grandes vacances* – when the whole of Italy and France take their annual holiday. In the more remote areas you should book **accommodation** in advance, for the simple reason that there is rarely more than a single hotel in any village.

Average daily temperatures (°C) and monthly rainfall (mm)

	Jan	Feb	Mar	Apr	May	June	July	Aug	Sept	Oct	Nov	Dec
Ajaccio												
daily max (C°)	13	14	16	18	21	25	27	28	26	22	17	14
monthly rainfall (mm)	76	65	53	48	50	21	10	16	50	88	97	98

25

things not to miss

It's not possible to see everything that Corsica has to offer in one trip – and we don't suggest you try. What follows is a selective and subjective taste of the island's highlights, from wonderful food and superb beaches to dramatic mountains and atmospheric towns. They're arranged in four colour-coded categories to help you find the very best things to see, do and experience. All entries have a page reference to take you straight into the Guide, where you can find out more.

02 Filitosa menhirs Page **232**
Among the western Mediterranean's greatest archeological treaures, unique for their carved faces.

01 San Michele de Murato Page **105** • The most distinctive among dozens of thousand-year-old Pisan chapels still standing on the island, built of green serpentine and pale grey granite.

04 **Girolata** Page **168** • The only fishing village on the island still inaccessible by road, set against an extraordinary backdrop of red cliffs and dense maquis.

03 **Sundowner at A Casarelle, Pigna** Page **144**
Savour the mesmerizing views over the Balagne coast with a glass of organic rosé and plate of local olives and homemade pâté.

05 **Spelunca Gorge** Page **175** • Porto to Évisa: Corsica's most dramatic road journey.

06 **Boat trips from Bonifacio** Page **276** • Catch a *navette* from the harbour visited by Odysseus for the most imposing views of Bonifacio's chalk cliffs and *haute ville*.

07 **Site Naturel de la Capandula** Page **88** • Ruined Genoese watchtowers preside over the pristine northern tip of Cap Corse, protected as a nature reserve.

08 **Apéritif at L'Hôtel Les Roches Rouges** Page **172** Sublime sea views and a seductive *fin-de-siècle* ambiénce make this the perfect spot for a chilled muscat.

09 **Col de Bavella** Page **395** One of the island's defining landscapes: a vertical world of stretched pines and soaring granite escarpments.

10 **Plage de Roccapina** Page **268** • Exquisite turquoise cove in the far south, overlooked by a lion-shaped rock.

11 **The micheline train** Page **34** • Connecting the three main towns via the high mountains and some gorgeous coast – worth taking for the rattling ride alone.

12 **Plage de Saleccia** Page **109** • Soft, white-shell sand, turquoise water and not a building or road in sight.

13 **St-Florent** Page **97** • An ideal base for explorations of the northeast, with classy eating, spectacular scenery and a pervasively salty atmosphere.

14 **Calvi** Page **117** • Corsica's hallmark resort, framed by snow peaks and a spectacular blue gulf.

15 **The GR20** Page **369** • France's ultimate Grande Randonnée: ten to fourteen days of punishing gradients and magnificent landscape.

16 **Corte** Page 338 • The former seat of Paoli's independent government and still a nationalist stronghold, with loads of period charm and a high mountain setting.

17 **Nonza** Page 95 • Backed by vertiginous cliffs, photogenic Nonza is the most striking *village perché* on the western cape.

18 **Plage de Palombaggia** Page 286 • Some of the softest, whitest sand and bluest water in the whole Mediterranean, backed by ranks of umbrella pines.

19 **Route de la Corniche** Page 81 • From Bastia's high corniche, views extend across the Tyrrhenian Sea to the Tuscan islands and distant Italian coast.

20 **Corsican charcuterie** Page 39 • Allowed to roam wild and feed on roots and fallen chestnuts, Corsica's free-range pigs are the secret behind Corsica's wonderfully strong charcuterie.

21 **Les Calanches de Piana** Page **171** • A vast mass of red porphyry, eroded into dogs' heads, witches and devils: best viewed at sunset.

22 **Aléria Museum** Page **302** A bumper horde of delicately painted ceramics, jewellery, weapons and sculpture, unearthed at the nearby ancient capital.

23 **Évisa** Page **176** • Lush chestnut forests, fine mountain cooking and crisp air: the island's most congenial hill resort.

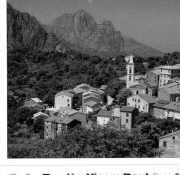

24 **Bastia Vieux Port** Page **69** • The twin campaniles of the Église St-Jean-Baptiste dominate the capital's crumbling Genoese harbour.

25 **La Plage d'Arone** Page **174** • Remote, blissfully unspoilt beach with great snorkelling and coast walks.

Contents

Using this Rough Guide

We've tried to make this Rough Guide a good read and easy to use. The book is divided into six main sections, and you should be able to find whatever you want in one of them.

Colour section

The front colour section offers a quick tour of Corsica. The **introduction** aims to give you a feel for the island, with suggestions on where to go. We also tell you what the weather is like and include a basic fact file. Next, our author rounds up his favourite aspects of the island in the **things not to miss** section – whether it's great scenery, amazing architecture or a special museum. Right after this comes a full **contents** list.

Basics

The Basics section covers all the **pre-departure** nitty-gritty to help you plan your trip. This is where to find out which airlines fly to your destination, what paperwork you'll need, what to do about money and insurance, about Internet access, food, security, public transport, car rental – in fact just about every piece of **general practical information** you might need.

Guide

This is the heart of the Rough Guide, divided into user-friendly chapters, each of which covers a specific region. Every chapter starts with a list of **highlights** and an **introduction** that helps you to decide where to go, depending on your time and budget. Likewise, introductions to the various towns and smaller regions within each chapter should help you plan your

itinerary. We start most town accounts with information on arrival and accommodation, followed by a tour of the sights, and finally reviews of places to eat and drink, and details of nightlife. Longer accounts also have a directory of practical listings. Each chapter concludes with **public transport** details for that region.

Contexts

Read Contexts to get a deeper understanding of what makes Corsica tick. We include an introduction to its history, plus a further-reading section that reviews dozens of **books** relating to the island.

Language

The **Language** section gives useful guidance for speaking Corsican and French, and pulls together all the vocabulary you might need on your trip, including a comprehensive food glossary. Here you'll also find a glossary of words and terms peculiar to Corsica.

Index + small print

Apart from a **full index**, which includes maps as well as places, this section covers publishing information, credits and acknowledgements, and also has our contact details in case you want to send in updates and corrections to the book – or suggestions as to how we might improve it.

Chapter list and map

- Colour section
- Contents
- Ⓑ Basics
- ❶ Bastia and northern Corsica
- ❷ The Balagne
- ❸ The northwest
- ❹ The Ajaccio region
- ❺ The south
- ❻ Eastern Corsica
- ❼ Central Corsica
- ❽ Long-distance walks
- Ⓒ Contexts
- Ⓛ Language
- Ⓘ Index

Contents

Colour section i–xvi

Colour map of Corsica iv
Where to go vii
When to go...x
Things not to miss....................................xi

Basics 9–56

Getting there 11
Red tape and visas 22
Information, websites and maps 23
Insurance 24
Health...26
Costs, money and banks........................27
Getting around..30
Accommodation 34
Eating and drinking 37
Communications 42
The media 44
Opening hours, public holidays and
   festivals 45
Outdoor pursuits 48
Crime and personal safety.....................51
Travellers with disabilities 52
Sex and gender issues 53
Travelling with children...........................54
Directory 55

Guide 57–404

**❶ Bastia and northern
   Corsica** 59–110
   Highlights 60
   A brief history 63
   Arrival and information 66
   Accommodation..................................66
   Place St-Nicolas 68
   Terra Vecchia 68
   Terra Nova 70
   Beaches 71
   Eating, drinking and nightlife 71
   Listings..74
   Moving on 75

Cap Corse 78
The eastern cape 81
The northern cape 87
The western cape 92
The Nebbio..96
St-Florent 97
Inland Nebbio....................................104
The Désert des Agriates.................107
Travel details 110

❷ The Balagne 111–156
   Highlights 112
   Calvi 117

Lumio 129
Algajola 131
L'Île Rousse 132
Inland Haute-Balagne 138
The Giunssani 148
Cirque de Bonifato 151
Galéria 151
La Vallée du Fango...........................154
Travel details 155

❸ **The northwest**.................157–190
Highlights 158
The Golfe de Porto...........................161
Porto 161
The northern gulf 166
The southern gulf 170
The Calanches 171
Piana 172
The Spelunca gorge........................175
The Golfe de Sagone 180
Cargèse 180
Sagone 184
Tiuccia 184
Vico and around...............................185
The Cinarca 188
Travel details 190

❹ **The Ajaccio region** 191–221
Highlights 192
A brief history....................................194
Arrival and information 195
Accommodation................................198
Place de Gaulle 199
Place Foch 200
Maison Bonaparte 202
The Citadelle 203
Eating, drinking and nightlife 204
Listings...207
Moving on 208
The Golfe d'Ajaccio 211
The Gorges du Prunelli 217
Travel details 220

❺ **The south**............................223–292
Highlights 224
The Golfe de Valinco 227
Porto-Pollo.......................................227
Filitosa 232

Olmeto 236
Propriano 237
Campomoro 240
The Alta Rocca.................................242
Fozzano 243
Ste-Lucie-de-Tallano 245
Levie 248
Carbini 249
Aullène and around 250
Quenza and around 252
Zonza 254
The route de Bavella 255
The Sartenais 257
Sartène...258
Bonifacio and around......................270
Porto-Vecchio and around 281
Travel details 291

❻ **Eastern Corsica** 293–319
Highlights 294
Solenzara 297
Ghisonaccia 297
Fiumorbo 298
Aléria 299
The Vallée du Tavignano 304
Castagniccia 307
The Casinca 317
Travel details 318

❼ **Central Corsica**................321–357
Highlights 322
The Vallée de l'Asco.........................325
The Niolo 331
Corte and around 338
The Venachese.................................347
Vizzavona and around 350
Ghisoni and around 352
Haut Taravo 355
Travel details 356

❽ **Long-distance walks** 359–404
Highlights 360
The paths: waymarks and maps 364
Accommodation, eating and
    drinking 365
Equipment 366
Health and safety 367
Costs and money.............................369

The GR20 369
The Tra Mare e Monti Nord 399
The Mare a Mare Nord 400

The Mare a Mare Centre 402
The Tra Mare e Monti Sud 403
The Mare a Mare Sud......................403

Contexts

The historical framework 407–419
The Corsican troubles:
  an overview 418–429

Corsican wildlife 432–438
Books 439–445

Language

The Corsican language 449
Corsican words and phrases.................449
French pronunciation 451

Learning materials 452
French words and phrases 450
A food glossary 456

Index + small print

Full index 465
Twenty years of Rough Guides 469
Rough Guide credits 470
Publishing information 470

Help us update 470
Acknowledgements 471
Photo credits 472

Map symbols

maps are listed in the full index using coloured text

═══	Major road	Lighthouse
═══	Minor road	Church (regional maps)
▦▦▦	Steps	Convent/Monastery
═══	Pedestrianized road	Airport
- - - -	Footpath	★ Bus stop
▬·▬·	Railway	P Parking
▪▪▪▪	Wall	Camping
— —	Ferry route	(i) Tourist office
‥‥‥	Waterway	⊠ Post office
─ ─ ─	Chapter division boundary	@ Internet access
	General point of interest	⊞ Hospital
▲	Peak	◉ Accommodation
	Pass	Building
	Escarpment	⊟ Church
↯	Viewpoint	Cemetery
◠	Cave	Park
▲	Refuge hut	Forest
	Waterfall	Marshland
■	Tower	Beach

Basics

Basics

Getting there 11

Red tape and visas 22

Information, websites and maps....................................23

Insurance...25

Health 26

Costs, money and banks 27

Getting around 30

Accommodation..34

Eating and drinking 37

Communications 42

The media 44

Opening hours, public holidays and festivals.................45

Outdoor pursuits 48

Crime and personal safety...51

Travellers with disabilities..52

Sex and gender issues 53

Travelling with children..54

Directory..55

Getting there

Flying is the fastest and most convenient – if not the most romantic – way to reach Corsica, whatever your point of departure. From the UK or mainland France, a direct flight to any of the island's four civil airports – Bastia (in the north), Ajaccio (in the west), Calvi (northwest) or Figari (far south) – takes between one and a half and two and a half hours, or just forty minutes for the short hop from Nice or Marseille on the French Riviera. With air fares lower than ever, travelling overland is worth considering only if you want to see some of France or Italy en route.

The cost of flights varies according to the **season**, peaking in the summer school holidays – the "Grandes Vacances" between mid-June and the end of August – and falling off in shoulder season (roughly Easter to mid-June and early September to the end of October). In the winter, when charter flights no longer operate, you'll have to rely on scheduled services from the Continent, the cost of which rises considerably on weekends and during national holidays, such as Christmas, Easter and New Year.

Air fares can be kept to a minimum by purchasing **charter tickets** from a package company, or combining a flight to one of the Riviera ports on a **low-cost airline** from the UK (such as Buzz, Go or EasyJet) with onward transport via a French domestic airline or ferry. Travelling to Corsica long-haul – from the US, Canada, Australia or New Zealand – you're unlikely to find an agent who will be able to book these kinds of tickets on your behalf, but there's nothing to stop you from buying your intercontinental ticket leg from a travel agent at home and the onward legs from the UK or France direct with the carrier.

Long-haul travellers should also bear in mind the potential savings of booking their intercontinental ticket through a **specialist flight agent** – either a consolidator, who buys up blocks of tickets from the airlines and sells them at a discount – or a discount agent, who in addition to dealing with discounted flights may also offer special student and youth fares and a range of other travel-related services such as insurance and car rental.

If Corsica is only one stop on a longer journey, another money-saving option might be a **Round-the-World** (RTW) ticket. None of

the island's airports feature on economy "off-the-shelf" RTWs, which route you through Paris, Nice or Marseille, but shop around and you should find a deal that will allow you to tack on the domestic flight to Corsica for a supplement.

Courier flights – in which you deliver a package in exchange for a heavily discounted ticket – are another way to keep your air fare as low as possible if you're flying long-haul. The disadvantage with these is that to get the best deals you have to book a maximum of three days before departure, but if you can be this flexible you stand to save a lot of money.

Booking flights online

By cutting out middlemen and other overheads, discount travel websites are frequently able to offer more competitive fares than those available on the high street. For long-haul travellers, the following list of sites is worth a browse. For travellers from the UK or Ireland, these addresses will be of less use than those of the budget airlines and package operators listed on pp.14 and 15.

Online booking agents and general travel sites

ⓦ **www.geocities.com/Thavery2000/** Has an extensive list of airline toll-free numbers and websites.

ⓦ **www.flyaow.com** Online air travel info and reservations site.

ⓦ **www.smilinjack.com/airlines.htm** Lists an up-to-date compilation of airline website addresses.

ⓦ **http://travel.yahoo.com** Incorporates a lot of Rough Guide material in its coverage of destination

countries and cities across the world, with information about places to eat, sleep, etc.
Ⓦ **www.cheaptickets.com** Discount flight specialists.

Ⓦ **www.lastminute.com** Bookings from the UK only. Offers good last-minute holiday package and flight-only deals.

Ⓦ **www.expedia.com** Discount airfares, all-airline search engine and daily deals.

Ⓦ **www.travelocity.com** Destination guides, hot Web fares and best deals for car rental and accommodation as well as fares. Provides access to the travel agent system SABRE, the most comprehensive central reservations system in the US.

Ⓦ **www.hotwire.com** Bookings from the US only. Last-minute savings of up to forty percent on regular published fares. Travellers must be at least 18 and there are no refunds, transfers or changes allowed. Log-in required.

Ⓦ **www.priceline.com** Name-your-own-price website that has deals at around forty percent off standard fares. You cannot specify flight times (although you do specify dates) and the tickets are non-refundable, non-transferable and non-changeable.

Ⓦ **www.skyauction.com** Bookings from the US only. Auctions tickets and travel packages using a "second bid" scheme. The best strategy is to bid the maximum you're willing to pay, since if you win you'll pay just enough to beat the runner-up regardless of your maximum bid.

Ⓦ **www.travelshop.com.au** Australian website offering discounted flights, packages, insurance, online bookings.

Flights from the UK and Ireland

The vast majority of British visitors travel to Corsica by direct charter flight – from the London airports of Gatwick or Heathrow, and regional airports such as Birmingham or Manchester – with the air fare included in the price of a package holiday (see p.13). If you buy your own ticket, however, and arrange accommodation and transport yourself, you can expect to save a bit of money.

Operating from early April until mid-October, **charter flights** are run by specialist airlines such as Britannia and Monarch, who sell blocks of seats in advance to tour operators, who then combine them with accommodation and sell them on as packages. Any left over unsold seats on the flights are cleared on behalf of the airlines by a consol-idator called Holiday Options (see below). If during the weeks before the departure date the tour companies think they may have unsold seats, they may also offer discounted "flight-only" deals. For this reason, the later you can leave buying a ticket, the more likely you are to come up with a cheap fare, although holding out for a last-minute bargain inevitably entails a degree of risk, particularly if you are travelling in high season. The only way to be sure of a seat on a charter flight, on the date you wish to travel, is to book well in advance, when tickets may be more expensive.

The best place to start looking for a charter air ticket is Holiday Options (see p.14), whose published return fares (to Bastia, Calvi, Ajaccio and Figari) range from around £175 off season to £245 in mid-August. In addition, they frequently advertise "short-notice" or "late-availability" flights for as little as £100 (often with bargain fly-drive or accommodation options thrown in). If Holiday Options is sold out, or has only standard fares on offer, try phoning around tour operators such as Voyages Ilena, Corsican Places, Simply Corsica, or others listed on p.15.

Charter flights to Corsica from the UK leave and return on Sundays; the ticket price should include all airport taxes. When booking, bear in mind which part of the island you intend to travel to first, and where any accommodation you may have pre-arranged is, or you could be faced with a long journey on arrival.

Outside the tourist season, from November until March, and at times when the charters are sold out, your only option will be to take a **scheduled flight**. No scheduled carrier flies direct from the UK to Corsica. However, Air France, British Airways and British Midland can all get you there, with a change of planes at either Paris, Nice or Marseille included in a single price. Of these, Air France offers the widest choice and best selection of discounts, with daily flights to three of Corsica's main domestic airports – Bastia, Ajaccio and Calvi – starting at around £200 for a return flight via Paris (Orly). BA offers comparable fares, routing you through one of the Riviera ports (Marseille or Nice).

The main disadvantage with scheduled routings compared with direct charter flights is that they take considerably longer. To the total flying time of around three hours (1hr 20min to Paris and 1hr 30min for the onward leg to Corsica, or 2hr to Nice and 45min to Ajaccio/Bastia), you have to add on another two or three hours (and sometimes more) for connections.

Apart from the annoying delays, the other downside with travelling scheduled is the extra **cost**. Standard scheduled tickets to Corsica start at around £200 return, rising to £440 in peak season (July and August). To cut costs, some travellers opt for a so-called "**double-ticket deal**", buying a heavily discounted ticket from the UK to Paris or one of the Mediterranean cities with a **budget airline** such as Go, Buzz or EasyJet, and the onward leg via a French domestic carrier such as Air Littoral, Compagnie Corse Mediterranée, Kyrnair, or Air Liberté. Most travel agents are happy to arrange this for you, but may point out that the saving on the cost of a through-ticket with BA or Air France brings with it a greater risk of delay or inconvenience; on double tickets, the first carrier is not contractually obliged to get you to your final destination, and will offer no compensation if a delay caused by them means you miss your connecting flight. Also, as EasyJet and the other budget airlines do most of their business over the Internet and telephone and do not pay agents' commission, it is worth bearing in mind that booking one of their tickets on the high street may incur a surcharge.

Travellers with more time than money on their hands might also consider the **rock-bottom option** of flying to the French or Italian rivieras with one of the budget airlines and catching a ferry or hydrofoil from there. EasyJet offers some amazingly low fares to Nice, and you can pick up equally cheap tickets with Ryanair to Genoa and Alghero (in Sardinia), from where regular boats sail to Corsica. Travelling this way it's possible to reach the island for as little as £100 return, but to do so you'd have to be sure of a prompt connection otherwise your net saving would disappear in hotel bills or on train tickets to and from whichever port the next boat happened to be leaving from when you arrived.

Finally, if you're offered a ticket to Corsica **via Paris from a regional airport in the UK**, check to make sure the onward leg to Corsica leaves from the same airport you arrived in. At the time of writing, only British

Airways flies from Manchester and Birmingham to Paris Orly, which is where all domestic flights to Corsica depart from; fly with Air France via Paris and you'll land at Charles de Gaulle (CDG) airport, leaving you an inconvenient, time-consuming trip across the city to pick up your plane to Corsica.

Flights from Ireland

No airline offers direct flights from Ireland to Corsica. From the **Irish Republic**, Aer Lingus operates **scheduled flights** direct from **Cork** and **Dublin** to Paris CDG (respectively once and five times daily), but you'll have to get from CDG to Orly airport on the other side of Paris to catch a flight to Corsica. The standard fare is €250 to Paris, though if you book early you may get one of the few seats at €175 return. Ryanair offers three flights daily from Dublin to Beauvais Tillé airport outside Paris for €125 return. Budget Travel organizes **charter flights** from Dublin to Nice for €250 (May to mid-Oct), while Go Holidays arranges them (April–Sept) from Shannon, Cork and Dublin to Marseille and Nice. Alternatively, you could fly to England with one of the low-cost airlines and pick up a charter flight from there (see p.12).

From **Northern Ireland**, British Airways flies directly from Belfast City to Paris CDG. Otherwise, a routing through London to pick up a charter is the best option.

Packages

In its simplest form, a **package holiday** is a combination of an air ticket and accommodation, for which you pay a single all-in price. As tour operators block book both flights and properties at least a year in advance, they pay lower rates than walk-in clients, which may – although not necessarily – mean better value for the customer. Although it can work out cheaper to make your own transport and accommodation arrangements, with competition as cutthroat as it is these days, the tour companies' mark-ups tend to be comparatively small and worth paying if you're short of time and/or not fluent enough in French to make all the phone calls yourself.

Aside from the hassle of making the arrangements, the main thing you pay for with this kind of holiday is the tour operators' local **contacts and knowledge**. Companies scour the island each year in search of the most attractive properties for their brochures. Having settled which ones best fit their portfolios, they then block book them for the whole season. This means you'd be lucky to find anywhere really special that hasn't already been snapped up (and even if you did, chances are it wouldn't cost much less than you'd pay booking it as part of a package).

In addition to the flight and accommodation, most operators offer **extras** such as car rental (aka "**fly-drive**"), sports facilities and flight upgrades. Again, it pays to compare their prices, and watch out, too, for late-availability deals, which sometimes include such extras in a single (and invariably unbeatable) package.

The **cost** of package holidays varies enormously – from company to company, depending on the kind of property you book and time of year you travel. The cheapest deals are usually for simple apartments in large holiday villages out of season. Self-catering chalets, with tiny kitchenettes, two bedrooms, living room and terrace, cost a notch more, followed by larger villas or cottages. A pool can double the cost of any place. If you're prepared to take the risk, **late-availability** deals can produce some superb packages, such as those offered by Holiday Options (see p.12). It is not unusual to see late-season fly-drive packages, offering a return air ticket and one week's basic accommodation including car rental for under £200 – impossible to match if you're booking independently.

The list on p.15 summarizes the tour companies who currently offer packages to the island from the UK, but smaller ones come and go. Apart from your local travel agent, the best places to hunt for their adverts are the travel pages of the Sunday newspapers, particularly the *Independent on Sunday*, the *Observer*, the *Sunday Times* and the *Sunday Telegraph*. Before booking with any travel company, ensure they are fully bonded – look out for the IATA or ATOL number given on the company's brochure.

Airlines in the UK

Air France ☎0845/084 5111,
ⓦwww.airfrance.co.uk.
British Airways ☎0845/77 333 77,
ⓦwww.britishairways.com.
British Midland ☎0870/607 0555,
ⓦwww.britishmidland.co.uk.
Buzz ☎0870/240 7070, ⓦwww.buzzaway.com.
Marseille from Stansted.
EasyJet ☎0870/600 0000, ⓦwww.easyjet.co.uk.
Nice from Gatwick, Luton and Liverpool.
Go ☎0870/607 6543 or 01279/666 388,
ⓦwww.goairways.co.uk. Nice from Bristol and
Stansted.
Ryanair ☎0870/600 0000,ⓦwww.ryanair.com.
Luton to Alghero in Sardinia – a cheap back route
to Corsica.

Airlines in Ireland

Aer Lingus ☎0818/365 000,
ⓦwww.aerlingus.ie.
British Airways ☎1-800/626 747,
ⓦwww.britishairways.com.
Ryanair ☎01/609 7800, ⓦwww.ryanair.com.

Flight and travel agents in the UK

Holiday Options ☎01444/244 411,
ⓦwww.holidayoptions.co.uk. The UK's most
promising source of discounted charter-flight
tickets, often combined with unbeatable fly-drive
and accommodation deals.
Real Holidays ☎020/7359 3938,
ⓦwww.realhols.co.uk. Knowledgeable London-
based Corsica specialists, dealing in charter and
scheduled flights, as well as packages with most
of the main operators.
STA Travel ☎0870/160 6070,
ⓦwww.statravel.co.uk. Worldwide specialists in
low-cost flights and tours for students and under-
26s, though other customers welcome.
Trailfinders ☎020/7628 7628,
ⓦwww.trailfinders.com. One of the best-informed
and most efficient all-rounders.

Flight and travel agents in Ireland

Aran Travel International Galway ☎091/562
595, ⓦhomepages.iol.ie/~arantvl/aranmain.htm.
Good-value flights to all parts of the world,
including the French Mediterranean ports.
CIE Tours International Dublin ☎01/703 1888,
ⓦwww.cietours.ie. General flight and tour agent.
Go Holidays Dublin ☎01/874 4126,
ⓦwww.goholidays.ie. Package tour specialists.
Joe Walsh Tours Dublin ☎01/676 0991,
ⓦwww.joewalshtours.ie. General budget fares
agent.
McCarthy's Travel Cork ☎021/427 0127,

www.mccarthystravel.ie. General flight agent.
Student & Group Travel Dublin ☏ 01/677 7834.
Student and group specialists.
Trailfinders Dublin ☏ 01/677 7888,
www.trailfinders.ie. One of the best-informed
and most efficient agents for independent
travellers.
usit NOW Dublin ☏ 01/602 1600,
www.usitnow.ie. Student and youth specialists
for flights and trains.

Package tour companies in the UK

Club Med ☏ 0700/007 007 or 0700/258 2633,
www.clubmed.co.uk. Child-friendly holidays in
purpose-built complex on Chiuni bay, near
Cargèse, with excellent watersports and tennis
facilities. See also p.183.
Corsican Affair ☏ 020/7385 8438,
www.corsicanaffair.co.uk. Fly-drive, hotel
packages and self-catering in a wide range of
attractive properties across the island.
Corsican Places ☏ 01424/460 046,
www.corsica.co.uk. Experienced, knowledgeable
Corsica specialists, offering tailor-made stays as
well as packages, in period properties and new
villas, at very reasonable prices.
Cresta Holidays ☏ 0870/161 0900. Basic hotel-
and-flight deals.
French Expressions ☏ 020/7794 1480,
www.expressionsholidays.co.uk. Upmarket
holidays in four-star hotels.
Mark Warner ☏ 020/7761 7100,
www.markwarner.co.uk. Watersports specialists,
with accommodation in beach-club-style hotels
and apartments, with special provision available
for kids.
Simply Corsica ☏ 020/8541 2205 or 8995 9323,
www.simply-travel.com. Currently the UK's
largest operator on the island, owned by Thomson
Holidays. Their portfolio includes a diverse range of
hand-picked properties, from classy hotels to villas
with pools, country cottages and seaside
apartments, and they offer unrivalled child-care
facilities (including a crèche and English-speaking
nannies). Check their brochure for special-interest
options: group walking, painting and wild flowers.
Vacances en Campagne aka The Individual
Traveller Company ☏ 01798/869 433,
www.indiv-travellers.com. A small number of
highly desirable self-catering properties, mostly
upscale, around Calvi and near beaches.
VFB Holidays ☏ 01242/240 310,
www.vfbholidays.co.uk. Flexible fly-drive
holidays with accommodation in various-star
hotels, small resort complexes and self-catering

properties (some with pools) all over the island,
including nine charming apartments in the remote
mountain village of Lama.
Voyages Ilena ☏ 020/7924 4440,
www.voyagesilena.co.uk. Star hotels and a wide
range of attractive self-catering accommodation at
particularly beautiful locations all over Corsica.
This small firm is among the oldest-established
and most knowledgeable operators on the island,
offering consistently good value.

Flights from the USA and Canada

From North America, Corsica is one of the
more obscure European destinations.
Discount travel agents – normally the mainstay of budget travellers – concentrate on
high-volume routes and are unlikely to be able
to ticket you beyond Paris, or perhaps Nice.
By all means give it a shot, but you'll probably end up paying a published fare to Corsica.

Whichever company you travel with, flying
to Corsica from North America will involve at
least one change of plane. Served by flights
from over thirty North American cities, **Paris** is
the most convenient gateway. It's also one of
Europe's cheapest destinations, thanks to stiff
competition between the dozen or so companies who fly there. For the onward leg to
Corsica, you'll have to purchase a second
ticket to Ajaccio, Bastia or Calvi with Air Inter,
Air France's subsidiary. This can be done
before you leave, or more cheaply on arrival in
France, although bear in mind that flights to
Corsica from the mainland are heavily sub-
scribed during the holiday season and should
be booked months in advance.

Fares also fluctuate according to the season, and are highest from around early June
to the end of August; they drop during the
"shoulder" seasons (Sept–Oct & April–May);
and you'll get the best deals during the low
season (Nov–March excluding Christmas).
Figure on the following approximate
winter/summer Apex return to Ajaccio,
Bastia or Calvi, based on midweek travel (flying on weekends ordinarily adds about $70
to the return fare): New York $765/$1135;
Washington $840/$1173; Miami $885/
$1195; Chicago $855/$1180; Houston
$885/$1249; LA or San Francisco $1160/
$1265.

Air France offers the most frequent service to Paris, and has the additional advantage of regular onward flights to Corsica on

its domestic subsidiary, Air Inter, although its fares tend to be on the expensive side. Other airlines with non-stop services to Paris from a variety of US cities are United, daily from Chicago, San Francisco and Washington DC; Delta, daily from Cincinnati, Atlanta and New York; TWA, daily from New York and three times a week from St Louis; and KLM, three to five times per week from Los Angeles, depending on the season. With all these carriers, agents should be able to book you a through-ticket to Corsica that includes the onward flight from Paris with a domestic carrier.

Bear in mind, too, that several airlines fly non-stop from North America to **Nice** and **Marseille**. Air France, for example, has a daily service to Nice from New York. Routes to these southern French cities cost on average between $200 and $300 more than flights to Paris, but you save nearly that much on the onward flight to Corsica, which is considerably cheaper.

An option well worth considering if you're on a tight budget is a **courier flight**. Standard return courier flights to Paris go for around $350, while last-minute specials can cost as little as $150. For more information contact: The Air Courier Association (℡1-800/282-1202, ⓦwww.aircourier.org or www.cheaptrips .com), Now Voyager ℡212/459-1616, ⓦwww.nowvoyagertravel.com); or the International Association of Air Travel Couriers (℡352/475-1584, ⓦwww.courier.org).

From Canada

The strong links between France and Québec's Francophone community ensure regular air services from Canada to **Paris**, from where you have to change onto a domestic carrier for the onward flight to Corsica.

Air France, Air Canada and Canadian offer non-stop services to Paris from the major Canadian cities. You can also fly non-stop to Lyon from Toronto, and fares (winter/summer) are very competitive (return to Paris from Toronto $830/$1225; from Vancouver $1125/$1645).

Package tours

Corsica is way off the beaten track for most North American **tour** operators. Your choices basically come down to a company arranging upscale tours and a couple of adventure-travel outfits that do hiking trips in Corsica (see below). If you're set on going with a package tour, you might want to consider contacting an operator in Britain (see p.13), where Corsica is a much more popular destination.

Airlines in the USA and Canada

Air Canada ℡1-888/247-2262, ⓦwww.aircanada.ca. Montréal, Toronto and Vancouver to Paris and Nice.

Air France USA ℡1-800/237-2747, Canada ℡1-800/667-2747, ⓦwww.airfrance.com. New York, Washington DC, Miami, Montréal, Toronto, Chicago, Houston, San Francisco and Los Angeles to Paris or Nice; connections to Ajaccio on Air Inter.

American Airlines ℡1-800/433-7300, ⓦwww.aa.com. New York, Miami, Dallas-Fort Worth, Chicago and Los Angeles to Paris.

British Airways ℡1-800/247-9297, ⓦwww.britishairways.com. Many North American cities to Paris and Nice (via London).

Canadian Airlines ℡1-800/426-7000, www.cd.air.com. Montréal, Toronto and Vancouver to Paris.

Continental Airlines domestic ℡1-800/523-3273, international ℡1-800/231-0856, ⓦwww.continental.com.

Delta Air Lines domestic ℡1-800/221-1212, international ℡1-800/241-4141, ⓦwww.delta.com. Atlanta, Cincinnati and New York to Paris.

KLM/Northwest Airlines domestic ℡1-800/225-2525, international ℡1-800/447-4747, ⓦwww.nwa.com. Los Angeles, Minneapolis and Detroit to Paris.

TWA domestic ℡1-800/221-2000, international ℡1-800/892-4141, ⓦwww.twa.com. New York, Boston, St Louis and Washington to Paris.

United Airlines domestic ℡1-800/241-6522, international ℡1-800/538-2929, ⓦwww.ual.com. Chicago, Washington DC, Los Angeles and San Francisco to Paris.

US Airways domestic ℡1-800/428-4322, international ℡1-800/622-1015, ⓦwww.usairways.com. Daily non-stop flights to Paris from Philadelphia.

Discount travel companies in the USA and Canada

Air Brokers International ℡1-800/883-3273, ⓦwww.airbrokers.com. Consolidator and specialist in Round-the-World tickets.

Airtech ☎1-877/247-8324 or 212/219-7000,
ⓦwww.airtech.com. Standby seat broker; also
deals in consolidator fares and courier flights.
Council Travel ☎1-800/226-8624,
ⓦwww.counciltravel.com. Nationwide organization
that mostly, but by no means exclusively,
specializes in student/budget travel. Flights from
the USA only.
Educational Travel Center ☎1-800/747-5551
or 608/256-5551, ⓦwww.edtrav.com.
Student/youth discount agent.
High Adventure Travel ☎1-800/350-0612 or
415/912-5600, ⓦwww.airtreks.com. Round-the-
World and Circle Pacific tickets.
New Frontiers/Nouvelles Frontières ☎1-
800/677-0720, ⓦwww.newfrontiers.com. French
discount-travel firm based in New York City. Other
branches in LA, San Francisco and Québec City.
Skylink USA ☎1-800/247-6659 or 212/573-
8980, Canada ☎1-800/759-5465,
ⓦwww.skylinkus.com. Consolidator.
STA Travel ☎1-800/777-0112 or 1-800/781-
4040, ⓦwww.sta-travel.com. Worldwide
specialists in independent travel; also student IDs,
travel insurance, car rental, rail passes, etc.
Student Flights ☎1-800/255-8000 or 480/951-
1177, ⓦwww.isecard.com. Student/youth fares,
student IDs.
TFI Tours International ☎1-800/745-8000 or
212/736-1140, ⓦwww.lowestairprice.com.
Consolidator.
Travac ☎1-800/872-8800,
ⓦwww.thetravelsite.com. Consolidator and
charter broker with offices in New York City and
Orlando.
Travelers Advantage ☎1-877/259-2691,
ⓦwww.travelersadvantage.com. Discount travel
club; annual membership fee required (currently
$1 for 3 months' trial).
Travel Avenue ☎1-800/333-3335,
ⓦwww.travelavenue.com. Full-service travel
agent that offers discounts in the form of rebates.
Travel Cuts Canada ☎1-800/667-2887, USA
☎1-866/246-9762, ⓦwww.travelcuts.com.
Canadian student-travel organization.
Worldtek Travel ☎1-800/243-1723,
ⓦwww.worldtek.com. Discount travel agency for
worldwide travel.

Tour operators in the USA and Canada

Adventure Center ☎1-800/228-8747,
ⓦwww.adventure-center.com. Hiking and "soft
adventure" specialists offering Corsican village
treks (around $1000 for 15 days).

Butterfield & Robinson ☎1-800/678-1147,
ⓦwwwbutterfield.com. Luxury tour of the island's
highlights, with stays in four-star hotels and
gourmet meals. Eight days from $4200.
Infohub ⓦwww.infohub.com. Eleven-day guided
cycling holidays from $2550.
Vacances en Campagne ☎1-800/327-6097.
Short-term rentals of châteaux and country
houses, from around $670 a week.
World Expeditions ☎1-800/567-2216,
ⓦwww.worldexpeditions.com. Self-guided
trekking holidays from $600.

Flights from Australia and New Zealand

There are no direct flights from Australia or
New Zealand to Corsica – the best you can
do is fly direct to Paris and change planes
there for Ajaccio, Calvi or Bastia. If you qualify for student/youth discounts, it's best to
book through an agent such as STA (see
p.18). Fares tend to be cheaper from mid-
January to the end of February and during
October and November, increasing during
high season (May–Aug and Dec–Jan). Some
airlines, such as Alitalia and Air France, offer
free transfer flights within Europe that can
get you to Corsica. Others have competitive-
ly priced add-on fares from Paris and Rome
from around Aus$385/NZ$450.

Air France flies from Sydney and Auckland
to Paris (Charles de Gaulle) via Jakarta and
Singapore at least once a week from around
Aus$2025/NZ$2275, and will throw in a
"side-trip" to Bastia or Ajaccio. Marseille and
Paris can also be reached more cheaply on
Aeroflot's bi-weekly service from Sydney via
Moscow for Aus$1650, but you'll have to
add on the cost of the onward flight to
Corsica from there. The same applies to the
dozen or so other international airlines that
fly to Paris, and whose agents will gladly
book a through-ticket to Corsica before you
leave. Your best chance of finding out which
one is currently offering the most competitive
fares is to ring around the agents listed
below, or to check the travel agents' ads in
the travel sections of the weekend newspapers. Also worth a browse are the online
resources listed on p.11.

Some **Round-the-World** routings allow
Corsica as a side-trip, using a combination
of airlines. Generally, six free stopovers are
offered by participating carriers, with additional stopovers for around Aus$100 each in

Australia and New Zealand. Fares start at Aus$2450/NZ$3430. Possibilities include UA's "Globetrotter", Air New Zealand/KLM/Northwest's "World Navigator", and Qantas/British Airways' "Global Explorer".

Airlines in Australia and New Zealand

Aeroflot Australia ☎02/9262 2233, ⓦwww.aeroflot.com. No NZ office.
Air France Australia ☎02/9244 2100, New Zealand ☎09/308 3352, ⓦwww.airfrance.com.
Alitalia Australia ☎02/9262 3925, ⓦwww.alitalia.com.
British Airways Australia ☎02/8904 8800, New Zealand ☎T800/274 847, ⓦwww.britishairways.com.
Singapore Airlines Australia ☎13 10 11, New Zealand ☎09/303 2129, ⓦwww.singaporeair.com.
Thai Airways Australia ☎1300/651 960, New Zealand ☎09/377 3886, ⓦwww.thaiair.com.

Flight agents in Australia and New Zealand

Budget Travel New Zealand ☎09/366 0061 or 0800/808 040, ⓦwww.budgettravel.co.nz.
Destinations Unlimited New Zealand ☎09/373 4033.
Flight Centres Australia ☎13 31 33 or 02/9235 3522, New Zealand ☎09/358 4310, ⓦwww.flightcentre.com.au.
Northern Gateway Australia ☎08/8941 1394, ⓦww.northerngateway.com.au.
STA Travel Australia ☎1300/733 035, ⓦwww.statravel.com.au, New Zealand ☎0508/782 872, ⓦwww.statravel.co.nz.
Student Uni Travel Australia ☎02/9232 8444, ⓔaustralia@backpackers.net.
Trailfinders Australia ☎02/9247 7666, ⓦwww.trailfinders.com.au.
usit Beyond New Zealand ☎09/379 4224 or 0800/788 336, ⓦwww.usitbeyond.co.nz.

Specialist tour operators in Australia and New Zealand

Abercrombie and Kent Australia ☎03/9536 1800 or 1300/851 800, New Zealand ☎0800/441 638, ⓦwww.abercrombiekent.com.au. Tailor-made upmarket tours, with stays in select hotels.
Adventure World New Zealand ☎09/379 9755, ⓔadvaki@hot.co.nz. NZ agent for Peregrine; see below.

Peregrine Adventures Australia ☎1300/854 444, ⓦwww.peregrine.net.au. Guided trekking holidays of various lengths and levels of comfort, with groups of 6–14 people.

By rail and sea from the UK and Ireland

The **Channel tunnel** has slashed travelling times between London and Paris, which in turn has led to a proliferation of cut-rate deals on regular train and ferry or hovercraft crossings. Given the low cost of charter flights, and the inconvenience and distances involved with travelling overland to Corsica, it is not surprising that very few British visitors approach the island by rail.

If you do opt for the **train**, you'll first have to choose between the tunnel and the sea crossing routes to Paris. From there, you can then take either a standard train south to Nice, Toulon or Marseille, or the superfast TGV (*Train à Grande Vitesse*). From the **Riviera ferry ports** there is then a choice of slow and fast services to Corsica.

Eurostar

Eurostar's **high-speed passenger service** to Paris Gare du Nord via the **Channel tunnel** departs seven to nine times daily from London Waterloo. Standard-class return fares for the three-hour trip range from £85 to £225, but special offers can bring prices down to as low as £55, even in the height of summer. Tickets can be bought directly over the phone from Eurostar; most travel agents; many rail stations in Britain; through SNCF (Société Nationale des Chemins de Fer – the French rail company) in London; from Waterloo International and Ashford ticket offices, from the new Eurostar shop and dedicated website (see p.19 for details).

Eurotunnel

The most convenient way of taking your car across to France is to drive to the **Channel tunnel**, load your car on the **train shuttle** and be whisked under the Channel in 35 minutes, emerging at Sangatte, France, just outside Calais. The sole operator, Eurotunnel, offers a continuous service with up to four departures per hour (only one per hour midnight–6am). Because of the frequency of the service, you don't have to buy a ticket in advance – though this might be advisable in midsummer or during school holidays. You must arrive at least 25 minutes before departure, and the target loading time is just ten minutes. Once inside the carriages, you can get out of your car to stretch your legs during the crossing. Tickets are available though Eurotunnel's Customer Service Centre (see below), or from your local travel agent. Fares are calculated per car, regardless of the number of passengers. Rates depenc on the time of year, time of day and length of stay (the cheapest ticket is for a day-trip, followed by a five-day return); it's cheaper to travel between 10pm and 6am, while the highest fares are reserved for weekend departures and returns in July and August. For example, if you book months ahead, a fourteen-day trip at an off-peak time starts at £80 (per car) in the shoulder season, rising to £120 in peak season. Alternatively, there's a wide range of ferry/hovercraft crossings (see below).

Ferry services

Crossing the Channel **by sea** instead of the tunnel can bring the overall cost of your train ticket to Corsica down slightly (by around £20), but takes considerably longer. Services leave London Victoria at 7.15am to connect with the cross-Channel ferries or hovercrafts at Dover or Folkestone, and onward trains on the other side from Calais and Boulogne, arriving in Paris Gare du Nord around 5.15pm.

Rail services across France

For the route down to the Côte d'Azur from Paris, the French national rail company, SNCF, offers a choice between the regular **express** and the superfast **TGV**, which takes around six and a half hours less to reach Marseille. Given that tickets cost the same on both, it makes sense to book early enough to avcid the slow train.

By taking Eurostar and the TGV, it's possible to reach Nice in only ten hours from London (not including the time it takes to cross Paris) for a fare of around £120 return. Note that the cheapest tickets are not open to holders of **rail passes** such as the Eurodomino and Interail; you also have to reserve them within 65 days of your return journey.

Motorists who don't want to drive far once in France can take advantage of SNCF's **Motorail**, putting the car on the train in Calais for Nice, Marseille or Toulon. This is a relatively expensive option: Calais–Nice, for example, costs £830–1150 return for one car, depending on the season. Bookings and timetable information are available through the International Rail Centre in Victoria and Rail Europe or via the Motorail website (see below).

Cross-Channel and rail services

Brittany Ferries UK ☎0870/901 2400, Republic of Ireland ☎021/427 7801, 🌐www.brittanyferries.co.uk. Poole to Cherbourg; Portsmouth to Caen and St Malo; Plymouth to Roscoff and to Santander (March–Nov/Dec); Cork to Roscoff (March–Oct only).

Hoverspeed ☎0870/240 8070, 🌐www.hoverspeed.co.uk. 24 daily departures. Dover to Calais and Ostend; Newhaven to Dieppe.

Eurostar ☎0870/160 6600, 🌐www.eurostar.com.

Eurotunnel ☎0870/535 3535, 24hr recorded departure info ☎0891/555 566 50p per minute, 🌐www.eurotunnel.co.uk.

Hoverspeed SeaTrain Express ☎0870/524 0241, 🌐www.hoverspeed.co.uk.

Irish Ferries UK ☎0870/517 1717, Republic of Ireland ☎01/661 0511, 🌐www.irishferries.com. Dublin to Holyhead; Rosslare to Pembroke, Cherbourg and Roscoff. Continental services March to end Sept.

Motorail UK ☎0870/584 8848, France ☎00 33 17 32 52 67 75, 🌐www.motorrail.com.

Norse Merchant Ferries UK ☎0870/600 4321, Republic of Ireland ☎01/819 2999, 🌐www.norsemerchant.com. Belfast and Dublin to Liverpool.

P&O Portsmouth ☎0870/242 4999, 🌐www.poportsmouth.com. Portsmouth to Cherbourg, Le Havre and Bilbao.

Rail Europe ☎0870/584 8848, 🌐www.raileurope.co.uk.

Sea France ☎0870/571 1711, 🌐www.seafrance.com. Dover to Calais.

Stena Line UK ☎0870/570 70 70, Republic of Ireland ☎01/204 7777, 🌐www.stenaline.co.uk. Rosslare to Fishguard; Dun Laoghaire and Dublin to Holyhead; Belfast to Stranraer.

Southern Ferries ☎020/7491 4968. Agents for SNCM Ferrytérranée.

UK rail enquiries ☎08457/484 950.

Via Mare ☎020/4560 7431, 🌐www.viamare.com. Agents for Corsica Ferries.

Ferry connections

Route	Company	Frequency	Length of Crossing	Single Fare		Period of Operation
				Foot	Small Passenger Car	
Ferry crossings from France						
Marseille–Ajaccio	SNCM	3–7 weekly	11hr overnight, 4hr 30min (NGV) –7hr daytime	€26–40	€50–100	year round
Marseille–Bastia	SNCM	1–3 weekly	10hr overnight or daytime	€26–40	€50–100	year round
Marseille –L'Île Rousse	SNCM	1–3 weekly	11hr 30min overnight	€26–40	€50–100	June–Sept
Marseille –Porto-Vecchio	SNCM	1–3 weekly	14hr 30min overnight	€26–40	€50–100	June–Sept
Marseille –Propriano	SNCM	1–5 weekly	9hr 30min	€26–40	€50–100	March–Sept
Nice–Ajaccio	SNCM	1–6 weekly	12hr overnight	€15–25	€40–110	year round
Nice–Bastia	SNCM/ Corsica Ferries	3–24 weekly	6hr–6hr 45min	€15–25	€40–110	year round
Nice–Calvi	SNCM/ Corsica Ferries	2–5 weekly	2hr 45min (NGV) daytime	€15–25	€40–110	year round
Nice–L'Île Rousse	SNCM	4–6 weekly	7hr overnight, 2hr 45min (NGV)– 5hr daytime	€15–25	€40–110	June–Sept
Toulon–Ajaccio	SNCM	1–4 weekly	10hr overnight	€26–40	€50–100	April–Sept
Toulon–Bastia	SNCM	1–3 weekly	8hr 30min overnight	€26–40	€50–100	April–Oct
Ferry crossings from Italy						
Genoa–Bastia	Corsica Marittima	2 weekly	5hr 45min –11hr	€15–27	€40–75	June–Sept
	Moby Lines	2–4 weekly	6hr	€15–28	€37–76	April to mid-Sept
La Spezia–Bastia	Happy Lines	5–7 weekly	5hr	€15–27	€40–73	May–Sept
Livorno–Bastia	Corsica Ferries	1–3 daily	4–7hr	€16–28	€40–78	June–Sept
	Corsica Marittima	1–5 weekly	1hr 50min (NGV)– 3hr 30min	€15–27	€40–75	April–Oct
	Moby Lines	2–5 weekly	4hr	€15–28	€37–76	April to mid-June
Livorno –Porto-Vecchio	Corsica Marittima	1–2 weekly	7hr 30min– 10hr 30min	€15–27	€40–75	June–Sept
Piombino–Bastia	Moby Lines	1 daily	3hr 30min	€15–28	€37–76	July to mid-Sept
Santa-Teresa-di- Gallura (Sardinia) –Bonifacio	Saremar Corsica Ferries	2–4 daily 2–4 daily	1hr 30min 1hr 30min	€7–8.5 €7–8.5	€20–28 €20–28	year round year round
Savona–Bastia	Corsica Ferries	1–3 daily	3hr	€16–31	€40–105	June–Sept
Savona–Calvi	Corsica Ferries	2–3 weekly	6hr 30min	€16–31	€40–105	June–Sept
Savona–L'Île Rousse	Corsica Ferries	2–3 weekly	6hr	€16–31	€40–105	June–Sept

Ferries to Corsica from France and Italy

Corsica has six ferry ports (Bastia, L'Île Rousse, Calvi, Ajaccio, Propriano and Porto-Vecchio), served by three ports on the French Riviera (Marseille, Toulon and Nice) and six in Italy (Savona, Genoa, La Spezia, Livorno, Piombo and Santa-Teresa-di-Gallura in Sardinia). From France, crossings take between 6hr (Nice–Bastia) and 13hr 30min (Marseille–Porto-Vecchio overnight) on regular ferries, and from 2hr 45min (Nice–Calvi) to 4hr (Nice–Ajaccio) on the superfast NGV hydrofoils (*Navire à Grande Vitesse*), which travel at a brisk 37 to 43 knots. Coming from the UK, Marseille is the obvious port to head for, but if you want to catch an NGV, you'll have to press on further up the coast to Nice. Both regular and NGV services are run by two companies: SNCM Ferrytérranée and Corsica Ferries (see below). Fares on their NGVs are around the same as on regular ferries, with both varying according to whether you travel in a blue (off-peak), green (mid-season), white (high-season) or red (peak-season) period.

One-way tickets to all ports in Corsica for reclining passenger seats, for example, on services from Marseille and Toulon cost €26–40, or €15–25 from Nice (return fares cost exactly double). Babies go free, while reductions of various degrees are available to children aged 4 to 12, young persons aged 12 to 25, senior citizens and for large families with four or more kids. You can also pay extra for a four-, two- or single-bed cabin (with or without shower and toilet). **Cars** are charged according to their length and height, with tariffs increasing dramatically (by around three times) in red periods. For a small car under 3.8m long and 2m tall, expect to pay around €40–110 from Nice and €50–100 from Marseille or Toulon; cars and passengers are charged separately. **Motorbikes** cost from €26–60, and **bicycles** €14 at any time of year.

On top of the advertised price of your ticket, note that you have to add on hefty **port taxes**, which vary from €3–5.50 per person per crossing, plus **vehicle tax** from €5.50 to €7.60 if you're driving.

Comparatively few British travellers approach Corsica **from Italy**, but ferry services from the six Italian ports are frequent throughout the summer and often less expensive (their red and white periods tend to be much shorter). Taking around 2hr 30min by NGV, the shortest, least expensive crossing is from Livorno to Bastia; tickets for foot passengers cost €15–27 one way, with a supplement of €7 if you opt for the NGV. Charges for (small) cars on the same route range from €40 to €75. There is also a port tax for Italy: €2.30 per person, plus €5.35 for a car. Most of the companies (see below), do special offers that can bring the overall price down, particularly if you're travelling as a family or in a group.

Bear in mind that during peak periods demand for ferry tickets to Corsica from both mainland France and Italy can far exceed supply. Book as far in advance as possible, particularly if you intend to take a car across, as vehicle places often sell out months ahead. **Reservations** can be made either through your local travel agent or directly with the ferry companies, over the telephone or Internet (their websites all have English versions and you can pay by credit card; see below for addresses). Most of the ferry companies also have **agents in the UK** whom you can contact for timetable information and bookings. If you do arrange your ticket through them, however, check at the outset for any additional charges: some levy a stiff booking fee for bookings under £100.

Ferry companies in France and Italy

For contact details of ferry company offices in their Corsican ports, see the relevant accounts in the Guide section of this book.
Corsica Ferries ☎00 33 4 92 00 43 76, 📠www.corsicaferries.com. In the UK their agents are Via Mare ☎020/4560 7431, 📠www.viamare.com.
Corsica Marittima Contact SNCM below. 📠www.corsica-marittima.com.
Happy Lines 📠www.happylines.it.
Moby Lines ☎00 33 1 55 77 27 00, 📠www.mobylines.com. UK agents: CIT ☎0891/71551 (50p/min).
Saremar 📠www.saremar.it.
SNCM Ferrytérranée ☎00 33 8 36 67 95 00, 📠www.sncm.fr. UK agent: Southern Ferries ☎020/7491 4968.

By bus

For any die-hard who might want to take a coach to Corsica, there is a direct service to

Nice, which takes 24 hours and is operated by **Eurolines** (164 Buckingham Palace Rd, London SW1 ☎0870/514 3219, ⓦwww.eurolines.co.uk), leaving once a week from London Victoria Coach Station from June to October. Fares start at around £100 return, with small reductions for under-25s and students.

Red tape and visas

Citizens of EU countries, Japan, New Zealand, Canada and the United States do not need any sort of visa to enter France for a stay of up to ninety days. Nationals of all other countries, including Australia, must obtain a visa before arrival in Corsica.

If you do need a visa, you have a choice of three types (all of which are valid from date of issue): a transit visa (£5–8), which is valid from one to five days; a short stay (*court séjour*) visa (£15–20), valid up to thirty days after date of issue; and the long stay (£29–90), which allows multiple stays of ninety days over three years (maximum of 180 days in any one year). Prices vary according to the countries of issue and whether or not you ask for a single or (more expensive) multiple-entry visa.

To **obtain a visa** you'll need an application form (available from the consulate or embassy), a passport valid for at least six months from your intended date of arrival in France, a ticket or verification of travel, and the visa fee (see above). Obtaining a visa from your nearest French consulate (the addresses of the major French embassies and consulates are given below) is fairly automatic, but check the hours before turning up, and leave plenty of time, since there are often queues (particularly in London in summer). Australians can obtain a visa on the spot in London.

For stays of longer than ninety days you are officially supposed to apply for a *Carte de Séjour*, for which you'll have to show proof of income at least equal to the minimum wage. However, EU passports are rarely stamped, so there is no evidence of how long you've been in the country, and if your passport is stamped you can legitimately cross the French border, to Italy for example, and re-enter for another ninety days.

French embassies and consulates abroad

Opening hours for most French embassies and consulates are Mon–Fri 9am–1pm.

Australia 492 St Kilda Rd, Melbourne, VIC 3001 ☎03/9820 0921; 31 Market St, Sydney, NSW 2000 ☎02/9262 5779.

Canada 42 Promenade Sussex, Ottawa, ON K1M 2C9 ☎613/789-1795; 1 pl Ville Marie, Bureau 22601, Montréal, Québec, QC H3B 4S3 ☎514/878-4385; 25 rue St-Louis, Québec, QC G1R 3Y8 ☎418/694-2294; 130 Bloor St Wt, Suite 400, Toronto, ON M5S 1N5 ☎416/925-8041; 1201–736 Granville St, Vancouver, BC V6Z 1H9 ☎604/681-4345.

Ireland 36 Ailesbury Rd, Dublin 4 ☎01/260 1666.

Netherlands Smidsplein 1, 2514 BT Den Haag ☎070/312 5800; Vijzelgracht 2, 1000 HA Amsterdam ☎020/624 8346.

New Zealand 1 Willeston St, PO Box 1695, Wellington ☎04/472 0200.

UK 59 Knightsbridge, London SW1X 7JT ☎020/7201 1000; 7–11 Randolph Crescent, Edinburgh ☎0131/225 7954.

USA 4101 Reservoir Rd NW, Washington, DC 20007 ☎202/944-6195; Park Square Building, Suite 750, 31 St James Ave, Boston, MA 02116 ☎617/542-7374; 737 North Michigan Ave, Olympia Center, Suite 2020, Chicago, IL 60611 ☎312/787-5359; 10990 Wilshire Blvd, Suite 300, Los Angeles, CA 90024 ☎310/235-3200; 934 Fifth Ave, New York, NY 10021 ☎212/606-3689; 540 Bush St, San Francisco, CA 94108 ☎415/397-4330.

Information, websites and maps

The foreign branches of the French Government Tourist Office give away maps and glossy brochures, including lists of Corsican hotels, campsites, sports facilities and public transport services. In Corsica every major town and large village has a tourist office, or *Office du Tourisme* (OT), addresses of which are detailed throughout this guide. Usually only open in summer (May–Sept), these offices give out specific local information, including free town plans, lists of leisure activities, bike rental and countless other things. Many tourist offices also publish hotel and restaurant listings, as well as driving and walking itineraries for their areas, and post daily weather forecasts, useful if you're hiking or sailing.

French government tourist offices abroad

Australia 25 Bligh St, 22nd Floor, Sydney, NSW 2000 ☎02/9231 5244, ⓕ9221 8682, ⓔifrance@internetzy.com.au.
Canada 1981 av McGill College, Suite 490, Montréal, PQ H3A ☎514/876-9881, ⓕ845-4868, ⓔmfrance@attcanada.
Ireland 10 Suffolk St, Dublin 1 ☎01560/235 235, ⓕ01560/679 0814, ⓔfrenchtouristoffice@mdlf.com.
Netherlands Prinsengracht 670, 1017 KX Amsterdam ☎0900/122 2332, ⓕ020/620 3339, ⓔinformatie@fransverkeersbureau.nl.
UK 178 Piccadilly, London W1V 0AL ☎09068/244 123 (premium-rate line costing 60p per min), ⓕ020/7493 6594, ⓔpiccadilly@mdlf.co.uk.
USA 444 Madison Ave, 16th Floor, New York, NY 10022-6903 ☎212/838-7800, ⓕ838-7855, ⓔinfo@francetourism.com; 9454 Wilshire Blvd, Suite 715, Beverly Hills, Los Angeles, CA 90212 ☎310/271-6665, ⓕ276-2835, ⓔfgtola@juno.com; 676 North Michigan Ave, Suite 3360, Chicago, IL 60611-2819 ☎312/337-6339.

Online resources

http://perso.wanadoo.fr/euromail/cormed01 .html A gateway to more than 600 Corsica or Corsica-related sites, with an exhaustive subject directory and some snappy graphic hotlinks. The most comprehensive information bank on the island currently online.
www.internetcom.fr/corseweb Corseweb's well-integrated site is essentially a platform for booking accommodation (hotels, gîtes and summer lets), accessed through a glossy region-by-region overview of the island.

www.corsematin.com Extracts – in French – from Corsica's best-selling daily paper.
www.napoleon.org Everything you ever wanted to know about Napoléon (and a lot more besides), with plenty of juicy links for Bona-philes.
www.chez.com Corsican folk-dance gigs and festivals, entered via a burst of hellish electronic oompah music.
www.sitec.fr/iledebeaute Myths and legends of the island, along with profiles of some of those who've shaped its history.
http://membres.tripod.fr/polog2marco Published by a hiking fanatic, this small but interesting site focuses on the prehistoric, religious and mysterious geological hot spots of the deep south.
www.sitec.fr/imuvrini This site, devoted to Corsica's most popular music group, the staunchly nationalist I Muvrini ("The Mouflons"), includes interviews with co-founders the Bernardini brothers, and audio snippets from their 1999 "Leia" tour.
www.caladisole.com/giramondu The website of pop polyphony group Giramondu features extracts from the best-selling latest album in RealAudio or (less troublesome) MP3 format.
http://perso.wanadoo.fr/d.aubin/cpa.htm An astonishingly comprehensive collection of old postcards from 1900 to 1940 showing everywhere from Ajaccio to Zicavo as they haven't looked for decades, as well as some fine portraits of local bandits and village characters.

Maps

Roads in Corsica are impeccably well signposted (even if the signs are frequently defaced by graffiti), and with the maps in this book you should be able to find your way around the places covered in the Guide. All the same, for motorists and cyclists, some kind of additional route map is essential.

Michelin's distinctive yellow 1:200,000 (1cm = 2km) map #90 is the benchmark publication, featuring every motorable road on the island on a sheet that's tough, well folded and with hand-shading to emphasize the topography. It's also unbelievably cheap – if you book a package holiday you'll probably be sent a complimentary one along with your tickets and accommodation details – and readily available at newsagents and bookstores across the island, as well as through the outlets listed below.

For a more comprehensive topographical picture of individual regions, IGN's beautifully produced **TOP Séries Bleues** maps are second to none. Drawn to a scale of 1:25,000 (1cm = 250m), they cover Corsica in 21 separate sheets. Just about every feature you could wish to identify – from footpaths and springs, to prehistoric monuments, different kinds of woodland, rock formations and beaches – are highlighted, and the contour lines are backed up with easy-to-read shading. The only catch is that they cost €9 each in France (or £8–9 if you buy them in the UK). All of the map suppliers listed below stock the IGN TOP series, but they don't necessarily charge the same prices (when you take into account postage surcharges), so shop around.

More specific advice on maps for **walkers** is featured on p.364.

Map outlets

UK and Ireland

Blackwell's Map and Travel Shop 50 Broad St, Oxford OX1 3BQ ☎01865/793 550, ⓦhttp://maps.blackwell.co.uk/index.html.
Easons Bookshop 40 O'Connell St, Dublin 1 ☎01/873 3811, ⓦwww.eason.ie.
Heffers Map and Travel 20 Trinity St, Cambridge CB2 1TJ ☎01865/333 536, ⓦwww.heffers.co.uk.
Hodges Figgis Bookshop 56–58 Dawson St, Dublin 2 ☎01/677 4754, ⓦwww.hodgesfiggis.com.
James Thin Booksellers 53–62 South Bridge, Edinburgh EH1 1YS ☎0131/622 8222, ⓦwww.jthin.co.uk.
The Map Shop 30a Belvoir St, Leicester LE1 6QH ☎0116/247 1400, ⓦwww.mapshopeicester.co.uk;15 High St, Upton-on-Severn, Worcestershire WR8 0HJ, ☎0800/085 4080, ⓦwww.themapshop.co.uk.
Maps Worldwide Datum House, Lancaster Road,

Melksham SN12 6TL ☎01225/707 004, ⓦwww.mapsworldwide.co.uk.
National Map Centre 22–24 Caxton St, London SW1H 0QU ☎020/7222 2466, ⓦwww.mapsnmc.co.uk.
Newcastle Map Centre 55 Grey St, Newcastle-upon-Tyne, NE1 6EF ☎0191/261 5622.
Stanfords 12–14 Long Acre, London WC2E 9LP ☎020/7836 1321, ⓦwww.stanfords.co.uk, ⓔsales@stanfords.co.uk. Maps available by mail, phone order, or email. Other branches within British Airways offices at 156 Regent St, London W1R 5TA ☎020/7434 4744, and 29 Corn St, Bristol BS1 1HT ☎0117/929 9966.
The Travel Bookshop 13–15 Blenheim Crescent, W11 2EE ☎020/7229 5260, ⓦwww.thetravelbookshop.co.uk.
Waterstone's Queens Building, 8 Royal Ave, Belfast BT1 ☎028/9024 7355.

USA and Canada

Adventurous Traveler Bookstore 102 Lake Street, Burlington, VT 05401 ☎1-800/282-3963, ⓦwww.adventuroustraveler.com.
Book Passage 51 Tamal Vista Blvd, Corte Madera, CA 94925 ☎1-800/999-7909, ⓦwww.bookpassage.com.
Distant Lands 56 S. Raymond Ave, Pasadena, CA 91105 ☎800/310-3220, ⓦwww.distantlands.com.
Elliot Bay Book Company 101 S Main St, Seattle, WA 98104 ☎1-800/962-5311, ⓦwww.elliotbaybook.com.
Forsyth Travel Library 226 Westchester Ave, White Plains, NY 10604 ☎1-800/367-7984, ⓦwww.forsyth.com.
Globe Corner Bookstore 28 Church St, Cambridge, MA 02138 ☎1-800/358-6013, ⓦwww.globecorner.com.
Maplink 30 S. La Patera Lane, Unit #5, Santa Barbara, CA 93117 ☎805/692-6777, or toll-free ☎800/962-1394, ⓦwww.maplink.com.
Omnimap 1004 South Mebane St, PO Box 2096, Burlington, NC 27216-2096 ☎336/227-8300, ⓕ227-3748, ⓦwww.omnimap.com.
Open Air Books and Maps, 25 Toronto St, Toronto, ON M5R 2C1 ☎416/363-0719.
Rand McNally ☎1-800/333-0136, ⓦwww.randmcnally.com. Around thirty stores across the US; dial ext 2111 or check the website for the nearest location.
The Travel Bug Bookstore 2667 W Broadway, Vancouver, BC V6K 2G2 ☎604/737-1122, ⓦwww.swifty.com/tbug.
Ulysses Travel Bookshop 4176 St-Denis, Montréal ☎514/843-9447.

World Wide Books and Maps 530 West Broadway, Vancouver, BC V5Z 1E9 ℡604/879-3621 or 687-3320, Ⓦwww.itmb.com.
World of Maps 1235 Wellington St, Ottawa, ON K1Y 3A3 ℡800/214-8524 or 613/724-6776, Ⓦwww.worldofmaps.com.

Australia and New Zealand

The Map Shop 6–10 Peel St, Adelaide, SA 5000 ℡08/8231 2033, Ⓦwww.mapshop.net.au.

Mapland 372 Little Bourke St, Melbourne, Victoria 3000 ℡03/9670 4383, Ⓦwww.mapland.com.au.
MapWorld 173 Gloucester St, Christchurch, New Zealand ℡0800/627 967 or 03/374 5399, Ⓦwww.mapworld.co.nz.
Perth Map Centre 1/884 Hay St, Perth, WA 6000 ℡08/9322 5733, Ⓦwww.perthmap.com.au.
Specialty Maps 46 Albert St, Auckland 1001 ℡09/307 2217, Ⓦwww.ubdonline.co.nz/maps.

Insurance

Even though EU health care privileges apply in France, you'd do well to take out an insurance policy before travelling to cover against theft, loss and illness or injury. Before paying for a new policy, however, it's worth checking whether you are already covered: some all-risks home insurance policies may cover your possessions when abroad, and many private medical schemes include cover when abroad. In Canada, provincial health plans usually provide partial cover for medical mishaps overseas, while holders of official student/teacher/youth cards in Canada and the USA are entitled to meagre accident coverage and hospital in-patient benefits. Students will often find that their student health coverage extends during the vacations and for one term beyond the date of last enrolment.

After exhausting the possibilities above, you might want to contact a specialist travel insurance company, or consider the travel insurance deal we offer (see box below). A typical travel insurance policy usually provides cover for the loss of baggage, tickets

Rough Guides travel insurance

Rough Guides offers its own travel insurance, customized for our readers by a leading UK broker and backed by a Lloyd's underwriter. It's available for anyone, of any nationality and any age, travelling anywhere in the world.

There are two main Rough Guide insurance plans: **Essential**, for basic, no-frills cover; and **Premier**, with more generous and extensive benefits. Alternatively, you can take out **annual multi-trip insurance**, which covers you for any number of trips throughout the year (with a maximum of 60 days for any one trip). Unlike many policies, the Rough Guides schemes are calculated by the day, so if you're travelling for 27 days rather than a month, that's all you pay for. If you intend to be away for the whole year, the Adventurer policy will cover you for 365 days. Each plan can be supplemented with a "Hazardous Activities Premium" if you plan to indulge in sports considered dangerous, such as skiing, scuba diving or trekking.

For a **policy quote**, call the Rough Guide Insurance Line on UK freefone ℡0800/015 0906; US toll-free ℡1-866/220-5588 or, if you're calling from elsewhere, ℡+44 1243/621 046. Alternatively, get an online quote or buy online at Ⓦwww.roughguidesinsurance.com.

and – up to a certain limit – cash or cheques, as well as cancellation or curtailment of your journey. Most of them exclude so-called dangerous sports unless an extra premium is paid: in France this can mean scuba diving, whitewater rafting, windsurfing and trekking, though probably not kayaking or jeep safaris. Many policies can be chopped and changed to exclude coverage you don't need – for example, sickness and accident benefits can often be excluded or included at will. If you do take medical cov-

erage, ascertain whether benefits will be paid as treatment proceeds or only after return home, and whether there is a 24-hour medical emergency number. When securing baggage cover, make sure that the per-article limit – typically under £500 – will cover your most valuable possession. If you need to make a claim, you should keep receipts for medicines and medical treatment, and in the event you have anything stolen, you must obtain an official statement from the police.

Health

No visitor to France requires vaccinations of any kind, and general health care in Corsica is of the highest standard. There are hospitals in all the main towns, and smaller places like Porto-Vecchio have clinics serving the surrounding area. EU nationals can take advantage of the French health services under the same terms as the residents of the island, as long as you're in possession of a form E111, application forms for which can be picked up at most major post offices. However, because the French health system provides subsidized rather than free treatment, travel insurance – covering health plus loss or theft of baggage – remains essential.

Under the French social security system, every hospital visit, doctor's consultation and prescribed medicine is charged – though in an emergency you won't be presented with the bill up front. Although all employed French people are entitled to a refund of 70–75 percent of their medical expenses, this can still leave a hefty shortfall, especially after a stay in hospital (accident victims even have to pay for the ambulance or helicopter that takes them there).

To find a **doctor**, stop at any *pharmacie* and ask for an address. Consultation fees

should be around €20–25, and after the visit you'll be given a *Feuille de Soins* (Statement of Treatment) for later documentation of insurance claims. **Prescriptions** should be taken to a *pharmacie*, which is also equipped, and obliged, to give first aid, for a fee. The medicines you buy will have little stickers (*vignettes*) attached to them, which you must remove and stick to your *Feuille de Soins*, together with the prescription itself. In serious **emergencies** you will always be admitted to the local hospital (*centre hospitalier*), whether under your own steam or by ambulance.

Costs, money and banks

On February 28, 2002, the euro superseded the franc français as France's sole legal tender. Euro coins come in eight different denominations, from 2 euros down to 1 cent. There are a total of seven euro notes, all in different colours and sizes, denominated in 500, 200, 100, 50, 20, 10 and 5 euros. In common with the rest of France, most Corsicans still find the new currency a little confusing and you'll often be quoted prices in francs. Menus and hotel tariff cards also tend to list rates in both currencies, which makes life a lot easier for British visitors, in particular, as the French franc rate was a lot simpler to convert than is the euro.

Costs

With a cost of living only slightly higher than the UK's, Corsica is no longer the exclusive luxury destination it used to be. That said, it can be disconcertingly easy to spend more money on the island than you might have intended. Aside from the obvious fact that most commodities have to be imported by sea or air, the main reason for this is Corsica's economic dependence on tourism, which ensures that from June until September prices of almost everything in demand by visitors – principally accommodation – rocket, allowing the locals to make enough cash during the short summer season to see them through the winter. However, your trip need not cost you a fortune, and throughout this book we highlight ways to help you enjoy the island on a minimum budget.

Unless you've prearranged somewhere to stay as part of a package holiday (see p.15),

accommodation will probably constitute your main expense, particularly if you come in July and August. The majority of hotels charge €35–65 for a double room. As a rule of thumb, places on the coast tend to be more expensive, with the best-value deals in the mountains of the interior, where there's far less seasonal price variation. Cheap *pensions* are rare, and where this type of accommodation exists it is listed in the Guide. Staying in campsites can be a money-saver as long as you stick to the basic sites found in rural areas (around €10–12 per day for two people, one tent and a car) and avoid the flashy three-star complexes along the coast, which can cost almost as much as a hotel. Travelling around the island out of season, you'll also find hoteliers ready to offer reductions, especially if you agree to stay for a couple of nights or more.

As for **food**, in any town you'll find restaurants with three- or four-course meals for

Rates of exchange and currency conversion

For up-to-the-minute rates of exchange go to: ⓦ www.oanda.com/convert/classic

Euros	UK£	US$	Can$	NZ$	Aus$
€1	£0.65	$0.99	$1.49	$2.00	$1.75
€5	£3.23	$4.94	$7.47	$10.00	$8.76
€10	£6.46	$9.89	$14.04	$20.00	$17.53
€15	£9.70	$14.83	$22.40	$30.00	$26.30
€20	£12.93	$19.77	$29.89	$40.00	$35.00
€30	£19.40	$29.66	$44.82	$60.00	$52.58
€40	£25.86	$39.54	$59.76	$80.00	$70.10
€50	£32.32	$49.43	$74.70	$100.00	$87.63
€100	£64.66	$98.86	$149.00	$200.00	$175.27

between €10 and €16, and the island is full of pizzerias where you can eat for even less than that. Picnic fare tends to be surprisingly expensive, especially if you buy cheese, charcuterie and other treats from Corsican speciality food outlets. Also worth bearing in mind is the expense of drinks in bars and cafés, particularly those situated on the beaches (*paillotes*), and the cost of wine in restaurants, which can easily double your bill.

Public transport costs around €18 for 100km, whether you're travelling by buses or by the *micheline* train (Bastia–Ajaccio is currently around €24). Petrol prices are amongst the highest in Europe, at €1.15 per litre for leaded ("Super") and €1.05 for unleaded. Car rental will set you back anything upwards of €225 per week, depending on the season (see p.30 for more details). Mountain bikes (VTTs) cost about €13–15 per day, and motorbikes start at around €50–60 per day for a 125cc Yamaha.

Museums and monuments won't prove too much of a drain on your resources, for the simple reason that there are relatively few on the island. Most charge between €3 and €5 and give discounts for holders of ISIC cards or to under-26s on presentation of a passport.

Thus, a **minimum daily requirement** (for food and accommodation only) would be around €35–40 per person, if camping and doing your own catering; a couple staying in budget hotels and eating in cheap restaurants could live comfortably on about €50–60 per person. Move around much, however, and you could easily find yourself spending considerably more than that. Finally, bear in mind local attitudes to money. Living on a rock-bottom budget – camping rough, eating nothing but bread and cheese, and avoiding bars and cafés altogether – is unlikely to endear you to the locals, who love to joke about *les mangeurs des tomates* – those die-hard backpackers and campervan tourists that are so eager to save money they miss out on one of the things Corsicans are deservedly most proud of: their wonderful cuisine.

Carrying your money

Traveller's cheques, one of the safest ways of carrying your money, are available from almost any of the principal banks, whether you have an account there or not. There's usually a service charge of one percent on the amount purchased, though some go as high as five percent (your own bank may offer cheques free of charge provided you meet certain conditions). Thomas Cook, Visa and American Express are the most widely recognized brands. In recent years, Thomas Cook traveller's cheques have been the best deal for British visitors to Corsica, as the Société Générale changes them without charging commission.

Make sure to keep the purchase agreement and a record of cheque serial numbers safe and separate from the cheques themselves. In the event that cheques are lost or stolen, the issuing company will expect you to report the loss forthwith to their office in your home country (you'll be given a freephone number when you buy the cheques); most companies claim to replace lost or stolen cheques within 24 hours.

Eurocheques – formerly the cheapest and most convenient way to pay on the continent – are no longer widely accepted in Corsica, not even by the large banks.

Credit and debit cards and ATMs

All over Corsica the major **credit cards** are almost universally accepted, enabling you to pay for meals, hotel bills, shopping and petrol – just watch for the window stickers. Visa – known as *Carte Bleue* in France – is the most widely recognized, followed by MasterCard (sometimes called EuroCard), with American Express and Access ranking considerably lower – only the Crédit Agricole bank provides facilities for Access, and many restaurants and hotels won't accept it because of the huge commissions they have to pay. Whichever card you have, always check in advance that the hotel or restaurant will accept it.

You can, of course, also use your credit card to withdraw money from banks, and **automatic cash dispensers** (ATMs or *distributeurs de billets*) during or outside normal banking hours. The commission tends to be higher – for example 4.1 percent instead of the 1.5 percent at home for Visa cards, but this can be well worth the convenience. The transaction itself takes a few seconds; your PIN number should be the same as the one you use for your bank at home, but check with your credit card company before you leave. Also, because French credit cards are smart cards, some ATMs refuse foreign plastic and may tell you that your request for money has been denied. If that happens, just try another machine. All ATMs give you the choice of instructions in French or English. Note that **post offices** in larger towns and villages tend to have ATMs these days, and many sub-post offices in out-of-the-way places also give cash advances on Visa credit cards – very handy if you run out of money in areas such as Cap Corse, where there are no machines.

Debit cards can also be used in ATMs, or to pay for goods and services if they carry the appropriate Visa or Maestro symbol or there's an "edc" (European acceptance) sign. You will be charged around one percent or a minimum of £1.50 to use your debit card in an ATM.

If you intend to use your credit or debit card as your principal means of obtaining cash while you're away, check before you leave that your daily or weekly limits are adequate, and confirm your card issuer's transaction charges. You should also take along a supply of traveller's cheques or currency in case the card is lost or stolen. Bear in mind, too, that credit cards are essential if you intend to rent a vehicle, as you'll need one to fill out the mandatory deposit docket (*caution*).

A compromise between traveller's cheques and plastic is **Visa TravelMoney**, a disposable pre-paid debit card with a PIN which works in all ATMs that take Visa cards. You load up your account with funds before leaving home, and when they run out, you simply throw the card away. You can buy up to nine cards to access the same funds – useful for couples or families travelling together – and it's a good idea to buy at least one extra as a backup in case of loss or theft. There is also a 24-hour toll-free customer assistance number (☏0-800-90-11-79 or go to ☹ http://usa.visa.com/personal/secure_with_visa/lost_your_card.html#numbs). The card is available in most countries from branches of Thomas Cook and Citicorp. For more information, check the Visa TravelMoney website at ☹ http://usa.visa.com/personal/cards/visa_travel_money.html.

Wiring money

Having money wired from home using one of the companies listed below is never convenient or cheap, and should be considered a last resort. It's also possible to have money wired directly from a bank in your home country to a bank in Corsica, although this is somewhat less reliable because it involves two separate institutions. If you go along this route, your home bank will need the address of the branch bank where you want to pick up the money and the address and telex number of the Ajaccio or Bastia head office, which will act as the clearing house; money wired this way normally takes two working days to arrive, and costs around £25/$40 per transaction.

Agents

American Express Moneygram
☹ www.moneygram.com. UK & Republic of Ireland ☏ 0800/6663 9472, USA & Canada ☏ 1-800/926-9400, Australia ☏ 1800/230 100, New Zealand ☏ 09/379 8243 or 0800/262 263.
Thomas Cook ☹ www.us.thomascook.com. UK ☏ 01733/318 922 (Belfast ☏ 028/9055 0030), Republic of Ireland ☏ 01/677 1721, USA ☏ 1-800/287-7362, Canada ☏ 1-888/823-4732.
Western Union ☹ www.westernunion.com. UK ☏ 0800/833 833, Republic of Ireland ☏ 1800/395 395, USA & Canada ☏ 1-800/325-6000, Australia ☏ 1800/649 565, New Zealand ☏ 09/270 0050.

Banks and exchange

Standard **banking hours** are Monday to Friday 9am to 4pm or 5pm, with most branches closing at noon for a couple of hours; some are also open on Saturdays 9am to noon. All are closed on Sunday and public holidays. The usual commission rate is one to two percent on traveller's cheques and a flat-rate charge on cash transactions (a €5 charge is not uncommon). As a rule of thumb, the high-street banks – Crédit Agricole, Crédit Lyonnais and Société Générale – give much better value than the privately run **bureaux de change** around the island.

Getting around

The overwhelming majority of visitors to Corsica come with their own vehicle or else rent one for the duration of their holiday. Given the manifest inadequacies of public transport – at least outside peak season, when services to most areas are drastically scaled down – this isn't surprising. But with a little flexibility and forward planning you can still reach all but the most remote corners of the island by bus or train, and throughout the Guide we've included information to help you on your way. Quite apart from reducing the overall cost of your trip, by travelling on public transport you'll be doing your bit to minimize pollution on an island that strains to cope with the extra tourists in summer.

Journey times and frequencies for buses, trains and ferries are given in "Travel details" at the end of each chapter, but bear in mind that timetables tend to change annually; you can always check schedules at a tourist office, or by phoning the transport company direct.

By car

For visitors used to the comparatively restrained roads and traffic manners of northern Europe, driving in Corsica can come as a rude shock. Once you're off the smooth national highways (*Routes Nationales*, prefixed with N), the constantly twisting *routes départementales* (prefixed with a D) present their fair share of hazards, not least of all **Corsican drivers** themselves, who race rally-style around the bends and habitually overtake in perilous situations. For this reason, expect to meet vehicles approaching at speed in the middle of the road, even on blind corners and brows of hills. If you find yourself with a local car breathing down your neck, pull over and let it pass at the first opportunity; nothing annoys Corsicans more than being held up by a cautious tourist in a rented car. Note, also, that the mountain and corniche roads are pitted with great potholes, while pigs or goats present further dangers.

EU and US **driving licences** are valid in France. If the vehicle is rented (see below), its registration document (*carte grise*) and the insurance papers must be carried (they are usually stored in the glove compartment of rental cars). In Australia, international driv-ers' licences can be purchased from the RAC (Royal Automobile Club) offices in most major towns and cities, and from the AA (Automobile Association) in New Zealand.

The French law of *priorité à droite* – **giving way** to traffic coming from your right, even when it is coming from a minor road – is gradually being phased out. It is sometimes respected in built-up areas of Bastia and Ajaccio, however, so you still have to be vigilant in towns, keeping a lookout for the yellow diamond on a white background that gives you right of way, until you see the same sign with an oblique slash, which indicates that vehicles emerging from the right have right of way. At **roundabouts** the cars on the roundabout have priority. *CÉDEZ LE PASSAGE* means "Give way", a *STOP* sign means come to a complete halt.

Speed limits are 110kph (68mph) on two-lane highways, 90kph (56mph) on other roads in non-urban areas, and 60kph (37mph) in towns. **Fines** for exceeding the speed limit by 1–30kph range from €150 to €1000, and are exacted on the spot, with only cash accepted. There are no toll roads in Corsica.

As for **fuel**, note that in remote country areas – such as Cap Corse and the interior – petrol stations are especially scarce, so remember to fill up in the towns. Unleaded fuel (*sans plomb*) is available everywhere.

Car rental

Given the competitive rates on offer, **renting a car** can work out cheaper than you think. In 2002, rock-bottom prices for a small hatchback were typically around £130–150/US$200–240 per week.

See p.455 for useful driving vocabulary.

To rent a car in Corsica you have to be over 21 (and in some cases over 25) and have been in possession of a clean licence (ie with no more than six points) for at least one year. All the international rental companies are represented on the island, with branches at the airports and in major towns, and there are numerous local firms, too. Some of these offer better deals than their larger competitors, although it can sometimes be difficult for non-French speakers to obtain quotes and details in advance. One local outfit worth phoning, however, is Rent-a-Car, based at the *Hôtel Kallisté* in Ajaccio (see p.207), whose staff all speak fluent English.

Another option is to look into the **fly-drive** deals offered by tour operators and consolidators (see p.11), who sometimes tack on a week's car rental to their discounted flights for as little as £100/US$160. Members of frequent-flyer clubs (such as British Airways' Executive Club) may also have access to special discounts, while passengers on British Midland are entitled to a ten percent discount on Avis cars.

When phoning a car rental company for a quote, ensure the price you're offered includes the following: unlimited mileage, collision damage waiver (check on the level of excess you are liable for if you cause any damage), theft protection, third-party insurance, licensing fee (aka "road surcharge") and airport surcharge. If you intend to share the driving with someone else, make sure they're eligible, and ask how much it will cost to name them as a second driver (usually around £15/US$25 extra per driver per week). Other points to clarify before booking might be whether or not it is possible to drop the car off in a different place to where you picked it up (and, if so, how much this costs), and whether you get a better deal by paying two or more weeks in advance.

If you **break down** in a rented vehicle, contact the rental company via the emergency number you'll have been given when you collected the car (it usually appears somewhere in the documents wallet). If you're in your own vehicle, consider taking out **extra insurance cover** for emergency recovery; in the UK, this typically costs around £59 for a fortnight. Look into the RAC's European Motoring Assistance (☎0800/550 055, ⓦwww.rac.co.uk), the AA's Five-Star Europe cover (☎0800/444 500, ⓦwww.theaa.co.uk)

or Europ Assistance (☎0645/947 000, ⓦwww.europ-assistance.com).

As in your home country, if you have an accident, exchange registration numbers (*numéros d'immatriculation*) with any other drivers involved. Break-ins should be reported to the local police in order to make an insurance claim, and in the event of an accident you are also obliged to complete a *constat à l'aimable* (jointly agreed statement), which your car insurers or rental company should give you.

Agencies in UK

Autos Abroad ☎0870/066 7788, ⓦwww.autosabroad.co.uk.
Avis ☎0870/606 0100, ⓦwww.avis.co.uk.
Budget ☎0800/181 181, ⓦwww.budget.co.uk.
Europcar ☎0845/722 2525, ⓦwww.europcar.co.uk.
Hertz ☎0870/844 8844, ⓦwww.hertz.co.uk.
Holiday Autos ☎0870/400 0099, ⓦwww.holidayautos.co.uk.
National ☎0870/536 5365, ⓦwww.nationalcar.com.
Suncars ☎0870/500 5566, ⓦwww.suncars.com.
Thrifty ☎01494/751 600, Northern Ireland ☎028/9445 2565, ⓦwww.thrifty.co.uk.

Agencies in Ireland

Argus ☎01/490 4444, ⓦwww.argus-rentacar.com.
Atlas ☎01/844 4859, ⓦwww.atlascarhire.com.
Avis ☎01/605 7500, ⓦwww.avisworld.com.
Budget ☎01/9032 7711, ⓦwww.budgetcarrental.ie.
Europcar Republic of Ireland ☎01/614 2800, ⓦwww.europcar.ie.
Hertz ☎01/676 7476, ⓦwww.hertz.co.uk.
Holiday Autos ☎01/872 9366, ⓦwww.holidayautos.ie.
SIXT ☎1850/206 088, ⓦwww.irishcarrentals.ie.

Agencies in North America

Alamo USA ☎1-800/522-9696, ⓦwww.alamo.com.
Auto Europe USA ☎1-800/223-5555, Canada ☎1-888/223-5555, ⓦwww.autoeurope.com.
Avis USA ☎1-800/331-1084, Canada ☎1-800/272-5871, ⓦwww.avis.com.
Budget USA ☎1-800/527-0700, ⓦwww.budgetrentacar.com.
Dollar USA ☎1-800/800-4000, ⓦwww.dollar.com.
Enterprise Rent-a-Car USA ☎1-800/325-8007, ⓦwww.enterprise.com.

Europe by Car USA ☎1-800/223-1516,
ⓦwww.europebycar.com.
Hertz USA ☎1-800/654-3001, Canada ☎1-800/263-0600, ⓦwww.hertz.com.
Kemwel Holiday Autos USA ☎1-800/422-7737,
ⓦwww.kemwel.com.
National ☎1-800/227-7368,
ⓦwww.nationalcar.com.
Thrifty ☎1-800/367-2277, ⓦwww.thrifty.com.

Agencies in Australia

Avis ☎13 63 33, ⓦwww.avis.com.
Budget ☎1300/362 848, ⓦwww.budget.com.
Dollar ☎02/9223 1444 or 1800/358 008,
ⓦwww.dollarcar.com.au.
Hertz ☎13 30 39, ⓦwww.hertz.com.
National ☎13 10 45, ⓦwww.nationalcar.com.au.

Agencies in New Zealand

Apex ☎0800/939 597, ⓦwww.apexrentals.co.nz.
Avis ☎0800 655 111 or 09/526 2847,
ⓦwww.avis.co.nz.
Budget ☎0800/652 227 or 09/976 2222,
ⓦwww.budget.co.nz.
Hertz ☎0800/654 321, ⓦwww.hertz.co.nz.
National ☎0800/800 115 or 03/366 5574,
ⓦwww.nationalcar.co.nz.
Thrifty ☎09/309 0111, ⓦwww.thrifty.co.nz.

Agencies in Corsica

ACL Rent-a-Car ☎04 95 51 34 45,
ⓦwww.rentacar.fr.
Avis ☎04 95 23 56 90, ⓦwww.avis.fr.
Budget ☎04 95 35 05 04,
ⓦwww.budget-en-corse.com.
Citer ☎04 95 70 16 95, ⓦwww.corse-auto-rent.fr.
Europcar ☎04 95 30 09 50,
ⓦwww.europcar.com.
Hertz Locasud ☎04 95 23 57 04,
ⓦwww.hertz.fr.

By bicycle

Corsica is no soft option for cyclists, but if you're in good shape you'll enjoy the challenge of the island's convoluted routes and long climbs. The main disadvantage is the traffic, combined with the narrowness of the roads. In summer, you'll also have the fumes to contend with, as well as the ferocious heat. All in all, it's a better idea to come in mid-season – May–June and Sept–Oct – and aim to avoid the traffic as much as possible.

> For more on **mountain biking** in Corsica, see "Outdoor pursuits" on p.49.

If you want to **bring your bike** from home, flying is by far the easiest way; provided you box it in the prescribed way, most airlines will transport it free of charge. Car ferries also carry bicycles for free, but the French railway SNCF charges a flat fee of €25 for transporting your bike, which cannot be taken on the train you're travelling on; usually there's a three- or four-day time-lag between your arrival at a given place and your bike's arrival. If you are taking your own bike from the UK, it's a good idea to join the **Cyclists' Touring Club** (Cotterell House, 68 Meadrow, Godalming, Surrey GU7 3HS ☎0870/873 0060, ⓦwww.ctc.org.uk), which will suggest routes and supply advice to members; they also run a particularly good insurance scheme. The cost of membership is £27 a year (£16.50 for students, the unemployed and under-12s).

A handful of companies around the island rent **cycles**, usually mountain bikes, *vélos tous terrains* (*VTT*) in French. Rates are fairly standard, at €13–15 per day, or €80 per week, with small discounts of fifteen to twenty percent out of season. You're also usually required to leave a credit card docket or around €300–450 in cash as a deposit (*caution*). See p.455 for useful cycling vocabulary.

Mountain bike (VTT) rental companies in Corsica

Ajaccio BMS Location, Port Tino Rossi ☎04 95 21 33 75 or 04 95 24 56 55; Corse Évasion, Montée St-Jean ☎04 95 20 52 05, ⓦwww.corsicamoto.com; Locacorse, 10 av Beverini-Vico ☎04 95 20 71 20, Ⓕ04 95 20 44 52; Rout'Évasion, 10 av Noel Franchini ☎04 95 22 72 87, Ⓕ04 95 22 46 69.
Bastia Objectif Nature, rue Notre-Dame-de Lourdes ☎04 95 32 54 34.
Calvi Location Ambrosini, rue Villa-Antoine ☎04 95 65 02 13.
Porto Porto Location, opposite Spar supermarket ☎04 95 26 10 13.
Propriano TCC Sarl, 25 rue Général-de-Gaulle ☎04 95 76 15 32; Location Valinco, 25 av Napoléon ☎04 95 76 11 84.

By motorcycle

Corsica is perfect **motorcycle** terrain, and during the summer its roads are teeming with tourers (most of them from Germany). If you've come without your own vehicle or can't afford to rent a car, you might consider **renting a bike**. This used to be relatively inexpensive compared to car rental, but today's high insurance premiums have pushed most of the smaller operators out of business, and forced prices to often prohibitive levels.

Bikes can be rented at various towns and resorts around the island, and the choice of vehicles on offer is pretty standard; only the prices vary. Cheapest of all, at around €30–35 per day, is a 50cc moped. While these are fine for nipping to and from the beach, they tend to struggle on the hills, which effectively writes off most of the island except the eastern plain. Nor do they tend to have any luggage-carrying facilities. For a trip into the interior or around the coast, you'll need at least a Vespa-style 100cc scooter. Starting at around €40 per day (or €200 per week), these can comfortably carry a rider and pillion passenger on level ground, and will make it over even the highest mountain passes if you're riding solo. Trials-style 125cc bikes are also widely available, though they cost upwards of €50–60 per day (€230–250 per week); anything larger than that – such as a Yamaha XTE 600cc – will set you back €70–85 (or €360–375 per week).

In addition to the daily rental rate, you'll need to leave a hefty **deposit** (*caution*) of around €800–1000. Rather than accept a cheque or cash, most companies these days prefer to swipe a credit card through their machine and keep the docket as security, tearing it up if you return the bike in a satisfactory condition.

Rental vehicles take some rough treatment, so check yours thoroughly before you ride off to make sure the brakes, lights and horn work. You should also check for any scratches or bumps with the owner present. The cost of renta generally includes a helmet, and covers third-party insurance, but not damage incurred to the vehicle in any accident – another reason to ride defensively. Crash your bike, and you'll almost certainly have to foot the bill. Theft is another problem – every year, rented scooters are stolen from car parks above beaches. For this reason, owners should issue you with a strong D-lock (*anti-vol*) or chain, which you fasten around the front wheel.

This, however, will at best only act as a deterrent, so be sure to use the steering lock

as well each time you park up. If the bike does get stolen, notify the rental company and local police immediately. In theory, the company should be covered by their insurance for theft, but check this before you leave their office; some insist on retaining most or all of your deposit if a bike disappears.

Motorcycle rental companies in Corsica

Ajaccio Cyrnos Location, *Hôtel Kallisté*, 51 cours Napoléon ☎04 95 51 61 81 or 04 95 23 56 36, Ⓦwww.cyrnos.net; Locacorse, 10 av Bévérini-Vico ☎04 95 20 71 20; Moto Corse Évasion, Montée St-Jean ☎04 95 20 52 05, Ⓦwww.corsicamoto.com; BMS Location, Port Tino Rossi ☎04 95 21 33 75.

Bastia Plaisance Service Location, Port Toga ☎04 95 31 49 01.

Bonifacio Corse Moto Services, quai Nova ☎04 95 73 15 16.

Calvi Location Ambrosini, rue Villa-Antoine ☎04 95 65 02 13.

Porto-Vecchio Suzuki Garage, route du Port-de-Plaisance ☎04 95 70 36 50.

Propriano TCC Sarl, 25 rue Général-de-Gaulle ☎04 95 76 15 32; Location Valinco, 25 av Napoléon ☎04 95 76 11 84.

By bus

Buses are Corsica's principal form of public transport, but, as most Corsicans own at least one car, demand outside the tourist season is minimal (for the most part, only visitors, students, pensioners and migrant workers use the buses). Even in summer, services on many routes are infrequent, to say the least, and if you rely purely on buses to get around your travels will be limited to a handful of arterial routes – between Bastia and Ajaccio (via Corte), Ajaccio and Porto-Vecchio (via Propriano, Sartène and Bonifacio), and Porto-Vecchio and Bastia (via Aléria) – along with a couple of routes in Alta Rocca and the northwest coast to and from Porto (via Cargèse).

In rural areas, the timetables tend to be constructed to suit working and school hours, which means there's often just one bus a day in any direction, departing at a dauntingly early hour. To confuse matters, virtually each route is covered by a different company, making it frustratingly difficult to obtain accurate timetable information. In theory, tourist offices should have up-to-date schedules (*horaires*) but you can't guarantee it.

The easiest way to work out which company serves which towns is to consult the "Travel details" section at the end of each chapter; this will include a brief outline of the region's main routes and contact numbers for the bus operator. Most accounts in the Guide section also list transport information.

Fares on Corsican buses are high, though the vehicles themselves are comfortable enough and kept in good condition. Trunk routes are served by large coaches, while the mountain villages of the interior and the northwest coast are connected by modern minibuses.

By train

Corsica's diminutive, bone-shaking **train**, the *micheline* or *trinighellu* (little train), crosses the mountains from Ajaccio to Bastia via Corte, with a subsidiary line running from Ponte Leccia, north of Corte, to Calvi. Constructed at the end of the nineteenth century, the 230-kilometre line, which boasts 32 tunnels, follows a rattling and precarious route across the mountains, transporting around 800,000 passengers each year. Plans are afoot to revamp completely the track and rolling stock, which will significantly increase the speed of services, but at the time of writing travelling by rail was still slower than the bus. All the same, it's an unmissable trip that you should try to do at least once, if only in one direction; the scenery is wonderful from start to finish, and there are plenty of tempting spots to get off and walk along the route. The line's most impressive feat of engineering is the famous pont du Vecchio at Vivario, designed by Gustave Eiffel in 1825. Crossing it, you get a matchless view across to the dizzying new pont du Vecchio road bridge, completed in 1999, with a span of 222m and a height of 137.5m. A short way further south, at Vizzavona, the line plunges into the watershed, which it crosses by means of a 3916-metre-long tunnel.

Tickets cost about the same as the buses (€23 for Ajaccio–Bastia and €27 for Ajaccio–Calvi). ISIC card-carrying students are entitled to discounts; bicycles go for free.

If you intend to make several journeys by train, consider investing in a **Carte Zoom**, which entitles you to unlimited rail travel over a seven-day period for a flat rate of €45; this also covers free use of CFC left-luggage (*consignes*). The cards are available from any station on the Corsican railway.

Timetables can always be checked at the stations, at local tourist offices or over the phone using the numbers listed throughout the guide. For 24-hour recorded timetable information call ☎04 95 32 80 60.

Accommodation

Protection of the natural environment and traditional architecture has always been a cornerstone of the Corsican nationalist agenda, and as a consequence the island holds few unsightly modern developments of the kind that nowadays blight much of the Mediterranean. Even around the popular resort beaches of Porto-Vecchio, building styles are for the most part low-rise and restrained, with few large and intrusive hotels and a correspondingly high number of private rental properties. Those visitors unable to afford such comforts have little alternative but to pitch in the many campsites that spring up in June.

Where good-value, inexpensive places to stay exist, you'll find them reviewed in the Guide, alongside the best accommodation choices at the top and bottom of the range, from farm campsites to luxury four-star resort hotels. Wherever you choose to stay, it's advisable to book ahead, especially during the "Grandes Vacances" – from mid-July to the end of August – when the French and Italians take their holidays en masse. The Language section at the back of this book (see p.447) should help you make your reservation, as few hoteliers or campsite managers speak any English.

In the event that all the places reviewed by us for the area you're in are full (*complet*), your best bet would be to visit the local tourist office and ask for their free accommodation brochure (*guide des hébergements*). These list virtually everywhere within reach and worthy of note, complete with a little photo, contact details, current prices and a rundown of facilities. Once you've settled on a place, the tourist officer should also help make the reservation if your French isn't up to the phone call.

Hotels

By comparison with the UK, hotel accommodation in Corsica represents extremely good value for money – at least outside the mid-July to August peak season.

Establishments are graded on a scale that rises to four stars. Room rates reflect the number of stars, but it's worth remembering that most places offer a spread of differently priced options of varying degrees of comforts, outlined in a list which you'll be presented with at reception.

It's unusual to find rooms costing less than €35, and those that do tend to be basic; they'll probably have a washbasin (*lavabo*), and sometimes a bidet, but little else. The shower (*douche*) and toilets (WC) will be outside on the corridor (*à l'étage*).

At the **one-star** level you can expect to pay €35–50 for a double, perhaps with a shower and toilet but probably not a bath-

tub. **Two-star** places, with fully en-suite facilities and often a small balcony, charge around €50–75. **Three-star** hotels usually cost between €75 and €100, for which you should enjoy a spacious double room with bathroom, television, large terrace or balcony, and access to a pool.

Breakfast can add €5–9 per person to a bill (if it's included you'll be told at check-in time), though you'll be under no obligation to have it and will invariably do better buying your own pâtisserie at a bakery and taking it to a café. The cost of **dinner** in a hotel's restaurant can be a more important factor to bear in mind when picking a place to stay. Some hotels insist you opt for half board (*demi-pension*), particularly in peak season. This may or may not be a good deal, depending on the quality of the restaurant and how much access to the main menu your half board entitles you.

Single rooms are typically one third cheaper than doubles, so sharing always keeps down the cost. Some hotels will provide extra beds (*lits supplémentaires*) for three or more, charging around 25 percent per bed. Note that many hotels are **open only in summer**, usually from May to September – we've indicated in the Guide those establishments that close for the winter. The ones that do stay open in winter often offer discounts to off-season visitors.

Chambres d'hôtes and ferme-auberges

Some of the most congenial private accommodation in Corsica is offered in small, rural bed-and-breakfast establishments, or **chambres d'hôtes**. There are dozens of places dotted around the island where you can stay as a fee-paying guest in someone's home, usually in a newly converted wing or modern annexe of a farmhouse. As you'd expect, the experience is more personal, especially in those places where evening meals are offered, giving you a chance to get to know your hosts. Room tariffs are not cheap, averaging from around €50–75 for two, including breakfast, but for many visitors, particularly those keen to practise their French, the off-the-beaten-track locations and warm Corsican hospitality give *chambres d'hôtes* the edge over most hotels.

Ferme-auberges, literally "farm-inns", are similar to *chambres d'hôtes*, but with the emphasis being essentially on the food: classy Corsican speciality dishes, made from locally produced ingredients. The hosts may, or may not, offer rooms, but if they do you'll be able to stay in one only if you have dinner. For this reason, prices are given as half board (*demi-pension*), which covers the room, breakfast and evening meal.

Rented houses

If you're planning to stay a week or more in any one place, it might be worth considering **renting a house**. The easiest and most reliable way to do this is through a package company before you leave home (see p.15), as holiday firms tend to acquire the pick of the properties in any given area. Alternatively, contact **Relais régional des gîtes de ruraux** in Ajaccio (77 cours Napoléon, BP 10, 20000 Ajaccio ☎04 95 10 54 30, ⓦwww.gites -corsica.com; Mon–Sat 10am–6.30pm) for a brochure, or check their website, then simply reserve a place for any number of full weeks over the phone or online. Other holiday villa websites worth a browse include: ⓦwww .guidevacances.com/gites/corse.html and ⓦwww.mylinea.com/gites/.

Finally, you can wait until you arrive in Corsica and ask any local tourist office for a list of properties to rent (*locations de partic- ulier*) in their region. For somewhere large enough to accommodate a family of four to five, expect to pay from €325 to €450 per week off season, or €450 to €800 in the school holidays. The rates may be less expensive than renting a villa through an agency, but there's obviously the risk that nothing will be available when you need it.

Bear in mind, too, that gîtes and other rented houses are normally available only on a week-to-week basis.

Gîtes d'étape and refuges

Corsica has dozens of gîtes d'étape and refuges situated at crucial stages along the main hiking trails (see p.365). Although designed primarily for walkers, anyone can stay at them and in several remote villages of the interior and northwest coast they often constitute the only budget accommodation.

Gîtes d'étape are essentially hikers' hostels offering basic accommodation, usually in four- to six-bunk-bed dormitories with communal hot showers and toilets; some also offer fully en-suite doubles, at far cheaper rates than comparable hotels. When demand is high, you'll have to share the dorm with others, but during off-peak periods the wardens (*gardi- ens*) try to put clients in separate rooms for the price of a single bed (around €10). Half board is generally offered for around €30 per person, and may even be obligatory. It's rare to find a gîte that's not kept in immaculate condition, and many have attractive terraces or gardens. Self-catering facilities are always provided, and included in the cost of the bed, but most walkers opt for half board, which can work out good value. As a rule, you can also **camp** in the garden for around the same price as a cheap campsite. Unlike hotels, the peak periods for gîtes are the walking sea- sons, from late May until early July and through September, when you should reserve a bed as far in advance as possible.

Situated in remote mountain locations, well away from roads, **refuges** are hikers' huts, converted from shepherds' crofts or ancient stone dwellings. While some provide little more than a roof, others have fully equipped kitchens, dining rooms, common dormitory and toilets. Most also have a bivouac area nearby where you can bed down outdoors or pitch a tent. Along the GR20, refuges are manned from late May until mid-September by *gardiens* who also collect the daily fee (€9 per bed or roughly half that for campers and bivouackers). Places in refuges are allo- cated on a first-come, first-served basis, and cannot be reserved in advance.

All refuges and gîtes d'étape are marked on the large-scale IGN maps; you'll also find listings for the gîtes d'étape, complete with full contact details, in our coverage of the island's long-distance walks (see p.359).

Camping

Practically every locality has at least one **campsite** to cater for the thousands of French, German and Italians who spend their holiday under canvas or in recreation vehicles. The cheapest – costing around €10–14 per night for a couple, tent and car – are small, family-run farm campsites (known as **campings à la ferme**), which offer basic amenities in attractive settings. They tend to be a much more pleasant experience, and better value, than the supe- rior categories of campsite dotted around the coast, where you'll pay prices similar to those of a one-star hotel for facilities such as bars, restaurants, tennis courts and swimming pools. People spend their whole holiday in these places – if you plan to do the same, and particularly if you have a caravan or a big tent, it's wise to book ahead. Throughout the Guide, we've picked out the best sites in each area, basing our choices on the attractiveness of the setting (and cleanliness of the washrooms); standards of both can vary enormously, particularly during the congested summer months.

Lastly, a **word of caution**: never camp rough (*camping sauvage*) on anyone's land without first asking their permission: it's illegal. Camping on beaches is also technically against the law, though a lot of people do it in remote areas such as the Désert des Agriates and Littoral Sartenais. Wherever you camp, be careful with **fires**, as the maquis burns quickly.

Eating and drinking

In common with their Continental compatriots, Corsicans take their food and drink very seriously indeed. At 12.30pm sharp, a mini rush hour in towns across the island heralds the return of workers home, or to a local restaurant, for a leisurely three-course meal, whose dishes may well be the subject of avid discussions throughout the afternoon. The quality and authenticity of Corsican cuisine, in particular, can provoke passionate feelings: a former president of the Chamber of Agriculture was murdered recently for his stand against battery pig farming (see box on p.40), while a wine adulteration scandal at Aléria in 1975 led to a bloody armed siege (see p.301).

For some visitors, the islanders' attitude to food can seem obsessive at times, but it does ensure that standards in restaurants are generally high, and prices low. Even travellers on tight budgets should be able to afford to eat in pizzerias, and you'll be missing out on one of the region's undisputed highlights if you don't sample a full-scale Corsican speciality meal at some point.

On the whole, **vegetarians** can expect an easier time than they might in mainland France. Several Corsican standards – including *omelette à la menthe*, stuffed aubergines and *cannelloni al brocciu* – are vegetarian dishes that you'll find on menus everywhere; and there are always plenty of meat-free options on offer in pizzerias. Remember the phrase "*Je suis végétarien(ne). Est-ce qu'il y a quelques plats sans viande?*" ("I'm a vegetarian. Are there any non-meat dishes?"). **Vegans**, however, should probably forget about eating in Corsican restaurants and stick to self-catering.

For a **glossary** of food and drink terms see p.456.

Breakfast and snacks

A typical café **breakfast** in Corsica consists of a croissant or pain au chocolat (the barman will usually leave a basket of pastries on your table and bill you according to how many you eat), served with hot chocolate or coffee. In coastal resorts, you'll find many places offering *petit déjeuner complet*, with half a baguette, butter and jam, fruit juice and a croissant for around €5–9 per person. Hotels invariably do set breakfasts for guests, too, but charge more and their dining rooms are often less appealing than a sunny café terrace.

At **lunchtime**, and sometimes in the evening, you may find cafés and small bistros offering *plats du jour* (chef's daily specials) from between €9 and €12, or *formules*, a limited or no-choice menu. Croque-monsieur or croque-madame (variations on the toasted ham-and-cheese sandwich) are offered at cafés and street stands, along with *frites*, panini (filled and

37

toasted French sticks), *glaces* (ice creams), slices of pizza, *bruscetta*, and all kinds of fresh sandwiches. Cafés in the mountains will make you up a *casse-croûte*, a huge sandwich often filled with a generous slice of *lonzu* (cured ham) or local *saucisse*, and *fromage corse* (local cheese). Most restaurants also offer a wide range of mixed **salads** from €5–8, although the standard of these varies enormously. A much safer bet is generally a plate of Corsican charcuterie or cheese, served with fresh bread and a small *pichet* of wine for €9–12.

Crêpes, thin pancakes with fillings, served up at ubiquitous *crêperies*, are popular lunchtime food – at least among tourists. The savoury buckwheat variety (often called *galettes*) provide the main course; the sweet white-flour ones, dessert. They taste nice enough, but are usually poor value in comparison with a restaurant meal; you need at least three, normally at over €4.50 each, to feel full. **Pizzerias**, serving pizzas usually *au feu de bois* (wood-fired) are also common. With most pizzas costing between €7 and €11, they offer better value for money than *crêperies*, but quality varies greatly – look before you leap into the nearest empty seats.

For **picnics**, local shops and supermarkets can provide you with almost anything you need from fruit, avocados and tomatoes, to pâté, cheese, yoghurt and salad oils, and a visit to a *rôtisserie* or charcuterie is always rewarding. Cooked meat, ready-made dishes, quiches and assorted salads can all be bought by weight from the latter, or you can ask for *une tranche* (a slice), *une barquette* (a carton) or *une part* (a portion).

Salons de thé, though few and far between, serve cakes and ice cream and a wide selection of teas. They tend to be a good deal pricier than cafés, as you pay for the swish decor, and they generally have a more female clientele and ambience. **Pâtisseries** also do wonderful cakes and local sweet delicacies such as chestnut cake and *fiadone* (see p.461), as well as some savoury snacks such as pizza and *tartelettes* (mini-quiches) and *canistrelli* (Corsican speciality-style biscuits).

Full-scale meals

During the tourist season, when the island seems to sport as many **restaurants** as it does pleasure boats, there's no reason why you shouldn't eat consistently well for a fraction of what you'd pay at home. The only problem is knowing where to find value for money. The resorts, in particular, are littered with places churning out indifferent microwave meals for large groups of undiscerning tourists.

Throughout the Guide, we've reviewed dependable restaurants and auberges (inns) to suit every budget. However, many change hands and have their ups and downs, and it's always worth asking locals or French people you meet for recommendations. This is the Corsican equivalent of commenting on the weather in Britain and may well elicit strong opinions. Above all, don't be afraid to take a chance on somewhere off the beaten track if it's been recommended. Many of the island's most acclaimed restaurants are lost deep in the maquis, without signs to show you the way. Dependent on word of mouth for their predominantly local custom, they are often classed as *ferme-auberges* (farm-inns), where top Corsican cuisine, made entirely from fresh, locally grown ingredients, is served in appropriately rustic surroundings.

With all *ferme-auberges*, and in touristy areas in high season, it's wise to make **reservations** – easily done on the same day. In small towns and villages, and during the winter, it may be difficult to find something open after 10pm, though in the larger resorts there's always at least a pizzeria open until midnight through the summer. Don't forget that hotel restaurants are usually open to non-residents, and are often good value.

Prices, and what you get for them, are posted outside restaurants. Normally there's a choice between one, or more, *menus fixes* – where the number of courses is predetermined and choice is limited – and choosing individually from the à la carte menu. The least expensive option is usually the **menu fixe**. At the bottom of the range, these revolve around standard dishes such as *cannelloni al brocciu*, lasagne, or fried fish of some kind (*friture du golfe* is common), and cost on average around €15–17.50. Further up the scale, there's usually a *menu Corse* that can be by far the best-value way of sampling regional cuisine, running to five or more courses that usually include delicious local charcuterie and *fromage*.

The *plat du jour*, often a regional dish, might well be featured on the *menu fixe*, but for unlimited access to the chef's specialities you'll have to go **à la carte**, where you can expect to pay upwards of €9 for the main course. A perfectly legitimate tactic is to order just one course instead of the three or four. You can share dishes or go for several starters – a useful strategy for vegetarians. In Corsica, as in the rest of France, any salad (sometimes vegetables, too) comes separate from the main dish, and you will be offered coffee, which is also charged extra, to finish off the meal. Your Corsican hosts may also offer you a small glass of eau de vie, local firewater, on the house to round off your meal. Fish, incidentally, is sold by weight; the price quoted represents the cost per 100g, so check how much it will come to before the waiter disappears with it into the kitchen or you could get a nasty shock when your bill arrives.

Unlike most Mediterranean countries, Corsica has a fair selection of traditional **desserts**, the majority of them milk-and-egg-based concoctions such as *fiadone* (tart made with soft cheese) which locals love to soak in spirit and flambée. In more serious Corsican restaurants and quality pâtisseries, you'll also come across *beignets*, little fritters made from chestnut flour and often stuffed with ewe's cheese (*brocciu*). Run-of-the-mill French desserts – crème caramel, chocolate mousse or a piece of fruit – are also widely available, although rarely as good.

Service compris or *s.c.* means the **service charge** is included. *Service non compris*, *s.n.c.*, means that it isn't and you need to calculate an additional fifteen percent. **Wine** (*vin*) or a **drink** (*boisson*) is unlikely to be included, though occasionally it is thrown in with cheaper menus (*menus fixes*). When ordering wine, ask for *un quart* (0.25 litre), *un demi-litre* (0.5 litre), *une carafe* (a litre) or *un pichet* (a jug). You'll normally be given the house wine unless you specify otherwise.

It is regarded as self-evident that large family groups should be able to eat out together, and Corsicans are, on the whole, very well disposed towards **children** in restaurants, not simply by offering reduced-priced children's menus but in creating an atmosphere that positively welcomes kids. That said, you'll find locals intolerant of undisciplined behaviour; screaming children invariably provoke disapproving looks and gruff comments in Corsican if left unchecked.

Corsican specialities

Whereas French cuisine traditionally relies upon complicated recipes and a large number of often unlikely ingredients for flavour, in Corsica freshness and simplicity are considered the essence of good cooking, with the emphasis more on quality than process.

For any important family meal, **meat** will invariably form the main course. Wild boar (*sanglier*) is probably the dish most closely associated with Corsica, whose forests remain well populated, despite the seasonal onslaught from camouflaged *chasseurs*. These days, however, if you see *sanglier* on a menu it's more likely to be free-range pork than real boar. Pigs, who feed on the chestnuts that were once the staple food in many regions such as Castagniccia, are reared in huge numbers to make **charcuterie**, which in Corsica has been elevated to an art form. Wherever you go you'll find a bewildering selection of cured meats on offer: *prisutu* (smoked ham), *figatellu* and *fitonu* (long liver sausages eaten chilled or grilled), *coppa* (shoulder), *lonzu* (smoked fillet), *salamu* (spicy salami-style sausage), *valetta* (cheek), *boudin* (hard sausage) and *fromage de tête* ("head cheese", made from seasoned pigs' brains). Most *charcutiers* are happy for you to taste, and artisanal meat outlets are dotted all over the island where you can sample the full gamut before buying.

Other typically Corsican meat dishes include *cabri de lait* (suckling kid), veal (served with local olives) and, in the winter hunting season, slow-cooked game stew (*tianu*). At this time, many auberges will also feature locally shot **game** on their menus: roast woodcock (*bécasse*), partridge (*pédrix*) and blackbird (*merle*) pâté. To accompany a meat dish, you might be offered some kind of fresh pasta (tagliatelle is a favourite), or *pulenta* (polenta), a stodgy mash made from chestnut or maize flour, which can be fried or sweetened with caster sugar, and eau de vie or liqueur.

As you'd expect, **seafood** predominates on the coast. Reduced fish stocks in the waters around Corsica (the result of overfishing) mean that supplies are notoriously irregular and prices high. But you can bank on finding red mullet (*rouget*) and sea bream (*loup de mer*) during the summer, as well as a great variety of shellfish – the best crayfish (*langouste*) comes from around the Golfe de St-Florent, whereas oysters (*huîtres*) are a speciality of the eastern plain. **Trout** (*truite*) are fished from the unpolluted rivers and are a popular alternative to meat dishes in inland areas.

Authentica: the real thing?

The cult of authenticity is something you'll encounter in different forms throughout Corsica, an island gripped by notions of regional and racial purity. In recent years, however, the struggle to define what is "pure Corsican" has spilt onto supermarket shelves. In the early 1990s, sales of that most Corsican of products – charcuterie (cured meats) – took a tumble when it was revealed that some seventy percent of the island's cured meat output came from factories that sourced their pork from Brittany and Spain.

Outraged by the revelation, around 250 farmers got together to form an organization called **Authentica**. In return for the right to use a special stamp of quality, its members agreed to conform to an exhaustive list of criteria guaranteeing that their primary ingredients were locally produced, their animals reared free-range and fed on organic feed (such as wild chestnuts), and their produce free of all artificial additives.

Visitors can purchase the results of Authentica's efforts through its chain of accredited **shops** on the island. Although far from cheap, their stock, sporting the sought-after stamp, ensures the highest standards:

Ajaccio Délices et Santé, 7 cours Napoléon.
Calvi A Casetta, 16 rue Clémenceau.
Porto Hibiscus A Spusatella, La Marine.

Porto-Vecchio L'Orriu, 5 cours Napoléon.
Propriano Bocca Fina, rue des Pêcheurs.

Mountain cooking is dominated by dairy produce, particularly the soft ewe's cheese known as **brocciu** (pronounced "broodge"), produced only in the winter. You'll come across it stuffed into aubergines, *cannelloni* and omelettes with mint, or deep-fried in dainty little fritters (*beignets*). During the summer months, supplies of ewe's milk dry up and cow's milk is used instead: the result is an inferior product known as *brousse*, which doesn't taste nearly as good. In the high sheep-rearing Niolo and Asco regions, hard cheeses are also widely produced, and these can be excellent.

In addition to the desserts mentioned previously, look out for Corsica's wonderfully tangy **jams** (*confitures*), made from fig and walnut, fig and almond, lemon, clementine or chestnut. The island also boasts six varieties of AOC (*appellation d'origine contrôlée* – see box above) **honey**; those derived from the maquis flowers tend to be more subtly scented than the more full-on chestnut-flower honey, which you'll find on sale at roadsides in Castagniccia for a short period in late summer.

Drinking

Cafés and bars line the streets and squares of Corsica's towns and tourist resorts, and these are where you'll likely do most of your drinking, whether as a prelude to food (*apéritif*) or as a sequel (*digestif*). Bars tend to be dark, functional places, whereas cafés are more open, often featuring a terrace where you can sit and watch life pass by. Every bar or café displays a price list with progressively increasing prices for drinks at the bar, at the table or on the terrace.

Wine (*vin*) is the regular drink, with rosé the type produced in greatest volume in Corsica. *Vin de table* is generally drinkable and always inexpensive; restaurant mark-ups for quality wines, on the other hand, can be very high for a country where wine is so plentiful. In bars, you normally buy by the glass, and just ask for *un rouge*, *un blanc* or *un rosé*; *un pichet* gets you a jug. For more on Corsica's wines, see the box opposite.

Belgian and German brands account for most of the **beer** you'll find. Draught beer (*bière à la pression*) is the cheapest alcoholic drink after wine – ask for *un demi* (25cl) – while bottled beer is exceptionally cheap in supermarkets. A brand to look out for, both as *pression* and bottled in the shops, is **Pietra**, a delicious (purely Corsican) beer based on chestnut flour. The same company recently launched a white beer alternative, similar to German *weissbier* but flavoured with local maquis herbs; it's refreshing and delicious, but pricy.

Strong alcohol is drunk right through the day, the most popular drink being strong aniseed-based *pastis*, especially the local brand, **Casanis**. Brandies and eaux de vie are always available – the latter comes in a variety of flavours, such as *prune* (plum) and *cerise* (cherry), and is usually distilled locally in the villages. In many small restaurants and bars you'll be offered these free. You may also be offered **Cedratine** and **Myrthe**, which are locally made, sweet liqueurs.

On the **soft drink** front, you can buy cartons of unsweetened fruit juice in supermarkets, though in cafés the bottled nectars such as *jus d'abricot* (apricot) and *jus de* *poire* (pear) still hold sway. Some cafés serve tiny glasses of fresh orange and lemon juice (*orange/citron pressé*); otherwise it's the standard fizzy cans. Bottles of **mineral water** (*eau minérale*) and spring water (*eau de source*) – either sparkling (*pétillante*) or flat (*plate*) – abound, but you'll probably find yourself simply refilling your empty bottles from roadside springs (*fontaines* or *sources*), provided they don't carry the warning "*Non Potable*" (unsafe to drink). That said, tap water (*eau du robinet*) is of a particularly good quality in Corsica, deriving originally from the fresh mountain streams.

Coffee is invariably espresso and very

Corsican wines

The reputation of Corsican wine has, over the years, been dogged by scandal. In spite of optimum soils and growing conditions, the output at the top end of the market has lagged well behind the prodigious quantities of wine pouring from the *vin de table* vineyards on the eastern plain around Aléria. Of 100 square kilometres under cultivation, only about ten enjoy *appellation d'origine contrôlée* (abbreviated throughout this book as AOC) status, the international mark of quality.

Nevertheless, several labels have gained a deservedly strong reputation over the past decade or so, and are well worth hunting out. Featured on the tourist office's much-plugged *Routes des Vins*, the best of them all cultivate traditional Corsican vine stock, or *cépage*: la **malvoisie**, responsible for the fine whites of Patrimonio; le **nielluccio**, which yields a deep red similar to Tuscan chiantis (try Antoine Arena or Yves Leccia in Patrimonio, Domaine de Toraccia in Porto-Vecchio; or Clos Reginu in Calvi); and le **sciaccarello**, behind the pick of Ajaccio's reds (look out for Domaine Comte Péraldi, or Clos d'Alzeto).

Especially popular with foreign visitors (although often undeservingly maligned by some French wine critics) are the delicious **muscats** of Cap Corse. A rich, sweet, amber-coloured dessert wine that Corsicans love to offer as an *apéritif* (some also sing its praises as an accompaniment for strong ewe's cheese). Although it's grown in a relatively small area, with more or less exactly the same mix of *cépages*, the variation in soils ensures that no two are exactly the same. One of the great pleasures of touring the Cape and Patrimonio regions is tasting your way through them. Pick of the crop, however, are the elusive Clos Nicrosi, Clos Gentille and Domaine de Gioielli – all small, family-run concerns of under two square kilometres.

Corsica has nine AOC regions; the most famous being Sartène, Patrimonio, Cap Corse and Ajaccio. Enthusiasts can pick up *Route des Vins* leaflets at any local tourist office, which list the top *domaines* in each area. All of them welcome visitors and offer tasting (*dégustations*), when you can sample their range, beginning with white and rosé, and working through the reds to end on a muscat (if they produce one). As Corsican wines are bottled following a short fermentation period in the barrels, the vast majority do not improve over time and are best drunk after a year or two. If you do taste a *vin de garde* ("wine for keeping"), you'll be advised of it at the time. There's no obligation to buy, but few visitors will leave a good vineyard without at least one or two bottles.

Enthusiasts would do well to get hold of a copy of *L'Esprit Corse*, a special edition magazine, published (in French only) by the Corsican federation of wine growers, which gives detailed background on the island's nine *grands terroirs d'AOC*. You can order one by fax on ℗04 95 32 87 81 or online at ©civ@vinsdecorse.com.

strong. *Un café* or *un express* is black, *un crème* is white, *un café au lait* (served at breakfast) is espresso in a large cup or bowl filled up with hot milk. Ordinary tea (*thé*) is Liptons' tea-bag tea nine times out of ten; to have milk with it, ask for "*un peu de lait frais*". Herb teas (*infusions*) are served in every café and can be a refreshing alternative. The more common ones are *vervaine* (verbena), *tilleul* (lime blossom) and *tisane* (camomile). *Chocolat chaud* – hot chocolate – unlike tea, can be had in any café.

Communications

Post offices are found in the centre of all towns and most sizeable villages. The queues in them may be longer than you're used to, but mail services are otherwise conducted with typically French efficiency. Letters and postcards usually reach the UK in three or four days, and the US in a week or so, depending on where you post them. The same high standards do not, however, apply to phone boxes, which the mobile phone revolution seems to have catapulted into a perpetual state of neglect. Considering the high costs of phone cards and the number of booths out of action, you'd be well advised to bring your own mobile if you have one. As for email, be warned that the island lags well behind the rest of France, with Internet cafés few and far between outside Ajaccio and Bastia.

Mail

Post offices – *postes* or PTTs – are generally open Monday to Friday 9am to noon and 2 or 2.30pm to 5pm, plus 9am to noon on Saturday. However, don't depend on these hours: in the major towns you might find the main office open throughout the day, whilst opening and closing times vary enormously in the villages.

You can have letters sent to you by **poste restante** at any main post office on the island. The addresses of the principal offices are: cours Napoléon, Ajaccio 20000, and av Maréchal-Sebastiani, Bastia 20200. To collect mail you'll need a passport, and should expect to pay a small charge. If you're expecting mail, it's worth asking the clerk to check under *all* your names, as filing systems tend to be erratic. The quickest international service for **sending letters** is by *aérogramme*, sold at all post offices. Ordinary **stamps** (*timbres*) are sold at any *tabac* (tobacconist). If you're sending **parcels** abroad, try to check prices in the various leaflets available: small *postes* may need reminding of the huge reductions for printed papers and books, for example.

Telephones

To make domestic and international phone calls from any telephone box (*cabine*), you'll need a **phone card** (*télécarte*), available for €7.50 (for fifty call units) and €14.75 (for a hundred units) from post offices and most *tabacs*. By pressing the button showing two little flags joined by an arrow, you should be able to get English instructions – when the option is given. In the majority of Corsican call boxes, however, the LCD displays still give instructions only in French: *décrochez* (pick up the receiver); *introduire votre carte ou faire numéro libre* (insert your card or dial freephone number); *patientez SVP* (please wait); followed by *numérotez* (dial). From the moment the call goes through, the window shows the number of units remaining on your card. When these run out, it will read *crédit épuisé*, at which point you can either end your call or **insert a new card**. To do this, press the green button and wait for the message *retirez votre carte*, at which point you should withdraw the used card; you should insert your new one only when the display reads *nouvelle télécarte*.

To call **Corsica from abroad**, dial ☎00 33 plus the nine-digit number (omit the first 0). To call **abroad from Corsica**, the country codes are as follows:

Britain ☎00 44

Ireland ☎00 353

USA and Canada ☎00 1

Australia ☎00 61

New Zealand ☎00 64

Time

Corsica is one hour ahead of Greenwich Mean Time, six hours ahead of Eastern Standard Time, and nine hours ahead of Pacific Standard Time. This also applies during daylight saving seasons from the end of March to the end of September.

Useful telephone numbers within Corsica

Ambulance ☎15

Fire ☎18

Police ☎17

Weather For the coast ☎08 36 68 08 20; for the mountains ☎08 36 68 04 04; calls are charged at €0.34 per minute.

Time ☎36 99

International operator For Canada and the USA ☎00 33 11; for all other countries ☎00 33 followed by the country code.

International directory assistance For Canada and the USA ☎00 33 11 12; for all other countries ☎00 33 12 followed by the country code.

French directory assistance ☎12

For **domestic calls** within Corsica and France, whatever the distance, you should dial all ten digits. Charges vary according to the time of day and day of the week, with the cheapest times Monday to Friday 9.30pm to 8am, and Saturday 12.30pm to 8am, or any time on Sunday.

For **international calls**, dial ☎00, wait for a tone, dial the country code (see box above), then the area code (minus its initial 0) and finally the subscriber number. By far the cheapest way to call abroad is with a standard French **télécarte**, which allows you to call any EU country, and the US, for €0.30 per minute or €0.25 off peak (Mon–Fri 7pm–8am, or 8pm Fri until 8am Mon). To make a **reverse-charge international call**, dial ☎00 33 followed by your country code (see box above), which will put you through to the international operator.

You can also make international calls using a **telephone charge card**, opening an account before you leave home; calls will be billed monthly to your credit card, to your phone bill if you are already a customer, or to your home address. Note, however, that the charges for these are considerably higher than calling from a standard call box.

An alternative to dialling internationally from a *cabine* is to use the booths at main post offices, where you pay after making the call. If you do this, make sure you count your units, which are clearly displayed – mistakes can be made in calculating the bill.

Mobile phones

Most UK **mobile phone** network providers offer coverage in Corsica, although unless you've a top-of-the-range package you'll have to contact them to get it switched on; there may be a charge for this. You are also likely to be charged extra for incoming calls when abroad, as the people calling you will be paying the usual rate. If you want to retrieve messages while you're away, ask your provider for a new access code, as your home one won't work in Corsica.

It is unlikely that mobiles bought for use inside North America will work outisde the US and Canada, unless it's a tri-band phone. Most mobiles in the UK, Australia and New Zealand use GSM which works well in Europe.

For further general information about using your phone abroad, check out ⓦwww .telecomsadvice.org.uk/features/using_your _mobile_abroad.htm.

Email

The Internet revolution has yet to hit Corsica in a big way, partly due to the fact that ownership of personal computers is very low on the island, but also because of the predominance of English on *Le Net*, as it's known in French. It is, however, considered pretty chic to have an email address and increasing numbers of hotels and other businesses are online.

In the Guide, we list details of places offering **Internet access**, but cybercafés are still pretty thin on the ground and you'll more often than not have to rely on your hotel's connection, if it has one. Opening a **free Internet account** for use while you're away is easy: head for www.hotmail.com or www.yahoo.com.

The media

With the island so often in the national spotlight, local media is closely scrutinized in Corsica, especially the daily newspaper, *Corse-Matin,* which you'll come across in even the most remote villages. Interest in foreign affairs, however, even those of Continental France, tends to lag well behind preoccupation with insular events, which partly explains the widespread indifference to French national news coverage, whether in the Paris-based papers or television.

Newspapers and magazines

The Corsican newspaper with the widest circulation is the **local daily**, *Corse-Matin*, printed by Nice-Matin. The occasional headlining nationalist atrocity aside, it's a typical regional paper, with far more coverage of local events than national or international news, and is really only useful for listings. Of the **national dailies** *Le Monde* (daily except Mon) is the most intellectual and respected, with no concessions to entertainment (such as pictures), but written in an orthodox French that is probably the easiest to understand. *Libération* (daily except Mon) is moderately left-wing and colloquial, with good selective coverage. All the other nationals are firmly on the right. British newspapers and the *International Herald Tribune* are intermittently available in the larger resorts, and in Ajaccio and Bastia.

Weeklies, on the *Newsweek/Time* model, include the wide-ranging, left-leaning *Le Nouvel-Observateur* and its rightist counterweight, *L'Express*. The best and funniest investigative journalism is in *Le Canard Enchaîné*, but it's almost incomprehensible to non-natives. For a detailed look at the island's political and economic life, hunt out a copy of *Corsica*, a glossy that tackles the issues of the day head-on – the first popular publication in Corsica's modern history to do so.

Television

You get both **French and Italian television** in Corsica. French is slightly better quality, although marred by an unbearable amount of advertising. The third channel – **FR3** – features Corsican regional programmes, with a local news bulletin every lunchtime and evening and a sporadic schedule of documentaries. Italian television is less widely available; the RAI channels are the best, featuring documentaries and good news coverage. Many hotels also have **satellite** channels, featuring a choice of English-speaking stations.

Radio

There are a few local **radio** stations in Corsica, many of them broadcasting within a tiny area. The best of these is Bastia's RCFM (Radio Corse Frequenza Mora; 103FM), broadcasting in French and Corsican and playing a good variety of music, including traditional folk music and modern Corsican bands.

The **BBC World Service** broadcasts around the clock, but for best reception in Corsica tune in on short wave from 7pm on

6195kHz or 9410kHz. Atmospheric conditions permitting, you can also pick up the World Service on FM, via Radio Riviera in Monaco, on 106 and 106.5.

Opening hours, public holidays and festivals

Basic hours of business are 8am till noon and 2pm till 6pm; almost everything in Corsica – shops, museums, tourist offices, most banks – closes for a couple of hours at midday. In remote parts of the island, lunch breaks tend to be lengthier and opening times less reliable. Food shops all over the island often don't open until midway through the afternoon, closing around 7.30pm or 8pm, just before the evening meal.

The standard **closing days** are Sunday and Monday, and in small places you'll find everything except the odd boulangerie shut on both days. **Museums** are not very generous with their hours, tending to open around 10am, close at noon until 2pm or 3pm, and then run through until 5pm or 6pm – opening hours from mid-May to mid-September are generally slightly longer than during the rest of the year. Museum closing days are usually Monday or Tuesday; sometimes both. Most churches are open all day; if you come across one that's locked, you can ask for the key at the local mairie (town hall).

Public holidays

There are twelve national holidays (*jours fériés*), when most shops and businesses, though not museums and restaurants, are closed.

January 1 New Year's Day
Easter Sunday
Easter Monday
Ascension Day (forty days after Easter)
Pentecost (seventh Sunday after Easter, plus the Monday)
May 1 May Day/Labour Day
May 8 Victory in Europe Day
July 14 Bastille Day
August 15 Assumption of the Virgin Mary
November 1 All Saints' Day
November 11 Armistice Day
December 25 Christmas Day

Festivals

Aside from the nationally celebrated **religious festivals**, such as the Assumption of the Virgin Mary, local saints' days are celebrated in Corsican towns throughout the year, and often include fireworks and processions. Many events are music- and arts-based affairs, with outdoor concerts and film festivals boosting the local tourist industry. There are also a few local **country fairs**, where you can hear traditional Corsican singing and purchase regional specialities.

Of the innumerable Catholic feast days, the most fervent are the **Easter** celebrations, almost invariably featuring a parade across town bearing a statue of the Virgin or of Christ, followed by Mass and a street party with fireworks and music. Many of these rituals also include a procession called a *granitola*, an ancient rite whereby a line of penitents forms a spiral as it moves through the town. The most intense of all Corsican religious ceremonies is the **Catenacciu** in Sartène, an Easter procession led by a penitent who drags a cross through the streets in imitation of Christ's walk to Golgotha.

Of the island's plethora of **folk festivals**, one that is definitely worth attending is the September *Santa di u Niolu* in Casamaccioli, a riotous event involving much drinking, singing and gambling. Corte's *Ghjurnate di u Populu Corsu* summer festival brings together nationalist separatists from all over Europe for a week of concerts and political speeches, although its place as the island's top choral festival has been lost to Calvi's excellent *Rencontres de Chants Polyphoniques*, featuring a cappella groups from all over the world. Mediterranean folk **music festivals** take place at various locations throughout the summer, and there's a jazz festival at Calvi every June.

Festivals and events

Just about every sizeable village and town in Corsica these days hosts its own festival, whether tagged onto some kind of local produce (olives, almonds, chestnuts) or a musical theme. In addition to cultural events, the calendar below features the island's major religious occasions: saints' day celebrations and the processions at Easter time by Corsica's masked brotherhoods (*confraternités*). These, of course, are free, but for anything involving staged performances, expect to have to pay upwards of €15 for tickets, which should be booked well in advance through local tourist offices.

February

Rencontres du Cinéma Méditerranéan Bastia, first fortnight of February. Movies old and new from around the Mediterranean basin.
Rencontres du Cinéma Italien Bastia, first week. Pre-release gala screenings, classic Italian films and appearances by stars from across the water.

March–April

Rencontres du Cinéma Espagnol Bastia. Spanish cinema comes to town for the whole of March.
Notre-Dame-de-la-Miséricorde Ajaccio, March 18. Religious procession led by the city's patron saint and protectoress. See p.200.
Fête de la Bande Dessinée Bastia, first week of April. Exhibition of international cartoon art, dominated by Belgian and French styles. For a taster, go to:
ⓦ http://perso.wanadoo.fr/rene.viale/f/pres1.html.
La Cerca Erbalunga (see p.83), **U Catenacciu** Sartène (see p.258), **La Granitola** Calvi (see p.126); Good Friday.
Corsica's sombre Easter rituals involve archaic candlelit processions by masked and robed brotherhoods.
La Passion du Christ Calvi, Easter weekend. Contemporary theatrical re-enactment of the Crucifixion, accompanied by sublime polyphony from the group A Filetta – a spine-tingling event even if you're not a Christian. See p.126.

May

Fête du Christ Noir Bastia, May 3. The "Black Christ", found floating in the waves and the patron saint of local fishermen, is carried around Terra Nova. See p.72.

June

Fiera di u Mare Solenzara, first week of June. Fishing, sailing, jet-ski races and seafood cooking competitions centred on the marina. See p.297.
St-Érasme Bastia, Ajaccio and Calvi, June 2. Fishermen's festival celebrated with a Mass and harbour firework displays. See p.126.
Notre-Dame-des-Neiges Col de Bavella, June 5. Mass pilgrimage to the miracle-working Madonna on one of Corsica's highest mountain passes. See p.255.
Festival du Jazz Calvi, third week of June. A week of top-drawer jazz performances by internationally renowned musicians on a stage below the citadel, with night-long jam sessions in the bars lining the quai Landry. See p.126.
Festimusica L'Île Rousse, third weekend of June. Corsican, Sardinian and Tuscan folk music performed on an open-air stage in the centre of town. See p.132
San Ghjuva Corte, third weekend of June. Corsica's former capital celebrates Saint John's day with recitals of polyphony against the backdrop of the citadel. See p.338.

July

Festivoce Pigna. Celebration of Corsican polyphony revolving around the Casa Musicale. See p.143.
Fiera di u Vinu Luri, first weekend of July. Wine and handicraft festival at the heart of the Cap Corse muscat region. See p.93.
Relève des Gouverneurs Bastia, end of first week of July. Historical re-enactment of the French Governor's arrival in the citadel, involving lots of flag waving and military drumming. See p.74.
Fête du Livre Corse L'Île Rousse, third and fourth weeks of July. Corsica's only literature festival. See p.132.
Foire de l'Olivier Montegrosso, July 15–16. Hugely popular event celebrating the olive tree and all things made from it.
Interlacs Corte, July 15–16. One of the world's greatest fell races, with contestants running from Lac de Nino over the Brêche de Capitello and around the head of the Restonica Valley. See p.344.
Nuits de la Guitare Patrimonio, last week of July. International guitar festival showcasing a range of styles, from classical to Gypsy jazz and

blues. Past performers have included John MacLaughlin and local Macaferri maestro, Rudolf Rafëlli. See p.104.

Rencontres Théâtrales Olmi-Capella, last week of July and first week of August. A fortnight of theatre by amateur and professional actors in the remote Giunssani region, with nature-bases scenery. See p.150.

August

Festival de Musique Erbalunga, first week of August. Jazz, flamenco, classical and Corsican polyphony around this picturesque port on Cap Corse. See p.83.

Film festival Lama, first week of August. Wonderful open-air f lm festival held in the most unlikely setting of an idyllic Balagne village. The theme is always "*Le cinéma à la campagne, et la campagne au cinéma*", with all the films set in rural societies. See p.137.

Country fair Col de Prato, Castagniccia, first week of August. Traditional rural fair with animal showing, local handicraft and fresh produce competitions and polyphony singing (including the rarely performed Chiama e Respondi duels). See p.315.

Foire de l'Amandier Aregno, end of first week of August. Music, food stalls and general revelry loosely associated with almonds. See p.143.

Porto Latino St-Florent, mid-August. The Nebbio lets its hair down South American style, with gigs by Cuban and other Latin bands in the square. See p.95.

Violin Festival Sermano, near Corte, third weekend of August. Shows by fiddlers from across Europe (notably Ireland), along with music and dance workshops on the village square. A warm-hearted event that's run on a non-profit basis, so the gigs are free. See p.307.

Fêtes Napoléoniennes Ajaccio, mid-August. Processions and parades in period garb, followed by son et lumière in the Jardin du Casone to celebrate Napoléon's birthday.

L'Assomption Bastia, Ajaccio and Calvi, August 15. Son et lumière in the citadels.

September

Notre-Dame-de-Lavasina Lavasina, September 8. Sombre candlelit procession on the beach and a midnight Mass, in honour of a miracle-working Madonna painting housed in the local church. See p.81.

Santa di u Niolu Casamaccioli, September 8–10. Arguably Corsica's oldest and best-known festival, featuring duels of Chiama e Respondi singing in the village bar. See p.337.

Rencontres de Chants Polyphoniques Calvi, around September 14–18. Hosted by top polyphony group, A Filetta, this four-day music festival of a cappella music from around the world is the one not to miss. See p.127.

October

British film festival Bastia, first week of October. The last of the capital's annual film festivals showcases the best of British cinema, old and modern.

Musicales de Bastia Bastia, first fortnight of October. Eclectic mix of live music at venues around the town, principally the municipal theatre and bandstand on the place St-Nicolas.

Festiventu Calvi, last week of October. Hundreds of kites and twenty thousand visitors attend Calvi's fastest-growing festival, held on the beach. See p.127.

November

Fête du Marron Évisa, mid-November. The largest of several chestnut bashes, providing a chance to gather nuts in the woods with locals and sample some of the wonderful specialities made in the village. See p.176

Outdoor pursuits

Corsica's varied landscapes and exceptionally mild climate make it ideal for out-door pursuits of all kinds. Over the years the Parc Naturel Régional and numer-ous private activity centres have developed an impressive infrastructure for exploiting the island's potential as an adventure sports destination. Marked foot-paths form an extensive network of long-distance trails – to which we devote a separate chapter on pp.359–404 – and there are plenty of equestrian centres from where you can explore the countryside on horseback. For the more adven-turous, mountain biking, climbing and canyoning are also well established, with marked routes and guides on hand at several key locations. In addition, a string of diving schools around the coast offer the chance to sample the island's superb underwater life, which ranks among the most varied in Europe. The one catch with the Corsican adventure sport scene is cost. The seasonal nature of most outdoor pursuits on the island means that instructors and equipment providers tend to charge highly for their services; wherever possible, bring your own gear with you.

Hiking

Hiking (*la randonnée pédestre,* or *la rando* for short) is without doubt the best way to explore Corsica's amazing interior and remote stretches of coast, and there are nearly 1000km of marked trails to help you do just that. For a full rundown of the routes, as well as tips on planning, equipment and safety, see Chapter 8 "Long-distance Walks".

Climbing

While not possessing the same allure as the Alps, Pyrénées or Gorges de Verdon in Provence, Corsica offers an impressive range of commendable climbing routes, from short cliff pitches to a number of classic *grandes voies*. Moreover, the **rock** – with a few exceptions – is solid.

For short climbs, the island's cream-tinted **chalk cliffs** are arguably the most reward-ing. Dotted along a seam running from L'Île Rousse (on the northwest coast) to Solenzara (on the east coast), these are grouped in three main areas: the Nebbio, Ponte Leccia and Solenzara. Pick of the crop are the chalk escarpments at **Caporalino**, Pietralba (in the Ostriconi Valley near Ponte Leccia), but there are also some wonderful pitches around **Patrimonio** and in

the **Désert des Agriates**. In the southeast, the **Falaise de Monte Santu**, just north of Solenzara near the hamlet of Penna, offers around fifty routes of varying degrees of diffi-culty, all of them with superb sea views.

The best known of the island's most demanding climbing sites, the *grandes voies*, are at **Bavella**, in south Corsica. However, you'll find less-frequented routes at several other sites around the island: **Bonifatu**, above the Carozzu refuge; around the lakes at the head of the **Restonica Valley**, near Corte; the famous north cliffs of **Capo d'Ortu**, rising sheer behind Porto on the west coast; and over the red flanks of **Paglia Orba**, the island's shark-finned peak.

To date, only one dependable **climbing guide book** to Corsica has been published in English: the excellent *Corsica Mountains* by Robin G. Collomb (West Co, UK), avail-able through all branches of Stanfords in the UK (see p.24) as well as Ⓦ www.amazon .co.uk. Most of the classic routes are cov-ered in detail, and there are plenty of techni-cal tips for more proficient and adventurous climbers. In Corsica itself, you can pick up numerous climbing guides in French. Try *Les 100 Plus Belles Courses de Corse*, a good all-rounder by Henri Agresti and Jean-Paul Quilici (Éditions Danoël). For the three big cliffs of the south, *Sari, Conca et Zicavo* by Michel Charles and Jean-Paul Quilici (published and sold locally) is indispensable, while if you intend to tackle any of the *grandes voies* of the interior, around Paglia Orba or Monte Cinto, *Corsica: Escalades Choisies* by Pierre Pietri is the one to go for. Bavella, on the other hand, is best covered in Jean-Paul Quilici's definitive *Le Massif de Bavella* (published by Edisud).

Less confident climbers may wish to employ the services of a **qualified high-mountain guide** (*guide de haute montagne diplômé*). There are only three on the island, all of them well known and thoroughly dependable: Jean-Paul Quilici, who lives at Quenza (☎04 95 78 64 33); Pierre Griscelli, *gardien* of the Carozzu refuge, Bonifatu, on the GR20 (☎04 95 30 82 51 or 04 95 44 01 95); and Pierre Pietri, expert on the Cinto massif and its environs (☎04 95 32 62 76).

Canyoning

An adventure sport that's been catching on fast in Corsica over the past three or four years is **canyoning**, which involves following the course of a river or stream (usually downhill) on foot. Where the water descends steeply, the route may require ropes and abseiling skills (and occasionally even tobog-gans). For anyone into climbing and swim-ming (at the same time), this offers the ulti-mate buzz.

Basic **equipment** for canyoning comprises a wet suit (*combinaison*), canoeing helmet (*casque*), wet sacks and training shoes (*ten-nis*); for more challenging routes, you'll also need quality ropes, harnesses and karabin-ers. Given the potential dangers involved, it's better to hook up with a guide company, who can also rent out the necessary equip-ment. One proven outfit is Corsica Trek in Porto (☎04 95 26 82 02 or 04 95 26 21 21, ℱ04 95 26 12 49), who offer a range of graded routes, from a leisurely half-day descent of the calanches de Piana (€40) to a ten-hour climb down the precipitous Faille de Revinda, between Piana and Cargèse (€70).

Other prime canyoning spots on the island include: the Falcone and Ladroncellu stream gorges around **Bonifatu** (southwest of Calvi); the **Fangu Valley**; the Spurtellu ravine near **Porto**; and the Fiumicelli and Polischello gorges in **Bavella**.

The greatest **danger** faced by canyoneers in Corsica are sudden and dramatic in-creases in water level caused by heavy rain-

fall. The non-porous granite rock drains water very quickly, and streams, particularly those in narrow defiles, can fill up at aston-ishing speeds. It is therefore not advisable to attempt severe routes in wet or unsettled weather.

Mountain biking

Given the terrain and state of most of the roads in Corsica, **mountain bikes**, which the French call VTTs (*vélos tous terrains*), have the edge on standard touring cycles as the tool of choice, allowing you to sidestep the congestion and follow forest tracks and old mule paths into the interior. In recent years the island has become a mecca for VTT enthusiasts of all abilities, and along the marked footpaths you're unlikely to encounter the disapproving looks reserved for off-road cyclists in Britain.

The most promising **routes**, which we've highlighted in the guide, are mostly in the south – around the Forêt de l'Ospédale, Bavella and the Coscione Plateau. The jeep tracks of coastal Sartenais, between Campomoro and Tizzano, also offer stun-ning rides, as do sections of the Tra Mare e Monti Sud long-distance hiking path between Porticcio and Propriano (see p.403). In the north, the Désert des Agriates, between St-Florent and L'Île Rousse, has a rugged coastal path and network of tracks winding through some of the island's most memorable scenery. Serious mountain bik-ers should seek out Didier Richard's two VTT route guides (for North and South Corsica), which describe fifty of the island's best off-road possibilities, illustrated with reliable contour maps.

In view of the toughness of the trails (and the relative scarcity of shops supplying spares for bikes), you might prefer to **rent a bike** from one of the main towns and tourist resorts. A list of established rental firms appears on p.32.

Horse riding

The experience of riding Corsica's hidden bridleways and galloping across immense windswept beaches is one that few horse lovers should pass up. The island's old equestrian culture nearly died out after World War II, but has been revived over the past decade or two by the appearance of several excellent **centre équestres**, within reach of the main tourist areas, which offer half-day, full-day or even longer treks. Standards of horsemanship are consistently high, and you won't find an animal that's not in top condition. In fact, few horses are ever sold; Corsicans pride themselves on keeping their horses at home until they die.

For a full day's guided excursion, count on €65–75, or €900–1000 for a week.

Accredited horse-riding centres in Corsica

Jacques Abbatucci "Fil di Rosa", 20150 Serra-di-Ferro ℡ 04 95 74 08 08, Ⓕ 04 95 74 01 07. Riding school on a beef and arable farm outside Porto-Pollo, on the north side of the Golfe de Valinco.

L'Albadu Jean Pulicani, ancienne route d'Ajaccio, Corte ℡ 04 95 46 24 55. Half-day rides and bathing in the roadless Tavignano Valley, and longer routes into the centre (including to the exquisite Lac de Nino and a week-long loop to the Désert des Agriates from Corte). Friendly, family-run place, which also offers inexpensive accommodation. See p.340.

Antoine de Rocca Serra 20170 Levie ℡ 04 95 78 41 90, Ⓕ 04 95 78 46 03. Rides from the heart of Alta Rocca, in the forests and mountains around the prehistoric ruins of Pianu di Levie.

Arbo Valley chez François Vascovali, Saleccia, Monticello, near L'Île Rousse ℡ 04 95 60 49 49. One of the island's top centres. Their *pièce de résistance* is a trip out to Saleccia, where you get to swim with the horses on one of the island's most beautiful and remote beaches.

Ferme Équestre Baracci 20110 Propriano ℡ 04 95 76 08 02 or 04 95 76 19 48. Day-trips or longer jaunts (3–15 days) from the Gulf of Valinco. Their speciality, unique to this centre, is the *traversée de la Corse*, which takes riders across the island's watershed in a fortnight (€1220). They also take groups down the roadless coast between Propriano and Bonifacio (€910). See p.239.

A Madunina à Sartène Sartène ℡ 04 95 73 42 89. Trips around the distinctive Cagna massif, across the vineyards of the Rizzanese Valley and to the remote beaches beyond Campomorro.

Pierrot Milanini Hameau de Jalicu, 20122 Quenza ℡ 04 95 78 63 21. One of the few centres at altitude, on the lower slopes of the isolated Coscione Plateau. €100 per day, includes bed and meals in a somewhat ropy gîte d'étape. See p.252.

L'Ostriconi Pierre-Jean Costa, Lama, Balagne ℡ 04 95 48 22 99. Perfectly situated for stunning rides into the Désert des Agriates and around the dry east side of Balagne.

Christian et Claude Perrier Domaine de Croccano, 20100 Sartène ℡ 04 95 77 11 37, Ⓕ 04 95 73 42 89, Ⓔ christian.perrier@wanadoo.fr. Renowned stud farm 3km north of Sartène in the heart of the Rizzanese wine region.

Diving

Thanks to a virtual absence of pollution and factory fishing, not to mention some enlightened marine-life management, Corsica's coastal waters rank among the cleanest and clearest in the Mediterranean, supporting a profusion of underwater life that's matched by few other regions in Europe. Whether you're an experienced diver or a novice, you'll be spoilt for choice, both in terms of dive sites and schools. The island currently boasts nearly thirty accredited diving centres, where you can rent state-of-the-art equipment and boats, and gain expert advice on local sites and conditions.

Surface **water temperatures** fluctuate hugely throughout the year, from around 14°C in February to a balmy 25°C in August. September and early October are also good months for diving, with maximum water temperature rarely dipping below 20°C. **Visibility** varies according to the weather, but 25m is about average, rising to nearly double that in perfect conditions. Winds can prove problematic, whipping up choppy seas and swells at any time of the year around exposed headlands, particularly around the island's two most spectacular diving areas, the Réserve Naturelle de Scandola (on the northwest coast) and the Îles Lavezzi (near Bonifacio).

The island's underwater **landscape** mirrors that of its mountainous interior, with sheer drops plunging to depths of around 700m along stretches of the wild west coast. Coating the contorted granite rock formations underwater is a vibrant array of sea life: colourful anemones, vibrant gorgonian corals and an amazing wealth of fish. Among the many species unique to the Mediterranean is the **brown grouper** (*mérou*), whose characteristic fat lips and massive speckled body (which can grow up to more than 1m in length) are a common sight in the crystalline waters around the Îles Lavezzi. Other kinds of fish routinely spotted by divers off Corsica include moray eels, John Dory, forkbeards, damselfish, scorpion fish, and the excuisite turquoise-and-red rainbow wrasse.

Several **wrecks** lurk off the coast; among them an American B-17 bomber that crashed in Calvi bay after being shot down by a German fighter in 1944, and a Luftwaffe Heinkel-111, which lies just beyond the breakwater at Bastia harbour. The best source of information on **dive sites** are the staff at local **diving centres** (see below), who can advise you on the most rewarding places to dive – given the prevailing weather conditions and your level of experience. They can also rent you all the equipment you'll need, arrange transport and instruction, usually for an all-in package rate, and will refill your bottles for a fee if you've brought your own.

Typical **costs** for a single dive range from €30 to €40 (plus €10 for gear rental); most centres also offer discount cards for three or more outings. After an initial, slightly more expensive introductory dive – or *plongée baptême* – beginners can also undertake **training courses** for the compulsory certificates required to cive, including the internationally recognizec PADI qualification. Fees for the PADI open-water course, after which you're entitled to dive accompanied by an instructor to a depth of 20m, range from €300 for level I to €450 for level II.

Whoever you dive with, be sure to respect the marine environment. Don't feed the fish (not even grouper, whom divers around Bonifacio have traditionally attracted with boiled eggs), as it can upset their metabolisms. Try to keep your feet away from underwater plants while wearing fins: the sudden sweep of water caused by a flipper kick can be enough to destroy coral. And control the speed of your descent, because enormous damage can be caused to marine life by divers landing hard.

Selected diving centres in Corsica

Atoll *Auberge A Cheda*, 2km north of Bonifacio ☏ 04 95 72 03 83, ℻ 04 95 73 17 72.
Calvi Plongée Citadelle Thalassa Immersion, 2 rue St-Jean, Bastia ☏ 04 95 31 78 90.
CESM Le Roya beach, St-Florent ☏ 04 95 37 00 61, ℻ 04 95 37 09 60.
École de Plongée de L'Île Rousse Port de Commerce, L'Île Rousse ☏ 04 95 60 36 85, ℻ 04 95 60 45 21.
Génération Bleue marina, Porto ☏ & ℻ 04 95 26 24 88.
Hippocampe Plage de la Chiappa, near Palombaggia beach, Porto-Vecchio ☏ & ℻ 04 95 70 56 54.
Porto Pollo Plongée Porto Pollo, Golfe de Valcinco ☏ & ℻ 04 95 74 07 46.

For details of other centres, consult the relevant section of the Guide; most outfits can be contacted through their local tourist office. Note that advance reservations are essential during July and August.

Crime and personal safety

Despite Corsica's reputation for violence and extremist politics, you are unlikely to encounter any trouble during your stay on the island. Petty crime is minimal, though it makes sense to keep a close eye on your valuables in the crowded tourist resorts. If you should get robbed, hand over the money promptly and start dialling the cancellation numbers for your traveller's cheques and credit cards. Cars are rarely stolen but tape players and luggage left inside are vulnerable to thieves – especially at beach car parks. Try not to leave any valuables in sight, and make sure you have insurance (see p.25).

There are two main types of French police (popularly known as *les flics*): the **Police** Nationale and the **Gendarmerie Nationale**. For all practical purposes, they are indistinguishable; if you need to report a theft, or other incident, you can go to either. A noticeable presence in Corsica is the **CRS** (*Compagnies Républicaines de Sécurité*), a mobile force of heavies posted here to handle demonstrations and the terrorist threat, with whom you should have no contact unless you inadvertently get caught up in a riot.

The police have the right to demand identification from any citizen, so if you want to avoid all possible hassle, make sure you're able to produce your passport, or something equally incontrovertible, on the spot. For driving violations such as speeding, the police also have the right to impose on-the-spot fines (see p.30). Should you be arrested on any charge, you have the right to contact your nearest consulate, which is likely to be

in Marseille (see below). People caught smuggling or possessing **drugs**, even a few grams of marijuana, are liable to find themselves in jail, and the consulate will not be sympathetic.

Emergency numbers

Ambulance ☎15
Fire service ☎18
Police ☎17

Consulates in Marseille

Britain ☎04 91 53 43 32
Canada ☎04 91 37 19 37
Ireland ☎04 91 54 92 29
Netherlands ☎04 91 25 66 64
USA ☎04 91 54 92 00

Travellers with disabilities

France has no exceptional record for providing facilities for disabled travellers, and Corsica lags far behind other regions in this respect. Accessible hotels do exist in the major resorts, and ramps or other forms of access are gradually being added to museums, but the situation is far from satisfactory. The organizations listed below can provide various forms of useful information.

Useful contacts

France

APF (Association des Paralysés de France) 17–21 bd Auguste-Blanqui, 75013 Paris ☎01 40 78 69 00. A national organization with regional offices all over France, which can provide lists of accessible accommodation.
CNFLRH (Comité National Française de Liaison pour la Réadaption des Handicapés) 236 bis rue Tolbiac, 15013 Paris ☎01 53 80 66 66. Information service for disabled travellers, with details of accessible accommodation, holiday centres, etc. Also distributes various useful guides, including one to Corsica.
Handi Cap Évasion ⓦhttp://handy.univ-lyon1.fr. An organization set up to aid disabled hikers, with the help of an ingenious wheelchair called "Joelette". Check out this French-language website for news, views and info on forthcoming

trips into the Corsican mountains.

UK and Ireland

Access Travel 6 The Hillock, Astley, Lancashire M29 7GW ☎01942/888 844, ⓦwww.access -travel.co.uk. Tour operator that can arrange flights, transfer and accommodation. This is a small business, personally checking out places before recommendation. They can guarantee accommodation standards in a range of countries, including France. ATOL bonded, established seven years.
Holiday Care 2nd Floor, Imperial Building, Victoria Rd, Horley, Surrey RH6 7PZ ☎01293/774 535, Minicom ☎01293/776 943, ⓦwww.holidaycare.org.uk. Provides free lists of accessible accommodation abroad. Information on financial help for holidays available.
Irish Wheelchair Association Blackheath Drive, Clontarf, Dublin 3 ☎01/833 8241, ⒻFAX833 3873, ⒺEMAILiwa@iol.ie. Useful information provided about

travelling abroad with a wheelchair.

Tripscope Alexandra House, Albany Rd, Brentford, Middlesex TW8 0NE ☎ 0845/7585 641, ⓦ www.justmobility.co.uk/tripscope, ⓔ tripscope@cableinet.co.uk. This registered charity provides a national telephone information service offering free advice on UK and international transport for those with a mobility problem.

USA and Canada

Access-Able ⓦ www.access-able.com. Online resource for travellers with disabilities.

Directions Unlimited 123 Green Lane, Bedford Hills, NY 10507 ☎ 1-800/533-5343 or 914/241-1700. Tour operator specializing in custom tours for people with disabilities.

Mobility International USA 451 Broadway, Eugene, OR 97401, voice and TDD ☎ 541/343-1284, ⓦ www.miusa.org. Information and referral services, access guides, tours and exchange programmes. Annual membership $35 (includes quarterly newsletter).

Society for the Advancement of Travelers with Handicaps (SATH) 347 5th Ave, New York, NY 10016 ☎ 212/447-7284, ⓦ www.sath.org. Non-profit educational organization that has actively represented travellers with disabilities since 1976.

Travel Information Service ☎ 215/456-9600. Telephone-only information and referral service.

Twin Peaks Press Box 129, Vancouver, BC WA 98661 ☎ 360/694-2462 or 1-800/637-2256, ⓦ www.twinpeak.virtualave.net. Publisher of the *Directory of Travel Agencies for the Disabled* ($19.95), listing more than 370 agencies worldwide; *Travel for the Disabled* ($19.95); the *Directory of Accessible Van Rentals* ($12.95) and *Wheelchair Vagabond* ($19.95), loaded with personal tips.

Wheels Up! ☎ 1-888/389-4335, ⓦ www.wheelsup.com. Provides discounted air fare, tour and cruise prices for disabled travellers, also publishes a free monthly newsletter and has a comprehensive website.

Australia and New Zealand

ACROD (Australian Council for Rehabilitation of the Disabled) PO Box 60, Curtin ACT 2605 ☎ 02/6282 4333; Suite 103, 1st Floor, 1–5 Commercial Rd, Kings Grove 2208 ☎ 02/9554 3666. Provides lists of travel agencies and tour operators for people with disabilities.

Disabled Persons Assembly 4/173–175 Victoria St, Wellington, New Zealand ☎ 04/801 9100. Resource centre with lists of travel agencies and tour operators for people with disabilities.

Sex and gender issues

Corsican attitudes to gender are fairly typical of the European Mediterranean. In most aspects of life, men and women outwardly conform more closely to Italian norms than to those of the mother country. When in public, women are expected to look feminine and glamorous; men tend to be under less pressure to look good, but where cars and motorbikes are concerned, size definitely matters.

Sex before marriage, while fast becoming the rule, is still regarded as a source of shame when it comes to daughters, whom most families will pressure to be at least engaged before they sleep with a boyfriend. No such opprobrium surrounds the sexual behaviour of men, who are encouraged to "play the field" once over the age of consent (18). This doesn't mean, however, that **sexual harassment** is common: on the contrary. Unlike across the Ligurian Sea, where any

woman dressed in summer clothes can expect a constant barrage of cat calls and hisses, men are invariably polite, with staring regarded as rude. If you feel you've been insulted in the street, don't be afraid to make your feelings known.

Rape is no more of a risk in Corsica than anywhere else, but as ever when travelling you should be on your guard when walking around at night, especially on unlit beaches and along dark lanes.

Gay and lesbian

Corsicans remain much more conservative in their attitude to homosexuality than do their compatriots on the Continent. Gay and lesbian islanders eschew the "we're here, we're queer!" stance of northern Europe and North America in favour of a low profile – which means lots of lavender marriages and creeping off under cover of night to the maquis and deserted beaches. With the exception of Ricanto beach, near Ajaccio airport (where you'll find the island's only out gay bar), you won't often encounter overt cruising, and when you do chances are it'll be someone from outside the island. At the same time, Corsica has long been a popular destination for discreet gay couples and no one is likely to raise much more than an eyebrow if you ask for a double bed when checking into a hotel.

The same doesn't apply to expressing affection in the street. Women can get away with holding hands and walking with arms around each other, but gay men can expect hostile comments if they do the same.

Travelling with children

Corsica is an easy place to travel with children of any age: the flight there is short, transfers from the airport quick and easy and the climate – especially in June and September – perfect for little ones. Kids will be well received everywhere and babies and toddlers, in particular, will be made a fuss of. The traditional pleasures of bucket, spade, sand and sea are never far away, which is just as well as the island has few purpose-made attractions. That said, throughout the Balagne region of the northwest you'll regularly come across signs advertising donkey rides, and if you're anywhere near Ajaccio a visit to the tortoise sanctuary, "A Capulatta", is guaranteed to be a big hit. Elsewhere, keep an eye out for aquariums (in Porto and Bonifacio) and boat rides (from resorts across the west coast).

Train and bus **travel** is free for the under-4s, or half-fare for 4- to 12-year-olds. Excursion boats also offer reductions for kids, as do museums and most other places charging admission.

Travelling by rented car, a **baby seat** is a must for infants. Rental and holiday companies can arrange to have one ready on arrival (for a an extra charge), but you may find their French fittings unfamiliar, or that the seats themselves are the wrong size, which can create added stress – so bring your own if you have one.

Accommodation shouldn't be a problem. Hotels generally welcome accompanied children and most have rooms with three or four beds (also charged extra). Self-catering villas, apartments and cottages also tend to be well geared up for kids, with high chairs, boxes of toys and a shelf of weathered French picture books. Most of the prime properties with pools get block booked by package companies (listed on p.15), but there are plenty more listed in handouts available at tourist offices (for more on how to book this kind of accommodation, see p.34).

Package operators go out of their way to attract families and all offer reductions for kids, typically of ten percent for under-12s in low and mid-season. Infants under 2 years go for £30–50 – roughly the cost of the airport tax. Rates are far from standard, however, and parents would do well to compare the small print in the brochures before booking. Some firms – notably the ones listed below – also offer dedicated **child-care facilities**, such as crèches, English-speaking nannies or special watersports instruction, albeit at a price.

On the whole, Corsican **beaches** are extremely safe, with gently shelving sand and very little swell, surf or undertow. One hazard parents should always look out for, however, are **anemones** – the little brown spiky balls that lurk on underwater rocks, and whose spines can lodge themselves under the skin and cause painful wounds.

As in other Mediterranean regions of Europe, children stay up late in Corsica, especially in the summer. It's very common for them to be running around pavement cafés or restaurants and your kids will no doubt enjoy joining in.

For those travelling with **babies**, international brands of formula milk and jars of the usual mush are available everywhere, as are disposable nappies (*couches-culottes*, or *couches à jeter* in French). Pampers and Huggies are ubiquitous, but the supermarket own-brands are of a higher standard than most sold in the UK, and a good deal cheaper.

One final word of advice for parents considering a package holiday: pick properties within easy reach of the airport to keep the transfer times down, which can spare a lot of hassle at the start and end of your stay.

Useful contacts

UK and Ireland

Club Med ☎0700/007 007 007,

ⓦwww.clubmed.co.uk. Specializes in purpose-built holiday resorts, with kids' club, entertainment and sports facilities on site. See also p.15.
Mark Warner Holidays ☎0870/770 4222, ⓦwww.markwarner.co.uk. Watersports-oriented holiday vacation campus on the west coast of Corsica, with children's entertainment and childcare included.
Simply Corsica ☎020/8541 2200, ⓦwww.simply-travel.com. Upmarket tour company (see p.15) that can provide qualified, English-speaking nannies to come to your villa and look after the children. They also have a crêche near Propriano, in southern Corsica.

USA

Families Welcome 92 N Main St, Ashland, OR 97520 ☎1-800/326-0724 or 541/482-6121. Vacations for parents and kids.
Rascals in Paradise 2107 Van Ness Ave, Suite 403, San Francisco, CA 94109 ☎415/921-7000 or 1-800/872-7225, ⓦwww.rascalsinparadise.com. Can arrange scheduled and customized itineraries built around activities for kids.
Travel With Your Children 40 Fifth Ave, New York, NY 10011 ☎212/477 5524 or 1-888/822-4388. Publishes a regular newsletter, *Family Travel Times* (ⓦwww.familytraveltimes.com), as well as a series of books on travel with children including *Great Adventure Vacations With Your Kids*.

Directory

BEACHES are public property within 5m of the high-tide mark; it's illegal to camp on them, however. Some beaches are protected areas, where you are prohibited from climbing on the dunes. And beware of goats – an aggressive hazard in many out-of-the-way spots.

CIGARETTES are the only consumer items cheaper than in mainland France.

CONTRACEPTIVES Condoms (*preservatifs*) are prominently displayed on pharmacy counters, and there's an increasing number of dispensing machines in public places. You

need a prescription for the Pill (*la pilule*).

ELECTRICITY is 220v, using plugs with two round pins.

EMERGENCY NUMBERS Ambulance ☎15, fire service ☎18, police ☎17.

LAUNDRY Self-service laundries in Corsica are thin on the ground; details are given in the "Listings" sections of the relevant accounts. You could discreetly do your own in your hotel room, though technically it's forbidden to wash clothes in hotels.

LEFT LUGGAGE *Consignes* are found in the ports and train stations, charging around €4.5 per item per day, although at the time of writing most were closed for security reasons.

PHOTOGRAPHIC FILM is more expensive in Corsica than the UK, so bring as much as you'll need. Slide (*diapositif*) and professional films such as Astia, Provia and Velvia are available only in Ajaccio, Bastia, Calvi, Porto-Vecchio and Propriano. Processing of both is done on the mainland within 24hr on weekdays, but be warned that it costs double what you probably pay at home.

TIME French summertime begins on March 28 and finishes on September 26, and is therefore an hour ahead of Britain for most of the year, except in October, when times are the same. Corsica is six hours ahead of Eastern Standard Time, and nine hours ahead of Pacific Standard Time.

TOILETS Outside public toilets are virtually nonexistent. Corsicans regard providing loos for visitors as a service to be paid for rather than a civic responsibility. Every bar has one – even if only a primitive, hole-in-the-floor affair – but you'll be expected to order a drink before using it. Ask for *les toilettes,* or *le WC* – pronounced "vay-say".

WORKING IN CORSICA Opportunities for working in Corsica are very limited, even for travellers from EU countries. Casual work in the service sector – in campsites, hotels, bars and on beaches – is plentiful, but it tends to go to French students over for the summer (*saisoniers/saisonières*). Cleaning and labouring is the preserve of Moroccan or Algerian guest workers, or else illegal immigrants from east European countries such as Poland or Romania, who work for less than the national minimum wage, le SMIG. That said, if your French is fluent and you speak another European language, especially German, you should be able to pick up some kind of temporary job in early June (campsite reception is a always worth a try), though don't expect it to pay well.

Guide

Guide

1 Bastia and northern Corsica 59–110

2 The Balagne 111–156

3 The northwest 157–190

4 The Ajaccio region 191–221

5 The South 223–292

6 Eastern Corsica 293–319

7 Central Corsica 321–357

8 Long-distance walks 359–404

Bastia and northern Corsica

CHAPTER 1 # Highlights

✱ **Sunset at the Vieux Port, Bastia** – Enjoy a sundowner with swifts screeching over tumbledown Genoese tenements and the twin campaniles of L'Église St-Jean-Baptiste. See p.69

✱ **Muscat** – The heavily scented dessert wine produced in Cap Corse is the ideal foil for Corsica's pungent ewe's cheese. See p.78

✱ **Le Sentier du Douanier** – Wildly scenic coast path taking in deserted watchtowers and the marine reserve of Capandula. See p.88

✱ **Centuri-Port** – Snug stone fishing harbour renowned for its seafood restaurants. See p.91

✱ **St-Florent** – Hub of the fertile Nebbio region, fringed by kilometres of deserted coastline and mountains. See p.97

✱ **San Michele de Murato** – The high watermark of Pisan church architecture on the island, made of polychrome stone. See p.105

✱ **Ferme-Auberge Campu di Monte** – Sumptuous *cuisine du terroir* served in an appropriately gorgeous rural setting. See p.106

✱ **Agriates beaches** – Jump on a boat to the island's most spectacularly remote beaches – Loto and Saleccia – in the Désert des Agriates. See p.109

Bastia and northern Corsica

Bastia, nowadays capital of the *département* of Haute-Corse, was the capital of the entire island under Genoa's colonial administration, and it was the Genoese who laid the foundations of northern Corsica's prosperity by encouraging the planting of vines, olives, chestnut trees and other more experimental crops – there's a village called Sparagaghjiu (Asparagus) in the hills above St-Florent. The long-term result of this development was that the peasant farmers of the north tended to be not just better off than their southern counterparts, but also politically more ambitious. Thus, when Pascal Paoli recruited his rebel armies it was on this region's downtrodden rich that he concentrated his efforts, rather than on the downtrodden poor of the south. Even today there's a palpable difference in the political climate of the island's two halves, with northerners tending to see themselves as more radical, energetic and enterprising.

A thriving freight and passenger port, **Bastia** is the point of arrival for many visitors, and it can be a rather depressing experience at first, with industrial sprawl on the way into town from the airport, high-rise blocks stacked up the hillsides above town, and no decent beaches. Yet, while Bastia lacks the appeal of sleek Ajaccio, this is the town to visit if you want to get to grips with modern Corsica, for a quarter of the island's population lives and works here and in the immediate surroundings. Moreover, despite suffering considerable damage in World War II, the city has retained its Italian character, especially around the **Vieux Port**, a horseshoe of vertiginous buildings dominated by the towers of the Église St-Jean-Baptiste and bulk of the Genoese citadel.

The nearest beaches are to the south along the unremarkable stretch of coast known as **La Marana**, which adjoins the **Étang de Biguglia**, a huge lagoon that's a haven for migrating birds, and the beautiful Pisan church of **La Canonica**. To the north of Bastia, a single road follows the shore of the long rocky peninsula of **Cap Corse**, giving access to some exceptionally beautiful and unspoilt stretches of coast, as well as a string of diminutive ports, of which **Erbalunga** and **Centuri–Port** are the pick. At the base of the cape's finger, on the western side, lies **St-Florent**, a snug little resort holding most of the north's accommodation outside the capital. The hinterland of St-Florent, the **Nebbio**, is famed for the wines produced near **Patrimonio**, for dramatically sited

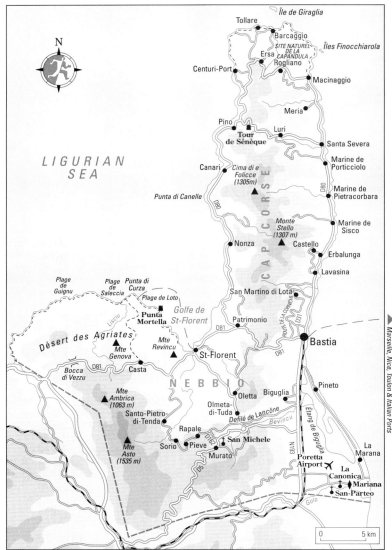

upland villages such as **Oletta** and **Santo-Pietro-di-Tenda**, and for the finest Romanesque churches on the island: Santa Maria Assunta, on the outskirts of St-Florent; and the chapel of San Michele, near Murato. West of St-Florent lies the uninhabited **Désert des Agriates**, a vast semi-barren expanse covered in massive clumps of rock, stands of cactus and the ruins of ancient stone granaries. The coast here is generally wild and inaccessible, though the beaches of

Saleccia and **Loto**, reachable by excursion boat from St-Florent, are amongst the finest in Corsica.

Public transport in the region is generally better than elsewhere on the island, but that isn't saying much. Corsica's train, the *micheline*, threads south from Bastia a little way, passing the Étang de Biguglia, but doesn't serve anywhere else covered in this chapter. Buses aren't common, but you can get one up into Cap Corse or the Nebbio at certain times of the week, and daily to St-Florent, while during the summer services run along the north coast to Calvi, skirting the southern fringes of the Désert des Agriates.

Bastia

Paradoxically, the dominant tone of Corsica's most successful commercial town, **BASTIA**, is one of charismatic dereliction, as the city's industrial zone is spread onto the lowlands to the south, leaving the centre of town with plenty of aged charm. This charm might not be too apparent from the vast **place St-Nicolas** and the two boulevards parallel to it, which, though flanked by faded Art Deco shop fronts, are choked with expensive cars and busy shoppers. But to the south of here lies the old quarter known as the **Terra Vecchia**, a tightly packed network of haphazard streets, flamboyant Baroque churches and lofty tenements, their crumbling golden-grey walls set against a backdrop of maquis-covered hills. **Terra Nova**, the historic district on the opposite side of the old port from Terra Vecchia, is a tidier zone that's now Bastia's yuppie quarter, housing the island's top-flight architects, doctors and lawyers.

Young upper-crust Bastiais always used to be sent to Italian universities for their education, a traffic that has had a marked effect on the city's tradition of professional success and on its cultural life – it's here that you'll find Corsica's only purpose-built theatre. Modelled on Milan's La Scala, it was regularly visited by the great Italian opera stars, and nowadays, even though some of the gloss has gone, the place fills up for occasional concerts by touring companies, or for one of Bastia's film festivals. Nothing packs in the crowds quite like the recurrent nationalist rallies, however, for Bastia is something of a centre for dissidence. Discontent with the way the city is run is a constant feature of life here, as highlighted in 1989, when Bastia's civil servants rioted over the mysterious disappearance of local government funds – the disturbances culminated soon after with the razing of the local tax office by a nationalist-terrorist bomb. Highly politicized and busily self-sufficient, Bastia may make few concessions to tourism, but its grittiness makes it a more genuine introduction to Corsica than its longtime rival on the west coast.

A brief history of Bastia

In the twelfth century, when Corsica was under Pisan control, wine was exported to the Italian mainland from **Porto Cardo**, forerunner of Bastia's **Vieux Port**. Moorish raids made the area too vulnerable to inhabit, however, and it wasn't until the Genoese ascendancy that the port began to thrive. At first the colony was governed from the former Roman base at Biguglia, to the south, but in 1372, when the fort was burned down by Corsican rebels, the Genoese abandoned the malarial site in favour of Porto Cardo, a spot close to Genoa and within easy trading distance of the fertile regions of the eastern plain, Balagne and Cap Corse. Before the end of the decade the governor, Leonello Lomellino, had built the *bastiglia* (dungeon) which gave the town its name; ramparts were constructed high on the escarpment above the port, and Genoese families, attracted by offers of free building land, began to settle within the fortifications in an area which became **Terra Nova**.

The sixteenth century saw the rise of a new class of merchants and artisans, who settled around the harbour on the site of Porto Cardo, the area now known as **Terra Vecchia**. The boom lasted until 1730, when Bastia was raided by an army of four thousand peasants, following similar attacks on Aléria and the Balagne settlements. Provoked to desperation by the corrupt despotism of the Genoese republic, the *paesani* went on the rampage for three days, annihilating most of the population of Terra Vecchia, who lacked the protection of the upper-class inhabitants of Terra Nova. Peace was finally restored by the intervention of the bishop of Aléria, but the remaining Genoese merchants promptly left for the safer ports of Bonifacio and Calvi, and Bastia went into decline.

During the **Wars of Independence** (1729–96) Bastia became a battleground. Pascal Paoli coveted the town for its strong position facing Italy, but it took two attempts and the efforts of the British fleet to take the citadel – the second assault was led by Nelson and Hood, who, though outnumbered by two to one, overcame the defenders in a long and difficult siege. In 1794, in the wake of this victory, Bastia became home to English viceroy Sir Gilbert Elliot, who lived here for the two years of the Anglo–Corsican alliance. Bastia's hour of glory was short-lived, however, as the French finally gained full control of Corsica in 1796, and the island was divided into two *départements*.

Despite the fact that in 1811 Napoléon appointed Ajaccio capital of the island, initiating a rivalry between the two towns that exists to this day, Bastia soon established a stronger trading position with mainland France. The **Nouveau Port**, created in 1862 to cope with the increasing traffic with France and Italy, became the mainstay of the local economy, exporting chiefly agricultural products from Cap Corse, Balagne and the eastern plain. During **World War II** Bastia was the only town on Corsica to be severely bombed – ironically, by the Americans. On the day after the island's liberation in 1943, a squadron of B52s belatedly launched an aerial attack against the non-existent Germans, Von Senger und Etterlin's Ninth Panzer Division having already completed its withdrawl across the Ligurian Sea. With many people in the streets celebrating the retreat, civilian casualties exceeded the total sustained throughout the occupation and many buildings were destroyed, including much of the old governor's palace; the consequences of the bombing can still be seen in Terra Vecchia.

Today, Bastia's population has grown to forty thousand, with the long-standing industries of freight handling and small-scale manufacture providing most of the employment, augmented by the burgeoning bureaucracies of local government. The city has also become a hotbed of nationalist activity, with more than its fair share of political assassinations and bombings in recent years; among these was the explosion in July 1996 in the Vieux Port, which killed a prominent Cuncolta leader. However, the worst tragedy since the war occurred on May 5, 1992, when a stand in the **Furiani stadium**, home of Corsica's top football team, Sporting Club de Bastia, collapsed during a European Cup tie with arch rivals Olympic de Marseille. Seventeen supporters died in the disaster and more than 1300 were injured. Those responsible have yet to be brought to justice, while the issue of compensation for the victims has become embroiled in scandal and protracted legal cases.

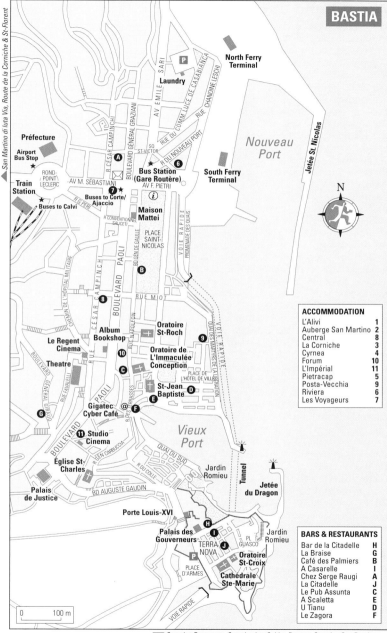

❶, **❷**, **❸**, **❹**, **❺** ▲ *Camping Casanova, Camping Les Orangers & Cap Corse*

BASTIA

◄ *San Martino di Iuta Via, Route de la Corniche & St-Florent*

North Ferry Terminal

P

Laundry

AV EMILE SARI

RUE CHANOINE LESCHI

RUE DU COMM LUCE DE CASABIANCA

SO ST-VICTOR

R DU NOUVEAU PORT

Préfecture

Airport Bus Stop

Ⓐ

R CESAR CAMPINCHI

BOULEVARD GENERAL GRAZIANI

ROND-POINT LECLERC

Train Station

AV M. SÉBASTIANI

Bus Station (Gare Routère)

❻

Nouveau Port

Jetée St. Nicolas

South Ferry Terminal

AV F. PIETRI

Buses to Corte/Ajaccio

R GEn DE GAULLE

R PERI

R CONVENTIONNEL SALICETI

❼

Ⓘ

Maison Mattei

PLACE SAINT-NICOLAS

N

Buses to Calvi

BOULEVARD PAOLI

Ⓑ

RUE MIOT

R CESAR CAMPINCHI

VOIE RAPIDE PROMENADE DES QUAIS

❽

Oratoire St-Roch

Album Bookshop

RUE NAPOLEON

❾

QUAI DES MARTYRS DE LA LIBERATION

VOIE RAPIDE

Le Regent Cinema

❿

Oratoire de L'Immaculée Conception

PLACE DE L'HÔTEL DE VILLE

ACCOMMODATION

L'Alivi	1
Auberge San Martino	2
Central	8
La Corniche	3
Cyrnea	4
Forum	10
L'Impérial	11
Pietracap	5
Posta-Vecchia	9
Riviera	6
Les Voyageurs	7

Theatre

St-Jean Baptiste

Ⓒ

Ⓓ

Ⓔ

Gigatec Cyber Café

@Ⓕ

Ⓖ

BOULEVARD GENERAL GIRAUD

RUE FAVALELLI

BOULEVARD PAOLI

R DES TERRASSES

Vieux Port

⓫ Studio Cinema

R EN CARBUCCIA

Église St-Charles

QUAI DU SUD

R DU COLLE

Jardin Romieu

Tunnel

Palais de Justice

BD AUGUSTE GAUDIN

Jetée du Dragon

Porte Louis-XVI

Palais des Gouverneurs

Ⓗ

Ⓘ

TERRA NOVA

Ⓙ

PL GUASCO

Jardin Romieu

P

Oratoire St-Croix

PLACE D'ARMES

Cathédrale Ste-Marie

VOIE RAPIDE

BARS & RESTAURANTS

Bar de la Citadelle	H
La Braise	G
Café des Palmiers	B
A Casarelle	I
Chez Serge Raugi	A
La Citadelle	J
Le Pub Assunta	C
A Scaletta	E
U Tianu	D
Le Zagora	F

0 — 100 m

65

▼ *Camping Esperanza, Camping Les Sables Rouges, Camping San Damiano,*
Étang de Biguglia, Poretta Airport, L'Arinella Beach, La Marana, Corte, Porto-Vecchio, Bonifacio & Ajaccio

Arrival and information

Bastia's Poretta **airport** (☎04 95 54 54 54, ⓦwww.bastia.aeroport.fr) is 16km south of town, just off the Route Nationale (N193); **shuttle buses** (☎04 95 31 06 65) into the centre coincide with flights, and enter town via Terra Nova, dropping passengers at the north side of the main square, place St-Nicolas, for €8 (one way). **Taxis** from the airport (☎04 95 34 07 00 or 04 95 32 70 70) cost €35.

Terminus for the *micheline* from Ajaccio, Corte and Calvi (via Ponte Leccia) is Bastia **train station** (gare SNCF) on the north side of town off the rondpoint Leclerc (☎04 95 32 80 60); the left-luggage room (*consigne*), behind the ticket counter, was closed as a security precaution when we last checked.

The same applies to the *consigne* in the smart new **ferry dock**, or **Nouveau Port**, a short way north of place St-Nicolas. The complex has two terminals – North (Nord) and South (Sud) – roughly 200m apart. Both have exchange counters (July–Sept 11am–5pm) and ticket hatches for the various ferry companies, in addition to the town's **cleanest public toilets**.

There isn't a proper **bus station** in the town, which can cause confusion, with services arriving and departing from different locations around the north side of place St-Nicolas. Rapides Bleus (☎04 95 31 03 79) services from Bonifacio and Porto-Vecchio via the east coast stop outside their travel agents opposite the post office (PTT) on av Maréchal-Sébastiani, whereas Beaux Voyages (☎04 95 65 11 35) buses from Calvi pull in outside the train station, as do Autocars Cortenais (☎04 95 46 02 12) three-weekly buses from Corte, via Ponte Leccia. Eurocorse Voyages (☎04 95 21 06 30) twice-daily services from Corte and Ajaccio arrive at a small square on the opposite side of av Maréchal-Sébastiani from the tourist office (see map) – which, confusingly, is referred to as the gare routière, even though it's little more than a lay-by. This is also the arrival point for suburban services, and for buses from Cap Corse, the Nebbio (including St-Florent) and Castagniccia. The shuttle service from the **airport** approaches town via the citadel and bd Paoli, dropping passengers outside the Préfecture building, on the opposite side of the roundabout from the train station. For a full rundown of Bastia's bus routes and companies, see "Travel details" at the end of this chapter.

Drivers should head for the large **car park** in the centre, beneath place St-Nicolas. It's expensive and often filthy, but is the only place you're guaranteed to find spaces; come armed with plenty of change for the ticket machine.

The **tourist office** is at the north end of place St-Nicolas (June–Sept 15 daily 8am–8pm; Sept 16–May Mon–Sat 8am–6pm, Sun 9am–1pm; ☎04 95 54 20 40, ⑨04 95 54 20 41; ⓦwww.bastia-tourisme.com). As well as the usual range of glossy leaflets, they hand out useful summaries of **bus timetables** for services to and from Bastia, and free fold-out **maps** of Corsica.

Accommodation

Bastia's passenger port receives twice as many visitors as Ajaccio's, but few linger in the city, preferring to head straight off to quieter corners of the island. This may in part explain the relative shortage of **hotel rooms**. Choice is particularly limited at the bottom end of the scale, so if you're on a tight budget think twice about spending a night here. Most of the classier places line the road to Cap Corse north of the port; the more basic ones are found in the centre of town, within striking distance of place St–Nicolas. Wherever you plan to stay, it's advisable to reserve well in advance.

There are also a handful of **campsites** located outside the town. The most convenient if you're relying on public transport are at Miomo, 5km north (buses every 30min Mon–Sat, hourly Sun, until 7.30pm, from the top of place St–Nicolas opposite the tourist office).

Hotels in the centre

Central 3 rue Miot ☎04 95 31 71 12, ℻04 95 31 82 40, ⓦwww.centralhotel.fr. Just off the south-west corner of place St-Nicolas. Recently refurbished rooms, with waxed walls and sparkling bathrooms. The welcoming *patronne*, Mme de la Paillonne, runs a tight ship, making this by far the most pleasant and best-value place to stay in the centre. Triples from €70. ④

Forum 20 bd Paoli ☎04 95 31 02 53, ℻04 95 31 65 60, ⓦwww.hotelforumwanadoo.fr. Dark, but well-appointed, hotel with a bar and various sizes of rooms (some on the small side), and a courtyard opening onto the backs of tenements. Don't be put off by the shabby entrance and loose handrails on the stairs, the interior is comfortable and the management unfailingly welcoming. ⑤

L'Impérial 2 bd Paoli ☎04 95 31 06 94, ℻04 95 34 13 76. Central, efficient two-star on the south side of town whose rooms are on the small side, but acceptable enough for a short stay. ④

Posta-Vecchia quai-des-Martyrs-de-la-Libération ☎04 95 32 32 38, ℻04 95 32 14 05, ⓔhotel-postavecchia@wanadoo.fr. The only hotel in the Vieux Port, and good value, with views across the sea from its (pricier) rooms at the front. Smaller, cheaper options are in the old block across the lane. ④

Riviera 1 bis, rue du Nouveau-Port ☎04 95 31 07 16, ℻04 95 34 17 39. Basic, and a bit noisy, but near the harbour. ④

Les Voyageurs 9 av Maréchal-Sébastiani ☎04 95 34 90 80, ℻04 95 34 00 65, ⓦwww.hotel-lesvoyageurs.com. Swish three-star opposite the post office, done out in pale yellow and with two categories of rooms: the larger, pricier ones have tubs instead of showers. No views to speak of, but fine for a night. ⑤

Hotels around Bastia

L'Alivi route du Cap, Ville Pietrabugno ☎04 95 55 00 00, ℻04 95 31 03 95, ⓦwww.hotel-alivi.com. Large three-star, 3km north of the city, with a pool, car park and private access to the beach. The rooms are light, spacious and all sea-facing with glorious views out towards the Tuscan islands from their terraces (especially lovely early in the morning). ⑧

Auberge San Martino place de l'Église, San Martino di Lota, 11km north of Bastia ☎04 95 32 23 68. Unpretentious, welcoming and typically Corsican auberge high above the corniche in the middle of a gorgeous old village, offering a handful of simple rooms (all en suite and an absolute steal at €38 for two including breakfast). There's no obligation to go for half board but given the hospitality most people do (see "Eating", p.72). The only drawback is you need your own transport to get here. Advance booking essential. ②

La Corniche San Martino di Lota, 11km north along the corniche road ☎04 95 31 40 98, ℻04 95 32 37 69, ⓦwww.lacorniche.com. Sunny rooms with superb vistas over schist rooftops and green hillsides to the sea, a pool and classy gourmet restaurant under plane trees (see "Eating", p.73). Part of the Logis de France chain, so its rates are very reasonable (down to €52 for a double in June). Closed Mon Oct–May. ⑤

Cyrnea Pietranea ☎04 95 31 41 71, ℻04 95 31 72 65. Congenial little two-star, 4km out of town on the roadside. All rooms are en suite, but only some overlook the water (from balconies where you can breakfast). You also get the run of a small garden, strewn with sun loungers, that falls to a secluded pebble beach. Good value given the location. ④

Pietracap route de San Martino ☎04 95 31 64 63, ℻04 95 31 39 00, ⓦwww.hotel-pietracap.com. Luxurious three-star set on a hillside overlooking the sea. The rooms open onto flowery terraces, most have lovely views, and there's a large pool set amid old olive trees. Take the first left after the *Alivi*. ⑦

Campsites

Casanova Miomo, 5km north along the route du Cap ☎04 95 33 91 42. Larger and greener than its neighbour, *Les Orangers*, but fractionally more expensive, and with a bar.

Esperenza plage du Pinède, route de Pineto ☎ 04 95 36 15 09. About 19km south of Bastia, beyond *San Damiano* (see below), with fewer facilities and poorly maintained toilet blocks, but cheap and close to the beach. Hourly buses in summer from the gare routière.

Les Orangers Miomo, 5km north along the route du Cap ☎ 04 95 33 24 09. Tiny site crammed onto narrow terraces, just off the main road. The cheaper of the pair in this suburb.

Les Sables Rouges 4km south, just beyond the turn-off for L'Arinella beach ☎ 04 95 33 00 65. Grotty and small, and for much of the year next to a noisy fairground, but slap on the beach and easily accessible by bus. Security could be a problem.

San Damiano Pineto, 10km south of Bastia ☎ 04 95 33 68 02. Huge, pricy 200-place site with top facilities, including a pool and Jacuzzi; take the road to the left across the bridge at Furiani roundabout (5km south on the N193). Buses as for the *Esperenza*, or you can jump on the train (the nearest station is Rocade). Open April–Oct.

The Town

Bastia is not especially large, and all its sights can easily be seen in a day without the use of a car. The spacious **place St-Nicolas** is the obvious place to get your bearings: open to the sea and lined with shady trees and cafés, it's the main focus of town life. Running parallel to it on the landward side are **boulevard Paoli** and **rue César-Campinchi**, the two main shopping streets, but all Bastia's historic sights lie within **Terra Vecchia**, the old quarter immediately south of place St-Nicolas, and **Terra Nova**, the area surrounding the **Citadelle**. Tucked away below the imposing, honey-coloured bastion is the much-photographed **Vieux Port**, with its boat-choked marina and crumbling eighteenth-century tenement buildings. By contrast, the **Nouveau Port** area, north of the *place*, is bland and modern, with little of interest other than restaurants, bars and a self-service laundry.

Place St-Nicolas

The most pleasant spot to soak up Bastia's Mediterranean atmosphere is **place St-Nicolas**. Lined by palms and pollarded plane trees, the long rectangular square is the social hub of the town. During the evening, with the Nouveau Port's gigantic white ferry boats forming a surreal backdrop, its cafés fill up with snappily dressed young Bastiais on their way home from work, while pensioners take leisurely *passeghiatas* under the trees. Apart from the camp marble statue of Napoléon in Roman emperor's garb, the square's only real sight is the wonderful Art Deco façade of the **Maison Mattei**, on the northwest side. This long-established wine merchants (July & Aug open till 10pm) sells liqueurs from all over the island, including the famous local quinine-based aperitif, Cap Corse.

Terra Vecchia

From place St-Nicolas the main route south into Terra Vecchia is rue Napoléon, a narrow street with some ancient offbeat shops and a pair of sumptuously decorated chapels on its east side. The first of these, the **Oratoire St-Roch**, is a Genoese Baroque extravagance, built in 1604 to reflect the wealth of the rising bourgeoisie. Particularly remarkable are its walls, which are covered with finely carved wooden panelling. The chapel also possesses a magnificent organ, decorated with gilt and wooden sculpture; and hardly altered since it was built in 1750.

A little further along stands the **Oratoire de l'Immaculée Conception**, built in 1611 as the showplace of the Genoese in Corsica, who used it for state occasions such as the inauguration of the governor. In later years, the English viceroy, Sir Gilbert Elliot, held parliamentary sessions here during the brief

Anglo-Corsican interlude. Overlooking a pebble mosaic of a sun, the austere façade belies the flamboyant interior, where crimson velvet draperies, a gilt and marble ceiling, frescoes and crystal chandeliers create the ambience of an opera house. The unusually narrow nave terminates at an elaborate polychromatic marble altar, over which hangs a copy of Murillo's *Immaculate Conception*. On the left stands a statue of the Virgin, which, on December 8, is paraded through the streets to the Église St-Jean-Baptiste. The sacristy houses a tiny museum (daily 9am–6pm; free) of minor religious works, of which the wooden statue of Erasmus, patron saint of fishers, dating from 1788, is most arresting.

If you cut back through the narrow steps beside the Oratoire de St-Roch, a two-minute walk will bring you to **place de l'Hôtel-de-Ville**, commonly known as place du Marché because of the **fresh produce market** that takes place here each morning (8am–1pm). At the south end of the square is the **Église St-Jean–Baptiste**, an immense ochre edifice whose twin campaniles, which loom dramatically above the Vieux Port, are Bastia's most distinctive landmark. Built in 1636, the church was restored in the eighteenth century in a Rococo overkill of multicoloured marble. Decorating the walls are a few unremarkable Italian paintings from Napoléon's uncle, Cardinal Fesch, an avid collector of Renaissance art (see p.204).

Around the church extends the oldest part of Bastia, an enclosed zone of dark alleys, vaulted passageways and seven-storey houses locked in isolation from the rest of town. Hidden among them, on the rue Castagno, is one of Corsica's few remaining synagogues, the **Beth Meir**. A plaque on its wall alludes to the anti-Semitism that was rife in Bastia during World War II, after which all but a handful of the town's Jewish population left. Since then, families of Moroccan immigrants have moved in to take their place as the district's underclass.

By turning right outside the Église St-Jean–Baptiste and following rue St-Jean, you'll come to **rue Général-Carbuccia**, the heart of Terra Vecchia. Pascal Paoli once lived here, at no. 7, and Balzac stayed briefly at no. 23 when his ship got stuck in Corsica on the way to Sardinia. Set in a small square at the end of the road is the **Église St-Charles**, an august Jesuit chapel whose wide steps provide an evening meeting place for locals.

The Vieux Port

The **Vieux Port** is the most appealing part of town: soaring houses seem to bend inwards towards the water, peeling plaster and boat hulls glint in the sun, while the south side remains in the shadow of the great rock that supports the citadel. Site of the original Porto Cardo, the Vieux Port later bustled with Genoese traders, but since the building of the ferry terminal and commercial docks it has become a backwater, deserted by day, when the clinking of yacht masts echoes around the marina. It's livelier at night, with the glow and noise from the harbourside bars and restaurants. These continue round the north end of the port along the wide quai-des-Martyrs-de-la-Libération, where live bands clank out pop classics for the tourists in summer.

The best view of the Vieux Port is from the **Jetée du Dragon**, the quay that juts out under the citadel. To build it, engineers had to destroy a giant lion-shaped rock known as the Leone, which formerly blocked the entrance to the harbour, and which featured in the foreground of many nineteenth-century engravings of Bastia. To reach the citadel from the quai-des-Martyrs, you can walk through the **Jardin Romieu**, a recently spruced-up, eighteenth-century terraced garden adorning the cliff on this side of the harbour. The steps leading through it bring you out at a little green, huddled below the bastion walls, that makes an ideal picnic spot.

Terra Nova

The military and administrative core of old Bastia, **Terra Nova** (or the **Citadelle**) lords it over the old port from its perch atop a sheer-sided rocky promontory. Beautifully restored over the past couple of decades, the quarter has a distinct air of affluence, and its lofty apartments and pastel colour-washed houses are now largely the preserve of Bastia's affluent set. The area is focused on **place du Donjon**, which gets its name from the squat round tower that formed the nucleus of the town's fortifications and was used by the Genoese to incarcerate Corsican patriots – Sampiero Corso was held in the dungeon for four years in the early sixteenth century. Next to the tower, a strategically placed terrace **bar** commands a magnificent view which, on a clear day, extends across the Tyrrhenian Sea to the Tuscan island of Elba.

The Palais des Gouverneurs and Musée d'Éthnographie Corse

Facing the bar is the impressive fourteenth-century **Palais des Gouverneurs**, Terra Nova's most prominent landmark. With its great round tower, arcaded inner courtyard and pristine peach-coloured paintwork, the building has a distinctly Moorish feel. During the Genoese heyday, the governor and the local bishop lived here with an entourage of seventy horsemen, entertaining foreign dignitaries and hosting massive parties. When the French transferred the capital to Ajaccio, it became a prison, and was then destroyed during Nelson's attack of 1794. The subsequent rebuilding was not the last, as parts of it were blown up by the allied bombardment (see box on p.416) in 1943, and today the restorers are trying to regain something of the building's former grandeur.

Part of the palace is given over to the **Musée d'Éthnographie Corse** (currently closed for renovation, but scheduled to re-open in 2003; daily: June 9am–6.30pm; July & Aug 9am–8pm; Sept–May 9am–noon & 2–6pm; last entry 45min before closing time; admission around €5), whose exhibition presents the history of Corsica from prehistoric times to the present day. Its vaulted chambers contain a motley collection of artefacts from rare rock specimens to Pascal Paoli memorabilia, an array that at first sight seems rather tired yet does include a handful of fascinating historical titbits, among them a diminutive Roman sarcophagus decorated with hunting scenes. Thought to have belonged to a child, it was discovered in Bastelicaccia, near Ajaccio, where it was being used as a horses' drinking trough. The remaining exhibits illustrate the island's history with old maps, engravings and documents, along with cases relating to key figures such as Sampiero, King Théodore and Nelson. On your way around, look out for the replica of Napoléon's death mask, and for the original "Moor's Head" **flag of Independence**, an emblem of obscure origins (see box on p.446).

Most visits to the museum wind up with a guided tour (price included in admission fee) of the renovated Genoese **dungeons** below the governor's palace. Although of little interest in themselves, the damp stone chambers are well worth a look if you can follow the French commentary, which describes in gruesome detail the conditions endured by the 350 or more inmates incarcerated here, many of them chained for days on end to the wet walls. Particularly poignant is the cell in which Resistance fighters were held and tortured by the Nazis during World War II; one actually cut out his own tongue rather than divulge the whereabouts of his comrades.

Terra Nova churches

Back in place du Donjon, if you cross the square and follow rue Notre-Dame you come out at the **Église Ste-Marie**. Built in 1458 and overhauled in the seventeenth century, it was the cathedral of Bastia until 1801, when the bishopric was transferred to Ajaccio. Inside, the church's principal treasure is a small silver statue of the Virgin (housed in a glass case on the right wall as you face the altar), which is carried through Terra Nova and Terra Vecchia on August 15, the Festival of the Assumption.

Immediatley behind Ste-Maire in rue de l'Evêché stands the **Oratoire Ste-Croix**, a sixteenth-century chapel decorated in Louis XV style, with lashings of rich blue paint and gilt scrollwork. It houses another holy item, the Christ des Miracles, a blackened oak crucifix, much venerated by Bastia's fishermen, which in 1428 was discovered floating in the sea surrounded by a luminous haze. A festival celebrating the miracle takes place in Bastia on May 3, when local fishing families carry it around Terra Nova. Beyond the church, the narrow streets open out to the secluded **place Guasco**, where a few benches offer the chance of a rest before descending back into the fray.

Bastia's beaches

Crowded with schoolchildren in the summer, the pebbly **town beach** in Bastia is worth visiting only if you're desperate for a swim. To reach it, turn left at the flower shop on the main road south out of town, just beyond the citadel. A better alternative is to head 1km further along the same road to the long beach of **L'Arinella** at Montesoro, the beginning of a sandy shore that extends along the whole east coast. A **bus** to L'Arinella leaves from *Café Riche* at the top of boulevard Paoli every twenty minutes; get off at the last stop and cross the railway line to the sea. There are a couple of sailing and windsurfing clubs here, plus a bar.

Leaving Bastia in the other direction, you will find sandy beaches about 1km along the road to **Cap Corse**, but these are rather polluted and the sea tends to be choppy.

Eating, drinking and nightlife

Lively place St-Nicolas, packed with cafés, is the place to be during the day, particularly between noon and 3pm, when the rest of town is deserted. For a more sedate atmosphere, head along boulvard Paoli and rue César-Campinchi, which are lined with chichi salons de thé offering elaborate creamy confections, local chestnut cake and doughnuts. Late-night clubbers can revive themselves with an early coffee and a pain au chocolat at one of the three cafés in place de l'Hôtel-de-Ville, which open at 4.30am for the market traders. You'll find that most cafés serve croque-monsieur at exorbitant prices, but for better-value **snacks** try the offbeat retro **kiosks** on place St-Nicolas, which sell hot dogs, crêpes, *panini* and tasty *casse-croûtes*. Numerous **pizza vans** are scattered about town until about 9pm (there's usually one outside the train station), evidence of a strong Italian influence that's also apparent in the predominance of pizzerias and pasta places crammed into the narrow backstreets behind the quai-des-Martyrs. The town also boasts some excellent yet inexpensive **restaurants** serving Corsican specialities, and fish is inevitably prominent: the posh places on the quai-des-Martyrs do the best *aziminu*, a Corsican version of bouillabaisse. Most of the good restaurants are to be found around the Vieux Port and on the quai-des-Martyrs, with a sprinkling in the citadel. The establishments listed below are open daily unless specified.

Drinking is serious business in Bastia. The **Casanis** pastis factory is on the outskirts of town in Lupino, and this is indisputably the town's drink – order a "*Casa*" and you'll fit in well. There are many bars and cafés all over town, varying from the stark, bright bars of Terra Vecchia, to the elegant, dimly lit cafés on place St-Nicolas, where you can sip hot chocolate on low leather seats. The best place to buy wine is *Grand Vin Corse* at 24 rue César-Campinchi; the obliging proprietor will fill up plastic bottles of muscat from the barrels for you.

Bastia doesn't offer much in the way of **nightlife**. There are a couple of cinemas, the island's only good theatre and a couple of cheesy clubs. The best source of information about all events is the daily local paper *Corse-Matin*.

Bars and cafés

Bar de la Citadelle In front of the Palais des Gouverneurs, Terra Nova. Basically a sandwich and ice-cream bar that would have little to recommend it were it not for the superb location overlooking the Vieux Port.

Café des Palmiers place St-Nicolas. One of the few along this stretch with comfy wicker chairs that catch the sun at breakfast time. Delicious fresh pâtisseries and attentive service.

Chez Serge Raugi 2 bis, rue Capanelle, off bd Général Graziani, at the north end of place St-Nicolas ☏ 04 95 31 22 31. Arguably Corsica's greatest ice-cream maker, from an illustrious line of local *glaciers*. Tables on a cramped pavement terrace or upstairs on an even smaller mezzanine floor. In winter, they also do a legendary chickpea tart to take away.

Le Pub Assunta 5 pl Fontaine-Neuve. Large, lively bar with a snooker table on its mezzanine floor and a terrace opening onto the old quarter. A good selection of draught beers, and live-music nights with local bands on Thursdays. Serves fast food indoors or on a shady terrace outside.

Restaurants

Auberge San Martino place de l'église, San Martino-di-Lota, 11km north of Bastia ☏ 04 95 32 23 68. This is one of the most convivial and best-value restaurants in the region, and reason enough to venture out along the corniche (a spectacular drive in itself: see p.81 for directions). Exposed beams, old farm tools and polyphony music set the tone. The food's copious, inexpensive and authentically local: anchovies à la bastiaise, game stews and wild boar lasagne, with homemade *migliaccoli* or *fiadone* for dessert. The tables indoors are more appealing than those outside in the *tonnelle* (plastic awning). Open all year.

La Braise 7 bd Hyacinte-de-Montrea/bd Général Giraud ☏ 04 95 31 36 97. Authentic Corsican pizzeria, decked out like the interior of a Castagniccian *séchoir*, whose succulent meat dishes and pizzas, cooked over wood grills with maquis herbs, have made its owner – a "Russian-Chuwawa-Indian retired boxer" – a local celebrity (check out the photos on the window of him posing with Belmondo and Coluche). The charcuterie (winter only) is wonderful, and the banana flambé a must. Count on €20 for the works, or €7–10 for pizzas. Closed Sun & Aug.

A Casarelle 6 rue Ste-Croix ☏ 04 95 32 02 32. Innovative Corsican-French cuisine served on a terrace on the edge of the citadel. The chef's specialities are traditional dishes of the Balagne, such as *casgiate* (nuggets of fresh cheese baked in fragrant chestnut leaves) or the rarely prepared *storzapreti* – balls of *brocciu*, spinach and herbs in tomato sauce. À la carte only; count on around €20–25 per head. Closed Sat & Sun lunchtimes.

La Citadelle 6 rue du Dragon, Citadelle ☏ 04 95 31 44 70. Gorgeous gourmet restaurant in the heart of Terra Nova. Mostly sumptuous French cuisine (*magret de canard à l'orange* is one of the chef's top dishes), served inside a vaulted cellar with mellow lighting and an old olive press in the corner. Prices are high for the area (€30.50 for the three-course *menu fixe*, or around €40 per head à la carte without wine), but you get what you pay for: this is one of the finest places to eat on the island. And be sure to leave room for one of their to-die-for desserts (the *mille-feuille aux fruits rouges* is sublime).

La Corniche San Martino-di-Lota, 11km north along the corniche road ☎ 04 95 31 40 98. Bastiais drive out in droves for the cordon bleu cooking served in this smart village hotel, situated high on a hillside with superb views out to Monte Cristo and Elba. The cuisine is a mixture of old family recipes and classy continental dishes given Corsican twists (eg *terrine de foie gras au muscat Cap Corse*). More standard local specialities and simple seafood dominate their popular €23 *menu traditionnel*. When booking, ask for a table on the terrace under one of the umbrella pines.

A Scaletta Vieux Port, entrance on the steps leading from the port to Église St-Jean-Baptiste. Down-to-earth seafood and Corsican standards served on a precarious balcony overlooking the boats (reserve early if you want to sit here). The

€18.50 menu's the one to go for, featuring fresh fish of the day, such as pan-fried sea bass or snapper, and a platter of Niolu cheeses. Not such a great option out of season, however, when the microwave takes over.

U Tianu 4 rue Rigo ☎ 04 95 31 36 67. Tiny, family-run restaurant with lots of atmosphere hidden in a narrow backstreet behind the Vieux Port. Their limited but excellent-value menus (€20–23) change daily but feature typical country dishes: *Figatellu* pâté, blackbird terrine, chickpeas with anchovies, mutton and lentil stew, sardines stuffed with *brocciu*, and *fiadone* soaked in homemade eau de vie.

Le Zagora 4 rue des Terrasses, Vieux Port ☎ 04 95 34 12 01. French-style Moroccan restaurant, with tables either in a tastefully ethnic interior or on a tiny balcony overlooking the harbour. Try their delicious *tagines* (€14), veal with plums and almonds, or chicken in olive sauce, washed down with mint tea. Around €20 per head. Closed Sun.

Nightlife

What there is of Bastia's **nightlife** centres around the bars, cafés and restaurants of the Vieux Port and place St-Nicolas. A couple of discos and cinemas add some variety to an evening, but you'll have to search hard for a crowded venue, as the preferred entertainment of Bastiais seems to be a quiet night in front of the television.

If there is a concert in Bastia it will almost certainly be held in the **theatre** in place Favalelli (☎04 95 34 98 00), west of rue César-Campinchi. Concerts of traditional Corsican singing and nationalist rallies are also regular events at the theatre and at the Chambre de Commerce off place de l'Hôtel-de-Ville – check out the fly posters scattered around town.

Of Bastia's two **cinemas**, the triple-screen Le Regent, just off the south side of rue César-Campinchi, shows new films, always dubbed into French, whereas the Studio, in nearby rue Miséricorde (see map for both), is a small outfit showing mostly subtitled foreign and art movies. The week-long Festival du Film et des Cultures Méditerranéennes takes place in the third week of November at the cinemas and the theatre, showcasing films, backed up by exhibitions, from all parts of the Mediterranean region. There's also a British film festival in the first two weeks in March, featuring fairly recent releases with French subtitles.

Nightclubs are few and far between. In the centre of town, the best is the long-established *St Nicolas*, underneath the *place* at 14 bd Général-de-Gaulle, whose music is more varied than the usual endless Europop. Out of town, *L'Apocalypse*, 10km along the La Marana stretch south of Bastia, is *the* disco to be seen at, but it attracts a mainly teenage crowd, and you'll need a car to get there. Entry is free and drinks extortionate at both, which keep going till dawn (closed Mon & Tues).

Summer firework displays are a regular occurrence, with the most spectacular show happening in place St-Nicolas on **Bastille Day** (July 14), when street parties are held all over town. A solemn procession heralds the **Fête de l'Assomption**, or le Quinze-Août (August 15), after which the Vieux Port becomes overrun by revellers. Other annual events include the **Fête du Christ Noir** on May 3 (see p.46), a **regatta** in June and the **Foire de Bastia** in July, which has stalls – mainly promoting local businesses – and live music in the evenings.

Listings

Airlines Air France, 6 av Émile-Sari ☎ 04 95 32 10 29 or 04 95 54 54 95; Air Inter, 6 av Émile-Sari ☎ 04 95 31 79 79. Both companies also have branches at Poretta airport.

Airport enquiries ☎ 04 95 54 54 54.

Banks and exchange Most of the main banks and automatic cash dispensers are on place St-Nicolas, at the bottom of bd Paoli, and on rue César-Campinchi. The main branch of the Société Générale (best for changing Thomas Cook traveller's cheques) is at the bottom of the square on rue Miot. American Express traveller's cheques are best changed at Crédit Agricole, which has a foreign-exchange counter in the arrivals hall of the gare maritime (terminal sud) in the Nouveau Port. One place to avoid is the Change at 15 av Maréchal-Sébastiani, opposite the post office (July & Aug Mon–Sat 9am–7pm), which charges a very stiff commission fee.

Bicycle and motorbike rental Locacycles, behind the Palais de Justice (☎ 04 95 32 30 64), rents bicycles by the day (€14) or for longer periods, as does Objectif Nature, rue Notre-Dame-de Lourdes (☎ 04 95 32 54 34). The only place in Bastia offering motorbike rental is Plaisance Service Location, Port Toga, at the north side of the Nouveau Port (☎ 04 95 31 49 01), which has bikes from 50cc to 400cc. Rates range from €50–80 per day depending on the size of the machine.

Bookshops The best-stocked bookshop and stationer is Album Librairie, at the top of rue César-Campinchi, which has a great selection of titles on Corsica.

Car rental Avis (Ollandini), 40 bd Paoli ☎ 04 95 32 57 30, airport ☎ 04 95 54 55 46; Europcar, 1 rue du Nouveau-Port ☎ 04 95 31 50 91, airport ☎ 04 95 30 09 50; Hertz, square St-Victor ☎ 04 95 31 14 24, airport ☎ 04 95 30 05 00; Rent-a-Car, Poretta airport ☎ 04 95 54 55 11. For central reservations of these and the island's other main rental companies, see Basics, p.31.

Diving Thalassa Immersion (☎ 04 95 31 78 90), 2km north of the centre (head past the marina and turn left at the Elf petrol station), or book through the shop of the same name, on rue

Napoléon, just behind the Vieux Port; Club Plongée Bastias, Vieux Port (☎ 04 95 33 31 28), works from their boat, moored on the north side of the harbour. Both outfits run trips to the famous Heinkel-111, just beyond the sea wall, and to the wreck of *La Cannonière*, about an hour's ride up the coast off Pietracorbara. Rates are around €35 per dive.

Ferry offices Corsica Ferries, 5 bis, rue Chanoine-Leschi ☎ 04 95 32 95 95, ℗ 04 95 32 14 71, or at the gare maritime ☎ 04 95 32 95 94, ℗ 04 95 32 95 55; Corsica Marittima, 15 bd Général-de-Gaulle ☎ 04 95 32 69 04, ℗ 04 95 32 69 09; Happy Lines, gare maritime, Nouveau Port ☎ 04 95 55 25 52; Mobylines, Sarl Colonna D'Istria & Fils, 4 rue Luce de Casablanca, just behind the Nouveau Port ☎ 04 95 34 84 94, ℗ 04 95 32 17 94; SNCM, Nouveau Port, BP 57 ☎ 04 95 54 66 66, ℗ 04 95 54 66 69.

Hospital Centre Hôpitalier de Falconaja, rue Imperiale, Lupino ☎ 04 95 55 11 11.

Internet access Gigatec, 8 rue Fontaine-Neuve, just above the Vieux Port, is one of Corsica's only Internet cafés; low light and high prices.

Laundry Lavoir du Port (daily 7am–9pm), two doors down from the big Esso petrol station, opposite the ferry dock's north terminal, charges €5.50 for a machine load (plus €1.50 for drying); cycles last around 40min.

Left luggage Both *consignes* in Bastia – in the arrivals hall of the gare maritime at the Nouveau Port (daily 8–11.30am & 2–7.30pm), and at the train station (daily 7am–10pm) – were closed at the time of writing as a security precaution.

Pharmacies Plenty on bd Paoli, or try Ricci-Luciani, at the top of place St-Nicolas, near the tourist office (Mon–Sat 8.30am–12.15pm & 2.30–7pm). In an emergency, call ☎ 04 95 31 99 17.

Post office The central post office is on av Maréchal-Sebastiani, between the train station and place St-Nicolas.

Taxis There is a taxi rank at the northern end of place St-Nicolas, next to the gare routière (☎ 04 95 34 07 00).

Train information ☎ 04 95 32 80 60.

Moving on from Bastia

As Corsica's busiest passenger ferry port, with road and rail connections to most parts of the island, Bastia is the north's main transport hub, and if you're travelling without the luxury of your own vehicle you're bound at some stage to pass through here. Obtaining information about departure times and points can sometimes be difficult, mainly because most services are run by private companies with offices scattered across town. The only place that keeps up-to-date timetables for all public transport services operating out of Bastia is the tourist office on place St-Nicolas (see p.66), where you can also get advice about onward journeys from other parts of the island, and towns and cities on the Continent.

By plane

Bastia's Poretta **airport** (℡04 95 54 54 54), 16km south of town, is served by direct flights from London (Gatwick and Stansted), Birmingham and several major French cities. The cheapest way to get there from the town centre is on the beige and blue shuttle bus, or *navette*, which departs to connect with flights from the Leclerc roundabout, in front of the train station. For precise times of the service, which costs €8 one way, call ℡04 95 31 06 65.

By ferry

Regular car and passenger **ferries** operate all year round between Bastia and the French ports of Nice and Marseille, with a less frequent service to Toulon. Also served in the summer months are the Italian ports of Genoa, La Spezia, Livorno, Savona and Piombino. In summer, be sure to reserve a place, especially if travelling by car. For details of ferry offices in Bastia see "Listings" on p.74. For more on routes, fares and timetables, see Basics, p.20.

By train

Corsica's famous narrow-gauge train, the **micheline** (see p.34), terminates in Bastia, and there are regular services from the town to stations along both branches of the line. During the summer (July 1–Sept 15), four trains run daily between Bastia and Ajaccio (€23), via Corte (€11), while for the rest of the year (Sept 24–June 30) only two services operate Monday to Saturday, with an additional two trains on Sunday. The schedule for the line connecting Bastia, L'Île Rousse and Calvi (€15) remains the same all year round, with two services running daily. Timetables are available from the train station and tourist office. For information, call ℡04 95 32 80 60.

By bus

Bastia is better connected by bus than any other town on the island, but finding out when and from where the services depart can be problematic (ask at the tourist office for their bus service résumé). Roughly speaking, buses to **Ajaccio**, and to smaller, rural destinations – including Patrimonio, Nonza, Cap Corse, Nebbio, St-Florent and Castagniccia – tend to operate out of the so-called gare routière, at the north end of place St-Nicolas behind the Hôtel de Ville, whereas services to the main towns start from less obvious spots. For **Bonifacio**, **Porto-Vecchio** and buses to the east coast, you pick up the bus from the roadside opposite the main post office on avenue Maréchal-Sébastiani. Services for **Corte** only, and **Calvi** (via **L'Île Rousse**), depart from outside the train station.

For a complete rundown of destinations reachable by bus from Bastia, see "Travel details" on p.110. Tickets for all services are available on the bus from the driver.

The poet-pilot's last flight

No writer in the history of French literature has enjoyed the mass popularity of **Antoine de Saint-Exupéry**, the author-aviator voted in 2000 as the most important *écrivain français* of the millennium. The only twentieth-century figure to have been depicted on French franc banknotes, and honoured with his own set of commemorative stamps, "Saint-Ex" owes his literary reputation to just five slim books – or more precisely, one very slim book. Written during World War II, **Le Petit Prince**, the story of a boy in flares and pointy shoes who befriends a rose and a fox on an asteroid called B-612, still sells a steady one million copies worldwide each year, having been translated into one hundred languages. This makes *The Little Prince* the best-selling French book ever written, a phenomenal achievement for a man lacking either the charisma of André Malraux or the intellect of Jean-Paul Sartre – his two closest rivals in the country's twentieth-century hall of literary fame.

One of the many romantic details of the author's life is that it ended enigmatically during a secret flight over occupied France in 1944. But few Saint-Ex aficionados could tell you that the place this flight began was Bastia's **Poretta airport**. Early in the morning on July 31, 1944, Saint-Exupéry's P-58 Lightning disappeared into a cloudless sky heading northwest towards the French coast on a high-altitude mission from which it would never return.

At the outbreak of war, the already famous author, with two decades of extreme flying across the Andes and Sahara for the Société Aeropostale under his belt, was posted to a long-range reconnaissance squadron, II/33 Group, for whom he flew many daring missions before being demobilized after the 1940 Armistice. Under Vichy, he lived quietly in the Unoccupied Zone until the death of one of his II/33 comrades – a pilot he'd flown with on airmail duty between Dakar and Casablanca before the war – galvanized Saint-Ex to fight the Nazis and the Vichy government.

Whether his decision to rejoin the war was an act of repentance, to restore honour lost through his tacit support for the Fascist occupation, remains a moot point among biographers. But in May 1943, after a brief spell in New York where he wrote *Le Petit Prince*, he received permission to fly once again for his old squadron, now re-formed under American command.

South of Bastia

It's easy to be put off by the industrial sprawl **south of Bastia**, but amidst the built-up areas are hidden some sights ideal for a half-day excursion – or as a scenic **alternative route to the airport**. At the Furiani junction, about 4km along the N193, you can turn off the main road to follow the stretch of coast known as **La Marana**, where holiday villages and villas back a sandy beach lined with pine woods. Between it and the N193 lies the **Étang de Biguglia**, a wildlife-rich **lagoon** named after the ancient capital of Corsica, now an unremarkable village on the slopes above the main road. The lagoon stretches as far as the **Roman site** of **Mariana**, 25km south of Bastia, where you can see the remains of a twelfth-century basilica and the superb **Pisan church** of La Canonica.

There is no public transport direct to Mariana. **Buses**, which leave from opposite the Bastia gare routière at 11.30am and 6pm in summer, take you along La Marana as far as Pineto. From here it's a good three-kilometre walk to the Roman site.

La Marana and the Étang de Biguglia

Traditionally the summer haunt of prosperous Bastia families, the sixteen-kilometre *littoral* known as **La Marana** (pronounced "la-mar*an*") is the begin-

Saint-Exupéry's return to active service, however, was to be short-lived. After a bad landing in which the notoriously non-conformist, irascible veteran flyer wrecked a P-58 Lightning, he was grounded. Already thirteen years over the limit for flying P-58s, his career looked at an end and would have been had not a Time-Life photo-journalist and great fan of Saint-Exupéry, **John Phillips**, pulled strings to get him back in the air. Phillips spent a month shadowing his hero at II/33 Squadron Allied Air Base in Alghero, Sardinia, and his evocative photographs graphically convey the mood of Saint-Exupéry's last summer, as he begrudgingly squeezed his middle-aged frame into modern flying suits and submitted to the indignities of radio head sets and English instructions from the control tower.

Over the years, Saint-Ex's depressed state in 1944 – his frequently articulated despair at "a world capable of producing perfect pianos off the assembly line but incapable of producing pianists" – has led to speculation that his death was suicide. Some weight was lent to the theory by the discovery off the coast of Marseille in 1999 of what experts now believe is the wreck of his P-58. The hunt for the plane began when a local fisherman landed a bracelet bearing the names 'Antoine' and 'Consuelo', the author's wife. Divers later located a Lightning's landing gear and a section of a tail fin. Yet German log books show no record of a P-58 being shot down, either by flak or fighter planes, on the day of Saint-Ex's disappearance, which some have interpreted as proof that the crash was intentional.

A **Commonwealth war grave and memorial** to the many other airmen and sailors who died in sorties out of Bastia in the last two years of the war stands 4km south of the city; look for the signpost off the west side of N193. In a well-groomed walled enclosure, rows of white tombstones stand engraved with the names of the deceased and, where known, the circumstances of their deaths. Just north of it are buried German soldiers killed in the battle of September 1943, while some of the many Berber *goumiers* who died fighting them were laid to rest in a small graveyard on the roadside, 1km northwest of St-Florent (see p.105). For more on the events of World War II in Corsica, see pp.416–417.

ning of the sandy stretch that continues more or less uninterrupted all the way down to Porto-Vecchio in the south. Largely the preserve of joggers, rollerbladers and windsurfers, the beach offers shady pine woods, restaurants and bars and, even though the sea is quite polluted due to boat traffic and the proximity to the town, it makes an agreeable excursion from Bastia when the heat gets too much. All this part of the coast is divided into holiday residences or sections of beach attached to bars, the latter freely open to the public.

Fed by the rivers Bevinco and Golo, the **Étang de Biguglia** is the largest lagoon in Corsica and one of its best **birdlife** sites, thanks largely to the reed beds bordering the water. Of the birds that nest in them, various species of warblers are most common – in summer you'll find reed warblers at the southern end of the lagoon, as well as moustached warblers and cetti warblers, with their distinctive loud repetitive cry. In winter, Biguglia is a stopoff point for migrating grey herons, kingfishers, great crested grebes, little grebes, water rails and various species of duck, such as the spectacular red-crested pochard, identifiable by its red bill, red feet and a bright red head.

Mariana

The Roman town of **Mariana**, just south of Étang de Biguglia, can be approached by taking the turning for the airport, 16km along the N193, or the more picturesque coastal route through La Marana.

Founded in 93 BC as a military colony, Mariana had become a Christian centre by the fourth century, when its basilica was built. The settlement was damaged severely by the Vandals and Ostrogoths in the fifth and sixth centuries, and by the time of the Genoese occupation Mariana had become so waterlogged and malarial that it had to be abandoned. Now the ruins and old Pisan church form an incongruous counterpoint to the space-age architecture of Poretta airport across the fields, whose constant traffic – both overhead and along the road – detract somewhat from the forlorn beauty of the place.

The houses, baths and basilica are now too tumbledown to be of great interest, but the square **baptistry** has a remarkable mosaic floor decorated with dancing dolphins and fish looped around a bearded Neptune – Christianized pagan images representing the Four Rivers of Paradise.

Adjacent to Mariana stands the church of Santa Maria Assunta, commonly known as **La Canonica**. Erected in 1119 close to the old capital of Biguglia, it is the finest of around three hundred churches built by the Pisans in their effort to evangelize the island. The perfectly proportioned edifice, modelled on a Roman basilica, is decorated outside with Corinthian capitals plundered from the main Mariana site and with plates of Cap Corse marble, their delicate pink and yellow ochre hues fusing to stunning effect. Carvings of animals and Celtic-like geometric bands also embellish the arch above the door. The interior has been recently restored in a very plain style, and is used for concerts and for Mass on religious festivals.

Marooned in muddy fields about 300m to the south of La Canonica stands **San Parteo**, built in the eleventh and twelfth centuries over the site of a pagan burial ground. A smaller church than La Canonica, it also displays some elegant arcading and stone sculpture – on the south side, the door lintel is supported by two writhing beasts reaching to a central tree, a motif of Oriental origins.

North of Bastia: Cap Corse

Until Napoléon III had a coach road built around **Cap Corse** in the nineteenth century, the promontory was effectively cut off from the rest of the island, relying on Italian maritime traffic for its income – hence its distinctive Tuscan dialect. Ruled by feudal lords who retained substantial independence from the island's governors, it maintained a peaceful existence that greatly influenced the character of the Capicursini, or **Cap Corsins**. For all the changes brought by the modern world, Cap Corse still feels like a separate country.

Forty kilometres long and only fifteen across, the cape is divided by a spine of mountains called the Serra, which peaks at **Cima di e Folicce**, 1324m above sea level. The coast on the **east side** of this divide is characterized by tiny ports or *marines*, tucked into gently sloping river mouths, alongside coves that become sandier as you go further north. The villages of the **western coast** are sited on rugged cliffs, high above the rough sea and tiny rocky inlets that can be glimpsed from the corniche road. Cap Corse remains virtually untainted by tourism: wild flowers grow in profusion on the mountainsides in spring, goats graze freely, fishing villages are quiet and traditional, and many of the inland slopes are occupied by vineyards, producing the fragrant **muscat wine** that's one of the cape's major exports. It's only in the last twenty years or so that hotels have appeared, with the highest concentration at **Macinaggio** and **Centuri–Port**, on either side of the northern tip. Unfortunately, though, much

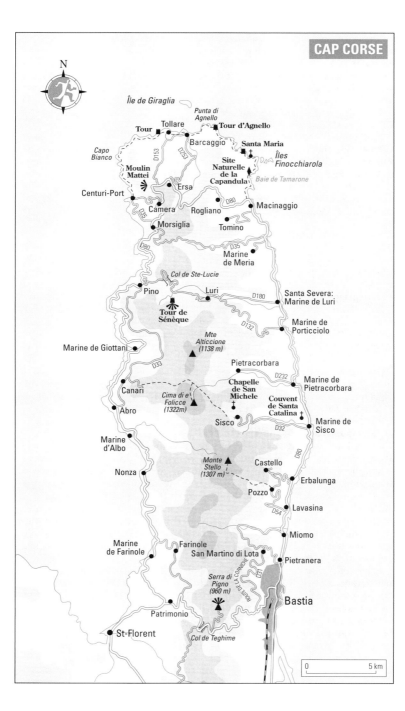

CAP CORSE

Île de Giraglia

Punta di Agnello

Tour d'Agnello

Tour   Tollare

Santa Maria

Barcaggio

Capo Bianco

Site Naturelle de la Capandula

Îles Finocchiarola

Moulin Mattei

Baie de Tamarone

Centuri-Port

Ersa

Camera   Rogliano

Macinaggio

Morsiglia

Tomino

Marine de Meria

Col de Ste-Lucie

Pino   Luri

Santa Severa: Marine de Luri

Tour de Sénèque

Marine de Porticciolo

Mte Alticcione (1138 m)

Marine de Giottani

Pietracorbara

Marine de Pietracorbara

Canari

Cima di e Folicce (1322m)

Chapelle de San Michele

Abro

Couvent de Santa Catalina

Sisco

Marine de Sisco

Marine d'Albo

Monte Stello (1307 m)

Castello

Nonza

Erbalunga

Pozzo

Lavasina

Miomo

Marine de Farinole

Farinole

San Martino di Lota

Pietranera

Serra di Pigno (960 m)

Bastia

Patrimonio

St-Florent

Col de Teghime

0   5 km

of the once verdant countryside has been blackened by fire (see p.116).

Many people tackle the hundred-kilometre corniche in a one-day tour from Bastia or St-Florent. A shorter alternative is to cut across the peninsula at Santa Severa, thereby getting a taste of the interior and a look at the spectacular **Tour de Sénèque**, where, according to popular legend, the Roman poet-philosopher Seneca spent his exiled years. Best of all, of course, would be to spend a few days here. If you're driving, bear in mind that petrol stations are few and far between, so fill up in Bastia.

Even more numerous than the Genoese watchtowers dotted along the shore of the cape are the **convents**, **churches** and in particular **Romanesque chapels** overlooking it. Cap Corse harboured some of the first Christian centres in Corsica, and this was the only region of the island where the Franciscan movement had any real influence. Elaborate marble **mausoleums** are also a common feature, often occupying lonely places on the inland hill-slopes and standing out strikingly white in a sea of green maquis.

Cap Corse transport

The main villages on Cap Corse are connected to Bastia's gare routière by **bus**, but services tend to be infrequent. Running up the east coast to Rogliano and Macinaggio, Transports Saladini's bus operates year round (Mon, Wed & Fri; ☎04 95 35 43 88), departing at 4pm from Bastia and arriving 1hr 15min later in Macinaggio; they also lay on two additional departures in summer, the first leaving Bastia early in the morning. For Luri, in the middle of the northern cape, there's Autocars Pavarini Jules' Wednesday-only bus (departs 4pm Bastia, arrives 4.50pm; ☎04 95 35 00 11). The other year-round service on Cap Corse is Transports Saoletti's bus to Canari (Mon & Wed; 1hr; €45; ☎04 95 37 84 05), which also departs at 4pm.

During August, you can complete the full *tour du Cap* by bus, thanks to Transports Micheli's convenient circular service from Bastia's gare routière to Erbalunga, Macinaggio, Centuri, Canari, Nonza, St-Florent and Oletta (Mon–Sat daily; ☎04 95 35 64 02).

A brief history of Cap Corse

Inhabited by various ancient civilizations – the Phoenicians, Greeks and Romans were all here – Cap Corse became significant in the tenth century, when the da Massa lords came over from Pisa and established fiefdoms across the region. By the following century Genoese settlers were being drawn to the cape's vineyards, and after Genoa's trouncing of Pisa at the Battle of Meloria in 1284, the feudal lords of Cap Corse became important – if intermittent – allies of the island's new rulers. Two local families shared most of the cape from this time – the da Mare clan held the north, whilst the da Gentile ruled the south, a situation that lasted into the late eighteenth century, when the French gained control of the island.

Although subject to the Genoese, the lords of Cap Corse were allowed a certain autonomy: largely ignored by the rest of the island, and well positioned for trading with the French and Tuscan ports, they were able to control their profits to a greater extent than their compatriots in the south. By the seventeenth century, Cap Corse was economically more successful than any other region in Corsica, but **piracy** was a huge problem for its tiny ports, which is why the coast is dotted with some thirty fortified watchtowers (see the box on p.103).

The late eighteenth and early nineteenth centuries saw an upsurge in emigration from the cape, as a shortage of agricultural land (brought about by a sharp rise in population) forced thousands of Capicursini to seek their fortunes in the colonies of South America and the Caribbean. Many of the emigrants grew rich on gold prospecting and coffee or sugar planting, and in time returned home to live in large villas, or *palazzi*, erected on their ancestral land. Known as *les maisons d'Américains*, these ostentatious country mansions, with their colonial-style colonnades and arches, lend a distinctively Central or South American feel to villages such as Rogliano, Morsiglia and Pino. Most are still in use, and during the summer welcome families from Puerto Rico or Venezuela, where Corsican colonies still exist – indeed, one former Venezuelan president was a Corsican.

Today, though wine continues to be a major export and nationalist politicians are promoting exploitation of the indigenous cedrat fruit, from which a liqueur and jam are made locally, tourism has become the only way to make real money. So far, however, it has been slow to develop on the cape, and there are few spots where concrete spoils the views.

The eastern cape

The **east coast** of the cape progresses from tightly packed villas immediately outside Bastia to lonely *marines* such as **Pietracorbara** in the north, via fishing villages such as **Porticciolo** and **Erbalunga**. The D80, which winds all the way around Cap Corse as far as St-Florent, is mostly built up within a short radius of Bastia (about the first 5km). You can, however, bypass the worst of the initial conurbation by following the wonderful "**Route de la Corniche**", which affords superb views over the town and Ligurian Sea out to the Tuscan islands of Elba and Monte Cristo. The easiest way to pick it up is to head west (left) from the top of place St-Nicolas, past the train station and straight up the hill; keep to the main road, bearing right onto the D231/D31 towards **Guaitella/Ville-di-Pietrabugno**. Once there, you're up on the corniche proper, whose first village of note is **San Martino-di-Lota**, site of two of the area's most appealing hotels and restaurants (reviewed on p.72).

Lavasina

LAVASINA, 5km north up the coast from Bastia on the main coast road (D80), grew up around a sanctuary created in the sixteenth century by one Danesi, who was given a painting of the Virgin which he donated to the sanctuary in lieu of payment for some merchandise. It became a place of pilgrimage in 1675, when a nun called Marie-Agnès, having disembarked from a boat to take shelter from a storm, prayed at the sanctuary and was promptly cured of her paralysis of the legs. Within two years the **Église Notre-Dame-des-Grâces** had been built to house the miraculous painting. An ugly rectangular grey clock tower, surmounted by a stiff statue of the Virgin, was added to the large pink building in the nineteenth century and effectively ruined the classical lines of the church. Inside, however, you might as well take a look at the famous **Madone de Lavasina**, which hangs above the great black and white altar. The painting, a melancholy work from the school of the Umbrian artist Pietro Perugino, is still believed to perform miracles and is the focus of a **festival** on September 8, involving a candlelit procession on the beach and a midnight Mass.

Next to the church, a granite panel indicates the head of the trail to **Monte Stello** (5hr); if you have a car, you can cut out the first part of this route (and save 2hr) by driving up to Pozzo, above Erbalunga. An account of the hike appears on p.84.

△ San Michele de Murato, Nebbio

Erbalunga

Built along a rocky promontory 3km north of Lavasina, the small honey-pot port of **ERBALUNGA** is the highlight of the east coast, with its old stone buildings stacked like crooked boxes behind a cosy harbour and ruined Genoese watchtower. A little colony of French artists lived here in the 1920s, perhaps drawn by the fact that the ancestors of the poet Paul Valéry came from the village, which has continued to attract a steady stream of admirers ever since. During the winter, well-to-do Bastiais frequent the harbourside restaurants, while in summer Erbalunga is transformed into a veritable cultural enclave, with concerts and art exhibitions adding a spark to the local nightlife.

A port since the time of the Phoenicians, Erbalunga was once a more important trading centre than Bastia or Ajaccio. With the increasing exportation of wine and olive oil in the eleventh century, it became the capital of an independent village state, ruled by the da Gentile family, who lived in the *palazzo* that dominates **place de Gaulle**. Its ascendancy came to an end in the 1550s, when long-running conflicts within the da Gentile camp finally broke the family's hold on this part of the cape, and in 1557 French troops destroyed the port, reducing the fifteenth-century tower to the ruined state it's in today.

Erbalunga is famous for its **Good Friday procession** known as the **Cerca** (Search), which has evolved from an ancient fertility rite. Starting at Église St-Érasme, at the entrance to the village, a procession of hooded penitents covers a distance of 14km, passing through the hamlets of Pozzo, Poretto and Silgaggia in the mountains and picking up people on the way. At nightfall, back in Erbalunga, the penitents form a spiral known as the *Granitola* (Snail); candles held high, they move to place de Gaulle and the spiral unwinds, while a separate part of the procession forms the shape of the cross.

Practicalities

Most of the village is closed to vehicles, but there's a **car park** on the left-hand side of the main road from Bastia, where the regular **bus** from place St-Nicolas stops. From here, the harbour is reached through place de Gaulle, where the mairie and the *palazzo* Gentile stand side by side. On the quayside, a couple of **bars** shaded by an enormous chestnut tree look out across the water to the tower.

The one **hotel**, the gorgeous *Castel Brando* (☎04 95 30 10 30, ℻04 95 33 98 18; April to mid-Oct; ❻), stands at the entrance to the square, shaded by a curtain of mature date palms, like the backdrop to a classic Visconti movie. It's an elegant, old, stone-floored *palazzo* with a lovely pool and its own car park. Period furniture and antique Corsican engravings fill the rooms and apartments, which are all air conditioned; those on the top floor have great views. Rates soar in July and August, but at other times you can spend the night here for under €70. Filling buffet breakfasts are served al fresco in the courtyard.

Pick of the harbourside **restaurants** is the renowned *Le Pirate* (☎04 95 33 24 20; Easter–Oct) for whose *cuisine gastronomique* well-heeled Bastiais flock here throughout the year. Seafood delicacies, such as spider crab (*araignée de mer*) and devilfish (*sarl*), dominate their menu, but vegetarians are well catered for with entrées from the *carte* – aubergines baked in parmesan or grilled vegetables with mozzarella. The house set menu costs around €30; à la carte courses range from €15 to €55. A less expensive option is *A Piazzetta* (☎04 95 33 28 69), in the tiny square behind the harbour, which does acceptable pizzas and has a generous selection of fresh pasta dishes from €10.50 to €18. In a similar price bracket, cheap and cheerful *Chez Antoine*, three minutes' walk north of the *Castel Brando* on the main street, does delicious *moules marinières* (for €7), as well as pizzas and a choice of *grillades*.

Castello

The thirteenth-century castle at **CASTELLO**, one of the many bases of the da Gentile family, stands 2km inland from Erbalunga, beyond the hamlet of Mausoleo. This ghostly village, dominated by the now-ruined castle, was the scene of a family feud that lasted a hundred years and split the da Gentile family into two factions. The strife began in 1450, when the lady of the castle, known simply as *La Sposetta* (The Little Wife), began an affair with one Guelfuccio, cousin of her husband Vinciguerra da Gentile. On discovery of this deception, Vinciguerra stabbed his errant wife to death, chased his cousin out of the castle and stormed off to settle with his brother in nearby Erbalunga. Here he built a new castle, which was wrecked in 1556 by the French, supported by members of the Castello branch of the da Gentile clan. Quick to retaliate, the Erbalunga side of the family, supported by the Genoese, launched an attack against Castello, an action that resulted in the total devastation of the port when the French struck back the following year. *La Sposetta* is generally thought to haunt Castello – presumably she also drops in on the da Gentile family's house, built in 1602 at the entrance to the hamlet.

To the south of the village on the road to **Silgaggia** stands the Romanesque chapel of **Notre-Dame-des-Neiges/Santa Maria di e Nevi**. Dating from the tenth century, it contains the oldest known **frescoes** in Corsica, beautiful portraits of saints painted in 1386. Having recently been vandalized, the chapel is no longer open to casual visitors, but in July and August you can book on to organized tours run by a very knowledgeable local guide, M Defendine (℡06 86 78 02 38; 2hr 15min; €10, children free), which start from Bastia or Erbalunga. Outside July and August, tours do run, but they're less regular – phone for more information (if your French isn't all that fluent, ask the management of the *Hôtel Castel Brando* in Erbalunga for help).

Monte Stello

The starting point for the climb up **Monte Stello** (1307m), the second-highest peak on Cap Corse (the highest is neighbouring Cima di e Folicce, 1324m), is the medieval hamlet of **Pozzo**, 3km from Erbalunga. From the summit, a superb panorama extends west across Golfe de St-Florent to encompass the island's main peaks, and east across the sea to the Tuscan coast. To enjoy the views, though, you'll have to set off early in the morning, as cloud invariably obscures the top of Monte Stello from 11am onwards. Allow around five hours for the round trip.

In Pozzo's square, a sign marked "Monte Stello 3h" points the way through the houses into the maquis, where the trail starts off clearly marked by arrows and daubs of blue paint. The first section of the hike climbs steeply west into the deep Arega stream valley, via the **Bergerie de Teghime**, reaching the windswept **Bocca di Santa Maria** pass, a distinctive niche in the Cap's watershed where you get your first hard-earned glimpse of the Golfe de St-Florent, after around 1hr 30min. From here it's another 1hr 40min and a 169-metre haul to the summit. Return by the same route.

For this walk we strongly recommend you take along IGN map #4347 OT Cap Corse. While most of the path is well waymarked, or cairned towards the summit, the maquis has overtaken some stretches, making it hard to follow in places.

Sisco

The landscape takes on a more desolate aspect as the coast road approaches **Sisco**, 6km north of Erbalunga, a *commune* made up of several hamlets scattered over the mountainside and the tiny seaside village of **MARINE DE SISCO**. The latter tumbles to a sandy beach, backed by a cluster of restaurants and two pleasant hotels. Of the pair, the old-fashioned *Hôtel de la Marine* (*"Chez Giuseppi"*; ☎04 95 35 21 04; Easter–Sept; ❸), is the less expensive, comprising rooms in terraced chalets that open onto a quiet garden behind the beach. There's no restaurant, but breakfast is served on the stone-floored verandah of the main house. If it's full, try the smarter, more modern *U Pozzu*, opposite (☎04 95 35 21 17, ℻04 95 35 27 19; ❹), whose welcoming proprietor speaks fluent English. Their restaurant offers a choice of two *menus fixes* (€15/17.50), with lots of fresh seafood à la carte (best accompanied by a bottle of rosé from the Lina Venturi-Pieretti vineyard at nearby Luri). An altogether more authentically Corsican place to eat, in fact one of the most reputed auberges on the island, stands 200m up the lane running inland from *U Pozzu*. In a down-to-earth little ground-floor restaurant, *A Stalla Sischese* (☎04 95 35 26 34; open all year), you can sample carefully prepared local specialities, including a succulent seafood salad, chestnut fritters, *ravioli al brocciu*, and a melt-in-the-mouth fresh *fiadone*; at lunchtime there's a choice of two menus (€18.50/23), or only the pricier one in the evenings. Advance reservation is recommended.

While in the area it's worth finding the time to visit the beautiful **Romanesque chapel of San Michele**, hidden on a hillside inland. From the main road, head 7km west up the D32 past *A Stalla Sischese* as far as the large but unremarkable Église St-Martin, where a right-hand turn signposted to San Michele will lead you north at contour level for 400m to the start of the rocky track (on your left). The elegant chapel, built in 1030 by Pisan masons, occupies a spectacular windswept hillside overlooking the Marine de Sisco, with Pietracorbara a misty ridge of buildings stretching to the north. On September 29, the Festival of St Michael brings pilgrims up from the surrounding hamlets to celebrate Mass here.

The Couvent de Santa Catalina

Back on the main coast road, the huge **Couvent de Santa Catalina** stands on a hillside high above the corniche, about 500m beyond Marine de Sisco. The convent is now an old people's home, but you can visit the church, which is reached by turning left off the main road, along a hairpin bend that doubles back to the building. (Ignore the turning next to the large stone statue of St Catherine, some 200m before, which leads to a dead end.) Built in the twelfth century, the graceless church, overshadowed by an ugly tower, was enlarged in the fifteenth century, when the hulking buttresses were added and the entrance widened to receive the pilgrims who came to see its famous relics. Comprising a piece of the clay from which Adam was made, an almond from Paradise, and one of Enoch's fingers, the relics were enshrined here in the thirteenth century by fishermen who, caught in a storm off Cap Corse, vowed to bring their holy cargo to the first church they came across if they were saved. This happened to be Santa Catalina; unfortunately, the relics are now kept in the mairie at Chioso and are not accessible to visitors. Perhaps the most impressive feature of the church's bare interior is the round crypt, dating from the 1200s and based – like nearly all round churches – on the Holy Sepulchre in Jerusalem.

Pietracorbara

The next village along the cape is **PIETRACORBARA**, 18km north of Bastia, whose beautiful beach – the only one of fine white sand on the cape –

marks the end of a broad river valley carpeted in shimmering reed banks. Overlooked by a ruined Genoese tower are a handful of houses, among them the *Hôtel-Restaurant Macchia e Mare* (℡04 95 35 21 26, ℻35 22 35, Ⓦwww.macchia-e-mare.com; ❸), a modern two-star with panoramic views over the bay from its north-facing restaurant terrace. Only four of the eight rooms overlook the sea. For campers there's the pricy but very well set up *Camping La Pietra* (℡04 95 35 27 49), 300m from the beach, which has a small shop and bar.

Porticciolo

Heading north along the cape, your arrival in **PORTICCIOLO** is heralded by the stark profile looming above the road of the **Tour de l'Osse/Torri di l'Ossu**. Formerly known as the Tour de l'Aigle (Eagle's Tower), it was re-named in the mid-nineteenth century after its foundations yielded a mass of mysterious skeletons. The village itself, once the cape's third-busiest harbour and important boat-building centre, is attractively compact and crumbling, with a tiny mooring for fishing boats jutting into the green sea. Its beach is rather marred by the proximity of the road, but the two **hotels** here offer peace and quiet, and make good bases for forays into the interior of the peninsula. The welcoming *U Patriarcu* (℡04 95 35 00 01; open year round ; ❸), on the south side of the village, is a stalwart period building with immaculate rooms overlooking the sea or the hills behind; half board (€48 per person) is obliga-tory in July and August. Further north, just off the main road down a narrow lane is the *Torra Marina* (℡04 95 35 00 80; May–Sept; ❹) better respected for its little restaurant than overpriced rooms. Served on a little stone terrace over-looking the water, in the shade of umbrella pines, seafood (all caught by the *patron*'s neighbour) dominates the €20 *menu fixe*.

Santa Severa and Tomino

At the little *marine* of **SANTA SEVERA**, 2km north of Porticciolo, the D180 cuts across the cape to Luri and the Tour de Sénèque (see p.93). The village holds less appeal than nearby Macinaggio (see p.87), but it does possess one of the island's most reputed vineyards, the **Domaine Venturi–Pieretti**, which has the distinction of being run by a woman – a rarity indeed for Corsica. At the little roadside *cave* just outside Santa Severa (April–Sept daily 10am–noon & 4.30–7pm) you can sample Lina Venturi-Pieretti's white, with its hints of cit-rus, the honey-scented muscat and spicy red, which in 1999 was the only *rouge corse* to be given three Hachette stars.

 Six kilometres beyond Santa Severa lies **Marine de Meria**, a collection of pastel-shaded cottages scattered around the base of a well-preserved watch-tower. From here it's 2km inland to the little *commune* of **TOMINO** (Tuminu), dubbed "the cradle of Christianity in Corsica" because the island's earliest Christians hid in caves on its hillsides during the Saracen raids of the sixth cen-tury. Sited on a windy, rocky spur, the *commune*'s main hamlet, **STOPIONE**, was once a serious rival to commercial Rogliano (see p.89), producing an excellent muscat wine. These days it lies boarded up and virtually deserted, but the **view** alone is worth the steep drive up the D353 from the *marine*. Following the hairpin road, which emerges on the left just before you enter Macinaggio, you'll soon come to the crest of the hill, where a Baroque chapel and a Genoese tower face each other before a tight cluster of houses. In the near distance, the Îles Finocchiarola and the Tuscan island of Capraia are visi-ble across the vast expanse of deep blue sea.

The northern cape

Macinaggio, northern terminus of the road along the east side of the cape, is also the largest settlement due north of Bastia, with a handful of hotels and restaurants, and one of the cape's few petrol stations. The only **bus** service to this somewhat isolated resort runs three times weekly (Mon, Wed & Fri) from Bastia's gare routière, and is operated by Transports Saladini (℡04 95 35 43 88).

The land between Macinaggio and **Barcaggio**, at the very tip of Corsica, forms part of a protected zone called the **Site Naturel de la Capandula**, and is a wonderful area to explore on foot, boasting some glorious **beaches**. Known as the "holy promontory" in Roman times because of its Christian settlements, the tip of the cape also has many ruined chapels, such as **Santa Maria**, near Macinaggio. Five kilometres inland, the eight hamlets of **Rogliano**, spectacularly spread out over the slopes, were for a few centuries the fief of the da Mare family, whose castles and towers lie dotted over the hills. On the western side of the northern tip, the chief focus of interest is picturesque **Centuri–Port**, where the much photographed horseshoe-shaped harbour shelters a string of seafood restaurants and the colourful boats that service it.

Macinaggio

A port since Roman times, well-sheltered **MACINAGGIO** was developed by the Genoese in 1620 for the export of olive oil and wine to the Italian peninsula, and in later years played its part in the wider history of the island. **Pascal Paoli** landed here in 1790 after his exile in England, whereupon he kissed the ground and uttered the words "O ma patrie, je t'ai quitté esclave, je te retrouve libre" ("Oh my country, I left you as a slave, I rediscover you a free man") – a plaque commemorating the event adorns the wall above the ship chandlers. **Napoléon** also stopped here on his way to Bastia as he fled from the Paolists in 1793, and in 1869 the empress Eugénie was forced by a storm to disembark here on her way back from the opening of the Suez Canal, before taking refuge in Rogliano – she had such a bad journey from Macinaggio up to Rogliano that on her return she ordered a new road to be constructed, known ever since as the "Chemin de l'Impératrice". There's not much of an historic patina to the place nowadays, but with its turquoise marina, line of seafront awnings and end-of-the-world feel, Macinaggio has a certain appeal; it also lies within comfortable walking distance of some of the island's most beautiful coastal scenery.

Another reason to linger here is to sample the superb **Clos Nicrosi** wines, grown in the terraces below Rogliano. Of all Corsica's top AOC labels, it's perhaps the hardest to find – not least because they pour any substandard years away rather than diminish the reputation of the property. But at their little shop on the north side of the Rogliano road, opposite the *U Ricordu* hotel, you can taste the *domaine*'s famously crisp white and heavily scented muscat.

Practicalities

Macinaggio has a little **tourist office** (June–Sept Mon–Sat 9am–noon & 2–7pm, Sun 9am–noon; Oct–May closed Sat pm & Sun; ℡04 95 35 40 34), on the first floor of a building on the harbourside, where you can pick up free map-leaflets for the Sentier du Douanier. They also keep timetables for the **boat trips** that run out to the nearby islands on board the *San Paulo* (℡04 95 35 07 09).

The least expensive place to **stay** is the recently renovated *Hôtel des Îles*, opposite the marina (℡04 95 35 43 02, ℻04 95 35 47 05; ❸), which also has a serviceable restaurant on its ground floor. All the rooms, though tiny, have showers and toilets; those at the front of the building overlook the port but get noisy at night, being above the most popular bar in the resort, so if you're a light sleeper ask for a room at the back. Otherwise try the more modern *U Libecciu*, down the lane leading from the marina to the Plage de Tamarone (℡04 95 35 43 22, ℻04 95 35 46 08; April–Oct, obligatory half board July & Aug; ❹); it's a modern building with no view to speak of, but the rooms are spacious and particularly good value in shoulder season. The three-star *U Ricordu*, on the south side of the road to Rogliano (℡04 95 35 40 20, ℻04 95 35 41 88, ⓦwww.hotel-uricordu.com; March–Sept, with obligatory half board Aug; ❽), is the most luxurious option hereabouts, with a swimming pool, sauna, tennis courts and over-the-top tariffs.

Macinaggio's only **campsite**, *U Stazzu*, lies 1km north of the harbour and is signposted from the Rogliano road (℡04 95 35 43 76; May–Oct). The ground is like rock, but it's cheap and there's ample shade and easy access to the near-by beach; particularly good breakfasts are also served in the site's little café.

Besides the hotel **restaurants** above, commendable places to eat in Macinaggio include the *Pizzeria San Columbu*, at the end of the port facing out to sea, which does a tasty seafood pizza; for a taste of local seafood, try *Les Îles*, the most dependable of a string of places with tables under awnings on the quayside, whose good-value €16 *menu fixe* features *soupe de poisson*, grilled *daurade* (gilt head) and *pâtisserie maison*. At the far north of the village a short way beyond the marina, *Chez Bellini* (℡04 95 35 40 37) is the other established favourite, with a €23 seafood menu.

Site Naturel de la Capandula

Macinaggio's town beach is seaweed-strewn and dirty, but you can get to some stunning stretches of white sand and clear sea by following the track at the north end of the marina to the **Site Naturel de la Capandula**. Covering 3.8 square kilometres of windswept maquis and pristine coast between Macinaggio and Bracaggio, the reserve, which encompasses the deserted Îles Finocchiarola and the Île de la Giraglia, can only be crossed on foot, via a coastal path that takes you through some wonderful scenery.

Although Capandula is off limits to motor vehicles, it is possible to drive the 2km from Macinaggio to the **Baie de Tamarone**, whose deep clear waters make it ideal for diving and snorkelling. The car park here also marks the start of the popular **coastal walk** through the reserve, known as the Sentier du Douanier after the Genoese customs officials who originally cut the path (see box).

Le Sentier du Douanier

The roadless northern tip of Cap Corse is among the few stretches of coastline on the island crossed by a waymarked path. Following the yellow splashes of paint, it's possible to walk all the way from Macinaggio to Centuri-Port (or vice versa) in seven to eight hours, taking in the picturesque Santa Maria and Agnello towers en route.

Although you can complete the **Sentier du Douanier** in a single long day, most walkers prefer to take their time, overnighting at Barcaggio (3hr) or Tollare (45min further on) before tackling the final, most spectacular stretch to Centuri-Port (4hr).

The **tourist office** in Macinaggio will furnish you with a free **map** and route description; otherwise get hold of a copy of IGN #4347 OT, which covers the entire path. Being mostly flat, the *sentier* presents no great physical challenges, although you should be aware of the force of the sun along this stretch of coast. In July/Aug, you'd have to set off at dawn and aim to rest up in the shade (of which there's precious little) between 11.30am and 4pm. **Water** can also be a problem as there are no springs: take along at least three litres per person.

For the less adventurous, there's a shorter **circular route** (1hr 30min–2hr), which begins at the Baie de Tamarone and takes in most of Capandula's highlights. From the car park, follow the Sentier du Douanier along the line of the bay and around the headland to a second beach, **Plage des Îles**. The sprinkling of barren islets offshore are known as the **Îles Finocchiarola**, after the wild fennel that grows in abundance over the rocks in the area. Hundreds of gulls and cormorants haunt this strip of coast, which, during March and June, is a stopoff for migrating **birds** from North Africa. If you're here at this time, look out for the elusive Audouin's gull, with its distinctive red bill encircled by a black band. Only 2500 pairs still survive in the Mediterranean, and they are a protected species here. Other types you might expect to see are the more common herring gull; the black-headed Mediterranean gull; and perhaps a Manx or Cory's shearwater. The islets are a nature reserve, visitable only between March and August, and fires and camping are strictly forbidden. **Boat excursions** run in July and August from the marina in Macinaggio; tickets cost around €15. The round trip includes a stop on the largest islet so that enthusiasts can do a spot of birdwatching.

Half an hour after leaving the Baie de Tamarone, you arrive at a stunning arc of turquoise sea known as the **Rade de Santa Maria**, site of an isolated Romanesque chapel. Raised on the foundations of a sixth-century church, the **Chapelle Santa Maria** comprises a tenth-century and a twelfth-century chapel merged into one, hence the two discrepant apses.

This bay's other distinctive landmark is the huge **Tour de Santa Maria**. Dramatically cleft in half and entirely surrounded by water, the ruined three-storeyed building was one of three *torri* built on the northern tip of the cape by the Genoese in the sixteenth century (the others are at Tollare and Barcaggio) as lookout posts against the increasingly troublesome Moorish pirates (see box on p.103). As Macinaggio grew in importance, the towers were also used by health and customs officers, who controlled the maritime traffic with Genoa. Pascal Paoli established his garrison here in 1761, having failed in his attempt to take Macinaggio, and contemplated building a rival port. Six years later, to undermine Genoa's position in the area, Paoli sent two hundred men under the command of Achille Murati to capture the neighbouring island of Capraia, which had belonged to Genoa since 1507. Murati's relatively easy victory marked the beginning of the downfall of the Genoese in Corsica.

A short way beyond the tower lie two beautiful little beaches – **Cala Genovese** and **Cala Francese** – both shining turquoise and well sheltered. If, instead of pressing on north, however, you turn south from the Chapelle Santa Maria and follow the track past a vine-covered hillside for around thirty minutes, you'll eventually arrive back at the Baie de Tamarone. Note that this circular walk can also be done in a clockwise direction by turning left out of the Tamarone car park instead of right at the start of the hike, and following the track inland to the chapel, and thence around the coast.

Rogliano

A cluster of schist-tiled hamlets scattered over a lush valley below the crags of Monte Poggio, **Rogliano** (Ruglianu), 7km up a series of hairpin bends from Macinaggio, ranks among the most picturesque *communes* in Corsica. Its constituent hamlets – Bettolacce, Olivo, Magna, Soprana, Vignale, Sottana and Campiano – were the base of the da Mare lords from the twelfth to the sixteenth century, and the ruins of their convents, towers and castles are distributed among them. However, the village's name, derived from the Latin *Pagus Aurelianus*, dates from the Roman era, when Rogliano presided over a busy trade with the Italian coast, while the oldest vines on the hillside are known to be of Carthaginian origin.

The easternmost and largest hamlet, **BETTOLACCE**, is dominated by the privately owned **Tour Franceschi**, an enormous round tower in remarkable condition. It also boasts an excellent **hotel**, the *Auberge Sant'Agnellu*, opposite (ⓣ & ⓕ 04 95 35 40 59; ⓦwww.hotel-usantagnellu.com; mid-April to mid-Oct; ➍), whose terracotta- and blue-washed façades overlook the valley. Extensively refurbished in 2000 (it was formerly the local mairie), the interior is decorated with antiques. There's also a wonderful terrace making the most of the views, where you enjoy fine *cuisine du terroir*, prepared with ingredients from the farm of the *patron*, M. Albertini's, brother: homemade chestnut pâté, *cannelloni al brocciu* and delicate *tarte aux herbes* for vegetarians.

Isolated in the valley some 500m beneath Bettolacce stands the ruined sixteenth-century **Église St-Côme-et-St-Damien**, accessible via the path leading opposite *Auberge Sant'Agnellu*. A curious rectangular bell tower stands separated from the nave, which is the oldest part of the church. **VIGNALE**, the hamlet above Bettolacce, is dominated by the crumbling ruins of the **Castello di San Colombano**, from which there's a magnificent view across the valley to Macinaggio. The castle was built in the twelfth century and became known as *U Castelacciu* (The Bad Castle) in the sixteenth, when Giacomo Santa da Mare abandoned the Genoese cause, switched his allegiances to Sampiero Corso and defected to the Franco-Turkish army. In 1553 the Genoese retaliated by destroying the castle, which was later restored, but it burned down in 1947.

From here a track leads 300m to **OLIVO** and the **Couvent St-François**, an imposing vine-covered building straight out of a Gothic romance. The convent and adjoining church, surmounted by a spindly clock tower, were built in 1520 by the Franciscans, who also restored them in 1711. They are now private property and closed to the public.

Barcaggio and around

To get to the very tip of Corsica, continue west along the D80 for about 5km, until you reach **Ersa**, where the D253 twists off northwards to **BARCAGGIO**, giving breathtaking views of the Île de la Giraglia. The *marine* (harbour settlement) is tiny – just a jetty, a couple of restaurants and a dozen houses built from the greenish local schist – but the setting is sublime and the **beach** wild and windswept. Curving east of the village to a headland crowned by a Genoese watchtower, it is set against a backdrop of austere, maquis-covered hills that are oddly reminiscent of the Scottish Highlands. You can leave your vehicle in the village **car park** (also a park for camper vans), from where a track leads through the dunes to a crystalline sea. The *La Giraglia* **hotel** (ⓣ04 95 35 60 54, ⓕ04 95 35 65 92; April–Sept; ➎) occupies a fantastic location at the north end of the village overlooking the tiny harbour (rooms 25 and 26 have the best views), though it's expensive for what it offers and doesn't accept credit cards. Nor does it have a restaurant, so if you fancy a **meal** your only options are *U Pescadore*, an ugly prefab hut on the jetty serving pricy fresh seafood dishes, or the better-value *Chez Néné* (ⓣ04 95 35 62 32; reservation essential July & Aug), 7km south of Barcaggio along the D253, which has a single set Corsican speciality menu at €17, served on a small terrace.

The northern extremity of Corsica is marked by the **Île de la Giraglia**, a green islet whose bare, rocky slopes sport a lighthouse and a sixteenth-century Genoese tower. The nearest settlement to it is **TOLLARE**, a neglected little coastal village of squat grey fishing cottages. Apart from the handful of holidaymakers who rent houses in the summer, hardly anyone ventures out here, but you can park up and paddle on the hamlet's tiny pebble beach.

Col de Serra and Camera

Further west along the main road, it's worth pulling over at the **Col de Serra** (365m) to admire the views and walk up to the famous **Moulin Mattei**, the round building with the coloured tiled roof on the hill above the road. Some considerate soul has installed a stone picnic table in the lee of this former windmill (restored by the Maison Mattei as tasting place for their quinine-rich aperitif, Cap Corse), from whose terrace you can admire the impressive panorama along the peninsula's north and west coasts.

Once over the col you soon come to **CAMERA**, the first hamlet of the *commune* of **Centuri** (pronounced "Chen*t*ori"), where the bizarre cylindrical turrets of the **Château de Bellavista** peer from the woods beneath the road. One of many so-called "*maisons d'Américains*" in this area, the castle (closed to the public) was built in the nineteenth century for Count Leonetto Cipriani, a mercenary in the service of the Duke of Tuscany, who later became a close friend of Napoléon. The smaller hamlet of **Canelle**, overlooking Centuri-Port and accessible from Camera along the road heading north or on foot from the port, is renowned for its enormous fig trees, whose drooping branches overhang the houses and shadow the road.

Centuri-Port

When Boswell arrived here from England in 1765, the former Roman settlement of **CENTURI-PORT** was a tiny fishing village, recommended to him for its peaceful detachment from the dangerous turmoil of the rest of Corsica. Not much has changed since Boswell's time: despite the annual tourist influx, and the rows of seasonal cafés and restaurants that have sprung up to cater for them, the village's petrified harbour still presents an arresting spectacle, its grey stone walls highlighted by the green serpentine roofs of the encircling cottages. The twenty or so boats bobbing around it are evidence of the village's ailing fishing industry. In years past, the local fleet was able to row to the fishing grounds just beyond the harbour wall and ceased work early in the autumn so as not to impinge on the lobsters' breeding season. But increased demand, modern nets and pollution from the asbestos mine at nearby Canari (see p.94) have all but wiped out in-shore sea life and these days the motorized boats are forced two or more hours further out, for ever diminishing returns. One of the few remaining residents of Centuri to have witnessed the economic revolution is retired fisherman Pierrot Tolanïni. Distinguished by his old salt's white beard and Breton fishing cap, Pierrot has become something of a celebrity since he was featured in a television documentary and magazine articles on the area: you'll come across him posing for photos next to the myrtle-wood lobster pots in the harbour, or regaling tourists with sea shanties on his accordion.

The only drawback to the settlement from the tourists' point of view is that the small pebble **beach** to the south is disappointingly grubby and not ideal for sunbathing. You can, however, reach some of the most pristine coast on the island if you're prepared to walk. Centuri-Port stands at the start of the wonderful **Sentier du Douanier**, the former customs officers' path, which winds all the way to Macinaggio via Tollare and Barcaggio in seven to eight hours. For more on the route, see the box on p.88.

Practicalities

There are plenty of small hotels occupying the former fishers' cottages around the quay. The best value and most pleasant among them is the *Du Pêcheur*, the salmon-coloured building at the back of the harbour (☎04 95 35 60 14; Easter to mid-November; ❸); its rooms are agreeably cool, with thick stone walls and green shutters on the windows, and it has a popular restaurant on the ground floor (menus €12.50–38). If it's full, try *Hôtel La Jetée*, to the left on the road as you arrive in Centuri (℡04 95 35 64 46, ℻04 95 35 64 18; April–Sept; ❸), whose rooms are ordinary and for the most part without sea views, but the cheapest in the village during high season. The *Vieux Moulin* (℡04 95 35 60 15, ℻04 95 35 60 24; March–Oct; ❹), opposite, is the most stylish option: a converted *maison d'Americain* with a wonderful terrace and attractively furnished en-suite rooms. For **campers**, choice is limited to the *Camping l'Isolettu*, 400m south along the D35 (℡04 95 35 62 81, ℻04 95 35 63 63; May–Oct), five minutes' walk from Centuri's scruffy little pebble beach.

Among the many **restaurants** around the port two stand out. Next door to the *Hôtel La Jetée*, the *U Cabalu di Mare* offers a cheap and cheerful selection of pizzas, omelettes, salads, sandwiches and three or four *plats du jour*, including the least expensive locally caught fish in town, which you can enjoy on a stone terrace above the harbour or indoors in a small bistrot. The service is particularly friendly and you get a complimentary aperitif on arrival. For more serious cuisine *capcorsine*, *A Macciotta (Chez Sker*; ℡04 95 35 64 46), on the lane running uphill from the rear of the harbour (to the left if you're facing away from the sea), is the best choice. *Menus fixes* start at €12.50, but for proper local lobster (cooked to perfection and served with homemade mayonnaise) you'll have to go for the €38 *menu poisson*, which also features anemones, squid salad and sea bass baked or pan fried with fennel. Both their terrace and cavernous fisherman's cottage interior can be cramped, so get there early.

The western cape

An altogether more sombre and dramatic landscape takes over once you've reached the western cape, with maquis-covered mountainsides plunging at increasingly steep angles into a coastline that's indented with few accessible coves. Winding high above the shore, the corniche route around it has terrified travellers since the time of Boswell who, having just arrived by boat in 1765, wrote in his journal: " . . . *such a road I never saw. It was absolutely scrambling along the face of a rock overhanging the sea, upon a path sometimes not above a foot broad*." Progress south down the cape is interrupted by a string of schist villages, stacked up the cliffsides above small *marines*. At **Pino** you can take a detour inland to see the **Tour de Sénèque**, while further south **Canari** holds another remarkable Romanesque church and a terrace with a superb view across the gulf. Just a few kilometres north of St-Florent, **Nonza** is perhaps the most photographed of all the *capcorsin* villages, perched high above a black sandy beach.

Morsiglia

With its medieval *torri* and terraced vineyards tumbling down an amphitheatre of hills to the sea, **MORSIGLIA** (Mursiglia) typifies the stark beauty of the western cape. Having suffered more than its share of out-migration since the 1950s, the village is hopelessly depopulated these days, but warrants a stop to admire its three splendid watchtowers (the last of six that originally stood here) and well-preserved eighteenth- and nineteenth-century *palazzi*. In 1765, Boswell spent the second night of his Corsican adventure in one of them. The pompous young dilettante was "much surprised" to find his host, Signor Antonetti's, house "quite an Italian one, with very good furniture, prints, and copies of some of the famous pictures". On a rainy Sunday morning, he was equally amazed that the locals seemed "afraid of bad weather, to a degree of effeminacy", until it was pointed out to him the reason for this was that most owned only one coat. Nowadays, with water shortages threatening to squeeze out the hundred or so remaining villagers who live here year round, the downpours that all too rarely sweep across this exposed tip of the peninsula are greeted with greater enthusiasm.

The droughts have been particularly tough on Eugène Paoli, one of Corsica's most famous *viticulteurs*, whose vineyards at Morsiglia have been cultivated continuously by the same family since 1768. Signposted from the corniche road, the **Domaine Pietri**, in the hamlet of Mucchieta (May–Sept Mon–Sat 10am–noon & 4–7pm; ℡04 95 35 60 93 or 04 95 35 64 79) produces equal quantities of muscat, white and red, but is perhaps most renowned for the latter, which has a wonderful aroma of dried fruits and blackcurrant.

Tour de Sénèque

At the first road junction south of Morsiglia, an east turn off the corniche in the direction of Luri will take you winding through pine woods to the Col de Ste-Lucie and thence up a badly potholed lane to the **Tour de Sénèque**. Set atop a pinnacle of black rock, the tower was built in the fifteenth century by the da Mare family, on the spot where Seneca is said to have lived from 41 to 49 AD, having been exiled for seducing the Emperor Claudius' niece. His rampant misconduct didn't stop there. During his exile, Seneca reputedly once came down from his rock in an attempt to ravage the Corsican women, for which he was attacked with nettles – hence, or so it is said, the profusion of the plants around the base of the tower. Whilst here he wrote a few appropriately bitter verses about the place:

What can be found so bare, what so rugged all around as this rock? What more barren of provisions? What more rude as to its inhabitants? What in the very situation of the place more horrible? What in climate more intemperate? Yet there are more foreigners here than natives. So far then is a change of place from being disagreeable, that even this place has brought some people away from their country.

It's a thirty-minute climb through the woods to the tower – well worth the effort for the views, which extend to both coasts of the cape and over the Monte Stello massif (see box on p.84). To pick up the trail, follow the motorable dirt track from the deserted school at the end of the *piste* towards the radio transmitter above you in the woods, then bear left along the path that peels from it after about five minutes. From here, it's a stiff ten-minute climb through the trees to the top, with the last 20m or so over exposed rocks.

Luri

Continuing south from the Col de Ste-Lucie, you soon come to the *commune* of **Luri**, surrounded by a delightful landscape of lemon trees and vineyards. At **PIAZZA**, Luri's central hamlet, the seventeenth-century **Église St-Pierre** houses a late sixteenth-century depiction of the life of St Peter against a background showing the local castles a hundred years or so before it was painted – the one on the left is the Tour des Motti, a precursor of the Tour de Sénèque, and on the right is the Castello di San Colombano, at Rogliano (see p.89).

Pino

A sense of the tropics pervades the air at **PINO** (Pinu), some 2km south of the turning for Luri. Palm trees grow up the cliff, and the houses, coloured pale pink, orange and yellow, feature turreted roofs and verandahs. Among the grander *maisons d'Américains* is one built by Antoine Liccioni, who, like many of his generation, left the village vowing not to return until he was rich. Liccioni, though, struck lucky, discovering seams of gold in both Venezuela and Brazil, and when he died it is said he owned half of Guyana.

Boswell, his luggage having been carried along the corniche on the heads of "a couple of stout women", arrived here in 1765, and promptly committed an atrocious gaffe: mistaking the house he was shown to for an inn rather than the home of a local worthy, he barked orders for what he wanted "with the tone which one uses in calling to the waiters at a tavern". His host, however, responded with un-Corsican equanimity and, instead of dumping the young aristo's dinner on his head, or worse, merely "smiled, saying with much calmness and good nature, *Una cosa dopo un altra, Signore.* One thing at a time, Sir".

You could stop in the village for a drink under the shade of the chestnuts and plane trees, or follow the steep road from just outside the village down to the *marine*, where a fifteenth-century **Franciscan convent** lies half-hidden amongst a jungle of bamboo. Although its outward appearance is grim, try to get inside for a look at the faded fifteenth-century frescoes above the entrance, featuring the Virgin flanked by saints Francis and Bernard.

Canari and around

Two corniche roads wind in tandem between Pino and Canari, along one of the most dramatic stretches of the Cap Corse coastline. The higher of the pair, the D33, is the more scenic, skirting through a string of isolated hamlets en route to **Canari**, this area's largest *commune*. **Buses** run out here from Bastia (daily in summer, with Transports Micheli ☏04 95 35 64 02; and Mon & Wed year round, with Transports Saoletti ☏04 95 37 84 05), but even in high summer the villages remain well off the tour coach trail.

Reason enough to make the detour off either corniche is the Romanesque chapel of **Santa Maria Assunta**, in the hamlet of **PIEVE**. Built at the end of the twelfth century and in an astonishingly good state of repair, it is noteworthy for the primitive sculpture lining the cornice beneath the roof – weird mask-like faces alongside strange beasts and stylized geometric patterns – among which was incorporated fragments of pre-Roman carving. The chapel is opened only once each year, on Ascension Day (August 15). Further up the hill, as indicated by a sign from the centre of the village, the gloomy Baroque **Église St-François**, formerly attached to a Franciscan monastery, harbours a fifteenth-century gilded panel of St Michael, on the left as you enter; a panel from the same altarpiece is set into the sacristy cupboard door. Also of interest is the sixteenth-century *Assumption of the Virgin* on the right of the nave, above the tomb of Vittoria da Gentile, who died in 1590 at a convent, no longer in existence, in Canari.

Pieve's other claim to fame is the little white campanile in its square, or more specifically the astounding **views** from the spot, which attract a trickle of picnickers in season. Standing on the east side of the *place*, the *Au Bon Clocher* (☏04 95 37 80 15; open year round; ➋) is a modest but congenial **hotel-restaurant**, offering simple rooms with sea views, showers, balconies and shared toilets. The restaurant downstairs serves mainly seafood specialities, ranging from expensive Centuri-Port lobster to a delicious fish soup that comes with mountains of croutons and mayonnaise for €10. Half board is obligatory in season.

The *Au Bon Clocher* makes an ideal base for a couple of long-ish day **walks** which the local council is seeking to promote. Waymarked and cleared annually, the best of these takes you up to **Cima a e Folicce** (1324m), the highest mountain on the cape. Following old transhumant paths up on to the watershed of the peninsula, the route is a stiff 3hr 45min climb which you should

Amianthus is a rare, fibrous rock with fire-resistant properties that were first discovered by the ancient Greeks. They are thought to have wrapped bodies with it for cremation, to prevent human ashes mingling with those of the wood. Unfortunately for the Cap Corse coastline between Canari and Nonza, where it is found in prodigious quantities, the pale grey mineral also used to be an essential ingredient in asbestos. During the 1950s and early 1960s, one million tonnes of the stuff were mined annually here, in a complex that would later be dubbed by its 320 ex-employees as "the White Hell".

For a while, the mining boom looked set to reverse the fortunes of this economically disadvantaged peninsula. But when cheap Canadian exports undercut the price of Corsican amianthus in 1965, the Canari mine was forced to close. It was then that the long-term costs of the project started to become apparent. With 98 percent of the extraction from the mine classed as *stérile*, or slag, untold quantities of pulverized toxic rock had been dumped via a vast silo into the sea. The impact on the local marine environment – including precious fish stocks – was catastrophic. Whole beaches, notably at **Marine d'Albo** and **Nonza**, were also ruined for decades by the pollution.

Another more sinister problem emerged in the years after the mine's closure, as former workers started to fall ill with a disease called *svetose*. Although similar to silicosis and linked to prolonged inhalation of toxic mineral dust, the condition is not officially recognized as an industrial disease, which meant that when former miners started to die from it their families weren't covered by insurance or entitled to any compensation. To this day, no one knows exactly how many people died.

attempt only in fair weather, starting early in the morning so as to avoid the convection clouds which mask the high ridges from 11am onwards most days. IGN #4347 OT covers the area and is widely available in local shops (at Nonza, Macinaggio and St-Florent).

South of Canari, the main corniche road cuts across a sheer mountainside horrendously disfigured by the Dantesque terraces of an **amianthus mine**, whose workings resulted in the dumping of untold quantities of toxic dust on the surrounding hillsides and beaches (see box above).

Nonza

Set high on a black rocky pinnacle that plunges vertically into the sea, **NONZA** is one of the highlights of the Cap Corse shoreline. The village was formerly the main stronghold of the da Gentile family, and the remains of the **fortress** still cling to the furthest rocks of the overhanging cliff. Nonza has a shady square, behind which you twist your way through stone-tiled houses and bougainvillea bushes to reach the ruined fortress and the more impressive green **watchtower** nearby. In 1768 the tower, one of the few on the island built in Paoli's time and not by the Genoese, witnessed one of the greatest con tricks in military history. The French, having succeeded in taking over the rest of Cap Corse, closed in on the Nonza garrison, which was under the command of one Captain Casella. Fearing that Casella's tenacity would lead them to their deaths, the Corsican troops absconded, leaving him to defend the tower single-handed. This he did, using a system of cables to maintain constant fire from a line of muskets and a single cannon, until the disheartened French offered a truce. Old Casella demanded that his army be allowed to parade out in dignity, and duly emerged alone and on crutches, brandishing his pistol, to the amazement of the besieging army.

Nonza is also famous for **Santa Julia**, patron saint of Corsica, who was mar-tyred here in the fifth century. The story goes that she had been sold into slav-ery at Carthage and was being taken by ship to Gaul when the slavers arrived. A pagan festival was in progress, and when Julia refused to participate she was raped, tortured and crucified; the gruesome legend relates that her breasts were then cut off and thrown onto a stone, from which sprang two springs, now enshrined in a chapel by the beach. To get there, follow the sign on the right-hand side of the road before you enter the square, which points to the **Fontaine de Ste-Julie**, down by the rocks.

Reached by a flight of six hundred steps, the long grey **beach** is thus coloured as a result of pollution from the asbestos mine up the coast. The local council has banned bathing here (allegedly because of the undertow). However, it's worth the walk down to the beach for the view of the tower alone, which looks as if it's about to topple over into the sea.

The only **accommodation** in the village is the *Auberge Patrizi* (☎04 95 37 82 16; ❹), attached to the big restaurant below the church. Its rooms occupy an attractively converted stone house, five minutes' walk down a steep flight of steps towards the beach. For much of the season, the best room, which has a gorgeous terrace with sweeping views across the gulf to the Désert des Agriates, tends to be block booked by agencies, but it's worth checking to see if any of their self-catering studios are free.

The Nebbio

Named after the thick mists that sweep across it in the spring and autumn, the **Nebbio** (Nebbiu) has for centuries been one of the most fertile parts of Corsica, producing honey, chestnuts and some of the island's finest wine. Officially, the region includes the barren **Désert des Agriates**, further west, but essentially the Nebbio comprises the amphitheatre of rippled hills, vineyards and cultivated valleys that converge on St-Florent, a region nick-named *A Conca d'Oro* (The Golden Shell) by Pascal Paoli because it encom-passed all the wealth of the area. Nourished by the headwaters of the **Aliso River**, its many beautiful villages, perched on pale green bluffs of schist that jut from the gently sloping sides of the basin, are swathed in greenery, with finger-thin bell towers pointing from their midst. In spite of their proximi-ty to the coast, tourism has made little impact on these scattered settlements, which remain largely dependent on agriculture and EU subsidies. The one major development in recent times has been the shift to **viticulture**: some of the wines produced around the *commune* of **Patrimonio** rival those of Sartène, and *caves* offering wine tastings (*dégustations*) are a feature of the whole region.

St-Florent at the base of Cap Corse – a bishopric until 1790 and now a chic coastal resort – remains the Nebbio's chief town and best base, while villages such as **Olmeta–di–Tuda** and **Oletta**, being close to Bastia, are lively and well-populated places, especially in the summer, when families move up to the cooler mountains from the city. The two most notable historic sites in this part of the island are the Pisan church of **Santa Maria Assunta**, just outside St-Florent, and the diminutive **San Michele de Murato**, close to the chapels strewn across the valley between **Rapale** and **Santo–Pietro–di–Tenda**.

The principal **public transport** serving the Nebbio is Transports Santini's bus from Bastia to St-Florent (see p.110 for details).

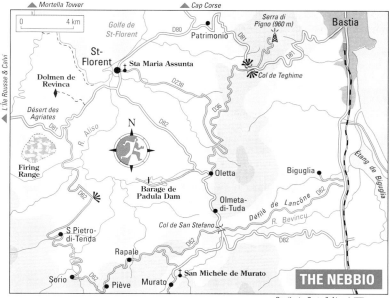

Mortella Tower ▲ Cap Corse

0 ___ 4 km

L'Île Rousse & Calvi

Golfe de
St-Florent

Serra di
Pigno (960 m)

Bastia

D80 Patrimonio D81

St-
Florent + Sta Maria Assunta

D238 Col de Teghime

Dolmen de
Revinca

Désert des
Agriates D81

R. Aliso D82

N

Barage de
Padula Dam

Oletta Biguglia

Olmeta-
di-Tuda

Défilé de Lancône D62

Col de San Stefano R. Bevincu

D82

S Pietro-
di-Tenda

Rapale

Sorio Piève Murato ↑ San Michele de Murato

THE NEBBIO

Étang de Biguglia

Bonifacio, Corte & Ajaccio ▼

St-Florent

Viewed from across the bay, **ST-FLORENT** (San Fiurenzu) appears as a bright line against the black tidal wave of the Tenda hills, the pale stone houses seeming to rise straight out of the sea, overlooked by a squat circular citadel. It's a relaxing town, with a decent beach and a good number of restaurants, but the key to its success is the **marina**, which is jammed with expensive boats throughout the summer. Neither the tourists, however, nor indeed St-Florent's proximity to Bastia, entirely eclipse the air of isolation conferred on the town by its brooding backdrop of mountains and scrubby desert.

In Roman times a town called **Cersunam** existed on the site where the Santa Maria Assunta stands today, 1km east of the present village. Few traces remain of the settlement, which in the mid-fifteenth century was sidelined by the port that developed around the new Genoese citadel. St-Florent proceeded to prosper as one of Genoa's strongholds, largely through the export of olive oil produced in its fertile hinterland, but later went into decline as its population – ravaged by malaria, Moorish pirates, and continual battles between the Corsicans, the French and the Genoese in the mid-sixteenth century – dwindled to 65. The town was also fought over during the struggles for independence in 1769; and it was from here that Paoli set off for London in 1796, never to return.

St-Florent is little more than a village and you won't find a great deal to see here, but there are lots of relaxing cafés to laze in. **Place des Portes**, the centre of town life, has tables facing the sea in the shade of plane trees, and in the evening it fills with strollers and *pétanque* players. In **rue du Centre**, which runs west off the square, parallel to the seafront and marina, you'll find a string of inviting restaurants, shops and wine-tasting places – be sure to sample the sweet, maquis-scented muscat from Cap Corse.

To reach the **citadel**, walk down rue du Centre and turn into place Doria, from the far side of which a lane runs up through the houses to the car park in front of the bastion. Unique in Corsica for its circular shape, the *torrioni*, as it's known locally, was built in 1439 for the Genoese governors, but was bombarded for two days by Nelson's fleet in February 1794 and reduced to a virtual ruin. Substantially renovated in 1998–99, it's today worth a visit primarily for the beautiful views of the hills of the Nebbio and the mountains of Cap Corse, disappearing into mists up the coast.

The nearest **beach**, Plage de la Roya, is a windy stretch of seaweed-strewn sand to the west of town – less than ideal for bathing as the sea is rather murky. To get there, cross the bridge through the marina (see map) and follow the path over the spit. Alternatively, jump on one of the seasonal **excursion boats** which run out of St-Florent marina to the superb beaches across the bay in the Désert des Agriates. The *U Saleccia* (☎04 95 36 90 78) and *Popeye* (☎04 95 37 19 07) leave at regular intervals throughout the day, returning around 4pm; tickets cost €12 for the round trip. For more on plages de Loto and Saleccia, see p.109.

Practicalities

Transports Santini buses (☎04 95 37 04 04) run from Bastia's gare routière to St-Florent twice daily – except Sundays – leaving at 10.30am and 5.30pm between June and September, and at 11am and 6pm during the rest of the year (except Oct–May Wed & Sat, when they leave at noon & 5.30pm), pulling into the vil-

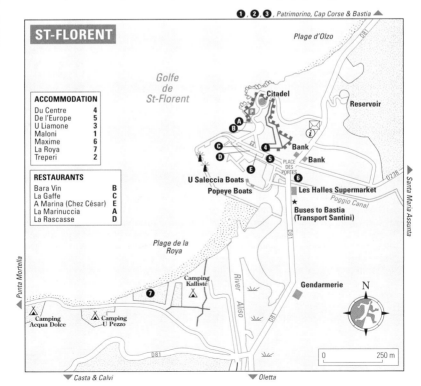

❶, ❷, ❸, Patrimorino, Cap Corse & Bastia

ST-FLORENT

Plage d'Olzo

Golfe de St-Florent

Citadel

Reservoir

ACCOMMODATION

Du Centre	4
De l'Europe	5
U Liamone	3
Maloni	1
Maxime	6
La Roya	7
Treperi	2

Bank

Bank

PLACE DES PORTES

RESTAURANTS

Bara Vin	B
La Gaffe	C
A Marina (Chez César)	E
La Marinuccia	A
La Rascasse	D

U Saleccia Boats

Popeye Boats

Les Halles Supermarket

Poggio Canal

Buses to Bastia (Transport Santini)

Santa Maria Assunta

Plage de la Roya

River Aliso

Camping Kalliste

Gendarmerie

N

Punta Mortella

Camping Acqua Dolce

Camping U Pezzo

Casta & Calvi

Oletta

0   250 m

lage car park, behind the marina. This is also the departure point for the return buses to Bastia, which from June to September leave at 7am and 2pm, and at 6.50am and 1.30pm from October until May. The journey takes one hour.

Bus times vary a little from year to year, but can be checked at the **tourist office**, at the top of the village (July & Aug Mon–Fri 8.30am–12.30pm & 2–7pm, Sat & Sun 9am–noon & 3–6pm; Sept–June Mon–Fri 9am–noon & 2–5pm, Sat 9am–noon; ☎04 95 37 06 04), where you can also get free **maps** of St-Florent and its environs, as well as the usual range of glossy leaflets on the area. The **post office** next door will change traveller's cheques (for a 1.2 percent commission) if they are in euros or dollars, but not sterling. Both the Société Générale and Crédit Agricole **banks**, off place des Portes (Mon–Fri 9–11.45am & 2–4.30pm), have bureau de change counters and hole-in-the-wall cash dispensers that accept MasterCard and Visa.

Les Halles de St-Florent, on the bridge, is the best **supermarket** in the area, and is open on Sundays in the summer. There's a **pharmacy** two minutes up the small unmarked road leading east off place des Portes towards the Santa Maria Assunta cathedral. You'll find a cluster of **telephones** in the marina car park in front of the square. **Motorcycles** are available for rent from Sun Folies, at the far west end of Plage de la Roya (☎06 13 07 39 83) for around €50–60 per day.

Accommodation

St-Florent is a popular resort and **hotels** fill up quickly, especially in the height of summer when prior booking is essential. A fair number of **campsites** are dotted west of the marina behind Plage de la Roya, becoming less expensive the further they are from town; unless stated otherwise, they're open May–Oct inclusive.

Hotels

Du Centre rue du Centre, 100m up the main street from *De l'Europe* ☎04 95 37 00 68, ☎04 95 37 41 01. Old-fashioned place of a kind that's fast disappearing on the island. Modest rooms, all en suite and with showers, kept impeccably clean by the feisty Mme Casanova. Ask for "*côté jardin*". ❸

De l'Europe place des Portes ☎04 95 37 00 33, ☎04 95 37 17 36. In a similar mould to the *Du Centre*, but in a slightly better location and with some sea-facing rooms. The downstairs bar, which stays open late, is the liveliest on the square. Good off-season discounts. ❸

U Liamone Next to the Elf petrol station on the route de Triperi ☎04 95 37 12 81, ☎04 95 37 19 00, ⓦwww.hotel-u-liamone.com. Dependable budget motel on the outskirts of town, with rooms looking across the road to the bay. Friendly hosts and informal atmosphere, although perhaps not such a great option for non-smokers. ❹

Maloni (formerly *Le Mogador*) On the Bastia road, 2km northeast of town ☎04 95 37 14 30, ⓦwww.lemogador.com. Until EU regulations forced it to close its kitchen, this used to be the only Kosher hotel in Corsica, run by a welcoming Jewish family with pan-Mediterranean roots. It's now an excellent little budget hotel, open to all,

with simple but pleasant en-suite rooms opening on to a leafy garden. The whole place is slightly frayed around the edges, which some will like. Rooms down to €35 or less in June & Sept. ❹

Maxime route d'Oletta, just off place des Portes ☎04 95 37 05 30, ☎04 95 37 13 07. Bright, modern hotel in the centre. The rooms, all with en-suite bathrooms and power showers, are on the small side but immaculate. Some have French windows and little balconies, but these overhang a smelly water course. No credit cards. ❹

La Roya plage de la Roya ☎04 95 37 00 40, ☎37 09 85, ⓦwww.hoteldelaroya.com. Since its recent face-lift, this three-star has become the smartest place in the area. The semi-open-air lobby, full of palms, Mediterranean pastels and plate glass, sets the tone. Beyond it, umbrella pines dot a huge lawn terrace and pool surrounded by a teak deck backing directly onto the beach. The thirty airy sea-facing rooms are spacious and quiet, and each has a large balcony. For a review of its gastronomic restaurant, see p.100. ❼

Treperi 1.5km northeast on the Bastia road, turn left immediately after the Elf petrol station and continue 500m uphill ☎04 95 37 40 20, ☎04 95 37 04 61, ⓦwww.hotel-treperi.com. Smart little two-star on a hilltop overlooking the bay, surrounded by vineyards and with panoramic views across the gulf and Nebbio from the room terraces. The grounds have tennis courts and a decent-size pool. Doubles drop to only €55 in June and Sept. ❼

Campsites

A Stella Marine de Farinole ☎ 04 95 37 14 37. Basic site that's slap on the beach in a remote spot, 5km northeast of St-Florent. The proximity of the sea ensures it's packed in high summer, but in May–June and Sept you'll have it virtually to yourself. A great base for exploring the area if you have your own transport.

Acqua Dolce route de la Plage de la Roya ☎ 04 95 37 08 63, Ⓕ 04 95 37 12 82. Unpleasantly

crowded in high summer, but otherwise a good choice, directly behind the cleanest stretch of the beach. Open all year.

Kallisté route de la Plage de la Roya ☎ 04 95 37 03 08, Ⓕ 04 95 37 19 77. The priciest site hereabouts, and thus the quietest despite being only ten minutes' walk along the beach from town. Right behind Plage de la Roya, with ample space and shade, and private access to the sand. There's also a café-bar serving fresh bread and croissant breakfasts in the morning.

U Pezzo route de la Plage de la Roya ☎ & Ⓕ 04 95 37 01 65. Very small site shaded by old eucalyptus trees, just down the road from *Acqua Dolce* and marginally cheaper than the competition. Has its own pizzeria.

Eating and drinking

Renowned for its crayfish (*langouste*) and red mullet (*rouget*), St-Florent has become popular with Corsican gastronomes over the past few years, largely thanks to the efforts of the establishments listed below. Dozens of other restaurants crowd the marina and its backstreets, enticing tourists with glossy photo menus and snazzy terraces, but as with most resorts, standards among them tend to vary widely from year to year. More consistent are the **cafés** lining the square, all of them with virtually identical prices and terraces where visitors and locals alike gather to watch the *passeghiata* and *pétanque*. For reviews of other recommended places to eat in the area, see the accounts of Oletta (p.105) and Murato (p.106).

Bara Vin place Doria. Popular tapas bar tucked away in a lively little square below the citadel. Dishes from €5 to €11 (for a full plate of *mezze*), and they do a great selection of Corsican AOC wines by the glass, served on stand-up barrel tops in the street.

La Gaffe On the harbour front ☎ 04 95 37 00 12. French seafood classics, such as grilled salmon dribbled with St-Jacques sauce, using only the freshest local fish. House specialities include sumptuous devilfish stew on a bed of tagliatelle and Cap Corse-style bouillabaisse (order a day in advance), offered exclusively à la carte. Their good-value four-course *menu fixe* is €22. Closed Tues, except July & Aug.

A Marina (Chez César) rue Nouvelle, on the harbourfront ☎ 04 95 37 15 33. Consistently good pizzas *au feu de bois*, grilled fish dishes, copious salads and several filling pasta options from around €10. A sound budget choice.

La Marinuccia place Doria, below the citadel ☎ 04 95 37 04 36. Traditional island seafood dishes – such as sardines stuffed with fresh ewe's

cheese, or wood-baked sea bass – served in optimum surroundings on a terrace jutting out into the sea off place Doria. Dependably good value for money, and their wine list features the elusive Clos Nicrosi blanc. *Menus fixes* at €18–20.

La Rascasse On the harbour front ☎ 04 95 37 06 99. One of the classiest addresses on the island, run by a talented young chef who has fast become the toast of sybaritic Bastiais. His menu is unashamedly gastronomic, dominated by imaginative spins on local seafood: cream of ray's wing, mussel and chestnut fritters, and lobsters sautéed in cured ham with tartlets of warm *brocciu*. Some of the finest cooking on offer in Corsica, though at a price: €40–50 per head for four courses.

La Roya route de la Plage de la Roya ☎ 04 95 37 00 40. Elaborate gourmet cuisine presented in three-star style, al fresco in a floodlit garden. Signature dishes include spider crab turnover with a squirt of Scotch, and fillet of St Pierre dressed in *prizuttu* ham. Menus range from €55 to a full eight-course *menu prestige* for €75; come armed with a good dictionary. Reservations essential.

Around St-Florent

The area around St-Florent offers plenty of opportunities for short excursions: the cathedral of **Santa Maria Assunta** is only a fifteen-minute walk from the

Mortella point and its famous tower can be reached on foot from St-Florent – a wonderful, mostly flat walk (2hr 30min–3hr) along some of the island's most scenic coastline. Set off early enough, and you can continue past the tower to Plage de Loto in the Désert des Agriates. The path is easy to follow, but you may want to take along IGN's #4348 OT (available at the Maison de la Presse newsagents on place des Portes in St-Florent).

The route begins at the far (west) end of Plage de la Roya, from where you follow the surfaced lane running behind the beach. With transport, it's possible to cut short the dull first stretch of this walk (2km) by driving or cycling as far as **Anse de Fornali**, a narrow inlet overlooked by a cluster of luxury villas where there's a small car park (note that the last 2km of the drive is via a severely rutted *piste*). From the car park, a sign points the way through the maquis to the start of the **Sentier du Douanier** (Custom Officers' Path). This hugs a highly convoluted, rocky coastline, studded with a string of tiny bays below the Domaine de Fonaverte, to round the **Punta di Cepo** headland fifty minutes further on from the car park. From here onwards, the coast is very beautiful, with plenty of idyllic coves for swimming. The IGN map implies the river mouths are open, but you can cross them easily on seaweed-covered sand bars. Winding due north, the final stretch from the crystal-clear, white-bottomed **Fiume Santu bay** to the tower takes around thirty minutes.

Most walkers turn around at the **Tour de Mortella**, but you can continue on to Plage de Loto by heading around the next promontory and following the path west as it cuts inland beneath the lighthouse. At the top of the rise, just after the trail starts to give ground, another path peels right, but you should ignore this and go straight on. **Plage de Loto** is reached after another good hour from the tower. Time your arrival well, and you might be able to catch a ride back to St-Florent on one of the two excursion boats than run here daily – ask at the marina before setting off. Two companies, *U Saleccia* (☎04 95 36 90 78) and *Le Popeye* (☎04 95 37 19 07), run **boat trips** from St-Florent marina to Plage de Loto. Tickets cost €10 (return) and can be booked the day before from June to September (when there are two departures daily).

town centre; also within easy reach are the **Tour de Mortella**, the creepy **Dolmen de Monte Recincu**, and the wonderful **beaches** of the Agriates coast.

Santa Maria Assunta

Situated in a lonely spot 1km east of St-Florent on the original site of the Roman settlement of Nebbium, **Santa Maria Assunta** – the so-called "Cathedral of the Nebbio" – is a fine example of Pisan Romanesque architecture, rivalled only by La Canonica at Mariana, its exact contemporary (see p.77). The route to it east off place des Portes is clearly signposted. In theory the cathedral should be left open from 5 to 8pm in July and August; at other times ask for the key at the tourist office (see p.99), bringing along a passport or some other kind of photo ID as security.

Deprived of its bell tower, which was knocked down in the nineteenth century, and set among pastures next door to a farmyard, the cathedral has a distinctly barn-like appearance. Built of warm yellow limestone, it's a superlatively elegant barn, though, and a close look soon reveals an unexpected wealth of harmonious detail: gracefully symmetrical blind arcades decorate the western façade, and at the entrance twisting serpents and wild animals adorn the pilasters on either side of the door.

In spite of some rather messy Rococo additions, the interior, too, is in essence plain. Carved shells, foliage and animals adorn the capitals of the pillars dividing the nave, at the back of which (to the left as you face away from the altar), you'll see a glass case containing the mummified figure of **St Flor**, a Roman soldier martyred in the third century for his Christian beliefs. Found among the catacombs of Rome with a vial of blood, signifying martyrdom, the soldier's remains were donated by Pope Clement XIV to the bishop of the Nebbio in 1771, and a gilded wooden statue stands as a further commemoration in the apse. The spacious nave also holds the tomb of **General Antoine Gentili**, a prominent supporter of Pascal Paoli during the struggles for independence.

Dolmen de Monte Revincu

One of the Nebbio's few surviving ancient monuments, the **Dolmen de Monte Revincu**, lies ninety minutes or so by foot southwest of St-Florent, lost in a scrub-covered gulley in the Désert des Agriates. The path starts around 2km out of town on the D81; cross the bridge over the Aliso River and follow the main road as it bends uphill through the hamlet of Fromontica. Just 250m beyond the second crossroads (roughly 3km out of St-Florent), a track zigzags downhill through the maquis to cross a stream, after which it climbs a steep spur, which it then follows before dropping into a gully on the far side. When you reach the point, 1.5km further on from the ridge, where two paths cross, turn left (southwest) and follow the waymarks to the dolmen, which crowns a rocky hillock. Once again, you'll find the going a lot easier with a copy of the IGN topo-map for the area, #4348 OT "Bastia and St-Florent" (available from the bookshops in town).

This megalithic tomb, made up of three roughly hewn stone slabs, is popularly known as the **Casa di u Lurcu** (House of the Ogre), after a gigantic creature with the head of a man and a wolf-like body that allegedly used to terrorize the locals by sucking the blood out of their cattle. One day, so the legend goes, the people decided to strike back. Gauging the monster's shoe size from his footprints, they made him some huge boots, which they filled with tar and left by his drinking place. Duly ensnared, the *Lurcu* tried to bribe the villagers with a special recipe for *brocciu*, a Corsican cheese, but the people suspected a trap and threw him into a ditch and buried him. Though it's not clear exactly when the stones were placed here, the legend dates them around 1500 BC.

Tour de Mortella

The ruined **Tour de Mortella**, isolated on the coast 7km west of St-Florent, is the most impressive piece of Genoese architecture hereabouts. Built around 1520 as an anti-piracy measure, the tower fell into disuse over time due to its inaccessibility, until the Corsican wars of independence, when it was reoccupied by French soldiers to guard the sea approach to the gulf. In February 1794, a British fleet under Lord Hood (which included the 64-gun *Agamemnon* commanded by a young Horatio Nelson) sailed in to blockade St-Florent, and were amazed when their two ships – a 74-gun and a 32-gun – were beaten off by the tower's three cannons, sustaining severe damage and suffering some sixty casualties. Only after two days of continual pounding from four guns placed on land (at a mere 137m from the tower), did the 38-strong French garrison surrender. As a result of the British bombardment, the tower was cleft in half, but its renovated ochre-washed walls still strike an impressive profile. More than two centuries later, towers modelled on this one still stand all over the world – from Key West in Florida to the islands of Mauritius – having been erected by the British as coastal defences. For more on "Martello Towers", as they were later re-named, see the "Pirates and watchtowers" box below, and the feature on Nelson in Corsica on p.120.

Pirates and watchtowers

Crowning rocky promontories and clifftops from Cap Corse to Bonifacio, the 91 crumbling Genoese watchtowers that punctuate the Corsican coast have become emblematic of the island's picture-postcard tranquillity. Yet they date from an era when these shores were among the most troubled in Europe. During the early fifteenth century, some five hundred years after the Moors had been ousted from the interior, Saracen **pirates** from North Africa began to menace the coastal villages, descending suddenly from the sea and making off with any valuables – including people – that could be shipped back to the Barbary states.

Held for ransom or sold as slaves, Christians were prime plunder for the pirates, and hundreds of islanders were abducted each year. Some did eventually return to their homelands, though not to resettle. Taking advantage of a law that allowed a slave to claim his freedom if he converted to Islam, former captives would set themselves up as traders in their new countries, or, more often, turn to piracy as a means to amass a fortune. For some reason, the latter vocation appealed particularly to Corsicans: records illustrate that, of the ten thousand or so pirates operating out of Algiers in the mid-sixteenth century, some six thousand were from the island. It is a little-known fact that most of the raids on Corsica during the Genoese era were perpetrated by former natives. Among these were such notorious figures as Mammi Pasha, the scourge of his birthplace, Cap Corse, and Piero Paolo Tavera, better known as Hassan Corso, one of two Corsicans who actually rose to become kings, or deys, of Algiers.

Pirate raids became so common by the end of the fifteenth century that many Corsicans left the coast altogether, retreating to villages in the hills. To protect those that remained, as well as the threatened maritime trade, the Genoese erected a chain of **watchtowers**, or *torri*, at strategic points on the island. Comprising one or two storeys, these squat, round towers measured 12–15m in diameter, with a single doorway 5m off the ground reached by a removable ladder. The towers were paid for by local villagers and staffed by watchmen, or *torregiani*, whose job it was to signal the approach of any unexpected ships by lighting a fire on the crenellated rampart at the top of the tower. In this way, it was possible to alert the entire island within an hour.

Piracy more or less died out by the end of Genoese rule in the mid-fifteenth century, but the *torri* remained in use long after, proving particularly effective during the Anglo-Corsican invasions 250 years later. The British were so impressed with the system that they erected a chain of 103 similar structures along the south coast of England and Ireland to ward off attacks by the French. Over time the same system spread to the far-flung corners of the British empire: India, Australia, Mauritius, the West Indies and USA still have intact **Martello towers**, as they were re-christened (recalling the name of the one near St-Florent that held off Lord Hood and Nelson's fleet). Perhaps the most famous *torri* of all though is the tower of Dun Laoghaire on the far side of the Liffy from Dublin, which was immortalized in the opening scene of James Joyce's *Ulysses*.

A tour of inland Nebbio

St-Florent may attract the bulk of visitors to the Nebbio, but the picturesque **villages** of its **hinterland** form the real heart of the region. Backed by a wall of sheer granite mountains, they cling to the sides of the spectacular **Aliso basin**, overlooking a vista of undulating vineyards that tumble to a deep cobalt-blue sea. Graffiti scrawled over any exposed rock face reminds you that this is a staunchly nationalist area; the Nebbio witnessed some of the fiercest fighting during the wars of independence against the French in the eighteenth century, and the spirit of resistance has never diminished.

Strung together by the winding D62, the villages of inland Nebbio can be visited in an easy day's drive from St-Florent. Aside from a handful of churches and **statue-menhirs**, they harbour few sights, but the constantly changing **views** make this round trip one of the most rewarding forays from the coast. Most people follow a loop from St-Florent, climbing the **Col de Teghime** and dropping down through **Oletta** to the **Col de San Stefano**, then up to **Murato**, and down again to **Santo-Pietro-di-Tenda** before heading back to St-Florent. If you're driving into the Nebbio from Bastia, you can join this loop at Col de Teghime or Col de San Stefano, the latter approached by the dramatic **Défilé de Lancône**; driving from St-Florent, the circuit may be shortened by taking the road straight up to Oletta. The Bastia to St-Florent bus, run by Transports Santini (℡04 95 37 04 04), follows the direct route over the Col de Teghime, stopping at Patrimonio on the way.

Patrimonio

Leaving St-Florent by the Bastia road, the first village you come to, after 6km, is **PATRIMONIO**, centre of the first Corsican wine region to gain *appellation contrôlée* status. Apart from the famous local muscat, which can be sampled in the village or at one of the *caves* along the route from St-Florent, Patrimonio's chief claim to fame is the sixteenth-century **Église St-Martin**, occupying its own little hillock and visible for kilometres around. Made of exposed brown schist and granite, it stands out vividly against the vineyards and weathered chalk outcrops to the north, but the interior was effectively ruined in the nineteenth century, when an elaborately painted ceiling and overdone marble altar were installed.

In a small clearing 200m south of the church, reached via the lane that drops sharply downhill from the crossroads, stands a two-metre-tall **statue-menhir** known as U Nativu, a late megalithic piece dating from 800–900 BC. The only limestone menhir ever discovered in Corsica, it was ploughed up in four fragments by a local farmer in 1964, restored and placed here under a small shelter. A carved T-shape on its front represents a breastbone, and two uncannily life-like eyebrows and a chin can also be made out.

Patrimonio's only other great asset is its annual open-air **guitar festival**, held in the last week of July, when performers and music aficionados from all over Europe converge on the village. Artists who put in regular appearances are Paris-based Corsican guitar supremo Rudolf Rafaëlli and *manouche* virtuoso Romane, two of France's leading exponents of Django-style Gypsy jazz.

Col de Teghime to Oletta

From Patrimonio the road climbs in a series of sharp switchbacks to the **Col de Teghime** (548m), where a memorial recalls the intense fighting that took place here prior to the withdrawal of the German army from Bastia in October 1943, and commemorating the troops who died here. Many of the fallen were

North African *goumiers* from the Berber areas of the Atlas Mountains; a cemetery full of gravestones bearing Arabic inscriptions stands on the outskirts of
St-Florent (2km northeast out of the town along the Bastia road).

From the col, it is possible to see the coastlines of both sides of the cape
(when it's not swathed in fog), with a stunning panorama of St-Florent and
Patrimonio spreading out to the west, while to the east you'll see Bastia, with
the glistening Étang de Biguglia stretching south. It's not unusual for the
weather to be entirely different on either side. For an even better view, follow
the Bastia road for another kilometre and turn left onto the D338, which leads
to the **Serra di Pigno**, a gentle climb of about 45 minutes – a massive television antenna marks the summit.

Oletta

The road south of the Col de Teghime will bring you after 10km to
OLETTA, where the eighteenth-century **Église St-André**, in the centre of
the village, has an ancient relief of the Creation (symbolized by a tree of life)
embedded in its recently renovated façade – a relic from the church that occupied the site in the twelfth century. Inside, there's a graceful triptych dating
from 1534, portraying the Virgin and Child flanked by SS John the Baptist and
Reparata. This used to reside in a local peasant's house until the Madonna
allegedly called out to the mother of the household to warn her that her baby's
cot had caught fire. Thereafter the triptych was transferred to the church, and
has been venerated as miraculous ever since.

The **square** outside the church witnessed one of the more gruesome
episodes in the Paolist insurrections of the eighteenth century, when a daring
rebel plan to seize Oletta from the French backfired. Eager to make an example of his Corsican prisoners, the French commander condemned the rebels to
a horrible death. After having their fingers crushed in a metal vice, they were
led naked to the square carrying torches of flaming wax, and forced to plead
forgiveness. The executioner then tore out their arms and kidneys, gashed open
their thighs, and finally tied them face upwards on a cartwheel, where they
were left to die.

If you feel like spending the night in Oletta, try *A Maggina*, at the entrance
to the village (☎04 95 39 03 68; April–Sept; ❷), which has three cosy en-suite
rooms with superb views over the Nebbio to the sea. Their **restaurant**, whose
terrace also enjoys a fine panorama, is worth a stop too, serving a good selection of local dishes such as duck and olives, roast lamb and veal *sauté*; their set
menus range from €19 to €24.

Le Col de San Stefano and Défilé de Lancône

The crossroads at the **Col de San Stefano** (349m), 4km south of Oletta,
marks the entrance to the **Défilé de Lancône**, a precipitous descent that hits
the main coast road 9km south of Bastia. Hewn out of the black rock, with
nationalist graffiti adorning the rock face at every lurching bend, the road
winds far above the River Bevinco, from whose bed the serpentine for the
church of San Michele de Murato was quarried. The Défilé is a road to be
treated with respect – numerous little shrines along the way testify to the fatal
smashes that have occurred here.

Murato

Continuing along the D5 instead of taking the Défilé, you soon pass the Pisan
church of **San Michele de Murato**, which sits on a grassy bluff high above
the Nebbio. Built around 1280, this late Romanesque building is notable for

its asymmetrical patterning of dark green serpentine and off-white marble, a jazzy counterpoint to the simple lines of the single-naved church, though these were damaged in the late nineteenth century, when the disproportionate bell tower was added. Outside, there's some sophisticated carving on the arches of the blind arcades and immediately beneath the roof, depicting gargoyles, wild beasts and human figures – look out for a relief on the north wall, showing an ashamed Eve reaching out to take the huge apple proffered by the serpent. Within the church you'll find less to catch the eye, although there's a faded fifteenth-century *Annunciation* frescoed on the arch of the apse. The church is always open to visitors.

MURATO, a kilometre or so south beyond the church, is one of the few well-populated villages in the Nebbio. Although not especially picturesque, it's a great place to pull over for a meal, with two commendable restaurants. Tacked on to the side of the church, *Le Monastère* (T04 95 37 64 18; menus from €15) serves delicious Corsica soup, chestnut fritters with lemon, roast kid and lamb in maquis herbs at tables on a grassy terrace overlooking the village. Murato is also renowned for its crusty round bread (*miches*) and plaited loaves (*scaccies* and *scacettes*), which you can buy in the boulangerie just down the road.

For top-class Corsican cuisine, however, you won't do better than the *Ferme-Auberge Campu di Monte* (T04 95 37 64 39; mid-June to mid-Sept daily; mid-Sept to mid-June Fri & Sat evening & Sun lunchtime). This farmhouse restaurant, perched on the mountain on the outskirts of the village, is renowned as much for its sublime location as the sumptuous mountain cooking of the *patronne*, Mme Juillard, whose specialities (many of them handed down from her grandmother) include traditional soft-cheese doughnuts, veal stews and fresh river trout. They offer a single set meal of unlimited portions for the all-in price of €40; reservation is essential, ideally at least a week ahead. Finding the auberge is something of a challenge: turn left at the *Victor Bar* in the village, and follow the road down to the river at the bottom of the valley; shortly after the bridge, an unsurfaced track (indicated with a sign) turns right off the road, heading 1.5km to the farm.

On from Murato

To continue the Nebbio tour, backtrack to the D162, which hugs the side of the Tenda massif as it runs west, snaking through villages built precariously on the lip of a shadowy forested valley. At **RAPALE**, a tiny ancient hamlet with castle-like houses built of schist stone, you can see the Romanesque chapel of **San Cesareo**, a green and white ruin hidden in the woods south above the village – it's a fifteen-minute walk.

Back on the main road, another 2km will bring you to **PIÈVE**. Set on a plinth in front of the church in the heart of this village are three well-preserved **stone menhirs**. Carved in the same minimalist style as the monolith at Patrimonio (see p.104), the 3000-year-old family group gazes out across the Aliso basin to the wall of cloud-fringed peaks to the west.

From Piève, the road twists through valleys along the River Aliso through Sorio and on to **SANTO-PIETRO-DI-TENDA**, an attractive red-stone settlement spread out under the shadow of the Mount Asto massif (1535m). An ancient chronicle recalls that a fierce battle took place on the mountain above the village some time in the tenth or eleventh century, when four thousand Moors were killed by a combined army of Spanish and Corsican troops, led by the Count of Barcelona. This defeat heralded the end of Muslim occupation of the island in the medieval era, but no traces of the momentous battle have ever come to light. These days the village's main point of interest is the tall Baroque

Église St-Jean, joined by a bell tower to the contemporaneous Chapelle Ste-Croix. The latter is closed to the public, but inside the church you'll find the most lavish decor in the Nebbio – elaborate trompe l'œil painting on the walls and a gloomy seventeenth-century *Descent from the Cross* above the altar, which has a wooden tabernacle displaying some fine marquetry on its pedestal.

If you follow the road for 12km until it joins the D81, it's only 7km further to St-Florent.

The Désert des Agriates

Bordered by 35km of wild and rugged coastline, the **Désert des Agriates** is a vast area of uninhabited land, a rocky moonscape interspersed with clumps of cacti and maquis-shrouded hills. The desert's limits extend eastwards to the Golfe de St-Florent, stretch west to the mouth of the Ostriconi River and down as far south as Santo-Pietro-di-Tenda. Although it might appear inhospitable, the desert has a long agricultural history, as its name implies – *agriates* means "cultivated fields". During the time of the Genoese, it was a veritable breadbasket: the Italian occupiers even levied a special wheat tax on local farmers (most of whom came from Cap Corse) to prevent any build-up of funds that might have financed an insurrection in the area. Every winter until the early years of this century, shepherds from the mountains of Niolo and Asco would move down with their flocks to the desert for the annual bartering of goat's and ewe's cheese, which they exchanged for olive oil and wheat cultivated on the Agriates. The grain was stockpiled in square stone storage huts known as *pagliaghju* or *paillers*, about twenty groups of which still exist and are nowadays used by hunters for shelter.

In the course of the eighteenth and nineteenth centuries, fires and soil erosion reduced the region to desert, and it was a total wilderness by the 1970s, when numerous crackpot schemes to redevelop the area were mooted. These included a proposal to convert it into a test zone for atomic weapons, and a plan to transform the entire coast into a purpose-built Club-Med-style tourist complex, complete with concrete holiday villages and a giant marina. In order to block these schemes, the government gradually acquired the Agriates from its various owners (among them the Rothschild family), designating it a protected site. Wildlife, however, remains under threat, not least from trigger-happy hunters. Various ecologically sound projects are currently under discussion, such as plans to introduce controlled breeding of the Agriates' **wild boar**, the purest type on the island due to the isolation of the area, but now endangered by illegal hunting. Other rare species, such as the huge orange and brown Jason butterfly, are also under threat of extinction, largely because of the fires that increasingly devastate the maquis (in September 1992, in a single day, 30 square kilometres went up in smoke, fanned by a mistral blowing onshore at 150kph). The maquis also harbours many species of rare birds, including bee-eaters, red-backed shrikes and cetti warblers.

Practicalities

Much the most relaxed way to penetrate the Désert des Agriates is to jump on one of the excursion **boats** from St-Florent. From their moorings in the marina (see map, p.62), the *Popeye* and *U Saleccia* shuttle passengers throughout the day to Plage de Loto, starting at around 9am and returning from 2pm until around 7.30pm, depending on the time of sunset and the weather. Tickets cost €10 (return) and can be booked in advance from the booths in the marina, where current timetables are posted. From Plage de Loto you can walk back to St-Florent in a little over three hours, or press on along the coast for another hour to Plage de Saleccia. For accounts of both beaches, see below.

Only one road, the D81, runs through the desert, skirting its southern limits between St-Florent and the junction with the N1197 Route Nationale near Ostriconi – the main artery between Bastia and L'Île Rousse/Calvi. In July and August, Autocars Santini's twice daily L'Île Rousse **bus** covers the route, which passes the only **accommodation** on the eastern side of the Agriates area. At the village of **CASTA**, 12km west of St-Florent, the *Le Relais de Saleccia* (℡04 95 37 14 60; Easter–Oct; ❸;) has ten modest en-suite rooms with terraces looking across a sea of undulating scrub to Monte Genova, the highest point in the desert. The couple who run it are very welcoming, and serve fresh local food in their roadside café-restaurant, which has a rear terrace that makes the most of the views.

The *Relais de Saleccia* stands near the start of the only motorable approach to the Désert des Agriates coast, an 11km **piste** winding north to Plage de Saleccia. Before venturing down it, enquire at the hotel about the state of the track, which even when it's in good condition can only be tackled by 4WD vehicles and mountains bikes (the latter are available from the *Relais* for €16 per day). Allow around three hours to cover the route on foot, or one hour by car or bicycle; and be sure to leave early in the day to avoid the heat, taking plenty of water.

The Désert des Agriates coast path

Over the past few years the old custom officers' *sentier* along the coast of the Désert des Agriates has been resurrected to provide footpath access to this pristine shoreline. Winding across wild headlands, crystalline coves piled high with bleached driftwood, and some of the most exquisite beaches in the western Mediterranean, it is – unlike the comparable Littoral Sartenais route in the far south of the island (see p.363) – well way-marked throughout. Before attempting it, however, consider the risks of **sunstroke and dehydration**: long stretches lack shade and there are very few sources of fresh water along the way (you'll need to carry at least three litres). Spring and autumn are the best times to walk; during the summer, temperatures are infernal.

The itinerary is broken into three easy stages, which can be covered in two days or, at a more leisurely pace, in three. Most people begin the route at St-Florent (following the path described in detail in the box on p.101), but there's no reason why you shouldn't start it at Ostriconi and walk from west to east instead. In this case, simply reverse the outline below; the stage timings are the same. Whichever direction you head in, take along the two IGN maps covering the Agriates coast: #4347 OT (Cap Corse) and #4249 OT (L'Île Rousse).

Stage One: St-Florent to Plage de Saleccia 4hr–4hr 30min. Key landmarks on this *étape* include the Fornali lighthouse, the Tour de Mortella, and the famous beaches of Loto and Saleccia. The only source of water and permitted camping place is the *U Paradisu* site, behind Saleccia beach (see p.109).

Stage Two: Saleccia to Plage de Guignu 2hr 30min. The wildest leg of the route, with some very rough maquis and no water sources until you reach the old *bergeries* of Alga Putrica at Guignu, where there's a welcome little gîte d'étape just above the beach (open April–Oct; reservation via the Syndicat Mixte des Agriates ℡04 95 37 09 86). Dorm beds cost €9 or you can pitch a tent for €5, for which you get the use of a small toilet block with cold showers.

Stage Three: Plage de Guignu to Ostriconi 5hr 30min. The path hugs the mostly rocky shore until forced inland around the crags north of Ostriconi beach (covered on p.135).

Approaching the desert by road from the opposite, western side (ie coming from L'Île Rousse), a good place to pull over is the *Auberge de Pietra Monetta* (☎04 95 60 24 88; ❸), situated 350m west of the D81/N1197 junction, just off the Nationale. It serves mainly local cuisine – such as wholesome bean soup, roast kid and lamb sautéed in maquis herbs – on an attractive terrace or inside the original eighteenth-century dining room. At the time of writing, the proprietors also offered a couple of inexpensive rooms (for €46 per person half board), but these may not be available in future except during high season, so phone ahead to check if you want to spend the night here. The nearest **campsite** in the area is at Ostriconi (see p.137), 4km further down the Route Nationale towards L'Île Rousse, where a spectacular beach (accessible by car) stands at the trailhead for the Agriates coastal walk described in the box opposite. You can get to both the *Auberge de Pietra Monetta* and Ostriconi via any of the buses running between Bastia and L'Île Rousse/Calvi (see "Travel details", p.110), but *not* by train (the line approaches the Balagne further west). With your own transport, another good springboard for the area would also be the village of **Lama**, one of the most attractive in northern Corsica (see p.137), 12km southeast.

More general **information** about the Désert des Agriates is available from the Syndicat Mixte des Agriates in Santo-Pietro-di-Tenda (Mon–Fri 9am–noon & 2–4pm; ☎04 95 37 09 86), and the tourist office in St-Florent (see p.99).

Désert des Agriates beaches

The Désert des Agriates coast is strung with gorgeous beaches, but none is more spectacular than **Plage de Saleccia**, 10km west along the coast from St-Florent – a kilometre-long curve of pearl-white sand and perfectly transluscent sea that's inaccessible by road. The majority of people who travel out to it (and be warned that there are lots of them in summer) do so in pleasure boats, or else via the horrendously pot-holed *piste* from Casta (see above), where you rent bicycles for the eleven-kilometre trip. It's also possible to walk via the coast path – a 4–4hr 30min trek from St-Florent (see box opposite). The excursion boats don't sail this far, but from the jetty at Plage de Loto it's only a gentle hour's walk around the headland. Just behind the beach, the *Camping U Paradisu* (☎04 95 37 82 51; mid-June to September) offers basic facilities in a scruffy site that's barely a notch better than bivouacking on the beach (which isn't allowed). Note that **swimming can be dangerous** off Saleccia; at certain phases in the tide, rips drag out unwary bathers – worth bearing in mind if you find yourself alone on the beach.

The same isolation that makes Saleccia so alluring today was the main reason it was chosen during World War II as a landing stage by the commander of the submarine *Le Casabianca*. From its base in Algiers, the sub made daring missions to the Corsican coast in 1942–43 to supply the fledgling Resistance. The one at Saleccia, though initially successful, ended in tragedy: having helped to transport the arms and munitions on muleback and hide them in remote locations around the desert, two of the *maquisards* left in charge of a truck's worth of supplies at a cottage near Casta were surprised by a patrol of Italian carabinieri. In the ensuing shoot-out, one of the patriots was killed; the other managed to slip away (he survived the war and later became the mayor of St-Florent). The beaches' historic associations may in part explain why Saleccia was used as a location for the World War II epic, *The Longest Day*, starring Robert Mitchum.

The other Agriates beach within easy reach, and thus deluged in summer by day-trippers, is **Plage de Loto** (or Plage de Lodo, as it's sometime spelled), to which the two excursion boats from St-Florent sail daily between June and September (see p.107). To see this magnificent site in all its deserted glory, therefore, you'll either have to get to it before or after the boats (a tall order in summer, when the first arrives by 10am and the last leaves around 7.30pm), or, better still, walk there out of season.

Walking the **coast path**, you'll cross several other, even more isolated, coves and beaches, the most striking of them **Plage de Guignu**, two and a half hours' west of Saleccia, where there's a small gîte d'étape run by the local nature conservancy council. Beyond the reach of all but the most tenacious trekkers and pleasure boaters, it's the most remote of the desert's large beaches and a perfect place to hole up for a few days (stays at the gîte are officially limited to four nights maximum).

Travel details

Trains

Bastia to: Ajaccio (2–4 daily; 3hr 10min–3hr 40min); Algajola (2 daily; 2hr 40min); Aregno-Plage (2 daily; 2hr 40min); Belgodère (2 daily; 2hr); Biguglia (2–4 daily; 10min); Bocognano (2–4 daily; 2hr 25min); Calvi (2 daily; 3hr); Corte (2–4 daily; 1hr 30min); L'Île Rousse (2 daily; 2hr 30min); Ponte Novu (2–4 daily; 50min); Ponte Leccia (2–4 daily; 1hr); Sant'Ambrogio (2 daily; 2hr 40min); Venaco (2–4 daily; 1hr 45min); Vivario (2–4 daily; 2hr); Vizzavona (2–4 daily; 2hr 10min).

Buses

The tables below summarize which bus companies cover which routes, how often they run and how long journeys take. Start by looking up your intended destination in the first table; then, using the company's acronym (eg EV or RB), go to the second table for more detailed route and frequency information. Precise departure times can be checked in advance either via the bus companies direct, or (if your French isn't up to that) Bastia tourist office (☎ 04 95 31 81 34).

Bastia to: Ajaccio (EV; 3hr); Aléria/Cateraggio (RB; 1hr 30min); Algajola (BV & EV; 1hr 55min); Calvi (BV & EV; 2hr–2hr 20min); Canari (TS &TM; 1hr 30min); Centuri (TM; 2hr); Corte (EV; 1hr 15min); Erbalunga (municipal buses & TM; 30min); L'Île Rousse (BV & EV; 1hr 40min); Luri (APJ; 50min); Macinaggio (TSD & TM; 2hr); Nonza (TM; 1hr

15min); Olmeta-di-Tudi (TS; 1hr); Patrimonio (TST; 30min); Porto-Vecchio (RB; 3hr); St-Florent (TST; 1hr); Santo-Pietro-di-Tenda; (TS; 2hr); Solenzara (RB; 2hr 10min).

APJ: Autocars Pavarini Jules ☎ 04 95 35 00 11. Bastia–Luri; year round 1 daily Wed only.
BV: Les Beaux Voyages ☎ 04 95 65 15 02 or 04 95 62 02 10. Bastia–L'Île Rousse–Algajola–Calvi; year round Mon–Sat 1 daily.
EV: Eurocorse Voyages ☎ 04 95 31 73 76. Bastia–Corte–Ajaccio; year round Mon–Sat 2 daily. Bastia–Ponte Leccia–L'Île Rousse–Algajola–Calvi; year round Mon–Sat 2 daily.
RB: Rapides Bleues ☎ 04 95 31 03 79. Bastia–Aléria/Cateraggio–Ghisonaccia–Solenzara–Porto-Vecchio; year round Mon–Sat (and Sun from mid-June to mid-Sept) 2 daily.
TM: Transports Micheli ☎ 04 95 35 64 02. Bastia–Erbalunga–Macinaggio–Centuri–Canari–Nonza–St-Florent–Oletta; Aug only, 1 daily Mon–Sat.
TS: Transports Saoletti ☎ 04 95 37 84 05. Bastia–Canari; year round 1 daily Mon & Wed.
TSD: Transports Saladini ☎ 04 95 35 43 88. Bastia–Rogliano–Macinaggio; year round 1 daily Mon, Wed & Fri.
TST: Transports Santini ☎ 04 95 37 04 04. Bastia–St-Florent; year round Mon–Sat 2 daily. St-Florent–Casta–L'Île Rousse; July & Aug 2 daily.

Ferries

For ferry details, see p.20 and p.75.

The Balagne

LIGURIAN
SEA

N

TYRRHENIAN SEA

MEDITERRANEAN
SEA

0   20 km

CHAPTER 2 # Highlights

* **Quai Landry, Calvi** – Sophisticated Riviera-style cafés, in the shadow of the Genoese bastion, with mesmeric views of the mountains – the perfect breakfast spot. See p.123

* **Calvi to L'Île Rousse by train** – The easy way to beach hop along the Balagne's magnificent coast. See p.129

* **Plage de Perajola** – Wilderness beach on the edge of the Désert des Agriates, with a campsite but little else. See p.137

* **Lama** – Flower-filled mountain village with two fine dining possibilities and dozens of rural gîtes to rent. See p.137

* **Sant'Antonino** – Crumbling "eagle's nest" village surveying a vast sweep of the Balagne. See p.142

* **Pigna** – The epicentre of the region's cultural revival holds numerous craft workshops and a café terrace to die for. See p.143

* **Auberge l'Aghjola, Pioggiola** – Rustic country inn with a table to match the spellbinding mountain scenery – an ideal base for explorations of the remote Giunssani region. See p.149

* **Walks in Galéria** – Climb into the hills around this lonely fishing outpost to experience the island's finest coastal landscapes. See p.153

②

The Balagne

M uch of Corsica's northwest is taken up by the **Balagne**, a region divided into Haute-Balagne – the coast between Calvi and L'Île Rousse, and its hinterland – and Balagne Déserte, the area south of Calvi. In the past the Haute-Balagne was the most fertile region of Corsica, famous for its prolific production of honey, fruit and wine, but nowadays – though it has its patches of lushness – a stark brightness characterizes the fire-devastated landscapes of the interior, with acres of gnarled olive trees and wavy vestiges of dry-stone walls intermittently breaking the pattern of pale orange rock. If you're approaching this region from the east, the first glimpse of its coast is an arresting sight, the turquoise and white stripes of sea and sand making a vibrant contrast with the mottled land.

Calvi, the Balagne's largest town and Corsica's third largest port, is also one of the most attractive places in Corsica, with its medieval citadel rising majestically from a stark granite promontory. Six kilometres of sandy beach, backed by a dark ribbon of pines, ensures its popularity as a summer resort, the seasonal influx being served by numerous hotels and a string of campsites. Tourist development has got a little out of hand to the east of Calvi, where private marinas and expensive holiday villages occupy much of the Haute-Balagne coast, but the beaches are outstanding, none more so than at the former Genoese stronghold of **Algajola**. A stunning white strand also forms the focal point of nearby **L'Île Rousse**, a beguilingly faded port built in the eighteenth century as a rival to Calvi.

Walks and hikes in the Balagne

In addition to the two major long-distance hikes originating in the Balagne (the GR20 and Tra Mare e Monti; see pp.369 and 398), a network of **footpaths** has recently been established between the region's three *communes*. Following the old mule tracks, or *chjappate*, that formerly linked villages, these wind across 200km of sea-facing hillsides, cloaked in beautiful olive groves and almond orchards; they're easy to follow and broken into manageable chunks (1hr 30min–3hr 30min), with a couple of longer routes connecting larger settlements. The paths are well marked with specially erected posts displaying the Balagne development council's cherry symbol, but you'll need a good map to make sense of them. In theory, the Pays Côtier leaflet, showing the trails on a monochrome map, should be available at local tourist offices, but they're like gold dust these days and you'll probably have to shell out for the more detailed **topo-guide** *Balagne* if you plan to do more than one of the hikes. The latter not only gives full-colour maps with the routes, but also good descriptions of the paths themselves. For more information, contact SIVU du Pays Côtier de Balagne, at the mairie in Avapessa (℡04 95 61 74 10 or 04 95 75 61 72).

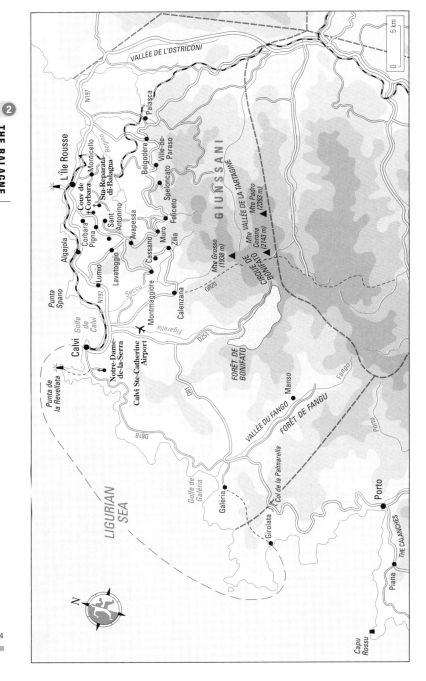

The hinterland of Haute-Balagne is a glorious landscape, with thousands of olive trees swathing the rocky slopes, and fortress villages such as **Sant'Antonino** and **Speloncato** crowning the hilltops, each one embellished with a Baroque bell tower. Many of these settlements are at the receiving end of government programmes aimed at reviving ancient industries and crafts, so you'll see functioning workshops in various places – indeed **Pigna** and **Feliceto** are practically run by their artisan communities. The area tourist office has included most of them on the so-called **Strada di l'Artigiani**, or Route des Artisans, which you can follow in easy day-trips from the coast; ask at any tourist office for the colour catalogue outlining the route.

The Monte Grosso massif, whose sheer granite spine dominates the horizon south of the Haute-Balagne, divides the coastal strip from the secluded **Vallée de la Tartagine**, a region of landlocked pine and chestnut forest known since ancient times as the **Giunssani**. With only a handful of depopulated villages hemmed in by towering peaks, this isolated valley system harbours some of the best hiking routes on the island. Its highest ridges are accessible via sections of the **GR20**, which skirts the Giunssani and presses southeast along the Corsican watershed towards the interior (see p.373). The official trailhead of the arduous ten- to fourteen-day route, however, is at **Calenzana**, in the hills southeast of Calvi. The village also marks the start of the more gentle ten-day **Tra Mare e Monti**, which zigzags south to Cargèse through some of the Mediterranean's most dramatic scenery. For more on both routes, see Chapter 8.

South of Calvi the terrain becomes increasingly grandiose, and the isolated coastal settlement of **Galéria** is well placed for excursions into some memorable landscapes. Inland, there's the **Vallée du Fango**, whose dense forests track the river to the base of towering Cinto Massif, or the spectacular **Cirque de Bonifato**, a ridge of jagged peaks (among them the red shark's fin summit of **Paglia Orba**) encircling another forested valley.

Transport in the Balagne

The Balagne has scarce **public transport**. **Buses** from Bastia serve just the main coast towns, and a minibus runs along the coast from Calvi to Porto.

The **train**, operating all year round, hugs the Haute-Balagne coast northeast of Calvi, veering inland beyond L'Île Rousse to Belgodère, before continuing on to Ponte Leccia, which has connecting services to Bastia and Ajaccio. It's a memorable journey from start to finish, rattling past a succession of turquoise bays and red-roofed hill villages, with the grey cliffs of Monte Tolo (1332m) as a dramatic backdrop. The last stretch before Ponte Leccia traverses the semi-desertified Ostriconi Valley, before passing through a long tunnel to penetrate the heart of the island at the confluence of the Tartagine, Asco and Golo rivers. In addition, a slower, even more rattly **tramway** train operates six times daily along the Balagne coast between Calvi and L'Île Rousse (mid-April to Oct), stopping at all the resorts, campsites and *villages de vacances* en route.

A brief history of the Balagne

Archeological digs in the Balagne have yielded evidence of settlements dating back to the sixth millennium BC. Early Neolithic peoples hunted and gathered along the coast, moving gradually inland during the late Neolithic period; by the Bronze Age, most settlements occupied more easily defensible hilltop sites. Tools and bones discovered in these suggest that their inhabitants both hunted (mainly a now-extinct species of mountain goat) and reared sheep for milk, establishing an agro-pastoral economy that would endure more or less unchanged for more than four thousand years.

Bushfires and the bovine connection

Each year, between 100 and 200 square kilometres of land are devastated by fire in Corsica (one fifth of the total surface area burned annually in France). All kinds of people have been blamed for starting the blazes – from lone pyromaniacs to cigarette-butt-chucking tourists – but the real culprits have only recently been singled out: **cows** or, more accurately, their owners.

The link between the annual infernos and the skinny cattle roaming the island's interior leads back to Brussels and the European Union's Common Agricultural Policy. In the late 1970s, the EU, attempting to reduce its milk lakes and butter mountains, introduced grants for dairy farmers to convert to beef and veal. Although they had never in fact produced much milk, the Corsicans responded by developing a sudden passion for cattle husbandry: within twenty years, the number of cows on the island nearly tripled from 29,000 to 80,000, bringing in a shower of lucrative **subsidies** from Brussels. Ironically, few of the recipients of EU money actually own any land – proof that you possess cattle is enough to secure entitlement. The cows, meanwhile, wander freely across communal areas of maquis, which the *faux éleveurs*, or "fake cattlemen" (also dubbed "the subsidy hunters"), routinely burn so that fresh shoots of grass will grow to feed their neglected animals. This technique has been used by pastoralists for centuries to provide food for cattle in long, dry summers, but their careful control of the fires meant that the amount of land damage was always sustainable.

That local cattle owners are behind the majority of bushfires has long been common knowledge in Corsica. However, it took a Fire Service study to bring the issue into the open. Dividing the island into blocks of four square kilometres, the *pompiers* kept detailed records of all fires reported and cross-referenced their findings with livestock ownership statistics. Soon patterns emerged, and it became possible to predict to within eighty percent of certainty when, where and in what weather conditions fires were most likely to occur.

In September 1994, when the bureaucrats in Brussels finally got wind of what was happening in Corsica, all EU aid to the island was suspended. The effects of the move were dramatic: bushfires fell to one tenth of the normal level that summer. Solving the problem in the long term, however, may be more difficult. EU subsidies bring in large sums of money for cattle owners, and any threat to their livelihood is bound to come up against stiff resistance. Nor is it only the farmers who benefit from the fires, but also builders (who restore damaged houses), foresters (to replant the trees) and, of course, firefighters (who welcome the overtime pay). Combine the financial disincentive with the customary Corsican mistrust of outside interference, and the future for the maquis looks black indeed.

Sweeping economic changes occurred in antiquity with the arrival of technologically advanced Phoenician and Etruscan traders, but the Balagne's agricultural potential was fully exploited only by the **Romans**, who began the cultivation of olives here in the fertile volcanic soil. Known since these times, and in various languages, as the "Pays de l'Huile et du Froment" (Land of Oil and Wheat), the region became the richest on the island, and a prime target for the Saracen raiders who menaced the Mediterranean in the medieval era. The attacks subsided under the rule of the **Pisans**, who constructed forts along the coast to keep the marauding Moors at bay. They also erected dozens of beautiful churches and chapels, whence the popular nickname "Balagna Santa". After the **Genoese** takeover in the thirteenth century, the citadels at Calvi and Algajola were built, and these new ports did a steady trade with Tuscany, the chief cargo being the local olive oil, which for hundreds of years enjoyed a reputation as the best in the Mediterranean.

Under the Genoese, the region was divided into semi-autonomous cantons ruled by the local nobility or **Sgio**, many of whom were highly cultured men who had been educated in Italy – a remarkable contrast to the wild *Sgio* of Sartène (see p.258). Furthermore, although class divisions were as strong as elsewhere in Corsica, the peasants of the Balagne were distinguished by their versatility, with many working as tailors or cobblers as well as farmers, and by their greater independence from their lords, in that they were allowed their own flocks. The result of this comparatively enlightened rule was that the people of the Balagne remained loyal to Genoa well into the eighteenth century.

The Balagne reached its apogee in the nineteenth century, but decline set in when emigration began in the early twentieth century and the small oil mills in the depopulated villages could no longer compete with industrialized producers. It wasn't until the 1950s, when Calvi and L'Île Rousse became popular tourist spots, that the local economy began to pick up, and hotels and holiday complexes mushroomed along the Balagne coast. More recently, the new N1197 road, linking Calvi to Bastia via Ponte Leccia, has improved communications with the rest of the island, while maritime traffic and flights to mainland France have increased in the last couple of years. Nevertheless, the economy of rural areas continues to struggle, in spite of attempts to develop small-scale wine and olive oil production with a modern irrigation programme; a telling fact is that the expensive new **Codole Dam**, inland from L'Île Rousse, has remained full to the brim since it was built because there has been so little demand for its water; the planned resorts hereabouts, for which the reservoir was constructed, have failed to materialize due to unwieldy local bureaucracy and the complexities of nationalist politics. Further setbacks to rural development have been the fires that have repeatedly devastated the countryside in recent years (see box on p.116), and an increasing number of nationalist-terrorist bombings such as the blast that destroyed Calenzana's main wine *cave* in 1987.

Calvi

Seen from the water, **CALVI** is a beautiful spectacle, its three immense bastions topped by a crest of ochre buildings, sharply defined against a hazy backdrop of snowcapped mountains. Below the citadel, a much-photographed strip of pastel-painted, red-roofed houses, belfries and spidery palm trees delineate the *basse ville*, with its yacht-crammed marina, from where the town beach sweeps in a graceful semicircle around the bay. Add a perpetually mild climate and Riviera-like atmosphere, and you can see why Calvi has been attracting tourists for quite a while.

A popular hangout for European glitterati since the 1950s, when *Tao's* nightclub kept the tangos playing till dawn (see box on p.126), Calvi in high summer has the ambience of a ritzy Côte d'Azur resort, with expensive quayside cafés whose clientele is drawn largely from the luxury yachts moored in the marina. A more down-to-earth holiday culture is never far away, though, thanks to the huge campsites that sprawl under the *pinède* (pine forest) to the east of the town, and the backstreets have their fair share of tacky souvenir boutiques.

Over the past few years, Calvi's cultural life has been considerably enriched by the numerous **festivals** that take place here. The best established of these is **Calvi Jazz**, which fills the bars lining the marina with big names from the international scene. September's **Rencontres Polyphoniques**, when traditional Corsican singers play host to some of the world's finest a cappella groups, also draws big crowds. **Festiventu**, in late October, sees the beach filled with hundreds of colourful kites and bizarre wind-powered contraptions. The town also hosts more authentic Balagne customs, principally Easter's **Granitola** procession of hooded penitents, and the October 12 celebrations for **Christopher Columbus** Day. Calvi is widely believed in Corsica to have been the birthplace of the great navigator, a debatable assertion proclaimed by roadside signs at the entrance to the town.

A brief history of Calvi

Calvi began as a fishing port on the site of the present-day *basse ville*, but like many of Corsica's coastal towns it was victim to relentless Vandal, Ostrogoth and Saracen raids between the fifth and tenth centuries. Until the Pisans conquered the island, no more than a cluster of houses and fishing shacks existed on the site. Only with the arrival of the Genoese did the town become a stronghold when, in 1268, **Giovaninello de Loreto**, a Corsican nobleman, built a huge citadel on the windswept rock overlooking the port and named it Calvi.

The republic of Genoa granted the town special privileges, such as freer trading rights and tax exemptions, in order to ensure the fidelity of the population who, in any case, were for the most part Genoese. This fidelity was tried in 1553 by a terrible combined siege of the Turks and French, earning Calvi its motto: *Civitas Calvi Semper Fidelis*. In 1758 Calvi refused to become part of independent Corsica, a stand for which it suffered in 1794, when Paoli made an alliance with the British. A fleet commanded by Nelson launched a brutal two-month attack, bombarding the walls from all sides and eventually forcing surrender. Nelson left saying he never wanted to see the place again, and nearly didn't, for during the attack he lost the use of one eye.

The nineteenth century saw a decline in Calvi's fortunes, as the Genoese merchants left and the French concentrated on developing Ajaccio and Bastia. One Victorian traveller described it as "a frowning fort with cracked, tottering ruins, worn and wasted by the rain". Later Calvi became primarily a military base, used as a point for smuggling arms and commandos to Occupied France in World War II, and has been a base of the **Légion Étrangère** (Foreign Legion) since 1962 (see box on p.122); you're bound to see groups of cropped-haired legionnaires in their characteristic white peaked *képis* and immaculate khaki uniforms strolling up and down the marina, watched by couples of similarly attired military police. Tourism, however, is now the essence of Calvi: the town became fashionable right after the war and has done good business as a holiday resort ever since.

Arrival and information

Ste-Catherine **airport** (℡04 95 65 08 09 or 04 95 65 88 88), served by daily flights from mainland France and weekly charters from the UK and other northern European countries during the summer, lies 7km south of Calvi; **taxis** (℡04 95 65 03 10 or 04 95 65 30 36) provide the only public transport into town, and fares shouldn't cost more than €14 during weekdays (or €16 evenings and on Sundays). The **train station** is on avenue de la République (℡04 95 65 00 61), close to the marina and the air-conditioned **tourist office** on quai Landry (June 15–Sept 30 daily 9am–7pm; Oct 1–June 14 Mon–Fri 9am–noon & 2–5.30pm, Sat 9am–noon; ℡04 95 65 16 67), whose staff are very helpful.

CALVI

ST-FRANÇOIS

Anse de Fontanaccia

La Maison Colomb

CITADELLE

Cathédrale St-Jean Baptiste

Oratoire St-Antoine

Caserne Sampiero

R. COLOMB

A

Port

AVE SANT-FRANÇOIS

PLACE DE L'OMBRE

RUE DE L'URUGUAY

VILAS SANT-ANTOINE RUE

PLACE CHRISTOPHE COLOMB

P

❶

Garage Ambrosini

❷ **Maison de la Presse**

AVENUE NAPOLÉON

Hôtel de Ville

Laundry

❸

B

BOULEVARD WILSON

R. ALSACE-LORRAINE

R. CLEMENCEAU

Tour du Sel

Port de Commerce

QUAI LANDRY

AVENUE GÉRARD MARCHE

D

Église Ste-Marie-Majeure

PL ST-CHARLES

❺

R. CLEMENCEAU

QUAI LANDRY

E

Boat excursions to Girolata

Beaux Voyages ★ Buses

LA PORTEUSE D'EAU

RUE JOFFRE

(i)

N

Train Station

❻

Marina

AVENUE DE LA RÉPUBLIQUE

AVENUE SANTA MARIA

◀ **C** , Galéria, Revellata & Notre Dame de la Serra

② THE BALAGNE | Calvi

◀ Marseille & Toulon ▶

◀ Nice & Genoa ▶

▶ Nice & Genoa

P

P

Laundry

Super-U

ROUTE DE SANTORE

Total Petrol Station

Beach

❼

BARS & RESTAURANTS

L'Abri Côtier	E
Chez Tao's	A
U Famale	C
U Minellu	B
Le Santa Maria	D

ACCOMMODATION

Les Arbousiers	8
BVJ Corsotel	6
Casa Vecchia	7
Du Centre	3
Christophe Colomb	2
Cyrnea	11
Grand Hôtel	5
Relais International de la Jeunesse "U Carabellu"	10
Le Saint François	1
Il Tramonto	4
La Villa	9

❽

ROUTE DE LA PIETRA MAGGIORE

0	50 m

❿ & Camping Bella Vista ▼

▼ ⓫ , Ste-Cat. Airport, L'Ile Rousse, Camping International & Camping La Pinède

More than a decade before his death at the battle of Trafalgar, a young and ambitious **Horatio Nelson** was gaining valuable experience fighting the French in Corsica on behalf of Pascal Paoli and his patriots. The unlikely alliance came about following the fall of Toulon in 1793, when the British, under Lord Hood, chose the island as a base for their Mediterranean fleet. Several ships were dispatched to blockade Corsica, among them Nelson's 64-gun *Agamemnon*.

Arriving off Cap Corse in the middle of winter, the British picked off a series of easy targets along the north coast before laying siege to the watchtower at **Punta di Mortella** (see p.102) and, later, the citadel at St-Florent, where they took a bloody nose before setting their sights on the tougher proposition of **Bastia**. In the course of the hard-fought 37 day siege that ensued, Nelson – who had during reconnaissance lied about the strength of the French defences in order to gain permission for an attack considered by his superiors as "most visionary and rash" – played a key role, overseeing the landing of cannon and manning of batteries. However, his small but resolute crew's contribution was never fully acknowledged. The army, whose commander had consistently refused to "entangle (himself) in any co-operation", stood by until the French surrender, whereupon it promptly marched on the town from St-Florent to steal Nelson's glory.

A still harder nut to crack was the French garrison at **Calvi**, to which the British turned their attention in June 1794. The landing of supplies and arms, at a cove southeast of the town behind the shoulder of hills backing the bay, was severely hampered by a fierce summer storm, which forced the ships to stand out for two days in raging seas, leaving the land force stranded. But the soldiers on shore had made good use of the delay, dragging cannons up the hills and digging into position.

The bombardment began on July 4. It was during the concentrated French counterfire that Nelson, eight days later, was struck in the face by stones and splinters thrown up after an enemy shell burst on the emplacement he was commanding. One laceration penetrated his eyeball, but the paragon of British stiff upper lip, writing to his senior officer that evening, reported only that he'd "got a little hurt".

Seemingly of more concern to Nelson at the time were the "shivering fits" bedeviling him and his men. The British hospital ship was by this stage crammed to the gunwales with malaria cases, stewed by the relentless mid-summer heat. Getting wind that the besiegers were succumbing to illness, the French sued for a short truce (time enough for the British to be further weakened and for reinforcements to arrive from the mainland) but their ruse didn't work. The cannonfire continued: in the four weeks preceding the surrender by a depleted and demoralized Gallic garrison on August 10, some eleven thousand cannon and around three thousand shells were launched at Calvi, reducing huge chunks of it to rubble (some of which has still not been cleared away). "The place is a heap of ruins," wrote Nelson.

On board the *Agamemnon* as it sailed back to Leghorn (Livorno), the future hero of Trafalgar finally wrote to this wife to inform her that the "slight scratch" he'd sustained three weeks earlier had resulted in the loss of sight in one eye. "(It) is grown worse, and is in almost total darkness, and very painful at times; but never mind, I can see very well with the other."

Among the many myths surrounding Britain's most illustrious admiral was that he wore an eye patch over his bad eye for the rest of his life. In fact, Nelson had a special shade made and fastened to his famous naval hat to protect his good eye from sun glare. In later years, he was able to put the bad one to good use. During the messy battle of Copenhagen in 1801, Lord Nelson, as he was by this time known, ignored orders from his Commander-in-Chief, Sir Hyde Parker, to discontinue action, saying to his colleague, "You know, Foley, I have only one eye. I have the right to be blind sometimes." Raising his spy-glass to his damaged one, he uttered the historic words "I really do not see the signal", and went on to win the decisive victory of the Baltic campaign.

Les Beaux Voyages' **buses** from Bastia and towns along the north coast stop outside the train station on place de la Porteuse d'Eau, whereas SAIB's minibuses from Porto pull in at the marina.

Ferries dock at the Port de Commerce, immediately below the citadel. For details of companies offering **car** and **motorbike rental** in Calvi, see "Listings" on p.127.

Car parking is easiest (and free) in the large roadside lot next to the marina, to the right of the main road as you approach town; otherwise, try the Super U car park further south (see map for directions).

Accommodation

There are a vast number of beds for tourists in Calvi, and **accommodation** is easy to find except during the jazz and choral festivals (see p.125), when you should book weeks ahead. Hotels range from inexpensive *pensions* to luxury hotels with pools and sweeping views of the bay. Prices are generally reasonable, apart from during high season, when they go through the roof. If you're on a tight budget, take your pick from the town's two excellent **hostels**, or the dozen **campsites** within walking distance of the centre. A full rundown of everywhere to stay in the town, complete with photos, current tariffs and contact details, features in the tourist office's free handout – useful in the unlikely event that our recommendations are all fully booked.

For reviews of **accommodation around Calvi**, see "Calenzana" on p.138.

Hotels

Les Arbousiers route de Pietra-Maggiore ☎ 04 95 65 04 47, ⒻX 04 95 65 26 14. Large, fading pink place set back from the main road, 1km south of town and 150m from the beach, with rooms ranged around a quiet courtyard. Particularly good deal mid and low season (June/Sept €33 per double). ❸

Casa Vecchia route de Santore ☎ 04 95 65 09 33, ⒻX 04 95 65 37 93, ⒺX info@casa-vecchia.com. Small chalets set in a leafy garden, 500m east of town, and 200m from the beach. In May, June and September doubles drop to €28; half board obligatory in July & Aug. A dependable budget option, though advance booking essential. Open May–Sept. ❸

Du Centre 14 rue Alsace-Lorraine ☎ 04 95 65 02 01. Somewhat institutional old *pension* occupying a former police station in a narrow, pretty street near Église Ste-Marie-Majeure and harbourside. Rooms are plain with shared WC. Among the cheapest options in town after the hostels (from €31 per double June/Sept), although prices rise to €42 and up in July and August. Open June–Oct. ❸

Christophe Colomb rue de l'Uruguay/place Bel' Ombra ☎ 04 95 65 06 04, ⒻX 04 95 65 29 65. Comfortable and spacious rooms, most with expansive views across the bay. There's also a bar, restaurant and off-road parking. Since the recent refurbishment, it's the most attractive upscale

place this close to the centre. Tariffs drop to €64 in June/late Sept. Open April–Oct. ❻

Cyrnea route de Bastia ☎ 04 95 65 03 35, ⒻX 04 95 65 38 46, ⒺX peretti.p@wanadoo.fr. Large budget hotel, 20min walk south of town or 300m from the beach. Good-sized rooms for the price, all with bathrooms and balconies (ask for one "*vue montagne*" to the rear). Outstanding value for money, even in high season. Open April–Nov. ❹

Grand Hôtel 3 bd Wilson ☎ 04 95 65 09 74, ⒻX 04 95 65 25 40, ⓌX www.grand-hotel-calvi.com. Characterful *fin-de-siècle* luxury hotel in the centre of town, with mostly period furniture and fittings. The rooms, though somewhat dowdy and in need of a lick of paint, are huge, and many have good views (as does the breakfast salon, which looks over the rooftops of the old quarter). Smaller than average tariff increases in high season. Open April–Oct. ❺–❼

Le Saint François pointe de Saint-François ☎ 04 95 65 03 61, ⒻX 04 95 65 30 01, ⓌX www.residence-st-francois.com. Tucked away just beyond the citadel, with sea views. Very central, reasonable prices (down to €46 per double in June/Sept) and clean, if a bit worn around the edges. You also get the use of a pool. ❺

Il Tramonto route de Porto ☎ 04 95 65 04 17. Another excellent little budget hotel, with rates down to €32 low season: ugly 1970s block from the outside, but the rooms are clean, comfortable and light. Definitely try for one with "*vue mer*"; there are little terraces and superb views over Punta della Revellata. ❸

La Villa 2km west of town along Chemin de Notre-Dame-de-la-Serra ☎04 95 65 10 10, ℱ04 95 65 10 50, ⓦwww.hotel-lavilla.com. Spacious cloisters, sunny mosaics, low terracotta roofs and arcades framing sea views give this luxury hotel on the hill above town, one of only a handful of four stars on the island, the feel of a Balagne monastery fused with a Roman villa. For €370 per night, you get the run of their Turkish baths, top-notch sports facilities and four pools (including one which seems to blend with the horizon), as well as an exclusive stretch of beach. And they've a heli-pad should you need one. ❾

White képis and winged daggers

Each year on April 30, ranks of immaculately dressed legionnaires from Calvi's Camp Raffali parade through town to celebrate "Camerone Day", commemorating a battle that, ironically, was among the worst defeats in French military history. Trapped in a cannon-scarred farmhouse on the road between Vera Cruz and Mexico City in 1863, a company of 63 men held out against an army of nearly three thousand long enough for an impor-tant arms column to reach their besieged comrades in the capital. Only three came out alive. The Camerone parade is the public face of a very private army unit: the enigmatic **2e Régiment Étranger de Parachutistes** of the **Légion Étrangère**.

The French Foreign Legion was formed in 1831 at the behest of King Louis Philippe as a means to employ gainfully the potentially troublesome hordes of economic migrants and excitable revolutionaries collecting in Paris at that time. Enticed by the promise of French citizenship in exchange for five years' service (an incentive that still exists today), the recruits were promptly packed off to fight in France's North African colonies. Expected to march 30km per day across soft sand carrying full packs, the first legion-naires were just as likely to perish from heat exhaustion and dysentery as battle wounds.

It was during this era that many of the clichés surrounding the Legion were coined; deserters were indeed buried up to their necks in sand to face the Saharan sun with their eyelashes sewn open, or dragged for days tied to mule carts. But in spite of the inhu-mane conditions, recruits continued to pour in. Many – like the American songwriter Cole Porter, English philosopher Arthur Koestler and the young Prince Aage of Denmark – did so for pure adventure; many more signed up to flee debt, prison or unhappy love affairs. Then, as today, the Legion offered **anonymity** for its recruits. For the first year of serv-ice, legionnaires are given a false name and there's an unwritten law that no one should be forced to answer questions about their past. Today, the Légion Étrangère comprises 8500 men from more than one hundred countries. The selection process they have to endure is among the toughest of its kind, beginning with an arduous three-week physi-cal fitness ordeal at the Legion's headquarters in Aubagne on the mainland, after which recruits are assigned to units all over the world.

The muscle-bound, crew-cut Rambo lookalikes you'll see swaggering around Calvi's quai Landry in their knife-edge creases and white *képis* are members of the Legion's elite force, hand-picked from the cream of the recruits. Based at Camp Raffali, on the southeast edge of town, the 2e REP earned its fame with a daring raid on Kolwezi, Zaire, in 1978, when three thousand expatriate civilians were rescued with ruthless effi-ciency from the midst of a communal massacre. Training of today's 1300 crack paras exploits the mountainous terrain of the Corsican interior and the varied coastal terrain near Calvi, where month-long courses culminate in 72-hour missions, during which recruits carry out high-altitude parachute drops, amphibious landings and simulate hostage rescues. Anyone who survives this basic training gets to wear the coveted green beret bearing the famous winged-hand-and-dagger emblem of the 2e REP. More often than not, however, it is the distinctive *képis* you'll encounter on the quai Landry, pulled more steeply over the eyes by Calvi's notoriously arrogant legionnaires than by those from regular regiments.

The Legion's headquarters at Camp Raffali opens its door to the general public twice each year: Camerone Day (April 30) and St Michael's Day (September 29).

Hostels

BVJ Corsotel 43 av de la République ℡ 04 95 65 14 15, ℻ 04 95 65 33 72. Huge youth hostel in prime position opposite the station and facing the sea. Very clean rooms for up to eight people (no double rooms), some with balconies, at €20.60 per bed. A superb deal in high season, but no off-peak discounts. Inexpensive meals served in an institutional canteen. Internet access available (residents only). Open March–Nov.
Relais International de la Jeunesse "U

Carabellu"** 4km from the centre of town on route de Pietra-Maggiore ℡ 04 95 65 14 16, ℻ 04 95 80 65 33. Follow the N197 for 2km, turn right at the sign for Pietra-Maggiore, and the hostel – two little houses with spacious, clean dormitories only at €25 per bed, looking out over the gulf – is in the village another 2km further on (along a track that's impassable for cars). Wonderful views from the terrace. Phone ahead to make sure it's open. May–Oct.

Campsites

Bella Vista 2km along the N197 from Calvi ℡ 04 95 65 11 76, ℻ 04 95 65 03 03. A large, quiet and friendly three-star site, 700m from beach. To get here, turn right at the sign to Pietra-Maggiore, and the campsite's another 1km along on the right-hand side. April–Oct.
Camping International 1km along the N197 near Prisunic supermarket ℡ 04 95 65 01 75. Well situ-

ated and shady, with more grass than most. The site's café is really lively on weekends. May–Oct.
La Pinède 2km east of Calvi between the beach and N197 ℡ 04 95 65 17 80, ℻ 05 96 65 19 60. Popular site in a pine forest, with bar, restaurant, supermarket, tennis courts and telephones. Catch the train out here, and ask the guard for two stops after Calvi. Open April–Oct.

The Town

Social life in Calvi focuses on the restaurants and cafés of **quai Landry**, a spacious seafront walkway linking the marina and the port. This is the best place to get the feel of the town, but as far as sights go there's not a lot to the *basse ville*. At the far end of the quay, under the shadow of the citadel, stands the sturdy **Tour du Sel**, a medieval lookout post once used to store imported salt. If you strike up through the narrow passageways off quai Landry, you'll come out at rue Clémenceau, where restaurants and souvenir shops are packed into every available space. In a small square opening out onto the street stands the pink-painted **Église Ste–Marie–Majeure**, built in 1774, whose spindly bell tower rises elegantly above the cafés on the quay but whose interior contains nothing of interest. From the church's flank, a flight of steps connects with boulevard Wilson, a wide, modern high street which rises to **place Christophe-Colomb**, point of entry for the *haute ville* or **citadel**.

The citadel

Beyond the ancient gateway to the **citadel**, with its inscription of the town's motto – *Civitas Calvis Semper Fidelis* (see p.118) – a narrow alleyway twists past the enormous **Caserne Sampiero**, formerly the governor's palace. Built in the thirteenth century, when the great round tower was used as a dungeon, the castle was recently restored and is currently used for military purposes, therefore closed to the public. The best way of seeing the rest of the citadel is to follow the **ramparts**, which connect three immense bastions. From each one the views across the bay to the mountains of the Balagne and Cinto massif are magnificent.

    Within the walls the houses are tightly packed along tortuous stairways and cobbled passages that converge on the diminutive **piazza d'Armes**, next to the Caserne Sampiero. Dominating the square is the **Cathédrale St-Jean-Baptiste**, set at the highest point of the promontory. This chunky ochre edifice, founded in the thirteenth century, was partly destroyed during the Turkish siege of 1553 and then suffered extensive damage twelve years later, when the powder magazine in the governor's palace exploded. Rebuilt in Greek cross form and surmounted by a black-tiled octagonal dome, the church became a cathedral in 1576, as the reconstruction was drawing to a close. **Inside**, to the left of the entrance, are three elaborate alabaster fonts, which date from 1568. Beside the ostentatious marble altar stands a finely carved eighteenth-century wooden pulpit, while beneath the dome lies the tomb of the Baglioni family, an illustrious Genoese clan who made their money from trade in the four-teenth century. In 1400 the hot-headed Bayon Baglioni is said to have saved the town from a treacherous pair who were plotting to hand Calvi over to the Aragonese. As he stabbed the traitors, he screamed "Libertà! Libertà!", a cry that became part of the family name and eventually, by a circuitous line of descent, the name of one of London's most famous streets, Liberty. If you look up, you'll see a line of theatre-like boxes screened by iron grilles under the roof of the cupola; built for the use of the noblewomen of the town, the grilles acted as protection from the commoners' gaze. In the apse there's a seventeenth-century wooden statue of John the Baptist, framed by a solemn triptych dated 1498 and attributed to the obscure Genoese painter, Barbagelata. The church's great treasure is the **Christ des Miracles**, which is housed in the chapel on the right of the choir; this crucifix was brandished at the marauding Turks dur-ing the 1553 siege, an act that reputedly saved the day.

North of piazza d'Armes, in a small patch of wasteland off rue du Fil, stands the shell of the building that Calvi believes was **Christopher Columbus's birthplace**, as the plaque on the wall states. The claim rides on pretty tenuous circumstantial evidence. Columbus's known date of birth coincides with the Genoese occupation of Calvi, at which time a weaving family by the name of Columbo lived in the town. Papers left by Columbus's son state that Christopher was the son of weavers, that he had two relations in the navy (there was indeed a Corsican sea captain named Columbo), who "came from the sea" (which could be interpreted as coming from the island of Corsica). What's more, Columbus is said to have taken Corsican dogs on his voyage, and he placed his first New World ports under the protection of popular Corsican saints. Believers claim that the Genoese deliberately burned the town archives in 1580 and renamed the street, formerly rue Columbo, in order to cover up the truth. The house itself was destroyed by Nelson's army during the siege of 1794, but as recompense a statue was erected on May 20, 1992, the 500th anniversary of his "discovery" of America; his alleged birthday, October 12, is now a public holiday in Calvi celebrated with fireworks and speeches.

On the east side of the citadel, it's a quick walk along the ramparts to Maison Pacciola, where Napoléon spent a night in 1793. Close by, the **Oratoire St-Antoine** is an unremarkable building dating from the early sixteenth century, but look out for a graceful grey granite **relief carving** above the door, featur-ing Anthony, patron saint of Calvi, flanked by St John the Baptist and St Francis.

The beach

Calvi's spectacular **beach** sweeps right round the bay from the end of quai Landry. Most of the first kilometre or so is owned by bars, which rent out sun loungers for a hefty price, but these can be avoided by following the track behind the sand to the start of a more secluded stretch. The sea might not be as sparklingly clear as at many other Corsican beaches, but it's warm, shallow and free of rocks. You can also swim and sunbathe off the rocks at the foot of the citadel, which have the added attraction of fine views across the bay.

Eating, drinking and nightlife

Eating is a major pastime in Calvi and you'll find a wide selection of restaurants and snack bars, although few offering good value for money. This is particularly true of the **fish restaurants** lining the marina, where a three-course seafood supper fresh from the bay can cost upwards of €40. As a rule, it's cheaper to eat in the backstreets of the *basse ville*, whose stairways and cramped forecourts hide a host of buzzing, inexpensive pizzerias and Corsican speciality places.

Cafés, complete with raffia parasols, are strung along the marina, becoming more expensive the nearer they are to the Tour de Sel. The best places are those closest to the beach, which also get the sun all day.

Calvi's **nightlife** is livelier than you might expect, with clubs opening up all over town in the summer; the best of the marina's nightspots is *Le Calypso*, at the far end of quai Landry under the citadel (summer only). There's also a summer open-air cinema, *Le Pop Cyrnos*, next to the Rallye supermarket on the N197, 1km out of town towards L'Île Rousse, which screens new releases (dubbed in French).

For **food shopping**, Calvi's two largest **supermarkets**, Prisunic and Super U, are both south of the centre on the main road (avenue de la République). You can also buy groceries at the small self-service *alimentation* on the corner of rue Joffre and rue Georges, above quai Landry (open Sun during the tourist season), or at the daily fresh produce **market** in the hall between rue Clémenceau and boulevard Wilson. For artisanal local specialities and other authentic souvenirs, the best shop in town is *Chez Annie*, at 5 rue Clémenceau, which stocks a huge range of wines, honey, charcuterie, liqueurs and *canastrelli* biscuits.

Restaurants

L'Abri Côtier On the quay, but entrance on rue Joffre. Mostly seafood dishes (such as sea bass with fennel and crayfish fresh from the gulf) and pizzas (from €8) served on a terrace looking out to sea. Their set menus (€12–20) and *suggestions du jour* are invariably the best deals; for vegetarians, there's a copious veggie platter.

Chez Tao's rue St-Antoine, in the citadel ☎04 95 65 00 73. Legendary nightclub (see box on p.126), now turned into an expensive piano bar offering fussy nouvelle cuisine and outstanding view of the bay. The only hints of its unusual history are the striking black and white photos of Russian aristos on the walls. Count on roughly €30 à la carte. June–Sept daily 7pm–midnight.

U Famale route de Porto, just outside the centre of town on the way to Punta della Revellata ☎04 95 65 18 82. Worth the walk out here for their delicious, beautifully presented Corsican specialities –

mussels or lamb simmered in ewe's cheese and white wine, a fine *soupe Corse*, and melt-in-the-mouth *fiadone*. Lovely views of the bay and Punta della Revellata too. *Menu* at €21 plus a full à la carte choice, and pizzas from €7.

U Minellu Off bd Wilson, nr Ste-Marie-Majeure. Wholesome Corsican specialities served in a narrow stepped alley, or on a shady terrace with pretty mosaic tables. Their menu features local charcuterie, baked lamb, *cannelloni al brocciu*, spider crab dressed "à la Calvaise", and a cheese platter – great value at €16.

Le Santa Maria Next to the Église Ste-Marie-Majeure, rue Clémenceau ☎04 95 64 04 19. Popular four-course tourist menu (€15.50), and particularly good paella (€17), served in an atmospheric little square in front of the church, with *pichets* of AOC house wine.

Festivals and events

Over the last decade Calvi has sought to reinvent itself as the island's culture capital through hosting a string of lively music **festivals** and **arts events**, over the summer and in the early autumn. One of the chief instigators of this renaissance was Jean-Témir Kéréfoff, son of the famous nightclub impresario, Tao, who saw a festival scene as the ideal way to assert a new identity for a town whose inhabitants feel perennially outnumbered – by tourists in the summer, and legionnaires in the winter months. The festivals generally don't pay performers, but instead offer a week's expenses-paid stay in a local hotel. Specific dates and details, for all the events listed below, are available through the Calvi tourist office (see p.118).

La Passion Good Friday. One of the island's most sombre Easter celebrations revolves around a procession of hooded penitents called *La Granitola* ("The Snail" in Corsican), which takes place on Good Friday. Starting at 9pm in Calvi's *basse ville*, the line of penitents, barefoot and carrying simple wooden crosses, winds and unwinds itself through the streets to the citadel, accompanied by an eerie chanting from the onlookers.

St-Érasme June 2. Fishermen's festival with firework displays in the harbour.

Festival du Jazz third week of June. One of the highlights of France's packed jazz calendar, featuring headline acts from all over the world.

Tickets for the formal evening gigs (available at the marquee on the north side of the marina, immediately below the citadel) cost around €25, but you can catch spontaneous free jam sessions, or *bœufs*, in the bars on quai Landry afterwards.

Citadella in Festa Ascension Day, August 15. A lively celebration of Corsican culture, with conferences, exhibitions of local crafts, and concerts culminating with a firework-spangled son et lumière at the citadel.

Rencontres d'Art Contemporain mid-June to early August. Exhibitions by local artists at various galleries in the citadel.

Tao

A rare Dionysiac interlude in Dorothy Carrington's classic but rather staid portrait of Corsica, *Granite Island*, occurs in a club in Calvi in the late 1940s:

The night was gathering impetus … it carried us with the rising moon into dark, unexplored, fathomless places. The music was hypnotic. No one resisted it; the dancers moved with a taut, controlled violence, the men crouching over their partners as if kindling a fire.

When Dorothy Carrington was being whisked off her feet by dashing legionnaires and "unnaturally quiet men from Calenzana", *Chez Tao's* (see p.125) was still owned and run by its founder, Tao, a charismatic Russian whose life story reads like the plot from a lurid picaresque novel. A handsome Tcherkess Muslim from the Caucasus, Tao came to Calvi via a convoluted odyssey that began with him fleeing slaughter following the defeat of his White Russian cavalry regiment in the Crimea. He escaped to Constantinople and scraped a living as a dancer, performing for the sultan and his harem. From Turkey he danced through the vaudeville theatres and ballrooms of Europe to Paris and eventually New York where, in 1928, he met **Feliz Youssoupof**, a rich Russian nobleman believed to be one of Rasputin's murderers. The two became firm friends and together decided to return to Paris, and then to Calvi.

The arrival of the exotic pair, together with their musical entourage, must have cut a dash in the (then) sedate Corsican town. Before long, peasants and fishermen from all over the island were flocking in to watch Tao's show, and to dance with the foreign thespians on the quayside (at that time women dared not venture out at night, so men danced with them "sailor style", as Dorothy Carrington puts it). His popularity was still running high when his benefactor left, and the resourceful Tao, now married to a local woman, was able to open a nightclub in the former chapel of a bishop's palace in the citadel.

Now run by Tao's son, *Chez Tao's* occupies the same sixteenth-century vault and still does a brisk trade during the season, but it's no longer a place where, in Dorothy Carrington's words, "masks and attitudes slip away". Far from it: posing and star-spotting these days preoccupy the majority of *Chez Tao's* summer punters. The local contingent, however, remain as "unnaturally quiet" as ever.

Rencontres de Chants Polyphoniques mid-September. Corsica's principal festival of song is hosted by renowned Corsican singer Jean-Claude Acquaviva and his wonderful polyphonies group, A Filetta, who share the stage with top a cappella performers from around the world. Regular workshops run throughout the fortnight.

Festiventu late October ⊕ 04 95 65 06 67, ⊛ www.festival-du-vent.com. Calvi psychs itself up for winter with a feast of kite flying and micro-light aircraft displays on the beach, as well as other weird attractions loosely connected to the theme of wind. Perfect for children.

Around Calvi

Surveying Calvi and its mountainous hinterland from a picturesque hilltop south of the town, the **Chapelle de Notre-Dame-de-la-Serra** is a popular picnic spot, and an obvious target if you fancy a short hike inland. To reach it by car, follow the Ajaccio road for 3km, then take the signposted left turn up the hill. An alternative route is the steep and rather slippery path that starts above *La Villa* hotel (see p.122): following the signposts off the main Calvi to L'Île Rousse road, drive or hike to the end of the lane running past the hotel, and follow the well-worn track that peels off left through the maquis for about twenty minutes until you see the chapel above you, set amid bulbous clusters of pale-pink granite.

Built in the 1860s over the site of a fifteenth-century sanctuary, the building boasts a fine parchment painting of the Immaculate Conception, but it's essentially the view that draws visitors – the great bastions of Calvi presiding over the perfect curve of the bay.

Boat excursions from Calvi

Catamarans, run by Colombo Line ⊕ 04 95 65 32 10, leave Calvi marina every day during the tourist season for Girolata, on the west coast, calling at **La Scandola** nature reserve and the **Calanches** rock formations of Piana en route (see pp.170 and 171). Much of this beautiful coast is off limits to visitors and can be seen close up only from the sea, which justifies the somewhat hefty ticket price. Full-day excursions, leaving at 9.15am and returning at 4pm, cost €46 (children aged 4–10 half price, babies free); the 2pm trip (return at 5.30pm) will set you back €38 (€19 for kids). Along the way, the boat chugs into gulleys, or *failles*, in the stark red cliffs, and you can occasionally glimpse marine life through the glass floor of the boat. It's a good idea to book the day before, and be prepared for last-minute cancellations if the weather looks unstable.

Listings

Airlines Air France or Air Inter Europe ⊕ 0820/820820; Air Littoral ⊕ 0803/834834; Compagnie Corse Mediterranée (CCM) ⊕ 08 36 67 95 20 or 04 95 65 88 60.
Airport enquiries ⊕ 04 95 65 88 88.
Ambulance ⊕ 04 95 65 11 91.
Banks and exchange All main banks and ATMs are on bd Wilson. The bureau de change on place de la Porteuse d'Eau, at the bottom of bd Wilson (June–Sept daily 9am–noon & 3–7pm), is one of several such places that change money outside normal banking hours (for a hefty commission fee).
Bicycle and motorbike rental Location Ambrosini, rue Villa-Antoine, on the left just west of place

Christophe-Colomb ⊕ 04 95 65 02 13. Well-maintained motorcycles (500–125cc; around €40 per day) and mountain bikes (€15 per day). Take along your credit card, which they'll need for the deposit.
Bookshops Halle de la Presse, at the top of bd Wilson on the left as you're heading towards the citadel, stocks a good selection of English titles.
Bus information Autocars les Beaux Voyages, Résidence Le Vieux Chalet, place de la Porteuse d'Eau ⊕ 04 95 65 11 35 or 04 95 65 15 02. Departure times can be checked at the tourist office (see p.118). Autocars SAIB ⊕ 04 95 22 41 99 or 04 95 21 02 07; no office in Calvi, buy your tickets on the bus.

Car rental Avis, Port de Plaisance ☏ 04 95 65 06 74; Budget, at the airport ☏ 04 95 65 88 34; Citer, l'Orée des Pins ☏ 04 95 65 29 99 or at the airport ☏ 04 95 65 16 06; Hertz, 2 av Maréchal-Joffre ☏ 04 95 65 06 64 or at the airport ☏ 04 95 65 02 96; Rent-a-Car ☏ 04 95 60 08 07.

Diving Calvi is one of Corsica's diving hot spots, with a wrecked American B-17 bomber from World War II at the mouth of the harbour (only 30m down), and more challenging underwater corridors full of marine life around the Punta della Revellata. The town's five diving centres are: Calvi Plongée Citadelle, in the marina ☏ 04 95 65 33 67; Club de Plongée Castille, marina ☏ 04 95 65 14 05; Hippocampe, at the foot of the citadel next to the fishing outfitters ☏ 04 95 65 46 66; École de Plongée Internationale de Calvi, next to the marina car park ☏ 04 95 65 42 22; JMB Diving, route de Donateo #42, Lot les Collines 9 ☏ 04 95 65 87 59.

Doctors Dr Michel Fade and Dr Brigitte Malter-Fade, 6 rue Joffre ☏ 04 95 65 03 20.

Laundry The cheapest self-service laundry is in the car park of Super U supermarket, av Christophe-Colomb (daily 8am–9pm); the one on bd Wilson has newer machines but charges top whack.

Left luggage The *consigne* at the train station (€3.50 per article per day; 6am–7pm) was closed for security reasons when we last checked.

Pharmacy Pharmacie Centrale, next to the *Rex Café*, bd Wilson, opens on Sunday during the tourist season.

Police Av de la République ☏ 04 95 65 33 30.

Post office At the lower end of bd Wilson.

Taxis At the airport and place de la Porteuse d'Eau ☏ 04 95 65 03 10 or 04 95 65 30 36.

Train information Gare de Calvi ☏ 04 95 65 00 61.

Moving on from Calvi

Calvi is a busy air and ferry port during the summer, as well as a year-round terminus for the *micheline* train, and is thus fairly well connected to mainland France and the rest of Corsica. Daily buses run along the recently revamped N1197/193 road link to Bastia via Ponte Leccia; transport services down the west coast from Calvi to Porto and beyond are less dependable. However you travel, check departure times and points in advance with the tourist office, or directly with the operator by telephone, as these tend to alter slightly from year to year. Bear in mind that timetables change during the off-peak period (late Sept–early June).

By plane

Daily flights to Paris and Nice with Air France, Air Littoral and Compagnie Corse Mediterranée (CCM) leave from Calvi's Ste-Catherine **airport**. Weekly charter flights from the UK (Gatwick and Stansted) also leave from here during the summer, and you can sometimes pick up one-way tickets on these through local agents, or by telephoning one of the charter operators in England, listed on p.14, who might offer you a fare for one of their unsold seats.

By ferry

Superfast Corsica Ferries and SNCM ferries to and from Nice run five times per week in each direction from July until mid-September, three or four times per week in April and May, three times a week in June, and twice each week or less from mid-September through the winter. The journey on the new NGV boats takes a mere 2hr 45min and costs €40–110 per vehicle, plus €15–25 per person depending on the time of year. To make a reservation (essential in peak season), go to SNCM's office in the port opposite the excursion boat stalls, or Corsica Ferries' agent, Les Beaux Voyages, in place de la Porteuse d'Eau ☏04 95 65 11 35 or 04 95 65 15 02.

By train

Two **trains** leave Calvi for Bastia daily (€15) – one early in the morning and the other in the afternoon – taking around three hours to wind along the

Balagne coast via L'Île Rousse. You catch the same trains to get to Ajaccio (€27), but have to change at Ponte Leccia onto one of the services running south from Bastia through Corte and Vizzavona – a spectacular journey that takes around four hours. In addition, smaller tramway trains shuttle up and down the coast six to eight times daily to L'Île Rousse, providing an unbeatable way to beach hop. A zone system of fares applies: if you're likely to use the service regularly, buy a carnet of ten tickets for around €8. Timetables (*horaires*) are available at the tourist office and the SNCF train station in Calvi.

By bus

Buses from Calvi run throughout the year to Bastia with Les Beaux Voyages (see "Listings" above) stopping at Lumio, Algajola and L'Île Rousse, and there's a quicker *navette* service to L'Île Rousse only from mid-May through to October. Beaux Voyages, buses also run to Calenzana, trailhead for the GR20 and Tra Mare e Monti hikes, and to Galéria. Ajaccio is more difficult to get to – you can either take a bus from the car park of Super U to Porto and then another bus from there the following day to the capital (both legs operated by Autocars SAIB, see "Listings" above), or take Beaux Voyages' Bastia service as far as Ponte Leccia, from where a connecting bus runs the rest of the way.

For a complete rundown of destinations reachable by bus from Calvi, see "Travel details" on p.156. Tickets for all services are available on the bus from the driver.

The Haute-Balagne coast

The **Haute-Balagne coast** may have been developed in recent decades, with purpose-built holiday villages and private marinas, but there are many unspoilt places to spend a pleasant few days in this corner of the northwest. East of Calvi, the N197 cuts inland through **Lumio**, a terraced village overlooking the gulf that boasts both an exceptional Romanesque church and the fascinating Centre d'Ethnographie et de Recherche Métallurgique, where you can watch steel being smelted and forged by traditional Corsican methods. One of the most pleasant places to stay in the area is **Algajola**, a few kilometres further along the coast road, a compact, relaxed resort with a golden half-moon beach. Beyond here, the distinctive red-tinged headland of La Pietra shelters the rather overrated and overrun town of **L'Île Rousse**, and a couple of outstanding beaches.

At regular intervals along the coast road, you can turn inland to visit the beautiful Haute-Balagne hill villages, the pick of which are covered in the section beginning on p.138.

Lumio

Lining a sun-drenched hillside above the Golfe de Calvi, **LUMIO** was in ancient times the centre of a sun-worshipping cult, and was known to the Romans as *Ortis Culis* or "Where the Sun Rises". The proximity of the busy Route Nationale, however, combined with the absence of a decent hotel, makes this a less than promising place to stay, though the views over the gulf are wonderful (particularly at sunset) and there are a couple of sights worth pulling over for.

One kilometre south of the village, on the N197, you'll pass the pale granite **Chapelle San Pietro** standing amidst a monumental cemetery. Founded in

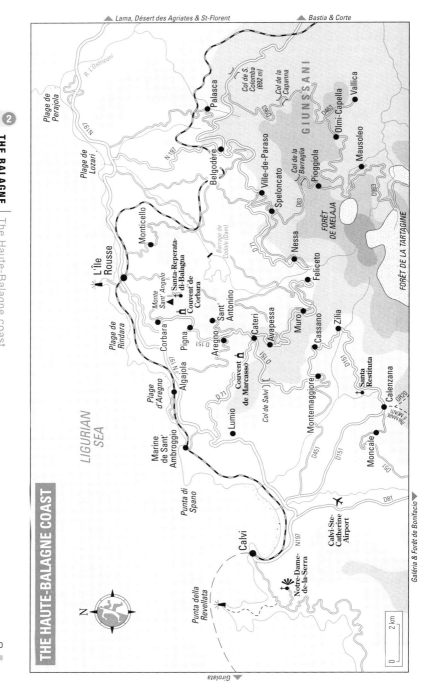

THE HAUTE-BALAGNE COAST

Lama, Désert des Agriates & St-Florent

Bastia & Corte

LIGURIAN
SEA

R. L'Ostriconi

Plage de Perajola

N197

Plage de Lozari

N197

Palasca

Col de S. Colomba (692 m)

D963

Col de la Capanna

D963

Vallica

Olmi-Capella

D463

Mausoleo

GIUNSSANI

Belgodère

Ville-de-Paraso

Col de la Barraglia

Spelontato

Pioggiola

D63

D963

FORÊT DE MELAJA

Barrage de Codole (Dam)

Nessa

D71

Feliceto

FORÊT DE LA TARTAGINE

Monticello

L'Île Rousse

Plage de Rindara

Corbara

Santa-Reperata-di-Balagna

Monte Sant'Angelo

Couvent de Corbara

Pigna

Aregno

Sant'Antonino

Cateri

Avapessa

Muro

Cassano

Zilia

D151

Plage d'Aregno

Algajola

Couvent de Marcasso

D151

Lumio

D71

Col de Salvi

Montemaggiore

Santa Restituta

Calenzana

GR20

TRA MARE E MONTI

D151

Marine de Sant' Ambroggio

Punta di Spano

D451

D151

Moncale

D51

Calvi-Ste-Catherine Airport

D81

Galéria & Forêt de Bonifacio

Calvi

N197

Notre-Dame-de-la-Serra

Punta della Revellata

Girolata

N

0   2 km

the eleventh century and rebuilt in the eighteenth, it retains some of its original Romanesque features, notably the palm-shaped capitals and geometric windows at the eastern end of the apse. The most outstanding feature, however, is the pair of grinning **lions** jutting from the façade above the door; it's thought they were originally intended to support a porch.

Just before you enter Lumio from Calvi on the Route Nationale you'll see a small sign marked "C Moretti, Couteaux d'art", which leads through the outskirts of the village to the **Centre d'Éthnographie et de Recherche Métallurgique** (Mon–Sat 2.30–6.30pm; ℡04 95 60 71 94; free). A team of young craftsmen, led by founder **Christian Moretti**, mine ore by hand in the mountains of Cap Corse and refine it through an extraordinarily involved process, replicating the methods used in Corsica from the late Iron Age to the end of the last century. A video illustrates the various stages, and you can watch the smiths in the forge. A selection of their work is on sale, from pocket-size pieces (€140) to long blades worked into olive-wood or bone handles (upwards of €1000) – not as expensive as they sound when you consider it takes the team a total of two and a half weeks to make a single small blade.

Algajola

Roughly midway between Calvi and L'Île Rousse, **ALGAJOLA** is Balagne's third largest resort, but a considerably quieter and less pretentious place than either of its more famous neighbours. Although the village gets as swamped as anywhere else along this coast during July and August, out of season you can expect to have the beach, Aregno–Plage, a kilometre-long curve of coarse sand beneath a picturesque Genoese citadel, pretty much to yourself.

Because of its exposed situation, Algajola has suffered the frequent attentions of hostile forces: in 1643, the Turks devastated its Genoese citadel, and in the 1790s Nelson assailed the town as a preliminary to the great Calvi siege. Despite such setbacks, the village did a steady trade in oysters and olive oil, and continued to be a major port on this part of the coast until L'Île Rousse developed towards the close of the eighteenth century. Its status was temporarily revived early in the twentieth century, when hotels were built over the old port, transforming it into a small but smart resort. However, decline set in after World War II, fuelled by the growing popularity of Calvi and L'Île Rousse.

Algajola consists of just one street, which begins alongside the beach, **Aregno–Plage**, and leads up to the **Citadelle**. Beyond the gates, the dominant building is the **Castello**, raised on its small promontory in the thirteenth century then heavily restored in the seventeenth, when the fortifications were added after the Turkish attack. For a hundred years, the fort served as the Genoese lieutenant governor's residence, and it is still an administrative building, so closed to the public. However, you can walk around the ramparts behind the castle, from where a path leads back down to the beach.

Algajola lies on the main bus and train routes between Bastia and Calvi, and is thus well connected by **public transport**, with regular services in both directions throughout the year.

Accommodation

Virtually every **hotel** in Algajola overlooks the sea. Although none can claim to be anything special, their rates are competitive, especially between Easter and June and from mid-September through October. **Campers** can stay at *Camping de la Plage*, at the north end of the beach (℡04 95 60 71 76 or 04 95 60 72 12), or the more attractive *Camping Panoramic*, 4km west on the N197 (℡04 95 60 73 13), which has wonderful sea views.

Le Beau Rivage Top of the beach ☎ 04 95 60 73 99, ⓕ 04 95 60 79 51. The same view as *L'Ondine*, but at more reasonable prices. Light, airy and modern rooms with tiled floors; those on the second storey have more spacious balconies. Cheaper options in the hotel's annexe. Obligatory half board peak season. ❸

L'Esquinade Next door to the post office by the citadel gates ☎/F 04 95 60 70 19. The best budget choice: clean en-suite rooms (ask for one on the *côté jardin*), with tariffs dropping to €43 off season. No restaurant, but the downstairs bar's cheery enough. ❹

L'Ondine 7 rue a Marina ☎ 04 95 60 70 02, ⓕ 04 95 60 60 36, ⓦ www.londine.com. A luxurious place boasting a garden, swimming pool and a panoramic view of the bay. Pricy half board (€77 per head) obligatory July & Aug. ❺

De la Plage Top of the beach ☎ 04 95 60 72 12, ⓕ 04 95 60 64 89. An old-fashioned place, caught in a 1950s time warp. Very good value given the size of the rooms and the views, but often booked (by groups of pensioners) in May, June and September. Peak season half board (€50/person) is obligatory. ❹

Saint-Joseph At the entrance to the village if you're coming from Calvi ☎ 04 95 60 73 90, ⓕ 04 95 60 28 74. Good-value, modern, chalet-style rooms, close to the sea and castle, with turquoise shutters opening onto a breezy courtyard-terrace with sun loungers. Rates drop to €50 per double in June/Sept. ❺

Stella Mare Above the train station ☎ 04 95 60 71 18, ⓕ 04 95 50 69 39. Smart little two-star in its own garden on the hillside above the village. Lovely sea views and large rooms (with terraces), though a notch more expensive than the competition. ❺

Eating

U Castellu In the little square behind the castle. Local standards (such as red mullet with fennel) served in a stone-vaulted room or on a cactus-lined terrace next to the citadel. Good-value *menu corse* for €17 (rounded off with a melt-in-the-mouth tiramisu *maison*), and a handful of *suggestions du jour* that often include "fish and chips" (sic).

La Vieille Cave Just inside the arched entrance to the square, on the left ☎ 04 95 60 70 09. A range of different menus, most under €20 and with more imaginative dishes than usual (spinach and fromage frais soup, scorpion fish *aux herbes du maquis* and onions stuffed with *brocciu* and charcuterie). They also do a great seafood selection à la carte, and the location's very pleasant, especially in the evenings.

L'Île Rousse

Developed by Pascal Paoli in the 1760s as a "gallows to hang Calvi", the port of **L'ÎLE ROUSSE** (Isula Rossa) simply doesn't convince as a Corsican town, its palm trees, neat flower gardens and colossal pink 1930s hotel creating an atmosphere that has more in common with the French Riviera. Yet, for all its artificiality, the place has become unbearably popular in recent years, receiving more ferries and packing in more tourists than the larger port of Calvi. The proximity of three large white-sand beaches is the main reason for the resort's popularity, together with its ultra-mild microclimate; thanks to the amphitheatre of hills that shelter the town from the cool winds blowing off the Haute Balagne's mountains, temperatures here average two degrees higher than Bonifacio and Porto-Vecchio, making this the hottest place in Corsica.

Pascal Paoli had great plans for his new town, which was laid out from scratch in 1758. He needed a port for the export of olive oil produced in the Balagne region, since Calvi was still in the hands of the Genoese, whose naval blockade was stifling the economy of the fledgling government. Originally the place was to be called Paolina, but the *Rubica Rocega* (Red Rocks) label had stuck from Roman times and L'Île Rousse it became. A large part of the new port was built on a regular grid system, featuring lines of straight parallel streets quite at odds with the higgledy-piggledy nature of most Corsican villages and towns. Thanks to the busy trading of wine and oil, it soon began to prosper and, two and a half centuries later, still thrives as a successful port. These days, however, the main traffic consists of holi-

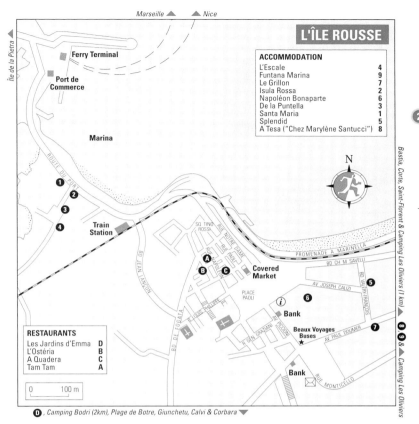

Marseille ▲ ▲ Nice

L'ÎLE ROUSSE

Ferry Terminal

Port de Commerce

Marina

Île de la Pietra

ACCOMMODATION

L'Escale	4
Funtana Marina	9
Le Grillon	7
Isula Rossa	2
Napoléon Bonaparte	6
De la Puntella	3
Santa Maria	1
Splendid	5
A Tesa ("Chez Marylène Santucci")	8

THE BALAGNE | The Haute-Balagne coast

Bastia, Corte, Saint-Florent & Camping Les Oliviers (1 km) ▶ ❽ ❾ & ▶ Camping Les Oliviers

Train Station

ROUTE DU PORT

BD JEAN LANÇON

BD DE FOGATA

RUE NOTRE DAME

SQ. TINO ROSSI

RUE PAOLI

PROMENADE A MARINELLA

BD CH M SAVELLI

AV JOSEPH CALIZI

BD VAL FRANÇOIS

❺

Covered Market

PLACE PAOLI

AV PICCIONI

RUE GÉN GRAZIANI

RUE LOUIS PHILIPPE

(i) ❻

Bank

Beaux Voyages Buses ★

AV PAUL DOUMER

❼

Bank

RUE MONTICELLO

N

RESTAURANTS

Les Jardins d'Emma	D
L'Ostéria	B
A Quadera	C
Tam Tam	A

0 100 m

❶ ❷ ❸ ❹ Ⓐ Ⓑ Ⓒ

Ⓓ , Camping Bodri (2km), Plage de Botre, Giunchetu, Calvi & Corbara ▼

---

daymakers. That the only town intended to be a Corsican success story makes its living from tourism as a classic French-style resort adds an ironic twist to Paoli's dream.

L'Île Rousse is connected by year-round **bus** services to Bastia and Calvi, with Autocars Les Beaux Voyages. The *micheline* **train** also stops here en route between Calvi and Ponte Leccia, where you can pick up connecting services to Ajaccio, via Corte and Vizzavona; and there are more or less hourly tramway services along the Balagne coast in the summer, starting at around 8pm and running until 6.30pm (frequent users of this service can save money by buying carnets of ten tickets for €8).

Arrival and information

The **train station** is on route du Port (☎04 95 60 00 50), 500m south of where the ferries arrive. Beaux Voyages' Bastia–Calvi **bus** stops in the town's main thoroughfare, **avenue Piccioni**, just south of place Paoli. The **tourist office**, on the south side of place Paoli (April–June & Sept–Oct Mon–Fri 9am–noon & 2–5pm; July & Aug daily 9am–1pm & 2.30–7.30pm; ☎04 95 60 04 35, ⓦwww.ot-ile-rousse.fr), hands out ferry and bus timetables. The **post office** is situated a five-minute walk to the east, in rue Monticello.

133

Ferries

Ferries between L'Île Rousse and mainland France depart from the Port de Commerce, 1km north of the centre. Between mid-June and the end of September, there are four to six daily crossings to Nice on the superfast NGV (2hr 45min), with additional departures on slower boats to Nice and Marseille (the overnight ferries taking up to 11hr 30min to reach the mainland). **Tickets**, which should be booked as far in advance as possible if you're travelling with a vehicle, can be bought from the SNCM agent, CCR (aka Tramar), on av Joseph Calizi (ⓣ04 95 60 09 56), or from the gare maritime (ⓣ04 95 60 11 30). For **fares**, see Basics, p.20.

Accommodation

Such a long season (May–Oct) means that L'Île Rousse fills up early in the year and it can be difficult to find a **hotel**, so be prepared to hunt around. Most places double or triple their prices in July and August (the period to which the tariffs quoted below apply), when half board is more often than not obligatory. For **camping**, you've a choice between two good sites close to town.

Hotels

L'Escale route du Port ⓣ04 95 60 27 08, ⓕ04 95 60 14 33. Two-star motel out near the port, with light air-con rooms, all en suite and with balconies. Plenty of parking. €60 off season. ⑦

Funtana Marina route de Monticello ⓣ04 95 60 16 12, ⓕ04 95 60 35 44. A modern hotel, 1km south of L'Île Rousse, with a pool and better than average views of the town and bay from its rooms. Reasonable rates out of season, but very expensive in July & August. March–Dec. ⑤

Le Grillon 10 av Paul-Doumer ⓣ04 95 60 00 49, ⓕ04 95 60 43 69. The best budget hotel in town, just 1km from the centre on the St-Florent/Bastia road. Nothing special, but quiet and immaculately clean. Half board in August (€47 per person), but at other times rates fall to €35 per double. April–Oct. ④

Isula Rossa route du Port ⓣ04 95 60 01 32, ⓕ04 95 60 57 32. Smallish rooms with en-suite bathrooms but no balconies, in a modern block on the seafront. Garden-side rooms are the least expensive; but no. 112 catches the sea breezes. From €55 in June/Sept. ⑤

Napoléon Bonaparte 3 place Paoli ⓣ04 95 60 06 09, ⓕ04 95 60 11 51. Converted *palazzo*, built in the eighteenth century, renovated in the 1930s, occupied by the king of Morocco during his exile in the 1950s, and garishly refurbished (in ice-cream pink) a decade ago. Now falling apart at the seams and undeserving of its three stars and high-season tariffs. That said, some rooms in the original (cheaper) wing have a certain faded charm; ask for no. 225, whose room-service bell has a button for the wine-cellar man. There's also a huge pool. April–Sept. ⑨

De la Puntella route du Port ⓣ04 95 60 04 34, ⓕ04 95 60 40 87. Offering smart little "studios" (rooms with four beds, kitchenette and bathroom), which are usually booked on a weekly basis during August; particularly good value for families. There's ample parking, and a 10am checkout. ③

Santa Maria route du Port ⓣ04 95 63 05 05, ⓕ04 95 60 32 48, ⓦwww.santamaria.com. Next to the ferry port, this is one of the larger and best-value three-star places. Their recently refurbished, air-con rooms have small balconies or patios opening onto a garden and pool, and there's exclusive access to a tiny pebble beach. Rates down to around €75 in June/Sept. Open all year. ⑦

Splendid 4 bd Valéry-François ⓣ04 95 60 00 24, ⓕ04 95 60 04 57. Well-maintained, 1930s-style building with a small swimming pool and some sea views from upper floors; very reasonable tariffs, given the location. From €50 in June/Sept. Open April–Oct. ⑥

A Tesa ("Chez Marylène Santucci") Lozari par Belgodère, 10km east of L'Île Rousse ⓣ04 95 60 09 55, ⓕ04 95 60 44 34. The principal attraction of this small auberge, a modern building lost in the countryside near the Barrage de Codole, is the fine Corsican cooking (see "Eating and drinking", p.136), but Mme Santucci has seven comfortable, neatly decorated en-suite rooms, at €46, and offers half board (€95 for two people). Follow the N197 towards Bastia for 7km and turn off onto the unnumbered lane running southwest from Lozari; the auberge is 2.5km further on your right. ③

Campsites

Camping Bodri 2km west on the Calvi road ⓣ04 95 60 10 86, ⓕ04 95 60 39 02. Separated from the beach by the train line, and well equipped with a laundry and a small pizzeria. It's also marginally less cramped in peak season than others in the area. You can get here direct by train (ask the conductor for "*l'arrêt Bodrî*"). June–Sept.

Les Oliviers 1km east of town ℡ 04 95 60 19 92, ℻ 04 95 60 30 91. Situated on a low hill overlooking the beach, but some pitches are a little too close to the Nationale for comfort. April–Sept.

The Town

All roads in L'Île Rousse lead to **place Paoli**, a shady square that's open to the sea and has as its focal point a fountain surmounted by a bust, *U Babbu di u Patria* (Grandfather of the Nation), one of many local tributes to Pascal Paoli. There's a pricy covered market at the entrance to the square, while on the west side rises the recently restored façade of the Église de l'Immaculée Conception. Between the two, a row of quintessentially French terrace cafés do a steady trade under rows of old plane trees. It was here at breakfast time on August 7, 2000, that the prominent nationalist politician, Jean-Michel Rossi, was murdered by five gunmen. With former Cuncolta leader François Santoni, he'd published a book blowing the whistle on corruption among Corsican paramilitaries and this was widely interpreted as the mob's response. Santoni was also gunned down the following year (for more background on these events, see "The Corsican Troubles", p.420).

From place Paoli, the three parallel streets of the **old town** run north to square Tino Rossi, where the Hôtel de Ville, formerly a military headquarters, displays the Corsican flag. Opposite stands a **tower** dating from before Paoli's time, but a plaque commemorating the Corsican hero has recently been placed on the wall.

To reach the **Île de la Pietra**, the islet that gives the town its name, continue north, passing the station on your left. Once over the causeway connecting the islet to the mainland, you can walk through the crumbling mass of red granite as far as the lighthouse at the far end. From here, the **view** of the town is spectacular, especially at sunset, when you get the full effect of the red glow of the rocks.

The beaches

Immediately in front of the promenade, the town beach is a crowded, Côte d'Azur-style strand, blocked by ranks of sun loungers and parasols belonging to the row of lookalike café-restaurants behind it. With your own transport, you're better off heading 3km west up the N197, where a signpost pointing right off the main road (next to the turning for *Camping Bodrî*) leads 300m downhill to a fee-charging municipal car park (€5 for the day; no shade) from where you can walk to two of the most beautiful beaches on the north coast. To your right as you face the sea, **Plage de Botre** is the more sheltered, backed by soft white dunes in which is nestled a smart but overpriced *paillote* dishing up crêpes and unadventurous salads. The sand is clean and the water crystal clear, but from late June onwards this normally isolated cove is swamped by campers from the nearby *Camping Bodri* (see p.134). A short walk further west around the rocky Punta di Ginebre, **Baie de Giunchetu** is a larger, though less picturesque, beach. Note that you can reach both of these by train: just behind Plage de Botre is a little request stop at which you can ask to be dropped by any of the services running between L'Île Rousse and Calvi.

Eating and drinking

Tourism has taken its toll here, hence the abundance of mediocre eating places. However, a few **restaurants** stand out, most of them in the narrow lanes of the old town. With your own transport, you might also consider heading inland to eat in one of the hill villages (see pp.138–148). The best **cafés** are those lining the south side of place Paoli, under a canopy of shady plane trees.

Le Grillon 10 av Paul-Doumer ℡ 04 95 60 00 49. High-ceilinged, blissfully cool air-conditioned hotel dining hall with a limited, but consistently good menu of mainly French dishes. Their *steak au roquefort* and cod in spicy Créole sauce are perennially popular, while for vegetarians there's a delicious courgette-and-basil pâté, rounded off with homemade honey-and-almond ice cream. Count on €20–27 per head.

Les Jardins d'Emma col de Fogata, 2km along the Calvi road just past Super U, on the left ℡ 04 95 60 49 07. This is the place to head if you fancy a more sophisticated meal but don't want to drive out to *A Tesa*. The cuisine is "*gastro-corse*" on a single four-course €30 menu that changes daily. House specialities include spider crab soup and sea bass stuffed with *brocciu*; and they do stupendous desserts.

L'Ostéria place Santelli. Tucked away on a quiet backstreet in the old quarter, this established Corsican speciality restaurant offers an excellent set menu (€16), featuring delicious courgette fritters, *soupe de nos villages*, tarragon-scented *gratin d'aubergines*, stuffed sardines and fresh pan-fried prawns. You can sit in a vaulted room adorned with farm implements or on the shaded terrace.

A Quadera 6 rue Napoléon ℡ 04 95 60 44 52. Sunny Mediterranean salads, quality charcuterie and imaginative seafood dishes such as king prawns flambéed in eau de vie, stylishly served inside an eighteenth-century town house with exposed stone walls. Their €15.50 menu offers great value for money.

Tam Tam rue Napoléon. Créole, Vietnamese and Antillaise dishes, based mainly on fresh local seafood, though with some lamb and chicken options. Try their deliciously spicy prawns or mussels in sweet and sour sauce (both available on the €15 *menu fixe*).

A Tesa ("Chez Marylène Santucci") Lozari par Belgodère ℡ 04 95 60 09 55. Wonderful *ferme-auberge* inland from L'Île Rousse that's among the most reputed Corsican speciality places on the island. All the ingredients are fresh from the garden or locally produced, and the portions copious. Their fixed menu (€35–46 per head depending on the dishes) includes an aperitif, five courses, wine, eau de vie and coffee. Advance reservation is essential. (You can also stay here: see "Hotels", p.134.)

Listings

Banks Several large banks are scattered around place Paoli, but the Société Générale, which charges no commission for changing Thomas Cook euro traveller's cheques, is on av Piccioni.

Bicycle rental Mountain bikes (VTT) are available for rent (€15 per day) at La Passion en Action, av Paul-Doumer ℡ 04 95 60 15 76.

Bus information Autocars Les Beaux Voyages (℡ 04 95 65 15 02 or 04 95 65 11 35) operates a year-round service connecting Calvi and L'Île Rousse with Bastia and Ajaccio, via Ponte Leccia (Mon–Sat 1 daily). Buses depart from in front of the *Bar Sémiramis*, on the junction of av Paul-Doumer and av Picconi, at 7.10am, or at 6pm heading in the opposite direction to Calvi. In winter, the timetable changes slightly, so check with the company or at the tourist office (see p.133) before you leave.

Car rental Europcar, place Paoli ℡ 04 95 60 30 11; Filippi Auto, route de Calvi ℡ 04 95 60 12 63; Hertz, place Marcel-Delanney ℡ 04 95 60 12 63.

Diving One of Corsica's best-known dive sites, a colossal rock draped in colourful corals, lies in the bay. Known as Le Naso, it's a prime spot for moray and conger eels. The town has two dive schools: recommended for advanced divers is Beluga, at the *La Pietra* hotel near the ferry dock (℡ 04 95 60 17 36); and the École de Plongée de L'Île Rousse, in a Portakabin near the ferry building (℡ 04 95 60 36 85), which caters particularly well for beginners and children.

Doctors Dr Guidicelli, rue Général Graziani ℡ 04 95 60 10 50; Dr Simeoni, Résidence Napoléon, av Joseph Calizi ℡ 04 95 60 26 00.

Horse riding Arbo Valley, 5km east (signposted off the main Bastia road, N197; ℡ 04 95 60 49 49 or 06 12 06 34 38), is an accredited riding centre offering short hacks and longer expeditions.

Laundry Rue Napoléon, one block down from *L'Osteria* restaurant (7am–10pm).

Left luggage The *consigne* at the ferry terminal has been closed for the past couple of years for security reasons.

Pharmacy On the corner of av Piccioni and rue Monticello.

Post office Rue Monticello, on the south side of town (Mon–Fri 8.30am–5pm, Sat 8.30am–noon; ℡ 04 95 63 05 50).

Taxis ℡ 04 95 60 04 35.

Train information Gare SNCF, route du Port ℡ 04 95 60 00 50. L'Île Rousse is on the main *micheline* line, and connected by two daily services to Calvi (30min) and Bastia (2hr 10min), via Ponte Leccia, where you can pick up *correspondances* to Ajaccio (3hr 30min). In summer, the tramway train also shuttles eight times daily to and from Calvi.

East of L'Île Rousse

Two excellent **beaches** indent the wild coastline **northeast of L'Île Rousse**. The first, the **Plage de Lozari**, is a long, semicircular sweep of coarse white sand, 7km out of town along the N197. A surfaced road signposted "Lozari" leads down to the shore and a discreet holiday village that brings crowds in summer.

Even more spectacular is the much-photographed **Plage de Perajola**, at the mouth of the Ostriconi River, where the rocky hills of the Désert des Agriates ripple north against a backdrop of turquoise sea, forcing the Route Nationale east up the depopulated Ostriconi Valley. To reach it, you have to turn north off the N1197, 10km east of L'Île Rousse, and join the disused corniche road; head past the campsite and *village de vacances* (see below) and continue for around 500m until you see a couple of lay-bys on the right of the road where you can leave your car. From here, a steep path cuts down through the maquis to the southwest side of the beach. Tourists from the holiday village spill over it in summer, but out of season this is a remote and windswept spot. The wilderness immediately to the north offers plenty of potential for **hiking**, although you'll definitely need an IGN map of the area (#4249 OT, ref C3/D3), as the waymarked **Désert des Agriates coast path** (see p.108) does not actually follow the coast; instead, it cuts inland at the first inlet you come to after Perajola (a narrow cove called the **Anse de Vana**, where there's a tiny beach), and follows the north side of a scrubby stream valley towards the Baie de l'Acciolu. This forms the concluding part of a superb three- to four-hour round route particularly favoured by equestrian centres in the area (see p.50), who lead horse treks into the heart of the desert from here.

Practicalities

The whole stretch described above is covered by Les Beaux Voyages' daily Calvi–Bastia–Calvi **buses**; ask for a ticket to Lozari or the *Village de l'Ostriconi*.

Inexpensive **accommodation** is available at the *Village de l'Ostriconi* itself, 1km inland from Perajola beach (T 04 95 60 10 05, F 04 95 60 01 47; ●), where simple bungalows cost €44–65 peak season, dropping to €26–50 in April, May and October (the pricier ones have bathrooms and kitchenettes). The same owners also have a large, well-shaded campsite (same phone; Easter–Oct), within walking distance of the beach: bring plenty of mosquito repellent, as the site borders a brackish lagoon, and be prepared towards the start of the season to wade through waist-deep water to reach the Perajola beach.

Lama

It's hard to picture the Ostriconi Valley, sweeping southwest from the edge of the Désert des Agriates into the mountains of the interior, as it must have looked three or more hundred years ago. Denuded by drought, overgrazing and repeated bush fires, its slopes now encompass some of the poorest agricultural land on the island. Yet in the seventeenth and eighteenth centuries the valley formed the centre of a booming trade in fine-quality olive oil, whence the profusion of Italianate *palazzi* at **LAMA,** an unexpectedly pretty village clinging to a granite spur high above the main road. Dozens of splendid *grandes maisons bourgeoises* still stand here, among them the Florentine **Casa Bertola**, with its distinctive arcaded belvedere, which belonged to the Corsican poet, Paul Bertola, in the last century.

Others have been renovated for use as holiday homes: the **tourist office** at the entrance to the village, which goes by the rather long-winded title of the Maison du pays d'accueil touristique de l'Ostriconi (Mon–Fri 9am–noon & 2–5pm, also 2–5pm Sat & Sun in July & Aug; ℡04 95 48 23 90) keeps a list of fifty or more **gîtes** for rent, many of them modern villas with sunny terraces, pools and dramatic views down the valley towards the sea. You can also stay at the *Auberge de Lama* (℡04 95 48 22 99, ℻04 95 48 23 77; ●), next door to the tourist office, a gourmet restaurant with a handful of rooms. The **food** here is resolutely "*gastro-corse*": *figatelli* (liver sausage) simmered in orange wine, entrecôte with myrtle liqueur sauce or pasta *maison* rolled in squid ink and *fruits de mer*. Menus start at €27. The other noteworthy restaurant is *Campu Latinu* (℡04 95 48 23 83), further up the hillside: turn right before the church and follow the road until you see a sign on your right. On lovely interconnecting stone terraces, shaded by olive trees with views over the village, you can enjoy a sumptuous *menu corse* (€25), featuring local dishes such as lasagne with *brocciu* and mint. Among their entrées are also a good choice of tempting vegetarian dishes, including delicate *beignets au fromage frais*, and tomato and mozzarella pâté.

Lama's cobbled, flower-filled lanes and arched passageways are ideal for a post-prandial stroll. Opposite the church, look out for the U Stallo (same hours as the tourist office), a photographic exhibition showing old images of the Ostriconi region. In summer, there's also a **swimming pool** (July & Aug noon–7pm, closed Thurs 3–7pm) on the far northern edge of Lama.

Inland Haute-Balagne

The fortress villages of **inland Haute-Balagne** are among the most picturesque on the island, their higgledy-piggledy terracotta rooftops and belfries presiding over an idyllic Mediterranean landscape of cypress-studded olive groves, backed by a dramatic wall of pale-grey mountains. Many of the settlements are nearly a thousand years old, having developed from the time of the Pisan occupation, when **Romanesque churches** such as the churches of San Trinita at **Aregno** and Santa Restituta at **Calenzana** were built. The rash of **Baroque churches** in the region emerged during the prosperous years under the Genoese, and some of them, such as the church at **Corbara**, warrant a visit for the sheer flamboyance of their decoration, even if Baroque isn't your thing.

A recent government redevelopment programme for the Balagne has meant the regeneration of certain traditional practices, including the production of olive oil using old presses. Young people are being encouraged to settle in the villages by the introduction of special grants for artisans willing to live and work here, and several places have their own musical and crafts societies – look out for posters advertising summer concerts in villages such as **Pigna** and **Belgodère**.

The only **buses** in the area run daily between Calvi and Calenzana (with Les Beaux Voyages – see p.156). The train stops near Belgodère, but to make the most of this beautiful area you need to have your own vehicle and be prepared to walk. Belgodère has some hotel accommodation, and there are more hotels at **Speloncato** and **Feliceto**.

Calenzana

Overshadowed by the great bulk of Monte Grosso and encircled by a belt of olive trees, the village of **CALENZANA** overlooks some of the most fertile

△ Speloncato

land on the island. Historically an economic rival to Calvi, it's still a thriving agricultural centre, renowned for its wine and honey, plus the village speciality, a little dry cake blessed with the tongue-twisting name of *cuggiuelli* (pronounced "koo-joo-*ell*-ee"), which you dunk in white wine. There's a less pacific side to Calenzana as well. In the eighteenth century it was known as a refuge for Paoli's freedom fighters, who weren't welcome in the Genoese stronghold of Calvi, and this century it gained a reputation for harbouring French gangsters; with Marseille a quick hop across the water, many prominent *milieu* members have retired here.

Lying close to the borders of the national park, Calenzana is renowned among hikers as the point of departure for the famous **GR20 hike**, whose ten-to fifteen-day haul through the island's mountain spine starts just above the village at the Oratoire St-Antoine. The chapel and its adjacent spring are also the trailhead for the shorter **Tra Mare e Monti** walk, which traverses a section of the national park as far as Cargèse. Accounts of both walks feature in Chapter 8, p.359.

The lively core of the village, the **Piazza Communa**, is a pleasant tree-lined square dominated by the heavily Baroque **Église St-Blaise**. Founded in 1691, the church boasts a sumptuous but dusty interior. Its centrepiece is a marble altar (1750), to the right of which stands a seventeenth-century tabernacle with a particularly ghoulish painted border.

The bell tower beside the church, built in the 1870s, stands on the "**Cimetière des Allemands**", the burial place of five hundred Austrian troops dispatched by their king, Charles VI, to help his allies the Genoese quell an uprising in January 1732. With no artillery to hand, the villagers are said to have hurled beehives, tiles and boiling oil from their windows, set flaming cattle loose in the alleyways, and then used makeshift weapons to pick off the Austrians as they fled through the old town. Only one hundred of the soldiers survived the massacre – a turnabout that played no small part in forcing the Genoese to capitulate at Corte the following May, three hundred years before the island's eventual independence.

Practicalities

Run by Les Beaux Voyages (☎04 95 65 15 02), **buses** between Calenzana and Calvi operate throughout the summer; off season, you can reach the village (in term time only) via the school bus – but this tends to run at inconvenient times (schedules available from the Calvi tourist office or by telephoning the above number). Most hikers walk or hitch the 12km of flat road from Calvi along the Bartasca river plain.

There are only two **hotels** in Calenzana, neither of them particularly appealing – unless you've just stepped off the GR. At the bottom of the village on the left as you arrive from Calvi, the *Monte Grosso* (☎04 95 62 70 15, ℻04 95 62 83 21; ❸), 48 rue du Font, is basic, with mostly shared toilets, and suffers from traffic noise in the summer. A sunnier and quieter option is the *Bel Horizon* (☎04 95 62 71 72; ❸), further up the hill opposite the church, which has comfortable rooms with views over the square or down across the village. Most long-distance walkers, however, check into the gîte d'étape *municipal* (☎04 95 62 77 13), just off the main road on the southern side of the village, which charges €9 per night for a place in its clean, new four-bed dorms, and around the same to camp in its garden under a grove of ancient olive trees. The rather impersonal complex has rudimentary self-catering facilities and bathrooms with power showers, but offers no meals. For breakfast you'll have to head back up the main street to the square where *Café Le Royal*, right opposite the church's bell tower, opens at 7am. The village boulangerie, which also opens early, stands 400m east of the square on the left past the pharmacy. To sample the famous *cuggiuelli* (see p.140), however, you'll have to hunt out the Corsican speciality pâtisserie, *E Fritelle*, up a narrow alley called U Chiasu on the left of the road as you leave Calenzana in the direction of Calvi.

Of the handful of **restaurants** in the village proper, only one is worthy of mention: *Le Calenzana "Chez Michel"* at 7 cours Blaise, opposite the church (☎04 95 62 70 25; open March–Dec), which assuages the monster appetites of its predominantly hiker clientele with groaning platefuls of delicious mountain cooking. Featured on set menus (€17–20), tender suckling lamb *aux herbes du maquis* with wheat-rolled potatoes is *the* house speciality, but they also serve a fine *terrine de figatellu*, pan-fried veal and beans, and a serious Corsican soup that comes complete with the bones. Vegetarians will have to make do with wood-baked pizzas.

With your own transport and a more flexible budget, this area's restaurant of choice, however, would have to be the *Ferme-auberge A Flatta* (☎04 95 62 80 38, ⓦwww.aflatta.com; ❼), tucked away 3km above Calenzana in a hidden side-valley at the foot of Monte Corona. To find it, bear right at the church and follow the signs until there's no more road. On an idyllic terrace beside a mountain stream, with the crags of the watershed only a stone's throw away, you can tuck into the tastiest local Corsican meat and fish dishes, grilled to perfection over a wood fire and accompanied by traditional sauces (veal in olive or foie gras, wild boar marinated in red wine, lamb sautéed in parsley and garlic, perch stuffed with *brocciu* and mint). For dessert, go for the dreamy honey parfait. The **rooms** upstairs are on a par with the cuisine, individually styled with luminous drapes and exposed beams. At around €100 for their standard doubles, rates are high in peak season, but drop to a more reasonable €70 in June and September. Advance booking (by phone or via their website) is essential.

Church of Santa Restituta

One of the most important places of pilgrimage in Corsica, the church of **Santa Restituta**, is set beside a shady grove of olive trees to the north of Calenzana, about 1500m along the D151. Dedicated to the martyred St Restitude, who in 303 AD, during the reign of Diocletian, was decapitated in Calvi for her Christian beliefs, the Romanesque church has been rebuilt many times but retains its attractive eleventh-century single nave. In the crypt you can see the fourth-century **sarcophagus** of the martyr. Discovered in 1951, it's a magnificent marble tomb, decorated with a figure of Christ and adorned at each end with strikingly human faces. During the thirteenth century, the sarcophagus was covered by a cenotaph decorated with **frescoes** depicting St Restitude and her fate against a tableau of Calvi, which are displayed nearby. The key to the church is kept by the owner of the *tabac*, just down from the village square, behind the church hall (*cazzasa*).

Calenzana to Cateri

The D151, which winds beyond Calenzana across a spur of the Monte Grosso massif to **Cateri**, strings together several of the region's prettiest villages, in particular **Cassano** and **Montemaggiore** with superb views of the mountains to the south. Northwest from Calenzana, a little over 1km past Santa Restituta, is an essential stop for wine buffs – the **Domaine d'Alzipratu** – where you can taste and buy some of the island's finest wines (daily 8am–noon & 2–7.30pm; ☎04 95 62 75 47). However, it is olive cultivation, centred on the photogenic village of **ZILIA** (Ziglia), that provides the staple income for this area. The other chief source of employment is the unsightly **mineral water** plant on the outskirts, from where some eleven million bottles of naturally sparkling Zilia water are exported annually.

Cassano and Montemaggiore

The most worthwhile stop along the D151 is **CASSANO** (Cassanu), which boasts a unique village square in the form of a star and has an outstanding triptych (1505) in its seventeenth-century **Église de l'Annonciation**. Around 2km further northwest of the village, to the right of the main road as you're heading for Montemaggiore, look out for the Romanesque church of **San Raineru**, one of the Balagne's most enchanting buildings, reached via a rough path from the main road. Constructed by Pisan stoneworkers in the eleventh and twelfth centuries, the church has an intricate multicoloured façade topped by two heads flanking a little cross. Inside, three hideous sculpted faces look out from the cylindrical stone font.

Fountains, arcaded houses and ancient streets characterize the village of **MONTEMAGGIORE**, which occupies a rocky pinnacle 3km north of Cassano. The **Église St–Augustin**, in the main square, has some interesting seventeenth-century paintings and an organ dating from the 1700s, but can't compete with the view from **A Cima**, the rocky outcrop at the eastern end of the village – from here you can see the ruins of the old village of Montemaggiore and right across to Calvi, with the gigantic granite cliffs of Monte Grosso on the opposite side of the valley.

In the third week of July each year, Montemaggiore plays host to the **Fiera di l'Alivu**, which brings together the *commune*'s olive producers for a weekend of exhibitions and tasting. The proceedings are brought to a close with a prize-giving ceremony for the region's best oil of that year. For precise dates of the festival, contact the Calvi tourist office (see p.118).

Cateri

Seven winding kilometres after Montemaggiore, the D151 arrives at **CATERI**, which straddles the crossroads of the Balagne's principal routes. Tiny streets with overgrown balconies surround the requisite Baroque church, **Église de l'Assomption**, a seventeenth-century edifice dedicated to the martyr St Bernin, whose tomb is the principal feature inside. The hamlet of **SAN CESARIU**, just below the village, is worth visiting for its Romanesque sanctuary, while 1km west of the village lies the oldest functioning Franciscan convent in Corsica, the **Couvent de Marcasso**, dating from 1621.

Cateri's only **hotel** is the *Auberge Chez Léon-U San Dume* (☎04 95 61 73 95, ☏04 95 61 79 31; ❸), a modern building whose rooms have en-suite showers and toilets and wonderful views. Their restaurant, *U San Dume*, is commendable, too, serving mainly seafood dishes on a terrace that makes the most of the location. This village is renowned as a cheese-making centre, and the best place to sample local specialities is the refreshingly unpretentious *La Lataria* (☎04 95 61 71 44), a converted dairy on the left of the crossroads as you leave the village. On a rear terrace that looks across half a dozen villages to the sea, you can order freshly made salads, charcuterie, succulent grilled veal in lemon sauce or *lasagna al brocciu*, rounded off with a stupendous homemade *fiadone*. There's also a little shop selling conserves and other local delicacies.

Sant'Antonino to Monticello

The hazy silhouette of the oldest inhabited village in Corsica, **SANT'AN-TONINO**, is visible for kilometres around, its huddle of orange buildings clinging like an crow's nest to the crest of an arid granite hilltop. The village was occupied in the ninth century, when the Savelli counts ruled from the now-ruined castle, and its circular layout of narrow cobbled lanes, vaulted passageways and neat stone houses has changed little over the past three hundred years. Recently voted one of France's most picturesque villages, Sant'Antonino has become something of a honey-pot destination, famed for its unrivalled 360-degree view of the Balagne. Out of season, however, the place has a forlorn air, with most of its houses locked or boarded up; the 110 permanent residents are mostly retired smallholders or artisans.

You can't drive up into Sant'Antonino, but there is a **car park** at the end of the road, just below the village. After a quick look at the sixteenth-century church, **Sant'Annunziata**, which boasts some attractive Baroque decor and a late eighteenth-century organ, head uphill into the warren of alleys above, where sooner or later you'll stumble across the wonderful A Stalla shop, which sells local produce; in addition to the pungent charcuterie and cheeses hanging from its rafters, there's olive oil, eggs, raisins, almonds and the delicious *cucciole* biscuits, made with chestnut flour.

For a substantial **meal**, try *La Taverne Corse* (℡04 95 61 70 15), overlooking the car park, whose €20 Corsican speciality menu includes five courses, served on a shady terrace with fine views of the hills inland. On the opposite side of the village, the more modest *La Belle Vue* (℡04 95 61 73 91) lives up to its name: the dishes on their superb-value €17 menu (charcuterie, mint and *brocciu* omelette, lamb or veal stew with beans, and local cheese) are all traditional and made with local ingredients.

For picnic food, call at Olivier Antonini's little produce stall, La Maison du Citron, at the entrance to the village just off the car park, where you can buy Balagne lemons, maquis-scented honey, village muscats, and citrus jams that are made according to recipes devised by the proprietor's mother twenty or more years ago.

Aregno

A kilometre further down the D151 lies the village of **AREGNO**, set amidst a blanket of olive, orange and lemon orchards that stretch down to the sea. The chief attraction here is the graceful Romanesque **Église de la Trinité et San Giovanni**, dating from the twelfth century and constructed, like San Michele de Murato in the Nebbio (see p.105), of chequered green, white and ochre stone. The triple-decker façade displays a fascinating diversity of stonework: an arch above the door is framed by two primitive figures; over these is a blind arcade decorated with geometric patterns and fantastic creatures; and right at the top there's a window surmounted by a couple of intertwined snakes and a crouching man holding his foot (believed to symbolize man paralysed by sin). Inside, on the north wall of the nave and to the right of the altar, are some arresting and well-preserved frescoes: the portraits at the top of the wall are the four Doctors of the Church, painted in 1458, and below them is St Michael lancing a dragon, from 1449. Since 1997, this village has played host to Corsica's only almond festival, **A Fiera di l'Amandulu**, which takes place at the beginning of August. Nut farmers and their families travel from all over the island to take part in cooking competitions.

Pigna

The tiny village of **PIGNA**, a compact cluster of orange roofs and sky-blue shutters set beneath the road 2km from Aregno, is home to one of the most successful restoration projects in the region. Combining the practical refurbishment of buildings with a revival of traditional culture, the project's achievements so far include the building of a new mairie out of earth, and the transformation of an old animal shelter into a lively theatre. Several **artisans' workshops** (open summer 10.15am–noon & 3–7pm) are good for browsing, with various craftworks for sale, including ceramics, engraving (*gravure*), musical boxes and instruments (namely flutes and the rare sixteen-stringed Corsican cittern), furniture and traditional woodcarvings.

The village follows an architectural plan typical of the Balagne, known as a *chjapatta* (hedgehog), whereby the streets branch out from the centre like spines. Pretty piazza d'Olmu and piazza Piazzarella provide glorious views of the sea, but your first visit will probably be to the central **Église de l'Immaculée-Conception**, built in the eighteenth century on a Romanesque base. A squat building with a giant façade flanked by a pair of stumpy campaniles, the church houses a magnificent organ that was restored in 1991 by local craftsmen.

In summer, the nearby open-air theatre hosts **concerts**, often featuring the ancient Moorish dance, the Moresc, which was traditionally performed to celebrate victory over the Saracens. Pigna is especially lively in early August when the **Festivoce** festival provides a forum for long nights of traditional a cappella singing in the outdoor amphitheatre, made from a renovated goat's shed. Concerts run by E Voce di U Comune, an association of artists and musicians dedicated to the promotion of Corsican literature, singing and art, are also held every Tuesday night in summer (or on Saturdays in winter) at the Casa Musicale (℡04 95 61 77 31 or 04 95 61 76 57, ℱ04 95 61 74 28), an old house that has been turned into a kind of musical inn at the edge of the village. These generally start at around 10pm and feature recitals by *polyphonies* singers, violins, harpsichord, citterns, and traditional percussion and wind instruments made from goats' horns. Admission is free, but most of the audience is drawn from Casa Musicale's restaurant, where you can enjoy quality Corsican charcuterie and main dishes such as *cabrettu a l'istrettu* (a kind of spicy kid stew) or delicious Cap Corse crayfish roasted in local olive oil and wild thyme, rounded off with homemade chestnut-flour deserts. Their terrace, with its panoramic view of the Balagne, is also an ideal spot for breakfast; non-residents pay €6 for a *petit déjeuner complet* of coffee, fresh bread, *canastrelli* biscuits, local honey and homemade fig-and-walnut jam. If you feel like **staying** the night, you can do so in the Casa's attractively decorated en-suite rooms (❹); they are all very pleasant, but "Sulana", on the first floor, has the added attraction of a huge terrace.

If they're full, try the village's little B&B, *A Merendella* (℡04 95 61 80 10; ❹), which has a handful of charming double- or triple-bedded rooms with shutters opening onto the valley; breakfast is included in the tariff. Finally, for a light snack or a sundowner, head through the winding alleyways at the bottom of the village to the wonderful *A Casarelle* café. At its tiny terrace, on furniture fashioned from old olive wood, you can order various tapas made from organic local produce (their baked aubergine pâté is a dream), washed down with *pichets* of chilled rosé *maison*. The views, which extend west across the Balagne to the coast at L'Île Rousse, are sublime, especially late in the afternoon.

Le Couvent de Corbara

One kilometre down the road from Pigna stands the little chapel of **Notre-Dame-de-Latio**, which houses a beautiful painting of the Virgin dated 1002. Opposite, a steep road leads up to the austere **Couvent de Corbara**, attractively framed by olive trees at the foot of Monte Sant'Angelo (see below). Founded as an orphanage in 1430, it was transformed into a Franciscan convent in 1456, badly damaged during the revolution of the 1750s, abandoned soon after, then restored in 1857 by the Dominicans. During World War I the

Davia Franceschini: Queen of the Moors

Corbara's Casa di Turchi is associated with the extraordinary story of **Davia Franceschini**, a member of the local ruling family who, in the late eighteenth century, rose to become queen of Morocco. According to the local version of events, Davia was the daughter of a poor charcoal-burner and his wife, who decided to seek their fortune on the mainland. Shortly before leaving Corsica, the girl came across a destitute old woman, half-dead with cold and hunger, to whom she gave food. The beggar returned the kindness by giving her a talisman, "La Main de Fatma", which she said would bring luck on her journey. In the event, the voyage to Marseille turned into a disaster as a storm broke the mast of the boat and swept it south to the Moorish coast, where the passengers were promptly imprisoned. It was at this point that the talisman came to Davia's aid: struck by the beauty of both the object and its wearer, the jailer took the young Corsican woman to meet his sultan, who immediately recognized the pendant hanging around her neck. It had belonged to a long-lost sister who had run away years ago to escape an arranged marriage with an ugly old merchant, never to be seen or heard of again. The sultan was smitten with Davia and they were married soon after. Her family was allowed to return to Corbara, where they lived in a grand house on the square.

This epic, however, is more fairy story than historical truth. In fact, the real Davia did not come from, and never even visited, Corsica. Born Marthe Franceschini in Tunis, she was the daughter of a couple abducted from Corbara by pirates in 1754 – an all-too-common occurrence at the time. Mother and child were both freed, only to fall into the hands of pirates a second time, and ended up in the Marrakech slave market. Eventually, Marthe, or **Daouia Lalla** as she was later known, entered the sultan of Morocco's harem and grew to become the ruler's favourite and most influential wife. After her death in the plague of Larache in 1799, her story was taken up and embellished by writers of exotic Oriental fiction, whence the more colourful yarn spun by the locals.

place was used as a prisoner-of-war camp. The Dominicans returned in 1927 and remain there today, running the place as a spiritual retreat. Inside the adjoining white church, of which the oldest part is the eighteenth-century **choir**, you can see the **tombs** of the Savelli family (see below) bearing the family arms – two lions holding a rose.

A mule track behind the convent leads to the summit of Monte Sant'Angelo (560m), a stiff one-hour walk. From the top you can see for kilometres across the Balagne and over the Désert des Agriates to the west coast of Cap Corse – on extremely clear days, it's even possible to see the Alps. Descend either by the same route, or by heading south to Sant'Antonino or east to Santa Reparata di Balagna.

Corbara

Fanning out over the Colline de Monte Guido, 2km beyond the convent road and 2km inland from the coast road, **CORBARA** is a quintessential Balagne town of small cubic houses clinging to a steep hillside. It served as capital of the region before the Genoese took over and founded the citadel at Calvi, and it still boasts the largest of Balagne's parish churches, the **Église de l'Annonciation**, a glitzy Baroque edifice built in 1685. Inside, the most overblown feature is the enormous swirling main altar flanked by two cloud-borne angels, which was constructed from Carrara marble brought over in the 1750s. The painted panels and carved furniture in the sacristy date from the fifteenth century and are relics of the church that occupied this site before the present structure. Two doors down from the church stands a grand house bearing the arms of the Franceschini family, who owned the village from the ninth to the nineteenth century. Known as the **Casa di Turchi**, it was built by Marthe ("Davia") Franceschini while she was married to the Sultan of Morocco (see box on p.145).

Occupying a rocky pinnacle below the village, the craggy ruin of **U Forte** was once the seat of the Savelli clan, the former overlords of this region. Founded in 1292 by Aldruvando, a vassal who had rebelled against Count Arrigho Savelli, the castle was completed in 1375 by Savelli's son, Mannone Savelli de Guido. When the castle was dismantled by the Genoese in the early sixteenth century, following a battle between the feudal lords and the republic, Savelli de Guido's descendants restored the nearby **Castel de Guido**, a fort founded in 816 by Guido de Sabelli, who was made Count of the Balagne by the pope after a victory against the Saracens. Here the Savellis ruled in an uneasy coexistence with the Genoese for two hundred years. Then, in 1798, this castle too was wrecked, on the orders of a political adversary of the Savelli family, one of whom was Paoli's chief administrator for the new town of L'Île Rousse.

Santa Reparata di Balagna and Monticello
From Corbara you can head back inland by the D263, which climbs up the side of the Regino Valley for 3km before reaching **SANTA REPARATA DI BALAGNA**, a terraced village of ancient crumbling buildings and arcaded streets that yield spectacular glimpses of the sea. The best viewpoint is the terrace of Santa Reparata, from where L'Île Rousse occupies the foreground. The church was built over a Pisan chapel and retains the eleventh-century apse, though the façade dates from 1590.

Four kilometres higher up the D263 lies **MONTICELLO**, fief of the great warlord Giudice della Rocca, whose thirteenth-century **Castel d'Ortica** sits on a rocky hillock to the north of the village, surrounded by a belt of olive trees. In the centre, the sole sight is the imposing **Maison Malaspina**, formerly owned by descendants of Pascal Paoli's sister, and yet another house in which Napoléon once spent a few days. One other famous former resident of Monticello was the English writer and comedian Frank Muir, who bought a house here called "A Torra" ("The Tower") with his wife, Polly, in the 1950s. In his autobiography, *A Kentish Lad*, Muir recalls many happy memories of the Balagne, among them "going on a tour and finding that we would rather be in Monticello than anywhere else on the island".

Cateri to Belgodère
To the south of Cateri the D71 swings through a region that's received a lot of government money to attempt to reverse the effects of the Balagne's recent dramatic depopulation (see p.117). Smaller-scale initiatives are in place, too, as you'll see at **AVAPESSA**, whose ancient watermill produces an olive oil that you can sample at *L'Alivu*, a restaurant set up by a community of young people trying to revive the local economy. Gîtes have also been opened in the vicinity – the mairie in the village square has details (☎04 95 61 74 10).

Muro
The next village along the route from Avapessa is **MURO**, once a hive of artisans, blacksmiths, silk weavers and wheelwrights. Nowadays it's part of the programme to revive old industries in the region, hence the two olive-oil mills straddling the river are working once again. Further evidence of former prosperity are the village's three churches. An elegant bell tower and an imposing façade decorated with statues distinguish the eighteenth-century **Église de l'Annonciation**, on the right as you enter the village. Inside, the usual profu-

sion of marble surrounds a **Crucifix des Miracles**, which in 1730 allegedly started bleeding during Mass and now attracts a steady trickle of penitents and pilgrims. The church opposite, **Santa Croce**, is much older, dating from the fourteenth century, and even more ancient is nearby **San Giovanni**, a partly ruined eleventh-century church, one of the oldest in Corsica.

Feliceto

Glass, wine and olive oil are the chief products at **FELICETO** (Filicetu), a village scattered over the banks of the River Regino, 2km east of Muro. The settlement is also famous for the purity of its water – a couple of *fontaines* 200m west of the centre provide a refreshing halt along the way. The inevitable Baroque church is **Église St-Nicolas**, its crypt containing the lavish tombs of local bigwigs; the next-door **Chapelle St-Roch** has a beautiful seventeenth-century wooden statue of Roch, patron saint of shepherds and horsemen, in a chapel beside the altar. If you're in the mood for a brisk walk, head for the building known as the **Falconaghja** (Eagle's Nest), an hour's climb along the footpath on the left as you leave the village heading north. A mayor of the village constructed this in the last century so he could keep an eye on his citizens with a telescope; later it became a hideout for passing outlaws, hence the alternative name, *Maison des Bandits*.

In the village, next to the hotel, is the **Domaine Renucci cave** (June–Oct daily 9am–noon & 2.30–6pm), where you can taste a highly perfumed rosé and one of northern Corsica's most highly regarded AOC reds, made from grapes grown in vineyards spread out below Feliceto.

Practicalities

Feliceto has one of the few **hotels** in these parts, the elegant *Mare e Monti* (℡04 95 63 02 00, ℻04 95 63 02 01; ❼; April–Oct), an enormous nineteenth-century *maison d'Américain* with a faded façade and plain stone-floored interior, fitted out with furniture handmade by the owner, M Renucci. Its eighteen rooms, gradually being restored in keeping with the building's period, are of modest size and have good views over the valley or rear garden, shaded by mature cedars.

The hotel has a small restaurant, but a more memorable **place to eat** is the *Osteria U Mulinu* (℡04 95 61 73 23; May–Oct daily except Tues), a restored olive-oil mill at the eastern end of the village. This inn is renowned throughout France thanks to the plate-throwing, whip-cracking and gun-firing antics of its eccentric *patron*, Joseph Ambrosini, and gets booked out weeks in advance during the summer, though it's still worth phoning ahead to see if they have a table free. The set menu is priced at €27.50, which includes an aperitif, a choice of desserts and as much of the house wine as you can drink. Reservation is essential.

Speloncato

Named after the caves and cavities that riddle the rocky prominence on which it sits, **SPELONCATO**, 6km from Feliceto and 33km east of Calvi, is one of the most appealing Balagne villages. A tight cluster of terracotta-red roofs crouched in the shadow of the Monte Grosso massif, it's dominated by the ruins of a convent of Santa Maria di a Pase, while the core of the place is a compact market square, **place de la Libération**. Opposite its café stands the stalwart **hotel** *Spelunca* (℡04 95 61 50 38, ℻ 04 95 61 53 14; ❹; open year round), former residence of Cardinal Savelli, an eighteenth-century papal minister whose corruption earned him the nickname *Il Cane Corso* ("The Corsican Dog"). The hotel doesn't have a restaurant, but you can **eat** very well across the road in the square at *Le Gallieni* (☎04 95 61 51 76), which serves a standard range of Corsican specialities on three set menus (€15–23). More serious cuisine is offered at the *Auberge de Domalto* (☎04 95 61 50 97; advance reservation essential), 6km below the village off the D71, where you can dine in a stylish eighteenth-century house overlooking the valley. At €27 for a *menu fixe* plus wine, this isn't a cheap option, but quality is guaranteed: house specialities include a delicious wild boar terrine, sea bream in cream of lemon sauce and homemade chestnut ice cream; and the *patronne* leaves the bottle of eau de vie on your table at the end of the meal.

Belgodère

BELGODÈRE, fourteen winding kilometres northeast of Speloncato, lies at the junction of the main inland routes and provides a possible base for the beaches around L'Île Rousse (see p.137), 15km northwest. The main Calvi–Ponte Leccia train also stops here, though the distance between the station and the village is too great to be covered on foot, and there are no taxis on hand. You can **stay** at *Hôtel Niobel*, 400m from the square on the edge of the village (☎04 95 61 34 00, ℱ04 95 61 35 85; ❹; April–Oct), a modern but cosy hotel with a good **restaurant**, whose large windows offer breathtaking views of the Balagne coast. Local specialities here include pork in chestnut sauce and veal stew.

There are a couple of churches in and around the village worth a look: the **Église St-Thomas** (San Tumasgiu) dates from the sixteenth century and houses a magnificent painted panel of the Virgin and Child (ask for the key in the café opposite); and the **Oratoire de la Madonuccia**, 500m from the square along the Speloncato road, harbours Corsica's oldest statue of the Madonna, placed here in 1387 to seal a reconciliation between Speloncato and the rival villages of San Columbano. Legend has it that the site was chosen because two bullocks who were transporting it between the opposing settlements stopped here and refused to move, which local people took to be a sign.

The best **views** of the surrounding area are to be had from the ruined **fort** on the edge of the village, reached via the archway between the two cafés on the square.

The Giunssani

The Giunssani is a spectacularly isolated part of the Balagne, enclosed by Monte Grosso (1938m) and Monte Padro (2393m), the northernmost high peaks of Corsica's mountainous spine. Rising in the cirque of Monte Corona, just south of Monte Grosso, the **River Tartagine** flows through its heart, fed on its northern flank by tributaries whose ravines are overlooked by four high-altitude villages and a scattering of more remote hamlets. Swathed in deep-green chestnut and oak forest, these are exquisitely picturesque but see surprisingly few visitors considering their proximity to the coast; most people who come here do so only for a day to take advantage of the **hiking trails** that thread around the lush sides and floor of the valley.

There are two **approaches** to the region. The first, giving an amazing view over the entire Balagne, is via the D63, which begins about 500m south of Speloncato, climbs up a high open route to the windswept Bocca di a Barraglia pass, and then plunges south, coming to a dead end in the base of the valley. The other route is along the D963, which branches off the N197 6km east of Belgodère, then drops down into the Tartagine Valley from the Bocca Capanna pass. If you're visiting the area as a day-trip from the coast, you could travel in on one road and out on the other, completing a loop that strings together the main settlements.

Pioggiola

Following the D63/D693 route in an anticlockwise direction, the first place you'll come to is **PIOGGIOLA**, a crown of yellow buildings nestled in a fold of hundred-year-old chestnut trees at an altitude of 1000m – which makes it one of the highest villages in Corsica. **Accommodation** is available in the ten-roomed *Auberge l'Aghjola*, just above the village proper (℗04 95 61 90 48, ℱ04 95 61 92 99; ❷), which ranks among the loveliest country retreats on the island. Although equipped with modern comforts (including a pool) the building has retained its original rustic feel, with wood and stone walls, but the real attraction here is the food, served on cool evenings at a heavy wooden table next to an open fire. Menus range from the basic €16 *menu berger*, comprising a plate of charcuterie, a plate of cheese and dessert, to the *menu de résistance* at €25, which might include house specialities such as haunch of wild boar baked in Cap Corse muscat, quails in a cream of mint sauce, or veal with wild cêpes. The restaurant is open to non-residents, but you have to book ahead, preferably the day before.

Walks in the Giunssani

Cut off by two of the highest motorable passes on the island, the **Giunssani** is a walker's and mountain biker's paradise, with an extensive network of well-marked and well-maintained trails leading through acres of pristine pine, chestnut and oak forest. The Parc Naturel Régional has produced a leaflet entitled *Giunssani: Oasis de Verdure*, detailing the routes on a monochrome section of the area IGN map, which you should be able to pick up at a tourist office. Otherwise, you'll have to shell out on two separate maps to cover the area (#4249 OT and #4250T).

Eight different **round walks** are featured in the leaflet, marked every 10m or so with splashes of orange paint. For a day-hike, try the five-hour route from Olmi-Capella to Vallica, which takes in a water mill, a Genoese bridge and bathing spots along the Tartagine River; or the five-hour loop from Pioggiola to Forcili and back, which skirts the cirque below Monte Tolu before dropping down to the Bocca di a Scoperta pass above Mausoleo. This latter hike can be extended by an hour to take in the San Parteo peak (1680m); an unmarked mountain path scales the east flank of the cirque and follows the ridge to the summit, from where you follow the spine of another ridge west to rejoin the waymarked trail to Mausoleo. The **Maison Forestière de Tartagine-Melaja**, at the very end of the D963, marks the start of another great five-hour loop that hugs the true right bank of the Tartagine, then climbs up to Mausoleo, before winding up the awsome Melaja Valley. After crossing the stream, you follow the path down until it meets the D963, which you keep to for the remaining 45 minutes back to the maison forestière.

In addition to these relatively easy *sentiers du pays*, Giunssani offers several **more challenging trails** that give access to the high ridges and peaks surrounding the basin. Deservedly the most popular of these is the six-hour climb up the head of the Tartagine Valley to Monte Corona (2144m), reached by following a chain of cairns through some rough alderscrub and boulders from the Bocca Tartagine (1852m). The final pull to the summit, described in detail in our account of the GR20 on p.373, is rewarded with an astonishing view of Monte Cinto's north face and most of the northwest of the island besides. Other rewarding routes take you to the **Bocca di l'Ondella** (1952m), 10km south, from where you can drop down to the Bergeries de la Tassineta in the Asco Valley. The routes to both these passes are ancient transhumance arteries used by shepherds and traders to reach the pastures of the west coast. They're fairly straightforward, though you definitely need to be equipped for altitude and sudden changes of weather (see our advice on pp.366–367).

Roughly midway between Pioggiola and its neighbour, Olmi-Capella, *A Tramula* (☎04 95 61 93 54; ❸), a huge modern building faced with local stone, is a newer hotel-restaurant that's fast developing a strong reputation for its comfortable en-suite rooms and fine Corsican speciality cooking, served on a spacious terrace overlooking the valley.

Olmi-Capella

Beyond Pioggiola the road divides, one branch of the D963 descending to the region's principal village, **OLMI-CAPELLA**, a cluster of sharp red roofs and mellow stone overlooking the Tartagine. In past centuries, many of the inhabitants of this village used to make their living as itinerant traders, selling top-notch Giunssani olive oil and leather shoes throughout the island; apparently their customers regarded them as *unti e fini* (unctuous and fine) – as much, presumably, for their slippery salesmen tactics and slick attire as their good manners and greasy mule packs. There's nowhere to stay here, but you can **eat** definitive Giunssani cooking at the *Auberge La Tornadia*, 2km east of the village in the direction of Pioggiola (☎04 95 61 90 93; April–Oct). Frequented as much by locals as visitors, this is a lively place that's full of atmosphere, with low wooden ceilings and old farm implements on the walls. Specialities include roast lamb, fresh pasta made with chestnut flour and, during the autumn, wild forest mushroom sauces; their home-baked biscuits and cakes are great, too. Expect to pay around €22–26 per head.

Vallica and Mausoleo

Carry on 3km further east from Olmi-Capella and you'll come to **VALLICA**, a sleepy village swamped in greenery that looks out to Monte Padro on the other side of the valley. Apart from the spectacular views, there's little of note here other than the nineteenth-century church.

The other branch of the D963 from Pioggiola descends to a junction for the ancient village of **MAUSOLEO**, the last of the Tartagine quartet, which boasts a fifteenth-century church containing an olive-wood statue of John the Baptist. Past the Mausoleo turning, the D963 twists through the spectacular gorges of the River Melaja to the banks of the Tartagine, terminating at the maison forestière and the **Forêt de la Tartagine-Melaja**. For a brief taste of the forest, you can follow various short marked paths from here; the principal major hikes are detailed in the box on p.152.

South of Calvi: Filosorma

From Calvi, two routes run south to **Galéria**, a tiny fishing settlement and summer resort situated about 25km down the coast. If speed is your main concern, the inland D81 is the better, cutting diagonally across the **Filosorma** region. An area of rolling, empty maquis overshadowed by the imposing north wall of the Paglia Orba massif – or *Grande Barrière* as it's known locally – this is one of the most sparsely populated corners of the island, largely due to the ravages of Muslim pirates in the fourteenth and fifteenth centuries, who burned some ninety villages to the ground and carried off their inhabitants as slaves to ports of North Africa; later, a succession of malaria plagues took their toll, while fierce fighting with the Genoese during Paoli's war of independence ensured the area's terminal decline by wiping out virtually all of its few remaining menfolk.

The D81 veers southwest just beyond Calvi airport at the village of **Suare,** in the Figarella Valley, from where the D251 continues southeast to penetrate a large forest of Laricio pines and evergreen oaks enclosed by some of the highest mountains in Corsica: the **Cirque de Bonifato**. The alternative, coastal route to Galéria is the D81B, which snakes around a relentlessly rocky shore via Argentella, the remote bay where de Gaulle planned to conduct nuclear tests in the 1960s (the plans were blocked by the first act of Corsican armed resistance against the French state since Napoleonic times: see p.422). This road rejoins the D81 at the River Fango, where a right turn brings you to Galéria and a left leads to the **Vallée du Fango**, one of the least-traversed areas of the island, worth visiting for the dramatic views of the *Grande Barrière* rising to its south.

Public transport through the area is limited to Autocars Les Beaux Voyages' seasonal minibus from Calvi to Galéria (July–Sept 15 Mon–Sat; ☎04 95 65 11 35), and Autocars SAIB's service (also seasonal) between Calvi and Porto (May 15–Oct 10 Mon–Sat 1 daily, Aug 1 daily; ☎04 95 22 41 99). Cycles and scooters can also be rented from Calvi (see p.127) and Porto (see p.163), though these are more expensive than those available in Ajaccio. If you have the time, the best way to explore this beautiful region is on foot, via the Tra Mare e Monti long-distance **footpath**, which runs from Calenzana, just south of Calvi, to Galéria, Porto and across the hills to Cargèse. For a fuller description of the trail, see p.397.

Cirque de Bonifato

A gigantic amphitheatre of red–grey crags and needles looming above a carpet of Laricio pines, the **Cirque de Bonifato**, 20km southeast of Calvi, forms an awesome gateway to the Corsican watershed. At few places on the island do the peaks surge so dramatically from the forest, rising from 200m to more than 2000m in only 7km. With the coast less than half an hour away, this is also among the most easily accessible mountain areas. The resulting traffic congestion can get unbearable in high summer, but at other times of year Bonifato provides an inspiring springboard for forays into the hills and woods.

The twisting road up the Figarella Valley comes to an abrupt end at a large paying **car park**, just beyond the *Auberge de la Forêt* (☎04 95 65 09 98; April–Oct; ❶), a gîte d'étape with a better than average restaurant on whose stone terrace you can steel yourself for the climbs ahead with sandwiches of local charcuterie, goat's cheese salad, *tarte aux herbes* and wild boar stews; set menus range from €18.50 to €21. Comprising a few spartan dorms with bunk beds, accommodation is basic but cheap: €14 per head, or €30 for half board (obligatory in August). You can also camp or bivouac (on very uneven ground) in the pines behind for €7.

Galéria

The only coastal settlement in the Filosorma, **GALÉRIA**, is believed to have been first settled by the Phoenicians in the sixth century BC, possibly even before the rise of Aléria on the east coast. Numerous Roman artefacts found in the vicinity, including fragments of an anchor discovered by divers here during the summer of 1992, have helped archeologists identify this as the site of ancient Kalaris, named on Ptolemy's map of the Mediterranean and a key port in classical times. Later, the anopheles mosquito ruled supreme, ensuring that the village remained malaria-ridden until the advent of DDT in the 1940s.

The auberge stands at the end of two liaison paths for the GR20. Trekkers for whom the first two stages of the famous *haute route* have proved too taxing use them to limp off the trail and back to Calvi. But the paths, waymarked with red and white splashes of paint, also make rewarding **day-walks** in themselves. Both begin a little over a kilometre further up the valley from the auberge: press on past the car park and follow the *piste forestière* along the true left bank of the Figarella River for 30min until you reach a bouldery stream crossing, marked with a PNRC signboard. From there, you can either head left and ascend the **Melaghia Valley** to the **Refuge d'Ortu di u Piobbu** (1570m; 2hr 30min–3hr); or else turn right and follow the path up the **Spasimata Valley** to **Refuge de Carrozzu** (1270m; 2hr 15min). The latter route boasts the more spectacular gorges, but the former leads to the foot of **Monte Corona** (2144m) – an extraordinary viewpoint which you can climb in a round trip of 2hr 30min from the refuge (for more on this ascent, see p.373).

With adequate equipment and the weather on your side, a superb two- or three-day round walk would be to combine the two by hiking up to Ortu di u Piobbu and then following the GR20 south over Capu Ladroncellu and the Bocca d'Avartoli to Carrozzu (arguably the most dramatic section of the whole GR), returning via the Spasimata Valley the next day.

Involving more than 2000m of altitude change in a day (or considerably more than that if you continue all the way to the summit of Monte Corona), neither of these two routes is likely to be much fun unless you're well equipped with lightweight gear and already fit. A softer option, though one which still requires around 600m of ascent, is the wonderful **round walk** from the auberge to the **Bocca di Bonassa** – a must for tree lovers as it takes in one of the western Mediterranean's few surviving ancient holm oak forests. Well waymarked throughout, the path starts just beyond the auberge (look for the PNRC signboard on the roadside), striking south (to the right) from the road and zigzagging uphill through the pines. After a couple of stream crossings, you ascend via a series of sharp switchbacks along the south-facing flank of a wooded spur, crossed at **Bocca di l'Erbaghiolu** (1258m). Having crested the ridgetop, the path contours west through the forest, descending sharply northwards just before reaching Bocca di Bonassa to join the **Tra Mare e Monti** trail. Turn left at the path junction and, once past a small **spring**, you can climb back up to 1153m to enjoy the magnificent views over the Cirque de Bonifato and Balagne Déserte from the pass. The best route down is to retrace your steps as far as the path junction (10min) and follow the main trail as it zigzags steeply down to the 700m mark, where it levels off for a leisurely descent through magnificent deciduous woods to the D251. A right turn at the road will take you, after a final kilometre, back to the auberge and car park. This long loop should take around four to five hours' walking.

As ever, bear in mind the potential dangers of mountain trekking, even on paths as well waymarked as these. Fatalities occur more or less annually in the Cirque de Bonifato, normally as a result of exposure. Weather can change very suddenly and, once above 1000m, near freezing temperatures are a risk at any time of year. Come prepared for the worst, especially if you attempt the higher sections along the GR20. And, whichever path you follow, take along IGN **map** #4149 OT, which covers all of the trails outlined above, except for the area around Ortu di u Piobbu, for which you'll need #4250 OT.

Since its renaissance as a low-key resort and diving centre in the early 1980s, Galéria's old granite core and beach, a compact curve of coarse sand ending at a fishing jetty, has acquired a scattering of modern houses, hotels and restaurants. But even in high summer the place never feels too crowded. Plage de Riciniccia, a dramatic sweep of red shingle 500m further northeast, attracts a fair number of visitors in season (most of them German naturists), but at other times of year remains blissfully empty.

Practicalities

Galéria's **tourist office** (June–Sept daily 9am–noon & 2–6pm; ☏04 95 62 02 27) is inconveniently situated at Maison a Torra, 4km away east at the junction of the D81 and D351 by the Cinque Arcate bridge. SAIB's west coast **buses** stop here en route between Calvi and Porto (mid–May to July & Sept to mid–Oct 1–2 daily; Aug 1 daily; ☏04 95 22 41 99 or 04 95 21 02 07). From July to mid–September, Les Beaux Voyages (☏04 95 65 15 02) also lays on a daily service which runs all the way to the church at the centre of the village. The **post office** next to the church doesn't have an ATM, but gives cash advances on credit cards.

Walks from Galéria

A waystage on the Tra Mare e Monti long-distance footpath, Galéria makes an ideal base for walks into some of the remoter corners of the northwest. You can trek to Girolata and back in a day via a ridge that gives a superb view of Paglia Orba and the Golfe de Porto, or climb to the top of Capu Tondu (839m), the eroded hill overlooking the village, for a fine panorama over the wild Balagne Déserte coast Both routes are covered on IGN **map** #4150 OT.

Galéria to Girolata

The hike from **Galéria** to **Girolata**, a tiny fishing village at the east edge of the Scandola reserve that can be reached only on foot or by boat (see p.127), is the fourth and most impressive stage of the ten-day Tra Mare e Monti trail. Winding from sea level up the Tavulaghu ravine and over the Capu Licchia ridge (700m) to the Gulf of Porto, the route takes in some of the finest scenery in Corsica, including the red volcanic crags of Scandola and the sugar-loaf Capu Rossu cliffs, 6km south across a deep-blue bay. You can do this hike at any time of year, though spring and autumn are best; if you attempt it in high summer, set off early in the morning, as much of the path is exposed.

The trail, waymarked with orange splashes of paint, is signposted from Galéria's gîte, from where you head up the surfaced road 200m, turning left again when you see a sign pointing through the maquis. After passing a small reservoir (30min), the footpath climbs the Tavulaghu, crossing from one side of the stream bed to the other as it makes for the head of the valley. The going gets tougher towards the top, with the trail zigzagging through dense vegetation and evergreen oak forest to the ridge, reached after three hours. From here the views are breathtaking as you follow the rocky spine due west, ascending to a maximum height of 784m at the **Bocca di Fuata pass** (4hr 40min). The round walk from Galéria to the col and back takes between six and seven hours. Alternatively, you can press on downhill along the base of the Cavone ravine to Girolata village (roughly 6hr), visible below. For details of **accommodation** in Girolata, see p.169.

Capu Tondu

A shorter but immensely enjoyable walk from Galéria is the ascent of **Capu Tondu**, the pyramidal peak overlooking the port. The trail climbs 839m in only a couple of kilometres, so don't attempt it in hot weather. Strong boots are also essential, as the waymarks cross lots of rough, exposed rock which can be very slippery in wet conditions; some simple hand holds may be required in places.

From the east end of the village's main street, follow the lane that turns south (to the right) before the main bend in the road. When you reach a junction in the lane 30m later, take a left turn, and then follow the lane as it bends right; keep going along the track for another 400m until the maquis begins. Just opposite an aluminium-roofed house, the path veers sharply uphill into the scrub. From here on it's a hard, steep climb all the way to the summit, following waymarks and cairns through dense maquis and, later, seams of rough rock. Allow 3hr 30min for the round trip.

Accommodation

Galéria has plenty of places to **stay**, ranging from dormitory accommodation for walkers in a pleasant gîte d'étape to swish self-catering chalets. There are also a couple of small hotels 1km east of the village in the lower Fango Valley (see below). Campers have a choice between the rudimentary *Camping Idéal* (ⓣ04 95 62 01 46), just behind the beach, and the better-equipped *Les Deux Torrents* (ⓣ04 95 62 00 67, ⓕ04 95 62 03 32, ⓦwww.2torrents.corsica-net.fr; June–Sept), 5km north on the Calvi road.

L'Auberge Opposite the school in the village centre ⓣ04 95 62 00 15, ⓕ04 95 60 00 63. Simple rooms with threadbare blankets and shared toilets above a restaurant. Inexpensive, but in the middle of the village with no views to speak of. ❷

Auberge Galéris Just behind the *Filosorma* ⓣ04 95 62 02 89. Half a dozen modest rooms with terraces in a modern concrete house, tucked away off the road. Breakfast available on request. Good value and friendly. April–Oct. ❸

Filosorma On the beach road in the centre of the lower village ⓣ04 95 62 03 45. Galéria's poshest hotel has comfortable sea-facing rooms, all with showers and toilets en suite. Pricy for the area. ❺

Gîte d'Étape 1km out of the village on the Tra Mare e Monti trail ⓣ04 95 62 00 46. A well-equipped gîte with thirty dorm beds (€13), hot showers and good self-catering facilities. Half board costs €30 per head; campers pay €6.50, which includes the use of a gas ring in the garden. Advance reservation (by postal payment of fifteen percent) recommended in May, June and September – the height of the hiking season.

Idéal Just behind the beach and *L'Alivu* restaurant ⓣ04 95 62 01 46. Basic rooms in a large modern building abutting a campsite. Shared toilets, but currently the cheapest option in the village. ❷

L'Incantu route de Calca ⓣ04 95 62 03 66. An unobtrusive complex of spacious studios and chalets with mezzanine floors, kitchenettes and sea-view terraces. Excellent value, particularly during the week. A good option for divers. ❹

La Martinella Behind the beach, near the *Loup de Mer* ⓣ04 95 62 00 44. Five immaculate rooms (all en suite and with fridges), some for up to four persons, opening onto a small garden with tables and views of the bay. Good off-season discounts. ❸

Stella Marina Opposite the *Restaurant Loup de Mer* ⓣ04 95 62 00 03, ⓕ04 95 64 02 29. The nicest place to stay in Galéria: a dozen large, light rooms set in a pleasant garden, backing on to virgin maquis. The top-floor rooms, with large terraces, have the best views over the bay. ❹

Restaurants

L'Alivu At the bottom of the village, where the road bends towards the marina. The best option if you're on a budget. Three courses for €12, or a fish-of-the-day dish, served under an old olive tree at the roadside.

L'Auberge Opposite the school in the village centre ⓣ04 95 62 00 15 or 04 95 62 03 00. Mountain charcuterie and meat dishes served in a stone-walled ground-floor *salon*; also fresh lobster and crayfish (which you have to order a day in advance). Menus at €14 and €20.

Sol e Mare Along the lane leading from the beach to the village centre. A safe bet for seafood: the *patron* is a fisherman. Splash out on the €20 menu, which offers fresh *crevettes* and sea bass grilled with fennel from the garden.

Stella Marina On the beach (see "Accommodation" above). Wood-grilled cuisine served in a modern building above the bay. *Langouste* is the chef's big speciality, but his apple pie *flambée à l'eau de vie* is to die for. Count on €23–30 per head.

La Vallée du Fango

Until the beginning of the twentieth century, the **Fango River**, which rises high on the flanks of Paglia Orba and flows west through a broad-bottomed valley into the sea at Galéria, served as a transhumant corridor between the winter pastures on the coast and the summer ones across the mountains in the Niolo Valley. The region's shepherds, known as the *Niulinchi*, would drive their flocks along the river banks and through the dense forests that still line the head of the valley to the famous Bocca di Capronale pass, ascending by means of a paved path that remains largely intact, although much less frequented these days.

Following in the footsteps of the *Niulinchi*, the **Tra Mare e Monti** trail (an account of which features on p.397) winds through the charred maquis and smooth boulders lining the Fango's right bank as far as the gîte d'étape of **TUARELLI** (see below), passing numerous *piscines naturelles* en route where you can pull over for a bracing swim. Traffic along the **D351** on the opposite bank tends to dry up once past the crossroads at **LE FANGO**, where a couple of hotels and restaurants serve travellers on the convoluted journey between Porto and Calvi (see below). But with the *Grande Barrière* forming an awesome backdrop in the east, the scenery grows steadily more astounding as you progress up the valley towards **MANSO**, a scattering of a dozen or so houses where there's a working olive mill but little else – the locals claim this as the most remote village in Corsica, with some justification.

Still more impressive views of the fin-shaped Paglia Orba and its adjacent peaks – the pierced Capu Tafonatu (2343m) and, to the left (north), Punta Minuta (2556m), part of the Cinto massif – lie in store if you continue past Manso to the tiny hamlet of **BARGHIANA**, above the confluence of the Candela and Fango rivers, site of an early-twentieth-century church dedicated to San Pancraziu, patron saint of shepherds. The narrow lane running next to the church (ie not the road that drops down to the river bridge) swings southwards through the village's chestnut orchards, eventually coming to an end 5km later at **Ponte di e Rocce** (aka Pont de Lancone). Depending on the condition of the *piste*, you may be able to drive on from here around the next spur, contouring across a steep hillside carpeted in lush deciduous woodland, to a second bridge. But from there on you'll need stout footwear and IGN map #4150 OT to tackle the remaining four-and-a-half-hour climb to **Bocca di Caporale** (1329m) – a superb ascent through holm oak woods. The route zigzags up via an ancient paved mule path that's a marvel in itself, with some stretches actually chiselled out of sheer rock. Once at the ridgetop, you'll be rewarded with a magnificent panoramic view over Paglia Orba and the Lonca Valley, enjoyed by only a tiny number of hikers each summer: in spite of being well cleared and waymarked, this is among the least frequented high trails on the island, and a good place to sight **mouflons**. You can follow it down to the un-staffed **Refuge de Puscaghia** on the far side of the pass, and thence over the Bocca di Guagnerola (1833m) into the Golo Valley, or south over the Col de Cuccaveca and Bocca a u Saltu to Évisa. However far you venture up this trail, a dawn start is recommended to avoid the heat and clouds that build up by early afternoon. Bear in mind, too, our advice on trekking safety (see p.367).

Practicalities

SAIB's seasonal Porto–Calvi bus will get you only as far up the valley as Le Fango, where two run-of-the-mill **hotels** – the *A Farera (Chez Zézé*; ☎04 95 62 01 87; ❸) and *Le Fango* (☎04 95 62 01 92; ❸) – offer modest en-suite rooms and Corsican speciality restaurants. Walkers following the Tra Mare e Monti invariably check in to the congenial **gîte d'étape** at Tuarelli (☎04 95 62 01 75; April–Oct), another one-and-a-half-hour's plod along the river bank, which has a small **campsite**. Beds cost €12 per head or €34 for half board. Served on a stone terrace overlooking the river, the restaurant offers good value for money given its remoteness and has a lively atmosphere during the trekking season.

Travel details

Trains

Two train services per day leave Calvi for Ajaccio and Bastia; they run year round, but on Sundays and public holidays a slightly different timetable applies. Check departure times at any gare SNCF, or call ☎04 95 65 00 61.

Algajola to: Ajaccio (2 daily; 3hr 45min); Bastia (2

daily; 2hr 30min); Belgodère (2 daily; 35min);
Corte (2 daily; 2hr); L'Île Rousse (2–10 daily;
20min).
Calvi to: Ajaccio (2 daily; 4hr); Algajola (2–10
daily; 20min); Bastia (2 daily; 2hr 45min);
Belgodère (2 daily; 50min); Corte (2 daily; 2hr
15min); L'Île Rousse (2–10 daily; 30min); Ponte
Leccia (2 daily; 1hr 40min).
L'Île Rousse to: Ajaccio (2 daily; 3hr 30min);
Algajola (2–10 daily; 15min); Bastia (2 daily; 1hr
50min); Belgodère (2 daily; 20min); Corte (2 daily;
1hr 45min).

Buses

The tables below summarize which bus companies
cover which routes, how often they run and how
long journeys take. Start by looking up your
intended destination in the first table; then, using
the company's acronym (eg BV or SAIB), go to the
second table for more detailed route and frequency information. Precise departure times can be
checked in advance either via the bus companies
direct, or (if your French isn't up to that) Calvi
tourist office (℡ 04 95 65 16 67).

Calvi to: Ajaccio (EV; 3hr); Bastia (BV; 2hr 15min);
Calenzana (BV; 30min); Galéria (BV/SAIB; 1hr); L'Île
Rousse (BV/EV; 40min); Lumio (BV; 10min); Porto
(SAIB; 2hr 30min).
Galéria to: Calvi (BV; 1hr); Porto (SAIB; 50min).
L'Île Rousse to: Ajaccio (EV; 2hr 30min); Algajola
(BV/EV; 10min); Bastia (BV; 1hr 50min); Calvi
(BV/EV; 25min); St-Florent (TST; 1hr).

BV: Autocars Les Beaux Voyages ℡ 04 95 65
15 02 or 04 95 65 11 35. Calvi–L'Île
Rousse–Bastia; year round 1 daily Mon–Sat.
Calvi–Galéria; July–mid-Sept 1 daily Mon–Sat.
Calvi–Calenzana; July to mid-Sept Mon to Sat 2
daily; mid-Sept to June timetable coincides with
school terms.
EV: Eurocorse Voyages ℡ 04 95 31 73 76. Calvi-
L'Île Rousse–Ponte Leccia–Corte–Vizzavona–
Ajaccio; year round 1 daily Mon–Sat.
SAIB: Autocars SAIB ℡ 04 95 22 41 99 or 04 95
21 02 07. Calvi–Porto; Aug 1 daily mid-May to
mid-Oct 1 daily Mon–Sat.
TST: Transports Santini ℡ 04 95 37 04 04. L'Île
Rousse–St-Florent; July & Aug 2 daily.

Ferries

For ferry details, see pp.20 and 134.

The northwest

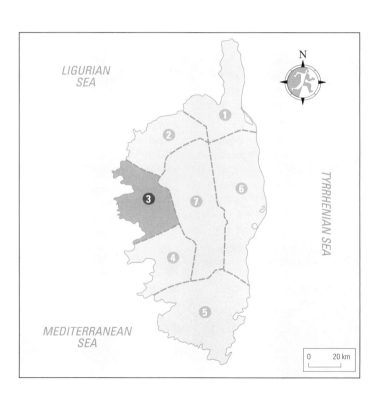

LIGURIAN
SEA

N

TYRRHENIAN SEA

MEDITERRANEAN
SEA

0   20 km

CHAPTER 3

Highlights

✳ **Plage de Gratelle** – For an amazing panorama of Capo d'Orto and the Calanches across the bay, come here at sunset time. See p.168

✳ **Girolata** – Extraordinarily picturesque village, set against red cliffs, though unreachable by road. See p.168

✳ **The Calanches** – Phantasmagorical rock formations in vivid red-tinged porphyry, best viewed from the footpaths. See p.171

✳ **Hôtel Les Roches Rouges** – *Fin-de-siècle* elegance and sublime vistas make this Corsica's top café-restaurant terrace. Call in for a chilled Cap Corse if nothing else. See p.172

✳ **Capo Rosso** – The Golfe de Porto's own pillar of Hercules is crowned by a lonely watchtower, which you can climb to – a superb walk. See p.174

✳ **Plage d'Arone** – White sand, turquoise water and an undeveloped hinterland of dense maquis – the best beach in the area. See p.174

✳ **Ascent of Capo d'Orto** – Arguably Corsica's ultimate viewpoint, accessible via a waymarked footpath. See p.173

✳ **Spelunca gorge** – More stupendous scenery culminating in the giant pines of the Forêt d'Aïtone. See p.175

✳ **Walk from Ota–Évisa** – Two of Corsica's prettiest hill villages, via Genoese packhorse bridges and a string of natural river pools. See p.177

The northwest

For sheer diversity of landscapes, nowhere else on the island compares with Corsica's **northwest** – the giant amphitheatre of mountains and valleys rearing up behind the gulfs of Porto and Sagone. Ringed by high peaks, this whole region – from the Palmarella pass in the north and the Col de Verghio in the east, to the Golfe de Sagone in the south – is believed to have been formed by lava flows from the Cinto massif, and its contorted rock formations retain a distinct air of cataclysm. The wild feel of the northwest, however, can be somewhat tempered by the volume of tourists who pour through from June until mid-September. Most of Corsica's one and a half million annual visitors will spend a day or so here at some stage in their holiday, and your enjoyment of the scenery will probably depend on the extent to which you are able to escape the crowds.

Thanks largely to its proximity to the Calanches, **Porto** village, at the easternmost extremity of the **Golfe de Porto**, has become the epicentre of the region's tourist scene, with a crop of hotels, campsites, restaurants and shops lining the narrow floor of a deep valley. Although a peaceful enough place out of season, traffic congestion and overcrowding at the height of the summer can make it a much less appealing base than some of the smaller villages dotted around the gulf. Reached via the breathtaking D81 corniche road, the **Col de la Croix** pass, northwest of Porto, marks the start of the well-trodden trail to the most picturesque of these, **Girolata**, the only permanently inhabited settlement in Corsica still unreachable by road. West of here stretch the spectacular cliffs of the **Scandola Nature Reserve**, a pristine red-granite promontory that supports a wealth of wildlife (both above and below the water level). The reserve is strictly off limits, but you can approach its fringes by boat or on foot, along one of the superb marked paths that wind high above the headland.

The region's principal attraction, however, has to be the **Calanches de Piana**, west of Porto on the opposite side of the gulf from Scandola. Made famous by the drawings of Edward Lear, this vast mass of twisted red- and green-tinged pinnacles, ravines and cliffs lies midway between Porto and its more sedate neighbour, **Piana**, whose pretty stone houses stand on the lip of a sheer drop with stunning views across the bay. Beyond it, the *falaises* of the westernmost Calanches peak at **Capo Rosso**, a vertiginous lump of pink rock crowned by a solitary watchtower, which overlooks the least-exploited beach hereabouts, **Plage d'Arone**.

Inland from Porto, the D84 and an old paved Genoese mule path wind through the towering **Gorges de Spelunca** to **Évisa**, a compact hill village and hiking centre clustered on a spur below the huge **Forêt d'Aïtone**. The

Genoese shipbuilding industry nearly finished this forest off four centuries ago, but the woodland has recovered and huge Laricio pines still loom over the main road to Corte, roamed by herds of semi-wild pigs. Temperatures drop as you approach the **Col de Verghio** via the highest motorable road on the island – gateway to the hidden Niolo Valley (covered in Chapter 7).

Back on the coast, the corniche road climbs high above Piana to the Col de Lava, then cuts inland to enter the **Golfe de Sagone** at **Cargèse**, an enchanting village with an unusual history of conflict and immigration from Greece. Lying within easy reach of the gulf's best beaches and coast walks, Cargèse makes a much better base than either **Sagone** or **Tiuccia**, two resorts further down the coast that boast a good range of amenities but little character. In this area, **Vico** and its surrounding hamlets, scattered over the steep slopes inland from the Golfe de Sagone, are the most rewarding targets for day-trips to the interior, offering glimpses of the watershed peaks between forests of chestnut and pine trees. Another possible diversion, which you could take en route to or from Vico, is a tour of to the wine-growing (and bandit-plagued) **Cinarca** district.

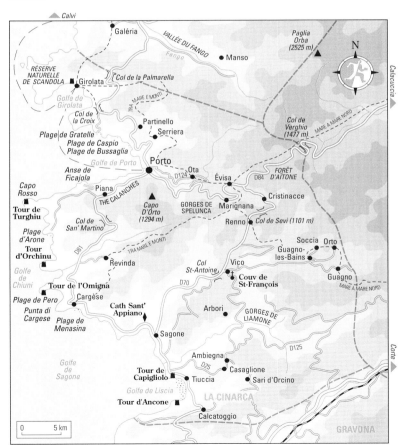

Public transport in the northwest region is limited to SAIB's daily **bus** service between Ajaccio, Cargèse, Porto and Ota, and Autocars R. Ceccaldi's daily bus from Ajaccio to Marignana, via Tiuccia, Sagone, Vico and Evisa. In summer, SAIB runs an additional service beyond Porto to Galéria and Calvi, and you can catch buses inland from Porto over the Col de Verghio to Niolu and Corte with Autocars Mordiconi.

Barely a straight stretch of road exists in this area, and surface qualities can vary as wildly as the scenery, so if you're driving take extra care, especially on the corniche road between Porto and Col de Palmarella, which sees more than its fair share of accidents.

The Golfe de Porto

The coast of the **Golfe de Porto** is one of Corsica's classic landscapes, famed above all for the corroded beauty of its red cliffs. Soaring sheer from a lapis-blue sea, the famous red-granite escarpments give way to layer upon layer of shadowy ridges that culminate in the shark's-fin peak of **Paglia Orba**, dominating the horizon to the east.

Porto, hidden in a niche at the end of the gulf, serves as the area's main resort. Although rather boxed in and cut off from the best of the views, the village does boast plenty of amenities, and is perfectly placed for day-trips. Northwest along the corniche road, a string of secluded coves punctuate the route to **Col de la Croix**, jumping-off place for wonderful walks to **Girolata**, an isolated fishing village on the edge of the **Scandola Nature Reserve**. Highlight of the southern gulf are the **Calanches**, 12km of dizzying pinnacles and ravines, ideally explored on foot, or at sea level by launch. A couple of superbly situated hotels make the nearby village of **Piana** a good alternative to Porto as a base, lying close to one of the island's most outstanding beaches, **Plage d'Arone**.

Porto

Before the tourist boom of the 1950s, virtually the only building in **PORTO** was an old Genoese watchtower, erected in the sixteenth century on an outcrop of granite where the river debouches into the gulf. Now the tower presides over a straggling rash of hotels, restaurants and shops, serving the hordes of visitors who pass through en route to or from the nearby Calanches. Overdevelopment, however, has been effectively held in check by the steep mountain slopes that hem in the village, and it is still the dramatic landscape of the gulf and its hinterland, rather than traffic congestion and jammed campsites, that leave the most lasting impressions. That said, you'd do well to time your visit carefully. Porto is so small that it can become claustrophobic in July and August, when overcrowding is no joke. Off season, the place becomes eerily deserted; the best months are May, June and September.

An avenue bordered by stately old gum trees, **route de la Marine**, links the two parts of the resort. A strip of supermarkets, boutiques, cafés and hotels 1km from the sea makes up the end of the village known as **Vaïta**, but the main focus of activity is the small **marina**, located at the avenue's end. Until the end of the nineteenth century Porto was used for exporting Laricio pines from the inland forests, and the route de la Marine was built to accommodate the great carts that used to haul the timber down from the mountains. Clustered around the great red rock that supports the tower, a nucleus of hotels and restaurants

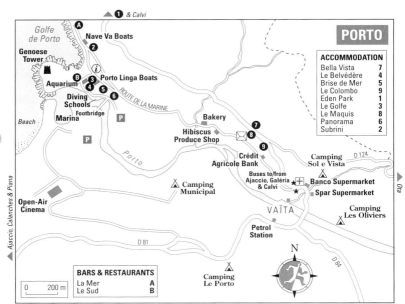

Camping Funtana al Ora, Évisa & Corte ▼

vie for views of the sea, while the rest of the buildings are crammed into what little space remains.

It's about a fifteen-minute walk from the marina up to the recently restored **Genoese Tower** (May–Sept daily 9am–8.45pm; €2.50, or €6.50 combined entry with the aquarium, see below), a squat, square, chimney-shaped structure, built in 1549, that was cracked by an explosion in the seventeenth century, when the construction was used as an arsenal. Renovated in 1993, it offers the village's best view of the churning sea. The ticket price includes a Walkman tour (French only), outlining the history of *torri* such as this and their role in the defence of the island against Saracen and pirate raids in centuries past.

Occupying a converted powder house down in the square opposite the base of the tower is the newly established **Aquarium de la Poudrière** (June–Aug daily 10am–10pm; €5.50, or €6.50 combined ticket with the tower), where you can ogle the various species of sea life that inhabit the gulf, including grouper, moray eels and sea horses. Kids under 7 are admitted free of charge, but might find the *Jaws*-style background music and light effects a bit unsettling.

The **beach** consists of a pebbly cove south of the massive rock supporting the tower. To reach it from the marina, follow the little road that skirts the outcrop, cross the wooden bridge over the River Porto on your left, then walk through the car park under the trees. Although it's rather exposed and the sea is very deep, the great crags overshadowing the shore give the place a vivid edge, and there's some great snorkelling to be had from the rocks to the south of the cove.

Arrival and information

Autocars SAIB's **minibus** from Calvi stops in front of the Banco supermarket car park at Vaïta, but leaves for the return journey from in front of the tourist office. Coaches to and from Ajaccio, also operated by Autocars SAIB, run all year round, stopping at the marina and opposite Banco supermarket; note that the afternoon departure to Ajaccio leaves two hours earlier (ie at noon) on Saturdays. Tickets can be bought on the bus. From July until mid-September, an additional service runs to Corte, via Évisa, with Autocars Mordiconi. For more on these services, see "Travel details" on p.190.

The well-organized **tourist office** is down in the little square behind the tower (May, June & Sept daily 9am–noon & 3–7pm; July & Aug daily 9am–7pm; Oct–April Mon–Thurs 2–6pm; ☎04 95 26 10 55, ℻04 95 26 14 25, ⓦwww.porto-tourisme.com). Among the many publications on sale here is a particularly useful one for hikers, *Balades & Randonnées dans le Golfe de Porto*, detailing the best day-walks (*boucles de journées*) in the area, with extracts from the relevant topo-maps – a bargain at €2.50. They also hand out an excellent free colour leaflet showing walks around the Calanches and Capo d'Ortu.

Porto doesn't have a year-round bank, but during July and August a temporary branch of the Crédit Agricole opens on route de la Marine, opposite *Hôtel Cala di Sol*. You can withdraw cash against debit and credit cards from its **ATM**, but the one outside the **post office**, further down the road on the right, is newer and more reliable. Otherwise, the only place to change money is the small bureau de change at the Spar supermarket up in Vaïta (daily June–Sept 9am–noon & 2–5.30pm), whose commission charges are steep.

Adventure sports and boat trips

The clear waters of the gulf offer superlative **diving** possibilities, with a string of outstanding sites along the Golfe de Porto from Capo Rosso to the tip of Scandola. Moreover, these are explored by only two schools, both working out of the marina next to the footbridge: the École de Plongée Sous-Marine "Génération Blue" (☎04 95 26 24 88, ⓦwww.generation-bleue.com) and the Centre de Plongée du Golfe (☎04 95 26 10 29 or 04 95 26 19 58, ⓦwww.plongeeporto.com). Both run courses for beginners and will take out more experienced divers with their own equipment for €30–40, plus €10 for gear rental; you can also fill your gas bottles here. In addition, the Centre de Plongée du Golfe offers good-value guided **snorkelling** trips around the base of Capo Rosso and Scandola (€25 per person), and they have unsinkable **canoes** for rent (€27 per half day, €38 per full day), ideal for paddling into the hidden coves around Porto.

For trips along the corniche or up to Ota and beyond, **mountain bikes** and **scooters** are available to rent at the café opposite the Spar supermarket (€15 per day for a mountain bike, €50 for an 100cc step-through).

Porto is perfectly placed for the increasingly popular sport of **canyoning** (see p.49), with a range of descents of varying difficulty down the steep stream gorges of the Spelunca Valley. Corsica Trek, based at Marignana, 17km east of Porto (☎04 95 26 82 02; see p.178), runs guided half- and full-day trips.

Tickets for the daily **boat excursions** to the Réserve Naturelle de Scandola via Girolata, and to the Calanches de Piana, are available in advance direct from the operators (not from the tourist office), who run stalls outside their associated hotels in the marina. Working out of the *Hôtel Monte Rossu*, just off the square, J.B. Rostini's Porto Linea carries only twelve people (April–Oct: for Scandola and Girolata, daily departures 9am and 2pm, €32; Calanches de Piana evening cruises daily 5.45pm, €18; ☎04 95 26 11 50). The rival Compagnie Nave Va, operating from the *Hôtel Cyrnée*, just behind the tourist office (April–Oct: Scandola and Girolata daily departures 9.30am and 2.30pm, €32; Calanches de Piana daily 6pm, €20; ☎04 95 26 15 16), has a much larger boat, which accommodates up to 180 people. Compagnie Nave Va also runs longer excursions that take in both the Calanches de Piana and Réserve Naturelle de Scandola (daily 2.30pm; 5hr; €40). Tickets should be booked at least a day in advance; both boats leave from Porto marina.

Accommodation

Competition among **hotels** is more cut-throat in Porto than any other resort on the island. During slack periods towards the beginning and end of the season, most places engage in a full-on price war, pasting up cheaper tariffs than their neighbours to entice the straggling tourists – all of which is great for punters. In late July and August, however, the normal sky-high rates prevail. At this time, queues for the three main **campsites** often trail along the main road, forcing many visitors further north along the gulf, where a string of quieter villages and beaches – notably Bussaglia and Partinellu – harbour a handful of smaller hotels and campsites. All the places listed below are marked on our map of Porto; the rates quoted apply to peak season. In the unlikely event of them all being full, ask at the tourist office for their *Guide Pratique*, which for once is exactly what it's called, with up-to-date listings for dozens of hotels and rented properties in the area. You might also consider spending the night in nearby **Piana** (see p.172), an altogether quieter village with lots more character and better views.

Hotels

Bella Vista Above the village on the Calvi road, just past *Le Maquis* ☎ 04 95 26 11 08, ⓕ 04 95 26 15 18, ⓦ www.hotel-bellavista.net. Pleasant, well-furnished rooms in an old pink-granite three-star with outstanding views of the mountains and sea. Also fully equipped studios, and a good restaurant. Obligatory half board in August. April to mid-Oct. ❻

Le Belvédère Porto marina ☎ 04 95 26 12 01, ⓕ 04 95 26 11 97. This three-star is the smartest of the hotels overlooking the marina, with great views from its comfortable rooms and terraces of Capo d'Orto. Reasonable rates given the location. ❺

Brise de Mer On the left of route de la Marine as you approach the tower from the village, opposite the telephone booths ☎ 04 95 26 10 28, ⓕ 04 95 26 13 02, ⓦ www.brise-de-mer.com. A large, old-fashioned place with very friendly service and a congenial terrace restaurant. Rooms at the back have the best views. April to mid-Oct. ❸

Le Colombo At the top of the village opposite the turning for Ota ☎ 04 95 26 10 14, ⓕ 04 95 26 19 90, ⓦ www.porto-tourisme.com/colombo. An informal, sixteen-room hotel overlooking the valley, imaginatively decorated in sea-blue colours with driftwood and flotsam sculpture. ❻

Eden Park 4km north of Porto on the Calvi road ☎ 04 95 26 10 60, ⓕ 04 95 26 17 74, ⓦ www.hotels-porto.com/edenpark. Porto's most luxurious hotel is set in its own grounds above Busaglia beach, with a palm-lined pool, piano bar and gourmet restaurant. April–Oct. ❾

Le Golfe At the base of the rock in the marina ☎ 04 95 26 13 33. Small, cosy and unpretentious; every room has a balcony with a sea view. Among the cheapest at this end of the village (down to €35 in shoulder season). Open May–Oct. ❸

Le Maquis At the top of the village just beyond the Ota turning ☎ 04 95 26 12 19, ⓕ 04 95 26 12 77, ⓦ www.hotel-du-maquis.com. A perennially popular, recently renovated budget hotel; rooms are basic, but comfortable enough, and they give good off-season discounts. Advance booking recommended; half board obligatory July and August. ❸

Panorama route de la Marine ☎ 04 95 26 11 05, ⓕ 04 95 26 10 15. The cheapest hotel in Porto (down to €20 in shoulder season), with only five rooms (shared toilets) backing on to the marina. April–Oct. ❷

Subrini Opposite the tower ☎ 04 95 26 14 94, ⓕ 04 95 26 11 57, ⓦ www.hotels-porto.com/subrini. A very comfortable three-star right in the centre of things, but with peaceful, air-conditioned rooms. Ideally placed for the sunsets behind Scandola. April–Oct. ❸

Campsites

Camping Funtana al Ora 2km up the Évisa road ☎ 04 95 26 15 48, ⓦ www.porto-tourisme.com/funtana-alora. Too far from the village if you're travelling without your own vehicle, but a shady, well-managed site close to some quiet bathing spots in the river. Mid-April–Sept.

Camping Municipal Behind the beach ☎ 04 95 26 17 76. The one to avoid unless you're counting every cent: stony ground and grubby washrooms. June–Sept.

Camping Le Porto On the right as you approach Porto from Piana ☎ 04 95 26 13 67. Further out of the village than the other sites, but smaller, and with plenty of shade. Mid-June–Sept.

Camping Sol e Vista At the main road junction near the supermarkets ☎ 04 95 26 15 71 or 04 95 26 10 79. A superb location on shady terraces ascending a steep hillside with a small café at the top. Great views of Capo d'Orto cliffs opposite, and immaculate toilet blocks. April–Nov.

△ Plage de Bussaglia

Eating and drinking

With a few notable exceptions (see below), the overall standard of restaurants in Porto is pitiably poor, with overpriced food and indifferent service the norm, particularly during high season. There are, however, a handful of exceptions, notably *Le Sud*, which serves some of the most succulent seafood in Corsica. If you're here during the summer and fancy eating somewhere less hectic than the busy pizzerias in the marina, head for *Chez Félix*, 4km up the road at Ota (see p.176). Porto also boasts one of the island's top artisanal food outlets, Hibiscus, on route de la Marine, where you can taste and buy a range of authentic charcuterie, cheese, jams and alcohol.

Le Maquis In the hotel of the same name. Honest, affordable home cooking in a warm bar or on a tiny terrace that hangs over the valley. Their good-value €17 menu includes delicious scorpion fish in mussel sauce.

La Mer Opposite the tower ☎04 95 26 11 27. One of the finest seafood restaurants in the area, with fish fresh from the gulf, imaginatively pre-pared and served in an ideal setting beside the tower. Set menus from €23.

Le Sud Along the walkway leading from the square to the marina ☎04 95 26 14 11. Arguably the best restaurant in Porto, thanks to their strict policy of serving nothing except the freshest local food – hence the limited menu (if the local fisher-men haven't landed anything, you won't find fish on offer). Simple and delicious cooking from around the Mediterranean ("*cuisine de tous les suds*") served on a stylish teak terrace overlooking the marina. Menu at €23, plus wine.

The northern gulf

The D81 north of Porto, a thirty-kilometre sequence of hairpin bends around the base of Monte Manganello, provides breathtaking views across the gulf to the Calanches and Capo Rosso, plus the opportunity to swim or dive at a string of coves along the way. Autocars SAIB's Calvi bus travels this route daily, but hitch-ing is fairly reliable in season, with droves of visitors driving from Porto to the two viewpoints at **Col de la Croix** and **Col de la Palmarella**. Alternatively, you could also **cycle** up to these passes, or ride by scooter (see box on p.163 for bike rental details). Better still, head out along one of the wonderful footpaths winding along the northern flank of the gulf (see box opposite).

Bussaglia

An abrupt left turn off the D81 about 5km west of Porto leads to **Plage de Bussaglia** (Bussaghia), the longest beach on this side of the gulf and the first you can get to by car. A sheltered curve of grey pebbles hemmed in by steep, scrub-by headlands, it's flanked by a pair of seasonal pizzerias. The one on the left as you face the sea, *Les Galets* (☎04 95 26 10 49), is among the best places in the region for seafood, fresh pasta and wood-baked pizzas, with a breezy sea-facing terrace that's popular with locals and visitors alike. Count on €15–20 à la carte.

You can also **stay** in Bussaglia, at the very pleasant *Hôtel L'Aiglon* (☎04 95 26 10 65, ☎04 95 26 14 77; April–Oct; ❸), a large pink-stone building with a relaxing terrace, restaurant and comfortable rooms that overlook the valley; their tariffs represent excellent value for money for this area, except in July and August, when half board is obligatory. Further down the road towards the beach, the more upmarket, three-star *Stella Marina* (☎04 95 26 11 18, ☎04 95 26 12 74; May–Sept; ❺) boasts fully air-conditioned rooms with terraces and a small pool. Once again, half board is obligatory in high season.

Partinello

Beyond the turning for Bussaglia beach, the corniche road crosses a dry stream bed (site of a famous roadside spring) and snakes up the folds of the scrub-covered hillside to sleepy **PARTINELLO**, set high above the shore under a

Porto is well placed for day walks around the gulf. In addition to the footpaths through the Calanches de Piana (see box on p.171) and the route to Girolata from Col de la Croix described on p.169, you can pick up the **Tra Mare e Monti** at Ota, 5km east, and follow its orange waymarks north over the Bocca San Petru (914m) and down the other side to Serriera – a classic trail giving some great views of the bay and its hinterland.

The path begins at the end of the lane next to *Chez Félix*. At the first sharp bend you come to (directly above *Chez Marie*), head straight on until the tarmac peters out into an old paved mule track. This bends around the base of Capo d'Ota via a succession of folds in the hillside and, after around an hour, begins a stiff ascent of the rocky Ravin de Vitrone to an unexpectedly green, sheltered depression lined with mature chestnut trees. There's a spring, **la fontaine de Pedua**, to the right of the path just after it levels off. A further thirty minutes' walk through the *châtaigneraie* from there brings you to the pass, at which point the trail plunges steeply downhill, affording impressive views of the northern gulf's peaks. When you reach a motorable *piste forestière*, around 1hr 15min from Bocca San Petru, turn left and follow it into Serriera. The main road lies another half an hour downhill from the village centre; with a pack and boots you shouldn't have any trouble hitching a lift back along the corniche to Porto. Allow 4hr 30–5hr 30min for this route, not including rest breaks, and as ever bear in mind the potential ferocity of the sun, especially in the south-facing Ravin de Vitrone, which heats up like an oven by mid-morning.

A shorter two- to **three-hour round route** begins from Porto itself, at the sharp bend in the Ota road above the *Sol e Vista* campsite (see map on p.160). Look for the cleared, waymarked path running west through the maquis (to your left if you've got your back to the valley) along the line of the hillside. Fifteen minutes into the walk you'll pass the entrance to the Grotta di a Petra Sorda cave. After around forty minutes, the path then splits: follow the one dropping left, which skirts the base of some cliffs before beginning a steep, zigzagging climb up the Ghineparu ridge, where you pass the bottom of the old chestnut orchard that flows all the way down the mountain from Bocca San Petru. After around an hour-long ascent, the trail peels right (east) off the ridgeline, drops gradually, and then veers into a sustained zigzagging descent back to the fork in the path you passed earlier. Return to the road via the same trail.

Both of these routes are well marked and easy to follow, but you shouldn't attempt them without some kind of **map**: either the booklet sold at the tourist office or, better still, **IGN #4150 OT**, which covers the whole of the gulf, including the Calanches and Capo Rosso.

carpet of green woodland and maquis. A friendly, inexpensive place to **stay** here is *Aria Marina* (☎04 95 27 30 33; June to mid-Sept; ❸), below the café–bar in the village centre, where half a dozen immaculate, inexpensive rooms (with showers and shared toilets) overlook the vegetable garden to the sea. There are also a couple of interconnecting family suites on the lower floor that are great value if you're travelling in a group of four or more. The **restaurant** is commendable, too, with a gorgeous terrace overlooking the gulf. Their good-value €15 menu features tempting local specialities such as *cabri* (suckling kid) on a bed of *pulenta* and pungent grilled *figatellu* served with chestnut pâté. Seafood lovers should splash out on the €20 *menu poisson*, featuring ray's wing in lemon sauce.

On the south side of the village, *Le Clos des Ribes* (☎04 95 27 30 36; €420 per week) is a posher option, whose luxurious studios (which can comfortably accommodate a family of four) have kitchenettes and verandahs; these are normally rented on a weekly basis, but you may be able to fix a rate for a night or two out of season – if you call in person, ask at the newsagent on the west side of the main road.

Plage de Caspio

The next turn left off the D324 from Partinello takes you down a broad valley to the popular **Plage de Caspio**, a steeply shelving mix of pebble and sand backed by a bar, 3km from the main road. You can rent "unsinkable kayaks" (€10/hr) for a potter along the coast or follow the gentle footpath that winds northwest around the headland from here to neighbouring Plage de Gratelle (see below). The cove also has a couple of small *paillotes* in season: the cheap and cheerful *Punta Rossa*, which does a little budget menu (€15) and pizzas (€7–10), and the more serious *U Caspiu*, which offers pricier Corsican seafood specialities such as octopus *à la mode corse* on a €23 menu.

Plage de Gratelle

A more enticing cove along this stretch is shingly Plage de Gratelle, just north of Caspio, accessible via a narrow signposted road at a point where the D81 widens, about 10km on from Partinello. The deep translucent sea and superb views of the Calanches and Capo d'Orto across the bay, which glow luminous red at sunset, make this one of the most attractive beaches in the area, though it's far from a well-kept secret and gets crowded in summer. Behind the beach, the *Bar-Restaurant Santa Maria* has a welcome shady terrace where you can order chilled Pietra beer and a range of salads, snacks and pizzas. Most of its clientele are drawn from the **campsite**, *E' Gratelle* (℡04 95 27 32 01), just up the lane, which is busy in season though all but deserted in June and September. Set on a steep hillside amid crumbling olive terraces, it is one of the most pleasant sites in the area, with a very friendly *patron* who keeps a modest stock of supplies, including quality wines and local cheeses, in his little shop.

The Cols de la Croix and Palmarella

A short distance beyond the Gratelle turning, the **Col de la Croix** (272m) has a strategically placed *buvette* with a wooden deck from which to enjoy the views west towards Scandola. It also marks the start of the **footpath to Girolata** via Cala di Tuara (see box). **Col de la Palmarella** (374m), a further 10km north along a gradually deteriorating corniche road, gives another panoramic view of the gulf and distant hills, and is a popular target for cyclists.

Girolata

Connected by a mere mule track to the rest of the island, the tiny fishing haven of **GIROLATA** has a dreamlike quality that's highlighted by its proximity to the sea and the vivid red of the surrounding rocks. For hundreds of years its few inhabitants lived a reclusive life, surviving on fishing and hardly communicating with the rest of the island. Then, in 1530, drama struck, when the notorious corsair Dragut was taken prisoner here by the Genoese general, Andrea Doria, who captured nine galleys. Dragut managed to bribe his way out of trouble, though, and returned eleven years later to wreak revenge by razing Girolata to the ground.

A sleepy place of only fifteen permanent inhabitants, Girolata comprises a short stretch of stony beach and a handful of houses overlooked by a stately seventeenth-century Genoese **watchtower**, built high on a bluff above the cove. For much of the year, this ranks among the most idyllic spots on the island, with only the odd yacht and party of hikers to disturb the settlement's tranquillity. From June through to September, however, daily **boat trips** from Calvi (see p.127), Porto (see p.163) and Cargèse (see p.181) ensure the village is packed during the middle of the day, so if you want to make the most of the grandiose scenery, and peace and quiet, walk here in the evening when the weather's cooled down and the light is at its best, and stay a night.

The path from Col de la Croix to Girolata ranks among the most popular walks on the island, and with good reason. Apart from affording wonderful views of Scandola and the gulf, it takes you past a small pebble beach that's great for snorkelling and, ultimately, leads to the postcard-pretty village of Girolata, where you can steel yourself for the climb back to the pass with a drink at one of the café-restaurants catering for the day-trippers who travel out by excursion boat from Porto and Calvi.

In recent years, the route has become synonymous with (in fact, re-named after) the larger-than-life character of Guy Ceccaldi, the ex-legionnaire who walks it six times each week to deliver the post from nearby Partinello. Since becoming the subject of two often repeated French television documentaries, the white-bearded "**Guy le Facteur**" has acquired a celebrity status he little dreamt of when he took the job on a dozen or so years ago. These days, bus parties drive out to applaud his arrival at Col de la Croix on his post-office-issue yellow moped, wearing his trademark 1960s army motorcycle helmet. Having swapped it for a long towel to protect him from the heat, Guy poses for photos or heads off straight off down the path at zealous speed, depending on his mood.

Signposted from the *buvette* at the pass, the path is easy to follow (even if Guy le Facteur isn't). Having passed the Funtana de Spana **spring** after fiteen minutes (the last source of fresh water before Girolata), it drops steadily downhill to **Cala di Tuara** (45min), a flotsam-covered cove offering sheltered swimming. The water here is clear and, as it's near the Scandola marine reserve, rich in sea life.

From the north end of the cove, follow the path bearing left around the headland rather than the one striking uphill – it's more scenic. The trail keeps climbing for fifteen minutes or so to crest a low pass, and then more or less contours around the headland, revealing ever more impressive views of Scandola as it does so. Eventually you'll round a corner and catch your first glimpse of Girolata through the maquis, its Genoese tower and turquoise anchorage set against the red cliffs behind. Allow one and a half hours to reach the village.

You can either return by the same path, or follow a more frequented orange-way-marked route over the top of the hill. This drops down to Cala di Tuara in around 1hr. For the rest of the climb from there back up to Col de la Croix, count on another 1hr.

From mid-May until the end of August, it's possible to pick up Autocars SAIB's **bus** back to Porto at 5.10pm from Col de la Croix, or from Curzu at 5.30pm (May 15–July 31 Mon–Sat 1 daily; Aug 1 daily). As ever, it's worth checking the times before you set off, as they tend to change slightly from year to year.

There are no hotels in Girolata, but you can stay at one of two **gîtes d'étape** that cater for the steady flow of hikers through here in the summer. Located on the beach, *La Cabane du Berger* (℡04 95 20 16 98; May–Oct; €28 per person for dorm bed half board) offers a choice of accommodation in dorms or small wood cabins in the garden behind (these accommodate two people); you can also put your tent up here. Meals are served in their quirky woodcarved bar, but the food isn't up to much. The same is true of the other gîte, *Le Cormorant*, among the houses at the north end of the cove (℡04 95 20 15 55; July & Aug; €28 half board), which has eighteen dorm spaces and a small restaurant overlooking the boat jetty. Unless you're staying at one of the gîtes (and thus obliged to pay for supper), you'll be better off paying a little extra to eat at one of the two restaurants just up the steps. With a teak terrace overlooking the beach, *Le Bel Ombra* is the pricier of the pair, offering local seafood specialities, including Scandola lobster fresh from the *vivier*. *Le Bon Espoir*, next door, is marginally cheaper, offering menus from €17 to €25. Note that neither restaurant accepts credit cards.

Girolata also has a little **shop** (March–Oct) selling staples for the trekkers who pass through on the **Tra Mare e Monti** (an account of which appears on p.399). Among the most memorable *étapes* of this ten-day trail is the one leading north from Girolata to Galéria via the Bocca di Fuata; for more on this walk, which takes around 3hr 30min, see the account of Galéria on p.151.

Réserve Naturelle de Scandola

The 700-square-kilometre **Réserve Naturelle de Scandola** (Scandula) is thought to takes its name from the wooden tiles (*scandule*) that cover many of the island's mountain houses, but the area's roof-like rock formations are only part of its amazing geological repertoire. The stacked slabs, towering pinnacles and gnarled claw-like outcrops were formed by volcanic eruptions 250 million years ago, and subsequent erosion has fashioned shadowy caves, grottoes and gashes in the rock. Scandola's colours are as remarkable as its shapes, the hues varying from the charcoal grey of granite to the incandescent reds and rusty purples of porphyry, striking a vivid contrast with the deep greens of the maquis and the cobalt-blue sea.

The headland and its surrounding water were declared a nature reserve in 1975, so **wildlife** is as varied here as anywhere in Corsica. Dolphins and seals thrive in the area, which also supports more than 450 types of seaweed and other sub-aquatic plants – including a rare type of photosynthesizing grass that grows at a depth of 35m due to the exceptional clarity of the water here – as well as some remarkable fish, such as the grouper, a species more commonly found in the Caribbean. Colonies of giant gulls and cormorants inhabit the cliffs, and you might see the odd **peregrine falcon** preying on the **blue rock thrushes** that nest on the bare ledges. Ospreys, extremely rare in the Mediterranean, are also found here, their huge nests of twigs crowning the pinnacles; there used to be only seven pairs, but careful conservation has increased the number to 24. Rare plants native to Corsica grow freely, such as the sea daffodil (*Pancratium maritimus*) and the *Senecio cineraria*, with its distinctive furry silver leaves.

Unfortunately for flora-spotters, however, the entire reserve is off limits to hikers, and can be viewed only from the sea, which for tourists means taking one of the daily **boat trips** from Calvi and Porto (see pp.127 & 163).

Starting the return trip from Calvi, the first port of call is the **Baie d'Elbu**, last refuge in Corsica of Europe's largest bat. Two kilometres south of here lies the **Punta Palazzu**, so called because of the soaring rocky towers that spring from the sea like a giant palace. Over the course of the last thousand years or so, the seaweed here has formed a thick white band around the base of the cliffs just above the surface of the water – a rare phenomenon that provides invaluable information about the changing sea level.

Beyond this point, the boat weaves through the narrow straits by **Île de Gargalo**, an islet created from volcanic lava where the most westerly point on Corsica is marked by a lighthouse.

The southern gulf

South of Porto, the D81 winds gently through the Piana pine forest before entering the spectacularly eroded terrain of the **Calanches**. The village of **Piana** itself, 12km along the route, has this area's main concentration of cafés, restaurants and hotels, and lies within easy reach of several rewarding day-hikes, among them the ascent of **Capo d'Orto**, the mountain whose sheer northern crags tower above Porto. On the seaward side of Piana, the panoramic **route de Ficajola** connects with the D824, a refreshingly smooth road leading to **Plage d'Arone**, the finest beach in the vicinity. En route, you pass the start of the footpath leading to **Capo Rosso**. Crowned by a Genoese watch-tower, this distinctive sugar-loaf lump of pink granite marks the southernmost extremity of the Golfe de Porto, of which its summit affords a sweeping view.

The Porto–Ajaccio **bus** (see p.190) stops at Piana, and will drop you at the *Roches Rouges* café in the Calanches given a little advance warning.

The Calanches

The **Calanches** derives its name from the Corsican word for "inlet" (*calanca*), but it is the vivid orange and red colours of the wind-eroded porphyry, rather than the creeks in the base of the cliffs, that leave the most lasting impressions of this UNESCO-protected site. Liable to unusual patterns of erosion, the rock forma-tions, some of which tower 300m above the water, were described by Maupassant as a "nightmarish menagerie petrified by the will of an extravagant god", and have long been traditionally associated with different animals and fig-ures. The most famous is the Tête de Chien at the north end of the stretch of cliffs, but elsewhere you might come across a Moor's head, a monocled bishop, a bear and a tortoise. An old local legend holds that these fantastic forms were the work of the Devil, who created them in a fit of rage after a shepherdess refused his amorous advances. Unable to punish her pure soul, he conjured the shapes of his enemies from the fiery rocks, among them the giant representations of the shepherdess and her fiancé that tower above the corniche road to this day.

Calanches walks

The rock formations visible from the road are not a patch on what you can see from the waymarked trails winding through the Calanches, which vary from easy ambles to strenuous stepped ascents. An excellent leaflet highlighting the pick of the routes against a colour segment of the IGN topomap is available free from local tourist offices. Whichever one you choose, leave early in the morning or late in the after-noon to avoid the heat in summer, and take plenty of water with you.

The most popular walk is the one to the **Château Fort** (1hr), which begins at a sharp hairpin in the D81, 700m north of the *Roches Rouges* café (look for the car park and signboard at the roadside). Passing the famous **Tête de Chien**, it snakes along a ridge lined by dramatic porphyry forms to a huge square chunk of granite resembling a ruined castle. Just before reaching it you arrive at an open platform from where the views of the gulf and Paglia Orba are superb. This has to be one of the best sunset spots on the island, but if you do come out here late in the evening bring a torch with you to help find the path back.

For a more challenging extension to the above walk, begin instead at the **Roches Rouges café**. On the opposite side of the road, two paths strike up the hill: follow the one on your left nearest the stream (as you face away from the café), which zig-zags steeply up the rocks, over a pass and down the other side to rejoin the D81 in around 1hr 15min. A hundred and fifty metres west of the spot where you meet the road is the trailhead for the Château Fort walk.

A small oratory niche in the cliff by the roadside, 500m south of *Les Roches Rouges*, contains a Madonna statue, Santa Maria, from where the wonderful **sen-tier muletier** (1hr) climbs into the rocks above. Before the road was blasted through the Calanches in 1850, this old paved path, an extraordinary feat of workmanship supported in places by drystone banks and walls, formed the main artery between the villages of Piana and Ota. After a very steep start, the route contours through the rocks and pine woods above the restored mill at Pont de Gavallaghiu, emerging after one hour back on the D81, roughly 1.5km south of the starting point. Return by the same path.

The Calanches have long been the west coast's top tourist site, and the road that winds through its granite archways en route to Piana gets jammed solid with coaches, cars and camper vans during July and August. One way to avoid the jams is to view the cliffs on a **boat excursion** from Porto (see p.163). Alternatively, get out on one of the marked trails that fans through the cliffs, crags and pine trees (see box on p.171).

Piana

With its terracotta roofs and ochre granite houses huddled on a belvedere overhanging the gulf, **PIANA**, at 438m above sea level, is both arrestingly picturesque and optimally placed for explorations of this dramatic coast. Yet it sees only a fraction of the number of visitors who descend on Porto – a fact all the more apparent after the through traffic has died down at the end of the day. The village, or more accurately a long-defunct medieval castle 4km south, was the seat of the Seigneurs de Leca, whose rule came to a bloody end on March 29, 1489, when they revolted against Genoese occupation and were brutally massacred for their audacity, along with the entire male population. Two centuries elapsed before Piana recovered. Not until the decline of the Genoese was the settlement rebuilt and reoccupied. Most of the buildings that today crowd its narrow paved alleyways – including the picturesque **Église de Saints de Pierre et Paul**, venue for an Easter *Granitola* procession (see p.337) – date from the settlement's late-eighteenth-century renaissance, when nearly 800 people lived here, farming the vineyards, fruit orchards and *châtaigneraie* that formerly spilled down the hillside.

Practicalities

The views across to Scandola from the village are in a class of their own, and there's no more civilized a place from which to savour them than the terrace of *Les Roches Rouges* (℡04 95 27 81 81, ℻04 95 27 81 76; April–Oct; ❼), an elegant old *grand hôtel* rising from the eucalyptus canopy on the outskirts. Having lain empty for two decades, the turn-of-the-century building was restored with most of its original fittings and furniture intact, and possesses loads of *fin-de-siècle* style. The rooms are huge and light, with large shuttered windows, but make sure you get one facing the water (those on the opposite side overlook the car park). Non-residents are welcome to drop in for a sundowner on the magnificent rear terrace, or for a meal in the fresco-covered restaurant, whose *menus gastronomiques* (at €23, €30 and €46), dominated by local seafood delicacies such as Scandola lobster and crayfish, are as sophisticated as the ambiance.

On the hillside above, the more modern *Capo Rosso* (℡04 95 27 82 40, ℻04 95 27 80 00, ✉caporosso@wanadoo.fr; ❽) boasts still more impressive views and all the trappings of a luxurious four-star (including a large pool and gourmet restaurant), yet lacks the allure of the *Roches Rouges*.

Of the more modest places to stay down in the village proper, the faded *Hôtel Continental* (℡04 95 27 89 00; ❷), the old house with blue shutters opposite the Coccinelle supermarket near the square, offers the best value for money. It's a little eccentric and frayed around the edges, with mostly shared bathrooms, but the management is friendly and there's a secluded garden to the rear where the *patronne* serves breakfast. If it's full, the best fallback in this bracket is the *Mare e Monti* (℡04 95 27 82 14; April–Oct; ❸), on the Porto side of the village, which has good views from its sea-facing en-suite rooms, though be warned that the so-called "*vue montagne*" ones actually overlook the road.

For those on tight budgets, the *Gîte d'Étape du Belvédère* (℡04 95 27 84 03; ❷), on the west edge of the village, offers dormitory bunk beds (€15 per person) and simple double rooms (toilets *à l'étage*; ❷) in addition to ample **camping** space on a grassy terrace overlooking the gulf. Run by a Corsican-Russian couple, this place is quirky, but clean and great value given the location. To find it, follow the main Cargèse road for 300m until you see a sign on your right.

If your wallet won't stretch to a meal at the *Roches Rouges*, your best bet among the many little **restaurants** clustered around the square is *Le Casanova*, on the east side of place de la Coletta opposite the church. Steps up the side of a little stone building lead to a snug dining room where the €15 *menu corse* features a delicious grilled *figatellu*. For dessert, try their melt-in-the-mouth nougat ice cream with raspberry coulis.

Full listings for everywhere to stay in the area, as well as the handy leaflet detailing the local footpaths, are available from Piana's **tourist office**, the *syndicat d'initiatif* (June–Sept Mon–Fri 9am–6pm, Sat & Sun 9am–1pm; Oct–May Mon–Fri 9am–4pm; ☏04 95 27 84 42, ⓦwww.sipiana.com), housed in the grand Neoclassical mairie above the square.

Around Piana

Piana serves as a convenient springboard for two of Corsica's benchmark **walks**. The ascent of **Capo d'Orto** (1294m) – the massive, sheer-faced horn of granite dominating the gulf – begins just east of the village. To scale the region's other Herculean pillar, **Capo Rosso**, you'll have to drive west along the D824. Just after the hamlet of **Vistale**, a winding side road (the D624) peels right off the main road, looping 350m downhill via a series of tight hairpins to the **Anse de Ficaghiola**. Reached after a five-minute walk down a stairway from the road's end, the tiny jetty here, hemmed in by the bottom of the Calanches tumbling almost vertically into the sea, serves as an anchorage for Piana's lobster fishermen. It's possible to snorkel from a minuscule pebble beach to explore the base of the surrounding cliffs, but keep an eye on the swell and passing excursion boats.

The main reason most people follow the D824, however, is to reach the beautiful **Plage d'Arone**, at the end of the road, where there's a better than average campsite and a couple of well-situated beachside restaurants.

Capo d'Orto

From Porto, you have to crane your neck to see the tooth-shaped escarpments of **Capo d'Orto** (1294m), Corsica's most imposing coastal peak, which looms above the head of the Spelunca Valley. Its north and west faces, and those of the massif's subsidiary summits – Capo Vittellu and the Tre Signore – still harbour unexplored rock walls up which new climbing routes are opened every year. But the approach from the more gently shelving western side is a popular forest walk via an old paved mule track, with a final section following cairns over exposed rock. The main incentive to do it are the vast panoramic views from the summit, which even by Corsican standards are extraordinary, taking in the entire gulf and central watershed.

Free **maps** outlining the route are available from local tourist offices; otherwise try to get hold of IGN #4150 OT. Don't rely on the **water** sources marked on either, which can run dry in summer; bring at least three litres per person in warm weather. Highly exposed and largely treeless, the summit of Capo d'Orto is no place to be in a storm; even a light rainfall can render the easy scramble to the top tricky in places. In dry conditions, however, the route offers no technical obstacles.

The round trip from **Piana** takes about five hours. You can save yourself a dull thirty-minute plod at the start by driving 1.5km east along the D81: just after the sharp bend at the Pont de Mezzanu, look for a stony *piste* cutting off the road to the right, where you can park. Following the track along, you'll then arrive at a **football pitch**; walk diagonally across it to a little **footbridge**, on the far side of which you should turn right, as shown by a signpost. From here a well worn *sentier muletier* presses east up the right bank of a stream under a dense cover of pine trees. After 45 minutes, it starts to zigzag more steeply northeast up a side valley, reaching a low saddle pass, **Bocca di Piazza Monica** (910m), where you meet another path (from the *Roches Rouges* café in the Calanches). Head right at this first junction and keep following the orange way-marks east around the line of the hill until you arrive at another signpost point-ing the route left, over bare rock, towards the summit, visible shortly after. From the hollow on the far side of the pass, a long sequence of **cairns** threads a steep-ening route through the rocks to the top, reached after 3hr 15min from the car park. Allow 1hr 30min–2hr for the descent by the same route.

Capo Rosso

The spectacular red mountain at the extremity of Porto's gulf, **Capo Rosso**, is crowned by a little Genoese watchtower, the **Tour de Turghiu**, which it's possible to walk to in a three-hour round trip – a route rewarded by stupen-dous views. The waymarked trail begins 7km west of Piana along the D824, as indicated by a blue and yellow *conservatoire du littoral* panel. Passing deserted *bergeries* and stone terraces that until the 1950s were occupied in winter by shepherds from Piana, the path gradually steepens into a stiff climb on its approach to the summit, but involves no technical difficulties and should be accessible to anyone over the age of 9 or 10 in reasonable physical shape. The tower itself has recently been renovated and contains a small fireplace, which means you can bivouac in it and thus be up here for sunset, when the panoramic views, encompassing the entire gulf and Paglia Orba massif, are at their most memorable.

Plage d'Arone

Continue along the D824 for another 6km after the start of the Capo Rosso path and you'll reach stunning **Plage d'Arone**, where the submarine *Le Casabianca* (see p.197) made its first landings of arms and supplies for the Corsican maquis in February 1943. A memorial statue on the roadside recalls the names of the local *maquisards* and members of the mission from Algiers code-named Pearl Harbour who took part in the *débarquement*, which nearly became a fiasco after the submarine and partisans on land managed to confuse the date of the operation. In the absence of a reception committee from Piana, Captain Jean L'Herminier had to give orders to hide his cargo of 450 Sten guns and 60,000 rounds of ammunition in a ruined shepherds' hut, where it was later found and dispersed to remote sites in the hills. A interesting coda to this story is that, years after the war, it transpired that a patrol of Italian conscripts had in fact stumbled upon the cache, but elected to keep it a secret to spare local villagers the inevitable reprisals, and themselves punishment for having missed the landing in the first place.

Behind the beach is a large, leafy and impeccably clean **campsite**, *Le Camping d'Arone* (☎04 95 20 64 54; June–Sept) with a shop and path leading through the maquis to the dunes. If it's closed, you can ask to pitch your tent in a grove to the rear of the *Casabianca* restaurant, on the far right side of the beach as you face the sea. On a terrace overlooking the sand, they serve inexpensive wood-grilled pizzas, brochettes, fresh salads and a full menu of Corsican specialities and seafood; count on €17.50–25 per head for three courses.

The **beach** itself can get crowded in summer, but tracks lead through the rocks on either side of it to secluded coves. Snorkellers and anglers should head right, where the surfaced road leading down to the *Casabianca* forks, then follow the dirt track that plunges into the maquis at a sharp left-hand bend; ten minutes' walk further down this path brings you to a rocky promontory where the water is crystal clear and the sea bed shelves steeply down, giving glimpses of many kinds of fish and underwater plants.

Inland from Porto

The coast around Porto may be spectacular, but it's positively tame in comparison with the jaw-dropping scenery immediately **inland**. Slicing into the craggy spine of the island, the Spelunca Valley snakes from sea level to the **Col de Verghio**, draped in thick pine forests. Its defining feature, however, is the awesome **Spelunca gorge**, whose colossal granite cliffs can be approached either by the D84 or along the smaller D124, via the attractive village of **Ota**, the administrative centre for the area and the best base for hiking in the valley. From here you can ascend the gorge along an ancient mule track, pausing at the Genoese bridges and crystalline bathing pools en route to **Évisa**, a resort situated in the lap of the mountains, or less frequented **Marignana**, whose lively gîte d'étape is well sited for explorations of the wild country to the west. Both villages serve as bases for visits to the **Forêt d'Aïtone**, which borders the road to the windswept **Col de Verghio**, the highest point in Corsica traversable by road.

For those without transport, the Ajaccio–Porto **bus** passes through Ota. During July and August there's also a daily service to Corte that calls at Évisa before scaling the pass into the Niolo; timetables for these are available from tourist offices, or you can call the companies direct; see "Travel details" at the end of this chapter.

The Spelunca gorge

Cleaving from the coast to the edge of the island's watershed, the **Spelunca gorge** is a formidable sight, its bare granite walls, 1000m deep in places, plunging into the green torrent created by the confluence of the rivers Porto, Tavulella, Onca, Campi and Aïtone. The sunlight reflecting off the rock walls creates a sinister effect that's heightened by the dark, jagged needles of the encircling peaks. Not surprsingly, local legend has it that the gorge was hewn by the Devil in a terrible rage.

The most dramatic part of the gorge is best viewed from the road, which hugs the edge for much of its length, but you can explore some beautiful side-valleys and riverbanks by striking out on foot along the old path between Ota and Évisa (see box on p.175).

Ota

Isolated on a verdant ledge 5km east of Porto, **OTA** is dominated by **Capo d'Ota** a colossal domed rock whose overhanging summit looks like it's about to topple onto the village. Generations of kids here have grown up believing that the only reason it doesn't is because the rock is held in place by monks tugging on long chains. As a ploy to get them to eat their greens, the children are also told that the ecclesiastical strongmen are sustained in their task by spinach *bastelles*, or pasties, delivered to them each week by an old lady on a donkey.

If you're in the area to hike, this village makes a much better base than Porto. An overnight stage on the Tra Mare e Monti trail, it boasts two excellent **gîtes d'étape**: *Chez Félix* (℡04 95 26 12 42), where you can bed down in clean and cosy dorms for €9 per night, and *Chez Marie* (*Le Bar des Chasseurs*), just down the road (℡04 95 26 11 37), which is equally well maintained. Given the choice, however, the former has the edge thanks to its wonderful **restaurant**, whose terrace affords a sublime view of Capo d'Orto on the opposite side of the valley. The food is great, too – ranging from local specialities such as lamb stew and grilled veal or wild boar (featured on the €18 *menu corse*), to more adventurous couscous dishes – and their deliciously cool draught beer is more than welcome if you've just hiked up from the river.

Évisa

The bright-orange roofs of **ÉVISA** emerge against a lush background of chestnut forests about 10km from Ota, on the eastern edge of the gorge. Situated 830m above sea level, the village sees a steady stream of hikers passing through on the two long-distance trails that converge here, and makes a pleasant stop for a taste of mountain life – the sky is blue, the air crisp and clear, and the food particularly good.

Buses to Évisa leave Ajaccio up to three times daily except Sunday, via Sagone and Vico; the service runs year round, with a slightly reduced schedule outside school terms. Timetables can be consulted at most tourist offices in the area, or by telephoning Autocars R. Ceccaldi (℡04 95 21 01 24 or 04 95 21 38 06).

The best place to **stay** is the rambling *La Châtaigneraie*, on the west edge of the village on the Porto road (℡04 95 26 24 47, ℻04 95 26 23 11; April–Oct; ❸). Set amid chestnut trees, this traditional schist and granite building has a dozen smart, cosy rooms (with and without toilets) in an annexe around the back of the main building. On the front side, a pleasant little restaurant serves mountain cooking such as wild boar stew with *pulenta* made from local chestnuts. The young *patronne* is American, so English is spoken. The *Hôtel du Centre*, opposite the statue in the centre (℡04 95 26 20 92; no credit cards; closed 15 Oct–Jan; ❸), is a pleasant fallback, with small rooms but an excellent Corsican speciality restaurant on its ground floor; the €23 menu features the chef's renowned *sanglier* (wild boar) steak in chocolate sauce, and a melt-in-the-mouth chestnut *parfait*. Half board (€85 for two) is obligatory here from June through to September; if you plan just to eat, be sure to reserve a table before 5pm. At the other end of the village, *Hôtel l'Aïtone* (℡04 95 26 20 04, ℻04 95 26 24 18; ❸–❺) is a large country hotel with a wide range of differently priced rooms, swimming pool, and relaxing bar-restaurant that enjoys a reputation both for gastronomic prowess and its fine views; the atmosphere here is best around early evening, when you can watch the sun set behind the gorge from their terrace. Otherwise, there's the more modest *U Pozzu*, opposite (℡04 95 26 22 89; ❹), run by the same family, which has a handful of light and airy rooms.

Walkers overnighting on the **Tra Mare e Monti** or **Mare a Mare** long-distance routes (covered in Chapter 8; p.396), tend to check into the cheerful *Gîte d'Étape Sarl u Poggiu* (℡04 95 26 21 88; April–Oct; ❶), at the bottom of the village, just off the waymarked path. Bunk beds in its clean dorms cost €13, but most people opt for the half board as the food, grilled on a old oven in the garden, is excellent. If you're **camping**, however, you'll have to press on up the Col de Verghio road to the *Camping Acciola* (℡04 95 26 23 01), a small site with a café-bar and great views of the mountains and sunset. It's roughly 3km out of Évisa: take the D84 for 2km, and turn right at the T-junction towards Cristinacce; the site lies another 400m on your left.

The wild pine-covered mountains around Évisa and the Spelunca Valley offer inexhaustible walking possibilities, from leisurely streamside rambles to the dizzying ascent of Paglia Orba (described in the "Long-distance Walks" chapter on p.377). Most of the routes are well waymarked and frequented, but to penetrate the more remote areas you'll definitely need a copy of the area IGN **map** #4150 OT.

An enjoyable half-day appetizer is the walk to neighbouring **Marignana**, which takes you in a sweeping loop across the Tavulella Valley, through some of Évisa's decaying *châtaigneraie*. The trail, waymarked in orange, begins just under 1km southwest of the village centre along the D24, past the gîte d'étape: look for the *piste* heading straight on at a prominent bend in the road. From here, the clear orange waymarks will lead you down through the woods – which open intermittently to reveal great views of Capo d'Orto and the Tre Singore over the gorge – to cross the river via a somewhat precarious cable bridge. From here they climb up the opposite bank to the deserted village of **Tassu** and, once clear of the ruins, contour west around the hillside, passing some giant dead chestnut trees before emerging on the road next to the gîte d'étape at Marignana (see p.176). Allow around 1hr 30min for this walk, and the same for the return leg back to Évisa.

Much the most popular walk in the area, however, is the one leading from **Évisa to Ota**, which drops down to the Spelunca gorge via dense forest of chestnuts and holm oak via a cobbled Genoese mule track. Clearly marked with orange splashes of paint, the route is basically easy-going, though from Ota you may prefer to hitch back to Évisa rather than climb back up the valley.

To pick up the trail, follow the road west of the village as far as the **cemetery** next to the *Hôtel La Châtaigneraie*, where a path marked "Ota–Évisa" descends sharply over the lip of the gorge into thick maquis interspersed with pines and moss-covered oak trees. About one third of the way down the valley, you pass an eternal spring on the left where you can fill your bottle; from here, the path descends through an endless series of sharp switchbacks, emerging after around an hour and a half at the picturesque Genoese **Pont de Zaglia**, a row of alders leaning across the confluence of the Aïtone and Tavulella. This is a good place for a swim, and a side track heads northeast up the Spelunca from the bridge, giving access to less-frequented bathing spots. Hugging the left bank of the stream, the path then cuts through the rocks below the most spectacular cliffs in the gorge to the confluence of the Onca and Spelunca, reached after around two hours. You can either cross the road bridge here and head up the Onca Valley to a chain of beautiful deep-green pools that are perfect for swimming, or else turn left onto the road, follow it for five minutes, and then skirt the village football pitch on your right to pick up the onward trail to Ota. This keeps to the left bank of the river until it reaches another beautiful Genoese bridge, the **Ponte Vecchiu**, from where the path gradually ascends the north flank of the valley to the village.

This last section of the walk, between the Pont de Zaglia and Ota, is the most scenic, and makes a very pleasant, undemanding two- to three-hour round hike from Ota. Following the route in this direction (ie from west to east, starting at Ota), you should follow the main road past *Chez Félix* and the church: the path starts just below the road on the edge of the village.

Marignana

Eclipsed by more accessible Évisa on the opposite flank of the Spelunca gorge, **MARIGNANA** presides over one of the northwest's sleepier side valleys. The vast chestnut woods enfolding it give some indication of how well populated and prosperous the village was until the mid–twentieth century, but since then economic decline has squeezed out all but a hundred or so stalwarts. What lit–

tle work there is here these days revolves around pig rearing (this remains a famous charcuterie-making centre) or else the trickle of walkers passing through on **the Tra Mare e Monti** and **Mare a Mare** trails.

The route followed by both paths from Cargèse, a two-day trek southwest across the Bocca d'Acquaviva, was precisely the one along which agents of the **Pearl Harbour Mission** were led in 1942, having landed by submarine and made contact with local partisans at Revinda (see p.183). The Nesa family who sheltered them spent the rest of the war hiding from the Italian carabinieri in the forest and maquis, supplied by the villagers of Marignana. A plaque on their house just above the centre of the village recalls their contribution to the mission that would eventually give rise to an island-wide Resistance movement. More background to these events appears on p.174, p.197 and p.416.

In addition to the many footpaths winding out of Marignana to the high ridges above the valley, the main incentive to come here is the excellent *Ustaria di a Rota* (℡04 95 26 21 21; **❶**), on the village's northern outskirts. The **accommodation** – in large dormitories or half a dozen double rooms in a separate annexe up the lane (**❸**) – is a bit ragged around the edges and less appealing than the wonderful atmosphere of the downstairs bar and dining hall, where you can enjoy local charcuterie and specialities such as wild boar or kid stew and traditional *pulenta*. The views across the treetops from the front terrace over Capo d'Orto to the sea are great, too, and there's also a small concert hall where in summer the gîte hosts cultural shows and concerts.

For a full rundown of the many **walking trails** in the area, contact the owner of the gîte, Paul Ceccaldi, who runs an outdoor activities centre, Corisa Trek, and is a fount of knowledge about the more obscure paths hereabouts, as well as the best **canyoning** itineraries in and around the Spelunca Valley.

The Forêt d'Aïtone

Thousands of soaring Laricio pines, some of them as high as 50m, make the **Forêt d'Aïtone** the most beautiful forest in Corsica. Incorporating the mountainous Forêt de Lindinosa, it reaches 1391m at its highest point – the Col de Salto – and extends over ten square kilometres between Évisa and the Col de Verghio. Well-worn tourist paths cross the forest at various points, but human disturbance is not yet great enough to upset the balance of local **wildlife**, even if the Aïtone foxes have become quite tame owing to visitors feeding them. Wild boar and stoats thrive here while, high up in the remoter parts of Lindinosa, mouflon are sometimes seen. Birds sighted in the forest include eagles, sparrowhawks and goshawks, and if you're lucky you may spot a Corsican nuthatch, a unique species distinguished by a black crown and a white stripe over the eye. The most exotic creature to haunt these parts is a rare, large and savage cat known as a **ghjattu volpe** – literally "cat-fox". A few years ago, a haul of illegal game from Corsica was uncovered by French customs, amongst which one of these cats was discovered. However, sightings of the creature in the wild are extremely rare.

Some of the oldest pines in the forest are approaching five hundred years old. Fine-grained, strong and very resistant to weathering, the Laricio was highly valued by the Genoese for ships' masts and furniture, and it was they who first built a road down the valley to the coast, later upgraded by the French using convict labour. Throughout the nineteenth century, forests all over Corsica were regularly decimated, as the island has the very best specimens of this species, which only grows in forests higher than 1000m. When the British artist and poet Edward Lear came here in the 1860s, he noted with regret "the ravages of [the] hatchets: here and there on the hillside are pale patches of cleared ground, with piles of cut and barked pines . . . everywhere giant trees lie prostrate".

Théodore Poli was 20 years old in 1817, at a time when the French administration was conscripting young men all over the island in an attempt to curb banditry. A brigadier from Poli's village of Guagno, in an act of spite, neglected to inform Poli that he was due for national service, thereby making him a deserter – an offence on which the French were especially harsh. Poli shot the man in revenge and, in true outlaw tradition, took to the maquis, where his confederation of some 150 bandits soon elected him "Roi des Montagnes". A bandit constitution was drawn up, whereby Poli was named Théodore II, after Théodore I, who had briefly ruled Corsica some sixty years earlier. Hiding out in the Aïtone forest, Théodore and his gang proceeded to terrorize the neighbourhood, imposing a heavy "tax" on the rich and the clergy, while exempting the poor. Becoming ever more ambitious, these self-styled champions of the downtrodden poor whipped up anti-French feeling wherever they could, raiding the gendarmeries for arms and even gunning down the local executioner of Bastia when he refused to participate in anti-French demonstrations. In 1827 the Roi des Montagnes' rule came to an abrupt end – lured into a forest glade by a beautiful woman, he was shot dead by one of his many enemies.

One of the most popular short **walks** goes to the **Belvédère**, a great natural balcony giving magnificent views across the copper-tinted rocks of the Spelunca gorge. To reach it, look for the a wide lay-by on the left-hand side of the road, 5km northeast of Évisa. A signpost pointing left indicates the well-trodden route through the forest. Following the unsurfaced forest track that peels left a little further up the main road, you can also drop down to the **piscine naturelle d'Aïtone**, one of the more accessible bathing spots in the forest, where the river crashes through a series of idyllic pools and falls.

Col de Verghio

Forming the northeastern limits of Forêt d'Aïtone, **Col de Verghio** (1477m), gateway to the remote Niolo Valley, presents a bleak spectacle, its denuded hillsides scarred by centuries of deforestation and overgrazing. After the long drive up here, along an endlessly winding road scattered with pine cones and foraging pigs, the pass comes as a bit of a disappointment (not least of all for the bus parties of pensioners who pour into the windswept car park to find there isn't a toilet). From the *col* you can, however, strike out on foot along the marked mountain trail leading north towards the Bergeries de Radule, roughly an hour away. Minutes into the walk, the views improve dramatically, with vistas of Punta Licciola and the lower slopes of the red, wedge-shaped **Paglia Orba** opening up to the north. Keep going long enough and you'll eventually hit the GR20, which winds past a succession of translucent turquoise natural pools up the Golo Valley to the **Refuge Ciottulu di i Mori**, springboard for the ascent of Paglia Orba and the adjacent giant rock archway, Capo Tafonata. Accounts of both this stretch of the path and the route up the mountain, feature in the "Long-distance Walks" chapter on p.375.

Immediately below the Col de Verghio is one of Corsica's few **ski stations**, an incongruously ugly concrete edifice that sees few visitors in winter, as these days there's rarely enough snow to keep it in use. Desperate for customers, the entrepreneurial owner "re-directed" the GR20 through his establishment some years back with a couple of tins of red and white paint. His decaying hotel-restaurant thrived briefly until the Parc Naturel Régional got wind of what he'd done and removed the misleading marks. Since then, the PNRC has rubber-stamped the re-route, but the *Hôtel Castel di Verghio* (☎04 95 48 00 01;

May to mid-Oct) remains a blot on an otherwise beautiful landscape. Facilities here include a grim **refuge** (**❶**), housed in an adjacent block, with a fenced enclosure where you pitch tents (make sure you close the gate to keep the pigs out at night); an equally insalubrious **gîte d'étape** (dorm beds €15); and a spartan **hotel** (**❸**). The food served in the downstairs restaurant is nothing special, either, but the views over Monte Cinto and the Niolo from its huge fishbowl windows are magnificent. Trekkers can **re-provision** from the modest selection of groceries and other basic supplies sold at the bar.

The Golfe de Sagone

Long curves of sandy beach characterize Corsica's largest gulf, the **Golfe de Sagone**, which stretches 40km from Capo di Feno up to the Punta di Cargèse. The gulf lacks the wild allure of much of the west coast, with new holiday villages, bungalows and campsites springing into existence every year, but its resorts make acceptable bases for a few days if you have your own transport. Tucked into the Golfe de la Liscia at the easternmost indent of the gulf, **Tiuccia** occupies the most sheltered spot, with a fine golden beach close by. North of here, **Sagone** thrives as a centre for scuba diving and watersports, but it can't match the appeal of **Cargèse**, a lovely and increasingly chic clifftop village at the northern tip of the bay.

Bounded by a curtain of pale grey peaks, the gulf's depopulated **hinterland** is among Corsica's least-explored areas. Once past **Vico**, its only sizeable settlement, the main road splinters into a network of narrow lanes winding to near-deserted hill settlements, several of which feature on the **Mare a Mare**'s Variant footpath (outlined on p.401). The region, however, is better known among Corsicans as a bastion of extreme nationalism. It was a separatist group from here that gunned down the island's Préfet, Claude Érignac, in 1998 while he was leaving the opera with his wife in Ajaccio. The principal suspect for the murder, a goatherd from the Cargèse district called Yvan Colonna, is still thought to be at large in the hills above Vico.

Cargèse

Sitting high above a deep-blue bay on a cliff scattered with olive trees, **CARGÈSE** (Carghjese) exudes a lazy charm that attracts hundreds of well-heeled summer residents to its pretty white houses and hotels. The locals, many of them descendants of Greek refugees from the Peloponnese in the seventeenth century (see box opposite), seem to accept this inundation and the proximity of a Club Med complex with generous nonchalance, but the best time to visit is September, when Cargèse empties and you can wander around its winding, flower-filled lanes, dripping with fig trees, bougainvillea and palms, in peace.

Two **churches** stand on separate hummocks at opposite sides of the valley head: one Catholic and one Orthodox, a reminder of the old antagonism between the two cultures. Built for the minority Corsican families in 1828, the **Catholic church** is one of the latest examples of Baroque in Corsica and has a trompe l'œil ceiling that can't really compete with the view from the terrace. The **Greek church**, however, is the more interesting of the two – a large granite neo-Gothic edifice built in 1852 to replace a church that had become too small for the congregation. Inside, the outstanding feature is the **iconostasis**, a gift from a monastery in Rome, decorated with icons painted by monks from Mount Athos and brought over from Greece with the original settlers in the late seventeenth century. Behind it, the graceful *Virgin and Child*, to the right of the altar, is thought to date from as far back as the twelfth century. The frescoes lining the side walls were recently restored, giving the church a rather too vibrant look. Mass is held here once each fortnight by the local priest, Monseigneur Florent Martiano. A Greek-Albanian raised in Calabria and educated in Paris, Père Florent is the only Catholic priest in the world permitted, according to a papal decree issued by Pope Paul VI, to pronounce both Greek Orthodox and Latin rites.

Practicalities

There's an unusually helpful **tourist office** on rue Dr-Dragacci (daily: July–Sept 9am–noon & 4–7pm; Oct–June 3–5pm; ☎04 95 26 41 31), which can provide you with a map of the area and will help you find accommodation; it also sells tickets for the **boat trips** up to the Calanches and Girolata (see p.168), leaving at 9am daily in summer and costing around €35.

Buses running between Ajaccio and Porto pull in for a ten-minute pit stop at the *Bar des Amis*, in the village centre. Two services a day operate all year

---

The Greeks of Cargèse

Some 730 Greek settlers from Mani, in the southern Peloponnese, originally landed on Corsica in 1676, fleeing the Muslim attacks and persecution that followed the conquest of Crete seven years earlier. They came as part of a Genoese plan to weaken Corsican resistance by colonizing the island with different nationalities; the deal involved the payment of a large sum of money in return for guaranteed protection from any hostile Corsicans who might object to their presence. The Greeks were allowed to maintain their own customs, including their Orthodox religion (though they had to recognize the supremacy of the pope), but were forced to Italianize their surnames: thus Papadakis and Dragakis became Papadacci and Dragacci, two prominent names in the village to this day.

The first settlement was 4km northeast of Cargèse at a place they called **Paomia**. Within a year they had built five hamlets, proving so successful as farmers that they began to incur the wrath of the locals, who resented Genoa's patronage. Peace came to an abrupt end in 1715, when Paomia was ransacked by Corsican patriots enraged by the Greeks' refusal to take up arms against their Genoese benefactors. After much bloodshed, the Greeks were forced to take refuge in Ajaccio, where they remained for forty years until the arrival of the French brought temporary peace to the island.

Their deliverance came in the form of **Count Marbœuf**, an ambitious French nobleman who in 1773 attempted to integrate the communities by forming a united regiment of Greeks and Corsicans, and offered the Greeks Cargèse as compensation for the loss of Paomia. Unfortunately, the building of 120 family houses and a castle for Marbœuf again provoked the locals, who in the same year descended from the hills to burn the castle and drive the Greeks into hiding in the towers of Plage de Pero. In 1793 the Greeks were attacked once more: their village was burned to the ground and they had to flee to Ajaccio. Four years later, only two-thirds chose to return. Gradually the Corsicans came to join them in their reconstructed village, marking the beginning of an uneasy coexistence which, largely through intermarriage, eventually led to integration. In the nineteenth century the Corsicans built their own church, after which the Greeks built one opposite and adopted some Catholic rites as a gesture towards integration.

There are still three hundred Greek families in Cargèse, well assimilated into the Corsican way of life but still observing the Greek liturgy and conducting weddings in the traditional Greek style, with the bride and groom crowned with vine leaves and olive branches. Also distinctively Greek is the **festival** of St Spiridion on December 12, when fireworks light up the village, and the Easter Monday blessing of the village, when all the women dress in black, the lights in the village are extinguished and the villagers form a candlelit procession to the church.

round from Monday to Saturday in either direction, with an additional departure on Sundays during the summer. Timetables can be consulted at any tourist office, or telephone Autocars SAIB (☎04 95 22 41 99 or 04 95 21 02 07); note that services on Saturdays leave one hour earlier than during the week.

Cargèse is well stocked with **shops**, including a large Shopi supermarket just off the place St-Jean at the top of the main street, rue Colonel-Fieschi, where you'll also find a handy ATM. There are other **ATMs** at the BPPC bank just past *Le Continental*, at the Crédit Agricole on rue Colonel-Fieschi, and at the **post office**, on the lane opposite the Spar down in the middle of the village.

Accommodation

Ranging from mountain refuges a day's walk into the hills to beachside villas with their own pools, accommodation in Cargèse is plentiful and, on the whole, good value – at least outside school holidays.

The nearest **campsite** is *Camping Toraccia*, 4km north along the main road (☎04 95 26 42 39; May–Oct). Well shaded under olive groves, its best pitches are at the top of the hill, looking inland towards Capo Vitullo (1331m); they also have simple wood cabins that can be rented on a daily basis out of season (❷), or by the week from late June to August.

Bel' Mare 400m south of the centre on the Ajaccio road ☎04 95 26 40 13 or 04 95 26 48 24, ⓦ www.belmare.net. Twenty spacious en-suite rooms in a modern block, steeply stacked down the hillside on the edge of the village, all recently refurbished and with sweeping sea views from their balconies; the restaurant upstairs is also pleasant. A bit overpriced in season, but down to a reasonable €52 in June/Sept. ❻

E'Case Revinda ☎04 95 26 48 19. Wonderful little gîte d'étape, converted from an old stone farm, high up in the hills behind Cargèse. A waystage on the Tra Mare le Monti and Mare a Mare Centre, it's ten minutes' walk from the nearest road but you can drive as far as Revinda (see p.183): head north on the D81 and take the first turning right after the junction for the Club Med complex at Chiuni. From Revinda village, walk past the church and turn right at the crosspaths after 5min. Dorm facilities are spartan, but you can camp in the garden and use the self-catering kitchen. Superb views and walking possibilities. They also offer copious Corsican meals. Advance reservation essential. ❶

Le Continental Top of the village, near the turning for Plage de Pero ☎04 95 26 42 24, ⒻO4 95 26 46 81, ⓦ www.lecontinental.com. Mostly sea-facing rooms (with shared toilets) overlooking the main road just past place St-Jean. Clean and effi-

cient, but worth considering only if the other places are booked. ❺

De France rue Colonel-Fieschi ☎04 95 26 41 07. The rock-bottom option: a bit dark and noisy (the front rooms open onto the main road), but unbelievably cheap, even in August. ❷

Les Lentisques Plage de Pero ☎04 95 26 42 34, Ⓕ04 95 26 46 61. Very congenial, family-run three-star with a large, breezy breakfast hall and ten simple rooms (fully en-suite and sea-facing), set in the dunes just behind the beach. There's also a big pool. Good value. ❹

Punta e Mare Up the lane past the Shopi supermarket ☎04 95 26 44 33, Ⓕ04 95 26 49 54, ⓦ www.corsica.net/punta-e-mare. Secluded, unpretentious hotel tucked away on the quiet outskirts of the village. Ample parking and the rooms, though on the small side, are well kept. Handy if you're heading off on one of the trails. ❹

St Jean Overlooking the crossroads ☎04 95 26 46 68, Ⓕ04 95 26 46 27). Smart rooms, some with sea views, mezzanine floors and self-catering facilities. Rates down to €45 per double off-peak. ❺

Thalassa Plage de Pero ☎04 95 26 40 08, Ⓕ04 95 26 41 66. Among the oldest-established places in the area, this attractive hotel is set right behind the beach, amid swaths of vegetation. Hospitable owners, but no credit cards. ❹

Eating

Le Cabanon de Charlotte In the marina. One of the best places in the area for seafood, served in a wooden cabin with a raised deck and teak furniture overlooking the jetty. Menus from €15 to €20, or you can go for their fresh fish of the day. Starters include locally made charcuterie and

Cargèse's only Greek salad.

A Piaghja Plage de Pero. A well set up *paillote* slap on the beach, offering a range of moderately priced *menus fixes* and filling *bruschetta*; they leave you with a jug of quality olive oil to help yourself.

Le St Jean place St-Jean. A dependable, busy

hotel restaurant at the top of the village serving a wide selection of island specialities, grilled seafood, pizzas and salads on a roadside terrace.

Around Cargèse: beaches, watchtowers and Revinda

Much the most spectacular beach in the area is the **Plage de Pero**, 1.5km north of Cargèse – head up to the place St-Jean roundabout and take the left fork down to the sea. Backed by a couple of seasonal cafés and terraces of holiday villas smothered in palm trees, it's large enough to absorb the crowds that descend here in summer and boasts a better than average *paillote*, *A Piaghja* (see "Eating", p.180). An enjoyable **walk** leads west along the headland to the seventeenth-century **Tour de l'Omigna**, from whose ramparts you get a fine view up the coast to Capo Rosso. The path begins at the end of the road running behind Plage de Pero: pass through the green gate and follow the orange waymarks along a broad *piste* until you reach a rather smelly sewerage treatment tank. Bear left here and then follow a narrower path through the maquis, past a little *bergerie* and its adjacent oven and threshing circle. The route takes around 1hr 30min there and back, and is easy to follow. It's especially rewarding in windy weather, when the rocks north of the tower are great for wave watching and scrambling.

The other beach within walking distance of Cargèse is the **Plage de Menasina**, a pretty cove with turquoise water 2km south along the main road. Although only a stone's throw from the highway, it's secluded, gently shelving and well sheltered.

Plage de Chiuni and Tour d'Orchinu

North around the headland from Pero lies another broad sweep of white sand enfolded by a pair of maquis-covered headlands, the **Plage du Chiuni**, reached by turning off the main D81 6km north of Cargèse. The presence of a large Club Med campus behind it ensures the sand is usually crowded, but you can escape the watersports scene by heading along an old shepherds' track to the **Tour d'Orchinu**, which crowns the steep hill overlooking the bay. The quickest, though far from driest, way to pick up the trail is to wade at low tide across the stream at the west end of the beach and turn left onto the *piste* at its far side. With a car, however, you can drive the long way around: follow the lane back past the holiday village, taking your first left and then, 1km later, another left turn; ignore the *piste* running left 500m later, and instead bear right along the track following the stream bank, which brings you after another 1km to the far side of Chiuni beach. A green gate marks the **start of the path,** which is well cleared and waymarked throughout, although a stiff 172-metre climb. After thirty minutes of steady ascent through the maquis, you'll arrive at a col with a little ruined *bergerie*, just before which a narrower path continues up to the ruined tower. Scramble through the vegetation below the badly ruined *torri*, and you'll be able to look down on the little **Golfe de Topiti**, where the submarine *Le Casabianca* (see p.197) made its first historic landing in 1942. Chiuni was the intended disembarkation point, but it's just as well the sub's commander, Captain Jean L'Herminier, picked the wrong bay by mistake. Had the agents and radio operator landed where they should have they'd have walked straight into an Italian garrison camped behind the beach.

Revinda

The tiny hamlet of **REVINDA**, a scattering of half a dozen or so houses huddled on a high balcony overlooking the bay, was the place the members of the

Pearl Harbour mission (see p.197) first made contact with local partisans. Having crept through the maquis under cover of darkness, they ran into the local curé, Père Toussaint Mattei, riding his donkey at dawn to Mass. When the team explained they'd just arrived by submarine from Algiers, the priest sheltered them in the church until arrangements could be made to guide them across the mountains to Corte. A plaque on the wall of the tiny church records these events, which less than a year later would snowball into the liberation of Corsica. A motorable side road winds off the main D81 to Revinda, giving increasingly spectacular views of the gulf, though degenerating towards its end into a badly rutted *piste*. You can use it to reach a string of lovely sunset picnic places, or press onto the village proper from where a path leads ten minutes uphill to the **Gîte d'Étape E'Case** (see p.182), a gorgeous little mountain refuge and hostel with camping space and self-catering facilities.

Sagone

SAGONE, 13km east of Cargèse, was a bishopric and important fishing port until marauding Saracens destroyed the town in the sixteenth century. Today, however, the only evidence of its past glory is the cathedral of **Sant'Appiano**, a crumbling medieval ruin just off the main road 1km north of the village. The settlement proper comprises a string of tired-looking hotels and restaurants, slightly redeemed by the long sandy beach spread out in front of them. Despite its minimal charm, Sagone gets pretty crowded in high season, principally on account of the watersports facilities offered along the beach.

The resort is served by Autocars SAIB's buses between Ajaccio and Porto (see p.190 for details).

Practicalities

Accommodation is strung out along the main road through the centre of the village. *Hôtel Cyrnos*, next door to Immeubles Les Mimosa in the centre (℡04 95 28 00 01; ❹), is functional but nothing special – it is, however, the base for the Centre Subaquatique (same phone number), whose staff can guide you to the excellent **dive** sites around the Ponte Leccia, a headland with a sheer underwater drop of 80m. A better option if you're looking for somewhere with more character close to the beach is *La Marine*, an attractive stone building on the side of the Ajaccio road (℡04 95 28 00 03, ℻04 95 28 03 98; closed Jan; ❺). The best **campsite** in the area, *Camping Sagone*, lies 3km inland on the road to Vico (℡04 95 28 04 15, ℻04 95 28 08 28; May–Oct). There are plenty of seafood **restaurants** and pizzerias dotted along the highway, but for classier local cuisine, head 2.5km inland along the Vico road to *Le Ranch* (℡04 95 28 07 30), a country auberge where you can enjoy the best of local charcuterie and traditional dishes such as courgettes fritters with mint and *brocciu*, stuffed cabage and meat dumplings made with fresh *herbes du maquis*; the *patronne* offers a single set menu, priced at €19.

Worth considering if you're staying in Sagone is a **boat trip** to Girolata and the Scandola reserve. Departing from the *Ancura* restaurant at 8.30am, the trips cost €35 (half price for children) for a full day; the boats are narrow enough to penetrate several of the most impressive breaches in the red cliffs and sea caves around Porto, and return via the Calanches at around 5pm. Tickets should be reserved the day before (℡04 95 28 04 13).

Tiuccia

TIUCCIA, 25km north of Ajaccio at the northern end of the Golfe de la Liscia, comprises a ribbon of modern buildings strung around a half-moon bay.

It has a trio of minor historic sights – two seventeenth-century Genoese watchtowers and the ruined **Castello di Capraja**, seat of Giudice della Cinarca – but its strong points are the spectacular **Plage du Liamone**, a huge sweep of coarse, steeply shelving sand around the headland to the north, and the more sheltered **Plage du Stagnone**, at the southern end of the bay.

Autocars SAIB's Ajaccio–Porto **buses** (see p.190 for details) stop on the main road in the centre of the village. If you have your own vehicle, however, the best place to **camp** is the three-star *Les Couchants*, 3km out of Tiuccia on the D25 to Casaglione (℡04 95 52 26 60; May–Oct), which occupies an attractive site in fields overlooking the valley to the sea. Alternatively, head 3km south along the Ajaccio road to *La Liscia* (℡04 95 52 20 65, ℻04 95 52 25 29; April–Oct), another large and well-equipped site with a disco, shop and snack bar. It lies close to the largest **hotel** in the area, the *Motel Les Sables de la Liscia* (℡04 95 52 51 50, ℻04 95 52 26 12), a huge campus of pastel-painted concrete apartments and beachside pavilions slap on the beach. You can pick up rooms here for under €50 per night in shoulder season, but during July and August they're rented out by the week.

Vico and around

Vico, the old capital of the Sagone region, crouches in the mountains 15km northeast of the coast. Although there's not much to see in the village proper, its café-lined squares and authentically Corsican atmosphere may tempt you to pull over if you're heading inland, while the **Couvent St-François**, on its outskirts, may appeal to Christian travellers seeking a spot of tranquillity. To the north, the **Col de Sevi** provides fine views across the mountains, or you can strike east and visit the thermal springs at **Guagno-les-Bains**. For a really vivid taste of the interior, however, press on up some of the island's most winding roads to the dramatically situated hamlets of **Soccia** and **Orto**, perched on a ledge in front of the crags of Monte Sant'Eliseo, from where you can walk to the popular beauty spot of **Lac de Creno**.

The only public transport in this region is Autocars R. Ceccaldi's **bus** between Ajaccio and Marignana (see p.190), which goes via Vico and the Col de Sevi.

Vico

Dominated by the dome of La Sposata, **VICO** lies at the base of a high wooded valley, remaining invisible until the final approach. For two hundred years the village was the residence of the bishops of Sagone after their settlement was destroyed by the Saracens in the tenth century. It went on to become the seat of the Da Leca clan, a Cinarchesi family who ruled the district in the fifteenth century. One day in 1456, 23 members of this rebel family were put to death by the Genoese governor Spinola, who had their throats cut out on the slopes east of town, where they were left to die a lonely death. Gian' Paolo da Leca escaped this massacre and in 1481 founded the only surviving remnant of Vico's past: the **Couvent St-François**, a great white building encircled by vivid green chestnut woods and gardens, 1km along the road to Arbori. Worth a look here is the seventeenth-century church (daily 2–6pm), whose chief treasures are the carved **chestnut furniture** in the sacristy and the wooden figure of Christ above the altar, which predates the fifteenth-century foundation of the monastery and is thought to be the oldest in Corsica. The dozen or so monks resident here also run a **gîte d'étape** (see below).

Practicalities

On the outskirts as you head out towards the convent, the *Hôtel U Paradisu*, (℡04 95 26 61 62, ℻04 95 26 67 01; April–Dec; obligatory half board July & Aug ❹) is a serviceable, old-fashioned two-star that's part of the Logis de France chain. Its rooms are simply furnished but comfortable, and overlook the valley; there's a fair-sized pool and a restaurant on the ground floor. An alternative place to stay and eat is the family-run *Ferme-auberge "Pippa Minicale"* (℡04 95 26 61 51; ❸), at the junction of the D70 and D23 on the Évisa road. Don't be put off by its unpromising exterior: the restaurant's single menu (€18) features superb local cuisine made from ingredients produced on their own farm, including succulent lamb and herb stews and pungent ewe's cheeses.

Rooms at the Couvent St-François (℡04 95 26 83 83; ❶) are offered on a gîte d'étape basis, principally to walkers and those wishing to spend time in retreat here.

Col de Sevi and Renno

Aside from the obvious draw of the mountain views, a drive up to the **Col de Sevi** gives you an unadulterated taste of rural Corsica. By regaining the D70 north of Vico, you'll start the ascent along a high, maquis-clad ridge. A detour 5km along will bring you to the former chestnut- and apple-growing village of **RENNO**, spectacularly set amidst swathes of orchards and *châtaigneraies* – be sure to taste the marvellous pippins that are sold in summer along the roadside. At first sight solely populated by pigs and chickens, the village hosts the annual **St-Roch fair** (August 16–18), a traditional country jamboree which involves selling livestock, honey- and chestnut-related products, as well as the usual pastis-imbibing.

Back on the D70 it's not far up to the **Col de Sevi** (1110m), the pass that links the Liamone Basin with the Porto Valley. From up here there's a tremendous **view**, but for an even better panorama of the region, climb to the summit of **L'Incinosa** (1510m), the peak to the right (southeast) of the pass; marked intermittently by cairns, the route keeps strictly to the ridgeline, ascending 300m in only 2km. Don't attempt this climb in wet weather or when visibility is poor.

Guagno-les-Bains

The inland route from Vico, the D23, crosses the Liamone River at the Pont de Belfiori and continues east through a densely wooded valley dotted with tiny hamlets and animal enclosures, finally reaching river level again after 12km at **GUAGNO-LES-BAINS**. A couple of hot springs were first exploited here in the eighteenth century, when illustrious personages such as Pascal Paoli made the trip by mule to take a thermal bath. The spa was renovated quite recently and is open from May to October. Visitors stay in the village's one hotel, the *Hôtel des Thermes* (℡04 95 26 80 50, ℻04 95 28 34 02; May–Oct; ❺), the only three-star in central Corsica, boasting a pool, tennis court and gourmet restaurant.

The village lies on the magnificent variant of the **Mare a Mare Centre** long-distance footpath, whose orange waymarks you can follow for a lovely riverside **walk**. From the hotel, continue north along the D323 for 200m and cross the bridge; on its far side you'll see the markers leading left alongside the river. These will take you to a small footbridge and thence into deep deciduous forest – one of the best-preserved holm oak woodlands on the island. Having crossed a second footbridge (this one over the Liamone), the path then veers northwards up the steep spur of hill, easing off when it reaches a pronounced belvedere from where you can look up a roadless side valley towards the peaks of the distant watershed. Contouring around the south flank of the hill, the waymarks wind west from this point towards the *fontaine* at the entrance to **Letzia**, reached after two hours.

Soccia

A long climb up the side of the valley from Guagno-les-Bains via Poggiolo brings you to **SOCCIA**, one of western Corsica's most remote villages. Draped across a high wooded spur against a backdrop of blue-grey crags, it is one of the few settlements in the region with a healthy permanent population, a fact

Walk to Lac de Creno and Monte Sant'Eliseo

High up in the lap of the watershed, **Lac de Creno**, or Lavu di Crenu in Corsican, is the only altitude lake on the island surrounded by Laricio pine trees. Thus screened from the winds off the surrounding hills, it forms an oasis of green, dotted with clumps of scarlet lotus flowers and surrounded by grassy banks that make perfect picnic places. In high summer, this idyllic spot sees a stream of refugees from the coastal heat, but at other times of year the paths to it, from the villages of Soccia and Orto, remain relatively empty.

The most gentle and direct of the two approaches is the one **from Soccia**, which takes 1hr 30min–2hr (allow 2hr 30min–3hr 30min there and back). You can drive as far as a car park above the village, overlooked by a large cross, where there's a seasonal *buvette* serving drinks and snacks. Waymarked with yellow paint blobs, the route rises gradually from the outset, arcing northeast above the *bergeries* de l'Arcate, visible on the valley floor.

After around an hour you pass the turning for **Monte Sant'Eliseo** (1511m), a pyramidal peak and superb viewpoint crowned by a little chapel that's the object of a mass pilgrimage in August. To reach the summit, follow the path that doubles back to the right of the Lac de Creno trail until it reaches the shoulder of the hill, where another path cuts more steeply up the ridgeline (on your left), drifting steadily off the ridge before switching southwards for the final steep climb to the top. This extension adds around 1hr–2hr to the walk, but is well worth it for the extraordinary panorama, which encompasses a great sweep of the watershed peaks and west coast.

Back on the main lake path, the first landmark after the turning for the Monte Sant'Eliseo path, just after entering the pine woods, is the **Funtana di a Veduvella spring**, which can run dry by the end of the summer. The only dependable water source of the route is at the lake itself, another ten minutes' walk along the trail.

A much less frequented footpath to Lac de Creno begins across the ridge from Soccia at **Orto**. Although considerably more strenuous, with more than double the altitude gain of the main path, it crosses more varied scenery and yields right from the start magnificent views up the Fiume Grosso Valley to snow-flecked Monte D'Oro. The trailhead is at the top of the village, just beyond the old *lavoir*, or laundry tub. Note that the lake path has **yellow waymarks**; follow the orange ones that start close by (peeling away to the left) and you'll find yourself crossing the hill to Soccia instead of ascending towards the lake. After an initial climb through exposed maquis (hot work by mid-morning), the path drifts to the right, rising at a more gradual gradient through chestnut woods. A series of zigzags bring you to the ridge, where a **cross** flags the start, shortly after, of the path up to Monte Sant'Eliseo (see above). The lake path, meanwhile, continues left, contouring across the hillside to join the other route from Soccia. Allow 2hr 30min–3hr for the return trip from Orto.

To make a **day-long round walk** out of the above routes, string them together, beginning at Soccia, and, after taking in the Lake and Monte Sant'Eliseo, dropping down to Orto. From there you can follow the orange waymarks of the Mare a Mare Centre Variant back to Soccia in an hour, although to get back to the car park above the village you'll have one last climb to tackle. A worthwhile investment if you attempt this longer walk is IGN **map** #4251 OT, which highlights the footpaths in red.

attributable in part to the popularity of the walks to Lac de Creno and Monte Sant'Eliseo, which begins at a car park just above it. Even if you're not here to hike, however, Soccia, with its ancient stone houses, crisp light and sweeping views over the valley, makes an ideal target for a trip inland.

Run by a welcoming young couple, *A Merendella* (℡04 95 28 34 91, ℻04 95 28 35 03), in the centre of the village, is the perfect spot to stop for lunch. On a grassy rear lawn looking across the valley, you can enjoy plates of superb homemade charcuterie and cheeses, or go for their €15 menu, changed daily. The service is cheerful and the cooking careful and refined, using fresh local organic produce. They also have a few cosy, smart rooms (❸), in the building across the lane from the restaurant terrace. The only other **place to stay** here is the larger and less appealing *U Paese* (℡04 95 28 31 92, ℻04 95 28 35 19; ❸), down the hill on the D123, whose rooms, in a modern building looking down the valley towards Guagno-les-Bains, all have little balconies and views.

Orto

Just over the mountain from Soccia, the tiny village of **ORTO**, reached via the D223 from Poggiolo, stands in every sense at the end of the road. A dense cluster of crumbling granite houses overshadowed by the crags of Monte Sant'Eliseo, it harbours a vestigial population of pensioners, reliant on grocery vans and visits from younger relatives on the coast for their survival. The minuscule *Café de la Paix*, at the bottom of the village, encapsulates the essence of the place, its gloomy interior (complete with a mural of a very young-looking de Gaulle) little changed since the 1950s.

Most visitors who come here are walkers following the **Mare a Mare Centre's Variant**, which passes through en route to Soccia. Another waymarked path winds from the old laundry tank at the top of the village through the maquis and chestnut woods to Monte Sant'Eliseo and Lac de Creno (see box on p.187) – a less-frequented version of the popular day-hike.

The Cinarca

Contained within mountains approaching 1000m high to the north and south, the **Cinarca** forms the hinterland to the Golfe de Sagone north of Ajaccio. Once the seat of the powerful Cinarchesi, a family of corrupt self-titled nobles who ruled the country in the thirteenth century, the region is today renowned for its *appellation contrôlée* wine, produced near the banks of the River Liscia, in a cluster of sleepy villages along the **Route des Vins**. A tour of the Cinarca can easily be made in about two hours, passing through **Calcatoggio** en route to the chief village of the region, **Sari d'Orcino**, an appealing little place set deep in the verdant countryside. From here you continue through the villages of **Casaglione** and **Ambiegna** before returning to the coast road.

The villages

Two kilometres from the main D81, just over 20km north of Ajaccio, **CALCATOGGIO**'s bleached houses rise from a jungle of vineyards and orchards, creating a scene that's typical of the Cinarca. The terraced hillside location overlooks the azure Golfe de la Liscia, and there are more fine views if you continue for about 1km beyond the village and then turn right along the D101, descending to the sinuous corniche of the Liscia Valley.

The medieval **Cinarchesi**, a loose association of feudal lords, many of them distantly related, controlled wide tracts of the wilder southern half of Corsica, maintaining an especially tight grip on the Cinarca region. The most famous of these chieftains was Sinucello della Rocca, better known as **Giudice della Cinarca**, described by fifteenth-century historian Giovanni della Grossa as "one of the most extraordinary men who has ever existed on the island".

Born in Olmeto in 1219, Giudice began his career allied to the Genoese, but he refused to give up his feudal rights and become a vassal to the republic. Constantly battling against the rival Cinarchesi from his base in the castle of Istria, he managed to gain effective control of the whole of the south of the island, and at one point was able to summon all the region's lords and chieftains to form a national assembly before the Genoese eventually had him chased out of Corsica. Thereupon Giudice took up the Pisan cause, distinguishing himself at the Battle of Meloria in 1284, the naval engagement that was Pisa's downfall. After that he returned to the mountain fastnesses of Corsica to resume his war on Genoa and his neighbouring warlords.

It was during this period that Giudice (meaning "judge" or "governor") set himself up as a figure of public authority, arbitrating vendettas, forcing the rich to pay high taxes, and punishing wrongdoers and enemies with extreme brutality – blinding his adversaries was a favoured tactic. He consolidated his position by allowing a greater degree of freedom to the burgeoning peasant bourgeoisie than was accorded by other Cinarchesi tyrants, and married off his six daughters to local counts to ensure the continuation of his power. In 1289 and 1290 the Genoese launched two massive and unsuccessful attempts to overthrow Giudice, who by this time was nearly blinded by venereal disease, yet he was captured only when betrayed by one of his many illegitimate sons. Thrown into a common prison on the French mainland, he died of fever in 1307.

Dorothy Carrington, in her book *Granite Island*, recalls a popular folk tale concerning Giudice. According to the story, the mighty warlord, who started life miserably poor and hunchbacked, fell in love with a wealthy and beautiful widow named Sibilia, whom he asked to marry him. On receiving her refusal, Giudice threatened to abduct her, whereupon the lady asked him to her castle at Istria. But the invitation was a trap and on arriving there the young suitor was imprisoned. To rub salt in the wound it is said that Sibilia had him thrown into an iron cage in her dungeon and "paraded herself in front of him, in all her loveliness, stark naked". However, Giudice bribed the guards to set him free and soon exacted a cruel revenge. Capturing the castle, he took Sibilia in the same cage to a nearby mountain col and prostituted her to passers-by until she perished of hunger and humiliation. The story is mostly myth, but retains a few bones of historical truth: Giudice (neither poor nor hunchbacked) did indeed court a beautiful widow, Sibilia de Franchi, who had him thrown into prison for a reason that has been lost over time. When the insulted nobleman eventually escaped from her clutches, he restored his honour by committing Sibilia to a place that was, in the words of a chronicler, "less than honest".

③

Passing through Sant'Andrea d'Orcino and Canelle, two villages nestled close together amidst vines and fig trees, the road threads its way up to **SARI D'ORCINO**, a village composed of two hamlets stacked up the slopes of Punta San Damiano. In the second, Acqua in Giu, the parish church's terrace gives a panorama of the whole of the Cinarca, its green carpet of fruit trees sliced by the river, which you can see flowing into the Golfe de la Liscia. Just beyond the village, you can stop and **taste wine** at the Clos d'Alzeto, owned by Pascal Albertini (☎04 95 52 24 67; free); there are no set times, as a rule, for visiting. North of Sari d'Orcino, the D1 skirts a high rocky wall for 3km as far as **AMBIEGNA**, an elegant village bordering the Liamone Valley and a soaring pine wood. Head south from here along the D25 for 3km to **CASAGLIONE**, an ancient cluster of silvery stone buildings grouped around a church that houses a painting of the Crucifixion dated 1505. From here it's a gentle meander back down to the coast.

Travel details

Buses

The tables below summarize which bus companies cover which routes, how often they run and how long journeys take. Start by looking up your intended destination in the first table; then, using the company's acronym (eg ARC or SAIB), go to the second table for more detailed route and frequency information. Precise departure times can be checked in advance either via the bus companies direct, or (if you're French isn't up to that) the tourist offices at Porto (℡ 04 95 26 10 55) and Cargèse (℡ 04 95 26 41 31).

Évisa to: Ajaccio (ARC; 1hr 45min); Sagone (ARC; 1hr 20min); Tiuccia (ARC; 1hr 30min); Vico (ARC; 45min).

Porto to: Ajaccio (SAIB; 2hr); Calvi (SAIB; 3hr); Cargèse (SAIB; 1hr 15min); Col de la Croix (SAIB; 1hr); Curzo (SAIB; 40min); Galéria–Fango cross-roads (SAIB; 2hr 20min); Ota (SAIB; 2hr); Partinello (SAIB; 30min); Piana (SAIB; 15min).
Vico to: Ajaccio (ARC; 1hr 15min).

ARC: Autocars R. Ceccaldi ℡ 04 95 21 01 24 or 04 95 21 38 06.
Ajaccio–Sagone–Vico–Évisa–Marignana; Mon–Sat 1–3 daily.
SAIB: Autocars SAIB ℡ 04 95 22 41 99 or 04 95 21 02 07.
Ajaccio–Tiuccia–Sagone–Cargèse–Piana–Porto–Ota; Aug to mid-Sept Mon–Sat 2 daily, Sun 1 daily; rest of year Mon–Sat 2 daily. Porto–Partinello–Col de la Croix–Le Fango (near Galéria)–Calvi; mid-May to Oct Mon–Sat 1 daily.

The Ajaccio region

LIGURIAN
SEA

N

TYRRHENIAN SEA

MEDITERRANEAN
SEA

0   20 km

CHAPTER 4

Highlights

* **Ajaccio market** – Browse or buy top-quality fresh produce – cheese, charcuterie, wine and chestnut cakes – from around the island. See p.203

* **Musée Fesch** – The most important collection of Renaissance art in France outside Paris. See p.204

* **A Cupulatta** – Tortoise sanctuary inland from Ajaccio – a must for kids. See p.210

* **Hotel-Restaurant Le Belvédère** – Bird's-eye views of the gulf and central range, and great regional cuisine. See p.217

* **Plage de Verghia** – Silver sand and perfectly translucent water edged by pines. See p.215

* **Cala d'Orzu** – Totally unspoilt beach on the remotest stretch of Ajaccio's gulf. See p.215

The Ajaccio region

jaccio is Corsica's largest town, capital of the *département* of Corse-du-Sud and seat of the island's Assemblée Régionale; yet – with its palm trees, street cafés and yacht-filled marina – the image it immediately projects is that of the classic French Mediterranean resort. Modern blocks are stacked up behind the town, but they do little to diminish the visual impact of its warm yellow-toned buildings and sturdy citadel, set in a magnificent bay and framed by a shadowy mountain range. Unlike Bastia, Ajaccio makes most of its money from tourism, a fact partly attributable to its own attractions, to its proximity to the west coast's wonderful beaches, and to its having been the birthplace of Napoléon Bonaparte. The prime Napoleonic sites – the Maison Bonaparte and the Salon Napoléonien – are not, however, the best of Ajaccio's cultural assets: that distinction goes to the Musée Fesch, which boasts France's most important collection of Italian paintings outside the Louvre.

The **Golfe d'Ajaccio**, an ethereal vista of mist-shrouded mountains by day, is transformed at night into a completely different but equally evocative scene by the lights of the bay's sprawling tourist developments. Flung out at the northern tip of the gulf, beyond the hotels, the islets known as the **Îles Sanguinaires** are perhaps the most popular excursion from the town, rivalled by **Porticcio** on the gulf's southern shore, a ribbon resort popular with sporty Ajacciens. Of greater appeal to most visitors are the secluded beaches that punctuate this side of the bay towards **Capo di Muro**, ideal targets for a picnic and a swim. Inland from Ajaccio, the craggy **Gorges du Prunelli** edge the river as far as **Bastelica**, birthplace of Corsican freedom fighter Sampiero Corso, but an uninspiring village that owes its popularity to the nearby Val d'Èse ski station.

Apart from the train line to Bastia and a few long-distance bus connections, **public transport** in this region is confined to a few shuttle services past the holiday complexes of the Rive Sud, the gulf's southern shore.

Ajaccio

Edward Lear claimed that on a wet day it would be hard to find so dull a place as **AJACCIO** (Aiacciu), a harsh judgement with an element of justice. The town has none of Bastia's sense of purpose and can seem to lack a definitive identity of its own. On the other hand, it's a relaxed and good-looking place, with an exceptionally mild climate (the average temperature for the year is 17°C), a wealth of cafés, restaurants and chic shops.

Golfe de Sagone

LA CINARCA

Ucciani
Tortoise Sanctuary
'A Cupulatta'

N193

GRAVONA Bastelica

Gravona

Rochers
des Gozzi

Appietto

Gorges du
Prunelli

Station de
Val d'Ese

Golfe de
Lava

Alata

Tolla

D27

Capo
di Feno

Punta Pozzo
di Borgo

Bge de Tolla
Ocana

Prunelli

PRUNELLI

Chât de la Punta
Les Millellis

Ajaccio

Bastélicaccia

D3

Eccica-Suarella

Punta
della
Parata

D111

Campo
dell'Oro
Airport

Cauro

N196

Tour de Capitello

Col
St-Georges

Santa-
Maria-
Sicché

Îles
Sanguinaires

Golfe
d'Ajaccio

Porticcio

D55

D302

Plage
d'Agosta

Col de Belle Valle

ORNAÑO

Tour de L'Isolella

Bisinao

Plage de Ruppione
Plage de Verghia

Pietrosella

Port de Chiavari
Anse de Portigliolo

D55

FORÊT DE
CHIAVARI

Punta di a Castagna

Col de
Cortone

Côti-
Chiavari

D355

N196

Capo di Muro

Cala d'Orzu

Capu
Neru

N

0   5 km

Napoléon gave Ajaccio international fame, but though the self-designated Cité Impériale is littered with statues and street names relating to the Bonaparte family, you'll find the Napoleonic cult has a less dedicated following in his home town than you might imagine. The emperor is still considered by many Ajacciens as a self-serving Frenchman rather than as a Corsican, and from time to time their disapproval is expressed in a dramatic gesture – such as painting his statue yellow, as happened a few years ago. Napoléon's impact on the townscape of his birthplace wasn't enormous, either. Spacious squares and boulevards were laid out during Ajaccio's brief spell as island capital, but Napoléon's efforts did little to alter the intrinsic provinciality of the place, and Ajaccio remains memorable for the things that have long made it attractive – its battered old town, the pervasive scents of fresh coffee and grilled seafood, and the encompassing view of its glorious bay.

A brief history of Ajaccio

Although it's an attractive idea that Ajax once stopped here, the name of Ajaccio in fact derives from the Roman *Adjaccium* (place of rest), a winter stopoff point for shepherds descending from the mountains to stock up on goods and sell their produce. This first settlement, to the north of the present town in the area called Castelvecchio, was destroyed by the Saracens in the tenth century, and modern Ajaccio grew up around the citadel that was founded in 1492 by the **Bank of St George**, a Genoese military organization that handled the administration of Corsica. Built to intimidate the local nobility, who had been launching regular assaults on the oppressive Genoese, the citadel was packed with Ligurian immigrants and remained off limits to Corsican settlers for half a century. In 1553, the Corsican patriot Sampiero Corso took control of the citadel, having sided with the French, but within six years the former rulers had returned, inaugurating a period of expansion fuelled in part by an influx of people fleeing Moorish raids on the surrounding countryside. The town's population rose from 1200 to 5000 between 1584 and 1666, a period that saw the reinforcement of the citadel, the construction of a new cathedral and the improvement of the **port**, which by 1627 was doing a better trade than Bastia, at that time a far more important military and political centre. None the less, the infertility of the immediate hinterland kept many Ajacciens in extreme poverty and made the town reliant on imports of Genoese olive oil and wheat, while trading restrictions imposed on the town's merchants fostered resentment among the rising bourgeoisie.

Yet, when Pascal Paoli launched his first campaign for an independent republic in 1739, the Ajacciens stayed faithful to their Genoese masters. In 1796, however, the **French** finally prevailed, and the ramparts were demolished on the orders of Napoléon. In its new role as capital of Corsica, Ajaccio expanded more rapidly than ever before and maintained its economic momentum right through the nineteenth century, largely due to the success of the wine trade. Since World War II – when Ajaccio, a centre for Resistance fighters, was the first Corsican (and thus French) town to be liberated – the tourist industry has become the most important income-provider.

As the capital and seat of French government in Corsica, Ajaccio sustained its share of nationalist attacks during the troubled 1980s and 1990s. The most notorious was the murder in February 1998 of Préfet Claude Érignac, France's most senior representative on the island, who was gunned down while leaving the opera with his wife. However, separatist *attentats* rarely (if ever) affect tourists. The only outward signs of the unrest you're likely to come across are the heavily armed CRS police who routinely patrol the port and streets around the gendarmerie and Assemblée Régionale, and the façade of the Palais de Justice, which is periodically sprayed with automatic gunfire.

Arrival and information

Served by regular direct flights from France, northern Europe, and North and West Africa, Ajaccio's **airport**, Campo dell'Oro (☎04 95 23 56 56), is 6km east around the bay. All of the island's main car rental companies have offices lined up outside the terminal building (see "Listings", p.207), and metered taxis queue up here at flight times (the fare into town is around €25). For budget travellers, shuttle buses (three per hour 6.30am–10.45pm; ☎04 95 23 29 41; €5 one way) run into the centre via the train station and stop on cours Napoléon, the main street – buy your ticket on the bus and stamp it in the machine behind the driver's cab.

Long-distance buses pull in at the bus station (**terminal routière/gare maritime**), next to the port de Commerce, a five-minute walk from the centre. Ferries from the mainland also dock in this gleaming modern complex, where you'll find Ajaccio's least expensive left-luggage facility (€1.80 per article per day, but closed due to security threats last time we checked), a bureau de change, and the cleanest **public toilets** in town. The SNCF **train station** (☎04 95 23 11 03), however, lies almost 1km north along boulevard Sampiero, a continuation of the quai l'Herminier.

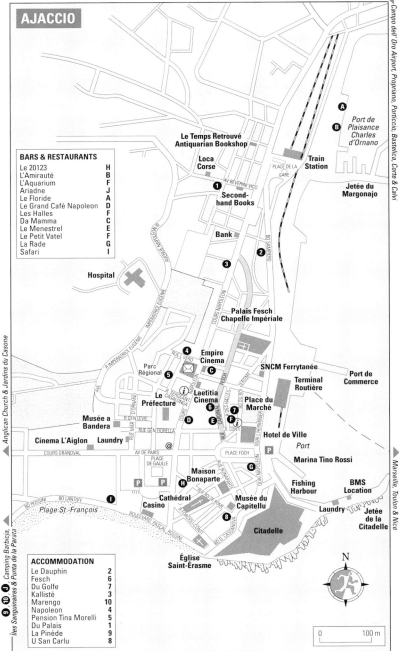

AJACCIO

Les Millelli & Camping Les Mimosas

Campo dell'Oro Airport, Propriano, Porticcio, Bastelica, Corte & Calvi

Anglican Church & Jardins du Casone

Camping Barbicaja, Îles Sanguinaires & Punta de la Parata

Marseille, Toulon & Nice

BARS & RESTAURANTS

Le 20123	H
L'Amirauté	B
L'Aquarium	F
Ariadne	J
Le Floride	A
Le Grand Café Napoleon	D
Les Halles	F
Da Mamma	C
Le Menestrel	E
Le Petit Vatel	F
La Rade	G
Safari	I

ACCOMMODATION

Le Dauphin	2
Fesch	6
Du Golfe	7
Kallisté	3
Marengo	10
Napoleon	4
Pension Tina Morelli	5
Du Palais	1
La Pinède	9
U San Carlu	8

Le Temps Retrouvé
Antiquarian Bookshop

Loca Corse

Second-hand Books

Bank

Hospital

Palais Fesch
Chapelle Impériale

Empire Cinema

SNCM Ferrytanée

Port de Commerce

Terminal Routière

Parc Régional

Laetitia Cinema

Le Préfecture

Place du Marché

Musée a Bandera

Cinema L'Aiglon

Laundry

Hotel de Ville

Port

Marina Tino Rossi

Maison Bonaparte

Place de Gaulle

BMS Location

Cathédral
Casino

Musée du Capitellu

Fishing Harbour

Laundry

Jetée de la Citadelle

Plage St-François

Citadelle

Église Saint-Érasme

Port de Plaisance
Charles d'Ornano

Train Station

Jetée du Margonajo

Place de la Gare

N

0   100 m

Car parking is a nightmare year round. You'll spare yourself a stressful tour of the town's one-way system by stumping up the fee for one of the large *parkings* on quai l'Herminier, close to the Hôtel de Ville, or under place du Diamant/place de Gaulle. Alternatively, head straight through the centre and west along the route des Îles Sanguinaires: there's nearly always plenty of (unshaded) space outside the cemetery, from where you can jump on a municipal bus back to the centre.

The **tourist office** on place du Marché, behind the Hôtel de Ville (May, June, Sept & April Mon–Sat 8am–7pm, Sun 9am–1pm; July & Aug Mon–Sat 8am–8.30pm, Sun 9am–1pm & 4–7pm; Oct–March Mon–Fri 8.30am–6pm, Sat 8.30am–noon; ℡04 95 51 53 03, ⓦwww.tourisme.fr/ajaccio), hands out large free glossy maps and has timetables for checking departure times. Anyone planning a long-distance hike should head for the office of the **Parc Naturel Régional Corse** (or PNRC), 2 rue Sergeant-Casalonga, around the corner

Le Casabianca

The long quayside connecting Ajaccio's two pleasure ports, where ferries and cruise liners today dock, was the scene of Corsica's most glorious hour in World War II, when it became the first patch of Metropolitan France to be liberated from occupation by Axis forces. On September 14, 1943, the submarine **Le Casabianca**, under the command of **Capitain du Vaisseau Jean L'Herminier**, sailed into the harbour from Algiers with 109 troops from the élite Bataillon de Choc. Witnessed by a jubilant crowd, it was the culmination of an extraordinary year for the submarine and its crew.

The 1500-tonne vessel was named after 12-year-old Giocante de Casabianca, who died at Aboukir in 1798 when he refused to leave his father's ship after it had been attacked by Nelson (giving Felicia Hemans her inspiration for the poem beginning "The boy stood on the burning deck . . . "). Having narrowly escaped the scuttle of the French fleet at Toulon, Le Casabianca limped across the Mediterranean to Algiers, where its commander petitioned naval bigwigs for useful employment (an uphill task as its torpedo tubes had been irreparably damaged).

In the end, the sub's cumbersome size and impaired state were to prove its greatest assets. Unable to free more serviceable vessels from the Mediterranean theatre, allied naval command asked L'Herminier to run secret missions to Corsica, where a Resistance network was to be established ahead of the Allied invasion.

Following a successful first landing of agents at Topiti creek, near Cargèse on the west coast (the famous "Pearl Harbour" mission, see p.174), *Le Casabianca* completed six further *débarquements*, dropping men, arms, munitions, supplies, money and radios, later deployed to transmit radio intelligence on the movements of occupying forces and, following the Italian armistice, mount attacks on the retreating German army.

The audacity with which the commander approached the Corsican coast under cover of darkness, hiding until the dead of night on the sea bed and resurfacing to dispatch the submarine's cargo using perilously unstable rubber boats, made L'Herminier a war hero. His memoirs, published as *Le Casabianca*, were a best-seller in the 1950s and remain in print to this day, while streets and the quayside where he landed in Ajaccio in September 1943 have been renamed in his honour.

The last vestiges of the submarine itself, however, have fared less well. Formerly installed within the courtyard of the Governor's Palace in Bastia, the conning tower was scrapped in 1999 and removed to the Air Force base at Solenzara where it now languishes in rusting obscurity – much to the chagrin of local *anciens combattants*, who are campaigning to have it restored to its rightful pride of place in front of Bastia museum.

from the *préfecture* on cours Napoléon (Mon–Fri 8am–noon & 2–6pm; ☎04 95 51 79 00), where you can buy topo-guides, maps, guidebooks and leaflets detailing regional trail networks, and check the latest weather reports for the mountains. They are also a good source of advice on how to combine different stages of their long-distance footpaths, and will help you sort out gîte d'étape accommodation and transport to the trailheads.

Accommodation

Ajaccio suffers from a dearth of inexpensive **accommodation**, but there are a fair number of mid- and upscale places scattered around town, chiefly along cours Napoléon and the coast road leading to the Îles Sanguinaires. Whatever your budget, it's essential to **book ahead**, especially for weekends between late May and September, when beds are virtually impossible to come by at short notice. All those places listed below are open year-round unless specified otherwise.

Hotels

Le Dauphin 11 bd Sampiero ☎04 95 21 12 94, ☏04 95 21 88 69. No-frills place opposite the port de Commerce, above a bar that's straight out of a French *policier*, complete with wide-screen TV, pinball machine and old men sipping pastis under a cloud of Gauloise smoke. Various categories of rooms, some on the grotty side for the price, but their budget options in an adjacent building (with shared showers and toilets) are among the cheapest beds in town (at €50 per double most of the year). Tariff includes breakfast. ④

Fesch 7 rue Cardinal-Fesch ☎04 95 51 62 62, ☏04 95 21 83 36. One of the oldest-established hotels in Ajaccio, and famous as the site of a (bloodless) armed siege in 1980, when it was occupied by fugitive nationalist guerrillas and their French secret service hostages. Following a recent re-fit, all rooms are bright and modern with air-con and TVs; balconies cost extra. ⑤

Du Golfe 5 bd du Roi-Jérôme ☎04 95 21 47 64, ☏04 95 21 71 05, ⊛www.hoteldugolfe.com. Large, well-appointed three-star whose slightly pricier (sound-proofed) front rooms overlook the market square and bay. Reasonable value given the location, and handy for ferry port, bus & train stations. ⑤

Kallisté 51 cours Napoléon ☎04 95 51 34 45, ☏04 95 21 79 00, ⊛www.cyrnos.net. Recently revamped third-floor hotel right in the centre, with plenty of parking space. Sound-proofed rooms for up to four people, all with cable TVs and bathrooms. Internet facilties in lobby, and the staff speak English. The best choice in this category. ④

Marengo 12 bd Mme-Mère ☎04 95 21 43 66, ☏04 95 21 51 26. A ten-minute walk west of the centre, up a quiet side-street off bd Mme-Mère. Slightly boxed in by tower blocks, but a secluded, quiet and pleasant small hotel (with only 16 rooms) away from the city bustle. Open mid-March to mid-Nov. ③

Napoléon 4 Lorenzo Vero ☎04 95 51 54 00, ☏04 95 21 80 40, ⊛www.hotel-napoleon-ajaccio.com. Characterless three-star tucked just off cours Napoléon. The rooms are dark and on the small side – a bit of a squeeze for three but comfortable enough as doubles. ⑥

Pension Tina Morelli 1 rue Lambroschini ☎04 95 21 16 97. Old-style French B&B, on the first and fourth floors of a dark tenement off cours Napoléon. Basic comforts, but at €45 for demi-pension (obligatory), you'll not find anywhere cheaper to stay and eat in the town centre. Book well ahead as it's invariably full. No credit cards. ②

Du Palais 5 av Bévérini-Vico ☎04 95 22 73 68. Comfortable mid-scale place, a 10min walk north of the centre, within easy reach of the train station. The rooms are on the small side and most have shared bathrooms, but they're impeccably clean; count on €20 extra for en-suite, and ask for one at the rear of the building if you want peace and quiet. ④

La Pinède route des Sanguinaires ☎04 95 52 00 44, ☏04 95 52 09 48. Most secluded and peaceful of the swish star hotels out towards Les Îles Sanguinaires, 4km west of the town centre. It's 300m from the beach (up a narrow lane signposted right off the main road as you head out of town), but with great views of the gulf, a large pool and tennis court. ⑧

U San Carlu 8 bd Danielle-Casanova ☎04 95 21 13 84, ☏04 95 21 09 99. Sited opposite the citadel and close to the beach, this three-star hotel is the poshest option in the old town. Well-appointed rooms, own parking facilities, and a special room for disabled guests in the basement. ⑥

Campsites

Le Barbicaja 4.5km west along the route des Sanguinaires ☎04 95 52 01 17. Crowded site, but close to the beach and easier to reach by bus (#5 from place de Gaulle) than *Les Mimosas*. Open April–Oct.

Les Mimosas 3km northwest of town ☎ 04 95 20 99 85, ℗ 04 95 10 01 77. A shady and well-organized site with clean toilet blocks, friendly management and fair rates. It's a long trudge if you're loaded with luggage so take a taxi which should cost around €12–15. Open May–Oct.

The Town

The core of the old town holds the most interest in Ajaccio: a cluster of ancient streets spreading north and south of **place Foch,** which opens out onto the seafront by the port and the marina Tino Rossi. Nearby **place de Gaulle** forms the town centre and is the source of the main thoroughfare, **cours Napoléon**, which extends parallel to the sea almost 2km to the northeast. Lined with chic boutiques, stores and brassy cafés, this is Ajaccio at its posiest – an endless procession of designer clothes, clipped poodles and huge motor-bikes. West of place de Gaulle is the town beach where Ajaccio's beau monde top up their tans, overlooked from the north by the honey-coloured citadel.

If you're intending to work your way around all of the town's museums and galleries, it's worth investing in a **Passemusée**. Costing €10, the pass covers the six main sights and is valid for seven days; you can buy them at the tourist office and at the admission desks of the museums themselves.

Around place de Gaulle and the new town

Place de Gaulle – otherwise known as place du Diamant, after the Diamanti family who once owned much of the property in Ajaccio – is the most useful point of orientation, even if it's not much to look at, being just a windy concrete platform surrounded by a shopping complex. The only noteworthy thing on the square is the huge **bronze statue** of Napoléon at the southern end: nicknamed *L'Encrier* (The Inkstand), this pompous lump was commissioned by Napoléon III in 1865, and shows Napoléon clad in Roman garb on horseback, surrounded by his four brothers.

The only museum in this part of town, **A Bandera**, is a short way north of the square, in rue Général-Levie, behind the *préfecture* (May–Sept Mon–Sat 10am–noon & 3–7pm; Oct–April Mon–Fri 9am–noon & 2–6pm; €3.85). Scruffy and underfunded, this small military museum houses few objects of note, and is only likely to be of interest if your French is up to the lengthy written explanations that accompany the pictorial exhibits. An English guide may be borrowed from the desk when you buy your ticket, but this translates only a fraction of the material set out on the walls.

The first room is devoted to prehistoric times, with a model of a Bronze Age settlement or *castellu* alongside bronze daggers and pottery fragments; the more interesting second room deals with the Moorish raids, displaying beautiful ivory-handled stilettos (small daggers) and several pictures of flamboyantly dressed corsairs. Among them is the notorious Dragut, a Moorish pirate who allied himself with the French during the campaign of 1553, when Sampiero Corso recaptured Corsica from the Genoese. The Wars of Independence are covered in the third room, featuring statutes drafted by Pascal Paoli and Sir Gilbert Elliot during the Anglo-Corsican alliance of 1794–96. The last room has a section on World War II and the Corsican Resistance, though the highlights are the press cuttings and photos presenting the island's **bandits** as genial, popular, local heroes and showing notorious figures such as Spada hobnobbing with aristocratic ladies in forest glades.

Devotees of Napoléon should take a stroll 1km up cours Grandval, the wide street rising west of place de Gaulle and ending in a square, the **Jardins du Casone**, where gaudily spectacular son et lumière shows take place in summer.

On the way you'll pass the **Assemblée Nationale**, an enormous yellow Art Deco building fronted by a jungle of palms and a couple of armoured police vans. An impressive **monument** to Napoléon dominates the square – a replica of the statue at Napoléon's burial place, Les Invalides in Paris, standing atop a huge pedestal inscribed with the names of his battles. Behind the monument lies a graffiti-bedaubed **cave** where Napoléon is supposed to have frolicked as a child.

Place Foch

Once the site of the town's medieval gate, **place Foch** lies at the heart of old Ajaccio. A delightfully shady square sloping down to the sea and lined with cafés and restaurants, it gets its local name – place des Palmiers – from the row of mature palms bordering the central strip. Dominating the top end, a fountain of four marble lions provides a mount for the inevitable statue of Napoléon, this one by Ajaccien sculptor Maglioli. A humbler effigy occupies a niche high on a wall south of the fountain, above a souvenir shop – a figurine of Ajaccio's patron saint, **La Madonnuccia**, her base bearing the text *Poserunt me custodem* ("They have made me their guardian"). The image dates from 1656, a year in which Ajaccio's local council, fearful of infection from plague-struck Genoa, placed the town under the guardianship of the Madonna in a ceremony that took place on this spot. Ajaccio was saved on that occasion and again in 1745, when *La Madonnuccia* was paraded around the ramparts to dispel the Anglo-Sardinian fleet bombarding the city – whereupon the enemy beat a miraculous speedy retreat. If you're here on March 18 you can witness Ajaccio's big event, the **Fête de la Miséricorde**, in which the statue is conveyed through the old town as a prelude to a big party and firework display.

Taking up the northern end of place Foch, the **Hôtel de Ville**, with its prison-like wooden doors, was built in 1826. The first-floor **Salon Napoléonien** (June 15–Sept 15 Mon–Sat 9–11.45am & 2–5.45pm; Sept 16–June 14 Mon–Fri 9–11.45am & 2–4.45pm; €2.29) consists of two rooms that are really only for dedicated Napoléon fans. A replica of the ex-emperor's death mask takes pride of place in a chamber bedecked with velvet, crystal chandeliers and a solemn array of Bonaparte family portraits and busts. Next door, the smaller medal room has a batch of minor relics – a fragment from Napoléon's coffin, some earth from his garden, and part of his dressing case – plus a model of the ship that brought him back from St Helena, and a picture of the house where he died.

South of place Foch

The **south side of place Foch**, the former dividing line between the poor district around the port and the bourgeoisie's territory, gives access to **rue Bonaparte**, the main route through the latter quarter. Built on the promontory rising to the citadel, the secluded streets in this part of town – with their dusty buildings, bistros and bar fronts lit by flashes of sea or sky at the end of the alleys – retain more of a sense of the old Ajaccio than anywhere else. Of the families who lived here in the eighteenth century, one of the most eminent was the **Pozzo di Borgo** clan, whose house still stands at 17 rue Bonaparte, its façade adorned by trompe l'œil frescoes. Carlo Andrea Pozzo di Borgo was a distant cousin and childhood friend of Napoléon, but was later to become one of his bitterest enemies. A supporter of Paoli, he was elected to the Corsican legislature and became president of the Council of State under the short-lived Anglo-Corsican rule of 1794–96. Described as "a man of talent, an intriguer", Pozzo was not content with this domestic position and in 1803 he became the ambassador to Russia, later befriending Wellington, with whom he fought at Waterloo. He went on to become a favourite at the English court, where Queen Victoria referred to him affectionately as "Old Pozzo".

Napoléon and Corsica

"M de Choisel once said that if Corsica could be pushed under the sea with a trident it should be done. He was quite right. It is nothing but an excrescence." This sentiment, expressed by Napoléon to one of the generals who had followed him into exile on St Helena, encapsulates his bitterness about his birthplace. Corsica's opinion of its most famous citizen can be equally uncomplimentary.

The year of **Napoléon's birth**, 1769, was a crucial one in the history of Corsica, for this was the year the French took over the island from the Genoese. They made a thorough job of it, crushing Paoli's troops at Ponte Nuovo and driving the Corsican leader into exile. Napoléon's father, **Carlo**, a close associate of Paoli, fled the scene of the battle with his pregnant wife in order to escape the victorious French army. But Carlo's subsequent behaviour was quite different from that of his former leader – he came to terms with the French, becoming a representative of the newly styled Corsican nobility in the National Assembly, and using his contacts with the French governor to get a free education for his children.

At the age of 9, Napoléon was awarded a scholarship to the Brienne military academy, an institution specially founded to teach the sons of the nobility the responsibilities of their status. The French were anxious to impress their values on the potential leaders of a now dependent territory, and with Napoléon they certainly appear to have succeeded. Give or take a rebellious gesture or two, this son of a Corsican Italian-speaking household used his time well, leaving Brienne to enter the exclusive École Militaire in Paris. At the age of 16, he was commissioned into the artillery. When he was 20, the Revolution broke out in Paris and the scene was set for a remarkable career.

Always an ambitious opportunist, he obtained leave from his regiment, returned to Ajaccio, joined the local Jacobin club and – with his eye on a colonelship in the Corsican militia – enthusiastically promoted the interests of the Revolution. However, things did not quite work out as he had planned, for Pascal Paoli had also returned to Corsica.

Carlo Bonaparte had died some years before, and Napoléon – though not the eldest son – was effectively the head of a family that had formerly given Paoli strong support. Having spent the last twenty years in London, Paoli was pro-English and had developed a profound distaste for revolutionary excesses (it was his determination to keep the guillotine out of Corsica that, as much as anything else, led him into the later failed experiment of union with Britain). Napoléon's French allegiance and his Jacobin views antagonized the older man, and his military conduct didn't enhance his standing at all. Elected second in command of the volunteer militia, Napoléon was involved in an unsuccessful attempt to wrest control of the citadel from royalist sympathizers. He thus took much of the blame when, in reprisal for the killing of one of the militiamen, several people were gunned down in Ajaccio, an incident that engendered eight days of civil war. In June 1793, Napoléon and his family were chased back to the mainland by the Paolists.

Napoléon promptly renounced any special allegiance he had ever felt for Corsica. He Gallicized the spelling of his name, preferring "Napoléon" to his baptismal "Napoleone". And, although he was later to speak with nostalgia about the scents of the Corsican countryside, and to regret he did not build a grand house there, he returned only once more to the island (after being forced to dock here during his return voyage from Egypt) and put Ajaccio fourth on the list of places where he would like to be buried.

Maison Bonaparte

Napoléon was born in the colossal **Maison Bonaparte**, on place Letizia, just off the west side of rue Bonaparte (May–Sept Mon 2–6pm, Tues–Fri 9am–noon & 2–6pm, Sat 9–11.45am & 2–6pm, Sun 9am–noon; Oct–April Mon 2–6pm, Tues–Sat 10am–noon & 2–5pm, Sun 10am–noon; €4). The Bonaparte family first appeared in the chronicles of Ajaccio in the fifteenth century, when they lived in a house that was demolished in 1555 by the French attack on the citadel. This later residence, acquired piecemeal over the years, passed to Napoléon's father Carlo in the 1760s and here he lived, with his wife Letizia and their family, until his death. Soon after, in May 1793, Letizia and her children were driven from the house by Paoli's partisans, who stripped the place down to the floorboards. Requisitioned by the English in 1794, Maison Bonaparte became an arsenal and a lodging house for English officers, amongst whom was Hudson Lowe, later Napoléon's jailer on St Helena. Though Letizia subsequently paid for its restoration with an indemnity given to those Corsicans who had suffered at the hands of the English, her heart wasn't in the job – she left for the second and last time in 1799, the year Napoléon stayed here on his return from Egypt. Owned by the state since 1923, the house now bears few traces of the Bonaparte family's existence, and barely warrants the admission charge unless you have a penchant for Napoleonic memorabilia.

The visit begins on the second floor, but before you go up look out for the wooden sedan chair in the hallway – Letizia was carried back from church on it when the prenatal Napoléon started giving her contractions, and it's one of the very few original pieces of furniture left in the house.

Upstairs, an endless display of portraits, miniatures, weapons, letters and documents gives the impression of having been formed by gathering together anything that was remotely connected with the family and unwanted by anyone else. Amongst the highlights of the first room are a few maps of Corsica dating from the eighteenth century, some deadly "vendetta" daggers and two handsome pairs of pistols belonging to Napoléon's father. The next-door Alcove Room was, according to tradition, occupied by Napoléon in 1799 when he stayed here for the last time, while in the third room you can see the sofa upon which the future emperor first saw the light of day on August 15, 1769. Adjoining the heavily restored long gallery is a tiny room known as the Trapdoor Room, whence Letizia and her children made their getaway from the marauding Paolists.

The Cathedral and St-Érasme

Napoléon was baptized in 1771 in the **Cathedral**, around the corner from Maison Bonaparte in rue Forcioli-Conti. It was built in 1582 on a much smaller scale than originally intended, due to lack of funds – an apology for its diminutive size is inscribed in a plaque inside, on the wall to the left as you enter. The interior is interesting chiefly for a few Napoleonic connections: to the right of the door stands the font where he was dipped at the age of 23 months; and his sister, Elisa Bacciochi, donated the great marble altar in 1811. Before leaving, take a look in the chapel to the left of the altar, which houses a gloomy Delacroix painting of the Virgin holding aloft the Sacred Heart.

Further down the same road stands **St-Érasme**, a Jesuit chapel built in 1617, then dedicated to the town's fishermen in 1815. Should you find it open, inside you can see some model ships, a statue of St Erasmus and a pair of wooden Christs.

Musée Capitellu and the Citadelle

A left turn at the eastern end of rue Forcioli-Conti brings you onto boulevard Danielle-Casanova. Here, opposite the citadel, an elaborately carved capital marks the entrance to **Musée Capitellu** (May–Oct Mon–Wed 10am–noon &

2–6pm; €4), a tiny museum mainly given over to offering a picture of domestic life in nineteenth-century Ajaccio. The house belonged to a wealthy Ajaccien family, the Bacciochi, who were related to Napoléon through his sister's marriage, though he doesn't figure at all here. The collection will appeal to anyone with a special interest in art and antiques, but others may find the steep entrance fee poor value for money.

Watercolour landscapes of Corsica line the walls of the first room, which also contains a marble *Madonnuccia* whose head was cut off with a sabre during the French Revolution. A bust of Sampiero Corso, a common adornment of smart nineteenth-century households, dominates the second room, with some elegant copies of figures of Venus from Herculaneum. The glass display cases hold the most fascinating exhibits, however, which include a rare edition of the first history of Corsica, written by Agostino Giustiniani, a bishop of the Nebbio who drowned in 1536, and the 1796 *Code Corse*, a list of laws set out by Louis XV for the newly occupied Corsica. The last room contains a bronze bust of a chubby-cheeked Pascal Paoli, and a striking painting titled *Sunrise over Bavella*, attributed to Turner's nephew.

Opposite the museum, the restored **Citadelle**, a hexagonal fortress and tower stuck out on a wide promontory into the sea, is occupied by the military and closed to the public. Founded in the 1490s, the fort wasn't completed until the occupation of Ajaccio by Sampiero Corso and the powerful Marshal Thermes from 1553 to 1558. During World War II it was taken by the Italians and used as a prison, whose most famous inmate was a young paratrooper captain called **Scamaroni**. Dispatched to Corsica from North Africa by de Gaulle in January 1943, he set up radio posts in the Ajaccio area (including one in the projection room of the largest cinema in town) and used them to broadcast information about enemy troop movements prior to the invasion later that year. But Scamaroni would never see the island's liberation. Betrayed by the forced confession of a fellow radio operator, he was captured and incarcerated in the citadel. However, despite being subjected to days of appalling torture, the war hero did not divulge any names of his contacts. Instead, he slit his throat and wrists with a length of electric wire, daubing on the walls of his cell with his own blood the words, "*Je n'ai pas parlé, vive la France. Ajaccio, 19 Mars, 1943.*" Like many martyrs of Corsica's liberation from the Axis, Scamaroni's name has been immortalized in street and square names all over the island.

The citadel overlooks the town beach, **Plage St-François**, a short curve of yellow sand facing the expansive mountain-ringed bay. Several flights of steps lead down to the beach from boulevard Danielle-Casanova. A little further down the promenade, the parking lot in front of the municipal sports centre hosts a weekly **flea market** each Sunday morning, starting at around 9am.

For the **nicest beach** within easy walking distance of the town, press on past the exercise area and gendarmerie to **Plage Trottel**, which is larger and much cleaner that Plage St-François.

North of place Foch

Immediately **north of place Foch** behind the Hôtel de Ville, **square César-Campinchi** is the venue for the island's largest **fresh produce market**, held here daily except Monday (between 6am and 2pm), and an essential part of Ajaccien life. Alongside the usual array of cut flowers, vegetables and fruit laid out under colourful stripy awnings are stalls selling artisanal delicacies such as barbary fig jam, honey *aux fleurs du maquis*, wild boar sauces and ewe's cheese from the Niolo, as well as muscat wines and myrtle liqueurs. The goods on sale are not cheap, but the quality is consistently high, and the cafés lining the west side of the square are among the liveliest breakfast spots in town – ideal for crowd-watching after you've finished browsing.

Behind the market, the principal road leading north is **rue Cardinal-Fesch**, a delightful meandering street lined with boutiques, cafés and restaurants. Halfway along the street, set back from the road behind iron gates, stands the **Palais Fesch**, home of Ajaccio's best gallery, the **Musée Fesch** (April–June & Sept Mon 1–5.15pm, Tues–Sun 9.15am–12.15pm & 2.15–5.15pm; July & Aug Mon 1.30–6pm, Tues–Thurs 9am–6.30pm, Fri & Sat 10.30am–12.15pm, Sun 10.30am–6pm; Oct–March same hours, but closed Mon; €5.34). Cardinal Joseph Fesch, whose image in bronze presides over the courtyard, was Napoléon's step-uncle and bishop of Lyon, a lucrative position from which he invested in large numbers of paintings, many of them looted by the French armies in Holland, Italy and Germany. A highly cultured man with an eye for a bargain, he bequeathed a thousand paintings to Ajaccio on the condition that an academy of arts was created in the town. His wishes were contested by Napoléon's brother Joseph, who turned a quick profit by dispersing much of the collection on the art market. Luckily for Ajaccio, however, Renaissance art was less highly regarded in those days than in later years, so many of the more valuable works remained here.

The collection is housed on four storeys; if you're pushed for time, skip the basement – which harbours an uninspiring assortment of Napoleonic memorabilia – and head, via the temporary exhibition room on the ground floor, to **Niveau** (Level) **3** upstairs where the cream of the sixteenth- and seventeenth-century Italian works are displayed. The paintings are ordered chronologically, starting in the gallery immediately to the right of the stairhead and progressing in an anticlockwise direction. In this first room hangs one of Fesch's greatest treasures, Sandro Botticelli's exquisite *Virgin and Child*, painted when the artist was just 25 years old. Dating from a later period, Titian's smouldering *Man with a Glove*, at the end of the corridor, is shown opposite Veronese's *Leda and the Swan*, an uncompromisingly erotic work for its time. **Niveau 4** is given over primarily to seventeenth- and eighteenth-century paintings, where the absence of the Dutch masters sold off by Napoléon's brother is most keenly felt. Highlights here include Poussin's *Midas à la Source du Pactole*, in the first gallery on the right after the stairs, and a vibrant array of still lifes, notably Giuseppe Recco's *Ray on a Cauldron with Fish in a Basket*, noted for its subtle mix of silver-tinged hues. The largest gallery on this floor, **La Grande Galérie**, houses a collection of outsize canvases, of which Gregorio de Ferrari's *La Sainte Famille* is the most famous.

You'll need a separate ticket for the **Chapelle Impériale** (same hours; €1.52), which stands across the courtyard from the museum. With its gloomy monochrome interior the chapel itself is unremarkable; the interest lies in the crypt, which holds the remains of various members of the Bonaparte family. It was the cardinal's dying wish that all the Bonaparte family be brought together under one roof, so the chapel was built in 1857, and the bodies subsequently brought in – as recently as 1951, Charles Bonaparte was reburied here, alongside Letizia, Cardinal Fesch and half a dozen other Bonapartes.

Lucien Bonaparte laid the first stone of the adjacent **Bibliothèque Municipale**, which contains a huge collection of rare antique books. You're not allowed to handle any, but are welcome to browse and read periodicals and magazines on the long, polished table stretching down the middle of the chamber.

Eating, drinking and nightlife

At mealtimes, the alleyways and little squares of Ajaccio's old town become one large, interconnecting restaurant terrace lit by rows of candles. All too often, however, the breezy locations and views of the gulf mask indifferent cooking

△ Place Foch, Ajaccio

and inflated prices. With the majority of visitors spending merely a night or two here in transit, only those places catering for a local clientele attempt to provide real value for money. Stick to the places reviewed in the listings below, though, and you shouldn't go far wrong.

Bars and **cafés** jostle for pavement space all over town but especially along cours Napoléon, which grows more old-fashioned and sedate as it approaches the place de Gaulle. If you fancy sipping a drink with a view of the bay, try one of the flashy cocktail bars that line the seafront beyond the citadel on boulevard Lantivy, but expect to pay for the privilege. For **breakfast**, you can't beat the row of workers' cafés along the west side of boulevard du Roi-Jérôme, which look onto the square César-Campinchi and the morning marketplace.

What **nightlife** there is in Ajaccio consists chiefly of eating and drinking, though there are four **cinemas** (see "Listings", p.207), a busy municipal **casino** on boulevard Lantivy (Pascal Rossini), and a few Eurotrashy **discos**, whose only outstanding features are their extortionate entrance charges. Of these, *Le Duplex*, on Ricanto beach out near the airport, is the most consistently lively and liberal, with a monthly gay night and visiting DJs.

North of the centre, in the district of Brasilia, the arts centre A l'Aghja, 6 chemin de Biancarello (T04 95 20 41 15), hosts theatre performances, world-music gigs and Corsican *polyphonie* singing, mostly on Friday and Saturday nights starting at 9pm. It's hard to find, but is the only venue in town where you can escape synth maestros and "club-style" crooners; head for Brasilia bus stop and ask the way from there, or take a taxi (€12 approximately). The tourist office posts details of forthcoming events.

Cafés and bars

Le Grand Café Napoléon 10 cours Napoléon, opposite the *préfecture*. Allegedly the oldest café in town, with Second Empire decor and a *troisième âge* clientele, most of them in suits and shades. The bar inside was the scene of a famous shootout during World War II, when a cell of key Resistance members was disturbed by the Italian caribinieri and forced to flee guns blazing.

Le Menestrel 5 rue Cardinal-Fesch. Dubbed "*le rendez-vous des artistes*" because local musicians play here most evenings after 7pm; café jazz, traditional mandolin and guitar tunes, with the odd *chanson* singalong number. Popular with bus parties of pensioners.

La Rade 1 place Foch. The most congenial of the cafés fronting the Port de Plaisance, and an ideal spot for crowd-watching over a chilled pastis.

Safari 18 bd Lantivy. One of a row of lookalike cocktail bars next to the casino, overlooking the promenade. Good for a breezy coffee, and for watching Ajaccio's beau monde strut their stuff on Saturday nights.

Restaurants

Le 20123 2 rue Roi-de-Rome T04 95 21 50 05. Decked out like a small hill village, complete with *fontaine* and parked Vespa, the decor here's a lot more frivolous than the food: serious Corsican gas-tronomy (from charcuterie starter to chestnut-flour flan desserts) featured on a single €26 menu. Top-notch cooking, and organic AOC wine. Closed Mon, except in July & Aug.

L'Amirauté Port de Plaisance Charles-d'Ornano T04 95 22 48 22. Right on the quayside, looking across a clutter of yachts and cruise liners to the mountains. Both the food (salads, grilled fish, Corsican speciality *plats du jour*) and atmosphere are quintessential Ajaccio, and for once the prices are restrained. Count on €18–23 à la carte. Closed Sun & Mon evenings.

L'Aquarium rue des Halles T04 95 21 11 21. One of the best places in town for *friture du golfe* and other fresh fish dishes – everything comes straight from the adjacent covered market. Set menus €11–32. Closed Mon, except July–Sept.

Ariadne route des Sanguinaires, near *Barbicaja* campsite T04 95 52 09 63. The oldest and most cheerful of Ajaccio's many beachside *paillotes*, with a wooden *pied dans l'eau* terrace opening straight on to the sand, and a consistently lively ambiance. World cuisine dominates the menu (dishes from Cuba, Morocco, Mali, the Caribbean and Laos) and there's usually live music (salsa/reggae/soukous) from 8.30pm. Most main courses €12–17. Open Easter–Oct Tues–Sun. You can get there from place de Gaulle on bus #5.

Le Floride Port de Plaisance Charles-d'Ornano

04 95 22 67 48. Sublime local seafood, including some of the less commonly served delicacies from the bay (such as *sar*, or devilfish), stylishly prepared and served in an airy first-floor dining hall overlooking the marina. Weekday lunchtimes are dominated by business clients, but the suits and mobile phones peter out in the evenings. If your budget can stretch to it, go for their €34 *menu poisson frais*. Closed Sat & Sun lunchtimes.

Les Halles rue des Halles ☎ 04 95 21 42 68. Open since 1933, and the favourite lunch venue for market stallholders and local office workers. They do a cheap and cheerful €14 menu with wild boar or fresh fish of the day, and a choice of omelettes and fresh pasta.

Da Mamma passage Guinghetta ☎ 04 95 21 39

44. Tucked away down a narrow passageway connecting cours Napoléon and rue Cardinal-Fesch. Authentic but affordable Corsican cuisine – such as *cannelloni al brocciu*, roast kid and seafood, on set menus from €10.50 to €22.50 – served in a stone-walled dining room or under a rubber tree in a tiny courtyard. Snappy service, convivial atmosphere, and the house wine's not bad, but their budget menus are less than exciting.

Le Petit Vatel rue des Halles. Authentically Corsican specialities, served on a crowded little terrace under awnings. Their set menus (€18 to €26) feature honey-roasted pork, lamb in red wine, trout stuffed with *brocciu à la menthe* and *gratin aubergine à la mozzarella* for vegetarians, rounded off by local cheeses and desserts.

Listings

Airlines Air France/Air Inter Europe, 3 bd du Roi-Jérôme, next to the *Hôtel du Golfe* ☎ 04 95 29 45 45; for reservations ☎ 0802/802802; Air Littoral ☎ 0825/834834; Compagnie Corse Méditerranée ☎ 0802/802802; TAT/British Airways ☎ 04 95 71 00 22.

Airport enquiries ☎ 04 95 23 56 56.

Banks and exchange Most of the main banks have branches on place de Gaulle or cours Napoléon, while the BNP is near the marketplace, on bd du Roi-Jérôme. The Société Générale, just up from the Parc Naturel Régional office on rue Sergeant-Casalonga, changes Thomas Cook euro traveller's cheques without commission.

Bookshops Maison de la Presse, 2 place Foch (☎ 04 95 25 81 18), stocks Ajaccio's best selection of new publications on Corsica, as well as a good range of international newspapers, including the *Guardian, Independent, New York Times* and *Washington Post*. Serious book, print and map collectors, and anyone with more than a passing interest in the island, should also make time for the wonderful Le Temps Retrouvé, at 1 rue Ste-Lucie (☎ 04 95 20 17 30, @ apiazzola@wanadoo.fr). Its owner, Alain Piazzola (Dorothy Carrington's former editor) has amassed a huge collection of rare books and other printed memorabilia – well worth a browse even if you're not buying. His prices are also a notch lower than those of Ajaccio's other secondhand bookshops, a couple of blocks away on rue Compte Bacciochi. See our town map for directions.

Bus information ☎ 04 95 21 28 01 (see "Travel details", p.220, for specific bus companies and their routes).

Car rental ACL Rent-a-Car is based at the *Hôtel Kallisté*, 51 cours Napoléon (☎ 04 95 51 34 45,

ⓦ www.rentacar.fr), and has a desk at the airport (☎ 04 95 23 56 36). Other companies include: ADA Location (airport ☎ 04 95 23 56 57); Avis-Ollandini, 1 rue Paul Colonna d'Istria (☎ 04 95 23 92 50, airport ☎ 04 95 21 28 01, ⓦ www.avis.fr); Budget, 1 bd Lantivy (☎ 04 95 35 05 04, ⓦ www.budget-en-corse.com); Citer, bd Lantivy (☎ 04 95 51 21 21, airport ☎ 04 95 21 18 68, ⓦ www.corse-auto-rent.fr); Europcar, 16 cours Grandval (☎ 04 95 21 05 49, airport ☎ 04 95 23 57 01, ⓦ www.europcar.com); Hertz-Locasud, 8 cours Grandval (☎ 04 95 21 70 94, airport ☎ 04 95 23 57 04, ⓦ www.hertz.fr).

Cinemas Ajaccio's four cinemas are dowdy old dinosaurs left over from the prewar era, complete with fire screens, sagging seats and ice-cream-selling usherettes. Unfortunately, ticket prices do not reflect their generally shabby state, but they offer an alternative to café crawling if you've an idle evening to kill. Those on cours Napoléon – The Empire, at no. 18 (☎ 04 95 21 21 00), the Bonaparte, down the road at no. 10 (☎ 04 95 51 27 98), and Laetitia, opposite the post office at no. 48 (☎ 04 95 21 07 24), screen mainstream French and Hollywood blockbusters. The latter also has an annexe, The Aiglon, around the corner at 14 cours Grandval (☎ 04 95 51 29 46), showing mainly arthouse and foreign films.

Diving Popular dive sites around Ajaccio include Les Dentis, a shallow shelf 200m offshore near the citadel; La Castagne, dramatic rock formations rich with underwater life on the southern extremity of the bay; and the Îles Sanguinaires, 12km west of town (see p.212). Winds and currents can be a problem in all three; for advice, transport and training, contact any of the following reputable diving clubs: Odyssée Plongée, Port de Plaisance

Charles d'Ornano ☎ 04 95 20 53 51; E. Ragnole, 12 cours Lucien Bonaparte, behind place Trottel at the west end of town; Plongée Nouvelles Frontières, route des Sanguinaires ☎ 04 95 21 39 65, ⓦ http://perso.clubinternet.fr/jmalamas; or Aquasub Center, *Hôtel Stella di Mare* on the route des Sanguinaires ☎ 04 95 52 01 68.

Ferry offices SNCM, terminal maritime ☎ 04 95 29 66 63, and quai l'Herminier (Mon–Fri 8–11am & 2–6pm, Sat 8–11.45am; ☎ 04 95 29 66 99). You can also access fares and timetable information via the ferry companies' websites: ⓦ www.sncm.fr and ⓦ www.corsicaferries.com.

Hospital Centre Hospitalier, 27 av Impératrice-Eugénie ☎ 04 95 29 90 90; for an ambulance, dial ☎ 15.

Internet access Game.Net, 2 ave de Paris, on the place de Gaulle; €5 per hour.

Laundry Just down the road from the Musée a Bandera at the bottom of rue Maréchal-Ornano, off cours Grandval; and in the marina Tino Rossi, next to the harbour master's office.

Left luggage Both left-luggage facilities – in the gare SNCF and terminal routière – are currently closed as a security precaution.

Motorbike rental Cyrnos Location, *Hôtel Kallisté*, 51 cours Napoléon ☎ 04 95 51 61 81 or 04 95 23

56 36, ⓦ www.cyrnos.net; BMS Location, port Tino Rossi ☎ 04 95 21 33 75; Locacorse, 10 av Bévérini-Vico ☎ 04 95 20 71 20; Moto Corse Évasion, Montée St-Jean ☎ 04 95 20 52 05, ⓦ www.corsicamoto.com.

Pharmacies There are several large pharmacies on place Foch and cours Napoléon.

Police rue Général-Fiorella ☎ 04 95 29 95 29; emergencies ☎ 17.

Post office 13 cours Napoléon (June–Aug Mon–Fri 9am–4.45pm, Sat 9am–noon; Sept–May Mon–Fri 9–11.45am & 2.30–4.45pm, Sat 9–11.45am; ☎ 04 95 51 84 65).

Sports facilities The Complexe Municipal Pascal Rossi, on av Pascal-Rossini (☎ 04 95 21 08 30), is Ajaccio's largest public sports centre, with a pool, gym, weights room and running track. The municipal tennis courts are out of town, on route des Sanguinaires (☎ 04 95 52 00 25).

Taxis The main taxi ranks are: on the north side of place de Gaulle (☎ 04 95 21 00 87); and on av Pascal-Paoli (☎ 04 95 23 25 70).

Telephones There are booths (*cabines téléphoniques*) all over the centre; phone cards are available in the post office, and at tobacconists and photography shops along cours Napoléon.

Train information Gare SNCF ☎ 04 95 23 11 03.

Moving on from Ajaccio

Ajaccio's ferry port is the second busiest on the island after Bastia, and its terminal routière on the quai l'Herminier forms the nexus of the long-distance bus network, so most independent travellers come here at some point to pick up onward transport.

By plane

Campo dell'Oro airport, 6km east of Ajaccio, is served by daily scheduled **flights** to cities on the French mainland, including Marseille, Nice and Paris on Air France/Air Inter, as well as weekly charter flights to northern Europe between April and October; Gatwick and Heathrow are the main destinations for British charter operators, but there are also weekly departures to Birmingham and Manchester. Details of airline companies with offices in Ajaccio appear in "Listings", on p.207. The cheapest way to get to the airport from town is on the shuttle bus (*navette*) that runs three times per hour from the parking lot next to the terminal routière (☎04 95 23 29 41 20; €5 one way); taxis cost around €25.

The airport itself is pretty basic, but it does have a Corsican speciality shop where you can stock up on last-minute presents.

By ferry

Most of the car and passenger **ferries** sailing out of Ajaccio go to Marseille, with less frequent departures to Toulon and Nice. SNCM operates one to two crossings to Marseille daily from July until mid-September, five to seven each week from then until the end of October and during late June, and three weekly for the rest of the year. The crossing takes seven hours by day and eleven hours on the night service, or four and a half hours on the superfast NGV 1, which sails only from June through to October. Tickets for foot passengers cost €15–40 per person, depending on the destination and time of year, and are available up to two hours before departure time from SNCM's counter inside the arrivals hall of the terminal maritime, or in advance at their office directly opposite on the quai l'Herminier (see "Listings", p.208) For more details, see Basics, p.20.

By train

Run by the Chemin de Fer de la Corse (CFC), the **train** trip from Ajaccio across the mountains to Bastia (3hr 15min–3hr 35min) ranks among the island's most memorable journeys, taking in the wild valleys and pine forests of the interior around Corte, and a string of sleepy village stations. At Ponte Leccia the line forks, with a branch veering northwest along the coast to L'Île Rousse and Calvi; taking 4hr 25min through to Calvi with a change at the junction, this route is longer, but even more scenic, with the added attraction of panoramic seascapes along the way. Four trains leave Ajaccio daily in summer for Bastia (€23), and between two and four in winter, depending on the day; Calvi (€27) is served by two departures all year round, although the timetables change between September and June. You can check the times at the tourist office, or by telephoning the station direct (☎04 95 23 11 03); the CFC doesn't as yet have a website.

By bus

Ajaccio is well connected by bus to other towns on the island, though finding out which one you need can be difficult, as the routes are all run by different companies. The tourist office on boulevard du Roi-Jérôme keeps a set of up-to-date timetables, and you can also get information at the terminal routière on quai l'Herminier, where all the operators have individual counters (open half an hour or so prior to departure). Their destinations and departure times are displayed on boards, and you can pay for tickets in advance as soon as the counter opens. This is a particularly good idea for services such as SAIB's Porto bus and others using minibuses, which tend to fill up quickly. They'll also look after your luggage for free. A full list of routes, along with telephone numbers for their operators, appears in "Travel details" on p.220.

Around Ajaccio

The maquis-carpeted ridge of hills north of Ajaccio, known as **Les Crêtes**, holds a few interesting possibilities for a half-day excursion, as long as you have your own transport. Chief of these is the **Punta di Pozzo di Borgo**, which provides an excellent view of Ajaccio and its bay and is reached by a road that takes you close to **Les Millelli**, the country residence owned (but seldom visited) by the Bonapartes. Walkers can take the gentle stroll west of town to **Monte Salario** to see the **Fontaine de Salario**. Further out of town, a new attraction that's certain to appeal to children is the **tortoise sanctuary**, "**A Cupulatta**", 17km northeast along the N193.

Les Millelli and Punta di Pozzo di Borgo

Enveloped in old olive groves on the hillside above Ajaccio, **Les Millelli** (daily except Tues 9am–noon & 2–6pm; €1.50) was the much loved, though rarely used, country retreat of the Bonaparte family. Letizia, Napoleon's mother, was forced to hide out in the house with the future emperor's sisters and uncle during the Paolist uprising of May 1793, and Napoléon himself famously stayed here with Murat six years later on his return from Egypt – but that's about the extent of the site's relevance. None the less, the house is a firmly established stage on the Napoleonic trail. It's a stolid, plain, eighteenth-century building whose real attraction is the surrounding terraced olive grove that overlooks the gulf – a pleasant picnic spot. Inside, there's just a small and dreary ethnographical museum. To reach Les Millelli, follow the main drag north out of town for around 1km and turn left onto the D61, marked to "Alata". A sign on the far side of the first large roundabout you reach, just under 1km beyond the turn-off, indicates the route up the hill.

If, instead of taking the turn to Les Millelli, you continue 6km further along the D61, you'll come to the Col de Pruno, where a left turn along a narrow twisting road will bring you after another 6km to the **Punta di Pozzo di Borgo** and its ruined **château**. Built by the Pozzo di Borgo family in 1886, the château was constructed with materials salvaged from the charred remains of Les Tuileries (Napoléon's residence in Paris), which burned down in 1871, and is the exact reproduction of one of its pavilions. An inscription on the wall states that it was built to preserve a precious souvenir of the home country; in reality, the Pozzo di Borgos – bitter enemies of the Bonapartes since the latter switched sides during Paoli's first exile – erected the replica to rub salt in their old rivals' wounds following the overthrow of Napoléon III. In the nineteenth century the family still owned everything round here, but virtually nothing remained of their native village, which was razed by pirates in 1594; a tower on the track up to the Punta is the sole vestige. From the terrace of the château you get fine **views** of the gulfs of Sagone and Ajaccio, and of Monte d'Oro and Renoso to the east.

La Fontaine de Salario

It's a five-kilometre walk or drive from Ajaccio, or a ride on the #7 bus from place de Gaulle, to the **Fontaine de Salario** (or Funta Salamandra), a spring on a 300-metre hill at the base of Monte Salario. Named after the salamanders that once crawled all over this part of the country, the spring affords another magnificent view of the Golfe d'Ajaccio. From here a trail leads up to **Monte Salario**, a thirty-minute walk.

A Cupulatta: the Tortoise Sanctuary

An essential destination for children and wildlife lovers is the new **Tortoise Sanctuary**, "**A Cupulatta**", at the hamlet of **Vignola**, 17km northeast of Ajaccio up the Vallée de la Gravona, on the N193, the main Corte road (daily: April, May & Sept–Nov 10am–5.30pm; June–Aug 9.30am–7pm; €7; Ⓦwww.acupulatta.com). In the short time it has been open, this sensitively designed breeding and research centre has become the largest of its kind in Europe, boasting 125 different species and around 2000 animals from five continents. All the indigenous tortoises, terrapins and turtles are represented, along with a number of exotic types such as the gargantuan Alligator tortoise (*Macroclemys temminckii*) and the unfeasibly ugly Matamata (*Chelus fimbriata*) from the Amazon region, which looks like a cross between a rotten log and a melting car tyre. The remaining species are considerably cuter, especially the newborns and the tiny terrapins you get to coo over on arrival.

A Cupulatta was the brainchild of **Philippe Magnan**, an accountant whose passion for reptiles nearly cost him his marriage, when the collection he started after the family dog brought a wounded tortoise home threatened to take over the house. Today, the whole family is involved in the management of the six-acre site, which has pioneered new breeding and feeding techniques.

The easiest way to get to A Cupulatta from Ajaccio by public transport is to jump on a train to **Carbuccia** station (4 daily; 20min), a twenty-minute walk from the sanctuary (head left out of the gare and follow the D129 until you reach the N193, where you should turn right; the site lies another 1km or so on your right). Alternatively, jump on any of the **buses** running between Ajaccio, Corte and Bastia.

The Golfe d'Ajaccio

West of Ajaccio, the **route des Sanguinaires** (as the D111 is known) hugs the coast for 12km, passing a succession of tourist developments and sandy beaches before coming to an end at the northern tip of the gulf, the **Punta della Parata**. This headland faces the cluster of crumbling granite islets called the **Îles Sanguinaires**, a miniature archipelago ideally seen from the sea. **Boat excursions** from Ajaccio, run by the company Nave Va from their cabin at the marina, leave around 2pm each day from May to September, stopping for an hour on the largest of the islands, Mezzo Mare; tickets cost €18.

Although the **beaches** along this stretch don't rate as highly as the more secluded strands of the southern gulf, they are more accessible to those without a vehicle. Regular **buses** from place de Gaulle follow the route: buses #1 and #2 go as far as Ajaccio's cemetery, whereas #5 will take you all the way to Punta della Parata, stopping at **Barbicaja**, **Scudo** and **Terre Sacré**.

The largest and most established resort along the southern arm of the Golfe d'Ajaccio – known as **La Rive Sud** – is **Porticcio**. Once a hangout for the rich and famous, the place nowadays has lost its elitist appeal and gets swamped by watersports enthusiasts and refugees from the heat of Ajaccio as soon as summer sets in. Quieter spots are found beyond Porticcio, where the coast is less developed and the scent of the maquis takes over, the shrubland clearing at intervals to reveal superb sandy beaches such as **Plage de Verghia** and **Portigliolo**. Genoese watchtowers again feature on every headland, the most prominent being the **Tour de la Castagna** and the enormous construction on **Capo di Muro**, the southernmost point of the gulf.

An alternative to the coast road is the inland route from Pisciatella, crossing a series of lovely mountain passes surrounded by maquis and dense woodland, through the belvedere village of **Côti-Chiavari** and then down to Capo di Muro.

Route des Sanguinaires

The first landmark along the coast west of Ajaccio, the **Chapelle des Grecs**, lies just beyond Plage Trottel. Built in 1632 by Artilio Pozzo di Borgo, it was allocated for the use of the Greeks in 1733, who settled in Ajaccio after being driven out of their small colony at Paomia by Corsican rebels (see p.181).

Ajaccio's characteristically ostentatious **cemetery** lies another kilometre west, its miniature streets of Neoclassical tombs stacked up the hillside like a ghost town. Bus loads of French pensioners pour through here during the holiday season to pay their respects at the **tomb of Tino Rossi**, France's answer to Bing Crosby, who was born in the town and crooned his way to superstardom between the 1940s and 1960s.

A good way to reach the remote, southernmost point of the Golfe de Sagone is to walk north of **Punta della Parata** along the coast as far as **Capo di Feno**, a route that has the added attraction of giving access to some fine, relatively unfrequented beaches. The distance of 15km takes about five hours one way, but you can turn around before the headland at one of the coves, making an easy two- to three-hour amble from Parata. The route doesn't involve any steep climbs, but there is some quite thick maquis to plough through, particularly towards the end, so you'll need to cover your legs.

Around 500m before the restaurant at Punta della Parata, on the land side of the main road, the trailhead starts at some municipal tennis courts. Park (or jump off the bus) here and follow the dirt track above the courts as it skirts the disused rifle range along the hillside, at an easy gradient. Once past a row of makeshift weekend cabins, the path narrows and scales a low headland. From here the route is a very pleasant, gentle walk through the maquis, with lovely sea views. The path starts to drop downhill after around one hour, descending to a beautiful, steeply shelving sandy cove known as **Anse de Minaccia** (also reachable via the D111B from Ajaccio), where there's a small *buvette* (beach bar). The next beach, **Cala di Fico** thirty minutes' walk further on, is just as beautiful and even quieter.

A wild promontory crowned by a Genoese watchtower, Capo di Feno is reached after another hour's walk along a rough path that keeps close to the rocky shoreline. From the top of the headland, a fine view extends north across the Golfe de Sagone to Cargèse, with the high peaks of the interior in the distance. Return by the same route.

The **beaches** start about 1km beyond the cemetery with **Barbicaja**, a usually crowded sandy stretch close to a large campsite of the same name (see p.198). **Marinella** (aka "Palm Beach"), another 2km on, is the next cove and the most popular, backed by bars and restaurants. About 4km further, **Terre Sacré** gets its name from the one-metre-high stone urn, containing the ashes of soldiers killed in World War I, that stands on the beach. **Cala Lunga** is the last strand, stretching as far as **Punta della Parata**, the narrow, rocky headland that was once connected to the Îles Sanguinaires. Tremendous views of the gulf reward the ten-minute clamber up to the **Tour de la Parata**, a twelve-metre-tall watchtower built of dark grey granite in 1608. One of the last of its kind erected by the Genoese to guard the coast against Barbary pirates, it sports the rusting remains of Corsica's first aerial telegraph, installed by the engineer Claude Chappe in the latter half of the eighteenth century.

Les Îles Sanguinaires

Composed of four humps of red granite, the **Îles Sanguinaires** might be named after Sagone or after *Sagonarri* (Black Blood), from the colour they turn at sunset. A protected site, the islands harbour large colonies of gulls, and it's forbidden to pick flowers or disturb nests on them.

The largest islet, **Mezzo Mare** (or Grande Sanguinaire), is topped by a lighthouse, where Alphonse Daudet spent ten days in December 1862. The experience marked him for life, inspiring one of his famous *Lettres de Mon Moulin*, in which he waxed lyrical about the islet's "reddish and fierce aspect", and instilling in him a preoccupation with the theme of isolation, which repeatedly resurfaced in his work. Tufts of gorse, a square watchtower (la Tour de Castellucciu) and crashing surf give the place a dramatic air, which is perhaps why Joseph Bonaparte wanted to be buried here, though his wish wasn't realized. In the nineteenth century, Mezzo Mare harboured a quarantine hospital for sailors and coral fishermen returning from the West African coast, to protect from tropical infections a town already in mortal fear of malaria. The ruins of the building, including its distinctively high wall, can still be seen.

Without the luxury of your own vessel, the only way to get a close look at Mezzo Mare is to join the daily **boat excursion** from Porticcio/Ajaccio run by the company Nave Va (℡04 95 51 31 31). One departure per day leaves Porticcio at 3pm and Ajaccio's Marina Tino Rossi half an hour later, stopping for an hour on Mezzo before returning by 6pm. Tickets cost €18.

La Rive Sud: the southern gulf

Capped with crumbling Genoese watchtowers, the three headlands of the Golfe d'Ajaccio's southern shore – the **Rive Sud** – separate a succession of sheltered bays, each lined with large sandy beaches. Those closest to town, grouped around the resort of **Porticcio**, are marred by modern holiday developments, but press on southwest down the D55, which keeps close to the convoluted coastline from its turning off the main N196 until the **Punta di a Castagna**, 22km south, and you'll soon escape the villa belt. Growing more spectacular at each bend in the road, the scenery culminates at **Capo di Muro**, the far southwestern extremity of the gulf, where a particularly impressive tower stands within walking distance of some gorgeous coves.

The Rive Sud resorts have a year-round **bus** service, operated by Sarl Casanova Transport (℡04 95 25 40 37), which runs around the bay to Porticcio and then on via Isolella to its terminus at Plage de Verghia (aka "Mare e Sole"). Six buses per day cover the route in summer (July–Sept), scaled down to just two (with one on Sat am, and none on Sundays) after the beginning of October. You can consult current timetables at the terminal routière and tourist office in Ajaccio, and at the bus shelters lining the route itself, or by phoning the company direct.

Porticcio can also be reached by **boat** from Ajaccio. A godsend in the summer when the main road around Campo dell'Oro gets very congested, the service, run by Nave Va, shuttles five times daily between Porticcio jetty and the Marina Tino Rossi; tickets cost €5 one way or €7 return.

No public transport serves the more isolated headlands beyond Verghia, to which you'll need to drive, walk or hitchhike. The same applies to the sinous inland route around Côti-Chiavari.

Porticcio

PORTICCIO, 18km around the bay from Ajaccio, has curiously little Corsican character considering its location, and the proximity of both the sea and maquis. This is due to the main road which scythes straight through the middle of the resort, and the greater than usual quantity of pastel-coloured concrete. Come summer, what little charm the place might possess evaporates altogether, as its beachside strip is overwhelmed by a constant stream of cars, gleaming motorbikes, joggers, rollerbladers, windsurfers and lapdogs. The reason so many Ajacciens drive out here is the **Plage de la Viva**, a wide sandy cove with a full-on watersports scene and great views of the gulf and city across the bay. For the many foreign visitors who rent holiday properties in the area, however, Porticcio serves as a convenient hub for trips down the coast to quieter corners. Grouped around a large car park behind the beach, the area's biggest supermarket, petrol station, bank (with ATM), boulangerie and collection of shops provide most essentials, as well as easy access to Ajaccio via the seasonal ferry and year-round bus link.

In the shopping complex, a small **tourist office** (May–Aug Mon–Sat 9am–1pm & 2.30–8pm, Sun 9am–1pm & 4–8pm; ☏04 95 25 01 01) holds a somewhat patchy accommodation brochure for the Rive Sud, as well as public transport timetables and contact details for diving schools and other watersports facilities in and around the resort.

Porticcio's top **hotel**, in fact one of the most luxurious places on the island, is the four-star *Le Maquis* (☏04 95 25 05 55, Ⓕ04 95 25 11 70, Ⓦwww.lhw .com/lemaquis; ⑨), a terracotta-roofed campus grouped around its own exclusive cove. Old farm implements and exposed beams lend a rustic theme to the interior, and each of the twenty luminous, individually styled rooms has panoramic sea views and large terraces. For a hefty €400 per night in season, you also get the run of outdoor and indoor pools and top-notch sports facilities. Mediterranean cuisine with a Corsican bias is served in their gourmet restaurant, *L'Arbousier*, against an appropriately exotic backdrop of the gulf and distant Îles Sanguinaires (set menu at €36 per head).

For **campers**, the four-star *Camping Benista* (☏04 95 25 19 30, Ⓕ04 95 25 93 70, Ⓦhttp://benista.free.fr; June–Sept), 2km north on the main road, is the swishest option, with a pool and footpath access to the beach. It's also handy for the airport. Much closer to town, and a good deal cheaper, is the *Camping Les Marines de Porticcio* (☏04 95 25 09 35, Ⓕ04 95 25 95 11; June–Sept), next to the Elf petrol station.

The Tour de Capitello

Overlooking the confluence of the Gravona and Prunelli rivers, the massive **Tour du Capitello**, 2km north of Porticcio, is one of the Golfe d'Ajaccio's defining landmarks. Before it was restored a few years ago, deep cracks in its side bore witness to the famous siege in 1793, when Napoléon and fifty men from the French fleet were stranded waiting for backup in preparation for an attack on Ajaccio. With only one cannon to protect them from the army of Corsican patriots, the defenders managed to hold out for three days – thanks to the same architectural design which so impressed Nelson when he was laying siege to the Mortella tower near St-Florent (see p.102). This was also the scene of Napoléon's reunion in 1793 with his mother, sisters and Cardinal Fesch, who, after travelling under cover of darkness from the Bonapartes' country house at Les Millelli (see p.209), embarked here for Toulon as the Paolist mobs searched for them across the water. Renovated in 1998, the tower stands on the spit dividing Porticcio from the gay and nudist end of Plage de Ricanto, close to the end of Campo dell'Oro's runway. It can be reached in an easy fifteen-minute walk: from the car park at the top of Porticcio beach, head right and skirt the edge of the Étang de Casavone until you see a path leading up to the tower from the end of the sand. The concrete ruins scattered around the building's base date from World War II, when it served as an important anti-aircraft battery, first for the Italians and, after September 1943, for the Allies.

South of Porticcio

South of Porticcio the D55 narrows in its progress along the coast, a high bank of maquis screening expensive villas and private beaches from the passing cars. Some 5km along, you'll come to **Plage d'Agosta**, a popular, wide, sandy beach sheltered in the south by the Punta di e Sette Nave, a narrow *presque'île* crowned by the **Tour de l'Isolella**. From the signposted turning for Isolella village at the roundabout on the main road (look for the row of shops on your right if you're heading south), a lane runs along the middle of the promontory giving access to a string of secluded holiday properties, between which tracks run down to little beaches. After 500m, the road reaches the turning (on your left) for the allées des Dauphins and des Dentis, which wind in a circle around the headland. It's worth pulling over here to follow the gentle path through the maquis to the **tower**, a well-preserved structure of exposed yellow granite giving fine views of the gulf. Like the others along this stretch of coast, it was built early in the seventeenth century to protect the hinterland from attack by North African pirates.

The best-value hotel in the area is the *Kallisté* (☏04 95 25 54 19, ℱ04 95 25 79 00; open Easter to mid-Oct; ➍), which stands on a hillside behind Plage d'Agosta (at the end of a badly rutted track). Located in a quiet spot with sweeping views, its rooms are light and airy and, off season, inexpensive for the area. For a sundowner, you won't find a more spellbinding location than the *Bar Oasis* (open June–Sept), down in Isolella village, whose beachside terrace enjoys superb views encompassing the entire northern watershed, from Monte Cinto and Paglia Orba to Monte Renoso.

A still more spectacular beach is **Plage de Ruppione**, a half-moon-shaped cove 8km south of Porticcio, with a sand bar that makes it especially safe for kids and snorkellers. Campers should make for the three-star *Le Sud* (☏04 95 25 40 51, ℱ04 95 25 47 39; May–Oct), one of the less expensive sites along this coast, situated on a pine-shaded terrace beside the main road. The quietest pitches lie at the top of the enclosure – an uphill trudge from the pizzeria, where you can tuck into huge pizzas *au feu de bois* with a wonderful view over the bay for under €10.

Plage de Verghia and Anse de Portigliolo

From here onwards, the coast becomes gradually less developed, with folds of woodland backing onto rocky headlands and golden coves. At **PORT DE CHIAVARI**, some 5km south of Ruppione, the beautiful **Plage de Verghia** is the scenic highlight of the Rive Sud, and a much less frequented beach with finer, whiter sand than its neighbours. Lying at the end of the Ajaccio bus route, it also boasts much the cosiest **campsite** in the district, *La Vallée* (☏04 95 25 44 66; May–Oct), set back from the main road under a long, narrow grove of eucalyptus trees. The shady terrace gets packed out in high summer, but at either end of the season remains pleasantly peaceful; the friendly *patron* and his family also run a well-stocked shop.

Once clear of Verghia, the D55 narrows and turns sharply inland towards Côti-Chiavari, deteriorating markedly on its approach to the **Anse de Portigliolo**, a delightful, almost circular sandy cove. Around 500m up the steep lane leading inland from the sea here, the *Hôtel Céline* (☏04 95 25 41 05, ℱ04 95 25 50 36; open Easter–Sept; ➍) is a very hospitable two-star whose most outstanding feature is its pool, which has fantastic views across the bay. The ensuite rooms, in a modern double-storeyed building, all have little balconies and there's a pleasant restaurant.

Capo di Muro

The Rive Sud draws to a dramatic climax at **Capo di Muro**, on whose sheltered northern flank a particularly picturesque watchtower rises from a dense cover of maquis. Follow the signboards off the main road and you'll drop down a rutted *piste* to a magnificent **beach** on the south side of the promontory called **Cala d'Orzu**. One of the two bar-restaurants behind it, *Chez Francis* (☏04 95 27 10 39; April–Nov), made international headlines when it was destroyed in an arson attack – not by separatist or Mafia guerrillas, as is normally the case in Corsica, but by undercover French police acting, or so it turned out, under direct orders from the state's most senior official on the island (see p.428). Since Préfet Bonnet's subsequent imprisonment, the infamous *paillote* has been restored to its former condition and is rebuilding its reputation as one of the area's top seafood restaurants, with prices to match its notoriety (€23 for grilled fish of the day). The neighbouring *Le Lago Bleu*, just up the beach, may not enjoy the same fame but offers far better value for money: fresh fish from the gulf for €17 or a bucket of moules-frites for €9.

Capo di Muro also has a couple of good **walks** to tempt you off the beach. From Cala d'Orzu, a 2hr 30min round trip leads to the **lighthouse** at the extremity of the bay, where a **Madonna statue** and little chapel overlook one of Corsica's most rugged coastlines. To pick up the path, you have to scramble across the rocks and little coves for around twenty minutes until you reach a motorable track running uphill to the hamlet of **Monte Biancu**, from where a clear route winds west through the maquis. Along the way, look out for an enormous rock formation nicknamed "Le Grain de Sable".

To reach the trailhead for the second walk, to the **Tour di Capo di Muro**, you'll need a car: backtrack from Cala d'Orzu, but instead of turning right when you reach the surfaced road, head left at the junction and follow the tarmac west along the brow of the headland as far as a little car park. From here, the clear path winds more or less along the ridgeline, crossing a number of side tracks en route where you may find yourself wandering into impenetrable maquis. Shortly after passing a ruined cottage, reached after just over an hour, the tower rises from the surrounding vegetation, its walls in a solid condition with a metal staircase giving access, via its interior, to a crenellated terrace. Return by the same route.

Côti-Chiavari and the inland route

Immediately behind Plage de Verghia at Port de Chiavari, the **D55** swings inland to begin its tortuous climb through the old holm and cork oaks of the **Forêt de Chiavari** to the ridgetops. As an alternative route over the headland, its merits are some of the best views of the region, and the very pretty belvedere village of Côti-Chiavari, where a dramatically sited (and particularly good-value) hotel offers one of this area's more tempting pit stops.

En route up or down the hill, keep an eye out for the gloomy ruins on the roadside, roughly 3km from the coast. These are the remains of an old prison camp, **l'ancien pénitencier de Chiavari**, dating from the Second Empire. Throughout the latter half of the nineteenth century convicts were interred in this lonely, malaria-infested clearing, where they served their time labouring in the surrounding vineyards and cork forest. A massive stone barn, which was used as a wine cellar, encapsulates the sinister feel of the place. Have a nose around the overgrown slopes beyond it and you'll come across several tunnels, caves and other intriguing ruins; the circular pit next to the main road was used for washing horses. Abandoned in 1906, the camp accommodated POWs in World War II, three of whose German inmates settled here after 1945 after their homelands were annexed by the Russians.

Another reminder of the last war stands at the centre of **CÔTI-CHIAVARI**: a bust mounted on brown marble recalling that this was the birthplace of Antoine Michel Bozzi, a Resistance radio operator who was captured and shot by the Italians only days before the liberation in 1943. Beyond the memorial in the shade of the roadside plane trees is the village's cheerful little **pizzeria**, *Les Platanes*, where you can re-fuel with copious wood-baked pizzas and fresh salads for €10–12, served on a terrace overlooking pale orange rooftops to the church and sea.

For the most imposing views of the gulf, however, press on another kilometre along the D55 to the lower edge of Côti-Chiavari and the *Hôtel-Restaurant Le Belvédère* (℡04 95 27 10 32, ℻04 95 27 12 99; ④). The building itself, made of pink-painted concrete that's clearly visible even from the seafront at Ajaccio, is a bit of an eyesore, but it boasts what must rank among the most sublime terraces in the Mediterranean. The cuisine is widely regarded as befitting the location: phone ahead to book (essential) and you'll be offered a choice of four set menus for €23 per head (not including wine), which might feature house specialities such as local king prawns, guinea fowl with chestnuts, or wild boar. Their sunny, gulf-facing rooms cost €46–61 in February, March and November, but for the rest of the year are only available on a half-board basis (€42–50 depending on the level of comfort and time of year). This is deservedly among the most popular addresses on the island and is more often than not fully booked, so reserve your bed as far in advance as possible; for a table, a phone call before noon of the same day should suffice.

The Gorges du Prunelli

A drive up through the **Gorges du Prunelli** provides an easy but immensely varied excursion inland from Ajaccio, as the landscapes change dramatically from gardens and orchards to the bare jagged granite of the gorges themselves. Two roads climb the opposite flanks of the valley for 20km before converging on the run-up to **Bastelica**, a mountain village with restaurants and hotels that is the main gateway to the **Val d'Èse** ski station. The road on the north side of the valley, the D3, passes through the villages of **Bastelicaccia** and **Ocana** on its way to the dam at **Tolla**, where the route becomes increasingly hairraising. To view the gorges from the other side, you can descend from Bastelica along the D27 via the **Col de Crichetto** and the attractive village of **Cauro**. The first route affords the best views, while the second is more easily negotiable by car; no public transport reaches these parts.

Bastelicaccia to Tolla

Fully cultivated since the nineteenth century in order to feed the growing population of Ajaccio, the plain around **BASTELICACCIA** has an air of cornucopian opulence, with its overflowing orchards of orange and lemon trees mingled with flower gardens and deep maquis. This is among the most pleasant places to stay within a short radius of Ajaccio, and one of the best local hotels is *L'Orangeraie* (℡04 95 20 00 09, ℻04 95 20 09 24; ④), situated 1km beyond the village amidst an orchard and a beautifully kept garden of palms and other Mediterranean plants (amid which there is also a small swimming pool). In addition to rooms, you can rent well-equipped studios here, sleeping two to four people, by the night or the week; advance booking is essential.

The scenery undergoes a dramatic change after Ocana, as high rock walls and pointed granite pinnacles begin to emerge from the greenery. **TOLLA**, a pretty village strung out on a ridge overlooking an immense reservoir of the **Lac de Tolla**, appears 2km further on. Trees abound: a bank of apple, walnut and chestnut orchards overhangs the valley in the approach to Tolla. Before you reach the village you can stop at the **Col de Mercuju** (716m), dominated by two great pyramids of rock rising from the circular hollow of the gorges, where a Corsican **restaurant**, *Chez Baptiste*, is set back from the road and overlooks the gorges. Opposite the restaurant a path leads down to a platform above the dam, affording an impressive view across the lake, and various gentle forest paths thread through the woodland lining the banks. **Pedalos** and canoes are available for rent here – a great way to cool down any overheated kids you might be travelling with.

Tolla itself is a lively place in summer, popular with Ajacciens who, returning to visit the family home, flock to the open-air pizzeria at the entrance to the village on the left. The only place to stay is a well-placed **campsite** down by the lake, *A Selva* (☎04 95 27 00 28; May–Oct), which also offers tasty Corsican cooking.

Once past Tolla, the landscape continues to be wild – rocky walls strewn with high maquis border the road, overlooked by the ragged crest of Punta di Forca d'Olmu to the south.

Bastelica

Set at 800m on the lower slopes of Monte Renoso, **BASTELICA** is a stark and unusually unprepossessing spot with a few rows of cold granite houses and an ugly modern church. It attracts a fair number of visitors, however, partly because of the nearby **Val d'Èse** ski station, and partly because it is the birthplace of Sampiero Corso (see box opposite), whose statue, dating from the 1890s, stands in the village centre. To visit the spot where Sampiero was born, walk up the road east of the church towards the adjoining hamlet of Dominicacci; take a left turn at the *U Renosu* restaurant, and then the first right up the lane running behind this building, which brings you to a T-junction; head right here and follow the backstreet for 20m or so; the house is on your right. The original building was burned down by the Genoese in 1554, but the façade of its replacement (1855) is adorned with an inscription that extols "the most Corsican of Corsicans, a famous hero amongst the innumerable heroes that love of the country, superb mother of male virtues, has nursed in these mountains and torrents".

Bastelica has remained a hotbed of nationalism. In 1980, it witnessed one of the more dramatic encounters between Corsican activists and the state when, on January 6, a group of RPR militants discovered three undercover Secret Service agents operating in the village. The men were captured and taken at gunpoint to Ajaccio's *Hôtel Fesch*, where they were held to draw attention to the French government's covert activities on the island. Paris, however, refused to negotiate with the Bastelica nationalists, whom they dubbed "racketeers and hostage takers", and ordered the storming of the hotel. On January 12, armed police liberated the three agents and seized the militants, who were subsequently tried and imprisoned on the mainland. Coming only a few years after the siege at Aléria (see p.301), the event enraged the FLNC and plunged the island into a period of spiralling violence during the early 1980s.

Accommodation and eating

Bastelica has a few **hotels** open in summer. The most central is the *Le Sampiero*, a large modern two-star opposite the church (☎04 95 28 71 99, ℱ04 95 28 74 11; ❹; closed Nov & Fri in winter), which enjoys uninterrupted views of the mountains from most of its rooms, and has a friendly bar on the ground floor. More comfortable is the slightly pricier *U Castagnetu*, past Sampiero's birthplace 1km north of the church (☎04 95 28 70 71, ℱ04 95 28 74 02; ❹), which has fifteen well-appointed rooms set amid chestnut trees, and stunning views over the valley from its sunny terrace. Half board is obligatory here in July and August. *Chez Paul*, 200m further along the same road (☎04 95 28 71 59; ❷), is more modest, offering simple but impeccably clean apartments by the night or week; it also has an excellent little **restaurant** where you can enjoy

"The most Corsican of Corsicans", **Sampiero Corso** was born into a peasant family in 1498 and first took up arms in 1517, when he entered the service of the Medici as a mercenary – a career followed by many of his poorer compatriots. Gaining himself a reputation for audacious ambition – he is said to have put forward a plan to assassinate Charles V in 1536 – he arrived in France in the company of Catherine de' Medici, and went on to distinguish himself in several campaigns, becoming renowned as the most valiant captain in the French army. At Perpignan in 1543 he saved the life of the future Henry II, husband of Catherine de' Medici, thereby ensuring his promotion in 1547 to colonel of the Corsican infantry. He returned to Corsica a proud and popular figure, and promptly married a young noblewoman named Vannina d'Ornano. The match was not approved of by her brothers, who saw their inheritance about to slip from their fingers – and their enmity was to have dire consequences.

Around this time the Genoese, suspicious of Sampiero's prestige, decided to lock him up for a spell, accusing him of having plotted an uprising against the republic. Their action engendered a hatred of Genoa that Sampiero was to hold for the rest of his days. It was the French declaration of war against Genoa in 1553, and their attempt to "liberate" Corsica from the despotic republic, that established Sampiero's legendary status. Setting out with Marshal Thermes and an expeditionary force of seven thousand mercenaries, amongst them a Turkish contingent led by the notorious Dragut, he managed a rapid takeover of Bastia, Ajaccio and Corte. Bonifacio and Calvi weren't such an easy proposition, however, being populated primarily by Ligurian settlers and thus more firmly entrenched as Genoese strongholds. Long and relentless sieges ensued, with Turkish ships ruthlessly bombarding the towns in a prelude to massacre and pillage.

The subsequent Genoese alliance with the Spanish resulted in Sampiero's return to the Continent in 1557, and two years later the treaty of Cateau-Cambresis gave Corsica back to Genoa. Sampiero passionately wanted independence for the island, but could not command the backing of France after strangling his wife, in Aix-en-Provence, after he found out she had betrayed him to the Genoese and sold most of his possessions. Escaping with some of her fortune, he returned to Corsica in 1564 to organize another revolt. He rapidly took over much of the island's interior but failed to take the ports, and enthusiasm for his cause soon diminished, a process doubtless hastened by the 2000-ducat price the Genoese put on his head. In 1567, Sampiero was decapitated in an ambush near Bastelica, a murder engineered by the Ornano brothers, who had never forgotten their grudge. His head was impaled on the town gate of Ajaccio, a warning to would-be rebels that ensured his martyr's status.

homemade charcuterie and traditional local dishes such as courgettes suffed with *brocciu*, wild boar pâté and veal in cêpe sauce, on excellent-value set menus of between €12 and €19. Bastelica is famous for its fine cheeses and charcuterie, and a good place to sample these is *Chez François Urbani*, next door to *Chez Paul*, which stocks a range of traditional local hams, sausages and ewe's cheese; the prices are much lower than you'll pay for the same stuff down on the coast, and quality guaranteed.

Bastelica to Cauro

On the way back down the main D27, there's the option of turning off the road 4km south of Bastelica to follow a parallel road which gives a stunning view of the gorges. If you're in a sturdy vehicle, you can enjoy even better views by taking the rough mountain track that branches off just before the junction at the **Col de Menta** (762m); this runs parallel to the D27, merging with it at the **Col de Crichetto**. The D27 is bordered by the **Forêt de Pineta**, whose carpet of Laricio pines, chestnut and beech trees makes it a good place for a picnic. From the maison forestière, 3km along the same road, it's a ten-minute marked walk to the **Pont de Zipitoli**, a single arc of Genoese stone spanning the River Èse.

After regaining the D27 at the **Col de Marcuggio** (670m), you descend through an increasingly pastoral terrain of vineyards interspersed by fields and folds of woodland. About 6km along from the col, just before the hamlet of Radicale, a bridge on a sharp left bend marks the start of a fifteen-minute trail to the **Cascade de Sant'Alberto**, a high waterfall hidden amidst the forest. **CAURO**, a pleasant but unremarkable village at the junction of the D27 and N169, has a good **hotel** – *Sampiero*, in the centre opposite the post office (☎04 95 28 44 84; ❹). Buses from Ajaccio to Bonifacio pass through here daily before crossing the **Col St-Georges**, 7km further south, where there's an excellent little roadside **restaurant**: in a small dining room behind a bar, the *Auberge du Col* serves traditional and tasty Corsican dishes such as cannelloni made with chestnut flour, and wild rabbit stew.

From Cauro, it's an easy 13km detour south to **SANTA MARIA SICCHÉ**, set amid dense swathes of coastal maquis just off the main road. The village would be a pretty but otherwise undistinguished place were it not for the fact that Sampiero Corso's wife, Vannina d'Ornano, was born here. The old stone house the couple lived in, the **Palazzo Sampiero** (1554), still stands; follow the lane leading left around the village church for about 500m and you'll see it on your left, marked with a plaque. Few Corsicans like to recall the fact, but the Corsos' marriage was brought to a violent end when Sampiero strangled Vannina after she had denounced him to the Genoese and run off with the family fortune to the Continent. The murder eventually led to his death in 1567: tipped off by the Italian authorities, her brothers ambushed and decapitated Sampiero near Bastelica, impaling his head on a stake at Ajaccio. Vannina's family home also still stands in the village, but it's harder to locate and unmarked: take the main road leading downhill past the church towards the highway for 300m – the house, a fifteenth-century tower, stands on the right, at the top of a black tarmac lane.

Travel details

Trains

For precise departure times, telephone Ajaccio station (☎04 95 23 11 03).

Ajaccio to: Bastia (4 daily; 3hr 15min–3hr 30min); Bocognano (4 daily; 50min); Calvi (2 daily; 4hr 25min–5hr); Carbuccia, for "A Capulatta" tortoise sanctuary (4 daily; 20min); Corte (4 daily; 1hr 45min–2hr); L'Île Rousse (2 daily; 4hr); Ponte Leccia (4 daily; 2hr 45min); Venaco (4 daily; 1hr 30min–1hr 45min); Vizzavona (4 daily; 1hr).

Buses

The tables below summarize which bus companies cover which routes, how often they run and how long journeys take. Start by looking up your intended destination in the first table; then, using the com-

pany's acronym (eg AR or SAIB), go to the second table for more detailed route and frequency information. Precise departure times can be checked in advance either via the bus companies direct, or (if you're French isn't up to that) Ajaccio tourist office (☎04 95 51 53 03). Leaving from Ajaccio, always aim to arrive at the gare routière well ahead of the departure time as tickets are not always available on the bus itself and, in season, may sell out.

Ajaccio to: Aullène (BE; 1hr 25min); Bastia (EV; 3hr); Bavella (AR/BE; 2hr 5min–3hr 15min); Bonifacio (EV; 4hr); Cargèse (SAIB; 1hr 10min); Corte (EV; 1hr 45min); Évisa (ARC; 2hr); Levie (AR; 2hr 45min); Olmeto (AR/EV; 1hr 35min); Porticcio (CA; 40min); Porto (SAIB; 2hr 10min); Porto-Vecchio (BE/EV; 3hr 10min–3hr 45min); Propriano (AR/EV; 1hr 50min); Quenza (BE; 1hr 45min);

Sagone (SAIB; 40min); Sartène (AR/EV; 2hr 15min); Ste-Lucie-de-Tallano (AR; 2hr 30min); Santa Maria Sicché (EV; 45min); Tiuccia (SAIB; 35min); Vico (ARC; 1hr 15min); Vizzavona (EV; 1hr); Zonza (AR/BE; 2hr 15min–3hr).

Cargèse to: Ota (SAIB; 1hr 30min); Piana (SAIB; 30min); Porto (SAIB; 1hr); Sagone (SAIB; 15min); Tiuccia (25min).

AR: Autocars Ricci ☎ 04 95 51 08 19.
Ajaccio–Olmeto–Propriano–Sartène–Ste-Lucie-de-Tallano–Levie–Zonza–Bavella; 1 daily Mon–Sat year round, with an additional departure weekday afternoons and Sun from July to mid-Sept.
ARC: Autocars R. Ceccaldi ☎ 04 95 21 01 24 or 04 95 21 38 06.
Ajaccio–Tiuccia–Sagone–Vico–Évisa–Marignana; 1 daily Mon–Sat year round, with 2 extra daily services in term time.
BE: Balési Évasion ☎ 04 95 51 25 56.
Ajaccio–Aullène–Quenza–Sonza–Bavella–l'Ospédale–Porto-Vecchio; July & Aug Mon–Sat 1

daily; Sept–June Mon & Fri only.
CA: Casanova Autocars ☎ 04 95 21 05 17 or 04 95 25 40 37. Ajaccio–Porticcio–Isolella–Plage de Verghia (Mare e Sole); Mon–Sat 2–6 daily.
EV: Eurocorse Voyages ☎ 04 95 21 06 30.
Ajaccio–Bocognana–Vizzavona–Vivario–Venaco–Corte–Bastia/L'Île Rousse & Calvi; Mon–Sat 1–2 daily. Ajaccio–Propriano–Sartène–Ste-Lucie-de-Tallano–Levie–Carbini–Zonza; June–Sept Mon–Sat 1 daily.
Ajaccio–Olmeto–Propriano–Sartène–Roccapina–Figari–Porto-Vecchio; Mon–Sat 2 daily year round, with additional service on Sun June to mid-Sept.
SAIB: Autocars SAIB ☎ 04 95 22 41 99 or 04 95 21 02 07.
Ajaccio–Tiuccia–Sagone–Cargèse–Piana–Porto–Ota; Sept–June Mon–Sat 1–2 daily; July & Aug 2 daily, including Sun and hols.

Ferries

For ferry details, see Basics, p.20.

The south

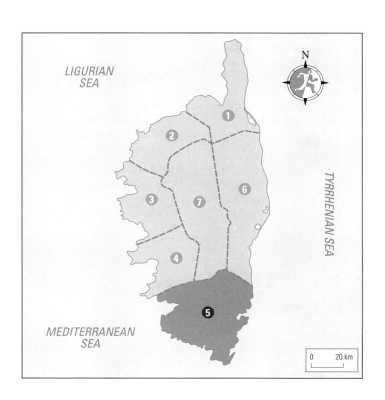

CHAPTER 5

Highlights

✱ **Plage de Cupabia** – Gem of a white-sand bay, hidden on the western arm of the Golfe de Valinco. **See p.229**

✱ **Filitosa** – Standing stones with clearly carved faces are the highlights of this unique, world-renowned prehistoric site. **See p.232**

✱ **Mountain cuisine** – Sample definitive regional cooking at the tables of *Kiesale* near Calzola, *A Pignata* at Levie and *L'Aiglon* in nonza. **See pp.235, 248** and **255**

✱ **Campomoro** – One of Corsica's most picturesque coastal villages, with a fine beach, huge watchtower and kilometres of deserted coast to the south. **See p.240**

✱ **Pianu di Levie** – Well-preserved megalithic remains, lost amid the gnarled oak woods of the Alta Rocca region. **See p.248**

✱ **Sartène** – Quintessentially austere Corsican town, whose buttressed-walled *vieille ville* overlooks the dramatic Rizzanese Valley. **See p.262**

✱ **Wine** – Spicy, robust reds with hints of maquis herbs are the speciality of the south's top vineyards, the Domaines de Torraccia and Fiumicicoli. **See pp.288** and **264**

✱ **Baie de Roccapina** – Stunning turquoise inlet overlooked by a lion-shaped rock formation. **See p.268**

The south

S ome of the most enduring evocations of Corsica's varied landscapes and culture − from Edward Lear's eerie etchings, to Prosper Mérimée's vendetta-yarn, *Colomba*, and Dorothy Carrington's occult explorations in *Dream Hunters of the Soul* − were inspired by **the south**, and this remains the most quintessentially Corsican corner of the island. Sparsely populated by comparison with the Ajaccio region, its rugged, inhospitable coastline and valleys support scattered villages where the old ways are never far from the surface. Vendetta may have been officially stamped out, but its roots still run deep. In recent years, long-standing family rivalries have repeatedly erupted into bloodshed, hiding behind the guise of nationalist-separatist score-settling, while organized crime, too, is rife, from petty racketeering of businesses in the resorts to high-level corruption.

The only evidence tourists tend to see of this malevolent undercurrent, however, are bullet-raked road signs, black graffiti and the odd bombed-out holiday home. It's the extraordinary landscapes that will leave the more lasting impression: the wild, maquis-backed coast beyond Campomoro, the striated chalk cliffs of Bonifacio, or the brooding, shadowy hinterland of Alta Rocca, with its vineyards, fragrant Laricio pine forests and backdrop of pale granite peaks.

The south is most famous, though, for its mysterious prehistoric standing-stone sites. Accorded World Heritage status by UNESCO, **Filitosa** is the best preserved of these, with carved menhirs strewn amid the ruins of three-thousand-year-old fortifications. A good base from which to visit the site is **Porto-Pollo**, a secluded seaside village at the northern end of the vast **Golfe de Valinco**. Alternatively, there's **Propriano**, a livelier modern port in the centre of the bay, offering the widest choice of hotels, shops and restaurants in the area. From here you can also explore the southern section of the Golfe de Valinco as far as picturesque **Campomoro**, or roam into the island's richest wine-producing country, taking in **Fozzano**, famed for its blood feuds and stalwart granite tower houses. A bit deeper inland, the region of **Alta Rocca** has an abundance of historic villages and prehistoric sites: the architecture of **Sainte-Lucie-de-Tallano** pays testimony to the wealth of the area's former overlords, the della Rocca family, while a visit to the Bronze Age ruins of the **Pianu di Levie** is an essential complement to the Filitosa trip. In the heart of Alta Rocca, the village of **Zonza** stands on the threshold of the south's major natural attraction, the sublime granite "needles" of **Bavella**.

Moving southwest, **Sartène** is in many ways the quintessential Corsican town, its history saturated with stories of vendetta and its stark, fortified buildings redolent of the harshness of life in the not-so-distant past. South of

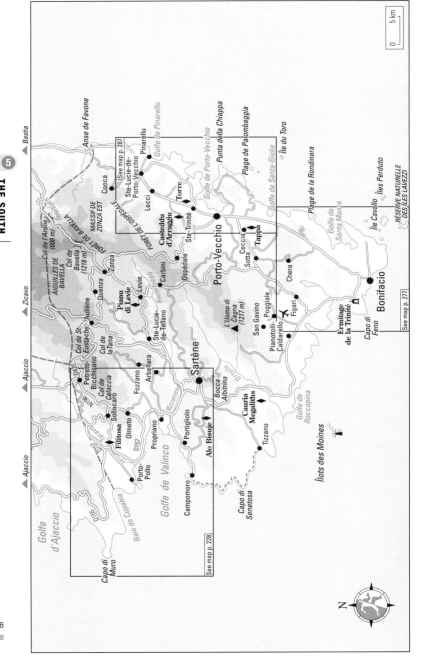

0   5 km

▲ Bastia

▲ Zicavo

▲ Ajaccio

▲ Ajaccio

Anse de Favone

See map p. 287

Conca

Pinarellu

Golfe de Pinarellu

Ste-Lucie-de-Porto-Vecchio

Lecci

Torre

Golfe de Porto-Vecchio

Punta della Chiappa

Plage de Palombaggia

MASSIF DE ZONZA EST

FORÊT DE BAVELLA

FORÊT DE L'OSPEDALE

Casteddu d'Arraggiu

Ste-Trinité

Porto-Vecchio

Golfe de Santa-Giulia

Île du Toro

AIGUILLES DE BAVELLA

Col de l'Arone (608 m)

Col de Bavella (1218 m)

Solbaro

Zonza

Quenza

Levie

Planu di Levie

Fiumicoli

Carbini

Ospédale

Ceccia

Sotta

Tappa

Plage de la Rondinara

Golfe de Santa Manza

Col de Ste-Eustache

Aullène

Ste-Lucie-de-Tallano

L'Uomo di Cagna (1217 m)

Chera

Golfe de Roccapina

San Gavino

Poggiale

Figari

Pianotolli-Caldarello

Île Cavallo   Îles Perduto

Île Lavezzi

RÉSERVE NATURELLE DES ÎLES LAVEZZI

Col de la Tana

Col de Celaccia

Petreto-Bicchisano

Fozzano

Arbellara

Sartène

D420

D57

Filitosa

Olmeto

SolJaccia

N196

Propriano

Portigliolo

Bocca Albitrina

Cauria Megaliths

Porto-Pollo

Golfe de Valinco

Rizzanese

Ortolo

Campomoro

Alo Bisuje

Tizzano

Capo di Senetosa

Îlots des Moines

Baie de Cupabia

Capo di Muro

Golfe d'Ajaccio

D155

D157

D157

Ermitage de la Trinité

Bonifacio

Capo di Feno

See map p. 277

See map p. 228

N

Sartène, a weird landscape of thick maquis and eroded rock outcrops makes an appropriate background for the **megaliths of Cauria** and **Alignement de Palaggiu**, Corsica's largest arrays of prehistoric standing stones.

Marking the southern extremity of the island, **Bonifacio** is one of the most dramatically sited towns in the whole Mediterranean, its old quarter sitting atop vertiginous white cliffs and almost severed from the mainland by a deep natural harbour. It's a popular holiday centre for Corsica's wealthier tourists, as is **Porto-Vecchio**, a former Genoese citadel that's close to the island's most beautiful, and popular, beaches and to the majestic forest scenery of the **Massif de l'Ospédale**.

The area is reasonably well served by **public transport**, with buses running year round, two to four times a day from Ajaccio to Porto-Vecchio, via Propriano, Bonifacio and Sartène. Daily buses also pass through the mountains from the west coast through Bavella and Zonza to Porto-Vecchio, but to visit all the prehistoric sites you will need your own vehicle.

The Golfe de Valinco

The most southerly of the four great bays indenting Corsica's west coast, the **Golfe de Valinco** gives easy sea access to two deep valleys – the Taravo and Rizzanese – that were among the first regions on the island to be settled. A stone's throw from the banks of the **Taravo River**, off the gulf's north shore, **Filitosa**'s prehistoric remains range from smoke-blackened early-Neolithic rock shelters to a fully developed Torréen castle, as well as the carved menhirs for which the site is renowned. The Taravo twists through a fertile flat-bottomed valley to join the sea near **Porto-Pollo**, a former fishing village overlooking the river mouth that's among the quietest resorts in this region. By contrast, **Propriano**, at the far east end of the bay, can feel overwhelmed in summer, although its busy marina and dramatic setting warrant at least a short visit en route to idyllic **Campomoro**, at the far southwest corner of the gulf. Crowned by a large watchtower, this village's perfectly curved bay and sandy beach make it among the most photogenic spots in the south; moreover, beyond it lies a rugged stretch of coast accessible only on foot, and thus deserted save for the odd hiker and pleasure boat.

Following in the footsteps of James Boswell, who travelled this way in 1765 to meet Pascal Paoli, most visitors enter the region via the **Col de Celaccia** before dropping down to **Sollacaro** (en route to Filitosa) or to **Olmeto** (on the main Propriano road, the N196). However, a much more scenic alternative is to take the coastal D155, threading its way around Capo di Muro in the Ajaccio region (see p.215) into the Golfe de Valinco. Aside from some amazing views of a totally unspoilt coastline, this badly potholed back road passes close to beautiful **Plage de Cupabia** – the area's best beach.

Porto-Pollo

On the northwestern edge of the gulf is **PORTO-POLLO** whose name derives from the Corsican *Porti Poddu*, meaning "troubled port" – a legacy of the pirate raids that ravaged the island's coast in former times. Today, the little harbour in this compact fishing village, 18km northwest of Propriano, provides sheltered moorings for yachts and the few fishermen who still venture out to supply the local restaurants with fresh langoustine from the gulf. Development here has been limited: barely a handful of hotels line the road behind the village's narrow beach and traffic is minimal, making this a peaceful base from which to visit

Filitosa, the Alta Rocca and Sartenais. In addition, the Golfe de Valinco's particularly clear waters have made the village one of Corsica's prime **diving** centres.

Practicalities

From June to September, **minibuses** provide the only public transport in the area, running between Propriano and Porto-Pollo. You can also get here direct from Ajaccio with Autocars Ricci (☎04 95 51 08 19), whose buses stop outside the *Hôtel L'Escale* on the main road.

The buses stop at various points along the road behind Porto-Pollo's beach, which is dominated by a string of mid-range **hotels**. Of these, *L'Escale* (☎04 95 74 01 54, ⓕ04 95 74 07 15, ⓔhotel-skle@wanadoo.fr; April–Sept; ➌), a bland modern place right behind the beach, is the least expensive, although its rooms lack sea views and half board is obligatory between July and mid-September. Only slightly pricier, *Les Eucalyptus* (☎04 95 74 01 52, ⓕ 04 95 74 06 56; April–Oct; ➌), on the opposite side of the road, has two categories of rooms: larger sea-facing ones with little terraces and three darker budget options around the back; they also offer plenty of off-road parking and a restaurant. Otherwise, try the smart, modern *Kallisté* (☎04 95 74 02 38 or 04 95 30 97 70, ⓕ04 95 74 06 26; ➍), the pastel-pink concrete building on the main street. Owned by a descendant of Pascal Paoli, it has large rooms and a quality restaurant serving mainly fresh seafood, though it's quite pricy, with menus starting at €20. Otherwise, you've *Le Golfe*, in a prime spot overlooking the marina at the far end of the village (☎ & ⓕ 04 95 74 01 66; April–Oct; ➍), with a handful of simple rooms opening onto the waterside. Half board is obligatory here in peak season, but at other times tariffs drop to around €50 for a double. Reception is to be found in the snazzy bar-restaurant next door, which boasts the biggest TV on this side of the gulf.

Other places worth considering if you've your own transport are M et Mme Tardif's lovely **bed and breakfast** in Sollacaro (reviewed on p.235) and the *Auberge U Mulinu* at nearby Calzola (see p.235), which lies just down the road to the area's most congenial **campsite**, the *Camping Kiesale* (see p.235). Closer to Porto-Pollo itself, the best options for campers are the central *Camping*

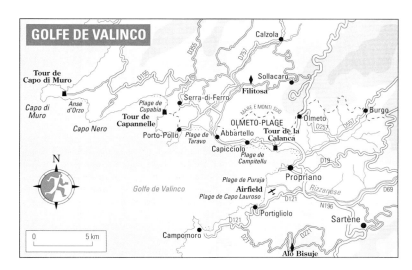

GOLFE DE VALINCO

Alfonsi (☎04 95 74 01 80; June to mid-Oct), at the entrance to the village, and the *Cyrnos*, behind the Plage du Taravo, 2.5km east (see p.231).

The *U Mulinu* and *Kiesale* at Calzola have the most commendable **places to eat** in the area. In Porto-Pollo, the *Escale* and *Kallisté* both have good restaurants, or you could try the cheaper *Le Pirate* on the beach, which includes tasty wood-grilled *brochettes de mer* and red snapper fillets on its good-value €14 menu.

Surfing and **windsurfing** equipment can be rented at the Centre Nautique de Porto-Pollo, at the entrance to the village. **Divers** are catered for by Porto-Pollo Plongeé (☎04 95 74 07 46), based in a Portakabin above the marina (accessible from the road). It runs dives to the spectacular Cathédrales, an underwater massif of rock pinnacles on the northern side of the gulf, as well as to some of the superb sites around Campomoro; rates start at around €35 per person for a guided dive. For more details on the underwater attractions in this area, go to their website ⓦhttp://perso.wanadoo.fr/portopolloplongee.

Beaches around Porto-Pollo

Staying in Porto-Pollo, you're spoilt for choice when it comes to **beaches**. Sandy southwest-facing coves scallop the entire north coast of the Golfe de Valinco, although getting to them can be tricky without some form of transport. Pick of the crop, and the least accessible, has to be gorgeous **Cupabia**, a twenty-minute drive (or enjoyable two-hour walk) northwest. Further east, you'll find acres of room at the sweeping **Plage de Taravo**, even in high summer, when the string of smaller strands lining the remaining stretch, skirted by the D157, tend to get swamped by campers from the sites dotted along the main road.

If sidestepping the crowds is a priority and you're happy to admire these beaches from afar, consider taking to the **Tra Mare e Monti Sud**, the way-marked footpath running along the maquis-covered ridges between Olmeto and the bed of the Taravo Valley. You can also use it to reach Cupabia from Porto-Pollo. For a general outline of the route, see Chapter 8, p.403.

Plage de Cupabia and the Tour de Capannelle

Lining the sheltered end of a deep blue bay against an amphitheatre of near-deserted hills, **Plage de Cupabia** is the most scenic of the Valinco region's beaches, yet sufficiently difficult to reach to have escaped large-scale development. To reach it **by car** from Porto-Pollo, take the first left (the D155) off the Propriano road and follow the bends uphill through the hamlet of Serra-di-Ferro (where you can pull over for the walk to the Tour de Capannelle; see below). Around 2km later you'll come to a junction, just after which a side road turns downhill to Cupabia, as indicated by a sign. The beach can also be reached on foot **via the Tra Mare e Monti Sud**, whose orange waymarks strike uphill from the roadside in the centre of Porto-Pollo (look for the wooden PNRC signboard from opposite the far northern end of the beach). Rounding the Punta Contra Grossa, the hill above the port, the path swings sharply northeast along the ridgetop towards to the village of Serra-di-Ferro. Five minutes after this bend, look for another (badly overgrown) path turning left into the maquis between two drystone boundary walls: this leads downhill via an old olive orchard to the sadly dilapidated **Tour de Capannelle**, reached around thirty minutes later and well worth the detour for the views over the bay. The orange waymarks, meanwhile, carry on past the turning for the tower and the *Village de Vacances Les Arbousiers* to Serra-di-Ferra, veering left at a PNRC signboard to begin a leisurely descent to the beach. Allow around two hours for the walk from Porto-Pollo, not including the diversion to the tower.

Cupabia bay, at the far western edge of the Golfe de Valinco, was the scene of an extraordinary, but now almost forgotten, episode during the Fascist occupation of World War II. Its remote situation, far beyond the reach of Italian searchlights, was exploited by the British SOE (Secret Operations Executive) to mount an undercover mission, code-named "Sea Urchin", whose aim was to co-ordinate resistance activities on the island and set up a radio link with the Free French command in Algiers. Three agents were selected for the job, led by **Fred Scamaroni**, a 29-year-old Corsican, personally chosen by de Gaulle, who had already made several clandestine trips to Vichy France, Algeria and London. Accompanying him were another Frenchman the radio operator Lieutenant Hellier – and SOE agent James Jickell, from Cardiff, Wales.

On the night of 6–7 June, 1943, the British submarine *Tribune* surfaced and the party was rowed ashore to a tiny beach on the rim of Cupabia bay called U Scogliu Biancu. They carried with them suitcases stuffed with clothes, replacement crystals for the radio set, weapons and a large sum of money – 600,000 French francs and US$500 – destined for the Corsican Resistance, which they hid under a bush. Having been forced to change their original rendezvous point, the team had quickly to make contact with the reception committee of local partisans waiting for them on the other side of Capo di Muro headland and split up, with Scamaroni riding to Ajaccio on a folding bicycle brought especially for the purpose. The other two walked to the capital.

Once they'd re-formed, the mission's first priority was to collect the bags hidden at U Scogliu Biancu. But by the time they returned to the tiny cove (by boat disguised as fishermen), they found that someone had beaten them to it: the suitcase containing the crystals, guns and money was missing.

In an area of uniform poverty such as this, sudden wealth was never likely to go unnoticed, and within a short time discreet inquiries around the local bars revealed that a 17-year-old shepherd boy had been seen wearing new clothes and flashing large-denomination notes around. When confronted at his home, the lad, who admitted he'd found the cases while setting nets to catch blackbirds, returned the mission's funds and gear. But before Scamaroni had time to count the bills, the boy slipped away to Bastia with 150,000 francs of the cash. He was, however, caught soon after in mid-spending spree by Resistance men in Bastia and returned to Côti-Chiavari to face the wrath of his father.

The mission may have begun in a picaresque fashion, but it ended tragically for most of those involved. Denounced by a double agent only two months after the landing, Fred Scamaroni slit his own his throat with a length of electrical wire in the dungeons of Ajaccio citadel rather than reveal the names of his accomplices under torture. Hellier was also caught by OVRA, the Italian gestapo, and shot on July 15, only a couple of months before the liberation. The shepherd boy, perhaps to redeem his dishonorable deception, signed up with the Free French army in September 1943 and was killed in battle on the Continent. Only the Welshman Jickell survived the war.

Only a scruffy campsite and a solitary *buvette* stand behind the long curve of soft white sand, which nevertheless sees a fair number of visitors in summer. To escape most of them, head right when you arrive at the beach and over the rocks at its far end to two secluded coves, where some driftwood structures and tall bushes provide more shade than you'll find on Cupabia proper.

Heading in the opposite direction, you can also walk south across the beach to pick up the old customs officers' path, **Le Sentier des Douaniers**, which leads past a little cove where you'll find a gate; beyond this, the path snakes through the maquis towards the Tour de Capannelle, reached after a steeper ten-minute climb though dense scrub.

Plage de Taravo

Two kilometres east of Porto-Pollo lies a second enormous stretch of sand, **Plage de Taravo** and the contiguous **Plage de Tenutella**, separated by a narrow tidal creek. This beach is busier than Cupabia due to the presence of a couple of campsites behind it (see below), but is large enough to absorb even the August deluge. You'll need a car to get there: the approach is via a kilometre-long *piste* which turns right (south) off the D757 2km out of Porto-Pollo – look for the sign for *Camping Cyrnos* (July to mid-Sept), a small site shaded by straggly poplars and lime trees, whose only plus is its proximity to the sand.

Olmeto-Plage

The stretch of coast between the mouth of the Taravo River and eastern extremity of the gulf, crossed by the winding D157, shelters a necklace of pretty beaches, all of them easily accessible by road. Traversed by the Tra Mare e Monti Sud trail, the hinterland is a rippling hillside littered with dozens of pastel-coloured holiday villas and a series of large, sheltered campsites strategically placed for easy access to the coves. In high season, the whole area, collectively known as **Olmeto–Plage**, becomes one large holiday centre, serviced by a disconcertingly busy road, but outside school holidays you can expect to have most of the beaches to yourself.

The main agglomeration of shops, hotels and restaurants is at **ABBARTELLO**, a ribbon development that begins at the southeastern end of the Plage de Tenutella and straggles along the main road, overlooking three small *criques* with lovely views across the gulf to Campomoro. Much the best-value place to stay here is the modern *Hôtel Abbartello* (☎04 95 74 04 73 or 04 95 21 96 09, ℱ04 95 74 06 17; mid-April to Sept; ❸), which offers some of the cheapest rooms in the area (down to €25 in shoulder season), most of them sea-facing, en-suite and with breezy terraces; those on the "*côté montagne*" have shared toilets. They also offer lovely self-contained studios that would accommodate a family of four or five, and in May and June rent out larger bungalows for maximum periods of three days. The sunny restaurant terrace, just above the beach, is one of the most idyllic spots for breakfast on the gulf. On the opposite side of the road, *Camping Chez Antoine* (☎04 95 76 06 06) is a small, basic and inexpensive site – ideal if you're passing through, but a lot less comfortable than the swish three-stars you'll see further along the main road to Propriano.

One of the largest of these, *U Libecciu* (☎04 95 74 01 28, ℱ04 95 74 28 44, ✉camping.ulibecciu@wanadoo.fr), lining a small, dark side valley above a bend in the D157, stands opposite the track down to **Cala Piscona**, one of the gulf's most beautiful beaches, though one to be avoided in high season if you want to keep clear of the crowds.

The next couple of coves, below the holiday campus at **CAPICCIOLO**, have become something of a British enclave, albeit a discreet one. You can spend a night here in style at the *Le Ruesco* (☎04 95 76 70 50, ℱ04 95 76 70 51; May–Oct; ❼), an exclusive, modern three-star built just beneath the beach, with luminous sea-facing rooms and large private balconies: ask for one on the first floor, which enjoy the best of the views over the gulf. Their *pied dans l'eau* restaurant, *L'Aria Marina*, which has a leafy terrace slap on the sand, makes a gorgeous breakfast venue and they also serve lunch and dinner of top seafood meals such as fresh crayfish and lobsters, though it's pricy.

The long golden beach east around the headland from Capicciola, the **Plage de Campitellu**, is a spectacular sight from above though a less enticing spot on closer inspection, swamped early in the season by German campers from the two sites behind it. Access is easiest via the broad road running to the sports pitch at the beach's southeastern end, which sweeps down to a large car park. En route, you pass the immaculately restored **Tour de Calanca**, privately owned and closed to the public.

At the eastern extremity of the gulf, close to Propriano, the **Plage de Baracci**, unsafe for swimming due to its formidable undertow, is backed by a large expanse of unsightly scrub on which you'll see the remains of a restaurant destroyed nearly a decade ago by nationalist bombers. For reviews of accommodation and the riding stables at Baracci, see p.239.

Filitosa

Eight thousand years of history are encapsulated by the extraordinary **Station Préhistorique de Filitosa** (Easter–Oct daily 9am–sunset; out of season by arrangement only; ☎04 95 74 00 91; €4), 10km inland from Porto-Pollo. Little is known about the peoples who inhabited this spot, a fact that adds an element of mystery to **FILITOSA**'s statue-menhirs, which glare amid meadows, gnarled old olive groves and patches of wild mint – a scene little changed since their creation. The site remained undiscovered until **Charles–Antoine Cesari** came upon the ruins on his farmland in 1948. He and **Roger Grosjean**, who was to become head of the centre for archeological research in Sartène, set about a full-scale excavation, discovering some menhirs lying face down in the maquis, others broken at waist level inside what is now known as the central monument (you can read an evocative firsthand account of the discovery in Dorothy Carrington's *Granite Island*; see p.439). When the digging was completed the menhirs were set into lines, and the site was opened to the public in 1954.

There's no public **transport** to Filitosa, but the Propriano to Porto-Pollo bus will take you as far as the D157/D57 junction, just before the Taravo bridge, from where you can hitch the remaining 6–7km; hitching is fairly reliable during the summer, when nearly all the traffic on these back roads is heading to or from the site.

A brief history of Filitosa

Filitosa was occupied from 6000 BC, when it was settled by **Neolithic** farming people who lived here in rock shelters. Flakes of obsidian, used to make arrowheads and only available from the Aeolian Islands and Sardinia, have been unearthed, indicating that the first Filitosans must have engaged in trade, but little else is known about them, other than the fact they were colonized some time between 3500 and 3000 BC by **megalithic** peoples from the East. Believed to have been missionary navigators, these early invaders came in search of converts to their faith, as well as land and metals, and were the creators of the first menhirs, the earliest of which were possibly phallic symbols worshipped by an ancient fertility cult. Later statues display stylized human features, making them quite distinct from nearly all other European menhirs of the megalithic period – such as those at Stonehenge and Avebury – which would seem to have been abstract expressions of devotion to a godhead rather than tributes to humankind. Most archeologists believe that the representational menhirs were memorials to dead chieftains and warriors. Grosjean, however, maintained that they were portraits of enemy **Torréeans**, who – most people agree – arrived in the Golfe de Porto-Vecchio from the eastern

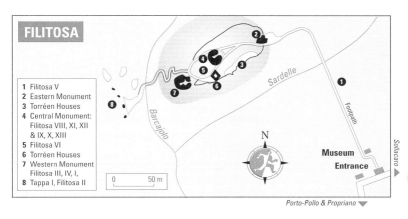

FILITOSA

1 Filitosa V
2 Eastern Monument
3 Torréen Houses
4 Central Monument:
   Filitosa VIII, XI, XII
   & IX, X, XIII
5 Filitosa VI
6 Torréen Houses
7 Western Monument
   Filitosa III, IV, I,
8 Tappa I, Filitosa II

0   50 m

N

Museum
Entrance

Sardelle

Barcajolo

Footpath

Sollacaro ▶

Porto-Pollo & Propriano ▼

THE SOUTH | The Golfe de Valinco

⑤

Mediterranean around 1700 BC. To back up his theory, Grosjean cites Aristotle, who claimed the ancient Iberians used to raise stones around the tombs of slain enemies; moreover, very few knives or daggers like the ones depicted have ever been found in megalithic sites on the island, nor at the time of the invasions did the farmers of Filitosa have the technology to make them.

As they settled, the Torréens built conical structures known as **torri** (towers) all over the south of Corsica. Again, no one is absolutely certain of their function; it's generally agreed that the smaller of these beehive-like towers are likely to have been used as places of worship to some divinity, though traces of ashes and bones in the vicinity also suggest these could have been where the Torréens burned or buried their dead. The larger *torri*, too small for human habitation, are thought to have served as stores for weapons or food, or perhaps as refuges or lookout towers.

When the Torréens conquered Filitosa around 1300 BC, they destroyed most of the menhirs, incorporating the broken stones into the area of dry-stone walling surrounding the site's two *torri*. Around the towers, the remains of which are the central and western monuments, they constructed a village of Cyclopean stone shacks – a complex known as a **casteddu**. As such *casteddi* became more numerous, their inhabitants were forced into attacking neighbouring settlements in order to protect their land and livestock. Grosjean believed that competition between the *casteddi* forced Torréen expeditions to migrate to northern Sardinia, which would explain the existence on that island of **nuraghi**, larger and more technically advanced versions of *torri*. A rival theory, however, suggests that the Torréens were in fact indigenous Corsicans who simply acquired their technical expertise from the Sardinian *nuraghi* builders.

The site

Vehicles can be left for free in the small **car park** opposite the main entrance. From there it's a five-minute walk to the site proper, which includes a small **museum** (best seen at the end of your visit) and a workshop producing reproduction prehistoric ceramics. Intrusive trilingual listening posts were recently installed at key positions, so get here early in the day if you want to escape the annoying recorded commentaries, which can severely detract from the natural beauty and haunting atmosphere of the site.

Filitosa V looms up on the right shortly after the entrance. The largest statue-menhir on the island, it's an imposing sight, with clearly defined facial features and a sword and dagger outlined on the body. Beyond a sharp left turn lies the oppidum or central monument, its entrance marked by the **eastern platform**, thought to have been a lookout post. The cave-like structure sculpted out of the rock is the only evidence of Neolithic occupation and is generally agreed to have been a burial mound.

Straight ahead, the Torréen **central monument** comprises a scattered group of menhirs on a circular walled mound, surmounted by a dome and entered by a corridor of stone slabs and lintels. Nobody is sure of its exact function.

Nearby **Filitosa XIII** and **Filitosa IX**, implacable lumps of granite with long noses and round chins, are the most impressive menhirs on the site – indeed Grosjean considered Filitosa IX to be the finest of all western Mediterranean megalithic statues. Filitosa XIII, the last menhir to be discovered here (the Torréens had built it into the base of the central monument), is typical of the figures carved just before the Torréen invasion, with its vertical dagger carved in relief – **Filitosa VII** also has a clearly sculpted sword and shield. **Filitosa VI**, from the same period, is remarkable for its facial detail. On the eastern side of the central monument stand some vestigial Torréen houses, where fragments of ceramics dating from 5500 BC were discovered; they represent the most ancient finds on the site, and some of them are displayed in the museum.

The **western monument**, a two-roomed structure built underneath another walled mound, is thought to have been some form of Torréen religious building. A steep flight of rough steps leads to the foot of this mound, where a tiny footbridge leads into the meadow, on the other side of which five statue-menhirs are arranged in a wide semicircle beneath a thousand-year-old olive tree. A bank separates them from a jumble of contorted, nobbly grey rocks – the **quarry** from which the megalithic sculptors hewed the stone for the menhirs. A granite block, marked ready for cutting, has been propped up on stakes to make a seat from which you can survey the site.

The **museum** is a shoddy affair, with poorly labelled exhibits and very little contextual information, but the artefacts themselves are fascinating. The major item here is the formidable **Scalsa Murta**, a huge menhir dating from around 1400 BC and discovered at Olmeto. Like other statue-menhirs of this period, this one has two indents in the back of its head, which are thought to indicate that these figures would have been adorned with headdresses like the horn that's been attached to Scalsa Murta. Other notable exhibits are **Filitosa XII**, which has a hand and a foot carved into the stone, and **Trappa II**, a strikingly archaic face. Explanatory notes and photographs around the walls sketch the progression of the excavations.

Inland from Filitosa

The lower Taravo Valley, a wide sweep of sparsely populated land patched with olive groves and old walled pastures, funnels **inland from Filitosa** towards the shadowy profile of the watershed peaks. Its principal village, high on the lip of the valley above the prehistoric site, is **SOLLACARO** (Suddacaru), which boasts the distinction of having hosted the first meeting of James Boswell and Pascal Paoli on October 21, 1765 (see box) – a plaque opposite the post office commemorates the occasion. The scene of the historic encounter, immortalized in Boswell's *Journal*, was a room in the top right-hand corner of a house which still stands above the main street: look for the prominently carved "1755" inscription on the wall. It is occupied by the same family who lived here back then – the former owners of the land at Filitosa, bought by the Cesaris only months before they discovered the menhirs in the late 1940s.

Dr Johnson's biographer courted men of genius as assiduously as he pursued women, and one of his early conquests was the Corsican patriot **Pascal Paoli**. In 1765, at the age of 25, **James Boswell** contrived to make the acquaintance of the great French philosopher Rousseau in Switzerland. The Corsicans, struggling to formalize their independence, had asked the author of the *Social Contract* to give them a new set of laws. In certain circles Corsica had something of the appeal that Greece was to offer Byron's generation sixty years later, and Boswell promptly suggested that Rousseau make him his ambassador to the Corsicans. He duly received a letter of introduction, which he was able to present to Paoli the following year.

The meeting was a far more nerve-racking experience for Boswell than his encounter with the philosopher. "I had stood in the presence of many a prince but I never had such a trial as in the presence of Paoli," he wrote. "For ten minutes we walked backwards and forwards through the room hardly saying a word, while he looked at me with a steadfast, keen and penetrating eye, as if he searched my very soul." A student of physiognomy, Paoli also feared an attempt on his life, so the close scrutiny was scarcely surprising, and it didn't hinder the development of a friendship that was to hold throughout Paoli's later exile in London.

The success of Boswell's book about his visit, *An Account of Corsica – the Journal of a Tour to that Island and Memoirs of Pascal Paoli*, helped launch his social and literary career in London, and commemorated a passion that endured throughout his life. In 1769, the year of the book's publication, he attended the first annual celebration of Shakespeare's birthday in Stratford-on-Avon, an event organized by the actor David Garrick. Boswell appeared at the celebrations dressed in the Corsican national costume and wearing in his hat a card that read "Corsica Boswell".

The village bar, *U Paese*, is a pleasant and welcoming place to re-fuel, serving delicious *bruschetta* made with local cheese and charcuterie. There's also a particularly good **bed and breakfast** place in the area: M et Mme Tardif's *chambres d'hôtes* (☎04 95 74 29 48 or 06 62 43 13 69; ●), situated 3km back down towards Filitosa. Signposted off the road, their house occupies a magnificent belvedere overlooking the valley, with modest but immaculately kept rooms (all en suite) opening on to a communal terrace. You can breakfast outside with the views, or in the family dining room upstairs.

Calzola

Two still more remote **places to stay and eat** are tucked away on the floor of the valley, near the hamlet of **CALZOLA**, reachable via the D757 from Porto-Pollo, the D457 from just below Filitosa, or on the scenic D302, which turns inland below Sollacaro and then winds downhill to the **Pont de Calzola**. Just next to the bridge (on its south side) stands the reputed *Auberge U Mulinu* (☎054 95 24 32 14, ⓕ04 95 24 30 09; ●), a restored water mill on whose riverside terrace you can enjoy traditional Taravo cuisine, notably wild river trout stuffed with *brocciu* and mint. Menus are priced at €15, €20 and €28. They also have fourteen rooms that are small and lacking character, but convenient if you decide to make the most of the wine list, which features the special Abbatucci *blanc*, produced just down the lane.

In addition to growing some of the area's finest wines, the neighbouring Abbatucci family run a deliciously down-to-earth **restaurant** and **campsite**, *Le Kiesale* (☎04 95 24 35 81 or 04 95 24 36 30; open year round), 500m beyond the *Auberge U Mulinu*. Having pitched your tent on one of their secluded, well-shaded terraces, you can order wonderful grilled organic lamb at the family restaurant, washed down with the *domaine*'s own wines, which here cost a fraction of what you pay for them in the shops. Nearly everything on the menu comes straight from the farm, except the wood-grilled fish of the day, which provides the ideal compliment for the Abbatuccis' prize-winning white.

If you're relying on **buses**, the good news is you can reach Calzola on Autocars Ricci's Propriano–Ajaccio service, which runs daily (except on Sundays) in July and Aug, and on Mondays, Wednesdays and Fridays the rest of the year.

Olmeto

Coming from Ajaccio and heading south, your first glimpse of the stunning Golfe de Valinco comes just below **Col de Celaccia** (583m), where a series of steep turns brings you down to **OLMETO**, situated 4km below the pass. With its grandstand view over Propriano, Olmeto was once a favourite spot with artists such as Edward Lear, and it remains a captivating place, close to the coast but far enough from Propriano to retain a village atmosphere, compromised only by holiday traffic clogging up the main road through the centre in summer. Once off the road, however, you're instantly hemmed in by lofty buildings and sleepy back alleys.

Contrary to appearances, life in Olmeto has not always been peaceful. The village was actually established on this high, easily defensible site to provide protection from the constant pirate raids that menaced the gulf from the fifteenth to seventeenth century; in 1617, fifty villagers were abducted and taken as slaves to North Africa. The village is also renowned for its bloody **vendettas**, some of which carried on well into the twentieth century; in *Granite Island*, Dorothy Carrington recalls meeting an old man who could name twenty people murdered there in his lifetime. Most famous of all the Corsican vendettas was the one instigated by **Colomba Carabelli**, the heroine of Mérimée's novel *Colomba*, who died here in 1861, aged 96, in the forbidding *palazzo* facing the mairie. Her reputation still attracts a few admirers, but what brings most tourists to Olmeto today are the views from the village's two main streets, which are linked by steep stairways, with the foundations of the houses vanishing into a valley whose olive groves once sustained the local economy.

Just before you enter the village, you'll notice the ruined **Castello di a Rocca** crowning an isolated peak on the opposite side of the valley. This inaccessible bastion was inhabited in the fourteenth century by Arrigho della Rocca, the fiery great-grandson of Giudice della Cinarca. Exiled to Spain in 1362, Arrigho enlisted the support of the king of Aragon and returned to Corsica ten years later, intent on taking over the whole island. He virtually succeeded, with only Calvi and Bonifacio holding out against him, and as count of Corsica ruled the island for four years until his death at Vizzavona in 1401, poisoned by one of his own vassals.

Practicalities

Straddling the busy N196, Olmeto is served by Eurocorse Voyages' regular **buses** between Ajaccio and Porto-Vecchio, which run via Propriano and Sartène, as well as Autocars Ricci's Ajaccio–Alta Rocca service. The **place to stay** here is *U Santa Maria – Chez Mimi* (T 04 95 74 65 59, F 04 95 74 60 33; March–Oct, obligatory half board in August; ❸), an old-fashioned inn next to the church with twelve spotless, bright rooms looking over the rooftops. Run by the inimitable Mimi, the hotel possesses loads more character than anything in Propriano and has a dependable little **restaurant** featuring locally reared lamb with wild mushrooms on its €18.50 menu.

Propriano

Bracketed by the promontory of Scogliu Lungu, the fine natural harbour of **PROPRIANO**, 71km southwest of Ajaccio, was exploited by the ancient Greeks, Carthaginians and Romans, but became a prime target for pirate raids and by the eighteenth century had been largely destroyed. The Port de Commerce, developed at the beginning of this century, now handles **ferries** to the French mainland and Sardinia, but still has an unfinished appearance. This is due in part to terrorist bombs: the post office, a symbol of the French administration and especially targeted for its isolated position here, has had to be rebuilt four times over the last thirteen years after nationalist attacks.

The amount of building work going on here also bears witness to the pace of change in Propriano, which has, in a little over fifteen years, metamorphosed from a sleepy fishing village into the service centre for an area capable of accommodating 23,000 visitors in peak season. Chief among the architects of this rapid transformation was the former mayor, Émile Mocchi, who ran the local town hall for more than two decades before being imprisoned on embezzlement charges – appropriately enough for an area long renowned for its corrupt officialdom and Mafia connections.

Propriano's internal politics don't seem to deter the tourists, however, who come for the beaches, the sailing, diving and other watersports. For people just passing through, the resort provides useful amenities (supermarkets and ATMs, for example) at the midway point between Ajaccio and Bonifacio.

Arrival and information

Ferries dock in the Port de Commerce, west of the town centre and ten minutes' walk from rue Général-de-Gaulle, the town's main street, which runs at right angles to the water. **Buses** pull into the little square in front of the church, reached via a flight of steps from the bottom of rue Général-de-Gaulle. The **tourist office** down in the marina (July & Aug daily 8am–8pm; June & Sept Mon–Sat 9am–noon & 3–7pm; Oct–May Mon–Fri 9am–noon & 2–6pm; ☎04 95 76 01 49) has up-to-date timetables for transport services all over the island, along with glossy accommodation brochures.

Accommodation

Propriano has a disproportionate number of tourist beds for its size and finding **accommodation** is rarely a problem, even during peak season. There are several good mid-range hotels in the centre of town, but with a car you might consider heading down the coast to Campomoro, or north around the gulf to more peaceful Olmeto-Plage (p.231) and Porto-Pollo (p.227).

Hotels

Arcu di Sole route de Baracci ☎04 95 76 05 10, ℻04 95 76 13 36. A large, modern pink building with green shutters, just off the main Ajaccio road, 3km west of town (turn inland by the Total petrol station). The ground-floor rooms have little balconies; those to the rear are pleasantly shaded. No views to speak of, but there's a garden pool, gourmet restaurant, tennis courts and mini-golf for the kids. April–Oct, half board obligatory in July and August. ⑤

Beach Hôtel av Napoléon ☎04 95 76 17 74, ℻04 95 76 06 54. Spacious and comfortable en-suite rooms, all recently refurbished, in a four-storey block overlooking the Port de Commerce/Plage du Phare. ⑤

Bellevue av Napoléon ☎04 95 76 01 86, ℻04 95 76 38 94. The cheapest central hotel, halfway down av Napoléon and overlooking the marina; all rooms have balconies with a view of the gulf and are cheerfully decorated; the bar is lively and frequented by locals. ④

Claridge rue Bonaparte ☎04 95 76 05 54, ℻04 95 76 27 77. A newish building in the middle of town, with comfortable rooms (from €50 in shoulder season) but grim views. March–Oct. ⑤

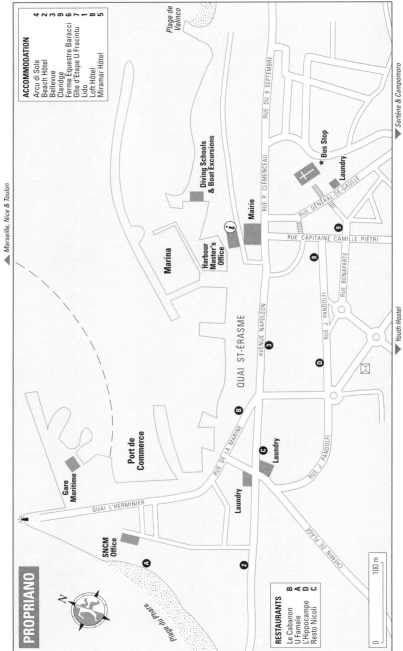

❹, ❺, ❻, ❼, Plage de Baracci, Porto-Pollo & Ajaccio ▲

▲ Marseille, Nice & Toulon

▼ Sartène & Campomoro

▼ Youth Hostel

PROPRIANO

Plage de Valinco

RUE DU 9 SEPTEMBRE

Bus Stop ★

Laundry

RUE P. CLÉMENCEAU

RUE GENERAL-DE-GAULLE

Mairie

Diving Schools & Boat Excursions

RUE CAPITAINE CAMILLE PIÉTRI ❾

ⓘ

Harbour Master's Office

RUE BONAPARTE

Marina

RUE J. PANDOLFI

❽

AVENUE NAPOLÉON

QUAI ST-ÉRASME

❸

Ⓓ

RUE J. PANDOLFI

Port de Commerce

Gare Maritime

QUAI L'HERMINIER

RUE DE LA MARINE

Ⓑ

Laundry Ⓒ

Laundry

SNCM Office

Ⓐ

❷

CHEMIN DE PLAGE

Plage du Phare

N

100 m

0

ACCOMMODATION

Arcu di Sole	4
Beach Hôtel	2
Bellevue	3
Claridge	9
Ferme Equestre Baracci	6
Gîte d'Étape U Fracintu	7
Lido	1
Loft Hôtel	8
Miramar Hôtel	5

RESTAURANTS

Le Cabanon	B
U Famale	A
L'Hippocampe	D
Resto Nicoli	C

Lido Between Plage du Phare and Plage de Puraja, on the west edge of town ☎04 95 76 06 37, ℻04 95 76 31 18. Dating from the 1930s, this low-rise hotel on the outskirts had a major face-lift recently, but still possesses more character than most of the competition. That said, its rooms, ranged around a cool courtyard with rear terraces jutting on the sand behind, are ridiculously over-priced in high season. ❽

Loft Hôtel 3 rue Capitaine. Camille-Piétri ☎04 95 76 17 48, ℻04 95 76 22 04. Former wine and flour warehouse imaginatively converted into a gleaming hi-tech hotel, with bright, clean rooms overlooking a car park. Good value. Mid-April to Sept. ❸

Miramar Hôtel route de la Grande-Corniche (a continuation of route de Baracci), 3km towards Ajaccio ☎04 95 76 06 13, ℻04 95 76 13 14. Splendid luxury hotel with a huge swimming pool, sauna, gardens and sweeping sea views from its air-con rooms. Not such a great option if you've mobility problems, though, as it has lots of steps. May–Sept. ❽

Gîtes d'étape and campsites

Camping Colomba 3km northeast along the route de Baracci ☎04 95 76 06 42, ℻04 95 76 27 52. Take the right-hand turning off the main road by the Total petrol station to reach this medium-sized, peaceful three-star with good facilities and plenty of shade – the best of the sites within walking distance of town.

Camping Lecci e Murta Portigliolo, 7km west on the Campomoro road ☎04 95 76 02 67, ℻04 95 77 03 38. Large, well-shaded site up a small side valley from Portigliolo beach, with grocery store, tennis courts and pizzeria. Very quiet in shoulder season.

Camping Tikiti 2km northeast towards the route de Baracci ☎04 95 76 08 32. Scruffier and more cramped than the nearby *Colomba*, but fine for a short stay and closer to town.

Ferme Équestre Baracci route de Baracci, 3km northeast of town ☎ & ℻ 04 95 76 19 48. Half-a-dozen small twin-bedded doubles (with or without toilets) next to one of the island's top riding centres. They also do good-value evening meals (€14; order in advance by 5pm). Friendly and certain to please if you like horses, but a bit far from town to reach on foot. ❹

Gîte d'Étape U Fracintu 7km northeast of Propriano at Burgo ☎04 95 76 15 05, ℻04 95 76 14 31. One of the largest hikers' hostels in Corsica, with sixty dorm beds and a couple of cheap double rooms (€35). Lovely views across the valley from its terrace, and right next to the Mare a Mare Sud trailhead. Advance booking essential. ❷

Beaches and boat excursions

The nearest **beach** to Propriano, **Plage du Phare**, lies a short way past the Port de Commerce. A steep crescent of yellow sand, it's surveyed by lifeguards during the summer but gets swamped at lunchtimes. Just around the headland, past the *Hôtel Lido*, **Plage de Puraja** is a much longer expanse of grey sand, backed by a big concrete hotel, that can seem pretty bleak in the heat. With more time, or your own transport, it's worth continuing around the coast to **Plage de Capu Laurosu**, a vast golden curve that rarely gets too crowded, at least if you're prepared to walk south beyond the aerodrome towards the **Plage de Portigliolo**, the beach's southern end.

North of Propriano, **Plage de Baracci** is less than ideal: locals avoid it because of the strong undertow and unsightly heaps of rubbish littering the wasteland behind. For an account of more appealing **Olmeto–Plage**, and the beaches lining the north shore of the gulf, covered by daily minibus from Propriano during the summer, see p.231.

An alternative way of reaching some of the less accessible stretches of the gulf is to take a **boat excursion** from the marina. Particularly recommended are those on the catamaran *Big Blue* and its sister cruiser, *Valinco*, in their "Mer et Maquis" tour. For bookings, go to their Portakabin at the far end of the marina past the tourist office. You are supplied with maps and photos for the walk up the coast from Campomoro (see box on p.241), at the end of which they'll collect you at a remote bay, Cala d'Agulia, around 4.30pm. They also operate a cruise to the far-flung Senetosa tower, enlivened by underwater music.

Restaurants

Le Cabanon route de la Marine ☎04 95 76 07 76. Gourmet fish restaurant, with terrace, at the west end of the marina towards the port. Their €13 lunch menu is excellent value, but the pricier options (€24–28) include more imaginative dishes such as king prawns in ginger.

U Famale Plage du Phare ☎04 95 76 43 06. Relative newcomer, at a prime spot with a terrace offering great views across the beach and gulf. The menu, featuring mussels à la crème, fish of the day and various *grillades*, is reasonably priced, and they do the full range of Fiumicicioli wines. Live Corsican music each evening.

L'Hippocampe rue Jean-Pandolfi ☎04 95 76 11 01. Tucked away behind the port, this is the best place for classy seafood at affordable prices, and their €22 menu offers unbeatable value for Propriano. Dine inside, where nautical bits and bobs provide the decor, or outside on a flowery roadside terrace.

Resto Nicoli av Napoléon ☎06 77 58 05 94. An Italian-style budget restaurant near the port, and just about the cheapest place to eat; the rock-bottom but generous €10 menu features *beignets de courgettes* and a complimentary liqueur for "nice customers", and they leave the cheese plate on your table.

Listings

Banks There are ATMs at the *poste* on the western edge of town, at the junction of rue du 9 Septembre and av Napoléon, and on rue Général-de-Gaulle.

Bus information For routes and frequencies, see "Travel details", p.291. Tickets for all departures are sold on the buses, which leave from in front of the church above rue Générale-de-Gaulle.

Diving Valinco Plongée (☎04 95 76 31 01) and U Levante (☎04 95 76 23 83), both in the marina. See also Porto-Pollo, p.227.

Doctors Dr Peninon, 11 av Napoléon ☎04 95 76 01 98; Dr Quilichini, 3 av Napoléon ☎04 95 76 00 96.

Ferries Services to Marseille and Toulon depart from the Port de Commerce between the last week of March and the end of September. Contact the SNCM, quai l'Herminier, for bookings ☎04 95 76 04 36, ℉04 95 76 00 98. For an idea of prices and frequencies, see p.20.

Horse riding The Centre Équestre de Baracci, 3km northeast on the route de Baracci, a five-minute walk from the Total station (☎04 95 76 19 48), offers guided rides for around €20 per hour on particularly beautiful horses especially bred for the island. They also do longer *randonnées* from €610 for a 7-night trip into the Sartenais *profond* to €1220 for a 17-day traverse of the whole island.

Hospital The nearest hospital with a casualty department is situated 6km southwest of Sartène, near Bocca Albitrina, just off the D21 (the back road to Belvédère).

Laundry Propriano has two self-service laundries (*laveries automatiques*): one just down from the tourist office on rue Général-de-Gaulle, the other opposite the Port de Commerce on av Napoléon.

Motorbike and mountain-bike rental Mountain bikes (*VTT*) and 50cc or 80cc scooters for rent through TCC, 25 rue Général-de-Gaulle (☎04 95 76 15 32), and Location Valinco (aka JLV), 25 av Napoléon (☎04 95 76 11 84); both also have a couple of 125cc trials bikes (€50–60 per day).

Pharmacy One on rue Général-de-Gaulle and another around the corner on av Napoléon.

Taxis There's a rank on rue Camille-Pietri, off the av Napoléon (☎04 95 76 11 03). Taxis charge €15–22 for the ride out to the trailhead of the Mare a Mare Sud at Burgo, depending on the time of day. Count on double that for Campomoro.

Campomoro

Isolated at the mouth of the Golfe de Valinco, **CAMPOMORO**, 17km southwest of Propriano, ranks among the most congenial seaside villages on the island. The main attraction here is the beach: 1km or so of gently curving golden sand and translucent sea, overlooked by an immense Genoese watchtower. In late July and August it's inundated with Italian families from the nearby campsites, but for the rest of the year Campomoro remains a sleepy place, with barely enough permanent residents to support a year-round post office. The village basically consists of one road, which turns left when it arrives at the beach and then runs in a curve around the bay, coming to a dead end below the promontory, which you can scale in ten or fifteen minutes to reach the **tower** (summer 9am–7pm; free), a lookout point surveying the entire gulf.

South of Campomoro stretches one of the wildest coastlines in Corsica: a windswept, sun-baked expanse of gently undulating maquis fringed by outlandish rock formations and empty beaches. The absence of a road into the area, nowadays officially protected as a regional nature reserve, means the only way to explore it is on foot, though there exist enough 4WD tracks to make it accessible to intrepid drivers, motorcyclists and mountain-bikers. This is also a stronghold of the Corsican wild boar, and a tangle of cartridge-strewn hunters' trails crisscrosses the deserted sea-facing slopes. Hikers, however, should stick to the recently inaugurated **coastal path**, or *sentier littoral*, which begins below the Campomoro watchtower and winds south through a string of flotsam-covered coves around Capo di Senetosa, crowned with a much-photographed Genoese tower, to Tizzano in 5hr 30min–6hr. Before setting off, get hold of a copy of the official accompanying leaflet, *De Campomoro à Senetosa*, available free from tourist offices in the area (and from most hotels). Aside from giving a detailed rundown of the history, flora and fauna of the path, it includes a helpful pull-out map. The more detailed and dependable IGN **map** covering the area is #4154 OT.

If you attempt to follow the route all the way to Tizzano, be prepared for some rough tussles with the maquis, which is made up of some particularly vicious gorse, mastic and juniper scrub. The path is cleared only once each year (by a lone Moroccan labourer) and gets muddled at several points with animal trails. You should also bear in mind the risks of **heat and dehydration**: there is only one spring before Tizzano and it shouldn't be relied upon. Lose your way once or twice and you could well find your water supply running dangerously low.

The path, waymarked with splashes of paint and the occasional rusting waymark posts or cairns, is easy to follow for the first 1hr 45min or so, as it threads through a series of dramatic granite outcrops eroded into phantasmagorical shapes. But once you've hit the **Anse d'Eccica**, a rather polluted bottlenecked cove backed by a scruffy little beach, the going gets markedly tougher. To pick up the trail again, head along the stream bed that winds inland for around 200m until you reach a waymark post, beyond which the trail plunges into tall, dense maquis. Climbing to a low pass over the ridge of the headland, it then drops down the other side to **Cala d'Arana**, a secluded cove where hunters have cobbled together tables, chairs and bivouac sites from driftwood.

After around 2hr 30min you'll arrive at one of the most beautiful beaches along the Littoral Sartenais, **Cala di Conca**, a small bay of soft white sand and turquoise water that can be reached by 4WD vehicles, which explains the numbers of people illegally camping wild here in high summer. There are a number of sheltered bivouac sites behind the beach, and a **spring**, the Funtana du l'Alcula (The Eagle Spring), ten minutes' walk further around the headland to the west of the beach, provides the only source of fresh water between Campomoro and Tizzano – look for the waymarked track striking to the left of the path.

Having rounded Capo di Senetosa, you can make a diversion, flagged by a waymark post at the pronounced bend in the path on the south side of the headland, to the wind-powered **lighthouse** and early seventeenth-century **Tour de Senetosa**, reached via a *piste* and, later, a roughly cairned path.

It takes another two and a half hours to cover the remaining leg to Tizzano, which is less well defined and cleared. The highlight of this section is **Cala di Tivella**, a secluded orange-sand beach with plenty of low trees behind it providing welcome shade. Beyond it, several false trails and stream channels may lead you off into the maquis or rocks along the shore. But keep pressing south and you'll eventually pass **Cala Longa**, a narrow cove with extraordinarily turquoise water, to meet the start of an unsurfaced *piste* that runs the rest of the way into Tizzano via the hamlet of Barcaju. Approaching the inlet, be sure not to wander off to the right down the lane leading to the fort, which is a dead end. A full account of **Tizzano**, and the onward path from there along the coast to Roccapina, appears on p.266.

Practicalities

A word of warning for car drivers: parking in Campomoro is a nightmare in peak season as there's only one small car park and tight restrictions apply on the road (enforced by wardens).

Holiday cottages and swish villas with pools make up most of the village's limited accommodation, so book well ahead if you plan to stay in either of its two **hotels**. *Le Ressac* (℡04 95 74 22 25, ℻04 95 74 23 43; April–Oct; ❹), about 100m behind the chapel, is a friendly family concern, with simply furnished, tiled rooms; those on the upper storey have balconies overlooking the bay or the olive groves behind. Half board (€110 for two) is obligatory between June and September; out of season, doubles here go for under €50. The other hotel, *Le Campomoro* (℡04 95 74 20 89, ℻04 95 74 20 89; ❺), overlooks the beach about 500m from the post office towards the tower. It's more formal and slightly pricier, but the rooms are pleasant and airy.

Much the more appealing of the two **campsites** in the village is *Camping Peretto Les Roseaux* (℡04 95 74 20 52; May–Oct), 500m from the post office down the lane running inland from the beach; it's fairly basic, but generally a lot more peaceful than *Camping Campomoro* (℡04 95 34 56 86), to the left of the road as you approach the village.

Campomoro's perennially popular lunchtime venue is *La Mouette*, opposite the church, which serves a selection of fresh salads, fish from the gulf and *plats du jour* from €10. Their busy terrace makes the most of its situation overlooking the beach, and towards the end of the day fills up with *pétanque* players and pastis-sipping spectators. For a more sophisticated meal, a better choice is *Le Ressac's* **restaurant**, which offers two *menus fixes*: one at €19, offering Corsican standards such as *cannelloni al brocciu*, squid, and lamb stew; and a pricier €28 *menu poisson*, which features the best of the day's catch from the local boats. They also do sumptuous *bouillabaisse* with half-a-dozen or more kinds of fish for €28 per person (order the day before).

For self-caterers, the *alimentation* (summer daily till 8pm) in the middle of the village opposite the post office stocks a better-than-average range of fresh fruit and veg, charcuterie, cheese, local wines, and other essentials (including bread, croissants and delicious *bastelles* from the baker's van).

The Alta Rocca

Winding inland from the Golfe de Valinco, the **Rizzanese River** dominates the varied geography of the **Alta Rocca**, a region of sprawling deciduous woods and deep valleys whose headwaters rise on the slopes of Monte Incudine, southern Corsica's highest peak. Together with the towering Aiguilles de Bavella, its domed summit forms the backdrop to one of the island's most distinctive micro-regions. From their trading posts on the coast, the Genoese were able to make little impression on its scattered villages, heartland of the rebellious Seigneurs della Rocca, who held sway over most of the south until the subjugation of the warlord Rinuccio della Rocca in 1510. The readiness of its inhabitants to take up arms in defence of their honour and independence, however, endured and it was this area more than any other that fixed the Romantic image of Corsica in the minds of outsiders during the nineteenth century: Prosper Mérimée set his best-selling vendetta novel *Colomba* in **Fozzano**, a definitively austere granite village in the hills overlooking Propriano, and some of the most notorious and fêted bandits of the era were the scourge of the maquis above Sartène. Later, in World War II, it was in the Alta Rocca that some of the fiercest Resistance fighting took place, as partisans armed with little more than pine-tree roadblocks and Sten guns inflicted terrible damage on German armoured divisions retreating towards the east coast.

The charms of the Alta Rocca's scattered villages today lie more in the pleasures of uplifting mountain views and café terraces on ancient stone squares than historic sights. But one monument merits a special excursion: the vestiges of prehistoric **Cucuruzzu**, near Levie, whose rock shelters and fortified towers rise from an extraordinary landscape of contorted oak forest and mossy boulders. Easily reachable from the coast, you could nip there in a day-trip from Propriano, breaking the journey at the **Domaine de Fiumicioli** (see p.264), source of what many regard as the island's finest wine, and picturesque **Sainte-Lucie-de-Tallano**, start of a lovely walk through the maquis to a deserted Pisan chapel.

Hotels are few and far between, concentrated mainly in the hill resort of **Zonza**, from where you can walk or drive to one of the island's defining landscapes, the massif of Bavella, with its soaring orange cliffs and pine forest. Further west, **Quenza**, huddled around its bare granite church, offers a more peaceful alternative, or you could base yourself in sleepy **Aullène**, high up on the edge of the Coscione Plateau, a grassy tableland in the lap of Monte Incudine to which shepherds formerly drove their flocks in summer.

It's possible to visit the most accessible of the Alta Rocca villages in a couple of days by car, but really to get to grips with this outstandingly beautiful region you should take to the **Mare a Mare Sud** hiking trail, which winds between Propriano and Porto-Vecchio in four to five days. Threading together the scenic highlights of the Rizzanese and its tributaries, the itinerary brings you at the end of each stage to a pretty village and gîte d'étape. Sections of the route are highlighted as short walks in this chapter. For tips on how to tackle all five stages, see the chapter on "Long-distance walks", p.403.

Three **bus** companies run through the Alta Rocca: operating year round, Autocars Ricci's service from Ajaccio goes as far as Bavella, via Ste-Lucie, Levie and Zonza; Balési's Évasion traverses the region via Aullène, Quenza, Zonza and Bavella en route to Porto-Vecchio; and Eurocorse Voyages connects Ajaccio and Zonza, stopping at Sainte-Lucie, Levie and Carbini. See "Travel details", p.291.

Fozzano

East of Propriano, the north flank of the Alta Rocca region is scattered with old stone villages, of which the best known is **FOZZANO**, 12km inland from Propriano and something of a tourist attraction due to its former reputation as a hotbed of vendetta. Its notoriety dates from the early eighteenth century, when the whole village became politically divided over the Corsican uprising against the Genoese, the lower village lining up behind the Carabelli and Bartoli families, the upper behind the Durazzo and Paoli clans. **Colomba Bartoli**, born a Carabelli, was a driving force within her faction and the most infamous example of the central role played by women in Corsican vendettas (see box on p.244).

In 1830, tension in Fozzano intensified after a quarrel outside the church culminated in three murders, with two victims coming from the Carabelli clan. When, a year later, a confrontation led to the death of another Carabelli, Colomba plotted an ambush in the maquis to murder three of the enemy, but the plan backfired and her son was killed. The result of the mayhem was that Fozzano was thrown into a state of siege: houses were barricaded up and children kept from school. When **Prosper Mérimée** came here in 1839, he talked to the ageing but fiercely rancorous Colomba, who had become something of a celebrity – Flaubert also paid homage to her. The Mérimée novel that came out of their encounter, *Colomba*, made the gang leader famous throughout France as a youthful, cold-hearted and beautiful heroine, a character far removed from the more brutal and ugly reality.

Fozzano's exceptionally high granite buildings and narrow streets are dominated by two towers: the fourteenth-century **Torra Vecchia**, on the left as you come from Arbellara, was the heavily fortified home of the Carabelli; **Torra Nova**, a Genoese construction built in 1548, was home to the Durazzo faction. It's possible to get inside the Torra Nova by asking for the key at the mairie in the main street, and at night the tower is dramatically lit.

At the edge of the village, south of Torra Nova, you'll find **Colomba's house** – the upstairs balcony is supposed to be where she heard the fatal gunshots far below in the maquis. Believing it to be only her enemies who had died, she

The Corsican vendetta

Corsica has long been renowned for its vendettas, or **blood feuds**, which in the past affected nearly every family on the island, dividing dozens of villages and resulting in the kind of body counts normally reserved for civil wars. First alluded to by the Roman chronicler Diodorus Siculus, the institution probably predates the arrival in the early medieval era of the Vandals and Ostrogoths, who are most often blamed by local historians for introducing *vindetta*. The heyday of the Corsican feuds, however, was during the Genoese occupation, when an average of 900 murders were reported annually from a population of only 120,000 – a homicide rate triple that of modern Manhattan. Later, King Théodore tried to tackle the problem by decreeing that anyone found guilty of a vendetta killing be tortured to death and publicly quartered, while Paoli went further, executing murderers and levelling their family houses to erect special "pillars of national disgrace". Vendettas might be sparked off for all sorts of reasons, but rarely did the original offence bear much relation to the gravity of the ensuing feud. At Venzolasco in Casinca, for example, the Sanguinettis and the Paolis committed 36 murders after an argument over a chestnut tree; 14 deaths resulted from the theft of a cock in Castagniccia; and one of the most notorious and long-lasting feuds in the south was provoked by a stray donkey.

To understand how such seemingly trivial incidents could unleash years (or centuries) of violence, it's necessary to appreciate the traditional importance in Corsica of family honour. In close-knit peasant communities, the respect shown to members of a family depended less on its material wealth than on how closely its members adhered to unwritten codes of conduct and morality. Essential for basic survival, unsullied honour ensured the goodwill and economic cooperation of others. Without it, life could be miserable, as one individual's personal dishonour necessarily implicated his or her entire family.

The most common way of shaming a family was through its women, who, while they rarely committed violent acts themselves, often played a seminal role in vendettas. Rape, seduction or elopement were extreme causes, but a feud could easily result if a man merely went for a walk with a girl without the permission of her father. More often, however, vendettas were started on purpose, usually with an act of clear provocation, such as the public humiliation of a female family member outside the village church. In what became known as the **attacar**, a young woman's headscarf would be torn off while she was leaving Mass to cries of "Dishonorata!" from onlookers; this would be met with an on-the-spot stabbing or shooting.

Lost honour was not irredeemable, and could be atoned for with a revenge killing. Thus, following an *attacar,* a solemn vow to avenge the injury would be made before the assembled family. If a murder had been committed, the victim's shirt would be

gloated to the passing Durazzo "there's fresh meat for you down there", and received the retort that there was some for her, too. The tombs of Colomba and her murdered son, Francescu, are in the nearby chapel.

Sainte-Lucie-de-Tallano

One of the most celebrated spectacles in the Alta Rocca is the view over the jigsaw roofscape of **SAINTE-LUCIE-DE-TALLANO**, perched on a green spur high above the Rizzanese Valley. Settled since pre-Roman times, the village was in the late fifteenth and early sixteenth century the stronghold of **Rinuccio della Rocca** who, in addition to being a fearsome thorn in the side of the Genoese, was an eminent patron of the arts, donating many paintings and pieces of Renaissance sculpture to the parish church in between his repeated, and increasingly desperate, attempts to oust the Italian occupiers.

removed, smeared with blood from the wound and nailed to the wall of the house, to be left there until revenge had been exacted. Meanwhile, all windows would be boarded up – both a defensive and symbolic gesture – and the men would allow their beards and hair to grow to indicate their involvement in the feud. From this moment on, no member of either family could live in safety, for the declaration of a vendetta implicated all the relatives of any victims, from brothers and fathers to in-laws and third cousins.

Among the most emotionally persuasive means of inciting the menfolk to avenge the death was the **voceru**, an impassioned funerary rite in which close female relatives of the deceased would gather around the corpse, stretched out on the family table, to sing. While the chorus wailed and tore their hair and faces, the chief singer, or *voceratricci*, would improvise four- or six-line verses mourning the loss and stirring up vengeful zeal among the men, seated in a back room banging their gun butts in time with the dirge. Often, the *voceru* would be followed by a dance called the *cara-colu*, in which the women would process around the table in darkness. And woe betide any of the men who failed to heed their wives' and daughters' call to arms. Cowards were subjected to **ribeccu** – cast out of their families and treated with looks of scorn and derision until they had settled scores with the enemy. In this way, vendettas could smoulder on indefinitely, only coming to an end if the murderer fled to the maquis to become a bandit (see box on p.246), or if a peace was brokered by the parish priest.

During the mid-nineteenth century, the Corsican vendetta excited the imagination of the French literary establishment, fuelled by a stream of lurid novels on the subject. The first of these was **Balzac**'s *La Vendette* (1830), but it was **Prosper Mérimée**'s phenomenally successful *Colomba*, inspired by the author's stay in the village of Fozzano (see p.243), that brought the subject to a mass reading public. Thereafter, a series of even more romanticized depictions of vendettas were penned by prominent writers – including **Alexandre Dumas** (*La Vendetta*; 1846) and **Guy de Maupassant** (*Un Bandit Corse*; 1877) – which over time actually provided role models for feuding Corsican villagers.

Officially, vendettas no longer exist in Corsica (the last one ended in a village near Ajaccio during the 1950s), but old habits die hard and family reputation and old rivalries still influence almost all major business deals, not to mention marriages and socializing in rural areas. Nationalist politics, too, have become increasingly vendetta-ridden. Reading the local press, you'll often come across the phrase *règlement de compte* ("settling of scores") to explain the politically motivated assassinations that have spiralled over the past few years.

Graceful balconied houses remain as a legacy of the wealthy families who once resided here, but Sainte-Lucie's chief treasures are housed in the Baroque **Église Paroissiale** next to the square. Attached to a column on the left inside the entrance, a finely worked marble bas-relief of the *Virgin and Child* was commissioned by Rinuccio della Rocca in 1498. There's also a marble font in the form of a hand, dating from the 1490s and bearing the della Rocca arms.

Behind the church stands the **Maison Forte**, a huge, impenetrable, grey-granite house built to shelter the population in times of danger. To reach the classic viewpoint over the village, walk north for five minutes to the **Couvent St-François**, founded by Rinuccio in 1492 and set squarely on a plateau

Les bandits d'honneur

The most romantic of all Corsican folk heroes is the bush bandit, or **bandit d'honneur**. Coined during the nineteenth century, the term was used to distinguish between common highway robbers and men who had taken to the maquis after committing a vendetta killing. Protected by impenetrable scrub and granite, these fugitives could survive for years in caves, ruins or makeshift shelters accessible only by a labyrinthine network of game trails.

The true *bandit d'honneur* never stole or murdered anyone except his sworn adversaries, and could rely on the support of local villagers in times of need. Wandering the maquis in a broad-brimmed hat, a gun slung over his shoulder and a dog at his heels, he was felt to epitomize the *âme corse*, or "Corsican soul" – the spirit of rugged defiance, pride and separateness with which islanders had traditionally engaged their colonial rulers. As such, the *bandits* were respected, and even revered: travellers, artists and famous authors would seek them out in their camps, wealthy women fell in love with them, and a spate of nineteenth-century novels romanticized their footloose lifestyles, steeped in the spirit of Jean-Jacques Rousseau's "noble savage". During a visit to the Lauretti brothers in their Fiumorbo hideout, for example, Flaubert wrote the following: "Great and valiant heart that beats alone in freedom in the woods . . . purer and nobler, no doubt, than most people in France."

While some *bandits* lived up to this ascetic ideal, many more took to drink, robbery, rape and murder, safe in the knowledge that they were beyond the reach of the *gendarmes*. In time, a new breed of outlaw emerged; one who adopted the wild life as a means to personal gratification rather than to escape the stringent ancestral code of vendetta. Playing on their reputation for ruthlessness, the new *bandits* – dubbed *bandits percepteurs*, or "tax-collecting bandits" – began to racket businesses and wealthy landowners. Far from being Corsican Robin Hoods, however, they are these days regarded as the precursors of the modern Mafia.

Around the turn of the century, the atrocities committed by *bandits* such as the Bellacoscia brothers (an account of whose career appears on p.352) spurred the police to mount a sweeping crackdown. Hideouts were raided, outlaws rounded up and imprisoned and their protection rackets rumbled. Today, there are no longer any bona fide *bandits d'honneur* remaining in the Corsican maquis, but their racketeering tactics, heroic self-image and hold over the local population have become distinguishing traits of the FLNC paramilitaries, who regularly invite journalists to their hideaways in the dead of night to be photographed wearing black jumpsuits and balaclavas, brandishing automatic weapons. (For more on the FLNC, see pp.421–431).

A biography of one of the first, and most notorious, Corsican *bandits*, Théodore Poli ("Le Roi des Montagnes") appears on p.179, while the story of Muzarettu, among the only traditional *bandits d'honneur* to have lived in the postwar period, is featured in the account of Sartène on p.263.

overlooking the valley. It was here that Dorothy Carrington, guided by a descendant of the della Roccas, re-discovered the art treasures collected by Rinuccio in the decade leading up to his death in 1510. Her initial hunch that the dust-covered canvases rotting in a ruined side chapel were the work of a master artist proved correct, although it took a "quest as intricate and stormy as any I undertook in Corsica", involving trips to Spain and Sardinia, to identify their creator. Rinuccio, Lady Carrington later speculated, must have commissioned the works while recruiting reinforcements for his war against the Genoese in neighbouring Sardinia, where the painter, a Spaniard by the name of Castel Sardo, was employed by the Franciscan Order at the time.

Sainte-Lucie's other claim to fame is a rare kind of rock called **diorite orbiculaire** – a greyish-blue stone with concentric rings of black and white, like a leopard pelt – which used to be quarried close by. The friendly *Bar Ortoli* opposite the war memorial at the bottom of the square displays some polished samples, but you can buy rough-cut lumps direct from the owner of the now-defunct quarry: head down the street from the bar and look for a sign saying "*Pierre Corse*" hanging from one of the houses on the right. It's the home of Mme Renucci who, before sealing the family shaft a decade or so ago, extracted four final tonnes of diorite which she sells to tourists for whatever she can get.

Chapelle St-Jean-Baptiste

From the edge of the Sainte-Lucie's square, you can just make out the red-tiled roof of the Pisan **Chapelle St-Jean-Baptiste**, nestled in the maquis a couple of kilometres down the hillside. The path to it, a section of the Mare a Mare Sud, makes a pleasant half-hour walk: follow the lane from the bottom of the square (the one running directly opposite the church) to the adjacent hamlet of **Poggio**, turning right (onto the D320) when you reach a T-junction; marked by a PNRC signboard for Fozzano, the orange-waymarked path starts shortly after on the left. The early eleventh-century chapel, perched on a high bluff jutting over the valley, is one of Corsica's best-kept medieval parish churches, dating from the start of Pisan occupation. Its interior today serves as a cattle shed, and is usually left open.

Practicalities

Autocars Ricci's bus calls at Sainte-Lucie en route between Ajaccio and Porto-Vecchio, via Bavella, Zonza, Levie and Propriano. Tourist offices in the region have timetables for you to consult; in Sainte-Lucie, ask at the *Bar Ortoli*.

The village sees few overnight visitors and has just two places to **stay**, one of which is the attractively converted gîte d'étape *U Fragnonu*, on the north edge of the village (℡04 95 78 82 56; obligatory half board ❷), which serves copious, traditional food. The other accommodation option is a little **bed and breakfast** place, *Chez Mme Antoinette Minchelli* (℡04 95 78 81 40; ❹), on the street between the *Bar Ortoli* and Mme Renucci's diorite sign, where you can stay in simple, spotlessly clean en-suite rooms to the rear of the building.

For a **meal**, try the *Pizzeria Santa Lucia*, next to the monument, which does inexpensive pizzas, salads and local cheeses, and whose terrace is the best place to watch the *pétanque* players next to the fountain. The streetside tables outside the *Bar Ortoli* provide another good vantage point from which to follow the comings and goings in the square, plus they serve fresh croissants for breakfast.

Levie

In the eighteenth century, **LEVIE** (Livia) was the capital of Alta Rocca, its Genoese families prospering from the fertile riverine countryside below. Today the village is rather dour, its main attraction being the proximity of the **Pianu di Levie** (see below), whose prehistoric sites provide much of the substance of the **musée départementale** (July & Aug daily 10am–6pm; Sept–June Mon–Sat 10am–noon & 2–4.30pm; €2) – at the time of writing in the process of being moved to a new building in the Quartier Pratu, below the main street on the north side of the village. The star exhibit is the so-called *Dame de Bonifacio*, a human skeleton discovered near Bonifacio and dated around 6570 BC, making this the oldest found in Corsica. The remains are those of a woman in her mid-thirties whose legs were badly crippled by old fractures; to have lived to such an age, she must have been cared for by her community. The other noteworthy artefact on display here is a beautiful ivory statue of Christ by a pupil of Donatello, given to Levie in the 1580s by Pope Sixtus V.

Practicalities

The only **accommodation** here is in the institutional **Gîte d'Étape Bienvenue à l'Alta Rocca** (℡04 95 78 46 41; May–Sept; €15 per bed) below the village centre beyond the gendarmerie; run by the local municipality, it's an untypically charmless place serving mediocre food.

You'll eat a lot better at the moderately priced *La Pergola* **restaurant** opposite the post office on the main street, which serves plain home cooking and will make charcuterie sandwiches on request. There's also a decent pizzeria, *Sorba*, a little further up the main street, serving the usual range of inexpensive wood-baked pizzas from €7 plus plenty of salads.

Lovers of quality regional cuisine, however, should note that one of the island's finest gourmet restaurants, *A Pignata* (℡04 95 78 41 90; April–Oct), lies close to Levie. It's hidden deep in serene countryside near Cucuruzzu, 5km west. Head 3km out of the village on the Sainte-Lucie road, turning right at the signpost for the Pianu de Levie archeological site. Roughly 1.5km further on the left you'll see a narrow, unsignposted lane marked by a couple of large wheely bins; the gateway to the auberge lies a short way further up the lane (don't look for a signpost – there isn't one). *A Pignata* earned its reputation through the sublime cooking of its *patronne*, Lily de Rocaserra; her son and daughter-in-law have since taken over the reins, but Lily keeps a careful eye on the kitchen. The family serves a single set menu, reasonably priced at €28 (including wine, five courses and eau de vie), and the food is refreshingly unpretentious, with everything from charcuterie to vegetables, jams and oil, made from ingredients produced on the farm. Advance reservation is essential, especially if you want to stay in one of their very pleasant **rooms**, which are rented out on a half-board basis (€52 per head for bed, breakfast and evening meal).

The Pianu di Levie

The most interesting prehistoric site on Corsica after Filitosa, the **Pianu di Levie** (daily: July–Aug 9.30am–8pm; April–June & Sept–Oct 9.30am–7pm; €5), is reached by taking the signposted road off the D268, 3km west of Levie. A further 4km will bring you to a field where you can park and buy your ticket – you get a ninety-minute cassette-guided tour of the site (or a printed booklet in English if you prefer) for no extra charge.

A fifteen-minute walk through a Tolkienesque tract of gnarled old oak trees brings you to the **Casteddu di Cucuruzzu**, the remains of a Torréen habitation dating from 1400 BC. Emerging from the forest and integrated into the chaos of eroded, moss-covered granite boulders, this is the best example of a *casteddu* in Corsica. The complex, dominated by a circular *torre* and surrounded by a thick high wall, was inhabited by Bronze Age artisans and farmers, who lived in the chambers surrounding the *torre* and in dry-stone shacks close by. The *casteddu* is entered by a steep and narrow stairway. Storerooms are ranged on the right, opposite a series of chambers with openings above to let the light in and the smoke out. Straight ahead, the *torre* has retained its vaulted roof of wide granite slabs, below which stones jutting out sideways from the walls suggest the existence of another floor. Stone tools, bronze belt links and domestic utensils, found in the course of excavations here, all point to the tower's having a functional rather than religious purpose. From the top you get a magnificent panoramic view of the region, from the needles of Bavella to the gulf of Propriano.

Another twenty minutes through the woods brings you to **Capula**, a site occupied from the Bronze Age until 1259, when its so-called **castle**, an impressive circular monument, was partly destroyed. Just below the entrance, look out for a headless menhir; other pieces of Bronze and Iron Age stonework are incorporated into the monument, mixed with hundreds of small granite bricks from the medieval period. About 200m beyond the castle, **Chapelle San Lorenzu**, a tiny thirteenth-century Romanesque building extensively restored in World War I, stands beside the ruins of an even older apsidal-ended chapel thought to date from the thirteenth century.

Carbini

South of Levie, the D59 runs 8km around the flank of a twisting valley to **CARBINI**, a tiny, depopulated village at the foot of the Ospédale massif. Heralding your arrival, a lone, square campanile, decorated with three storeys of graceful pierced arcades, is all that remains of the Église St-Quilico, which historians believe was the birthplace of the **Giovannalani**, an heretical off-shoot of the Third Franciscan Order that emerged midway through the fourteenth century in the wake of the Black Death. Popular belief has it that the sect used to end their services with mass orgies in front of the altar, but Dorothy Carrington, who visited the village in the late-1940s, showed this to be a scurrilous gloss added by biased chroniclers in later centuries. In fact, the Giovannalani espoused a far more pious way of life than the Order they sprang from. Fearing the spread of their popularity across the island, Pope Urban V resolved to stamp them out and dispatched a punitive expedition to Corsica in 1362. The papal troops were joined by local reactionaries who hunted the Giovannalani down and massacred them in two mass burnings – one here, at a rocky eminence above the village, and another near Ghisoni, further northeast. Carbini then had to be repopulated by families from Sartène, which explains why in subsequent centuries it was overtaken by a bloody vendetta.

The Romanesque **San Giovanni Battista**, next to the bell tower, was the precursor of St-Quilico (whose floor plan is discernible nearby); beautifully restored in the nineteenth century under instructions from Prosper Mérimée, the then inspector of historic monuments, it is decorated with geometric patterns, human forms and various odd beasts typical of the Pisan era. Crowned with a crucifix, the rocky hilltop rising above the houses to the south was where the Giovannalani were murdered in 1362; a path leads to the spot, from where the views across the valley extend to Bavella – especially evocative at sunset.

No trace remains of the eccentric *Hôtel des Nations* where Dorothy Carrington spent a lurid sojourn in 1948, but you can stop for a drink at the *Café du Centre*, under the limes on the main street, which has changed little since then. Other than that, the only facility for visitors is a small tap dispensing spring water – a welcome sight for hikers ambling through on the Mare a Mare Sud trail.

A stiff **walk** of around 1hr 45min takes you east from Carbini to a splendid viewpoint surveying the entire Alta Rocca. Look for the orange waymarks leading east off the main street towards the hamlet of Supranu. Once clear of the last houses, the route follows a *piste* for a short while before peeling left into the woods. Having crossed the *piste* again further on, it then starts to climb more steeply via an ancient paved mule track that zigzags through the forest at a comfortable gradient. Gradually, chestnut trees, beech and mountain oak start to give way to maritime pines, whose massive cones litter the path as you approach the ridge. At the point just before the *sentier* veers around a sharp bend, around 1hr from Carbini, keep an eye out for a large flat-topped boulder on your right – the views from it west encompass most of southern Corsica, from the Golfe de Valinco to Monte Incudine.

Return by the same route, or press on for another hour past Foce Alta (1171m) – from where you get an even more impressive panorama across the Straits of Bonifacio to Sardinia – to **Cartalavonu**, where there's an excellent little restaurant (reviewed on p.286). IGN **map** #4254ET covers the route.

Aullène and around

Set midway between the east and west coasts, at a crossroads of four main inland routes, **AULLÈNE** (Auddé), 40km northeast of Sartène, is a typical Alta Rocca hill village, its hub of weathered granite houses swathed in chestnut trees – the source of the village's long-gone prosperity. Pastoralism was the other traditional mainstay, and a network of old shepherds' paths still threads through the surrounding woods to the Plateau de Coscione, making this a prime spot for hikers.

Old-fashioned **accommodation** is offered by the *Hôtel de la Poste* (T & F 04 95 78 61 21; May–Oct; ②), on the main street just above the square. Occupying a late-nineteenth-century coaching inn, its rooms overlook the village rooftops and valley; they're basic, with toilets *à l'étage*, but impeccably clean and comfortable, and great value. Downstairs, a little restaurant is squeezed on to a leafy terrace raised above the road on which you can sample superb local charcuterie, pork dishes and other mountain specialities, including homemade chestnut-flour desserts. Half board here costs around €45 per head.

Apart from a meal at the *Hôtel de la Poste*, another reason to pause in Aullène is the seventeenth-century **Église St-Nicolas**, at the very top of the village, which harbours an unusual wood-carved pulpit supported by twisting sea monsters emerging from a Moor's head. Two theories account for this sculpture: the first holds that it symbolizes the defeat of the Saracens and Moorish pirates who penetrated deep into the interior of Corsica in the late-medieval era; the second is that the work depicts the migration of souls, carried (according to an image dating from antiquity) on the backs of dolphins. If the church is locked (more likely than not), ask at the mairie for the key.

Onwards from Aullène

Two spectacular mountain roads wind over the ridges beyond Aullène, one connecting the village with **Petreto-Bicchisano** on the main Ajaccio–Propriano road (N196), the other striking north towards **Zicavo** and the deep interior of the island. They're adventures in themselves by car, and offer arguably two of the best long-distance **cycling** routes in Corsica due to the relative absence of traffic, even in summer.

Heading **west**, the **D420** crosses the Chiuvone River just north of the village at the **pont d'Arina** and then rises through a dramatic rocky landscape, with enormous boulders dominating the road as far as the **Col de la Tana** (975m), 7km along. Beyond this pass, the route contours around the mountainside at the edge of a fire-damaged belt of pinewood, overshadowed by the pink granite bulk of the Punta di Tacculaja (1330m). At the **Col de St-Eustache** (995m), a further 3km, a fantastic view opens up north over the mountains to the Vallée du Taravo and beyond.

North of Aullène, an even wilder back road, the **D69**, skirts the fringes of the Plateau de Coscione, passing a string of converted *bergeries* and streams on its winding climb to the **Col de la Vaccia** (1193m). From the pass, you can look across the entire upper Taravo Valley to the grey summits of the watershed in the distance. A perfect place to enjoy the panorama is the rarely frequented *Auberge du Col de la Vaccia* (T06 84 75 70 27, F04 95 25 04 74; May–Sept; ❸). Seated outside on the terrace, or indoors next to an open fire if the weather's chilly, you can tuck into copious local cuisine on a four- or five-course €20–30 menu, or order filling gourmet snacks such as crêpes filled with wild mushrooms and ewe's cheese (only €3). Upstairs, half a dozen smart, recently refurbished rooms provide the last **accommodation** before Zicavo. Priority is given to guests opting for half board, so book ahead.

Serra di Scapomena, Zerubia and Sorbollano

At the head of the Rizzanese Valley, two charming hill villages straddle the main road between Aullène and Quenza, covered by Autocars Ricci's bus, but visited by surprisingly few outsiders. Hikers following the Mare a Mare Sud trail make up the majority of visitors to the first, **SERRA DI SCAPOMENA**, whose well-run **gîte d'étape** (T04 95 78 64 90; April–Oct) enjoys glorious views across the pale blue Bavella, Zonza and Ospédale massifs from its terrace and dorms. If you're driving, a small car park in the middle of the village, facing the magnificent panorama, makes a good picnic stop. Stock up beforehand with the best of local cheeses, wines and charcuterie at the village shop, Funtanedda, below the gîte.

Serra also has the only **campsite** in the area, the municipal *Camping de l'Alta Rocca* (T04 95 78 64 90; mid-June to Sept 15), situated 1km above the village – turn off the main road up the lane next to the gendarmerie. The Mare a Mare Sud runs right past it, making this a great base for day-walks in the area.

The only other **accommodation** hereabouts is Marie-Claire Comiti's lovely **gîte rural** (T04 95 78 73 64; ❸) in the minuscule village of **ZERUBIA**. It's fiendishly difficult to find: look for the signpost off the D420, 2km west of Serra di Scapomena, and when you reach the church follow the lane steeply uphill until you see the gîte on your left. The situation is superb – Corsica does not get any *plus profonde* than this – and Mme Comiti's cooking, based on old family recipes using only fresh local produce, is traditional and delicious.

The next village east of Serra, **SORBOLLANO**, marks the start of a spectacular, but rarely travelled, back route down the hidden **Rau di Codi Valley**, a tributary of the Rizzanese. Twisting around a sharp spur, the **D20** plunges through dense woodland to cross the stream at Ponte de la Nova. A short way beyond the bridge, at the hamlet of **Campu**, a PNRC signpost on the left of the road, marked "Santa Lucia", points the way to an idyllic **bathing place** at the confluence of two boulder-choked streams, a gentle ten-minute walk from the road. You'll know you've arrived when the path emerges from the woods at a footbridge across the river, underneath which a small coarse-sand beach makes a picturesque **picnic spot**. Note that you can also **walk** to this bathing spot from Serra di Scapomena in around 45min via the orange waymarked Mare a Mare Sud, which begins at the far northeastern edge of the village, after the war memorial and bar (look for the PNRC signboard). The path emerges from the woods on the D20, which you should follow downhill for 750m until you see the "Santa Lucia" sign on your left. Allow 1hr 15min for the climb back up again through the chestnut forest.

Quenza and around

Set on a rocky *balcon* smothered in pines and chestnut groves, with Bavella as a spiky backdrop, **QUENZA** – 13km east of Aullène, at an altitude of 820m – enjoys a spectacular location at the high end of the Alta Rocca, and a refreshing climate. Its inhabitants have traditionally been a mixture of shepherds from Conca on the coast (whence the denuded slopes above the village) and malaria-plagued Porto-Vecchiens. If you're merely passing through, make time for a visit to the fine Romanesque chapel of **Santa Maria**, located 300m southwest down the Serra di Scapomena road (D420). Built on a single-nave plan with a rounded apse in the year 1000, the building retains an ancient granite-tiled roof and some traces of fifteenth-century frescoes inside. It was founded long before Quenza had sprung up, perhaps because of the spot's remoteness from the pirate-ravaged coast. A further echo of Corsica's medieval struggle with North African raiders appears in the more modern **Église de St-Georges**, next to the *fontaine* in the centre of the village, whose pulpit is supported by twisting sea serpents and a Moor's head similar to the one in Aullène (see p.250). If the church is locked, ask at the bar opposite for the key.

Practicalities

Quenza lies along the route of Autocars Ricci's Ajaccio–Porto-Vecchio bus, which passes through daily in both directions. The village's only **hotel**, the *Sole e Monti*, lies just past the centre along the road to Zonza (T 04 95 78 62 53, F 04 95 78 63 88, W www.solemonti.com; ●). It's a large granite-fronted place, affiliated to the Logis de France chain, whose spacious en-suite rooms have small balconies overlooking the valley. The extrovert *patron*, M Balési, claims to have accommodated two British prime ministers over the years and his kitchen is regarded as one of the best in the Corsican mountains. On the small triangular garden out the front, you can enjoy the four-course €28 menu featuring local trout and free-range pork or lamb, rounded off with fiery homemade vin de myrthe.

Hikers passing through on the Mare a Mare Sud tend to hole up in the more modest **gîte d'étape**, *Corse L'Odysée* (T 04 95 78 64 05, F 04 95 28 61 91), 1km north of the village at the end of an appallingly rutted dirt track (follow the signs just beyond the *Sol e Monti*). The dormitory accommodation here is pretty basic, but you can have your own double room (with shared toilet) for €34; and the food, once again, is dependably good. Bank on €32 per head for bed, breakfast and evening meal if you sleep in one of the dorms, with an additional €3 per head if you opt for a double room.

To explore the country surrounding Quenza on **horseback**, head up the hill to Pierrot Milanini's stables (T 04 95 78 63 21 or 04 95 78 61 09), in the nearby village of **Jalicu**, 5km northwest. A day's pony trekking will set you back a steep €100, but the horses are in tip-top condition and the landscape's ideal for a good hack. The Milaninis also run an independent **gîte**: a combination of budget dormitory accommodation and classy half-board cooking for the excellent all-in price of €30 per head. With a little advance warning, non-residents can drop in for a meal (€23), served in the gîte's cavernous dining room with a open fire.

Forest walks don't come much more varied than this 4–5hr **round route**, which can be begun at either Zonza or Quenza. It follows the Mare a Mare Sud and its less often walked Variant routing in a broad triangle through a succession of remote stream valleys where you can swim and enjoy secluded picnics. Marked at regular intervals with orange blobs of paint, the itinerary is easy to follow and well cleared. Don't bother with an IGN map as the route roams over two separate sheets.

The waymarks begin to the right of the lane running behind Quenza's Église de Saint-Georges, emerging shortly after at another lane, which they follow for around 100m before turning right again. From here the route meanders due south at a largely level gradient to an estate known as **Campu di Bertu**, where tall fences enclose a 20-acre site set aside by the PNRC for the regeneration of a rare species of deer, *Cervus elaphus corsicanus*. Indigenous to the island, the deer was almost wiped out after World War II, and breeding pairs were imported from Sardinia in the 1970s to repopulate the Alta Rocca's woods.

Once past the deer enclosures, with the Aiguilles de Bavella rising to the north, bear left at a fork in the path and follow the waymarks steeply downhill to the **Rizzanese** (1hr 30min), turning right at the far side of the bridge. Having crossed a side stream on the left shortly after, the route then climbs steadily uphill to a **junction**, where you should **turn left** towards Zonza, as indicated by a PNRC signboard (if you head straight on here instead you'll arrive after twenty minutes at the Romanesque Chapelle de San Lorenzu and Bronze Age site of Capula, part of the Cucuruzzu pre-historic complex, described on p.248). Forty-five minutes beyond the junction, after a steady descent through thick mixed deciduous forest, the path meets a second river, the **ruisseau di Pian di Santu**, which the waymarks follow for a while before crossing to the right bank to begin a sustained climb to **Zonza**, reached 2hr 30min into the walk.

To pick up the onward trail from the village, head one kilometre down the D420 from the centre (past the *Hôtel Le Tourisme*), keeping an eye out for the start of the path on the left of the road. Crossing the **rau de St-Antoine** stream twenty minutes later, the path begins to climb steadily again, emerging on the D420 500m east of Quenza.

The Plateau de Coscione

The **Plateau de Coscione**, known as *U Pianu* (The Tableland) in Corsican, is the rugged roadless region north of Quenza, west of the mighty Monte Incudine Massif (2136m). For centuries, this wilderness of rolling grassland and bog, which remains well watered throughout the summer by thousands of mountain streams, provided rich grazing for the pastoralist communities of the coast, who used to drive their immense flocks of sheep and goats up here each year after the spring snow melt. Between June and September, up to seven hundred men and their animals would live here in seasonal settlements of ramshackle stone huts. With the demise of transhumance, however, Coscione became a total backwater. Nowadays, barely a handful of shepherds follow in their forebears' footsteps, and those that do drive their animals up here in trucks for the summer, leaving them to their own devices until the autumn.

The rutted 4WD tracks used by today's shepherds and cattle rearers crisscross Coscione from north to south, but to experience the region properly you'll have to leave your car behind and set out on foot. Comprising areas of lumpy green marshland where mist and cloud frequently sweep in from the surrounding granite ridges, the landscape of the plateau will feel oddly familiar to British visitors. This is somewhere you'll want to walk more for the atmosphere than the views, although approaching the region via the GR20, which traverses Coscione en route between Zicavo and Bavella, affords some fine panoramas of the interior mountains and Alta Rocca. Probably the easiest way to get a quick taste of the plateau is to drive in **from Quenza**. A narrow single-track lane winds north along the west side of an otherwise roadless valley, around the flanks of Punta Grossa to a deserted outdoor pursuits complex that was built in the 1980s as a service centre for skiers; in winter, Coscione's undulating hills can be carpeted in deep snow for months – ideal for *ski de fond* (cross-country skiing). From the car park, you can set off on foot to follow a clearly defined jeep track into the heart of the plateau.

For a detailed description of the northern approach to the Coscione Plateau, via the village of Zicavo and the Monte Incudine path, see p.356.

Zonza

Framed against the craggy *Aiguilles* of the Bavella massif, **ZONZA** looks like something off the top of a chocolate box, and its prominence on postcard racks and brochure covers ensures that this picturesque granite village is transformed during summer by the annual influx of tourists – hikers, climbers and horse riders, as well as a steady stream of motorists and backpackers. Its most illustrious visitors, however, were probably Muhammed V, Sultan of Morocco, and his son, who turned up here with three limousines in October 1952 after the family had been deposed in a coup d'état. The French Ministry of the Interior had requisitioned the village's now-defunct *Mouflon d'Or* hotel to accommodate the royals during their two-year exile. But the winter snow and rain got the better of them, and after only five months the sultan demanded that the government find him a place on the coast. Another hotel was subsequently occupied: the palatial *Napoléon Bonaparte* in L'Île Rousse.

Situated within easy striking distance of the most dramatic mountain scenery in the south, Zonza is well placed to use as a base for day-walks in the Alta Rocca (try the round route described in the box on p.253, beginning it here instead of Quenza). The village, which owes its sudden expansion in the nineteenth century to its strategic position straddling the region's main roads, is well served by daily bus connections to Porto-Vecchio, Ajaccio and the rest of the Alta Rocca.

Practicalities

Three scheduled **bus** services pass through during the summer. Autocars Ricci's coaches (☏04 95 51 08 19 or 04 95 76 25 59) leave from Ajaccio's terminal routière mid-afternoon via Propriano, Sartène, Ste-Lucie-de-Tallano and Levie, arriving here three hours later and returning early the next morning. From Porto-Vecchio Balési Évasion's daily minibus (☏04 95 70 15 55) leaves at 7am, and pulls in here an hour later en route to Ajaccio via Quenza and Aullène. You can also get to Zonza with Eurocorse Voyages' bus (☏04 95 21 06 30), which leaves Ajaccio at 4pm. Travelling in the other direction, this service departs Zonza before dawn. You can check timetables at the **tourist office**, Information Tourisme Alta Rocca (Mon–Fri 8am–6.30pm, daily in July and August; ☏04 95 78 56 33, ℱ04 95 78 44 77, ⓦwww.alta-rocca.com), just below the crossroads at the centre of the village (behind the war memorial), which also hands out leaflets for various Alta Rocca walks, including the one described on p.253. Topoguides for the **Mare a Mare Sud**, whose Variant passes through, are sold at the nearby *tabac*.

Zonza boasts a better-than-average crop of **hotels**, and an even more impressive array of **restaurants**. Pick of the bunch has to be the long-established *L'Aiglon*, on the main road (ⓣ04 95 78 67 79, ⓕ04 95 78 63 62; April–Dec; ❹). Some of its rooms are small and on the dark side, but all are individually decorated with local tapestries and collected textiles from around the world. Some have toilets *à l'étage*, so check when you book if this is important; families should request the lovely wood-lined suite on the top floor, which has its own rooftop terrace. Downstairs, the hotel restaurant is in a class of its own, serving some of the most sumptuous cuisine in Corsica. Locals travel up from the coast to eat their *plat de résistance*, "La Muntanela", a groaning selection of special mountain delicacies given a twist by the chef: baked green flan (*gratin de verdure*) stuffed with wild leaves, hazelnuts and *brocciu*; chestnut-flour polenta; grilled Alta Rocca *figatellu*; and sweet chestnuts steeped in black muscat, to name but a few. They also serve a stupendous sautéed organic veal in orange, and a dreamy choice of desserts (try the *tarte aux châtaignes* or *flan crémeux au coulis de fenouil*). Menus are priced at €25 and €28; count on €30–35 à la carte.

A notch pricier, and correspondingly more spacious, are the rooms at *Le Tourisme* (ⓣ04 95 78 67 72, ⓕ04 95 78 73 23, ⓦwww.hoteldutourisme.fr; April–Oct, half board obligatory in August; ❹), on the north edge of the village, set back on the side of the Quenza road. The interior recently had a major makeover and is now bright and modern. Their top-of-the-range options have the best views over the valley, but the smaller standard rooms are comfortable enough for a night or two. The restaurant, too, is renowned throughout the Alta Rocca, with menus from €13 to €24.50. House specialities include roast chicken stuffed with river shrimp – a rarely served local delicacy – and *stuffata*, a filling Corsican stew made with four kinds of meat. Otherwise, there's the pleasantly old-fashioned, more down-to-earth *L'Incudine*, at the opposite side of the village (ⓣ04 95 78 67 71; April–Oct, half board obligatory in August; ❸). It offers great value for money, with fourteen smart, modern rooms, recently refurbished, complete with air conditioning, en-suite bathrooms and views. The busy restaurant on the ground floor is renowned above all for its homemade mountain charcuterie, cheeses and succulent *grillades*, prepared *au feu de bois* in front of you by the *patron-chef*.

Zonza has two **campsites**. The nearest, *U Fuconu*, 1.5km out of the village centre, occupies a secluded spot just off the Quenza road. In addition to great views of the Aiguilles looming above the tree line, it has a pleasant on-site pizzeria. Set in a pine wood 4km out of the village on the D368, the main Ospédale/Porto-Vecchio road, is the somewhat less appealing *camping municipal* (ⓣ04 95 78 62 74), which lays on complimentary minibuses for backpackers.

The route de Bavella

The **route de Bavella**, between Zonza and Solenzara on the east coast, is perhaps the most dramatic road in all Corsica. Once across the **Col de Bavella** (1218m), marked by a statue of **Notre-Dame-des-Neiges** rising white above a pile of granite stones and petition plaques, an amazing panorama unfolds. Immortalized in the stretched etchings of Edward Lear, the serrated pinnacles of the **Aiguilles de Bavella** in the west dominate a surreal landscape of wind-twisted maritime pines, while on the eastern side of the valley the orange wall of the Crête de Punta Tafonata sweeps sheer above the treeline.

The vast escarpments towering above the Col de Bavella are riddled with way-marked **footpaths**, catering for all levels of fitness and competence. The three most spectacular are outlined below in order of difficulty. They're well marked and accessible to all – you'll only need a copy of IGM **map** #4253 if you want a fuller picture of the area. Car drivers should note that parking is limited at the *Auberge du Col*, starting point for two of the routes; leave your car instead at the large car park up at the col itself, next to the Notre-Dame-des-Neiges statue.

The most popular of the walks beginning at the *Auberge du Col* goes to the **Trou de la Bombe**, a circular hole in the Paliri crest of peaks between Punta Velaco (1483m) and Calanca Murata (1407m). From the spring next to the auberge, follow the GR20 for 800m, then take the first path to the right, signposted "Trou de la Bombe". The track rises through a wood as far as a ridge, then drops gradually before beginning a short climb to the hole, which emerges to the right. Those with a head for heights should climb right into the *tafoni* for the dizzying view down the sheer five-hundred-metre cliff on the other side.

Even more amazing views can be had from the summit of the adjacent peak, **Calanca Murata**, which you can scale after a steep, but technically straightforward haul from the head of the ravine just below Trou de la Bombe. Cairns mark the route, which threads its way up a sheer gulley immediately north of the main path, lined by gnarled pine trees. After ten minutes you emerge at a large natural balcony that makes a perfect **picnic place**. The pull to the top of the mountain through a narrowing chimney takes thirty to forty minutes. At no stage do you need to climb, and the views, which take in the entire Bavella massif to the west and a huge sweep of the eastern plains, are on a par with those from the island's major peaks.

The distinctive **red-and-white waymarks of the GR20** skirt the *Auberge du Col* and you can use them to explore some of the more rugged terrain flanking the pass. A varied three-hour return route leads you via an ancient transhumant artery (formerly used by shepherds from Conca to drive their flocks up to Monte Incudine and the Coscione Plateau) to the **Refuge de Paliri**, a mountain hut hidden on the far side of the Crête de Punta Tafonata. Paved for much of the way and keeping to man-

---

The hamlet of **BAVELLA** itself, a cluster of neatly painted tin- and stone-roofed cabins just below the col, 9km northeast of Zonza, was built in the early nineteenth century for the inhabitants of the Conca *commune*, who were granted the land by Napoléon III as a refuge from the summer heat of the lowland. Since then, the local *commune* has washed its hands of the settlement, which as a result lacks basic amenities, including electricity and mains water – the source of an ongoing dispute. It's a spot that can seem as eerie as it is serene, especially in winter, but the proximity of the mountains and long-distance trails (the GR20 makes one of its rare descents to road level here) makes this an ideal place to locate yourself for **hikes** in the area (see box). The *Auberge du Col* (℡04 95 72 09 87, ℻04 95 72 16 48; April–Oct; ❶) offers clean and comfortable **gîte d'étape** accommodation (€13 per bed), with the option of good-value half board (€30 per person) in their restaurant, where you can order plates of local charcuterie and cheese on a sunny terrace. A little further down the hill on the right, *Le Refuge* (℡04 95 72 08 84, ℻04 95 71 05 77; ❶), has four very basic rooms with shared toilets, and rough camping space under the pines around the back. Their homely little roadside restaurant offers simple but copious menus of local specialities, from €11.50 to €18, plus wine.

From the auberge, it's a steep descent through what's left of the **Forêt de Bavella**, which suffered a devastating fire in 1960 but still boasts some huge

ageable gradients, it's one of the less challenging sections of the GR20. From its bifurcation with the waymarks leading to Trou de la Bombe, the path plunges quite steeply downhill to join a *piste forestière* , then crosses a stream (whose banks you can follow uphill for five minutes to a wonderfully secluded **bathing spot**) before leaving the *piste* to start the stiff twenty-minute climb to **Foce Finosa** (1206m). The effort is rewarded with fine views over some desolate terrain to the south from the pass. Dropping downhill on the other side, you've another 45min of easy walking to reach the refuge, which has a water source, camping and bivouacking space and bunk beds for twenty people. From the rock platform behind it, scan the vast cliff to the north for the **Punta Tafonata di Paliri** (1213m), a large hole high up near the ridge line that's a popular target for rock climbers. Return by the same route.

Starting from the main car park at the col proper (not the *Auberge du Col*), a more taxing route takes you via a famous high-level Variant of the GR20 into the heart of the **Aiguilles de Bavella**, the giant rock towers looming above the road. Waymarked with yellow paint spots, the itinerary is known as "Le Variant Alpin" because of its imposing gradients and rocky terrain. Sheer and physical from the outset, it should only be attempted by adequately equipped, experienced walkers – and never in bad weather (the granite gets very slippery after even a light shower). Some simple hand holds are required on the tough initial ascent, which takes you from the col to the Bocca di u Truvunu, at the base of Tower I. For the next hour and a half or so you'll be climbing and descending across a mixture of pine-covered boulder fields, scree and steeply inclined slabs below Towers II and III, one section of which requires the use of a fixed stanchion cable. The waymarks then begin their final ascent to **Bocca di u Pargulu** (1622m), highpoint of the Variant Alpin, from where a magnificent view of the Incudine massif is revealed. You can either return by the same route (1hr 45min) or else drop very steeply down the far side of the valley from the pass to rejoin the red-and-white waymarks of the main GR20, which can be followed south-west (left) around the base of the Bavella needles and back up the Caca la Volpe ravine to the col – a dull plod of around 3hr 15min (from the path junction). For further advice on the kind of gear and precautions you'll need to take if you attempt the Variant Alpin from Bavella, see chapter 8.

Laricio pines. About 10km from the pass you'll come to the **Col de Larone** (608m), offering a grandiose panorama of the mountains and the **Forêt de Tova** in the north. Vast cliffs and rock falls tower on all sides as the road winds through a landscape reminiscent of the American Wild West, with dizzying drops to the River Solenzara, full of smooth white rocks and turquoise pools. Towards the bottom of the gorge, you can pull over in several places for a dip. For a review of the **campsite** and **places to eat** at the bottom of the valley, see p.297.

The Sartenais

The **Sartenais**, in Corsica's far southwest, is the wild tract of dense maquis fanning seawards from the district's main town, **Sartène**, which the French novelist Prosper Mérimée famously dubbed "la plus corse des villes corses" (the most Corsican of Corsican towns), famous for its feuds and austere, buttress-bottomed houses. Scattered with **standing-stone sites** and ghoulish rock formations, this is a region rich in folklore, much of it fragmented transmissions from ancient times, when the weird granite outcrops looming above the scrubland sheltered communities of hunter-gatherers and, later, Neolithic farmers. The settlements retained a healthy population until Saracen pirates made off with most of their inhabitants between the fifteenth and seventeenth centuries. Since then, the area has remained depopulated and desolate, save for the vineyards of the Fiumicicoli and Ortoli valleys, which produce the robust AOC wines that have made this a highly reputed wine-growing area.

The writings of Dorothy Carrington did much to fix popular impressions of the Sartenais as a mysterious and somewhat forbidding corner of the island. Many of her most valuable informants – traditional healers, bards and *mazzeri* ("dream hunters"; see p.290) – were old folk from the region's most remote villages. Life has moved on since Lady Carrington first travelled here in the late 1940s, but this remains an area with a peculiarly loaded atmosphere, heightened by the shadowy forms that emerge from the rocks around sunset time. Crossed by comparatively few roads, it is also one of the least developed parts of Corsica. You can literally walk for days along the **Sartenais coast**, between Campomoro and Roccapina, and not see a single inhabited building.

Public transport is frequent on the main road between Sartène and Bonifacio/Porto-Vecchio, but to reach the most interesting and atmospheric parts of the Sartenais you'll need your own vehicle, mountain bike or, best of all, sturdy walking boots.

Sartène

A "town peopled by demons" is how German chronicler Gregorovius described **SARTÈNE** (Sartè) in the nineteenth century, and the town hasn't shaken off its hostile image. Located near the coast and therefore vulnerable to foreign invaders, it was persistently attacked by pirates in the Middle Ages, and from the twelfth to the sixteenth century became the seat of the ferocious **Sgio** (from *signori*), feudal lords who preferred to implement justice without interference from the island's rulers and who thus turned Sartène into an asylum for refugees from the law of the state. A bloody **vendetta** in the nineteenth century sealed the town's reputation and left a legacy of tall, grim fortress houses. An insular outlook continues to this day, and outsiders can be put off by the implacable ambiance of the place. On the other hand, it's a smarter, better-groomed town than most in Corsica, with a perfectly preserved medieval heart that's blissfully free of ferro-concrete. One of the main reasons for this was the former communist mayor, who passed laws banning unsightly buildings, neon signs, and even overhead cables. Another is the money brought in from the Sartène **wine** – the best on the island.

Despite its turbulent history, the town doesn't offer many diversions once you've explored the enclosed **vieille ville** and paid a visit to the **Musée de la Préhistoire Corse**. The only time of year Sartène teems with tourists is at Easter for **U Catenacciu**, its highly charged Good Friday procession (see box on p.260).

A brief history of Sartène

Sartène was formed when, in the tenth century, the inhabitants of this region's agglomeration of hamlets were forced to congregate in one place by Saracen raids. In the twelfth century the **della Rocca** family held sway over the area with the consent of its Pisan governors, but when the Genoese took over in the thirteenth century, Sartène became a centre of discontent. The laws giving Genoa a monopoly on Corsica's trade were anathema to the local nobility, the **Sgio**, who continued to resist the Genoese until the final stand of Rinuccio della Rocca, defeated after a long struggle in 1510.

△ Sartène

Sartène's Good Friday ceremony of **U Catenacciu**, generally considered to be the most ancient ritual in Corsica, is a sombre enactment by hooded and masked brotherhoods of Christ's walk to Golgotha. The nocturnal procession through candlelit streets is headed by the **Grand Pénitent** or Pénitent Rouge, dressed in a scarlet hooded robe, who carries a heavy wooden cross and is chained on the ankle – *u catenacciu* means "chained one". In former times the volunteer was usually a bandit whose identity was officially known only to the priest. Anonymity is still guaranteed, and there's a waiting list of twelve years to take part, which means that some of the penitents are very old men. If the Grand Pénitent is too frail to shoulder the cross alone, he's helped out by the **Pénitent Blanc**, who follows behind, representing Simon of Cyrene. Behind him marches a troop of **Pénitents Noirs** bearing the statue of Christ on a bier. Accompanied by the continuous unearthly chanting of an ancient Corsican prayer, *Perdonu miu Diu*, the procession passes slowly from Église Ste-Marie through the streets of the *vieille ville*, ending up three hours later in place Porta, where they receive benediction at midnight.

In the past it was a dangerous event, as the penitents were often known murderers at whom onlookers would fling stones – though this was one time of year when a truce was observed between sworn enemies, so nobody got killed. It's still a rough affair, with a lot of pushing and shoving to get the best view among the throng of tourists, and shots are often fired into the air at the end of the ceremony, by which time excitement is running high.

It was not until early in the sixteenth century that Sartène became a Genoese administrative centre, and even then their tenure was deeply troubled. In 1565 Sampiero Corso's army destroyed the town after a 35-day siege, then the Genoese took it back, only to lose it again in 1583 to **Hassan Pasha**, the mad king of Algiers, who ransacked the town and abducted four hundred of its inhabitants, a third of the population. Thereafter Sartène remained faithful to Genoa, so much so that Paoli had a struggle to win its inhabitants to his cause in the fight for a Corsican republic.

The nineteenth century saw the re-emergence of the Sgio: recognized as members of the nobility by the French monarchy, these powerful aristocrats prospered under privileges granted by Napoléon III; and, whereas other parts of Corsica suffered depopulation and decline, the Sgio oversaw the development of a wine industry that still underpins the local economy. Today, the Rocca Serras and della Roccas continue to dominate the political life of the town, now the *sous-préfecture* of southern Corsica – France's second-largest *commune* – and the most important regional capital in the south after Ajaccio.

Arrival and information

If you're arriving in Sartène by **bus** you'll either be dropped at the top of avenue Gabriel-Péri (Eurocorse Voyages) or in the main square (Autocars Ricci). **Car parking** can be tricky thanks to the one-way system: the easiest place to leave your vehicle is in the lot next to the Super U supermarket at the bottom of town and walk up cours Soeur-Amélie (though you should check what time the gate closes).

The **tourist office**, on rue Borgu (summer Mon–Fri 9am–noon & 2.30–6pm; ☏04 95 77 15 40), can help you find accommodation in the area if the hotels listed below are full.

Accommodation

The nearest **campsite** to Sartène is the three-star *Camping Olva (Les Eucalyptus)*, 5km out of town towards Castagna on the D69 (☎04 95 77 11 58, ℱ04 95 77 05 68; May–Oct). Travellers without their own vehicle can telephone for a courtesy *navette* from either of the town's bus stops.

U Listincu 3km down the N196 ☎04 95 77 17 51. Simple but immaculately clean rooms in a modern building on the main road. Hardly the most appealing spot in the area, but fine for a night, and one of the cheapest options for miles in peak season. ❸

Les Roches av Jean-Jaurès ☎04 95 77 07 61, ℱ04 95 11 19 93. A large 1970s-style hotel on the edge of the old town, most of whose well-appointed, en-suite rooms command panoramic views of the Vallée du Rizzanese. It's invariably block booked by bus parties and billeted local gendarmes, so reserve well ahead. ❹

Rossi Hôtel (Fior di Riba) 1km west of town on the Propriano road ☎04 95 77 01 80, ℱ04 95 73 46 67. Plain, modern place next to *La Villa-Piana* (see below), with smart rooms and furnished studios for longer stays. Tariffs vary according to room size and proximity to pool. April to mid-Oct. ❹

La Villa-Piana 1km west of town on the Propriano road ☎04 95 77 07 04, ℱ04 95 73 45 65, ⓦwww.lavillapiana.com. The classiest option in this area, and good value, with lovely views from spacious front terraces, tennis court and a pool overlooking the Rizzanese. Doubles down to a bargain €45 in shoulder season. April–Oct 15. ❻

The Town

Place Porta – its official name, place de la Libération, has never caught on – forms Sartène's nucleus. Once the arena for bloody quarrels, it's now a well-kept square opening onto the valley. Somnolent by day, place Porta comes alive for the early-evening *passeggiata*, when it fills with snappily dressed townsfolk.

❶, ❷, ❸, ❹, *Propriano & Ajaccio*

SARTÈNE

ACCOMMODATION
U Listincu	3
Les Roches	4
Rossi Hôtel (Fior di Riba)	1
La Villa-Piana	2

Couvent de San Damiano

U STRITTONU

AVENUE JEAN-JAURÈS

Échauguette

Hotel de Ville

PLACE PORTA Église Ste-Marie

Autocars Ricci's Bus Stop

COURS BONAPARTE

Old Musée de la Préhistoire

Eurocorse Voyages Bus Stop

BORGU

St Sébastien

0   50 m

RESTAURANTS
La Cave Sartenais	C
Piazza Porta	D
A Tinedda	A
Zia Paulina	B

Zonza & Corte

THE SOUTH | The Sartenais

❺

Flanking the south side of place Porta is **Église Ste-Marie**, built in the 1760s but completely restored to a smooth granitic appearance. The chief interest here is historical – it was in this church that the warring families of nineteenth-century Sartène were forced to make their peace, though the truce often lasted only until they got outside again. Inside you can see the weighty wooden cross and chain used in the *Catenacciu* procession (see p.260), but otherwise the only notable feature is the Baroque altar, a present from the town's Franciscan monastery, no longer in existence.

Formerly the palace for the Genoese governor, the nearby **Hôtel de Ville** serves as an archway into the Santa Anna district of the *vieille ville*; the building is not open to the public and its archives have been closed since the 1880s, due to the endemic corruption of local politics, it's said.

The vieille ville

A flight of steps to the left of the Hôtel de Ville leads past the Maison de la Culture and cinema to the post office, behind which stands the ruined **échauguette**, a small lookout tower which is all that remains of the town's twelfth-century ramparts. This apart, the best of the **vieille ville** is to be found behind the Hôtel de Ville in the **Santa Anna** district, a labyrinth of constricted passageways and ancient fortress-like houses reached via the archway directly beneath the Hôtel de Ville, which rarely harbours any signs of life. Featuring few windows and often linked to their neighbours by balconies, these houses are entered by first-floor doors, a necessary measure against unwelcome intruders; dilapidated staircases have replaced the ladders that used to provide the only access. The main "road" across Santa Anna is rue des Frères-Bartoli, to the left of which are the strangest of all the vaulted passageways, where outcrops of rock block the paths between the ancient buildings. Just to the west of the Hôtel de Ville, signposted off the tiny **place Maggiore**, you'll find the **impasse Carababa**, a remarkable architectural puzzle of a passageway cut through the awkwardly stacked houses. A few steps away, at the western edge of the town, **place Angelo-Maria-Chiappe** offers a magnificent view of the Vallée du Rizzanese.

Vendetta in the vieille ville

In the villages of nineteenth-century Corsica it was common for blood feuds to start over something as trivial as the theft of a cockerel (see box on p.244), but Sartène's vendetta had its roots in a political dispute between the rich **Roccaserra** family of Santa Anna – supporters of the Bourbons – and the anti-monarchist Ortoli family of the poorer Borgo district. In 1830, on the occasion of the overthrow of the Bourbons in France, a group of Ortolis and their cohorts marched through Santa Anna to provoke the mayor, a royalist Roccaserra. In the ensuing fight Sebastien Pietri, a leading light in the Roccaserra clan, was killed and five of his comrades were wounded, which provoked an invasion of the town by a thousand Roccaserra allies from the mountains. The scene was witnessed by French chronicler A.C. Pasquin Valéry, who wrote, "The French are powerless against the nature, manners and passions of the Corsicans." After a series of violent confrontations in the maquis, where many members of both factions were killed, a mediator was brought in, a peace treaty drawn up and in 1834, at a Mass in Église Ste-Marie, the survivors of the vendetta were forced to swear to live in peace. Even then, street corners were guarded and windows bricked up, the feud relaxing only on the election of Napoléon III in 1848, when the children of the families were allowed to dance together at the celebrations.

Musée de la Préhistoire Corse

At the time of writing, the Musée de la Préhistoire Corse (June–Sept Mon–Sat 10am–noon & 2–6pm; Oct–May Mon–Fri 10am–noon & 2–5pm; €3) is in the process of being moved to a new building across town, due to open sometime in 2003. Spanning the period 6000 BC to 500 BC, its collection is dominated by fragments of terracotta pottery unearthed in Neolithic and Torréen sites across the island. Alongside these, however, are more accomplished fragments of decorated ceramics, obsidian arrowheads, polished granite axes and mattocks, gold jewellery and statuettes, as well as a pile of human bones deformed by fire, discovered near Bonifacio. A scale model of Cucuruzzu gives a good idea of what a Bronze Age settlement looked like and a statue-menhir has been coloured red as it would have been during the megalithic era.

Couvent de San Damiano

A ten-minute walk along the road to Bonifacio will take you to the **Couvent de San Damiano**, the building in which the *Catenacciu* penitent spends the night before the procession, when he has to be guarded from curious outsiders by police. One of the last of the old-style bandits, a formidable character called **Muzarettu**, died here in the 1940s at the age of 90, having been given refuge

---

Transitus and Le Choeur d'Hommes de Sartène

On October 4, 1996, an extraordinary concert took place in Sartène's **Couvent de San Damiano**. In the crypt of the nineteenth-century Franciscan church, the newly formed male voice choir of the village, dressed in black and standing in a tight semi-circle, celebrated St Francis of Assisi's day in truly traditional style by singing a choral work based on the saint's ascent to heaven. An original manuscript of the piece, **Transitus**, composed by the Italian friar **Pietro-Battista Farinelli da Falconara** in the late nineteenth century, had come to light two years before, enabling the Franciscans to revive a tradition that been dormant for over seventy years.

The concert was the consummation of a decade of work by Corsica's most famous singer and composer, **Jean-Paul Poletti**, who co-founded the hugely influential group **Canta U Populu Corsu** (The Corsican People Sing) in the mid-1970s. With their powerful renditions of traditional songs collected in the villages, Canta plucked *polyphonie* from near extinction and exploited its stirring harmonies and emotive associations as a rallying call for the nascent nationalist movement. Nine acclaimed albums later, however, the man dubbed "la plus belle voix de Corse" left the group to pursue formal music studies in Italy, where he became head chorister at the renowned Fiesole school in Siena.

More success followed Poletti's return from the Continent, notably his formation of the platinum-disc-selling *Nouvelles Polyphonies Corses* whose sublime harmonies opened the Winter Olympics at Albertville. But, away from the public eye, Poletti and the communist mayor of Sartène, Dominique Bucchini, were working to regenerate a grassroots choral tradition on their home patch. In 1987 they formed a school to promote what both regarded as an essential, but fast-disappearing, facet of village life. **Granitu Maggiore** ("granite" from the rock, and "major" after the chord) now boasts three choirs, the largest of them with 380 voices.

Transitus provided a perfect vehicle for the new choir formed from the cream of Granitu Maggiore's pupils, Le Choeur d'Hommes de Sartène. Since their recording of the long-lost score in 1996, the choir, comprising two local postmen, a Breton restaurateur and four students – in addition to Poletti himself – has toured all over Europe. Yet their most important gig remains the October 4 Mass at the convent of San Damiano, whose exceptional acoustics create the definitive setting for a piece of music that looks set to put Corsican choral music on the classical map.

by the monks. Cast out from his village for killing a nephew who had slapped his face, Muzarettu took to the maquis, then proceeded to terrorize the neighbourhood from his cave hideout near Propriano, where he hosted wild parties for the fishermen who brought him food and drink. A few more murders along the way kept him outlawed for many years, but as an old man he developed cancer and came to this convent to die; repenting his sins right at the very end, he was visited by the chief of police on his deathbed. The convent is now home to a brotherhood of Belgian monks and is out of bounds to the public, but there's a fine view of the valley from the outside.

Eating and drinking

Hotels may be thin on the ground in Sartène, but there is no shortage of restaurants, most of them cosy, traditional places in old stone buildings. A handful of inexpensive snack bars and pizzerias also line the main square, and are ideal for a light lunch or ice cream.

La Cave Sartenais place de la Libération. Directly beneath the Hôtel de Ville, and the most congenial place in town to taste and buy quality local wines. The three top *domaines sartenaises* – Saparale, Fiumicicoli and San Michele – are well represented, and there's a great selection of cheeses and charcuterie. June–Sept Mon–Sat 9am–8pm. Out of season, closed lunchtimes.

Piazza Porta place Porta. *Panini* (toasted sandwiches), fresh salads, crêpes and pizzas served at reasonable prices on tables in the *vieille ville*.

A Tinedda 5km northwest along the Propriano road ☏ 04 95 77 09 31. Definitive *cuisine du terroir* – *tripettes sartenaises*, *cannelloni al brocciu*, grilled local meat, *riz fermier*, and AOC wines – are the stock in trade of this pleasant, family-run *ferme-auberge*. You can eat in their intimate dining room or outside on a rear terrace facing the garden, where most of the chef's ingredients come from. The single *menu du jour* costs €25; advance reservation essential.

Zia Paulina rue des Frères-Bartoli, in the *vieille ville*. The perfect lunch venue, at the far end of an atmospheric narrow alleyway in the dead centre of the old town. Sartenais specialities dominate both their good-value €15 and €20 menus, and there's a generous selection of local wines to choose from.

Around Sartène

Littered across the southwest Sartenais is an extraordinary crop of **megalithic sites**, ranging from the flat-topped **Dolmen de Fontanaccia** at Cauria, the best-preserved prehistoric tomb on the island, to the enigmatic alignments of **Stantari** and **Renaggiu**, an impressive congregation of statue-menhirs. Further northwest, 258 standing stones of various sizes lie strewn amid the maquis at **Palaggiu**.

The coast hereabouts, most easily accessible via the D48 to Tizzano, is among the least developed on the island, with remote coves providing some excellent spots for diving and secluded swimming. From Tizzano's spectacular beach, **Cala di L'Avena**, you can follow a broken footpath south around the shoreline to the isolated **Plage de Tralicetu**, while to the north of the village, an equally wild coast stretches via some idyllic little bays to Capo di Senetosa and Campomoro (a route described in detail, in the reverse direction, on p.241).

Domaine Fiumicicoli

Wine buffs shouldn't leave the area without a visit to the **Domaine Fiumicicoli**, 7km north of Sartène on the D69, whose distinctive label design derives from the nearby **Spin'a Cavallu**, an immaculately preserved Genoese bridge spanning the Rizzanese. Spread over the hillsides beyond it, the Fiumicicoli vineyards turn out what Corsicans from this side of the mountains regard as the island's finest AOC wines. Their robust red is the perennial prize-winner, but you should also taste the *cave*'s unique ruby muscat, sold in chic little half bottles.

Alo Bisuje

Just west of Sartène, the prehistoric site of **Alo Bisuje** provides a taster of the archeological treats in store further south. It is reached by a quiet back road that leads eventually over the peninsula to Campomoro (see p.240): follow the N196 south as far as the Bocca Albitrina, branching right towards Tizzano, right again at the first fork, and then left at the second fork – 500m later – just beyond the hospital. The site, a scrub-covered mound on the right-hand side of the road, appears after 3km. Neolithic settlers occupied this rocky hillock around 1700 BC, before the arrival of the Torréens, building a double wall of Cyclopean boulders surmounted by a structure measuring 8m across and centring on a hearth.

The megaliths of Cauria

To reach the **Cauria** megalithic site you'll need to pick up the D48, 2km southwest of Sartène at the **Bocca Albitrina**, and follow it south towards Tizzano. Four kilometres along the route a left turning brings you onto the D48A, which winds through vineyards until eventually the **Dolmen de Fontanaccia** hoves into view on the horizon, crowning the crest of a low hill amidst a sea of maquis. A blue sign at the parking space indicates the track to the dolmen, a fifteen-minute walk away.

Known to the locals as the Stazzona del Diavolu (Devil's Forge), the Dolmen de Fontanaccia is in fact a burial chamber from the second phase of the megalithic era, around 2000 BC. This period was marked by a change in burial customs – whereas bodies had previously been buried in stone coffins in the ground, they were now placed above, in a mound of earth enclosed in a stone chamber. What you see today is the great stone table, comprising six huge granite blocks nearly 2m high topped by a slab, which remained after the earth rotted away.

The 22 "standing men" of the **Alignement de Stantari**, 200m to the east of the dolmen, date from the same period. All are featureless except the two distinctly phallic stones, which both have roughly sculpted eyes and noses, with diagonal swords on their fronts and sockets in their heads where horns would probably have been attached.

Across a couple of fields to the south you'll find the **Alignement de Renaggiu**, a gathering of forty menhirs standing in rows amid a small shadowy copse, set against the enormous granite outcrop of Punta di Cauria. Some of the menhirs have fallen, but all face north to south, a fact that seems to rule out any connection with a sun-related cult.

Palaggiu

The extraordinary **Alignement de Palaggiu**, the largest concentration of menhirs in Corsica, lies further south down the D48; 1500m past the Domaine la Mosconi vineyard (on your right, 3km after the Cauria turn-off), a green metal gate on the right side of the road marks the turning. From here a badly rutted dirt track leads another 1200m through to the stones, lost in the maquis, with vineyards spread over the hills in the half-distance. Stretching in straight lines across the countryside like a battleground of soldiers, the 258 menhirs include three statue-menhirs with carved weapons and facial features – they are amidst the first line you come to. Dating from around 1800 BC, the statues give few clues as to their function, but it's a reasonable supposition that proximity to the sea was important – the famous Corsican archeologist Roger Grosjean's theory is that the statues were some sort of magical deterrent to invaders.

TIZZANO (Tizza), the only permanently inhabited settlement on the Sartenais coast, brings the road to an end 3km south of Palaggiu. A scruffy collection of half-built holiday houses stacked around the sides of a steep headland, the village presents a much less arresting spectacle than its beach, **Cala di L'Avena**. Around the corner to the north, a narrow cove fitted with a jetty provides sheltered anchorage for a dozen or so fishing boats and yachts. It's overlooked from the opposite shore by the ruins of an intriguing fifteenth-century **fort**, built by the Genoese but destroyed in World War II, when it was used for explosives practice by trainee commandos (led, ironically, by a British agent).

Aside from Cala di L'Avena, the main reason you might want to venture down here is the **walk**. Interrupted by some of the island's most stunning shell-sand beaches and watchtowers, the coastlines in both directions are gloriously stark, roadless and unspoilt, although you need to be resilient to maquis scratches to explore them. For advice on how to set about the routes, see our

---

Coast walks from Tizzano

The coast path **north** from Tizzano to Campomoro via Capo di Senetosa is described in reverse (from north to south) on p.241, but there's no reason why you shouldn't attempt the route from this side. The same precautions apply in either case: take IGN **map** #4154 OT, and enough water to keep you going even if you lose the trail from time to time – more than likely on the first stretch at least (between Tizzano and Capo di Senetosa), which is poorly waymarked in places and frequently cross-cut by sidetracks.

Heading **south**, it's possible to follow the path without encountering any significant obstacles as far as the magnificent Plage de Tralicetu, but the beaches beyond there (notably the even grander Plage d'Erbaju and the gem of the Sartenais coast, Roccapina) are more easily approached from the south, via the main Propriano–Bonifacio road (see p.268).

That said, route finding is a problem at the very start: look for the orange paint mark on a rock at the far end of **Cala di l'Avena** beach, from where a rough path strikes uphill through tall maquis. Turn right when you arrive at a *piste* shortly after, which drops downhill to sea level and a small clearing: look for the **cairns** leading to the left across the rocks here. Without them you'd stand little chance of finding a way around **Capo di Zivia**, the headland extending southwest from Tizzano bay. The path becomes more clearly defined at the tip of the peninsula, winding south below Punta di a Botta. Just beyond a little cove called **Cala di Brija** (Witches' Bay), it meets the motorable *piste* arriving via the inland route from *Camping L'Avena* in Tizzano, which in turn gets muddled with a couple of parallel tracks in the maquis. Avoid the lowest one, which peters out at a cove, and you'll eventually round the corner to **Plage de Tralicetu**, a kilometre-long spread of coarse white sand and translucent water which you should reach 2hr 30min after leaving Tizzano.

The remaining stretch of the path to Roccapina, which recommences in the dunes behind the silver-sand cove at the far southern end of Tralicetu, **Plage d'Argent**, would be straightforward were it not blocked after thirty minutes by **La Domaine de Murtoli**, a private estate run as an exclusive holiday enclave and shooting reserve. You can run the gauntlet of gun-toting gamekeepers and skirt the estate, but given how much more easily accessible the beaches beyond it are by road, we recommend you approach them via the **Golfe de Roccapina**, covered on p.268.

box on p.241 (for the stretch between Campomoro and Tizzano) or opposite (for the leg to Roccapina).

The only **hotel** in Tizzano, the swish but unwelcoming *Du Golfe* (☎04 95 77 14 76, 📠04 95 77 23 34; Easter–Oct; ❼), is ideally placed overlooking the harbour. Its seventeen rooms are very smart, with terraces and great views out to sea, but the tariffs are ambitious, particularly in high season, when half board is obligatory. For campers, the basic *Camping L'Avena* (☎04 95 77 02 18; late-May to Sept) sprawls up the valley behind the beach – a peaceful enough spot in shoulder season, but crammed in high summer.

The cream of the day's catch landed on Tizzano's pint-size jetty is hauled straight up to the *Restaurant Chez Antoine* (☎04 95 77 07 25), just along the lane from the *Du Golfe*, whose terrace stands beside its own tiny beach. Depending on what the boats have brought in, their classy menu (€25) might include wood-grilled snapper, ray's wing in lemon sauce, or lobster, and given a day's warning they'll knock up a *bouillabaisse* with every edible kind of fish and crustacean available off the Sartenais coast for €38.

For more basic snacks and drinks there's the *Café Chez Julie*, opposite which a seasonal **shop** stocks essentials (June–Aug daily 8.30am–12.30pm & 4–7pm; May & Sept Mon–Sat 9am–noon & 4–7pm).

The far southwest: Sartène to Bonifacio

The far southwestern corner of Corsica, between Sartène and Bonifacio, is the island's least populated coastal lowland – a rolling expanse of archetypal Mediterranean scrub dotted with the odd vineyard and roadside auberge, but little else. Emblematic of its eerie grandeur, the **Uomo di Cagna** – a giant boulder eroded by the sea winds into the form of an old man wearing a hat – surveys the plain from the summit of the far south's highest mountain. Fishermen from the village of **Monaccia–d'Allène**, at the foot of the hill, used to use "u Uomo" as a beacon, turning back towards land whenever they lost sight of the figure.

In August 2001, the same remote village was dragged into the international spotlight when it witnessed the Mafia-style murder of former separatist-militant leader, **François Santoni**, who was shot dead by gunmen while attending a wedding at the parish church. Santoni had been on death lists since he split the nationalist party he used to head, A Cuncolta Naziunalista, and wrote two whistle-blowing books about the movement's links with organized crime. This, his home patch, has always existed on the violent margins of the law, its mainly poor pastoralist inhabitants little influenced by the more urbane, Italian-oriented merchant culture of nearby Bonifacio. For centuries it was subsumed in a bitter vendetta between a clan from the mountains (driven here themselves, it is said, by vendetta) and the indigenous shepherds who traditionally occupied the coastal plain. Inevitably, the big money nowadays pouring into the area with tourism has ignited old family rivalries, and many regard Santoni's assassination as a modern reincarnation of the wild southwest's age-old ways. For more background on the murder and its consequences, see "The Corsican Troubles" on p.427.

The region's main artery is the N196, which wriggles south from Sartène, veering eastwards at the col above **Roccapina**, one of Corsica's most arresting beaches. From there, the main road arcs across the coastal belt to **Figari**, the island's newest airport and arrival point of many UK charter flights. The rough swath of maquis south of the main highway is edged by a string of hidden beaches, the best of them accessible via **Pianotolli–Caldarello**. Two to four **buses** pass through daily en route between Ajaccio and Bonifacio and Porto-Vecchio; the same service, operated by Eurocorse Voyages (☎04 95 70 30 83), can be used to get within walking distance of Roccapina, but to reach the more remote campsites and coves beyond Pianottoli you'll need your own transport.

Roccapina

The great landmark of the journey around Corsica's southwest coast is the **Lion de Roccapina**, a lump of roseate granite weathered into the shape of a recumbent lion. Visible from a lay-by on the roadside, it presides over a dazzling turquoise-blue bay, the **Golfe de Roccapina,** a protected site whose dunes harbour no more than a desultory municipal **campsite**. The only way to reach it is via a rutted *piste*, which winds 2.5km downhill from the *Auberge Coralli* on the N196 (a request stop for Eurocorse Voyages' bus) to the *Camping Arepos-Roccapina* (☎04 95 77 19 30), an inexpensive, well-shaded site. It only really gets crowded from early July, but the shallow bathing, soft white sand and crystal-clear water of the bay beyond are only too visible from the highway, so don't expect to have Roccapina to yourself unless you come off-season.

To reach the old Genoese **watchtower**, head up the stony path that leads right off the main approach to the beach, and bear left when you reach a fork five minutes later (the right fork of this path will take you to the Lion de Roccapina, which is extremely dangerous to climb, regularly claiming lives in spite of the warnings posted around it). From the ridge, the views south across the cove, north up the wild Ortolo Valley and along the Sartenais coast, are superb. Immediately below the ridge, the immense white-sand beach around the headland from Roccapina, **Plage d'Erbaju**, can be accessed via a stony path from the ridgetop in around twenty minutes. The dunes behind it, patrolled by a herd of stray cows, are strewn with bushes of cinqfoil and twisted pines – the only shade for kilometres. Backed by the private estate of **Murtoli**, whose isolated houses you can just about discern on the far side of the bay, this beach is inaccessible by road and thus sees only a scattering of (mostly German nudist) visitors, even in high summer.

Roccapina and the Queen-Emperor's jewels

The Golfe de Roccapina witnessed one of the most notorious **shipwrecks** of the nineteenth century when, on the night of April 17, 1887, the luxury P&O steam liner *Tasmania* ran aground onto the treacherous Des Moines rocks a short way out to sea. En route to Southampton from Bombay, she was carrying in her holds a trunk whose contents were worth an estimated eight times the value of the entire ship – precious gems sent by the rajahs of India to Queen Victoria on her jubilee. Once they learned of the cargo, rescuers began to search for the trunk, but it was eventually picked up by crew members of a salvage vessel, the *Stella*, three weeks later. Local legend has it, however, that some of the jewels found their way into the possession of the *bandit* **Barrittonu**, who used to hide out in the hollows around the Lion de Roccapina. No one has ever proven this rumour to be true, though it is known that a purse of Indian diamonds sent as part of the gift to the Queen-Emperor was never recovered; its whereabouts are still the subject of speculation.

Pianotolli-Caldarello

Back on the main road, the first sign of civilization comes at **PIANOTOLLI-CALDARELLO**, the largest settlement between Sartène and Bonifacio. Two hamlets make up the village, and their names tell you everything about the locale: Pianottoli, the northern half straddling the highway, is derived from the word for "plain", and Caldarello, 1.5km south, means "extreme heat". There's nothing much to see in either, but a handful of unfrequented coves lie within easy reach, and if you're catching a plane from nearby Figari airport, a couple of **campsites** provide convenient places to spend your last night on the island. Three kilometres down the road to the sea, *Camping Le Damier* (℡04 95 71 82 95) is a large three-star site with a pizzeria and bungalows that are a steal (②) in low season. It charges more or less the same rates as the rival *Kevano Plage* (℡04 95 71 83 22, ℻04 95 71 83 83; April to mid-Oct), a short way down the lane. Both lie within easy walking distance of the secluded **Plage de Chevano**, a narrow sandy beach spread around a shallow turquoise bay, 500m further south.

To escape the campers who spill across it in season, head down the road directly opposite the entrance to the *Kevano Plage* and turn onto the second *piste* on your left (after around 1500m). This splits into two at a bend: take the right fork there and follow the track through the maquis to a small car park, from where footpaths run the rest of the way to a gorgeous string of little coves.

The only **hotel** in this area is the luxury *U Libecciu* (℡04 95 71 87 93, ℻04 95 71 86 54; ⑦), a recently built three-star backing onto its own exclusive beach, with a pool, tennis courts and eighty air-conditioned rooms. From the small jetty behind it you can rent sailing boats, windsurfers and waterskis. The hotel stands 2km south of Caldarello village; follow the signposts from the main road.

Figari

Cut in half by the main Porto-Vecchio to Ajaccio highway, the village of **FIGARI** sees a disproportionate amount of traffic thanks to its proximity to south Corsica's largest **airport**, spread over the floor of the valley below. Most charter and scheduled flights to northern Europe leave at civilized times, and visitors generally drive here on the day of their departure. If, however, you're travelling without the luxury of your own vehicle you'll have to get here via Eurocorse Voyages' Ajaccio bus or one of the *navettes* that run to the airport from opposite the marina in Porto-Vecchio to meet flights (more details of this service appear on p.285).

Overlooking the airport from the isolated village of San Gavino, 6km off the main road, *L'Orcu* (℡04 95 71 01 27; ③) is a quirky little **bed and breakfast** offering simple, clean rooms in an old granite house. The *patronne*, Mme Bartoli, cooks traditional family dishes, offered on a €25 menu that changes daily. Breakfast and dinner are served in the shade of an ancient tree outside. San Gavino is marked on the Michelin map (just): follow the signs to Poggiale from the main road and turn uphill at a sharp bed just southwest of the village church.

Another noteworthy Corsican speciality **restaurant** stands in Figari proper, at the Porto-Vecchio end of the village on the main road. *U Fuconu* (℡04 95 71 04 27) gets rave reviews for its pork fillets in honey, fresh lasagne and stuffed aubergine, rounded off with a selection of homemade chestnut-based desserts. The cooking is consistently careful, fresh and delicious, and the menus great value (at €12–18), making this one of the most tempting pit stops in the area.

Bonifacio and around

BONIFACIO (Bonifaziu) enjoys a superbly isolated situation at Corsica's southernmost point, a narrow peninsula of dazzling white limestone creating a town site unlike any other on the island. The **haute ville**, a maze of narrow streets flanked by tall Genoese tenements, rises seamlessly out of sheer cliffs that have been hollowed and striated by the wind and waves, while on the landward side the deep cleft between the peninsula and the mainland forms a perfect natural harbour. A haven for boats for centuries, the anchorage is nowadys dominated by a swish marina that attracts yachts from all around the Mediterranean.

Separated from the rest of the island by an expanse of maquis, Bonifacio has maintained a certain temperamental detachment from the rest of Corsica, and is distinctly more Italian than French in atmosphere. It has its own dialect based on Ligurian Italian, a legacy from the days when it was practically an independent Genoese town. The *haute ville* retains Renaissance features found only here and, with Sardinia just a stone's throw away, much of the property in the area is owned by upper-echelon Italians.

Such a place has its inevitable drawbacks: exorbitant prices, overwhelming crowds in August, and a commercial cynicism that's atypical of Corsica as a whole. However, the old town forms one of the most arresting spectacles in the Mediterranean, and warrants at least a day-trip. If you plan to come in peak season, try to get here early in the day before the bus parties arrive at around 10am.

A brief history of Bonifacio

It could be that Bonifacio's first documented appearance is as the town of the cannibalistic Laestrygonians in **The Odyssey**; Homer's description of an "excellent harbour, closed in on all sides by an unbroken ring of precipitous cliffs, with two bold headlands facing each other at the mouth so as to leave only a narrow channel in between" fits the port well. The unploughed land that Odysseus comes across inland of the harbour could be a reference to the plain beyond the Bonifacio promontory, and it's also possible that the Neolithic tribes that once lived in this area were the barbaric attackers of Odysseus's crew.

In Roman times there was a village on this site, but the town really came into being in 828 AD, when Count Bonifacio of Tuscany built a castle on the peninsula. Like other settlements on the Corsican coast, this one suffered continuous pirate raids, but its key position in the Mediterranean made various powers covet the port. Subject of a dispute between Pisa and Genoa in 1187, Bonifacio eventually fell to the Genoese, who then proceeded to massacre the local population and replace them with Ligurians, to whom they offered exemption from tax and customs duty in their ports. Two hundred and fifty families duly settled here, and soon the town developed into a mini-republic with its own constitution and laws, governed by elected magistrates called Anziani.

In 1420 **Alfonso V** of Aragon set his sights on Corsica, and for five months his fleet blockaded the port, hoping to starve the Bonifaciens into submission. Every citizen joined in the defence of the citadel, with clergymen, women and children flinging wooden beams, rocks and blinding chalk dust down on the attackers – they even tried to demoralize the enemy by pelting them with cheese, an action masterminded by one Marguerita Bobbia, whose ingenuity is commemorated by a street named after her in the old town. Eventually, a boat was built inside the citadel by the famished defenders, lowered onto the sea from the clifftop and dispatched to seek help from Genoa. Seven galleons were immediately sent to help the Bonifaciens, but they were delayed by contrary winds. Only by donning the armour of their dead soldiers, ringing all the church bells and parading around the town ramparts, were the last survivors of the siege able to buy the time needed for their Genoese rescuers to arrive. When the ships finally appeared, shortly after Christmas, the resolve of the Aragonese was decidedly weakened; they decamped shortly after. The Bonifacien bluff had turned the battle.

Another celebrated siege occurred in 1554, when the town was recovering from an outbreak of plague that had claimed two-thirds of the population. **Henri II** of France arrived with the Turkish fleet, led by the fearsome corsair Dragut. The town held on through eighteen days and nights of cannon fire, and then a member of the eminent Cattacciolo family was dispatched to Genoa to raise help. He was seized on his return by the Turks, who forced him to carry a forged letter refusing them the assistance of the republic, a ploy that brought about Bonifacio's surrender. The invaders pillaged the town, which was then rescued by Sampiero Corso. There followed a brief period of French rule, which came to an end when the Treaty of Cateau Cambresis returned Corsica to Genoa in 1559.

Thereafter the Genoese port enjoyed relative prosperity until the late eighteenth century, when the French gained control of the island. No longer permitted their special autonomy, the merchants moved away and the town suffered a commercial decline that was reversed really only with the advent of tourism.

Arrival and information

To get from **Figari airport**, 17km north of Bonifacio, you'll have to take a taxi into town – around €45 – as there's no *navette* service. Eurocorse Voyages' **buses** to and from Ajaccio and Porto-Vecchio use the car park by the **marina** as a terminal. Drivers can either pay to park here or leave their cars for free behind the nearby supermarket; there are also four more *parkings payants* up in the Bosco, at the west end of the *haute ville*, reached via avenue Générale-de-Gaulle. This is where you'll find the **tourist office** (July–Sept daily 9am–8pm; Oct–June Mon–Fri 9am–12.30pm & 2–5.15pm; ☎04 95 73 11 88, Ⓦwww.bonifacio.com), at the bottom of rue Fred-Scamaroni.

Accommodation

Finding **accommodation** can be a chore, as Bonifacio's few hotels are quickly booked up in peak season; so if you want to stay centrally, ring well in advance. Be prepared, too, for higher-than-average tariffs. With the exception of the *Araguina*, the nearest **campsites** are all a drive away, along the road to Porto-Vecchio.

Hotels

La Caravelle 35 quai J. Comparetti ☎04 95 73 00 03, Ⓕ04 95 73 00 41. Old-established place in prime location on the quayside, whose standard rooms are on the small side for the price. ❼

Centre Nautique The marina ☎04 95 73 02 11, Ⓕ04 95 73 17 47; Ⓦwww.centre-nautique.com. Chic but relaxed hotel on the waterfront, fitted out with mellow wood and nautical charts. All rooms are tastefully furnished and consist of two storeys connected with a spiral staircase. The best upmarket option in town, although their prices (€190 for a double in peak season) reflect the hotel's popularity among wealthy Americans. ❾

Des Étrangers 4 av Sylvère-Bohn ☎04 95 73 01 09, Ⓕ04 95 73 16 97. Simple double-glazed rooms

(the costlier ones have TV and air-con) facing the main road, just up from the port. Nothing special, but pretty good value for Bonifacio. April–Oct. ❺

Le Genovese The citadel ☎04 95 73 12 34, Ⓕ04 95 73 09 03, Ⓦwww.hotel-genovese.com. The only luxury hotel in the *haute ville*, hence the sky-high rates (from €230 per double in peak season). Views over the marina from some rooms and a newly installed pool with teak deck and furniture (for which they controversially demolished parts of the old town walls). ❾

Du Golfe Santa Manza ☎04 95 73 05 91, Ⓕ04 95 73 17 18, Ⓦwww.corsud.com. An unpretentious two-star in a lovely location. The rooms are plain but pleasant, and some have shuttered windows opening onto the gulf. Half board obligatory. ❼

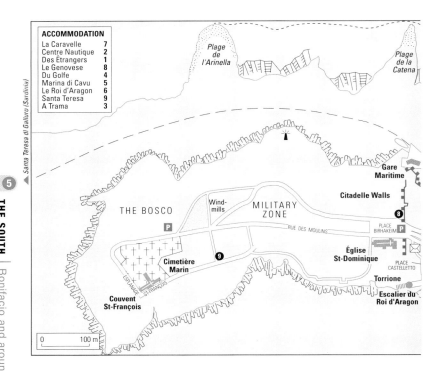

ACCOMMODATION

La Caravelle	7
Centre Nautique	2
Des Étrangers	1
Le Genovese	8
Du Golfe	4
Marina di Cavu	5
Le Roi d'Aragon	6
Santa Teresa	9
A Trama	3

Marina di Cavu Calalonga, 6km out of town ☎04 95 73 14 13, ⓕ04 95 73 04 82, ⓦwww.marinadicavu.com. One of Corsica's top luxury hotels, comprising a campus of sunny, colour-washed rooms swathed in oleanders and maquis on a hill facing Les Îles Lavezzi – a sublime location, with a pool and breakfast terrace that do it justice. Ultra-chic, but even so the peak-season rates (€213–350) are high. ⑨

Le Roi d'Aragon 13 quai J. Comparetti ☎04 95 73 03 99, ⓕ04 95 73 07 94. A recently revamped three-star overlooking the marina, with better-than-average off-season discounts. Some of the rooms are small, but the pricier ones have sunny interconnecting terraces looking across the port. ⑥

Santa Teresa quartier St-François ☎04 95 73 11 32, ⓕ04 95 73 15 99. Large (48-room) three-star on the clifftop overlooking Cimetière Marin, worth a mention for its stupendous views across the straits to Sardinia. Not all the rooms are sea-facing, though, so ask for "*vue mer avec balcon*" when you book. ⑧

A Trama 1.5km from Bonifacio along the route de Santa Manza ☎04 95 73 17 17, ⓕ04 95 73 17 79, ⓦwww.oda.fr/aa/trama. Discreet three-star, hidden behind a screen of maquis, palms, pines and drystone chalk walls. The rooms, all with private terraces, are grouped around a garden and pool, and there's a classy restaurant (*Le Clos Vatel*). Expensive (€161 per double) in high summer, but more affordable off season. Open all year. ⑨

Campsites

L'Araguina av Sylvère-Bohn, opposite the Total petrol station ☎04 95 73 02 96. Closest place to town, but unwelcoming, horrendously cramped and with inadequate washing and toilet facilities. Avoid unless desperate. April–Sept.

Campo di Liccia 3km north towards Porto-Vecchio, opposite *U Farniente* ☎04 95 73 03 09. Well shaded and large, so you're guaranteed a place. April–Oct.

Pian del Fosse 4km out of town on the route de Santa Manza ☎04 95 73 16 34. Big three-star site that recently had a makeover. Very peaceful and quiet in June and September, and well placed for the beaches. April to mid-Oct.

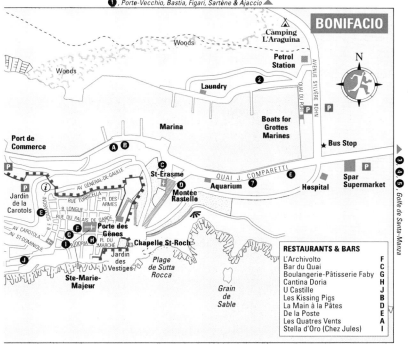

BONIFACIO

Camping
L'Araguina

Petrol
Station

Woods

Woods

Laundry

Marina

Boats for
Grottes
Marines

Port de
Commerce

★ Bus Stop

St-Érasme

QUAI J. COMPARETTI

AV GENERAL-DE-GAULLE

Aquarium

Hospital

Spar
Supermarket

Jardin
de la
Carotols

RUE TORRICELLA
PL DES
ARMES
R. LONGUE

Montée
Rastello

RUE DU PALAIS DE GARDE

AV CAROTOLA
AV ST-DOMINIQUE

Porte des
Gênes

Chapelle St-Roch

PL DU
MARCHÉ

Jardin
des
Vestiges

Plage
de Sutta
Rocca

Ste-Marie-
Majeur

Grain
de
Sable

RESTAURANTS & BARS	
L'Archivolto	F
Bar du Quai	C
Boulangerie-Pâtisserie Faby	G
Cantina Doria	H
U Castille	J
Les Kissing Pigs	B
La Main à la Pâtes	D
De la Poste	E
Les Quatres Vents	A
Stella d'Oro (Chez Jules)	I

The Town

Apart from the cafés, hotels and restaurants of **quai Comparetti**, the only attraction in the lower town is the marina's **Aquarium** (daily: May–Oct 10am–8.30pm; July & Aug open until midnight; €4), where all but the rarest creatures exhibited are caught fresh each year and released in the autumn, the giant blue lobster being the main highlight. At the far end lies the port, from which ferries depart for Sardinia and, in between, a cluster of restaurants and shops lies at the foot of **Montée Rastello**, the steps up to the *haute ville*.

The haute ville

Many of the houses in the **haute ville** are bordered by enormous battlements which, like the houses themselves, have been rebuilt many times – the most significant modifications were made by the French during their brief period of occupation following the 1554 siege, after they had reduced the town walls to rubble. Remnants of cannonshot-peppered buildings still scatter the *haute ville*, especially around the **Bosco** area at the tip of the promontory, where the barbed-wire fences around the military barracks and decaying German bunkers from 1943 all add to the war-torn appearence. The *haute ville* has been sparsely populated since the Genoese merchants moved out in the eighteenth century, and the precariousness of many of its buildings is no enticement to settle – on the southeast side the houses have no surrounding wall to protect them, and in 1966 one house fell into the sea, killing two people. Since then, various plans have been put forward to reinforce the cliff, but the state of the buildings is still a great problem.

From the top of the Montée Rastello steps, dubbed locally as the *grimpette* (literally "little climb"), you can cross avenue Général-de-Gaulle to **Montée St-Roch**, which gives a stunning view of the white limestone cliffs and the huge lump of fallen rock face called the **Grain de Sable**. At the **Chapelle St-Roch**, built on the spot where the last plague victim died in 1528, more steps lead down to the tiny beach of Sutta Rocca, which is great for snorkelling.

At the top of the Montée St-Roch steps stands the drawbridge of the great **Porte des Gênes**, once the only entrance to the *haute ville*. Through the gate and to the right, on place d'Armes, you can see the **Bastion de l'Étendard** (July & Aug daily 10am–9pm; April–June & Sept Mon–Sat 11am–5.30pm; €2), sole remnant of the fortifications destroyed during the siege of 1554. Inside is a small museum whose only noteworthy exhibit is a facsimile of the *Dame de Bonifacio*, a remarkably intact prehistoric skeleton of a woman found in a cave shelter near the town (the original is housed at the musée départementale in Levie: see p.247). You can also climb over the battlements to the tiny **Jardin des Véstiges**, which affords the *haute ville*'s best views of the cliffs to the east.

Back in the square, a few paces from the bastion lies **rue des Deux-Empereurs**, where at no. 4 you'll see the flamboyant marble escutcheon of the Cattacciolo family, one of many such adornments on the houses of this quarter. In 1541, the emperor Charles V, having been caught in Bonifacio by a storm, stayed in this house as a guest of Filippo Cattacciolo; after the departure of his illustrious visitor, Cattacciolo shot the horse he had loaned to him, on the grounds that nobody else was worthy to ride the poor beast after it had supported the ruler of half the known world. Opposite stands the house in which Napoléon resided for three months in 1793.

Cutting down to rue Palais-du-Garde brings you to **Église Ste-Marie-Majeure**, originally Romanesque but restored in the eighteenth century, though the richly sculpted belfry dates from the fourteenth century. The façade is hidden by a **loggia** where the Genoese municipal officers used to dispense justice in the days of the republic. If you look up you can see buttresses connecting the houses in the adjoining streets to the roof of the church – these were vital not just as support but also for draining rainwater into a huge cistern underneath the porch, which provided the town with water in times of siege and during the dry summers. The church's treasure, a relic of the **True Cross** said to have been brought to Bonifacio by St Helena, the mother of Constantine, was saved from a shipwreck in the Straits of Bonifacio; for centuries after, the citizens would take the relic to the edge of the cliff and pray for calm seas whenever storms raged. It is nowadays kept in the sacristy, along with an ivory cask containing relics of St Boniface. In the main body of the church the highlight is the marble **tabernacle** to the left of the door; decorated with a bas-relief carving of Christ supported by eight glum-faced cherubs, it's thought to have been created by a north Italian sculptor in 1565. The holy water stoup below it is a third-century **sarcophagus**, the sole Roman item in town.

Rue du Palais-de-Garde, which runs alongside the church, is one of the most handsome streets in Bonifacio, with its closed arcades and double-arched windows separated by curiously stunted columns. The oldest houses along here did not originally have doors; the inhabitants used to climb up a ladder, which they would pull up behind them to prevent a surprise attack, while the ground floor was used as a stable and grain store.

South of here, rue Doria leads towards the Bosco (see below); at the end of this road a left down rue des Pachas will bring you to the **Torrione**, a 35-metre-high lookout post built in 1195 on the site of Count Bonifacio's castle. Descending the cliff, the **Escalier du Roi d'Aragon**'s 187 steps (June–Sept daily 11am–5.30pm; €2) were said to have been built in one night by the Aragonese in an attempt to gain the town in 1420, but in fact they had already been in existence for some time and were used by the people to fetch water from a well.

The Bosco

To the west of the tower lies the **Bosco**, a *quartier* named after the wood that used to stand here in the tenth century. In those days a community of hermits dwelt on the spot, but the limestone plateau now lies open and desolate. The only sign of life comes from the military barracks – home of the IIième REP Foreign Legion Parachute Regiment until it decamped to Calvi – where a couple of hundred youngsters sweat out their national service. The entrance to the Bosco is marked by **Église St-Dominique**, a rare example of Corsican Gothic architecture – it was built in 1270, most probably by the Templars, and later handed over to the Dominicans.

Beyond the church, rue des Moulins leads onto the ruins of three mills dating from 1283, two of them decrepit, the third restored. Behind them stands a memorial to the 750 people who died when the troop ship *Sémillante* ran aground here in 1855, on its way to the Crimea, one of the many disasters wreaked by the straits.

The tip of the plateau is occupied by the **Cimetière Marin**, its white crosses standing out sharply against the deep blue of the sea. Open until dusk, the cemetery is a fascinating place to explore, with its flamboyant mausoleums displaying a jumble of architectural ornamentations: stuccoed façades, Gothic arches and classical columns. Next to the cemetery stands the **Couvent St-François**, allegedly founded after St Francis sought shelter in a nearby cave – the story goes that the convent was the town's apology to the holy man, over whom a local maid had nearly poured a bucket of slops. Immediately to the south, the **Esplanade St-François** commands fine views across the bay to Sardinia.

Eating, drinking and nightlife

Eating possibilities in Bonifacio might seem unlimited, but standards rarely befit the locations, especially when it comes to the chintzy restaurants down in the marina, few of which merit their exorbitant prices – the places in the *haute ville* generally offer better value for money. For much of the day and in the evening, the **bars** and **cafés** lining the quai Comparetti are the social focus, but for serious nightlife you'll have to head for *Via Notte* near Porto-Vecchio (see p.284).

Restaurants

L'Archivolto rue de l'Archivolto, just off the place de l'Église ☎04 95 73 17 48. With its candlelit, antique- and junk-filled interior, this would be the most commendable place to eat in the *haute ville* were the cooking a little less patchy and the prices fairer. But it still gets packed out: advance reservation recommended. Open Easter–Oct.

Boulangerie-Pâtisserie Faby 4 rue St-Jean-Baptiste, *haute ville*. Tiny local bakery serving Bonifacien treats such as *pain des morts* (sweet buns with walnuts and raisins), *fugazzi* (*galettes* flavoured with eau de vie, orange, lemon and aniseed) and *migliaccis* (buns made with fresh ewe's cheese), in addition to the usual range of spinach and *brocciu bastelles*, baked here in the

traditional way – on stone.

Cantina Doria 27 rue Doria ☎04 95 73 50 49. Down-to-earth Corsican specialities at down-to-earth prices, served in an old vaulted dining hall. Their popular three-course €14 menu – which includes the house speciality, aubergines *à la bonifacienne* – offers unbeatable value for the *haute ville*, though you'll soon bump up your bill if you succumb to the temptations of the excellent wine selection, featuring Domaine Toraccia (available in half bottles) and the sublime Abbatucci *blanc*.

U Castille rue Simon-Varsi, *haute ville*. Italian-style dishes based mainly on lamb, veal and fresh seafood – try their wonderful *terrine de sanglier*, fresh pasta *à la carbonara*, or tomato and mozzarella salads steeped in fresh basil. For vegetarians there's artichoke stuffed with *brocciu*, or juicy pizzas (the latter served in a separate *pizzeria* across the alleyway).

Centre Nautique The marina, in the hotel of the same name. Bonifacio's most chic breakfast venue: coffee, hot croissants, baguettes and freshly squeezed orange juice on a cool wood deck, with optimal views of the bastion across the marina. Well worth splashing out €10 for, but get here early for the best tables.

La Main à la Pâtes 1 place Bonaparte, at the bottom of the Montée Rastello. Three dozen different kinds of fresh pasta, with especially imaginative sauces: cocoa, mint or sea urchin. Not cheap, but you get what you pay for here, which makes a change in Bonifacio.

Marina di Cavu Calalonga, 6km out of town ✆04 95 73 14 30. Ultra-sophisticated gourmet restaurant, built around a huge granite boulder, which gives the designer dining hall an earthy feel – despite the proximity of the pool. Based on the freshest local fish and meat, the cooking's *haute gastronomie* and priced accordingly, with menus at €34 and €54.

De la Poste 6 rue Fred-Scamaroni. A cheap and cheerful pizza place serving oven-baked lasagne, spaghetti *al brocciu*, stuffed mussels and delicious pizzas (€7–10).

Les Quatres Vents On the quayside near the ferry dock ✆04 95 73 07 50. Lively little restaurant fronting the marina that's popular with locals and tourists alike. Their €17 menu – fish soup or charcuterie, *poisson du jour* or *lasagna al brocciu*, and dessert – is great value. Come early to get a table outside.

Stella d'Oro (Chez Jules) 23 rue Doria, near Église St-Jean-Baptiste. À la carte place with stone walls and wood beams, whose top-notch Corsican dishes include the definitive *merrizzane* (stuffed aubergine) – *the* local speciality. They also do a famous spaghetti in lobster sauce and ravioli *brocciu*. Most main courses €13.

Bars

Bar du Quai Marina. Run-of-the-mill café that's popular with locals, and an excellent spot for a croissant and coffee breakfast, as its terrace catches the morning sun and breeze off the water.

Les Kissing Pigs Next to *Le Goulet* restaurant at the top of the marina. Curiously themed wine bar boasting the world's largest collection of kissing pig photos and other snout-related ephemera. Open late.

Ferries to Sardinia

Ferries for Santa Teresa di Gallura, Sardinia, leave the gare maritime at the far southern end of the marina. Mobyline (✆04 95 73 00 29) and Saremar (✆04 95 73 00 96) operate ten to fourteen daily crossings between July 19 and September 1, reduced to between four and seven daily from March 3 to July 18 and September 2 to 29, with none for the rest of the year. The one-hour crossing costs €7–8.50, plus €20–28 per car. You can get tickets for both operators from Agence Gazano, Port de Bonifacio ✆04 95 73 02 47.

Listings

Airport Figari, 17km north of town, off the D859 ✆04 95 71 10 31.

Banks and exchange Societé Générale, 2 rue St-Érasme, at the foot of the steps to the *haute ville* has an ATM (as does the post office; see below). Avoid the bureaux de change dotted around town – they charge extortionate commission rates.

Bookshops There are a couple on the quai Comparetti, of which the Librairie-Papeterie Simoni is the largest, selling a range of imported newspapers, pulp fiction and guidebooks.

Car rental Avis, quai Banda-del-Ferro ✆04 95 73 01 28; Citer, quai Noel-Beretti ✆04 95 73 13 16; Hertz, quai Banda-del-Ferro ✆04 95 73 06 41. All of the above also have branches at Figari airport.

Diving Full information about the superb diving possibilities in the south of Corsica – including the famous "Mérouville" site where you're guaranteed a close encounter with huge grouper fish – is available from Bonifacio's three accredited schools: Atoll, at the *Auberge A. Cheda*, 2km north on the Porto-Vecchio road ✆04 95 73 02 83; Barakouda, 3km north on the same road ✆04 95 73 13 02; and Kallisté, in the harbour itself, reached via the roundabout 1km north of town – look for the sign by the Elf petrol station ✆04 95 73 53 66.

Hospital 1 route de Santa-Manza, at the entrance to town ✆04 95 73 95 73. For an ambulance, phone ✆04 95 73 06 95 or 04 95 73 06 94.

Laundry Laverie automatique, northeast side of the port.

Motorbike and mountain-bike rental Corse

Moto Services, quai Nova, on the north side of the port ☎ 04 95 73 15 16.
Pharmacy 17 quai Comparetti.
Police Route de Santa-Manza ☎ 04 95 73 00 17.

Post office On place Carrega in the *haute ville* (Mon–Fri 9am–noon & 2–5pm, Sat 9am–noon).
Taxis Louis di Meglio ☎ 04 95 73 02 86 or Nicole Horrach ☎ 06 62 35 79 50.

Around Bonifacio

The views of the citadel from the cliffs at the head of the Montée Rastello (reached via a pathway running left from the top of the steps) are impressive enough, but they're not a patch on the spectacular panorama to be had from the sea. Throughout the day, a flotilla of excursion **boats** ferries visitors out to the best vantage points, en route to a string of caves and other landmarks only accessible by water, including the **Îles Lavezzi**, a scattering of small islets where the troop ship *Sémillante* was wrecked in 1855. The whole experience of bobbing around to an amplified running commentary is about as touristy as Bonifacio gets, but it's well worth enduring just to round the mouth of the harbour and see the *haute ville* perched atop the famous chalk cliffs.

With more time, you can sidestep the crowds completely by heading off on one of the wonderful coast walks from the town: southeast towards the lighthouse on Capo Pertusato, Corsica's southernmost point; or west to Ermitage de la Trinité, an old convent with fine views across the straits to Sardinia.

With the notable exception of the horseshoe-shaped Plage de Rondinara,

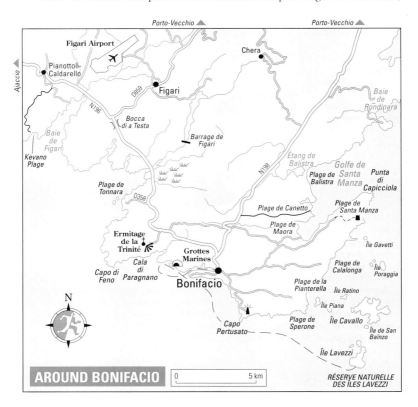

AROUND BONIFACIO

0   5 km

RÉSERVE NATURELLE DES ÎLES LAVEZZI

midway between Bonifacio and Porto-Vecchio, the beaches along this part of the coast are generally smaller and less appealing than most in southern Corsica, although those fringing the Golfe de Santa Manza, to the north, are set amid some fine scenery. Over the past two decades, this whole area has become the preserve of an international jet set, whose luxury villas, golf courses and helipads are sometimes the only blots on otherwise unspoilt islets and coves.

Ermitage de la Trinité

The **Ermitage de la Trinité**, 7km west of Bonifacio, off the N196, stands on a site that has been inhabited since prehistoric times and was a hermitage right at the beginning of the Christianization of the island. Heavily restored in the thirteenth century, the convent sits beside a terrace of olive trees, a backdrop of gigantic eroded outcrops lending it a brooding atmosphere. There's a fine view of Bonifacio from here, and an even better one if you follow the track to the left before you reach the building, which arrives at the **Mont de la Trinité** after about fifteen minutes' gentle climbing.

Boat trips to the grottes marines and the Îles Lavezzi

From the moment you arrive in Bonifacio, you'll be pestered by touts from the many boat companies running excursions out of the harbour. There are more than a dozen of these, but they all offer more or less the same routes, at the same prices.

Lasting between thirty and forty-five minutes, the shorter trips take you out along the cliffs to the **grottes marines** (sea caves) and *calanches* (inlets) below the old town; tickets cost €8–10 depending on the demand and how well you can haggle. The largest of the three caves, the **Grotte du Sdragonatu**, is worth the money on its own – a magnificent grotto where the water takes on an extraordinary violet luminosity and the rock walls, encrusted with stalactites and arches, glitter with the colours of amethyst, indigo and gold. Guides like to point out that when viewed from directly below, the hole in the roof of the chamber resembles the shape of Corsica.

Longer excursions out to the **Îles Lavezzi**, part of the archipelago to the east of the straits of Bonifacio, cost around €25. Most companies offer a shuttle (*navette*) service, allowing you to spend as much time as you like on the islands before returning.

Having passed the Grain de Sable, the Phare du Pertusato and the heavily guarded private island of Cavallo (where Sly Stallone has a holiday villa), the boats moor at the main island of **Lavezzi**, beside the **cimetière Achiarino**. Buried here are the victims of the *Sémillante* shipwreck of 1855, in which 773 crew members and soldiers bound for the Crimean War were drowned after their vessel was blown onto the rocks. The bodies were washed ashore over the following fortnight, but so disfigured were they that only one (that of the captain) could be identified; the rest are interred in unnamed graves. A stone pyramid on the western tip of the isle commemorates the tragedy, the worst ever shipwreck in the history of the Mediterranean.

Classified as a nature reserve since 1982, the island is home to several rare species of **wild flower**, such as the yellow-horned poppy, the white sea daffodil and the stonecrop, distinguished by its fleshy red leaves beneath heads of small blue flowers.

Further north, **Cavallo** and its adjoining islet, **San Bainzo**, were the sites of Roman quarries, which feature on most of the boats' half-day excursions; huge monolithic columns lie at the water's edge, cut from horizontal trenches in the rock nearby and discarded, seemingly in haste. The stone quarried here was not used in Corsica, but transported to the mainland to fuel the decadent building boom at the end of the Roman Empire. Most touching of the remains here is an image of Hercules Saxanus, the patron saint of hard labour, carved by slaves on the face of a large boulder.

Capo Pertusato

The deeply scored limestone cliffs southeast of Bonifacio culminate in the wide headland of **Capo Pertusato** (Pierced Cape), a steepish climb of about 45 minutes from Bonifacio. At the end of the walk you'll be rewarded with an incredible seascape embracing Sardinia, the crested islands of Lavezzi and Cavallo, and Bonifacio itself, just discernible to the west. Leaving town along the D58, almost immediately bear right along the D260, a narrow road hugging the cliffside as far as the **Phare du Pertusato**, the lighthouse at the edge of the point. Drivers should take extra care as the road out here is very narrow, with no room for passing and no barriers to protect your car from the chalk walls.

Beaches around Bonifacio

Visible from the north side of the *haute ville*, the nearest accessible beach coves to Bonifacio, **Plage de la Catena** and **Plage de l'Arinella**, are small and picturesque but catch a lot of flotsam and oil pollution from the passing maritime traffic. However, the **walk** to them is very pleasant, beginning at a track just before *Camping L'Araguina* (see map on p.277).

On Corsica's southernmost tip, reached via a narrow but easily motorable road, a trio of small coves are the most popular beaches in this area. The first, **Plage de Pianterella**, is also the dullest, backed by marsh. Walk south around the headland for fifteen minutes and you'll reach the more pleasant **Plage de Sperone**, a pearl-white cove with calm, shallow water that's ideal for children. Overlooking the transparent waters of the straits, with Sardinia only 12km away, is the island's top eighteen-hole **golf course** (Ⓦ www.sperone.net), 72 hectares of immaculate turf installed with the help of huge subsidies from the regional assembly. In January 1997 it made headlines when the former nationalist leader, François Santoni, and his then girlfriend, lawyer Marie-Hélène Mattei, were found to have extorted protection money from the golf club's owner. Santoni served a prison sentence for his role in the affair, but has since been murdered (see p.430).

A better place to escape the summer masses lies further around the coast at **Plage de Calalonga**. To get there, head east of town on the D58, and take the first turning right after around 3km. Passing a series of heavily guarded military communications complexes, this narrows rapidly, deteriorating into a badly rutted *piste*, at the end of which lies a tiny bulldozed car park.

For details of **hotels** in this area, see "Accommodation" on p.271.

The Golfe de Santa Manza

Marginally more enticing are the beaches lining the **Golfe de Santa Manza**, northeast of Bonifacio along the D58. The first of these, **Plage de Maora**, lies at the far west end of the gulf, reached by a lane running north off the crossroads of the D60 and D58. A narrow curve of pink granite grit with a small *buvette*, it's frequented mainly by tourists from the surrounding *villages de vacances*. Further around the bay, the views improve and the coves, backed by the road, attract increasing numbers of watersports enthusiasts as you approach the **Plage de Santa Manza**, where the route ends. Again, the beach itself is a bit of a disappointment, but it does give access to a wild stretch of coast that has plenty of potential for walking. Don't follow the most obvious path along the shore; instead, head inland along a *piste* marked "Passage Privé" (it isn't private, in fact), past the stone hut behind the beach and uphill for around twenty minutes as far as a fork. If you bear left here, you'll eventually come out, after around twenty to thirty minutes, at an old **watchtower**, from where the views along the coast and across to the Îles Lavezzi are wonderful.

A review of the gulf's most appealing **hotel**, the *Du Golfe*, appears on p.271.

Plages de Caneti and Balistra

Two of the least-frequented beaches in the Bonifacio region line the north coast of the Golfe de Santa Manza. With a backdrop of weathered chalk cliffs, **Plage de Caneti** is the most picturesque, but hard to reach. Heading north on the main Porto-Vecchio road, turn right directly opposite the *Camping di Licia*, 3km out of town, and follow the signs for the luxury four-star *Hôtel Capu Biancu*, until you reach a fork after 4.5km. Bear left here (not right, which will take you to the hotel) and drop down the south bank of a stream; the beach lies 500m further on.

Plage de Balistra is the next beach up the coast, 5km north of the Caneti turning down an unsurfaced road (look for the signpost on the main road). The largest and least crowded in this area, it is strewn with seaweed and backed by an *étang* (brackish lagoon) that's a breeding ground for some particularly rapacious mosquitoes, but don't let this put you off. The sand is soft and white, and the views across the bay fine.

Rondinara

A perfect shell-shaped cove of turquoise water enclosed by soft dunes and a pair of twin headlands, **Rondinara** looks like most people's idea of a paradise Pacific lagoon. Thankfully, it is also well off the beaten track, although the recent appearance of a surfaced road all the way to the beach could well change that. To see it at its most empty, get here early the morning. A large hoarding on the N198, 10km north of Bonifacio, indicates the way to "Camping Rondinara", 4km along the D158. Set back 600m behind the beach amid a scattering of (as yet) ineffectual saplings, the **campsite** (☎04 95 70 43 15, ⓕ04 95 70 56 79; mid-May to Sept) is spacious and well equipped, with its own (enormous) pool. Tariffs are also low, considering the location.

The Porto-Vecchio region

Nowhere on the island has been so thoroughly given over to tourism as the area around **Porto-Vecchio**, thanks to the wealth of white-sand beaches and turquoise bays that indent the coastline around this former Genoese port. Shaded by a canopy of pines, thousands of manicured holiday villas and *villages de vacances* carpet the headlands and hills behind the beaches, while the town itself, a seasonal ferry harbour, seems entirely populated by Italians in summer.

If you've wondered where those Seychelles-style beach shots might be that shine from every postcard rack on the island, head south from Porto-Vecchio to **Palombaggia**, Corsica's most-photographed beach, or to the translucent waters of **Santa Giulia**. Bear in mind, though, that these photos tend to be taken in winter, when the beaches are deserted, and that during the summer you won't be able to slot a postcard between the sun worshippers crammed onto them. The same goes for the bays north of Porto-Vecchio – **San Ciprianu** and **Pinarellu** – preludes to the near unbroken beach running from here all the way up the eastern plain to Bastia.

While you're in the area, make time for some of the **prehistoric sites** dotted around Porto-Vecchio: the Bronze Age settlements of **Torre** and the **Casteddu d'Araggiu** to the north, and the Torrean monuments at **Ceccia** and **Tappa**. The perfect antidote to the heat and bright light of the coast, the **Forêt de l'Ospédale** holds plenty of pine-shaded walks with fine views over the plains to Sardinia.

Porto-Vecchio is connected by regular **buses** to Bastia, via the east coast highway. You can also get here on direct services from Ajaccio, either via the mountain route through Ospédale, Zonza and Bavella (see p.291), or on the Route Nationale that loops south through Propriano and Figari. In addition, *navettes* run throughout the busy summer months from the town to the most popular beaches in the area, including Santa Giulia and Palombaggia.

Porto-Vecchio

Set on a hill in the most sheltered corner of a deep gulf, **PORTO-VECCHIO**, in the southeast of the island, was rated by James Boswell as one of in "the most distinguished harbours in Europe". Pleasure boats, yachts and international ferries still crowd the port, but trade has long given way to tourism as the town's *raison d'être*. Its popularity as a holiday centre derives more from the proximity of the island's most spectacular beaches, but you

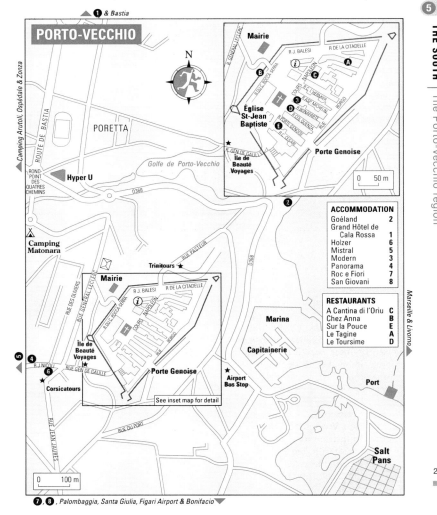

PORTO-VECCHIO

Camping Arutoli, Ospédale & Zonza

① & Bastia

Mairie

R.J. BALESI   R DE LA CITADELLE

Église St-Jean Baptiste

Porte Genoise

PORETTA

ROUTE DE BASTIA

Golfe de Porto-Vecchio

Île de Beauté Voyages

ROND-POINT DES QUATRES CHEMINS

Hyper U

D368

②

Camping Matonara

Trinitours ★

RUE PASTEUR

RUE DES OLIVIERS

RUE GÉNÉRALE LECLERC

Mairie

R.J. BALESI   R DE LA CITADELLE

Île de Beauté Voyages ★

⑤ ④

R.J. NICOLI

RUE GEN DE GAULLE

Corsicatours ★

Porte Genoise

Marina

Capitainerie

★ Airport Bus Stop

See inset map for detail

RUE JEAN JAURÈS

RUE DU PORT

0   100 m

Port

Salt Pans

Marseille & Livorno

ACCOMMODATION	
Goéland	2
Grand Hôtel de Cala Rossa	1
Holzer	6
Mistral	5
Modern	3
Panorama	4
Roc e Fiori	7
San Giovani	8

RESTAURANTS	
A Cantina di l'Oriu	C
Chez Anna	B
Sur la Pouce	E
Le Tagine	A
Le Toursime	D

⑦, ⑧, Palombaggia, Santa Giulia, Figari Airport & Bonifacio ▼

could do worse than spend an afternoon or evening here. Once beyond the unpromising outskirts – marred by roundabouts, light industry and patches of insalubrious marshland – things improve considerably as you approach the old **citadel** that still forms the hub of the town, with its leafy church square and picturesque backstreets, lined by restaurant terraces and designer boutiques.

Porto-Vecchio was founded in 1539 as a second Genoese stronghold on the east coast, Bastia being well established in the north. The location was perfect: close to the unexploited and fertile plain, the site benefited from secure high land and a sheltered gulf. Unfortunately, however, the Genoese hadn't counted on the mosquito problem, and within months malaria had wiped out the first Ligurian settlers. Sampiero Corso occupied the port for a brief period in 1564, having failed to take Ajaccio, but Genoa got it back a few months later, and things began to take off soon after, mainly thanks to the cork industry, which thrived until the twentieth century. Today a third of Corsica's wine is exported from here, but most revenue comes from the rich tourists who flock to the town each year.

Around the centre of town there's not much to see, apart from the well-preserved **fortress** and the small grid of ancient streets backing onto the main **place de la République**. East of the square you can't miss the **Porte Génoise**, which frames a delightful expanse of sea and through which you'll find the quickest route down to the modern **marina**, lined with cafés and hotels. Visible on the southern eastern fringes, a grid of shallow basins sporting rows of white mounds comprise the town's **salt pans**, or *salins*, which are open to visitors during the summer (mid-May to Sept daily 8am–8pm; ☎04 95 70 62 00; guided tours in French on the hour).

Arrival and information

Porto-Vecchio doesn't have a **bus** station; instead, the various bus companies stop and depart from outside their agents' offices on the edge of the old town. Coming from Bastia or the eastern plain (Solenzara or Aléria) with Rapides Bleus, you'll be dropped at the Corsicatours office on 7 rue Jean-Jaurès. The same firm also runs shuttle buses to and from Santa Giulia beach in the summer. Eurocorse Voyages operates the fast services to Ajaccio via Bonifacio, Sartène and Propriano, and its buses stop outside the Trinitours office on rue Pasteur, just north of the citadel; they also have a seasonal *navette* to Palombaggia (July & Aug only). Finally, the agents for Balési Évasion, whose minibus connects Porto-Vecchio with Ajaccio via Bavella and Alta Rocca, are Île de Beauté Voyages, at 13 rue Général-de-Gaulle. For more on services from Porto-Vecchio, see "Travel details" on p.291.

The town's efficient **tourist office**, just north of place de la République (July & Aug Mon–Sat 9am–8pm, Sun 9am–1pm; June & Sept Mon–Sat 9am–1pm & 3–6pm; Oct–May Mon–Fri 9am–noon & 2–6pm, Sat 9am–noon; ☎04 95 70 09 58, ⓕ04 95 70 03 72; ⓦwww.accueil-portovecchio.com) is the best place to check transport timetables. Its glossy brochure, *Destination Corse Sud*, is more thorough than usual, featuring aerial photographs of all the region's beaches in addition to the usual listings.

Accommodation

Finding somewhere to stay in Porto-Vecchio is only a problem during peak season, when prices approach those of neighbouring Bonifacio. **Hotels** are grouped around the old town, with a handful of more expensive places down in the marina and out of town on the coast, while **campsites** line the route north of the centre towards Pinarellu beach and Bastia, and along the road to Palombaggia.

Hotels in the town

Goéland Port de Plaisance ☎ 04 95 70 14 15, ℱ 04 95 72 05 18; ✉ hotel-goeland@wanadoo.fr. Very pleasant and good value, in an excellent seaside location looking across the gulf; large rooms, convivial atmosphere and welcoming owners. Tariff includes breakfast. ❼

Holzer 12 rue Jean-Jaurès/rue Jean-Nicoli ☎ 04 95 70 05 93, ℱ 04 95 70 47 02. Labyrinthine place with airless, boxed-in rooms, but immaculately clean and very central. ❺

Mistral rue Jean-Nicoli ☎ 04 95 70 08 53, ℱ 04 95 70 51 60. Comfortable mid-range hotel slightly removed from the noisy centre of town. Classier than the *Panorama* opposite, with the priciest rooms in a modern air-conditioned block across the road. ❹

Modern 10 cours Napoléon ☎ 04 95 70 06 36. The only hotel overlooking the square. Most rooms have shared toilets, but there are some en-suite options; particularly recommended are nos. 20 and 21 on the roof, which have gulf views. Tariffs are particularly good value in June and Sept. ❻

Panorama 12 rue Jean-Nicoli ☎ 04 95 70 07 96, ℱ 04 95 70 46 78. Simple place just above the old town run by an elderly couple, with parking spaces and various types of rooms (nos. 8 and 9 on the top floor are the cosiest, though without toilets). Not all that well maintained, but usually the cheapest in town. ❸

Hotels around Porto-Vecchio

The hotels listed below are marked on the map on p.287.

Grand Hôtel de Cala Rossa Cala Rossa, near Lecci di Porto-Vecchio ☎ 04 95 71 69 24, ℱ 04 95 71 60 11, ⓦ www.cala-rossa.com. Beautifully designed luxury hotel, occupying a secluded cove lined by turquoise water and a fine-sand beach, at the breezy northern end of the Golfe de Porto-Vecchio. Wooden decks, driftwood beams and traditional terracotta tiles set the tone, but the 52 air-con rooms, spread under the shade of umbrella pines across a 72-hectare site, are bright, private and modern. A large pool, good childcare facilities, fitness centre, Michelin-starred restaurant and 35-foot yacht number among the extras. Obligatory half board (€520 for two people) in July & Aug. ❾

Roc e Fiori Bocca dell Oro, 4km south ☎ 04 95 70 45 20, ℱ 04 95 70 47 61, ⓦ www.rocefiori.com. Ersatz Mediterranean-style "village" of fifteen luminous rooms, suites and apartments, painted in pretty lemon, pink and ochre pastels amid rock gardens on the hillside above the Palombaggia–Santa-Giulia strip. Very chic indeed, but not at all child-friendly and expensive in high season, when half board (€374 for two sharing) is obligatory. ❾

San Giovanni 2km south of the centre along the D659, towards Arca ☎ 04 95 70 22 55, ℱ 04 95 70 20 11, ⓦ www.hotel-san-giovanni.com. Thirty comfortable chalet rooms in extensive landscaped, flower-filled gardens. They've a good-sized pool, complimentary mountain bikes, Jacuzzi, sauna, tennis courts and a ping-pong table. Good value at this price, and peaceful. ❻

Campsites

Arutoli route de l'Ospédale ☎ 04 95 70 12 73. Large, well-equipped site located 2km northwest along the D368. Enormous swimming pool makes this a good option for families, and hikers on the Mare a Mare Sud, which passes nearby.

Asciaghju Bocca di l'Oro ☎ & ℱ 04 95 70 37 87. Pick of the bunch within striking distance of the beaches to the south. Rock-hard ground, but plenty of shade, clean toilet blocks and only 300m from secluded Asciaghju beach (see p.287). Mid-June to mid-Sept.

Les Jardins du Golfe 4km along the route de Palombaggia ☎ 04 95 70 46 92, ℱ 04 95 72 10 28. One of a string of large, well-equipped sites lining the road to the area's most popular beach. It's a state-sponsored project run by people with learning disabilities, and has a lovely atmosphere, a small shop and a snack bar.

La Matonara carrefour des Quatre-Chemins ☎ 04 95 70 37 05. A large site shaded by cork trees, with clean *sanitaires* blocks and washing machines. By far the best choice if you don't have your own vehicle, as it's within walking distance of the centre (see map, p.281), but don't come here without mosquito repellent.

Eating and drinking

With a few exceptions, most of Porto-Vecchio's eating establishments are substandard tourist traps, but there are a couple of decent addresses where you can enjoy quality seafood and local specialities at affordable prices, and cheap and cheerful pizzerias and pasta places are dotted around the centre. Cafés line place de la République and cours Napoléon, which runs along the east side of the square.

A Cantina di l'Oriu 5 cours Napoléon. Essentially a Corsican produce shop selling top-quality cheese, charcuterie, wine, honey, jams and other local delicacies, with a small terrace tacked on the side where you can order various *formules*. Get there for "Happy Hour" (6.30–7.30pm) when they offer plates of strong mountain ham, bread and a glass of wine for €5. At other times, count on €12–15 for plates of assorted cured meats and olives.

Chez Anna rue Camille-de-Rocca-Serra ☎04 95 70 19 97. Classy little pasta restaurant down an alleyway off the main square, where you can eat off starched white tablecloths *à la terrasse* or indoors. Try their delicious stuffed aubergines or fresh gnocchi with mussels. Menus around €20.

Sur la Pouce rue de la Porte-Genoise. Various *pani-ni* and other light snacks to take away for around €4, many using quality local cheeses (such as their delicious *panini "corse"*, with goat's cheese filling). A real find if you're on a tight budget.

Le Tagine rue de la Citadelle. Authentic Moroccan cooking, based mainly on lamb, couscous and fresh vegetables, served from terracotta gratin dishes in an attractively decorated first-floor room. Most main dishes around €15.

Le Tourisme Opposite the church ☎04 95 70 06 45. Pricier than most of the places around the square, but correspondingly more adventurous and stylish. Fragrant, light Porto-Vecchien specialities – such as mussels in fennel and pastis served on a bed of tagliatelle – are their strongpoint. Menu at €23, and there's a range of various good-value *formules* at lunchtime.

Bars and nightlife

Apart from when the Italians swamp the town in August, **nightlife** is fairly low-key, revolving around the cafés in the square. The few bars and nightclubs that stand out are listed below.

Pub Le Bastion Opposite *Le Tagine* restaurant on rue de la Citadelle. Claiming to serve three hundred varieties of beer, this bar has one of Corsica's only dartboards, and stages live music – cheesy local rock bands – most weekends.

A Ruscana route de Pinarellu, Ste-Lucie-de-Porto-Vecchio ☎04 95 71 5 42. Open-air cinema, 11km north along the main highway, showing different films each night in summer. Look for the posters at the tourist office in Porto-Vecchio.

Le Taverne du Roi Near the Porte Génoise, where you can hear more traditional music – a mixture of Corsican choral and folk tunes, and French standards, accompanied by guitar and piano.

Theatre d'Été Small open-air stage down behind the marina which hosts choral concerts and plays during the summer. Forthcoming events are advertised on posters around town, and in the tourist office.

Via Notte On the south edge of town ☎04 95 72 02 12, ⬤www.vianotte.com. Corsica's number one nightspot: a full-on Italian-oriented place that stages top Euro DJs in July and August (when admission charges and drink prices go through the roof) – about as sophisticated as the island's nightlife gets. To find it, head south of town on the Bonifacio road, cross the bridge and pass the Palombaggia turning, then take the second left after that, signposted for Bocca di l'Oru; the club's 500m further on.

Listings

Banks and exchange All the big banks have branches in the town centre and will change traveller's cheques. ATMs accepting Visa and other credit cards are available at the post office, Société Générale on the Quatre-Chemins cross-roads near the Super U supermarket, and on the south wall of the Super U itself.

Car rental Europcar, route de Bastia ☎04 95 70 14 50; Rent-a-Car, route de Bonifacio ☎04 95 70 03 40.

Diving CIP La Palanquée, Les Marines, 500m south of town on the Bonifacio road ☎04 95 70 16 53; Club Plongée Kallisté, Plage de Palombaggia ☎04 95 70 44 59; Sud Corse Loisirs, Santa Giulia ☎04 95 70 22 67. All the above can arrange trips to dive sites around the Îles Cerbicale, off Palombaggia, and the wreck of the *Pecorella*, lying 12m down at the north end of the gulf.

Internet access The tiny newsagents directly opposite the tourist office on the square offers Internet access for €3 per 30min.

Motorbike rental Corsica Moto Rent, 3km south on the route de Bonifacio ☎04 95 70 03 40. A range of bikes, from €45 per day for a 50cc scooter to €62 per day for a 125cc trials bike. They also have pricier 650cc machines. Considerable reductions for longer periods.

Mountain bike rental Années Jeunes, av Georges-Pompidou ☎04 95 70 36 50.

Pharmacy on the corner of rue de Gaulle and rue Général-Leclerc.

Taxis Accolta Taxis ☎ 06 07 21 88 39; Eric Bronner ☎06 12 54 58 38.

Moving on from Porto-Vecchio

Porto-Vecchio's proximity to Figari airport means this is the first port of call for many independent travellers. Thankfully, it's well served by **public transport**, so you shouldn't have to spend more time here than you need in order to catch a bus somewhere else.

By plane

Figari airport, 28km southwest, is served by weekly charter **flights** to various destinations in northern Europe, including London Gatwick, and by domestic departures to several cities on the French mainland. **Getting to Figari** without your own vehicle is straightforward during the summer, when a bus leaves from the marina to connect with flights; tickets cost €8 single (for precise timetable information, contact Transports Rossi on ☎04 95 71 00 11). At other times of year, you'll have to take a taxi (€45–55 depending on the time of day) or catch the Ajaccio bus to Figari village (see p.269) and arrange onward transport there.

By ferry

Car and passenger **ferry** services from Porto-Vecchio to Marseille and Livorno operate from mid-June to September, with none during the rest of the year. For a summary of destinations and costs, see "Basics", p.20.

By bus

Buses to **Ajaccio** via **Figari**, **Sartène** and **Propriano** are operated by Eurocorse Voyages, leaving two to three times daily (except Sun) from in front of the Trinitours travel agents on rue Pasteur. From June through to September you can also travel to the capital via a longer and more convoluted mountain route that takes you through **Ospédale**, **Zonza**, **Quenza** and **Aullène**; this service is run by Balési Évasion and leaves from outside Île de Beauté Voyages, 13 rue Général-de-Gaulle, at 7am. For **Bonifacio**, there are one to four buses each day with Eurocorse Voyages, taking thirty minutes. Rapides Bleus also run coaches up the east coast to **Bastia** (3hr) from outside the Corsicatours office, 7 rue Jean-Jaurès. Departure points for all of the above services are marked on the town plan on p.281.

   Bus tickets can be bought on the day from the driver. Note that in the winter timetables are scaled down slightly; departure times can be checked at any of the travel agents in town or at the tourist office. For outlines of frequencies and journey times, see "Travel details" at the end of the chapter.

   Finally, if you're spending any time in the area it's worth knowing that during July and August buses run out to the **beaches** around town. Operated by Rapides Bleues from their agency Corsicatours on rue Jean-Jaurès, the *navette* to **Santa Giulia** leaves four times daily; for **Palombaggia**, Eurocorse Voyages' bus departs twice daily from in front of the school opposite the Trinitours office on rue Pasteur; and there's one daily departure from the same place to **Pinarellu** via Cala Rossa with Autocars Bradesi. For precise timetable information, ask at the relevant agency.

Massif de l'Ospédale

Broadly covering the hinterland of the Golfe de Porto-Vecchio, limited in the northwest by the Massif de Bavella and in the southwest by the Montagne de Cagna, the **Massif de l'Ospédale** is a forested upland studded with enormous granite boulders. Although much of its forest was devastated by fire four or five years back, enough remains on the higher slopes to make this a rewarding area for short hikes, with spellbinding views across the gulf through the trees.

Leaving Porto-Vecchio by the D368 northwest of town, a twisty drive of 19km up the slopes will soon get you to **OSPÉDALE**, a village that has long been used as a summer retreat by inhabitants of the coastal belt. Plumb in the middle of the forest, within a backdrop of massive clumps of granite, it has a superb view over the Golfe de Porto-Vecchio to Sardinia. An ideal place to enjoy the panorama is the rear terrace of the **café** on the bend in the road at the top of the village.

You can sidestep the bus parties that tend to congregate here by heading out of Ospédale along the **Mare a Mare Sud** footpath, which peels left off the main road, 500m beyond the last houses (look for the PNRC signboard). Winding at a gentle gradient under the maritime pines, the orange waymarked path cuts southwest up the mountainside to the former *bergeries* of **CARTA-LAVONU** in around 45 minutes. The route offers no views to speak of, but concludes at the welcoming **gîte-d'étape-restaurant** *Le Refuge* (☎04 95 70 00 39; mid-March to Oct), where you can enjoy traditional Alta Rocca cooking – homemade charcuterie, wild-boar pâté, stuffed courgettes and lamb stew – served in a rustic dining hall around an open fire. Count on €27 for four-courses à la carte (there's no *menu fixe*). Most of the people who eat here are walkers, for whom basic dormitory **accommodation** is provided in four- to six-bed dorms (€12 per bed, or €30 per person half board).

Continue uphill from Cartalavonu, following the waymarks for another 45 minutes or so, and you'll walk clear of the forest across a rocky hillside to **Foce Alta** (1171m), one of southern Corsica's finest viewpoints. From one side of the pass unfolds the wild, spectacular Caracutu Valley and northern flank of the Cagna massif, while on the other the col overlooks the **Barrage de l'Ospédale**, a large reservoir supplying Porto-Vecchio with water.

Around Porto-Vecchio

Much of the coast of the **Golfe de Porto-Vecchio** and its environs is characterized by ugly development and marshland, yet some of the clearest, bluest sea and whitest beaches on Corsica are also found around here. The most frequented of these can be reached by **bus** from town in the summer (see "Moving on" p.284, or "Travel details" p.291); at other times of year you'll need your own transport.

South of Porto-Vecchio

Heading **south of Porto-Vecchio** along the main N198, take the turning signposted "Palombaggia" about 1km along and you'll find yourself on a narrow road winding around the coast. Three kilometres beyond Picovaggia village, the **Plage de Palombaggia** – a golden semicircle of sand edged by short twisted umbrella pines and red rocks – might be the most beautiful beach in Corsica were it not for the crowds, which pour across in such numbers that a wattle fence has had to be erected to protect the dunes. For **campers**, *Les Jardins du Golfe* (see p.283) has excellent facilities, but bring plenty of mozzie repellent if you stay here. At the southern end of the beach, the *Tamaricciu* (☎04 95 70 49 89) is probably the smartest *paillote* on the island, with a deck and huge supporting beams made entirely from teak. The service is slick, the food a cut above your average beach-shack fare (sunny salads, fresh pasta, wood-baked pizzas, *grillades* and char-grilled seafood), and the prices reasonable given the idyllic location.

A few kilometres further south along the same road takes you to the **Golfe de Santa Giulia**, a spectacular white-sand beach and turquoise bay that looks like something out of a Bounty advert (minus the palms). The presence of several sprawling holiday villages and facilities for windsurfing and other watersports ensure large crowds from early in the season, but the colours alone

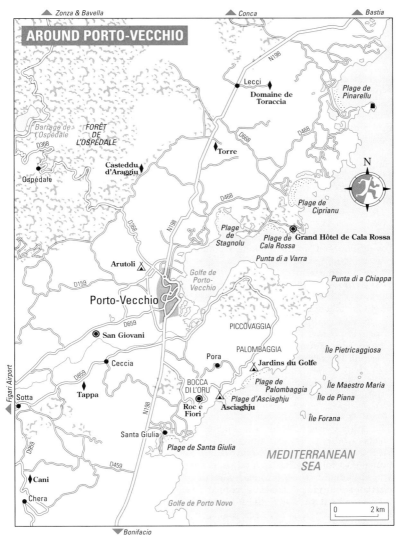

Lecci
Domaine de Toraccia

Plage de Pinarellu

Barrage de l'Ospédale   FORÊT DE L'OSPÉDALE
D368

Ospédale

Torre

Casteddu d'Araggiu

D468

Plage de Ciprianu

Plage de Stagnolu   Plage de **Grand Hôtel de Cala Rossa**
Cala Rossa

Arutoli ✕

Punta di a Varra

Golfe de Porto-Vecchio

Punta di a Chiappa

Porto-Vecchio

D159

D659

PICCOVAGGIA

San Giovani

PALOMBAGGIA

Ceccia

Pora   Île Pietricaggiosa

D859

Jardins du Golfe ▲

Île Maestro Maria

Tappa

BOCCA DI L'ORU   Plage de Palombaggia
Roc e Fiori   ▲ **Asciaghju**   Plage d'Asciaghju   Île de Piana

Sotta

Île Forana

Santa Giulia   Plage de Santa Giulia

MEDITERRANEAN SEA

D459

♦**Cani**

Chera

Golfe de Porto Novo

0   2 km

◀ Figari Airport

N

warrant a detour. Shallow and crystal clear, the water is especially good for little ones. The best **restaurant** here is *Le Santa Marina* (☎04 95 70 45 00), at the northern end of the bay, which serves refined, delicious gourmet seafood on a terrace overlooking the sea. For dessert, try their sublime *brocciu* and orange turnover. Menus range from €25 to €40.

A couple of smaller but equally beautiful (and generally less crowded) beaches lie **between Palombaggia and Santa Giulia**, backed by dunes and pine trees. The largest of them, **Plage d'Asciaghju** (sometimes spelt "Acciaju") has a small campsite and there's a gorgeous little hotel tucked away in the greenery at **Bocca dell Oro** (see "Accommodation" on p.283). Narrow access lanes and *pistes* peel off the main road around the headland at regular intervals, but the best way to enjoy these beaches is by walking along them; interpretative panels give rundowns of the local flora, which includes a wealth of juniper species that conservationists are attempting to protect by fencing off areas of the dunes.

North of Porto-Vecchio

North of Porto-Vecchio, the coast has been intensively developed, much of it for upmarket tourism, with self-contained *villages de vacances* and large villa complexes shielded from view by screens of recently planted pine trees. The first beach along this stretch, **baie de Stagnolu**, is the least appealing, backed by a large campsite, *Camping Golfo di Sogno* (℡04 95 70 08 98).

Just around the headland, **Cala Rossa** is a beautiful bay of reddish sand and turquoise water whose most secluded cove is annexed by the glamorous *Grand Hôtel de Cala Rossa* (see p.283). Large modern villas line up behind it, some of them very swish indeed, with landscaped gardens running right down to the beach, leaving little room for outsiders.

Development is rather less obtrusive at **baie de San Ciprianu**, a half-moon of white sand, reached by turning right off the main road at the Elf garage. A few years back, the FLNC destroyed one of the largest holiday complexes here, having removed all the residents in minibuses during the middle of the night. The most promising beach for day-trips in this area, however, has to be the **Plage de Pinarellu**, 7km further up the coast, with a long sweep of soft white sand overlooked by a Genoese watchtower. Hidden among the pine forest and lagoons at the far eastern end of the bay, *Camping Le California* (℡ & ℱ 04 95 71 49 24, ⊛ www.camping-california.net) is a swish three-star site with tennis courts, pizzeria and grocery store. It's a dull 1500-metre plod from Pinarellu village, but enjoys private access to a secluded cove just south of the main bay (colonized in summer by nudists from the neighbouring *centre nudiste*).

Beyond Pinarellu, north of the village of Sainte-Lucie-de-Porto-Vecchio (the turning for Conca), the **Côte des Nacres** runs from Favone to Solenzara. The beaches at the **Anse de Favone** and **Canella** are pretty average by Corsican standards, but they gain immensely from the backdrop of towering crags behind.

Conca

The largest village inland from Pinarellu bay is **CONCA**, renowned among hikers as the traditional finishing (or starting) point of the **GR20** (see pp.369–396). Scattered over a broad amphitheatre of maquis, with the crags of Punta d'Orto towering behind, it is livelier than most villages in Porto-Vecchio's depopulated, fire-scarred *arrière pays*, but holds nothing of sufficient interest to warrant a diversion from the nearby Route Nationale, beyond its role as walkers' gateway to the interior mountains.

The Domaine de Torraccia

A short way inland from Pinarellu, the hamlet of Lecci, straddling the main Porto-Vecchio to Bastia Route Nationale, marks the turning for one of Corsica's finest vineyards, the **Domaine de Torraccia** (℡04 95 71 43 50). It was founded in the mid-1960s by viticulturalist Christian Imbert. Produced with traditional vine stock and labour-intensive organic cultivation methods, his wines have become renowned throughout the island, particularly the red, labelled "Oriu". You can visit the vineyard (Mon–Sat 8am–noon & 2–6pm; free) and taste the *domaine*'s range in its cellar, where there's an engaging exhibition of old Corsican photographs to peruse. Pick of the vintages currently on sale (at bargain prices, considering what you'd pay for these wines in the shops) is the 2000 Oriu, among the few quality local wines that ages well.

Footsore GR20 veterans stagger straight to the gîte d'étape, *La Tonnelle* (☎04 95 71 46 55), at the bottom of the village. Beds here cost between €13 and €17 depending on the size of the dorm, and you can camp in the garden for €5. Breakfast and evening meals (€13; reserve in advance) are served in a spacious common dining room or rear terrace. Each morning, minibuses run down the valley from here to Porto-Vecchio and **Sainte-Lucie-de-Porto-Vecchio**, on the Route Nationale (where you can pick up buses to Bastia).

If you fancy pampering yourself after a fortnight of rough refuges in the mountains, head for the *Hôtel San Pasquale*, at the top of the village (☎04 95 71 56 13; ◑), which offers very comfortable studio apartments with large balconies, or smaller en-suite rooms, overlooking a sunny central courtyard. They don't do food, but the *U Chjosu* **restaurant**, a Corsican speciality place on Conca's main street, is only a short walk away.

Prehistoric sites around Porto-Vecchio

Sometime around 1500 BC, the megalithic people responsible for carving Corsica's famous figurative standing stones were displaced by more technologically advanced invaders. No one can say for sure where they came from, but the band of rolling maquis between the hills and coast around Porto-Vecchio is where most experts agree the warlike incomers first settled. Known by archeologists as the **Torréens**, they quickly colonized the southeast, erecting over the vestiges of their Stone Age predecessors fortresses of Cyclopean proportions – large dry-stone towers with corbel-vaulted roofs covering weirdly shaped curved rooms. The most fully preserved of these *torri* stands at the village of **Torre** itself, just north of Porto-Vecchio. Nearby **Casteddu d'Araggiu**, another Bronze Age settlement set higher on the mountain slopes above the gulf, is also worth a visit, and to complete the prehistoric tour you should go south of Porto-Vecchio to the sites of **Ceccia** and **Tappa**, also impressive legacies of the civilization that first brought metal working and knife-making skills to the island. Finally, a worthwhile side-trip from the main Porto-Vecchio to Figari road takes you south to the tiny hamlet of **Chera**, where a couple of enigmatic natural rock formations, known as **orii**, have become the objects of much local folklore.

Torre and the Casteddu d'Araggiu

Just follow the N198 north of Porto-Vecchio for 8km to reach **Torre**, which stands on its own at the end of a narrow lane running to the right (east) of the highway. Built against a massive granite rock and covered in broad stone slabs, the semicircular construction, an impressive if small-scale Torréen edifice, crowns a granite hillock above a tiny farming hamlet, and is thought to have been used as a crematorium.

The **Casteddu d'Araggiu** lies on the other side of the main road, about 4km up the D759; from the site's car park it's a twenty-minute stiff climb through maquis and scrubby woodland along a well-defined path. Erected around 1500 BC, the *casteddu* consists of a complex of chambers built into a massive circular wall of pink granite. The site is entered via a ten-metre-long corridor covered in stone slabs. Immediately to the left you'll see a small triangular enclosure, in the centre of which would have been a clay fireplace, a forerunner of the *zidda* (hearth) found in traditional Corsican households. Continuing in a clockwise direction you come to the *torre* itself, comprising a central chamber of which only the foundations remain. Past the tower, the next enclosure – measuring 10m across – also harbours the remains of a fireplace, and a little further on it's possible to make out a well built into the thick walls, beyond which stands another small hut with fireplace.

Ceccia and Tappa

The **Ceccia** site lies about 5km southwest of Porto-Vecchio along the D859, overlooking the tiny village of the same name. Set on a prominent spur, this isolated tower was raised around 1350 BC, possibly for scanning the surrounding countryside for invaders, or for cult purposes. Unlike other Torréen sites, no traces of dwellings remain here.

Mazzeri

Of all the occult phenomena recorded in Corsica – from vampire witches (*stregoni* and *strèga*), evil-eye (*occhiu*) healing, *orii* (see p.291), Christian sects and pagan cults – the strangest has to be the existence of **mazzeri**, dubbed by Dorothy Carrington in her book on the subject as "dream hunters". Also known as *colpadori* (from the Latin *culpi*, "to strike"), *mazzeri* (from the Corsican *ammazza*, "to kill") are those who possess the power to foresee death. They do this by slipping into the maquis in the dead of night and waiting silently, usually next to a stream, to kill the first living creature that passes. On retrieving the body, the *mazzeri* will recognize in its face, or hear in its death cries, the identity of a person they know well, usually someone from their own family or village, who will shortly die. If the *mazzeri* has only managed to wound the animal, the person concerned will suffer a grave illness, for the quarry temporarily harbours the spirit of the doomed individual.

Bizarrely, these nocturnal hunting expeditions rarely take place in the literal sense, for the realm of the mazzeri is that of dreams. Nevertheless, records exist of *mazzeri* who were known to leave their house at night in a state of trance and return covered in scratches from the maquis – whence another of their Corsican names: *sunnambuli*, or "sleepwalkers". Despite the ambiguity surrounding the nature of the hunting activities of the mazzeri, the outcome is invariably unequivocal. Once the death of an individual has been foretold, it always occurs, usually within a week or two, and certainly before a year has passed.

Although the *mazzeri* may have predicted the event and performed a symbolic or dream killing of the deceased's spirit, he or she is not held directly responsible, nor regarded as a murderer. In some villages they are actually held in high esteem for the protective role they play in a former pagan festival marked on the last night of July. At this time it is said that *mazzeri* from different villages form teams (*milizia*) to wage phantom battles (*mandrache*) against each other on lofty mountain passes dividing districts. Using an armoury of traditional weapons – knives, axes, lances, human bones and asphodel plants (known in Corsica as *fiori di morti*, "flowers of death") – they fight the opposition until one side is forced to retreat. Once again, although the killing occurs in the dream world the outcome is real enough, and any *mazzeri* slain in a battle on July 31 is destined to die within twelve months. Moreover, the village whose side loses the ghost battle will sustain more unexpected deaths during the year. For this reason, villagers all over the island still light fires outside churches and place knives above doorways on the last night of July, to ward off evil spirits.

All this may sound like mere folk myth, but *mazzeri* still exist in many areas (notably the far south around Sartène and Figari), albeit in far smaller numbers than a century ago. Recent interest by local ethnologists has unearthed a wealth of lore surrounding the phenomenon, and several erudite books and papers have been published – well worth hunting out if you're interested in the esoteric side of island life. Of these, Dorothy Carrington's *The Dream Hunters of Corsica* (see p.442) is the most detailed, but if your French is up to it ask in any good bookshop for the special edition of *L'Origine* magazine devoted to Corsican *mazzeri* and related subjects.

About 1km southwest of Ceccia down the D859, you'll find the **Tappa** *casteddu* signposted to the south of the road, opposite an abandoned farm building. Set on a granite mound about ten minutes' walk away, the site lies on private property and is approached on foot, passing through the gate and following the direction indicated. The surrounding wall is considered to be more recent than the rest of the *casteddu*, which was developed in the half-millennium prior to 1000 BC. A large *torre* at the southern end of the site consists of several small rooms around a central chamber. A ramp leads up to the main structure, entered by a narrow corridor, inside which another ramp winds up to a second level. The excavation of various clay pots, pounding implements and grindstones here has led archeologists to propose that this building was used for milling as well as storage.

The orii of Chera and Cani

Amidst the chaos of rocks by the side of the roads in southern Corsica, you occasionally come across large boulders whose overhanging crevices have been bricked in with masonry. Known as **orii** (*oriu* in the singular), these distinctive rock formations, whose name is thought to derive from the Latin for "granary", *horreum*, have been used for centuries to store grain and hay, and to provide shelter for animals. They crop up with surprising frequency in old folk songs and legends, suggesting they were at one time central to the life of rural communities; some have even been "Christianized" and are the focus of religious rituals.

One such *oriu* stands in the far-flung hamlet of **CHERA**, roughly midway between Porto-Vecchio and Bonifacio (turn south off the D859 at Sotta). The most famous of its kind, it overlooks the village from the top of a rocky outcrop, crowned by a crucifix. Local people believe the artificial cave sheltered their pastoralist ancestors when they fled here centuries ago to escape a vendetta in the mountains, since when it has been revered as a kind of guardian spirit of the Culioli clan. Dorothy Carrington – who was shown the *oriu* by one of the island's most renowned bards, the long-white-bearded Jean-André Culioli – was told it was haunted by a phantom goat whose hoofsteps could occasionally be heard trotting over the rock in the dead of night.

Even spookier is the *oriu* of **CANI**, 4km north down the valley from Chera (look for a hand-painted sign on the right, or east, side of the road). Pull over outside the farmhouses where the road ends and follow the track as it bends right; once over two stiles, you come to a breach in a wall, from where a faint trail cuts uphill through the woods to the *oriu*, perched on a rock platform above the tiny hamlet. An improbably contorted lump of granite with a strange high-pitched "roof", the structure looks like one of Salvador Dali's nightmares, and it's not hard to see why local people believe it was once inhabited by a witch. In fact, the last recorded resident was one Vinceguerra Pietri, the local landowner, who lived here until a ripe old age at the end of the nineteenth century.

Travel details

Buses

The tables below summarize which bus companies cover which routes, how often they run and how long journeys take. Start by looking up your intended destination in the first table; then, using the company's acronym (eg AR or RB), go to the second table for more detailed route and frequency information. Precise departure times can be checked in advance either via the bus companies direct, or (if your French isn't up to that) the tourist offices at Propriano (☎ 04 95 76 01 49), Porto

Vecchio (☎04 95 70 09 58) and Bonifacio (☎04 95 73 11 88).

Bonifacio to: Ajaccio (EV; 3hr 30min–4hr); Olmeto (EV; 2hr 20min); Porto-Vecchio (EV; 30min); Pianottoli (EV; 30–50min); Propriano (EV; 2hr 10min); Roccapina (EV; 1hr 10min); Sartène (EV; 2hr).

Levie to: Ajaccio (AR & EV; 2hr 45min); Bavella (AR; 30min); Sainte-Lucie-de-Tallano (EV & AR; 15min); Zonza (EV & AR; 15min).

Olmeto to: Ajaccio (EV & AR; 1hr 20min); Bonifacio (EV; 2hr 30min); Porto-Vecchio (EV; 2hr); Propriano (EV; 15min); Roccapina (EV; 55min); Sartène (EV; 35min).

Porto-Vecchio to: Ajaccio (EV, BE & AR; 3hr 30min); Aléria/Cateraggio (RB; 1hr 15min); Aullène (BE; 1hr 40min); Bastia (RB; 2hr 45min); Bavella (BE; 1hr 15min); Bonifacio (EV; 30min); Figari (EV; 15min); Ghisonaccia (RB; 1hr); Olmeto (EV; 1hr 45min); L'Ospédale (BE; 30min); Moriani (RB; 2hr 10min); Poretta (for Bastia airport; RB; 2hr 35min); Propriano (EV, BE & AR; 1hr 45min); Sainte-Lucie-de-Porto-Vecchio (for Conca; RB; 20min); Quenza (BE; 1hr 25min); Roccapina (EV; 2–4 daily; 50min); Sartène (EV; 1hr 25min); Serra di Scapomena (BE; 1hr 35min); Solenzara (RB; 40min); Zonza (BE; 1hr 5min).

Porto-Pollo (Marinca stop) to: Ajaccio (AR; 1hr 30min); Calzola crossroads (AR; 20min).

Propriano to: Ajaccio (EV & AR; 1hr 35min–1hr 50min); Bonifacio (EV; 2hr 15min); Olmeto (EV & AR; 15min); Porto-Vecchio (EV; 1hr 45min); Roccapina (EV; 40min); Sartène (EV & AR; 20min).

Roccapina to: Ajaccio (EV; 2hr 40min); Bonifacio (EV; 50min–1hr 35min); Olmeto (EV; 55min); Porto-Vecchio (EV; 1hr); Propriano (EV; 50min); Sartène (EV; 35min).

Sainte-Lucie-de-Tallano to: Ajaccio (EV & AR; 2hr 30min); Bavella (AR; 45min); Levie (EV & AR; 15min); Zonza (EV & AR; 45min).

Sartène to: Ajaccio (EV & AR; 2hr); Bonifacio (EV; 1hr 10min–1hr 55min); Olmeto (EV; 20min); Porto-Vecchio (EV; 1hr 10min–1hr 25min); Propriano (EV & AR; 15min); Roccapina (EV; 20min).

Zonza to: Ajaccio (BE & AR; 3hr); Bavella (BE & AR; 15min); Levie (EV & AR; 15min); Sainte-Lucie-de-Tallano (BE, EV & AR; 30min).

AR: Autocars Ricci ☎04 95 51 08 19 or 04 95 76 25 59.
Ajaccio–Olmeto–Propriano–Sartène–Sainte-Lucie-de-Tallano–Levie–Zonza–Bavella; July to mid-Sept 1–2 daily; mid-Sept to June Mon–Sat 1 daily.
Ajaccio–Calzola–Porto-Pollo–Propriano; July & Aug Mon–Sat 1 daily; Sept–June Mon, Weds & Fri 1 daily.

BE: Balési Évasion ☎04 95 51 25 56 or 04 95 70 15 55. Ajaccio–Aullène–Serra di Scapomena–Sorbollano–Quenza–Zonza–Bavella–l'Ospédale–Porto-Vecchio; July–Aug 1 daily; Sept–June Mon & Fri 1 daily.

EV: Eurocorse Voyages ☎04 95 70 13 83 or 04 95 21 06 30.
Ajaccio–Olmeto–Propriano–Sartène–Roccapina–Pianottoli–Figari (village)–Porto-Vecchio/Bonifacio; July to mid-Sept 2 daily; mid-Sept to June Mon–Sat 2 daily.
Ajaccio–Propriano–Sartène–Sainte-Lucie-de-Tallano–Levie–Zonza; Mon–Sat 1 daily.

RB: Rapides Bleus ☎04 95 31 03 79 or 04 95 70 10 36. Porto-Vecchio–Sainte-Lucie-de-Porto-Vecchio (for Conca)–Solenzara–Ghisonaccia–Moriani–Poretta (village)–Bastia; mid-June to mid-Sept 2 daily, mid-Sept to mid-June Mon–Sat 2 daily.

Ferries

For ferry details, see Basics, p.20.

Eastern Corsica

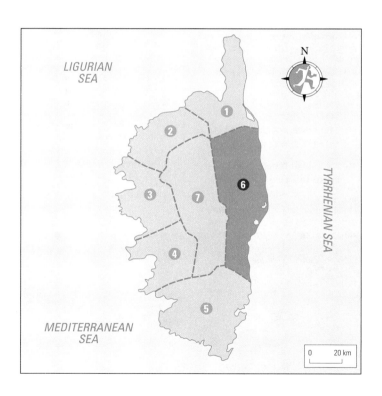

LIGURIAN
SEA

N

TYRRHENIAN SEA

MEDITERRANEAN
SEA

0   20 km

CHAPTER 6

Highlights

* **Musée d'Archéologie Jérôme Carcopino, Aléria** – A horde of ancient Greek and Roman artefacts, unearthed at the nearby ruins. See p.302

* **Restaurant Le Pieds Dans L'Eau, Étang de Diane** – Dine on fresh oysters straight from the lagoon. See p.303

* **Santa-Lucia-di-Mercurio** – Jewel in the crown of the Bozio's wild schist *villages perchés*, framed against a vast sweep of snow and granite. See p.307

* **Ascent of Monte San Petrone** – Hike to the summit of Castagniccia's holy mountain for superb views across the Tyrrhenian Sea and interior range. See p.314

* **Church door, Piazzole** – The finest example of Corsican folk art, carved by a repentant bandit. See p.313

* **Église de St-Jean-Baptiste, La Porta** – The island's most celebrated Baroque church, with a resplendent Rococo façade. See p.315

* **Maison de Pascal Paoli, Morosaiglia** – Evocative memorabilia relating to the founding father of Corsican independence, collected in the former family home. See p.315

6

Eastern Corsica

Comprising one hundred and fifty square kilometres of vine-striped plains backed by rippling mountains, the landscape of Corsica's **east coast** is restrained in comparison with the rest of the island. If you do visit the region it'll probably be to take advantage of the smooth, straight N198, the main north–south artery, from which windier side roads penetrate the more varied and rugged interior. That said, the *littoral oriental* – re-branded in recent years by the local tourist authority as the **Costa Serena** – does have its attractions, not least of which are several vast sandy **beaches**, where scattered resorts and a string of large self-contained campsites offer plenty of inexpensive accommodation.

Of the small seaside towns strung along the highway, **Solenzara**, at the head of the spectacular road leading to the Col de Bavella, is arguably the most appealing. North of here, beyond the desultory agro-town of **Ghisonaccia**, the hills recede and you move into the eastern plain proper, an enormous malaria-ridden swamp until the Americans sprayed it with DDT after World War II. Now enclosing kilometres of clementine orchards and vineyards, this patchwork of fields is punctuated by shimmering lagoons, of which the **Étang d'Urbino** and **Étang de Diane** are the largest, supplying plentiful oysters and mussels for local restaurants. Set on a rise between these *étangs* – where Corsica's longest river, the Tavignano, debouches into the sea – is the Roman capital of **Aléria**, whose ruins have yielded a wonderful collection of ancient ceramics, jewellery and weapons. The converted Genoese fort where they're now housed, in a small but excellent museum, is reason enough to pull off the highway, but there's also a decent beach close by and a few hotels straddling the main road.

Inland, the terraced villages of the **Fiumorbo** region afford sweeping views of the plain and the Tuscan islands offshore, or you could venture into the *villages perchés* of the **Vallée du Tavignano** and **Bozio**, either as a diversion on the drive to or from Bastia or as a route into the core of the island. A still more fascinating region to explore is **Castagniccia**, further north, its tunnelled roads twisting past waterfalls and through an enormous forest of chestnut trees that shelters the highest concentration of highland settlements in Corsica. There's only one hotel in the area, at **Piedicroce**, on the slopes of Monte San Petrone, scaled by an ancient pilgrimage path that makes the best hike in the area. North of Castagniccia lies the **Casinca**, a more compact region of delightful villages such as **Vescovato** and **Venzolasca**, which could feasibly be seen on a day excursion from Bastia.

Since the German army sabotaged the Bastia–Porto-Vecchio railway in 1943, **transport** around the east coast has been limited to the main highway. Rapides

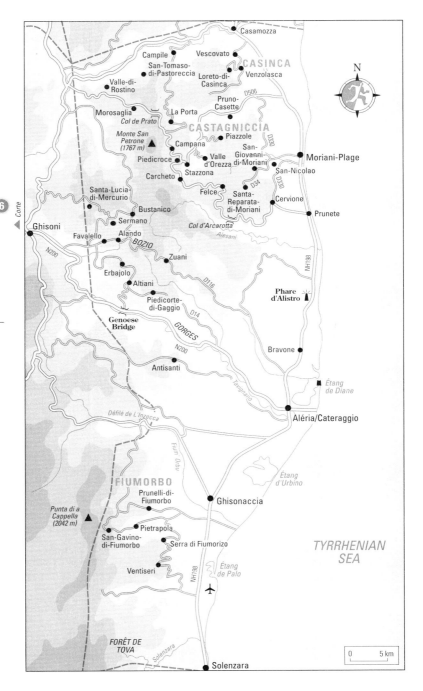

Bleus' **buses** pass twice daily along it, stopping at Solenzara, Ghisonaccia and Aléria (Cateraggio), but to penetrate the hinterland you'll need your own transport.

Solenzara

SOLENZARA might not be the most glamorous coastal resort in Corsica, but its endless sandy beach, hidden behind a strip of shops and busy marina, inspired Iggy Pop's French hit, *Sur la plage de Solenzara*, from the soundtrack of the movie *Arizona Dream*. The village's other claim to fame is that it lies at the junction of the **route de Bavella** (see p.255), one of the island's most spectacular mountain roads, whose lower reaches hug the river, giving access to numerous bathing and picnic spots.

There are a few **hotels** here as well: try the *Maquis et Mer*, on the main street (☏04 95 57 42 37, ℻04 95 57 46 85; ❺). A huge, old-fashioned three-star, it offers five categories of rooms (ask for one in the old wing, which has flagstone floors, an original granite staircase and pale blue shutters on the windows). A much cheaper and more cheerful option is the family-run *Orsoni*, further up the main street past the tourist office (☏04 95 57 40 25, ⓦwww.hotelorsoni .com; ❸), which has plain but impeccably clean rooms and a dependable restaurant on the ground floor. *La Solenzara*, above the beach north of the village (☏04 95 57 40 25, ℻04 95 57 46 84; ❺), is the most stylish place in the area, with high stucco ceilings, gilt candelabras and a gorgeous pool overlooking the sea; considering the location, facilities and atmosphere, it offers excellent value for money.

The **tourist office**, on the main street opposite the Prisunic supermarket in the centre (June–Sept daily 9am–noon & 5–7pm; Sept– June Mon–Fri 9am–noon; ☏04 95 57 43 75), can provide additional addresses in the unlikely event that these hotels are booked up. **Campers** have a choice between the *Camping de la Côte des Nacres*, set amid eucalyptus trees 1.5km north of Solenzara next to the river and beach (☏04 95 57 40 65; May–Oct), or the cheaper *U Rosumarinu* (☏04 95 57 47 66; June–Sept), 6km up the Bavella road in the middle of nowhere. If peace, quiet and scenery are more of a priority than sea and sand, this latter site, overlooking the stream and well placed for a bracing dip, definitely has the edge.

For a **meal**, you can take your pick from any of the hotel restaurants and pizzerias dotted along the main road or drive 4km along the Bavella road (D268) to the wonderful *Ferme-Auberge "A Pinzutella"* (☏04 95 57 41 18; *menus* €23–26), which serves fresh, simple Corsican specialities – such as roast kid, wild leaves and spinach in puffed pastry, and *brocciu* with strawberries from the garden – on a fabulous terrace looking up the valley.

Ghisonaccia

The one sizeable village between Solenzara and Aléria is dusty **GHISON-ACCIA**, whose pejorative "*accia*" suffix (meaning "bad") seems just as applicable today as it was when the town was a malarial bog. That said, the place has enjoyed a certain prosperity ever since the late 1950s, when pieds-noirs from Algeria bought much of the hitherto useless agricultural land in the area to plant vineyards. The wine they eventually produced became France's leading brand of cheap *vin de table*, stimulating a boom that lasted until the 1970s, when it was discovered that most of Ghisonaccia's farmers had been mixing sugar and dodgy chemicals into their wine to bump up production. Since then, the vines have been replaced by orchards of clementines, kiwis and other soft fruit, picked by the low-paid Arab agro-workers you'll see hanging around the main crossroads. The village's other main source of revenue, after tourism and farming, are the close-cropped national service lads from the nearby air-force base who fill the bars on weekends.

Practicalities

The less expensive of the two **hotels** here is the *De la Poste* (T & F 04 95 56 00 41; ③), just north of the crossroads, whose rooms are gloomy but acceptably clean. On the south side of the main street, the *Franceschini* (T 04 95 56 06 09, F 04 95 56 05 32), is an altogether ritzier affair, with recently refurbished en-suite rooms (some opening onto a roof terrace) and a smart bar-restaurant downstairs.

The nearest **beach**, Plage de Tignale, lies 4km east; it's clean and broad for the east coast, but gets inundated during the summer by thousands of Germans and Italians from the enormous **campsites** behind it. These are all flashy four-star places complete with restaurants, shops, coin-operated fridges and the like. The most homely of the bunch is the *Arinella Bianca*, reached via a signposted turning off the main beach road (T 04 95 56 04 78, F 04 95 56 12 54; May–Oct). A pleasant and relatively inexpensive place to **eat** at Plage de Tignale is *Les Deux Magots*, where you can enjoy locally caught seafood such as mussels and *loup de mer* on a breezy beach-side terrace.

Fiumorbo

The little-explored region of **Fiumorbo** (or Fium'orbo), immediately inland from Ghisonaccia, has been renowned for the independent spirit of its inhabitants ever since 1769, when a group of shepherds who had refused to submit to French laws were struck down in an ambush along the road to Corte. Thirty years later a coalition of royalist, Paolist and pro-British Corsican exiles organized another anti-French rebellion, which spread as far as the Sartenais before it was crushed by the French authorities. This tradition continued into the early nineteenth century, when an insurrection broke out and five thousand troops hired by Louis XVIII's government were unable to suppress the hordes of mountain people who seized control of the region. Eventually the ringleaders were either gunned down or deported to the French mainland by Général Morand, who was nevertheless obliged to accede to them an area of coastal land. By the end of the century the Fiumorbo had become notorious bandit country, ruled by outlaws who terrorized the villages, untouched by the police, but today this is one of the quietest, and most untroubled, parts of Corsica.

The region is reached by following the D244 west off the highway 2km south of Ghisonaccia, then turning onto the D145, a route that winds into the valley of the **River Albatesco**, a tributary of the River Fium'orbu ("Blind Waters") and location of the chief settlements of the region. Running between them, the old inter-village mule tracks have been exploited to create the **Mare a Mare Centre** long-distance footpath, which starts at the Pont de l'Abatesco, just south of Ghisonaccia, and penetrates the interior of the island via the Col de Laparo, a major landmark on the GR20.

Marking the end of the first stage of the walk, the **gîte d'étape** (T 04 95 56 70 14 or 04 95 56 10 89) in the village of **SERRA-DI-FIUMORBO** provides basic dormitory accommodation in a converted hydroelectricity station, with fine views over the eastern plain. To get there, you have to turn left off the D145.

Head straight on instead and you'll press up the Abatesco Valley to **PIETRAPOLA**, whose **thermal baths** attract sufferers from arthritis and rheumatic disorders throughout the year. The village is also thought to have been the site of an encounter between local bandits and a detachment of

Roman soldiers en route from Sardinia in 231 BC. Ambushed and relieved of their booty, the Romans pursued the Corsican robbers into the hills, only to nearly die of hunger and thirst trying to find a way down again. Eventually they discovered a spring at Pietrapola and survived, consecrating a special "Temple of the Spring" at the gates of Rome on their return. The façade of the village church, Santa Maria, sports a remnant of this era: an incongruous four-metre column salvaged from a Jupiter-Saturn temple that once stood in a now deserted forest glade above the village.

Another column from the same ruin has been incorporated into the tower of **PRUNELLI-DI-FIUMORBO**'s church, 7km northeast uphill from Pietrapola along the D45. Approached along an avenue of oak trees, with the austere peaks of Monte Renoso looming behind, this beautiful village is clustered like an eagle's nest on top of a hill. Again, the views are superb, but an additional reason to make the drive up here is a little **museum** set up by local amateur historians (Mon–Fri 9.30am–noon & 3–5.30pm, Sat 9.30am–12.30pm; free). Housed in the mairie, it comprises a modest but fascinating collection of Roman and other archeological artefacts, displayed alongside photographs of the ruined temples and Pisan chapels lost in the surrounding forest. In another room, is an array of World War II memorabilia, including evocative photos of the liberation. If there's no one at the mairie to let you into the museum, ask at the *Café Buttéa* next door for the key.

The Défilé de l'Inzecca

Northwest of Ghisonaccia, the D344 scythes straight across a broad tract of fruit orchards and vineyards towards a narrow niche in the wall of coastal mountains. Formed by the fast-flowing River Fium'orbu, the **Défilé de l'Inzecca** is a sheer granite trench bounded in the south by the needles of the Kyrie peaks, and in the north and west by the grey, snow-flecked east face of the Renoso massif. The road that winds through the gorge, leading from the coast to the village of **Ghisoni** (covered on p.352), provides one of the most spectacular approaches to the interior, cutting across dramatic pale green serpentine cliffs speckled with stunted trees. Below, colossal boulders choke the river, which has been dammed to form a reservoir for a small hydroelectricity station.

Aléria

Built on the estuary at the mouth of the River Tavignano, **ALÉRIA** was the capital of the Corsican province during the Roman era, remaining the east coast's principal town and port right up until the eighteenth century. Little is left of the historic settlement except the **Roman ruins** and the Genoese fortress, which stand high against a background of chequered fields and vineyards. A sizeable proportion of the local population is employed in farming oysters and mussels in the neighbouring **Étang de Diane**, formerly the Roman harbour. To the south, a strip of modern buildings flanking the main road makes up the modern village of **Cateraggio**, but it's the hilltop hamlet just west of here that holds most interest.

A brief history of Aléria

This area was first settled in 564 BC by a colony of Greek Phocaeans who had been chased from their land by the Persian invasion. Calling their new port Alalia, these Greeks initiated the island's trade routes around the

△ Musée d'Archéologie Jérôme Carcopino, Aléria

Mediterranean, selling the copper and lead they mined from the land, and the wheat, olives and grapes farmed here. In 535 BC the settlers managed to survive a battle with the Carthaginians, but were left considerably weakened as a colony. Eventually fleeing to the mainland, the Phocaeans established a new capital at Massiglia (Marseille), retaining Alalia as a trading link between their colonies in southern Italy, Greece, Carthage and Spain.

In 259 BC the Romans arrived and conquered what was left of the port, which was by that time controlled by Carthaginians. It wasn't until around 80 BC, however, that a naval base was built on the site they re-christened Aléria, which re-established its importance in the western Mediterranean. As the only town of significant size on the island, Aléria was named administrative capital of the province, and before long boasted a population of some thirty thousand. Under the orders of the emperor Augustus a fleet was harboured in the Étang de Diane and public buildings were constructed, including baths, a forum and a triumphal arch, the remains of which are visible today. Light industries also flourished during this period as Aléria developed into a thriving crafts centre, producing jewellery, ceramics and clothes. Honey and wax were also marketed, and seafood from the Étang de Diane was traded with the continent.

The Aléria siege

It may look like just another derelict, graffiti-covered ruin at the roadside, but the bombed-out Depeille wine cellar, 1.5km north of Aléria, was the site of the **Aléria siege**, an event seminal to the modern history of Corsica. On August 21, 1975, it was occupied by a group of armed nationalists, angry at its owners' part in a wine-adulterating scandal that threatened the livelihoods of many small-scale Corsican *viticulteurs*. Few of the militants, however, could have foreseen the violent outcome of their action, nor the dramatic impact it would subsequently have on the island's relations with the French government.

The **Depeilles** were one of around six hundred pied-noir families that settled on the east coast after Algerian independence in 1962, and who made sizeable fortunes from the vines they planted on newly reclaimed land in the area, helped by generous government subsidies. This and their North African origins made them unpopular with many locals, but the resentment never went beyond the odd piece of racist graffiti until it was discovered that many of the pied-noir farmers were doubling their wine output by illegally adding sugar and other chemicals to the grape juice. Frustrated by the government's apparent inability to stamp out the practice, armed commandos from the hitherto moderate nationalist organization the ARC (l'Action Régionaliste Corse), led by **Edmond Simeoni**, marched on the Depeilles's *cave*. With President Giscard d'Estaing on holiday, it fell to Michel Poniatowski, the minister of the interior and – unfortunately for the nationalists – a close associate of the Depeille family, to mount a response. Two days later, on August 23, 1250 police, four armoured cars and a couple of helicopters descended on the building. In the ensuing shoot-out two police officers were killed. Afterwards Simeoni was arrested and imprisoned in Paris (the campaign for his release would become the cause célèbre of the nationalist movement for decades to come), and riots erupted in Bastia, where another gendarme died.

The Aléria siege, the first direct confrontation between armed nationalists and the French authorities, marked a turning point in the struggle for Corsican autonomy, leading to the inauguration of the **FLNC** (Fronte di Liberazione Naziunale di a Corsica) in May 1976, and the first bombing campaign on the mainland. A full account of the nationalist armed struggle with the French state is featured in Contexts, p.421.

Aléria's Roman days came to an end in 410 AD, when the city was devastated by fire. Malaria epidemics put paid to many of the survivors and the town was all but finished off by Vandals later that century. Only at the start of the Genoese occupation in the thirteenth century was Aléria redeveloped, eventually becoming the seat of a bishopric with its own bastion, **Fort Matra**. When Theodor von Neuhof was received here in 1736 this was still one of the principal ports on the east coast.

The Musée d'Archéologie Jérôme Carcopino and ancient Aléria

The best place to begin your visit is the **Musée d'Archéologie Jérôme Carcopino** (May 16–Sept daily 8am–noon & 2–7pm; Oct–May 15 Mon–Sat 8am–noon & 2–5pm; €2), housed in Fort Matra. Pending the completion of building work on the ground floor, the collection – comprising remarkable finds from the Roman and Greek sites – is crammed into three interconnected rooms on the first storey of the fort, with ceramics, metal objects and jewellery forming the bulk of the exhibits.

The **first room** contains magnificent evidence of ancient Aléria's importance as a trading port. Hellenic and Punic rings and belt links are ranged alongside elaborate oil lamps decorated with Christian symbols, amphorae and some fragments of water pipes. In the first case on the left, a large Attic plate, depicting a faded red-grey elephant against a black background, takes up the middle of one display case, with various glazed dishes using the same painting method (red and black) ranged beneath. The real highlight of this first room, however, is a second-century marble bust of Jupiter Ammon, which was discovered near the forum.

Moving clockwise, the **second room** houses painted earthenware, Etruscan goblets, a number of exquisite Cretan-style vases from the fourth to third century BC, and more fine red and black ceramics in near-perfect condition. Most notable of the exhibits in the **third room** is a shallow-stemmed Attic bowl featuring a masturbating Dionysus, with twisting erotic figures on its rear face. Thought to date from 480 BC, this piece is attributed to master artist Panaïtos and ranks among the museum's most treasured exhibits (although you won't get to see its famous rear face as the curator recently removed the mirror formerly placed behind it, presumably in order to spare teachers accompanying school groups embarrassment).

Two remarkable drinking vessels, or "rhytons" – one representing the head of a mule and the other the head of a dog – feature in the longer **fourth room**, where you can also see finely worked Etruscan bronzes and delicate jewellery from the fourth to the second centuries BC. Encased here, too, are objects discovered in the tombs of ancient Aléria, one of which, uncovered in 1966, revealed a priceless collection of elegantly curved Greek swords, lances and daggers from the fifth century BC. Iron weapons, armour and hundreds of finely painted cups called "craters", one of which features a picture of *Hercules and the Lion* and another which represents Dionysus, this time overseeing the grape harvest, are also housed in this end room, near a ground plan of a fourth-century-BC tomb.

The Roman site

The proximity of the sea, the strong scent of wild tarragon and the arresting view of snowcapped mountains and Fort Matra create an appropriately epic backdrop to the **Roman site** (closes 30min before museum; admission by same ticket), a short way up the hill from the fort. It's believed that the core of the ancient cap-

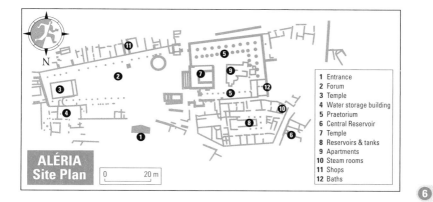

1	Entrance
2	Forum
3	Temple
4	Water storage building
5	Praetorium
6	Central Reservoir
7	Temple
8	Reservoirs & tanks
9	Apartments
10	Steam rooms
11	Shops
12	Baths

ALÉRIA Site Plan

0   20 m

ital would have extended from this ridge crest down to the Tavignano estuary and port, located east of the modern highway. Mérimée noticed signs of the Roman settlement here during his survey of the island in 1830, but it took over a century before systematic excavation work was undertaken. Begun in the late 1950s, this yielded the extraordinary finds how housed in the museum, but has since ground to a virtual halt. The fact that the bulk of the city remains buried, however, serves only to accentuate the site's romantic appeal.

First of the major discoveries at Aléria was Augustus's triumphal **arch**, which formed the entrance to the governor's residence – the praetorium – on the western edge of the **forum**, and which now dominates the ruins. In the adjacent **balneum** (bathhouse), a network of reservoirs and cisterns, the **caldarium** bears traces of the underground pipes that would have heated the room, and a patterned mosaic floor is visible inside the neighbouring chamber. To the north of the site lie the foundation walls of a large house, while at the eastern end of the forum the foundations of shops and the **temple** can be seen, alongside the ground plan of the apse of an early Christian church. Some vestiges of the Greek settlement – including an acropolis – have been discovered further to the east.

L'Étang de Diane and Plage de Padulone

During his exile on Elba, Napoléon kept in contact with his homeland by ordering boatloads of oysters from the **Étang de Diane**, the large saltwater lagoon just north of Aléria. Flushed daily by the mingling of tidal currants and in-flow of fresh water via the River Arena, the *étang* is freer of pollution now than it was two thousand years ago, when boatloads of oysters stacked in jars used to leave the teeming port for Rome. Prodigious quantities of the celebrated **Nustale oysters** are still hauled from the water here: 70 tonnes per year, plus 400 tonnes of mussels. For visitors, the unusual landscape and vivid light of the lagoon, fringed on its eastern flank by a long sandy beach, make it a pleasant place to break the journey up the coast.

To get there, follow the main road north for 2km until you see the derelict Depeille wine warehouse on your left, opposite which a narrow lane runs down to the western shore of the *étang*. There's no better place to sample the famously strong-tasting oysters than *Le Pieds Dans L'Eau* **restaurant** (☎04 95 57 04 55; menu at €25, plus plenty of à la carte options), resting on stilts above the water at the end of the lane. Their seafood platter – featuring clams, mussels and a terrine made from dried mullet's eggs called *poutargue* – is the kind of food one imagines the Romans must have feasted on when they farmed the *étang* two millennia ago. Yet the only discernible evidence of ancient occupation here is the tiny **Île des Pêcheurs**, at the northernmost corner of the lagoon, which was used for centuries as a shell dump and whose lonely house and boat sheds as a consequence stand on a brittle calcified crust.

The best places for swimming are the sandy eastern banks, which you can reach via the main road from the Cateraggio crossroads, the N200, which cuts in a straight line though rolling vineyards to the **Plage de Padulone**, 3km due east. A row of modest seafood restaurants and downbeat cafés overlooks the car park. Follow the beach north for 3.5km and you'll reach the Genoese **Tour de Diane**, which overlooks the mouth of the lagoon. Directly opposite, the **Île de Santa Maria** holds a tiny chapel and the ruins of an ancient quayside – all that remains of the port that formerly sprawled from the shores of the lagoon, now long since submerged. Just south of the tower, a waymarked **footpath** peels along the eastern shore of the *étang*, skirting the Domaine de Marestagnu vineyard to rejoin the beach a little under a kilometre from the roadhead – a round walk that should take you about two hours.

Practicalities

Aléria has a handful of good-value **hotels**. *Les Orangers*, just off the crossroads on the road to the beach (☎04 95 57 00 31, ℻04 95 57 05 55; June–Sept; ❷), offers the best value, with tariffs as low as €30 for a double room (with shared toilets) in high season (€45 for fully en suite). Just west of the main crossroads, look for the blue-and-white sign on the roadside advertising *chambres d'hôte* (☎09 12 04 51 80; ❸), where simply furnished rooms in a large modern house cost €50 (including breakfast). Alternatively, *L'Empereur* (☎04 95 57 02 13, ℻04 95 57 02 33; ❹), a big hotel around the corner just north of the crossroads on the highway, is clean and comfortable, and a good deal, with large motel-style rooms opening onto a central garden. Top of the range in this area is the recently refurbished three-star *L'Atrachjata*, a little further north (☎04 95 57 03 93, ℻04 95 57 08 03, ℗www.hotel-atrachjata.net; open all year; ❺), which is plush, fully air-conditioned, and fitted with most mod cons. Prices vary according to the size of rooms, but drop to as low as €54 off season.

One of the most pleasant **campsites** on the east coast lies 3km east of the Cateraggio crossroads: the *Marina d'Aléria* (☎04 95 57 01 42, ℻04 95 57 04 29; Easter–Oct) backs onto the beach and is well equipped, with facilities including washing machines and refrigerated lockers.

For **food**, you won't do better than *Le Pied Dans L'Eau* on the shores of the *étang*, reviewed above. The same owners also run the *Auberge Le Chalet*, on the roadside at the turning off the main highway for the lagoon, which serves an identical menu but lacks the atmosphere of its floating sister concern.

Vallée du Tavignano

Running northwest from Aléria, the **Vallée du Tavignano** forms an exhilarating approach to Corte, its craggy schist gorges and denuded slopes dotted with red-roofed villages. The N200, which tracks the river all the way, provides the quickest route to the centre of the island, but if you're in no hurry you could take the upland road through the **Bozio**, contouring around the north flank of the valley through a succession of picturesque *villages perchés*.

For a quick, easy and rewarding detour on your way across the eastern plain, though, **ANTISANTI**, 20km west of Aléria at an altitude of 700m, is hard to beat. In the twelfth century the village was an important stopoff point for merchants travelling between Corte and the coast. Resisting Pascal Paoli's revolution, it was burned down in 1753 and today consists of only one street, but there's a café from which, on a clear day, you can see all the way from the needles of Bavella and Monte Incudine to the islands of Elba, Capraia and Monte Cristo.

The gorge route

Following the course of the Tavignano, Corsica's longest river, the main Route Nationale (N200) from Aléria to Corte was recently upgraded and now forms Corsica's most direct link with the mountainous interior. Having meandered across the plains for 10km, it starts to wind under steepening schist cliffs overlooked by the villages of the Bozio. Look out for the fine triple-arched **Genoese bridge** spanning the river; it is nicknamed the "Pont Laricio" because it was once nearly washed away by a giant pine tree swept down in the spring floods. Around 8km further on, at the junction with the D314 (from Altiani), stands the tenth-century **chapelle San Giovanni Battista** – a tiny Romanesque edifice built of patterned stones alternating with plain blocks of granite.

The Bozio

Scattered across the bare ridges dividing the Vallée du Tavignano and Castagniccia, the **Bozio** comprises a wild, depopulated necklace of schist villages strung over spurs and rocky belvederes on the northern shoulder of the valley. A major crossroads in Roman times, when it formed a trade link between the mountains and coastal plains, the region today sees fewer visitors than perhaps anywhere else on the island. Yet as a route between Corte and Aléria, it holds considerably more appeal than the faster highway on the valley floor. Romanesque churches, many of them decorated with original medieval frescoes and stone carving, lie scattered around the villages, and the views across the Tavignano Valley to the central range are magnificent. An additional incentive to spend time in the area is the **Mare a Mare Nord**, which contours in tandem with the corniche through the villages, roughly following the course of the old paved Via Romana, between Poggio in the east and Santa-Lucia-di-Mercurio in the west. More details of the itinerary, highlighted on IGN map #4351 OT and waymarked at regular intervals with orange paint marks, appear on p.400.

Pressing inland from Aléria, the landscape starts to grow noticeably wilder at **PIEDICORTE-DI-GAGGIO**, a protuberance of red roofs with a central square that opens onto a panorama of the eastern plain. In the thirteenth century, while the island was being disputed by the regional superpowers Genoa and Pisa, this was the fief of the powerful de Gaggio family, the ruins of whose castle mingle with those of the Chapelle de Santa Maria on the Punta Gaggio (1189m), rising steeply above the village to the north.

About 4km further along the road, the crumbling tower houses of **ALTIANI** (a constriction of *alti piani*, or "high pine trees") cluster around a huge lump of grey granite. The village's focal point, the place Mauresque, is said to be so named because of a fierce fight that took place on the spot in medieval times with an army of Moorish raiders. After a long and bloody siege, or so the story goes, the Corsicans flew a white flag to seek terms. But the surrender would only be accepted on condition that all the women and girls of the village, then sheltering in the church, were handed over to the pirates. This insult only seems to have stiffened the resolve of Altiani's menfolk to fight on, because somehow the encounter ended with a massacre of the Moors in the square.

At 1851m, **Monte Piano Maggiore** is the highest point in the Bozio, and as magnificent a belvedere as you'd expect for a peak facing the full glory of Corsica's central range. Traversing pastureland and fire-damaged hillsides scattered with crumbling remnants of an era when this area was intensively farmed, the route is easy to follow and not all that strenuous, with a net altitude gain of only 570m. Aside from the views, the obvious reason to attempt it is that very few other people do; from the start, you should have the hillsides entirely to yourself, which – combined with the ruined huts, terraces and threshing circles encountered along the way – conveys just how wild and deserted the region has become since it was depopulated in the 1950s. Given the absence of fellow trekkers, it's all the more important to approach the route with caution: assess the weather carefully before you leave; make sure you've adequate clothing to cope with a sudden change in conditions (bearing in mind the culminating altitude of the route); and take along IGN **map** #4351.

The trailhead, which you can drive to, is marked by a lonely chapel high above **Bustanico**: from the village, follow the D15 uphill (signposted towards Carticasi) for a couple of kilometres until you reach the col, where a lane branches left (northwest). Keep to this for just under 3km and you'll arrive at the **Chapelle Sant'Antoine**, which crowns the ridge dividing the lush chestnut forest to the north from the more arid, scrub-covered terrain flanking the lower Tavignano Valley. This is as far as it's possible to go by car.

The path begins at the disused threshing area behind the chapel, following the ridgeline due northwest. Having crossed a flattened shoulder scattered with ruins, it then starts to contour around the summit of Punta di San Cervone, disappearing regularly into the mass of animal tracks and terraces that striate the mountainside. After roughly one and a half hours, however, you'll arrive at the **Caldone stream**, whose true left bank you climb along to reach the **Bocca Prova** (1353m). It was here in March 1757 that Pascal Paoli and his army got bogged down in deep snow on their way to relieve rebel forces besieged in the Couvent d'Alando.

From the col, a sharp 45-minute ascent brings you finally to the **summit**, dotted with wind-bent beech trees. On a clear day the view stretches all the way from Monte Incudine to Monte Cinto, and out across the Tyrrhenian Sea to the Italian coast.

Return by the same route; allow a total of **four hours** to complete the round trip from the Chapelle de Sant'Antoine and back.

ERBAJOLO (Erbaghjolu), the next village along the corniche, offers another fantastic view of the Rotondo massif on the far side of the Tavignano. From the end of the lane behind the church, you can walk a kilometre or so along a mule track to the remote Pisan chapel of **San Martino**, a gentle thirty-minute hike through the maquis.

From Erbajolo, the more scenic of the onward routes, the D14, follows the course of the ancient Via Romana across the ridgetops and down to the floor of the Zingajo stream valley. Having joined the D215, it then begins the short climb up to **FAVALELLO**, where the Romanesque church of **Santa Maria Assunta** harbours fifteenth-century frescoes. Three kilometres further on, **ALANDO** was the birthplace of Sambucuccio d'Alando, a legendary fourteenth-century leader of a popular movement against the region's despotic nobility. Alando is credited with the invention of the "Terra del Commune", an organization that between 1359 and 1362 united villages all over Corsica under one administrative body of elected magistrates. If you fancy stretching your legs, **walk** along the Mare a Mare Nord west from Alando to Sermano. Waymarked in orange, the old path drops down into the chestnut woods from the road (look for a PNRC signboard at the trailhead), crossing a series of pretty streams before climbing to Sermano, reached after 1hr 30min.

The corniche (D441), meanwhile, wriggles through one of the last remaining patches of greenery on this side of the valley as it approaches **BUSTANICO**, the village said to be the source of the War of Independence. It began in 1729 when an old man named Lanfranchi, or "Cardone", sparked off a local rebellion against the Genoese after a tax collector threatened to carry off all his possessions. Outraged at such injustice, fellow villagers rose up in his defence, triggering riots and raids all over eastern Corsica, culminating in the sack of Bastia in 1730. The village church has a graceful polychrome wooden figure of Christ, sculpted by a local craftsman in the eighteenth century.

Sermano, Santa-Lucia-Di-Mercurio and Tralonca

The most scenic stretch of the corniche brings you next to **SERMANO**, famous for polyphonic *paghjella* singing (see p.330), which is performed each year during the *Jour des Morts* festival at the Pisan chapel of **San Nicolao**. The chapel, fringed by stands of cypress trees, stands fifteen minutes' walk from the centre: follow the footpath descending from behind the houses on the opposite side of the road from the church. Before setting off, though, ask at the gîte d'étape for the key, which will allow you to see the naïve fifteenth-century frescoes of Christ, the Virgin, the Apostles and saints adorning the interior. Back up in the village centre, the **Église de l'Annunziata** incorporates fragments of a much older Romanesque chapel, which formerly stood on the hillside above – look for the strange mythical animals on the lintels of the north-side door. A waystage on the **Mare a Mare Nord**, Sermano also holds the area's only **accommodation**, in a tiny **gîte d'étape** (☎04 95 48 67 97), overlooking the main road at the western edge of the village, with only sixteen dorm beds and no camping space.

Perhaps the finest view of the whole Bozio region awaits 6km west of Sermano as you approach **SANTA-LUCIA-DI-MERCURIO**. From the top of a steeply shelving spur, the hamlet looks southwest up the Restonica and Tavignano gorges to the snowcapped peaks of the watershed, spread in a dramatic 2500-metre wall on the far side of the valley. The spectacle of the tiny campanile framed by the distant mountains is emblematic of the defiant nationalist spirit that has always been synonymous with this region, from the uprisings of the medieval era to the present day. It was in the neighbouring village of **TRALONCA** in 1996 that the FLNC staged its most infamous show of force of recent years, when 600 paramilitaries – wearing black balaclavas and armed to the teeth with automatic pistols, rifles, flame-throwers and rocket launchers – staged a *nuit bleue* to declare a cessation in hostilities against the French state. For more on this extraordinary event, which rebounded badly on both the armed separatist movement and the government ministers who'd covertly arranged it, see "The Corsican Troubles" in Contexts, p.420.

Castagniccia

Castagniccia, pronounced "Castaneetch", takes its name from the dense forests of chestnuts (*castagna*), first cultivated here by the Genoese in the fifteenth century, which later made this the richest and most densely populated part of the island. Today, many of the beautiful grey-green and silver schist hamlets perched on its ribbon-thin ridges lie virtually deserted or derelict, but the region remains a rewarding one to explore – particularly during the autumn, when whole valleys are carpeted in vivid gold and russet, and in wet weather, when wisps of mist and cloud cling to the lush canopy.

Castagniccia covers roughly a hundred square kilometres, extending south of the River Golo as far as the Bozio, and westwards just beyond the shadowy crest of Monte San Petrone (1767m), its highest mountain. Fuelled by a lucrative trade in chestnut flour and fine woodcarving, the region's golden era occurred during the Genoese peace between 1569 and 1729, when the majority of its opulent Baroque churches, convents, chapels and lofty stone houses were built. In the eighteenth century the arms industry thrived here as well, and its products found a ready market during the Corsican Revolution, during which Castagniccia was a bastion of support for Pascal Paoli (see box on p.316), a native of **Morosaglia**. Decline set in only towards the end of the nineteenth century, with the completion of the railways through the interior of the island. Easing the transport of timber to the coast, this hastened the process of **deforestation**, which ultimately undermined the area's traditional agro-pastoral economy, and stimulated an exodus to the coastal towns and French mainland. These days, Castagniccia comes alive only during August, when families return from Marseille to visit elderly relatives.

Exploring the Castagniccia requires a vehicle and some caution: although there's a larger concentration of roads here than anywhere else in the interior of the island, routes are extremely winding and narrow, with the added hazard of roaming pigs, cows and goats. Daily **trains** from Bastia stop in Casamozza and Ponte Leccia, but unless you're prepared to walk or hitch this isn't much help for exploring the area. Furthermore, hotels and restaurants are to be found only at **La Porta**, **Piedicroce** and **Cervione** – though you could always stay on the coast at Moriani-Plage and see the Castagniccia on a day's tour. There's a choice of routes into the region: from the east coast via Prunete or Moriani-

Porto-Vecchio & Bonifacio ▼

Plage; from the north, via Casamozza; or, from the west, through Ponte Leccia and Morosaglia.

Moriani-Plage

One of a string of virtually indistinguishable resorts along the coast north of Aléria, **MORIANI-PLAGE** is a bland strip of kitsch souvenir shops and cafés huddled around a crossroads on the N198. The one old building left standing is a tiny schist cottage facing the beach from where, as a plaque on its peeling wall recalls, a 14-year-old Pascal Paoli left for exile in Naples with his father in 1739. For a foray into Castagniccia, however, this is a convenient base, boasting the last decent beach before Bastia, a reasonable choice of accommodation, a large Champion supermarket (300m south of the crossroads), a Société Générale cash dispenser (the only one for kilometres if you're heading inland), a self-service laundry (on the road leading to the beach) and a small **tourist office** (Mon–Fri 9am–noon & 2–5pm; ☎04 95 38 73).

A dependable budget **hotel** here is *L'Abri des Flots*, set back a little from the beach (☎04 95 38 40 76, ℱ04 95 38 03 06, ⓦwww.moriani.fr; half board at €42 per person obligatory in July & Aug; ➋), whose plain but clean rooms all have shower-toilets attached. There's also a very pleasant little **chambres d'hôte** place, *A Casa Corsa* (☎04 95 38 01 40, ℱ04 95 37 07 11; ➌), 6km south of Moriani on the highway; just north of the Cervione turning (D71) look for a sign on the roadside indicating a lane running to the west off the main road – the guesthouse stands 150m along it. The hospitable owners, M and Mme Doumens, have five large en-suite rooms, all lovingly decorated with homemade quilts and family photos, and a flowery patio where breakfast is served.

For **campsites**, you've a choice between the flashy four-star *Camping Merendella*, 700m south of the crossroads (☎04 95 38 53 47; May–Oct), or the more modest *Camping Calamar*, 6.5km south at Prunete (☎04 95 38 03 54; May–Oct). The latter is situated right next to the beach amid an old olive grove, and ranks among the most congenial sites on the island; it's small, with only simple facilities, but is kept immaculately clean (the young *patronne* has even planted beds of aromatic herbs outside the toilet block), and has a sociable little snack bar that stays open late.

Inland from Moriani-Plage

A great place to make the most of the views from the east-facing flanks of the coastal hills lies a short way **inland from Moriani-Plage** along the D34. Signalled by the prominent bell tower of its church, the village of **SAN-NICOLAO** emerges after 6km of tight bends and dense chestnut woods. You can pull over here to admire the colourful decor and trompe l'œil in the seventeenth-century parish church, or continue 4km further uphill to the hamlet of **SAN-GIOVANNI-DI-MORIANI**, where the wonderful *Bar-Restaurant Cava* (☎04 95 38 51 14; June–Sept) serves wholesome Castagniccian specialities, including *migliacci* (goat's-cheese doughnuts), on an €18 set menu. Their terrace overlooks the Tyrrhenian Sea and all the Tuscan islands are visible; on a clear day you can make out the Italian coast.

One of the most isolated villages in Castagniccia, **SANTA-REPARATA-DI-MORIANI**, lies at the end of the D34, which winds southwest from San-Giovanni-di-Moriani into a dense chestnut forest. A good reason to venture up here is the excellent gîte d'étape *Luna Piena* (☎04 95 38 59 48), which makes a perfect base from which to explore a new network of **waymarked trails**.

Three excellent round walks of between two and a half and five hours begin at the village, taking in the old chapels, springs and *bergeries* (shepherds' huts) dotted about the surrounding forests and steep hillsides. Glossy leaflets giving details of the routes on a simple contour map are available free from the gîte. Beds in their two- or four-person dorms cost €10, or €27 for half board, which is a bargain considering the quality of the food served – Castagniccian specialities made entirely from local produce. Non-residents can also eat here by prior arrangement.

Cervione

From San-Nicolao, it's 5km south to the largest, busiest and most welcoming village of the Castagniccia, **CERVIONE**, whose houses, spread in an amphitheatre around the lower reaches of Monte Castello, tower over a sloping medieval square that's linked to the surrounding streets by a labyrinth of alleys and archways. Flanking the south side of the *placette* is one of the first Baroque churches on Corsica, the **Cathédrale St-Érasme**, founded in 1578 by St Alexander Sauli, who was ordained bishop of Aléria in 1570 and soon transferred the bishopric to Cervione to escape the malaria-ridden swampland of the plain. Reached via an arcaded entrance immediately behind it, the **bishop's palace and seminary**, once the residence of King Théodore (see box below), houses an ethnographical **museum** (May–Sept Mon–Sat 9am–noon & 2.30–6pm; €2) exhibiting various farm implements and religious statuary.

Théodore von Neuhof

Scorned by Corsican historian Chanoine Casanova as an "operetta king", **Théodore von Neuhof** was crowned king of Corsica on April 15, 1736, a unique title he was to hold for just eight months.

Théodore was an ambitious nobleman with a very colourful past. Brought up in the court of France where he was page to the duchess of Orléans, mother of the Prince Regent, he travelled around England, Holland and Spain, killed his best friend in a duel, and acquired a fortune through some rather dubious financial speculations. Captured by Moors in Tunis in the early 1730s and put into slavery in Algiers, he managed to bribe his way to freedom, and was soon sending word to a group of Corsican exiles in Livorno that he would provide them with aid in return for the crown of their troubled island. Impressed by his royal connections and fancy talk, and desperate for money and arms, the Corsicans agreed. Soon after, Théodore landed at Aléria, decked out in full Turkish regalia with a retinue of French, Italian and Moorish attendants, and was taken in state to the Couvent d'Alesani to be crowned King Théodore I of Corsica. His powers were severely constrained – a council of 24 men was appointed to advise him, and he was answerable to a Corsican parliament – but Théodore had plenty of opportunities for kingly behaviour. Living it up at the bishop's palace in Cervione, he distributed titles among the wealthier Corsicans, made increasingly exaggerated promises of arms for the liberation of his people, and organized a few ineffectual sieges and pointless military manoeuvres against the Genoese.

Mistrust amongst his ministers increased as the emptiness of his promises became obvious, and in November 1736 the king was forced to flee the island via Solenzara, disguised as a priest. Théodore didn't give up entirely on the Corsicans, however – in 1739 he returned with a small fleet but was deterred from landing by the French. Eventually Théodore returned to England, where he died in 1756 having accumulated massive debts. A plaque in London's Soho Square commemorates him: "Fate poured its lessons on his living head, bestowed a kingdom and denied him bread."

The museum, or the mairie next door, keeps the key for the elegant Romanesque chapel of **Santa Cristina**, a pleasant forty-minute walk from Cervione – take the road down towards Prunete (the D71) for about 600m, where a signpost shows the way down a narrow lane. Marvellous **frescoes** dating from 1473 decorate the twin apses: on the left side Christ is depicted with the Virgin, St Cristina and a kneeling monk; on the right, Christ is surrounded by the symbols of the Evangelists; and over the arch between them is a portrayal of the Crucifixion. A longer walk into the mountains starts from the west of the village: leave the square via the road running past the Bishop's Palace and bear right at the fork reached soon after. This brings you onto a lane leading 2km uphill to Notre-Dame-de-la-Scobiccia, a tiny Romanesque chapel containing a white marble Madonna statue washed up on the beach at Prunete. Just past the chapel, an old mule track peels right, cutting up the hillside to the Bocca Sambachi (998m); you can follow this path for literally hours along the ridgetop.

There is no hotel in the village, but the friendly *Trois Fourchettes* **restaurant** (☎04 95 38 14 86), in the square, does a great-value four-course menu featuring local charcuterie, *soupe corse*, pork filet with aubergines and cheese, plus dessert, all for €13 (including wine). Advance booking is recommended.

Cervione to Carcheto

South of Cervione, after about 12km of hairpin bends (many with dizzying drops and no barriers), comes **Vallé-d'Alesani**, from where a short detour down the D217/D317 leads to the **Couvent d'Alesani** (near the hamlet of **Piazzali**) where King Théodore was crowned (see box opposite). Founded in 1236, the Franciscan monastery is mostly a ruin, but its church holds a beautiful fifteenth-century Sienese painting known as the *Virgin and the Cherry*. The site is also associated with the infamous Giovannali sect, who sheltered here after the destruction of their monastery at Carbini (see p.249).

Back on the main road it's not long before you reach **FELCE**, whose Baroque church is decorated with simple yet arresting frescoes – on the ceiling you'll see the artist, palette in hand, floating among the clouds. Also of interest is the **tabernacle** above the altar, carved by a penitent bandit. Ask for the key at the mairie. Another reason to pull over here is the fragrant local-produce shop, A Coualina, run by Christine Bereni, on the outskirts of the village, where you can buy home-grown chestnut-pollen honey, free-range eggs, charcuterie, jams, tasty goat's and ewe's cheese and locally made baskets.

Beyond Felce, the road winds slowly up to the **Col d'Arcarotta**, dividing the Alesani Valley from the Caldone basin, the heartland of Castagniccia. Straddling the pass, the *Auberge des Deux Vallées*, one of the area's few gîtes d'étape (☎04 95 35 91 20; 15 June–Sept 4; €10 per dorm bed), takes in the best of the views, with Monte San Petrone dominating the skyline to the northwest. Its convivial wood-lined bar makes a good place for a pit stop, or you can sample typical Castagniccian cuisine (such as *figatelle*, roast pork or trout in cream cheese) in the restaurant. Served indoors or alfresco on the terrace (for a ten percent surcharge), menus are priced at €15–20, all featuring pork with *brocciu* and chestnut-flour fritters. Standing at a nexus of some enjoyable local footpaths, the auberge is also well placed for **walks** in the area. Ask in the bar for the *Sentiers de Pays* leaflet (*dépliant*), which gives you a rough idea of the routes and distances of the various paths. From the col, much the most rewarding option is the five-hour round walk to Stazzona and the mineral-water hamlet of Eaux d'Orezza (see p.313), taking in some of the region's best viewpoints and tracts of old chestnut forest.

The chestnut tree (*la chataîgnier* in French, **a castagna** in Corsican) grows in most areas of the island that lie between 500m and 800m, but only in Castagniccia – whose mild, moist climate and schist soils create the optimum environment – does it form such extensive forests. Planted in the fifteenth century by the Genoese, these were the linchpin of the local economy for more than four hundred years, providing fuel, carving and building material, pollen for bees and, most importantly of all, a ready source of food.

The first chestnut pods, or *pelous*, appear on the trees in mid-August, but the harvest doesn't usually start until two months later, while the leaves are falling. Removed from their spiky pods, the nuts are shelled and stored in special double-storey stone sheds called **séchoirs**, where they dry over the winter. Traditionally, the largest and most succulent were eaten whole, while the rest were taken to water-mills and ground into flour (*farina*). This formed the mainstay of the peasant diet in many areas of upland Corsica, where it was mixed with salt and water to make **pulenda**, a kind of polenta, or, on special occasions, baked into cakes and biscuits. Any surplus was bartered for olive oil and wine from the coastal villages.

During the late nineteenth century, the "chestnut economy" of regions such as Castagniccia went into free fall as acres of forest were felled for timber and to provide tannin for leather production. Still more trees died due to neglect as rural populations dwindled, while a virulent fungal disease has also taken its toll over the past decade. These days, *pulenda* and chestnut-flour cakes, served as gourmet specialities in expensive restaurants and souvenir boutiques, have become more a symbol of the islanders' traditional identity than eaten as daily staples; emigrants, for example, are still often sent parcels of flour from their family land by older relatives. The only apparent beneficiaries of the chestnut's decline are Corsica's wild pigs, who gorge themselves on the ungathered windfalls.

The first sizeable settlement below the pass is **CARCHETO**, set amidst an ocean of chestnut trees and giving a good view of Piedicroce across the valley. Carcheto's dilapidated **Église Ste-Marguerite**, set by a wood on the edge of the hamlet, is an eighteenth-century edifice packed with decaying examples of local work – luridly painted stucco covers the walls, portraying scenes from the Crucifixion, with an alabaster statue of the Virgin and Child providing a restrained counterpoint. If the church is locked, you can pick up the key from the *Refuge* hotel in Piedicroce (see below). Outside the church, a sign for "La Fontaine" directs walkers through the wood to a **waterfall**, which cascades through an opening in the trees – a fine spot for a dip and a picnic: follow the track indicated, heading straight on where the the main (motorable) trail switches sharply to the right (ignore the orange splashes of paint). You'll know you're going the right way when you pass a cemetery, followed by a spring.

Piedicroce

A cluster of hamlets comprising the commune of **Orezza** lies to the north of Carcheto, strung along the lower slopes of Monte San Petrone. During the mid-nineteenth century, this was the most densely populated *commune* in the whole of France, with 91 inhabitants per square kilometre. Today, however, barely 200 permanent residents live in **PIEDICROCE**, the area's principal village, whose **hotel**, *Le Refuge* (☎04 95 35 82 65, ℻04 95 35 84 42; closed mid-Oct to Nov; ❸), is the sole place to stay in the valley. Perched on a steep terrace, the building itself is a pink monstrosity, but its **restaurant** does excellent Corsican food, including Castagniccian specialities such as chestnut fritters with *brocciu* cheese.

Piedicroce's **Église de Saints de Pierre et Paul**, built in 1691, harbours a handful of mediocre sixteenth- and seventeenth-century paintings, and a restored organ that is reputedly the oldest in Corsica. A short way further north on the D71, the forlorn ruins of **Couvent d'Orezza** have profound historic resonance for Corsicans. A centre of resistance to the Genoese republic in the eighteenth century, the building hosted several *consulte* (rebel meetings): on April 20, 1731, twenty representatives of the clergy gathered to discuss whether violent rebellion was against the fundamental principles of Christian morality, and it was here that Paoli was voted commander-in-chief of the Corsican National Guard. Paoli also met Napoléon at the church in 1793 during an unsuccessful attempt to achieve a truce between their respective armies. The Germans finally destroyed the convent in 1943 after discovering it had been used as a Resistance arms dump.

Piedicroce's **tourist office** (mid-June to mid-Oct daily 9am–noon & 2–6pm; ☎04 95 35 82 54), opposite the spring in the middle of the village, stocks an impressive selection of books on Corsica, as well as the usual gamut of leaflets (including the handy *Sentiers de Pays* detailing the area's footpaths). Nearby, the *Café Oimeauz* serves fresh sandwiches and ice creams on a lovely terrace overlooking the valley; the baker's van passes by at around 10pm in time for a late breakfast.

Stazzona

STAZZONA, 2km downhill along the D506 from Piedicroce, was the centre of arms manufacture during the War of Independence – its name means "forge" in Corsican. From the 1850s onwards, however, it has made its money from the naturally sparkling **Eaux d'Orezza** spring: as the faded old hotel signs indicate, people used to come up here for the curative waters, among them Pascal Paoli, Napoléon Bonaparte, English aristocrats and colonialists from French Indochina. The local council, which owns the springs, gave up the enterprise in 1995 because sales were poor, but the celebrated Eau d'Orezza made a comeback in 1999, after a twenty-million-francs publicly funded relaunch. The gradual decline in the water's popularity this century was mainly attributable to its foul metallic taste; for this reason, a large part of the grant was spent on a new bottling plant, where the iron content of the water is reduced and its bubbles made smaller. To reach the new factory, which churns out 2500 litres per hour, continue down the hill for a couple of kilometres and cross the bridge, where a side road turns right.

Orezza, Piazzole and Pruno-Casette

While you're on this side of the valley, you could follow the D46 past the spring another 4km to **VALLE D'OREZZA**, where traditional smoking pipes and boxes are carved from olive and chestnut wood. Formerly this hamlet exported crafted wood objects all over Corsica, France and Italy; now only a handful of elderly artisans still live here, selling their work to visitors direct from tiny cottage workshops.

Somewhat grander Castagniccian wood carving adorns the door of the church at **PIAZZOLE**, reached by following the D506 down the valley for 4km until you see a sign pointing uphill to the right. One of Corsica's finest examples of **naïve folk art**, the door, painted in terracotta, peppermint and blue, is believed to have been the work of a repentant bandit as a act of atonement and gratitude to the villagers for sheltering him from the gendarmes. A recently installed panel nearby unpacks the elaborate symbolism of the carved panels, one of which features a self-portrait by the artist.

Visible all over Castagniccia and central Corsica, the craggy summit of **Monte San Petrone** (1767m) is one of the most thrilling viewpoints on the island, and is accessible on a comfortable four-hour round-hike (2hr 30min ascent, 1hr 30min descent) along a clearly marked trail. Each year in August, hundreds of local villagers, including a fair number of old folk, climb to the top for a special Mass, so the route is relatively easy going. That said, you'll definitely need sturdy footwear and a good pair of lungs, as the path gets steep and rocky towards the top.

The trailhead for the hike is at **Campodonico**, about 2km west of Couvent d'Orezza up a side road. Park your car in the lay-by at the entrance to the hamlet and head down the lane through the houses, turning right along the mule track that leads up the valley. From here, the trail – marked at regular intervals with splashes of orange or red paint – zigzags up to a scattering of **bergeries** (1hr 30min), where you should briefly quit the path and follow the hillside around to the north to get the best views of the mountains inland. All of northern Corsica's principal peaks are visible at this point, from the Cinto massif down to Monte Rotondo.

Once you've rejoined the marked trail, it takes around one hour to reach the summit, passing through beautiful birch woods and mossy boulders. The final thirty minutes are tough going, but the 360-degree panorama from the top, marked with a crucifix and a serpentine-stone carving of St Peter, is breathtaking. In clear weather you can see from the coast of Tuscany to Cap Corse, and across the swath of dramatic snowcapped mountains to the east.

Note that if you have the use of two vehicles or are happy to hitch, a good alternative descent leads north from the *bergeries* mentioned earlier along a clearly marked trail to the **Col de Prato**, a short way east of Morosaglia. Some hikers use this gentler, more shaded trail as an approach, but it isn't nearly as rewarding a route as the one described above (the beech cover obscures the views for most of the way).

Back down on the main road, a right turn will lead you north along the D506 down an imposingly deep valley towards the coast. At a tiny hamlet called **Rumitoriu**, roughly 10km north of the turning for Valle-d'Orezza, is the region's most pleasant **campsite**, the *Camping à la Ferme Les Prairies* (☎04 95 36 95 90). Spread over grassy terraces under stands of magnificent old chestnut trees, it's a rough-and-ready place with only basic facilities, but the views up the valley are lovely and the *patrons*, M et Mme Fontana, very welcoming; they also have a handful of simply furnished rooms in a new block on the edge of the site, costing around €50 in peak season.

For a classy Corsican speciality meal, continue north on the D506 for another 3km to the village of **PRUNO–CASETTE**, where the excellent *U Travone* (☎04 95 36 98 98) **restaurant**, occupying what looks like a large family house just below the road, offers menus at €20 or €28 (including wine). The latter features the house signature dish, stuffed trout, and as a starter you might be offered delicate *beignets* flavoured with wild mint, or an alternative main course of veal and olive stew, rounded off with quality local cheese and a *digestif*.

Campana

CAMPANA, 4km west of Piedicroce, merits a stop for its Baroque church of **Sant'André**, which houses a fine *Adoration of the Shepherds* attributed to the Spanish seventeenth-century painter Zurbarán. Renowned for its beautiful light (and, bizarrely, for the faintly demonic expression on the face of the boy carrying the eggs), the painting was given to the parish by a wealthy local resident in 1895. The key to the church is kept by an old lady who lives in the last house on the left as you face the village.

There's a great little **place to eat** here: the *Restaurant Sant'Andria* (☎04 95 35 82 26; open for lunch and dinner, except Sun out of season). The single €18 menu is definitively Castagniccian – local charcuterie or pâté, veal and olive stew, chard spinach with mint, strong ewe's cheese and chestnut flan for dessert – and the interior full of warm wood colours from the carved furniture and light streaming in through large windows overlooking the valley.

La Porta and Col de Prato

Thanks largely to the gigantic five-storey bell tower rising from its terracotta and grey schist rooftops, **LA PORTA**, 6km up the hill from here, is the most distinctive village in Castagniccia. Swathed in lush chestnut forest, with the granite crags of Monte San Petrone looming behind, its centrepiece is the spectacular **Église St-Jean–Baptiste**, erected in 1720 and widely regarded as the high watermark of Baroque architecture in Corsica. The church's grand façade gracefully unites all the principal features of Rococo. Inside the building are several noteworthy art treasures, including a resplendent trompe l'oeil ceiling, a gory depiction of the beheading of St John the Baptist (to the right as you face the altar) and, opposite this (on your left as you enter), *The Martyrdom of Sainte Elaulie* by Detouche, a student of Delacroix.

There is nowhere to stay in La Porta, but the *Restaurant de L'Ampigignani* (*Chez Elizabeth*; ☎04 95 39 22 00), down the road through the centre of the village from the church, is a good **place to eat**. It looks unpromising from the outside, but has a light and airy dining hall with magnificent views down the valley. The food is consistently good, too, and reasonably priced considering the quality; everything comes from the immediate vicinity, and is prepared according to traditional Castagniccian recipes (set menus €14–23, and pizzas from €7 to €11).

Heading uphill on the D205 out of La Porta will bring you to the **Col de Prato** (985m), the highest point on the roads of Castagniccia. From the col, a walk to the ruined **San Petrucolo** (a church founded as far back as the sixth century) can be done in half an hour. Follow the narrow track south in the direction of Monte San Petrone, then after 100m take the track on the right into the maquis – keep to this for a few steps, then strike left, and you'll see the chapel straight in front of you.

Morosaglia

MOROSAGLIA, a short way north of Col de Prato on the outside edge of Castigniccia, is renowned as the birthplace of Pascal Paoli. The family home, still owned by a descendant of the man Corsicans call "U Babu di a Patria" ("Father of the Nation"), has been given over to a small but interesting museum, the **Maison de Pascal Paoli** (daily except Tues: April–Sept 9am–noon & 2.30–7.30pm; Oct–March 9am–noon & 1–5pm; €2), signposted east of the village in the hamlet of Stretta. A video primes you for the tour of the house, whose exhibits comprise a small collection of letters, maps (by such cartographers as Thomas Jeffries), books (among them a first edition of Boswell's *Journal*) and other memorabilia, including the very first Corsican newspaper, printed in 1794, and the original Moor's head flag. Over the past decade or so, the museum has also acquired an impressive array of Paoli-related works of art: the famous portrait painted during his exile in London by Sir Thomas Lawrence (formerly housed in the British Museum); a contemporary copy of

"He smiled a good deal when I told him that I was much surprised to find him so amiable, accomplished and polite," wrote Boswell on first meeting **Pascal Paoli** in 1765, "for although I knew I was to see a great man I expected to find a rude character, an Attila king of the Goths, or a Luitprand king of the Lombards." By this time Paoli was 40 years old and famous throughout Europe, widely admired by the liberal intelligentsia of the time, among them Jean-Jacques Rousseau.

Paoli was born in **Morosaglia** (see p.315) with the cause of Corsican independence in his blood – his father, Giacinto, a doctor, was a first-generation rebel, one of the three primates elected in 1731 by the independent assembly. At the age of 14, Pascal accompanied his father into exile in Naples, where the boy became a keen student of political enlightenment. At the time of Gaffori's assassination, Pascal was a 29-year-old sub-lieutenant in a Neapolitan regiment, but his brother Clemente was in the thick of the rebellion. Appointed one of four regents after Gaffori's death, Clemente invited his younger brother to take over the position of **General of the Nation**, a title he accepted in **1755** and was to hold for the next fourteen years.

Paoli's intention was to drive out the Genoese by force of arms, but despite his military background he wasn't an experienced soldier, and was anyway always short of the necessary supplies. However, he proved to be adept in the art of government, giving the island a **democratic constitution** that anticipated that of the United States of America; founding the university at Corte; building a small navy that was strong enough to break the Genoese blockade; and establishing a mint, a printing press and an arms factory. Furthermore, the system of justice instituted by Pascal Paoli was effective enough to bring about a decline in vendetta killings.

Then in **1768** everything collapsed. The French moved in once more, this time intending to stay after having bought out the Genoese under the terms of the Treaty of Versailles. Determined to crush the rebels for good, the French overwhelmed the Corsican troops at **Ponte-Nuovo**, whereupon Paoli went into exile in London. However, his political life was not over.

In **1789**, at the start of the French Revolution, the people of Corsica were declared to be subject to the same laws as the revolutionary state, and it was in this changed political climate that Paoli returned triumphantly to the island in the following year. Initially he sympathized with the new republicanism, but the Corsican Jacobites – the Bonaparte family amongst them – owed too much to France to have much sympathy with separatist politics. Disagreements came to a head with Paoli's arraignment in June **1793**. His response was dramatic. Setting up an independent government in Corte, he approached the British government for help, who, having been driven out of Toulon by the French, were in search of a naval base in the area; and so there followed one of the more curious episodes of Corsican history.

The British sent **Sir Gilbert Elliot** to evaluate the situation, and agreement was quickly reached. English troops and naval forces moved in and after some fighting – during which the future Admiral Nelson lost the sight in one eye – the French moved out. A new constitution was drawn up that gave Corsica an attachment to the English Crown, but with a large degree of autonomy. It's questionable whether Paoli was ever entirely happy with the course of events, but he was in a difficult situation, as the guillotine was waiting for him if France ever regained control. There seems no doubt that he expected to be appointed viceroy of the island, and when Elliot was given the job things began to turn sour. The parliament of 1795 elected Paoli as president, but Elliot objected; soon after, rioting was provoked by a rumour that Paoli's bust had been deliberately smashed at a ball given in the viceroy's honour. When the English began talking again to the republican French, the game was over. In 1796 Paoli was persuaded to return to London, shortly before Elliot withdrew as Napoléon's army landed to secure the island for France.

Given a state pension, Paoli died in London in **1807** at the age of 82, a revered figure. He was initially buried in his place of exile – there's a bust of him in Westminster Abbey – but his ashes now lie in his birthplace.

a bust sculpted by Chapman for the memorial at Westminster Abbey; and Bainbridge's 1769 battlefield scene, bought recently for $25,000 from an American collection. Paoli's ashes, brought back from England in 1807, are entombed in a marble-lined chapel next door, revered as a shrine by Corsican nationalists.

Paoli was baptized in the Pisan-founded but extensively rebuilt church of **Santa Reparata**, reached via a path that starts 400m down the hill, behind the large house on the right side of the road. His brother Clemente, described by Dorothy Carrington as "a matchless marksman who prayed for his enemies' souls as he shot them down", lived out his retirement here, in the large mansion that's now the village school.

A couple of fine Romanesque chapels are to be found beyond Morosaglia. The nearer, **Santa–Maria–di–Valle–di–Rostino**, stands to the west of the D15, 5km along the road. Passing the village on your right, continue for 500m to reach the ruined chapel, accessible via a rough track. Dating from the tenth century, the apse displays some fine Pisan stonework created by narrow blocks interspersed with green and grey schist, adorned with slender columns and harmonious arcading. Amongst the primitive sculpture along the external roof band, Adam and Eve on either side of the Tree of Life feature most prominently. **San-Tommaso-di-Pastoreccia**, 10km north of Morosaglia at the end of the zigzagging route through Pastoreccia, is a half-ruined building of grey schist, dating from the tenth century, its interior enlivened by a series of sixteenth-century **frescoes.** Some are in very bad condition, but you won't have any difficulty picking out most of the Apostles and saints (a young St John stands out in a gold surround), or deciphering the scenes from the Passion and the Last Judgement.

The best **place to eat** in this area is an auberge called *A Stella di Rustino* (T04 95 38 77 09) in the village of **Valle-di-Rostino**, reached via the windy back road that turns right off the D71 at the Bocca a Serna, 2km below Morosaglia. Follow the D15B for 2km, and turn left at the first fork. The restaurant, occupying a new building at the entrance to the village, is run by a French Basque and his Parisian wife who pride themselves on their hospitality and delicious local speciality cooking. The house has two signature dishes: Corsican lasagne, with six kinds of meat (including pigeon and wild boar) cooked in wine and flavoured with strong ewe's cheese; and *tripettes* of veal. Two menus are offered: one at €23 and the other at €32, both including wine, coffee and *digestif*.

The Casinca

Bounded by the Golo and Fiumalto rivers, the **Casinca** covers the eastern slopes of Monte Sant'Angelo, an area swathed in olive and chestnut trees and embellished with stately villages. It's less popular with tourists than the Castagniccia, but is easier to get into if you haven't got your own transport, as a **bus** runs daily (except Sun) from Bastia to **Vescovato** and **Venzolasca**, many of whose inhabitants earn their living in the city. There's no accommodation on offer, but it's a small area and easily coverable in half a day.

The Casinca villages

CASTELLARE-DI-CASINCA, just 1km up the D6 from the main coast road, about 15km north of Moriani-Plage, affords a wonderful view of the eastern plain and has a beautiful tenth-century church, **San Pancrazio**, notable for its triple apse and for housing the mummified remains of St-Pancrace, who was martyred in Rome in 304 AD and later became the patron saint of Corsican bandits. About 1km further along the D206, a road off to the left leads to **PENTA-DI-CASINCA**, the second-largest village in the region. Its dark streets, crammed with lofty schist buildings dating principally from the fifteenth century, open out onto a large square, which gives another fine view across the plain.

Heading east for 1km along the D206 will bring you to a junction where an abrupt left turn leads onto the spectacular road flanking Monte Sant'Angelo. **LORETO-DI-CASINCA**, the next halt, and the area's most appealing village, perches on a spur overlooking all the villages of the Casinca, its long main street affording a panorama right across to Bastia – the terrace to the left of the church is the best place to make the most of it. A waymarked hike through the chestnut forest up **Monte Sant'Angelo** (1218m) starts 500m south of the village along a recently surfaced road, from the neighbouring hamlet of **Silverecio** – it's about ninety minutes' fairly strenuous climbing to the summit.

Some 500m north of the village you can cut back east by taking a right turn and following the road across a ridge for 2km until you hit the D237 again. A right here will bring you to **VENZOLASCA**, a remote and lofty village whose slender, lance-like church spire is conspicuous from a long way off. Venzolasca is one of the few places in Corsica where you still see men dressed in traditional black corduroy, complete with silver studs and gun belt.

From here it's a short drive down to **VESCOVATO**, set amongst chestnut trees and olive groves. Capital of the Casinca, this was an important place in the thirteenth century when the bishopric of Mariana was transferred here in a move to escape the malaria-ridden plain (*vescovato* means "bishopric" in Corsican). The bishopric remained until 1570, when it was relocated to the more important town of Bastia. The village is livelier than most places hereabouts – its busy central square, shaded by lines of ancient plane trees, even has an outdoor café, a rare find in these parts.

On the south side of the square, a family coat of arms indicates the house of the historian Filippini, whose *Historia di Corsica* (1594) is a principal source of medieval Corsican history. A further wander through the village reveals various plaques commemorating eminent visitors such as Mirabeau, but Vescovato's main sight is the church of **San Martino**, reached by climbing a flight of steps north of the square. Enlarged by the bishops of Mariana in the fifteenth century, the church contains a fine marble tabernacle, carved by a Genoese sculptor in 1441 and portraying two Roman soldiers sleeping against the tomb.

Travel details

Buses

The tables below summarize which bus companies cover which routes, how often they run and how long journeys take. Start by looking up your intended destination in the first table; then, using the company's acronym (eg RB or AC), go to the second table for more detailed route and frequency information. Precise departure times can be checked in advance either via the bus companies direct, or (if your French isn't up to that)

Bastia tourist office on ☏ 04 95 31 81 34. Most of the buses along the east coast are operated by Rapides Bleus.

Aléria (Cateraggio) to: Bastia (RB; 1hr 30min); Corte (ACT; 1hr 25min); Ghisonaccia (RB; 25min); Porto-Vecchio (RB; 1hr 20min); Solenzara (RB; 40min).
Ghisonaccia to: Aléria (RB; 15min); Bastia (RB; 1hr 45min); Porto-Vecchio (RB; 55min); Solenzara (RB; 15min).

Moriani-Plage to: Bastia (RB; 35min).
Solenzara to: Aléria (RB; 35min); Bastia (RB; 2hr 5min); Ghisonaccia (RB; 20min); Porto-Vecchio (RB; 40min).
Venzolasca to: Bastia (AC; 50min); Vescovato (AC; 10min).
Vescovato to: Bastia (AC; 40min); Venzolasca (AC; 10min).

AC: Autobus Casinca ☎04 95 36 70 64.

Bastia–Vescovato–Venzolasca Mon–Sat 1 daily.
ACT:Autobus Cortenais ☎04 95 46 22 89.
Aléria–Corte 1 Mon, Wed & Fri 1 daily.
RB: Rapides Bleus ☎04 95 31 03 79 or 04 95 70 10 36. Porto-Vecchio–Solenzara–Ghisonaccia–Aléria (Cateraggio)–Prunete–Moriani-Plage–Bastia mid-June to mid-Sept 2 daily; mid-Sept to mid-June Mon–Sat 2 daily.

EASTERN CORSICA | Travel details

Central Corsica

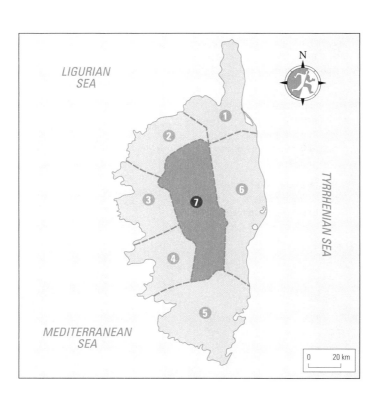

LIGURIAN
SEA

N

TYRRHENIAN SEA

MEDITERRANEAN
SEA

0   20 km

CHAPTER 7

Highlights

* **Monte Cinto** – Corsica's rooftop, and a step up from the surrounding landscapes, in every sense. Or try the ascent of Punta Muvrella, a real lung-stretcher, for the ultimate view of the island's highest peak. See p.329

* **Niolo cuisine** – Eye-wateringly strong ewe's cheese and mountain charcuterie – perfect picnic fodder. See p.333

* **Lac de Nino** – Scenery reminiscent of Tibet, with wild horses and snow peaks fringing the horizon. See p.336

* **Santa di u Niolu** – The interior's major religious festival, celebrated with ritual and polyphony singing. See p.337

* **Corte citadel** – Perched atop a twisted pinnacle of rock – the perfect emblem for *l'âme corse*. See p.342

* **Gorges du Tavignano** – Neck-craning cliffs and ancient pine forest, crossed by a medieval mule track. See p.344

* **Chapelle Sant'Eliseo** – The island's highest pilgrimage place and a superb viewpoint. See p.348

* **Hotel Monte d'Oro** – Creaking floorboards, the smell of bees' wax and *fin-de-siècle* decor – a hotel oozing period charm, slap on the watershed. See p.350

Central Corsica

W hen the FLNC (Fronte di Liberazione Naziunale di a Corsica) decided to stage a show of force – or *nuit bleue* – to underline its ceasefire in 1996, it was no coincidence that the location they chose lay deep in the centre of the island. Although thoroughly depopulated and at an all-time economic low ebb, the interior, with its granite mountains, swirling mists and dark tracts of pine forest, is far more expressive of Corsica's essence than the pastel and turquoise colours of the coast. Ajaccio and Bastia (or Paris and Marseille) may be where most islanders live these days, but it is to the villages of the mountain valleys that most return in August, and which they consider home.

For visitors, the big attraction of the island's core are its stupendous landscapes, and the best way to immerse yourself in them is to get onto the region's ever-expanding network of marked trails and forest roads. The ridge of mountains lining the watershed is closely tracked by the epic GR20, a route that can be picked up from various villages and is scattered with refuge huts. Other marked trails wind off the watershed to the surrounding summits. Of these, the island's two highest peaks – Monte Cinto and Monte Rotondo – provide the most compelling routes. For less experienced trekkers, there are also plenty of lower-altitude trails to exquisite glacial lakes and viewpoints over the valleys, while the region's roads, though often in disrepair, penetrate deep into the forests that carpet the mountain slopes.

Corte, set in a broad valley at the centre of the island on the main road between Ajaccio and Bastia, provides the perfect base to begin exploring, as it's well placed to reach anywhere covered in this chapter and has the bulk of the region's accommodation – elsewhere, it's rare to find more than one basic hotel or gîte d'étape per village. Capital of independent Corsica in the eighteenth century, Corte is a fortress town *par excellence*, with its walled citadel, set atop a twisted pinnacle of rock, piercing the landscape of overlapping mountains and forests. Despite being the second-ranking town of Haute-Corse, it's a peaceful, slow-moving place where old traditions die hard, making it a fascinating introduction to the mentality of the interior.

In the immediate environs of Corte the chief attractions are the spectacular **Vallée de la Restonica** and the parallel **Gorges du Tavignano**. A dramatic, recently upgraded road scales the former, giving access to the beautiful Lacs de Melo and Capitello, as well as one of the most famous stretches of the GR20, but you can escape the crowds by following the time-worn medieval mule path bordering the Tavignano River deep in the mountains.

Further north, another hi-spec, Euro-funded road penetrates a region of soaring peaks and wild forest that only a century ago was the domain of trans-

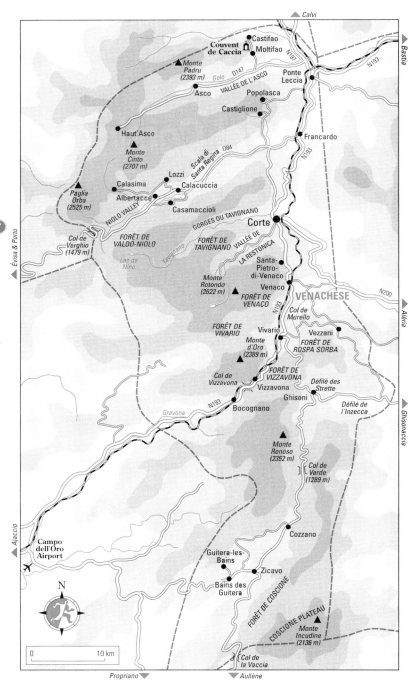

humant shepherds and the toughest alpinists. Dominated by the rugged north face of Monte Cinto, the higher reaches of the **Vallée de l'Asco** are encircled by a ring of 2500-metre mountains, many of which – including Cinto itself – may be approached via technically undemanding routes.

A more gentle path up Corsica's highest mountain begins in the adjacent valley of the **Niolo**, a sheep-rearing region that was isolated for centuries until legionnaires gouged a road up it a hundred years ago. Like Corte, the Niolo is an essential visit for anyone eager to understand *l'âme corse* – "the soul of Corsica" – so you might want to linger for a night or two in the main settlements of **Calacuccia**, **Albertacce** and **Casamaccioli**, not least to sample the region's famous mountain charcuterie and ewe's cheese, still made according to traditional methods.

The four great valleys north of Corte attract a far greater number of visitors than those south of the interior's capital, but there's some great walking to be had in the **Venachese**, where villages such as **Vivario** and **Vizzavona** stand amid some of the island's best-preserved forest. Edward Lear's trademark Gothic etchings perfectly captured the intense sense of verticality generated by **Monte d'Oro**, whose vast pyramidal summit dominates this part of the watershed. At its foot, the **Cascades des Anglais**, a sequence of turquoise pools and falls set amid some glorious old-growth forest, have been attracting tourists since the *bel époque* of the late nineteenth century, when aristocratic British expats used to catch the newly inaugurated railway up here to escape the heat of Ajaccio.

The *micheline* train still provides a convenient way to penetrate deep into the Monte d'Oro area, but to reach the high country further south and east you'll need a car. As a base camp for explorations of the whaleback Monte Renoso massif, the village of **Ghisoni**, at the head of the Fiumorbo Valley, is the obvious candidate, with the only decent hotel for miles. High above it, a decaying ski station, **E'Capannelle**, presides over the trailhead for the ascent, its lively gîte d'étape crammed with footsore GR20 hikers during the summer.

Pressing on south from Zicavo, you cross the watershed at aptly named **Col de Verde** – in many respects a more attractive walking base than E'Capannelle – to enter the head of the magnificent Taravo Valley. Nestling amid the swath of unbroken chestnut and pine forest spreading below the pass, the villages of **Zicavo** and **Cozzano** have both retained plenty of Corsican character, with ancient stone houses and a handful of congenial places to stay and eat. While lacking the alpine feel of Asco and the Restonica Valley, the scenery of the Haut Taravo is nonetheless imposing, while the trails through it have the advantage of being less frequented. One of the best is the two-day traverse of Monte Incudine, the final 2000-metre-plus peak in the south, which takes you across the rolling grassland of the Coscione Plateau – one of the island's most celebrated landscapes.

The Vallée de l'Asco

The **Vallée de l'Asco**, the northernmost (and wettest) of the interior's great valleys, was once a region of intensive pastoral farming, whose scattered population lived for centuries off small-scale cheese and wool production, supplemented by crops such as wheat, tobacco, linen and hemp. During the Genoese era, the *poix*, or pitch, made by the Aschesi from pine sap, caused the wholesale destruction of the area's forests, and today much of the landscape is denuded and bleak. Ringed by a string of 2000-metre peaks, the valley remains among Corsica's most remote enclaves; only in 1937 was Asco village connected to the road network, which was extended as far as the ski station by the French Foreign Legion in 1968. Today, the Aschesi, like most mountain communities, rely on the seasonal influx of hikers to make ends meet, along with modest sales of cheese and charcuterie, and their famously fragrant **honey**, produced in the ranks of ramshackle hives stacked up the hillsides.

The River Asco starts life as the Stranciacone, which rises at an altitude of 2556m on the lower slopes of **Monte Cinto**, Corsica's highest mountain, then flows through the village of Asco and on through a fantastic **gorge** before reaching the River Golo close to **Ponte Leccia**. In the upper valley, beyond Asco, the scenery is most alpine – up here mouflon roam in carefully protected zones, and bearded vultures and royal eagles are sometimes to be spotted in the magnificent **Forêt de Carozzica**. The road comes to an end 15km west of Asco at the semi-operational ski station at **Haut'Asco**, from where trails lead into the surrounding mountains.

No buses run to Haut'Asco, so you'll need your own transport to make a tour of the valley. Starting at Ponte Leccia, it's a good idea to detour up to the delightful villages of **Moltifao** and **Castifao**, before returning to the gorge and the road up to Haut'Asco.

Ponte Leccia, Moltifao and Castifao

Lying 19km north of Corte at the junction of road and rail routes to Bastia, Corte and the Balagne, **PONTE LECCIA** has little to recommend it beyond its supermarkets and service stations, where you may want to refuel before pressing on into the Vallée de l'Asco or Castagniccia. Outdoor sports enthusiasts might also wish to pay a visit to the office of In Terra Corsa, next to the village train station, which manages (and rents equipment for) the nearby **Via Ferrata** in the Asco Valley, and can also kit you out for kayaking trips on the rivers in this area.

The best-value place to stay hereabouts is the *Cabanella*, a down-to-earth **chambre d'hôte** just beyond the turning for Moltifao, 7km from the junction with the N197 (☎04 95 47 83 29; ➌). Breakfast is included in their good-value rates; count on an additional €15 for an evening meal of traditional home cooking (book in advance). Close by and run by the same family, the *Camping A Tizarella* (☎04 95 47 83 92; April–Oct) is a well-equipped, two-star site with plenty of shade and a pizzeria; it's easy to spot – look for the giant painted wooden flowers at the roadside.

A right turn along the D247 here will take you up the hillside to **MOLTIFAO**, an amphitheatre of old stone buildings set on a spur above the Asco Valley. Moltifao's church houses a beautiful sixteenth-century triptych and some sacristy furniture, including a wooden retable incorporating a fine primitive painting of the Virgin on a gold background.

Presiding over the pass above is the ruined **Couvent de Caccia**, a former Franciscan monastery built in the late Gothic style. Partially derelict, it nowadays serves as a cemetery for the nearby villages; the crucifixes, marble tombs, candles and flowers create an extraordinary atmosphere amid the exposed brickwork and lofty Gothic arches. Some of the tombstones outside the building bear the name "Stuart", which historians believe may have been brought to the area by Scottish mercenaries during the Wars of Independence. An ideal picnic spot from which to view the spectacular Mori massif, on the opposite side of the valley, is the grassy ledge below the ruin, reached by hopping through a gap in the fence where the road bends sharply towards the pass.

Via Ferrata, literally "Iron Way", is like rock climbing without the risk. Originally devised by the Italian army in the 1914–1918 war with Austria as a means to penetrate the least accessible cliffs and mountain summits lining the Dolomite frontier, it employs stanchion cables, ramps, fixed ladders and cemented rungs to ease movement over vertical surfaces, with climbers clipped onto steel ropes to ensure they won't fall. The result is that anyone with a head for heights can experience the kind of thrilling exposure normally the preserve of confirmed rock climbers.

In 1998, an entrepreneurial team of Corsican outdoor instructors installed a new route in the Asco Valley. Extending 350m (with a total elevation of 200m), **la via ferrata di a manicella**, 14km west of Ponte Leccia, is classed D+ according to the French scale, which means that only experienced enthusiasts can tackle it unaccompanied. However, In Terra Corsa, from their office next to Ponte Leccia station (℡04 95 47 69 48, ⍟www.interracorsa.fr), provides fully qualified guides to lead you through the succession of high rock ledges and weird *tafoni* formations. Under instruction, complete novices can follow the route in around 2hr 30min, rounding off the adventure with a celebratory dip in the natural pools of the Asco river afterwards.

For those wishing to work into the sport more gradually, In Terra Corsa also manages a much easier beginners' route, the **la via ferrata di a scaletta** (400 metres long, with an altitude gain of 200m).

Access to both sites is strictly controlled. Only people with the necessary equipment are allowed on them, and first-timers have to be accompanied by In Terra instructors. You can rent all the necessary **gear** (gloves, helmet, harness, caribiners, lanyards and dynamic ropes to break falls) from the company in Ponte Leccia for €11; **admission charges** are €5 per half day and €10 for a full day, which includes the cost of an instructor.

For more on the Asco routes, which are open year round, go to In Terra Corsa's website or the site of the French Via Ferrata society, where you'll find a review and description of the "a scaletta" at ⍟http://viaferrata.org/france/c3f27mani.htm.

Asco village and around

The valley proper begins at the **Gorges de l'Asco**, where overhanging rock faces of orange granite soar to 900m. There isn't much to **ASCO** itself, an austere little place 22km west of Ponte Leccia, famed in the eighteenth century as home of the *paceri* (peacemakers), a tribunal of locally elected magistrates who mediated between families involved in vendettas. Its location, however, couldn't be better: built up the left bank of the river, the village lies at the base of a grandiose crest of mountains, with the crags of Monte Padro immediately to the northwest and the Monte Cinto massif and Capo Bianco to the southwest. You can stay here at the welcoming *Ferme-Auberge d'Ambroise et Nicole Vesperini*, on the way into the village (℡04 95 47 83 53; May–Oct, half board €40 per head obligatory in July & August; ❸), which offers comfortable accommodation in small but cosy rooms, and excellent local cuisine in its **restaurant**, where a four-course meal will set you back around €23 (cards not accepted).

A wonderful – if well-known – **swimming spot** can be found on the riverbank below Asco, at the renovated fifteenth-century **Genoese bridge**, a listed historical monument; follow the narrow one-way road west through the village until you reach a potholed lane running sharply downhill. The water on either side of the humpbacked stone bridge is transparent green and fairly deep, but freezing cold even in midsummer. On its far side, an ancient, paved mule track strikes up the **Pinara Valley** towards the Col de Serra Piana – formerly the main line of communication with the Niolo Valley to the south. Twenty minutes into the walk, you find yourself deep in a wilderness of scrub and towering rock, with only semi-wild goats for company; press on for another couple of hours and you'll arrive at the disused **Bergeries de Cabane**, ancient shepherds' huts clinging to the foot of Capu Biancu (2562m), the notheastern-most summit of the Cinto massif and a prime spot for sighting mouflon.

Haut'Asco

Beyond Asco village, the D147 widens as it passes through the **Forêt de Carozzica**, a magnificent forest of maritime and Laricio pines, which extends up the valley walls as far as the 2000-metre contour. Hugging the river, the road passes clearings and pools ideal for a picnic and a swim, then becomes increasingly steep as it climbs to **HAUT'ASCO**, a ski station set amid acres of denuded meadows and lightning-stunted pines. Paid for largely by government grants, the unsightly chalet blocks and rusting ski lifts would be more tolerable if they were used regularly, but over the past few years there has been so little snow up here that the station has remained closed. During the summer, however, the place is popular with hikers, who come to tackle the ice-flecked crags of the Cinto massif, looming to the south, and it serves as a major reprovisioning stop for long-distance walkers following the **GR20**.

While you're here, keep your eyes peeled for a tiny bird scurrying up and down the trunks of the giant Laricio pines on the far side of the road from the *station*. Unique to the island, the Corsican nuthatch (*sitelle corse* in French) ranks among the rarest species of bird in Europe, with only an estimated 2000 breeding pairs left in the high pine forests of the Corsican interior. It was first "discovered" to be a separate species in 1883 by a British ornithologist, whence its Latin name, *Sitta whiteheadi*.

No-frills **accommodation** is available at the large and impersonal *Le Chalet* (☎04 95 47 81 08, ℱ04 95 30 25 59; May–Sept; ❸), which, in addition to standard chalet-style rooms with balconies, offers budget gîte d'étape dorm beds (€24 half board). If you can ignore the dusty car park in front of it, the downstairs terrace, where GR20 hikers nurse their aches and blisters, offers an inspiring view of Monte Cinto's forbidding north face. Worth a look in the wood-lined bar behind is the collection of evocative old black-and-white photos showing the Asco Valley's turn-of-the-century explorers, among them **Félix Von Cube**, the Austrian doctor who pioneered the first ascent of Monte Cinto, and several other of the island's major peaks, between 1899 and 1904. The food served in the adjacent **restaurant** is nothing to write home about, unless you've just staggered in from the hills, in which case forget their €15 menu in favour of the *carte*, which includes *Le Chalet*'s famous steak and chips.

Still more basic dormitory accommodation is offered at the PNRC **refuge**, behind the hotel, which also has a well-equipped kitchen and communal dining hall centred on a huge wooden table. Campers and bivouackers pitch amid the scant shelter of the pines and juniper bushes outside. A couple of kilometres back along the valley, the two-star *Monte Cintu* campsite (☎04 95 47 85 88; May–Oct) is a more popular option with drivers, offering more comfort on fairly level pitches under the pine trees, plus clean toilet blocks and electricity hook-ups.

The road up the Asco Valley takes you right into the heart of the mountains, and the ski station is a popular springboard for some exceptional high-altitude hiking, most notably the ascent of Monte Cinto. Nearly all of the trails in the area are well frequented and marked every 10m or so with paint splashes, but you should be prepared for sudden and dramatic changes of weather, particularly in August, when electric storms rip across the ridges most afternoons. IGN **topo-map #4250** is also essential, although you could get by with the Parc Naturel Régional's topo-guide of the GR20, which passes within a stone's throw of the roadhead.

Monte Cinto

A line of broken crags marking the high point of the crest dividing the Niolo and Asco basins, **Monte Cinto** (2706m) is the loftiest, if not the most handsome, mountain in Corsica, and as such attracts greater numbers of hikers than any other peak on the island. Even so, it's a long hard slog to the summit, and you need to be in good shape to complete the ascent in a day. The route from Haut'Asco, winding up the massif's wilder north face, is more varied and dramatic than the approach from the south (via the Niolo Valley), and is a much better option except in May and early June, when patches of eternal snow clinging to sheltered crevices can be treacherous. A spray-painted rock and regular red spots indicate the way from the ski station car park, from where the trail crosses the Stranciacone torrent, hugging the true right bank before peeling left into the Cirque de Trimbolaccio. Once across the little footbridge, the ascent steepens as the waymarks zigzag up the side of a spectacular ravine via a flank of steep, slabby rock. Once you've reached a spur at 2100m, look across the gorge to the "Leaning Tower", one of the Cinto Massif's most famous formations. From here, a sustained climb across a long scree field brings you to a saddle known as **Bocca Borba** (2207m), where there's a walled shelter under a prominent boulder. At this point, the path fragments into numerous trails which all lead southwest across the névé-encrusted cwm below the summit. Having skirted the semi-frozen **Lac d'Argentu**, you then press up a dramatic, steepening moraine to a ridgetop revealing for the first time superb views south over the Niolo Valley and west coast. However, another 45 minutes of stiff walking still lies ahead as the route drops down the far side of the ridge and then bends left (east), eventually cutting into a final steep climb to the summit across open boulders.

Allow at least **seven hours** for the trip to the top and back (4hr 30min of ascent and 2hr 30min of descent); and bear in mind the advice on mountain safety in Chapter 8 (see p.367). The weather on Monte Cinto can be treacherous at any time of year: a few years back, seven hikers died on the mountain in a freak snow storm in July, one of them only a few hundred metres from the ski station at Haut'Asco. Always check the latest weather report before you set off (see p.367) and carry enough warm, waterproof clothing to see you through a sudden deterioration.

Punta Muvrella

After Cinto, the most popular option for a day-hike is the strenuous ascent of **Punta Muvrella** (2148m), reached after a climb up a rocky ravine running west from the ski station (2hr 30min). The route follows that of the GR20 and is thus impeccably well waymarked with red-and-white flashes of paint as far as the pass, **Bocca a i Stagni** (2010m). From here you have to follow a straightforward cairned route leading to the right (northeast) up the ridgeline to the summit of the mountain, which offers unrivalled views of the Cinto massif's spectacular north face and, in the opposite direction, distant Calvi. In clear weather it's even possible to see the southern Alps rising from the French and Italian rivieras.

CENTRAL CORSICA | The Vallée de l'Asco

7

The Niolo

The Niolo – homeland of Corsican freedom, inviolable citadel from which the island's invaders have never been able to expel its mountain folk. This wild trench is unimaginably beautiful. Not a blade of grass, nor a plant; granite . . . nothing but granite.

Guy de Maupassant, *Un Bandit Corse* (1892)

The **Niolo** is the glacial basin of the upper reaches of the **Golo**, a river that rises on the flank of Paglia Orba and expires to the south of Bastia, 80km from its source. The region's name – a corruption of the Corsican *niolu*, meaning "sombre" or "afflicted" – is now more appropriate than ever, for fire has destroyed much of its forested land, leaving bleak landscapes of granite and shrivelled vegetation dotted with legalithic remains and weird boulders. Conifers and chestnut trees scatter the lower slopes of Monte Cinto, but of the great dark forest that once blanketed the whole basin all that remains is the **Forêt de Valdo–Niolo**, a swath of Laricio pines blackened by huge patches of fire damage.

Les polyphonies corses

A mode of entertainment and religious expression for centuries, *u cantu* – **polyphonic singing** – performed several important functions in traditional society. As recently as the 1960s village streets would still occasionally resound to the wild, searing incantation of the **voceru**, an improvised dirge sung by a woman in mourning for a loved one. In the more distant past, when the death of a son or husband often stemmed from a vendetta, its verses would register not only the pain of bereavement but also the urgency of revenge, aimed at spurring the surviving men to retribution.

Death and separation were also the taproots of **a paghjella**, the most distinctive kind of Corsican polyphony and the one which perhaps best reflects the wildness of the island's interior landscape and ways of life. Traditionally the preserve of shepherd communities of remote valleys such as the Niolo and Bozio, in it purest form *a paghjella* is performed by three male voices – the first (*a prima*) sets the pace for the chant, the second (*u boldu*) provides the base sound, while the third (*a terza*) sings the mesmerizing melody, heavily ornamented with improvised embellishments. Standing close together in a tight semicircle, with eyes closed and hands cupped over ears, the singers aim to create a single body of sound that transcends the sum total of its parts. Mass used to be sung this way in the island's ancient Romanesque chapels, but today you're more likely to hear *a paghjella* at staged concerts and festivals.

A third type of singing, known as **chiami e rispondi** ("questions and answers"), is the polyphonic form most closely associated with the Niolo Valley's famous religious celebration, **Santa di u Niolu**. It takes the form of a competition in which two male contestants have to improvise a dialogue in strictly rhyming verse to a repetitive air. They may sing about anything, but it's popular to aim abuse at the assembled company or else declaim about political issues. The one who first runs out of answers in this battle of wits is the loser.

During the twentieth century, the drift of rural populations into the towns and to the French mainland nearly killed off polyphony, but the form enjoyed a dramatic revival during the nationalist renaissance of the 1970s, when young singers such as **Jean-Paul Poletti** and **Petru Guelfucci** made a name for themselves performing patriotic songs at political rallies. Since then, several have formed groups to spread the nationalist message, mixing modern guitar, keyboard and percussion sounds with traditional harmonies. The most commercially successful of these has been the band **I Muvrini**, who these days play to packed houses in Paris as well as Bastia

The forest extends east of the frequently snowbound Col de Verghio, the highest motorable mountain pass in Corsica and one of two routes into the Niolo. The other one is the rocky corridor known as the **Scala di Santa Regina**, a vertiginous ravine some 21km long and 300m high, through which a road was built in the late nineteenth century. Until then, people had used hazardous goat and mule tracks (the *scala*) to get into this region, whose isolation and consequent inbreeding perpetuated the singularly tall, blond and blue-eyed appearance of the Neolithic tribes known as the Corsi, from whom the Niolins claim direct descent.

The Niolins have always made their living from the breeding of goats. Shepherds formerly lived a solitary, harsh existence, trekking over the mountains with their herds to the milder coastal plains for winter – mainly to Galéria on the west coast, but sometimes as far as Cap Corse – and returning to the high ground with their flocks in summertime. Some of the old, bare stone dwellings still litter the higher hillsides, but are mostly abandoned these days. The Niolo's craft industry has all but disappeared, too, though the production of local gastronomic specialities survives: a sharp goat's cheese and some renowned char-

and Ajaccio. Another name to look out for is **Les Nouvelles Polyphonies Corses**, a five-piece mixed-gender group of young singers who've collaborated with musicians from other parts of the world to forge a radically new, ambient reworking of traditional Corsican choral singing. Composed by Jean-Paul Poletti and produced by synth supremo Hector Zazou (of Voix Bulgares fame), their first album *Les Nouvelles Polyphonies Corse I* was an international World Music bestseller, while their second offering, *Paradisu*, a collection of sacred music produced by ex-Velvet Underground violinist John Cale, with Patti Smith, has also been highly acclaimed. The subject of a separate feature on p.263, Jean-Paul Poletti's latest group, **Le Choeur d'Hommes de Sartène** (Audvis), have chosen to break new ground by returning to the more traditional Christian context of choral music. The ensemble that has achieved the widest success internationally, however, has been **A Filetta**, the etherel singing and inspired arrangements of whose leader, Ghjuvan-Claudiu Acquaviva, can be heard on several major film soundtracks (among them *Himalaya*, about transhumant life in the Dolpo region of Nepal).

During the summer months, posters and banners advertise **gigs** by well-known nationalist-oriented bands – such as **Chjami Aghalesi** and **Canta u Populu Corsu** – at towns and resorts all over the island, and these are well worth attending. Rooting out pure, traditional polyphony singing, however, can be more difficult. One occasion you're sure to encounter the *crème de la crème* of Corsican singers is the annual four-day **Rencontres de Chants Polyphoniques**, held in Calvi in mid-September. Co-host of this event are A Filetta, who also perform each year in a highly charged re-enactment of the Crucifixion to celebrate Holy Week (see the festival calendar, p.46). Regular recitals also take place at La Casa Musicale in **Pigna**, Balagne (see p.143), while during the **Santa di u Niolu** festival Casamaccioli's village bar bursts at the seams with exponents of the rarely performed *chiami e rispondi*.

Failing that, splash out on a **cassette** or **CD**. Recommended titles include the ubiquitous *Voce di Corsica: Polyphonies* (Olivi Music/Sony), which features the island's six greatest living male voices performing a set of Corsican standards in a church in Bonifacio; *Per Agata* by the all-women ensemble Donasulana (Silex/Auvidis), whose renditions of old *voceri* and *lamenti* are sublime; and any recent recording by A Filetta, especially *Intantu* – an album of spine-tingling brilliance that covers the full spectrum from traditional *a paghjella* to recent ambient composition.

△ Citadelle, Corte

cuterie, which cures particularly well at this altitude. Ancient traditions, however, have an extra vitality in the Niolo, and some of the finest polyphony singing can be heard here (see box on p.330). In addition, improvised *chiami e rispondi* competitions are still held at Casamaccioli during the three-day **Santa di u Niolu**, a country fair that takes place around September 8.

These days tourism is making itself felt at the far-flung capital of the Niolo, **Calacuccia**, an exposed little place whose limited accommodation makes it the most promising base from which to explore the area. Apart from a trip to **Casamaccioli**, you could pause for a definitive Niolin meal at **Albertacce**, climb the southeast side of **Monte Cinto** or hike up the southern flank of the valley to Corsica's most exquisite altitude lake, **Lac de Nino**. To the north, the distinctive shark's fin summit of **Paglia Orba** offers perhaps the most compelling of all mountain ascents on the island, the springboard for which is a tiny mountain refuge at the head of the magnificent Golo Valley, a paradise of translucent pools and Laricio pine forest.

Calacuccia and around

CALACUCCIA, *chef lieu* of the Niolo region, benefits from its unusual location high on a south-facing slope at the heart of the valley's head. Looming behind, the Cinto massif forms a neck-craning backdrop, while below stretches the Lac de Calacuccia, a large reservoir built in 1968 to supply Bastia and the eastern plain. Bathing and sailing on the lake are forbidden, and locals insist the water has caused undesirable climatic changes in the valley – notably an increase in mist and humidity – but its rippled surface, shimmering with reflections of the surrounding peaks, is an undeniably beautiful sight.

Most visitors come to Calacuccia en route between Porto and Corte, pausing to sample its famous charcuterie and ewe's cheese before embarking on the long drive down the Scala di Santa Regina. But the village makes a good base for **walks**, not least the ascent of Monte Cinto and the coast-to-coast **Mare a Mare Nord**, which winds through on its way to the Col de l'Arinella and Tavignano gorge over the ridge to the south.

Aside from a scattering of inaccessible menhirs, the most notable historic monument here is the white-painted **Église de St–Pierre**, at the western exit of the village near the petrol station; inside, a seventeenth-century wooden statue of Christ forms the principal attraction. A kilometre further west on the main road, the **Couvent St–François–di–Niolu** is infamous as the scene of the **1774 Massacre**, when eleven local men (one of them only 15 years old) were crushed on cart wheels and hanged for their part in a rebellion against the French. The event is commemorated by a recently inaugurated memorial, while the anniversary of the atrocity, June 25, is marked by a small gathering with polyphony singing and speeches. Just how resonant a symbol the massacre remains for the island's nationalists is potently conveyed by a *paghjella* on the 2001 album *Intantu* by the group A Filetta, which begins with the lines: "If you ever travel through the Niolo, you'll see a convent/Tears still surround it, which time has never managed to efface". St-François-di-Niolu nowadays houses a gîte d'étape (see below).

Calacuccia practicalities

Calacuccia is served by daily **buses**, leaving Bastia at 4pm and arriving in Calacuccia at 6.30pm. From July until mid-September, an additional service runs between Corte and Porto via Calacuccia and Col de Verghio. Timetables are available at the village **tourist office**, 200m east of the centre on the Corte road, adjacent to the fire station (mid-June to Sept Mon–Fri 8am–noon & 2–7pm, Sat 8am–noon; ☎04 95 48 05 22).

The Parc Naturel Régional recently inaugurated an extensive network of marked footpaths in the Niolo, but by far the most popular mountain hike in the area remains the ascent of **Monte Cinto** (2706m), Corsica's highest mountain, via its southeast face. Although not nearly as dramatic as the approach from the Asco Valley (see p.329), this route, boulder-strewn for much of its length, ranks among the island's most frequented trails between mid-June, when the snow melts, and mid-October, when it returns with a vengeance on the high ridges.

To drive as close to the mountain as possible, take the D218 north out of Calacuccia, then turn right along a rough track at the hairpin bend just beyond the hamlet of **Lozzi**, some 6km along. A short way above the village lie two good campsites (reviewed on p.335), from where a motorable dirt track winds via another series of sharp switchbacks to a small car park – the de facto trailhead. Another 35 minutes on foot will bring you to the **refuge de l'Ercu** (1600m), which is open all year but staffed only between July and mid-September. If you're hiking all the way from Lozzi, allow around three hours to reach the refuge. This is where the ascent proper starts, and you should aim to be here shortly after dawn, particularly during the summer, when electric storms and rain frequently force hikers off the mountain by mid-afternoon. The climb to the summit takes between three and four hours, depending on how fit you are, and the views are sublime, taking in both coasts, the Tuscan islands and, even on very clear days, the Côte d'Azur and Alps.

For the best views of the Cinto massif itself, however, you have to scale the opposite, southern, side of the Niolo Valley. A broken mule track beginning at the Calacuccia dam cuts up the mountainside to the **Col de l'Arinella** (1592m), a pass separating the Golo and Tavignano valleys, from which there's a magnificent vista of the valley. To pick up the trail – a section of the **Mare a Mare Nord** long-distance footpath – cross the dam and follow the waymarks as they cut uphill across the switchbacks on an unsurfaced *piste*. Allow two hours for the climb to the col from the dam. Descend via the same route back to Calacuccia, or continue down the other side for an hour to the **refuge de la Sega**, where you can camp or bunk down in a swish new steel-and-wood chalet by the side of the stream. From here, the trail follows the Genoese paved mule path down the Tavignano all the way to Corte, reached in around four hours from the refuge.

If you feel more like a leisurely **low-altitude walk** than a full-on mountain hike, call in at the Calacuccia tourist office for a free copy of the Parc Naturel Régional's excellent *Balades en Corse: Niolu* leaflet (*dépliant*), which outlines five routes (of between 3hr 30min and 7hr) on a monochrome topo-map. Some, like the "Tour des Cinque Frati", involve stiff ascents, but most are leisurely ambles taking in some of the many prehistoric sites littering the valley floor.

Whichever route you choose, bear in mind the advice regarding mountain safety and equipment in Chapter 8.

Calacuccia has three **hotels,** the most comfortable of which is *L'Acqua Viva*, next to the petrol station as you leave the village on the road to Col de Verghio (☎04 95 48 06 90 or 04 95 48 00 08, Ⓕ04 95 48 08 82; ❹); its dozen rooms are well appointed, with en-suite bathrooms and balconies – the ones to the rear of the building have the best views (and escape the petrol fumes). Down in the centre of the village, the *Hôtel des Touristes* (☎04 95 48 00 04; May–Oct; ❸), a large, grey, granite building by the roadside, is a more old-fashioned affair that's little changed since the 1930s and remains popular mainly with hikers. In addition to standard hotel rooms (with or without attached toilets), they offer budget gîte d'étape accommodation in an adjacent annexe for €13 per head. Finally, just over a kilometre west on the

Albertacce road, the *Auberge Casa Balduina* (℡04 95 48 08 57, Ⓔjeannequilichini@aol.com; obligatory half board ❼), opposite the convent, has recently been upgraded to a smart two-star. The *patronne*, who speaks good English, has a fine table of local specialities (open to residents only), offering *charcuterie maison*, a famous white beans and ham soup, free-range veal steak with olives and chestnut *fiadone*.

A more atmospheric place to bunk down if you're walking lies a kilometre west of the village at the *Couvent St-François-di-Niolu* (℡04 95 48 00 11; open year round) – site of a famous massacre (see above) – which has large, well-fitted dorms and a refectory that's fully equipped for self caterers. The only catch is they don't offer evening meals, for which you'll have to plod back into Calacuccia or over to the *Auberge du Lac* at Sidossi on the lakeside (see below).

The two best **campsites** in the area – *Camping U Monte Cintu* (℡04 95 48 04 45; mid-May to Sept) and *L'Arimone* (℡04 95 48 05 51; mid-May to Sept) – lie next door to each other on a superbly situated natural balcony overlooking the valley, in the hamlet of Lozzi, 4km west on the D218. The latter also has a handful of inexpensive rooms (❷), and a basic pizzeria. Situated within easy reach of the trailhead for the ascent of Monte Cinto, both are well placed for early departures.

To sample the best of the valley's renowned cuisine, head 2km west of the village along the road that skirts the lakeside to the *Auberge du Lac* (℡04 95 48 02 73), in the hamlet of **Sidossi**, whose huge, luminous dining hall enjoys a near-perfect location on the water's edge, and serves authentic Niolin cuisine at reasonable prices; set menus range from €16 to €25, with homemade charcuterie, free-range lamb, wild mushrooms and local cheeses featuring prominently.

Albertacce and around

The row of low granite cottages comprising **ALBERTACCE**, 3km west of Calacuccia, makes an interesting contrast with the fortress houses found throughout the rest of the island – people hereabouts thought the mountains were protection enough against uninvited guests. For walkers, the village's modest **gîte d'étape** (℡04 95 48 05 60 or 04 95 48 08 05; €11 per head), on the side of the main road on the eastern edge of the settlement, provides adequate dorm beds and self-catering facilities, though you'd do better to eat at the wonderful *Restaurant U Cintu* (*"Chez Jo Jo"*; ℡04 95 48 06 87; May–Oct, and out of season with a couple of hours' warning), a short walk west. In a small family dining room, complete with TV in the corner, you can enjoy definitive Niolo home cooking – *charcuterie maison*, *ravioli-brocciu*, locally reared lamb in a rich stew, chestnut flan, cheese from a nearby *bergerie*, and eau de vie – on a superb-value €20 menu; they also do a simpler €13 menu, with only three courses (including the *plat de résistance* of the day). The atmosphere is informal and the couple who run the restaurant are hugely hospitable and deservedly proud of their regional cuisine.

A pleasant **short walk** leads west of Albertacce via the **Mare a Mare Nord**, which begins directly opposite the large roadside crucifix on the edge of the village, to the locals' favourite **picnic spot**. Follow the orange-waymarked path for twenty minutes or so and you'll round the hillside to reach the **Pont de Muriccioli**, where a small chapel and restored water mill overlook a particularly beautiful stretch of river (the Rau de Viru). You can swim in a series of deep natural pools and enjoy the dramatic spectacle of Paglia Orba's rugged summit rising at the head of the valley to the northwest.

Two of the best hikes in Central Corsica begin southwest of Calacuccia, at the head of the Niolo Valley. Crossed by the D84 on its way to Col de Verghio, this area is covered by the extensive **Forêt de Valdo-Niolo**, which comprises some of the island's finest Laricio pines, some of them more than 500 years old and 40m tall.

The classic trail hereabouts leads from the maison forestière at Poppaghia, 10km southwest of Calacuccia, to **Lac de Nino**, an exquisite high-altitude lake reached after a strenuous three-hour climb from the road. The path is well waymarked and frequented, but it's a good idea to get hold of the IGN topo-map 25, #4251 OT (ref A4/B4). The trail, marked with yellow splashes of paint, follows a mountain stream up to the **bergeries de Colga**, a gathering of stone shacks just above the tree line (1411m), then on – more steeply through a boulder-strewn landscape dotted with stunted elms – up to the **Col de Stazzona** (1762m), between Monte Tozzu (2007m) and Punta Artica (2327m). At the top of the pass there's a weird scattering of black, pointed rocks known as the **Devil's Oxen** – the story goes that the Devil was challenged by St Martin to plough a straight line and, upon failing, his oxen were turned to stone. The Devil hurled his ploughshare in a rage through the distinctively shaped red peak known as **Capu Tafonatu** ("Pierced Mountain"), the vast *tafonu* visible on the opposite side of the valley. It's only fifteen minutes further to the lake, which from June to September is home to herds of wild horses and pigs; in autumn, with a dusting of snow on the peaks, the scenery is reminiscent of Tibetan plateau pastureland. The surrounding marshy turf declivities, known as *pozzi* (meaning "wells"), are the remnants of lakes gouged by glaciers, which subsequently filled up with sediment.

The other recommended hike in the forest is a much easier two-hour return trip to the **Cascades de Radule**, where the River Golo, which has its source high up on Paglia Orba, plunges through a series of waterfalls, forming perfect natural pools. Although it is marked with red-and-white splashes, it's worth taking the IGN topo-map 25, #4250 OT (ref C1/D1). The trail (one of the rare easy-going stretches of the GR20) starts at the hairpin bend in the D84 known as Fer à Cheval ("Horseshoe"), 4km below the Col de Verghio. After around thirty minutes you emerge from the pine trees at the **bergeries de Radule**, a collection of shepherds' huts from where the path descends to the river and falls. The GR20 proper continues north, winding up the stream valley, and is well worth following for another couple of hours as far as the **refuge Ciuttulu di i Mori** (1962m), the usual night halt for mountaineers attempting Paglia Orba (for a description of this ascent, see box opposite).

With a car, another worthwhile foray from Albertacce is the seven-kilometre drive up the D318 to **CALASIMA**, Corsica's highest village, which is as remote and dour as you'd expect for a settlement at 1100m. The views over the Niolo improve if you press on west below the Cinque Frati ("The Five Brothers"; 1986m) to the **Grotte des Anges**, a sacred cave 8km out of Calasima, the approach to which is via an unsurfaced forestry track. It's worth enduring the ruts and bumps as far as the first sharp switchback, from where a clearly marked footpath winds north into the spectacular **Ravin de Straciancone**. Follow this for about an hour from the road and you'll pass through some majestic Laricio pine forest before emerging at the **bergeries de Vallone**, a remote café serving wonderful homemade Niolo charcuterie, cheese and wholesome soups. The hut, re-provisioned each day by mule, serves as a stopover on the GR20 and makes an ideal target for a walk into this magnificent roadless area. For a fuller review, see p.377.

Casamaccioli

Occupying the greenest part of the Niolo, **CASAMACCIOLI**, 5km from Calacuccia, lies south of the lake on the edge of a large *châtaigneraie*. Its small square, edged by enormous chestnut trees, is the setting for the **Santa di u Niolu** (see p.330), Corsica's most important religious festival, when thousands of pilgrims and expatriate natives descend on the village to celebrate the Nativity of the Virgin. The focal point of the event is a statue of the Madonna, **Santa Maria della Stella**, which miraculously transported itself here by mule in the fifteenth century after the convent in which it originally resided was burned down by Turkish pirates. Now venerated for her miracle-working powers, she is carried in procession through the village, but the most visually striking feature of the festival is the famous **Granitola**, when dozens of white-robed and white-hooded penitents, drawn from the village's various religious brotherhoods, or *Cunfraterna*, wind and unwind in spirals around a cross (a similar procession takes place in Calvi; see p.126). La Santa has a strongly secular aspect, too. Formerly, the event, held at the end of the first week in September, provided the main opportunity of the year for Niolites from remote villages to buy, sell and barter; in exchange for wool, meat, milk, cheese and charcuterie, they would obtain hardware, hats, horse tack, woodcarving, textiles, shoes and anything else that could not be manufactured in the mountains. Gambling was also central, and remains so to this day, with serious round-the-clock card sessions held in unlicensed home casinos. Afterwards, the participants celebrate, or

7

The ascent of Paglia Orba

The great red wedge of **Paglia Orba** (2525m), rising like a giant dorsal fin beside the pierced peak of **Capu Tafonatu** (2343m), is the Corsican watershed's most distinctive mountain. Thanks to the dizzying drops into the Fangu Valley and Filosorma from its vast northwest face, it is also a more challenging proposition than nearby Cinto. In fine, dry weather you don't need ropes or any technical expertise to attempt the ascent, but a good head for heights is essential, as some sections are notoriously vertigo-inducing.

The traditional **approach** to the mountain via the **Cascades de Radule** at the head of the Golo Valley (described on p.336) is itself a wonderful walk, passing stands of old Laricio pines, deep bathing pools, and eventually, high Alpine-style pastureland where you can usually spot mouflon grazing on inaccessible ledges. However, you'd have to be a strong climber indeed to cover this, the ascent to the summit and descent back to the roadhead afterwards, in a single day. Instead, most people bivouac at the **refuge Ciuttulu di i Mori**, perched on a natural balcony at the head of the Golo, and set off for the top the following morning (thereby increasing the chances of clear skies and good views).

The **route** begins immediately behind the refuge, climbing steeply up a huge rock choke towards a ridge known as **Col de Maures**. A short way before the pass, cairns rising to your right (north) up a deep corridor indicate the way through a series of huge granite blocks. Once you've arrived at a large ledge after around twenty minutes, the route steepens, progressing through some tight chimneys as far as a false summit, the western edge of the giant Paglia Orba tabletop. From here you drop into a little hollow known as "La Combe de Chèvres", carpeted in deep névés during early summer, before tackling the final haul to the top. Because the sides of Paglia Orba fall away so steeply, the views from the summit are even more dramatic than from Monte Cinto, extending far out to sea and across the entire northwestern watershed. Allow a good three and a half hours for the ascent from the refuge, and don't attempt the route if the rock is wet.

drown their sorrows, in the village bar – one of the few places in Corsica where you can still hear traditional improvised singing, or *chiami e rispondi* (see box on p.330). Outside festival time, however, the only noteworthy sight here is the small **Église de la Nativité**, where you can pay your repects to the crudely repainted and gold-crowned Santa Maria della Stella herself, and enjoy magnificent views of the Cinto massif to the northwest.

In Casamaccioli's tiny **gîte d'étape** beside the church (☎04 95 48 03 47), dorm beds cost €11 per night. You can use their self-catering facilities or, if you book in advance, opt for an evening meal (€15).

Corte (Corti) and around

Stacked up the side of a wedge-shaped crag, against a spectacular backdrop of brooding granite mountains, **CORTE** (Corti) epitomizes the spirit of dogged defiance and patriotism is never far from the surface. This has been the home of Corsican nationalism since the first National Constitution was drawn up here in 1731, and was also where **Pascal Paoli**, "U Babbu di a Patria" ("Father of the Nation"), formed the island's first democratic government later in the eighteenth century. Self-consciously insular and grimly proud, it can seem an inhospitable place at times, although the presence of the island's only **university** lightens the atmosphere noticeably during term time, when the bars and cafés lining its long main street fill with students. For the outsider, Corte's charm is concentrated in the tranquil **haute ville**, where the forbidding **citadel** – home to the island's premier **museum**, the Museu di a Corsica – presides over a warren of narrow, cobbled streets. Immediately behind it, the Restonica and Tavignano gorges afford easy access to some of the region's most memorable mountain scenery, best enjoyed from the marked trails that wind through them.

A brief history of Corte

Corte's reputation for belligerent independence was born in the ninth century, when the occupiers of the strategic post allegedly saw off a group of Saracen raiders. Later on, the Genoese rulers were constantly harried by the local nobles, culminating in 1419 with the takeover by **Vincentello d'Istria**, the king of Aragon's viceroy. After Vincentello's execution in 1434, Genoa ruled relatively undisturbed until the French expedition of 1553, when Corte happily succumbed to Sampiero Corso, though within six years the Genoese were back in charge, and were to stay in control for a long time.

By the early eighteenth century, Corsican nationalism was on the rise in Corte, its success due in part to the town's isolation from the occupied coastal towns. Following a local insurrection in 1731, a National Constitution was drawn up here at the first National Assembly, and in 1752 Gaffori was elected head of state in Corte. After Gaffori's assassination in 1753, Pascal Paoli returned from exile and from 1755 to 1769 made Corte the seat of his revolutionary government, which set up the first Corsican printing press and the **Università di Corsica**, the first university to be established on the island.

However, in 1768, under the terms of the Treaty of Versailles, France bought Corsica from the Genoese, and after the Battle of Ponte Nuovu the following year the period of Corsican independence was at an end. Under the French the town became insignificant, and it's only recently that it has acquired a slightly more exalted status as *sous-préfecture* of Haute-Corse and as the seat of

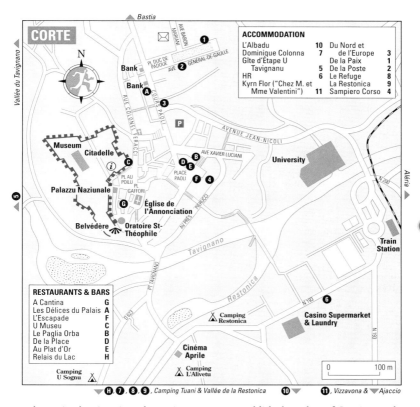

ACCOMMODATION

L'Albadu	**10**	Du Nord et	
Dominique Colonna	**7**	de l'Europe	**3**
Gîte d'Étape U		De la Paix	**1**
Tavignanu	**5**	De la Poste	**2**
HR	**6**	Le Refuge	**8**
Kyrn Flor ("Chez M. et		La Restonica	**9**
Mme Valentini")	**11**	Sampiero Corso	**4**

RESTAURANTS & BARS

A Cantina	**G**
Les Délices du Palais	**A**
L'Escapade	**F**
U Museu	**C**
Le Paglia Orba	**B**
De la Place	**D**
Au Plat d'Or	**E**
Relais du Lac	**H**

the revived university, whose aims are to re-establish the value of Corsican culture, partly through the compulsory teaching of the indigenous language.

Arrival and information

Buses from Ajaccio and Bastia stop in the centre of town on cours Paoli, the main street, and halfway along avenue Xavier-Luciani. The **train station** is at the foot of the hill near the university, from where it's a ten-minute uphill walk into town. If you're **driving**, the best place to aim for is the **free car park**, to the left at the top of avenue Jean-Nicoli, the road leading into town from Ajaccio and Aléria.

Corte's swish new **tourist office** is situated just inside the main gates of the citadel, near the museum (July & Aug daily 9am–8pm; June & Sept Mon–Sat 9am–1pm & 2–7pm; Jan–May Mon–Fri 9am–noon & 2–6pm, plus Sat in May; ℡04 95 46 26 70). In the same office you'll also find the desk of the Parc Naturel Régional Corse (same hours and telephone number), the best information bank in Corte for walkers.

Accommodation

Accommodation in Corte is plentiful and, with the exception of the smarter hotels hidden 2km southwest of town amid the lower reaches of the Restonica

Valley, costs a lot less than on the coast. One reason for this is the huge *Hôtel HR*, whose unbeatable rates pin down tariffs throughout the town at the lower end of the scale; the other is that the majority of visitors to the area come here equipped for the outdoors and prefer to **camp**.

The only time pressure for rooms exceeds supply tends to be during wet or stormy weather, when walkers descend in droves from the hills to escape the rain. In this case, ring around and if you still can't find a room, try *Le Torrent* in Santo-Pietro-di-Venaco (see p.348), which usually has vacancies.

Hotels

If you're travelling without a vehicle, bear in mind that most of the hotels and guesthouses situated out of town, including *L'Albadu* and those up the Restonica Valley (but not *Kyrn Flor*), will provide a complimentary pick-up from the station if you let them know the day before.

L'Albadu ancienne route d'Ajaccio, 2.5km south-west of town ☎ 04 95 46 24 55, ℉ 04 95 46 13 08. Simply furnished rooms with showers (shared toilets) on a working farm-cum-equestrian centre. Warm family atmosphere, beautiful horses, fine views and top Corsican speciality food, served *en famille* so you get to practise your French (at €38 per head, the half board is a bargain). Easily among the most congenial, and reasonably priced, *ferme-auberges* on the island. If you're driving, the easiest route is via the main Ajaccio road for 1500m, where a red-and-white sign points to the right (around the side of a building). Advance reservation essential. **②**

Dominique Colonna Vallée de la Restonica, 2km south of town ☎ 04 95 45 25 65, ℉ 04 95 61 03 91. The more modern of this pair of jointly owned luxury auberges, set amid pine woods next to the stream. With less character than its neighbour (see *La Restonica* below), but smart and efficient and with all the mod cons you'd expect of a three-star. Rates include use of the *Restonica*'s pool. Half board optional, even in high summer. Open mid-March to Oct. **⑥**

HR allée du 9-Septembre ☎ 04 95 45 11 11, ℉ 04 95 61 02 85. This converted concrete-block gendarmerie, 200m southwest of the SNCF train station, looks grim from the outside, but its 125 rooms are comfortable enough and its rates rock-bottom; bathroom-less options are the best deal. No credit cards. **②**

Kyrn Flor ("Chez M. et Mme Valentini") U San Gavinu, 3km south on the N193 ☎ 04 95 61 02 88. Friendly bed and breakfast with very pleasant en-suite rooms, a leafy garden and pool, although a little too close to the main road for comfort. Optional evening meals €23 (including wine); rooms from €24, with breakfast. **③**

Du Nord et de l'Europe 22 cours Paoli ☎ 04 95 46 00 33, ℉ 04 95 46 03 40, ⓦ www.hotel-dunord-corte.com. Pleasant, clean place right in

the centre. The variously priced rooms are basic but huge, and the building has oodles of charm, with a marble-floored entrance hall and high stucco ceilings. Reception in the *Café du Cours* next door. **②**

De la Paix 1 av Général-de-Gaulle ☎ 04 95 46 06 72, ℉ 04 95 46 23 84, ℮ socoget@wanadoo.fr. Large, smart and central, in an elegant part of town. Entirely refurbished in 1999, and now pitched primarily at tour groups. Their pricier rooms have large balconies and TVs. No credit cards. **④**

De la Poste 2 place du Duc-de-Padoue ☎ 04 95 46 01 37. The cheapest rooms in the centre (from €30 for WC *à l'étage*), in a huge old building that opens onto a quiet square just off the main drag. Comfortable enough, but on the gloomy side. **②** .

Le Refuge Vallée de la Restonica, 2.5km south-west of town ☎ 04 95 46 09 13, ℉ 04 95 46 22 38, ⓦ www.lerefuge.fr. Cosy, unpretentious hotel-restaurant at the roadside, with rooms overlooking the stream (the ones at the back are a touch noisy in spring, when the snowmelt raises the water level, but fine in summer), and a sunny terrace. April–Oct, half board obligatory (€115 for two). **④**

La Restonica Vallée de la Restonica, 2km south-west from town ☎ 04 95 45 25 25, ℉ 04 95 61 15 79. Sumptuous comfort in a wood-lined riverside hotel set up by a former French-national footballer, Dominique Colonna, who bought it after winning the lottery. Hunting trophies, old paintings, salon with open fireplace and leather upholstered furniture create an old-fashioned atmosphere, and there's a large pool and garden terrace. Half board obligatory in season (€125 for two). **⑤**

Sampiero Corso 1 av Président-Pierucci ☎ 04 95 46 09 76, ℉ 04 95 46 00 08. Good-value 1960s-style modern block, with spectacular views from the balconies. Breakfast included in the tariff. Inexpensive for a two-star. April–Sept. **③**

Gîtes d'étape and campsites

L'Albadu 2.5km southwest of town ☎ 04 95 46 24 55. Perfect little *camping à la ferme*, situated on a hillside above Corte. Basic, but much nicer than any of the town sites, and well worth the walk up here (the owners will show you a short cut that'll get you to the centre in 15min). For directions by road, see *Albadu*'s listing under "Hotels" above.

L'Alivetu faubourg St-Antoine ☎ 04 95 46 11 09. One of two sites definitely to avoid (the other is the *Batho* behind the citadel): crowded, noisy and with dirty toilet blocks.

Gîte d'Étape U Tavignanu ("Chez M. Gambini") Behind the citadel ☎ 04 95 46 16 85. Run-of-the-mill hikers' hostel with small dorms and a relaxing garden terrace that looks over the valley. Peaceful, secluded, and the cheapest place to stay after the campsites. Follow the signs for the Tavignano trail (marked with orange spots of paint) around the back of the citadel. €14 per bed (includes breakfast).

Restonica 500m south of the town centre. Middle-sized site on the riverside, close to town, with low terraces, plenty of shade and its own café-bar.

U Sognu route de la Restonica ☎ 04 95 46 09 07. At the foot of the valley, a 15min walk from the centre. Has a good view of the citadel, plenty of poplar trees for shade, and toilets in a converted barn. There's also a small bar (in summer) and a small restaurant (pizzas *au feu de bois* June–Sept).

U Tavignanu chemin de Balini, Vallée du Tavignano ☎ 04 95 46 16 85. The hiker's option: a tiny campsite next to the gîte d'étape of the same name (see above), accessible only on foot. Follow the road around the back of the citadel, cross over the river bridge and bear right; the site lies another 10min walk up a path.

Tuani 7km southeast, Vallée de la Restonica ☎ 04 95 46 11 62. Too far up the valley without your own car, but the wildest and most atmospheric of the campsites around Corte, overlooking a rushing stream, deep in the woods. Ideally placed for an early start on Monte Rotondo. Basic facilities, although they do have a cheerful little café serving good *bruschetta* and other hot snacks.

The Town

Corte has a very compact centre effectively consisting of one long street – **cours Paoli**. Lined with shops, banks, restaurants and cafés, this busy thoroughfare runs alongside the **haute ville**, which is reached by climbing one of the cobbled ramps on the west side of the cours, or by taking the steep rue Scoliscia from place Paoli.

At the north end of the *cours* lies **place du Duc-de-Padoue**, an elegant square of nineteenth-century buildings that's strangely out of place in this rough mountain town. Its statue, a grim bronze lump by Bartholdi, designer of the Statue of Liberty, is of Arrighi di Casanova, a general whose service under Napoléon earned him the title of duke of Padua; his ancestral home can be seen in **place Poilu** in the *haute ville*. Apart from this square, there is only one spot where you might want to hang around: **place Paoli**, at the southern end of the main street in the lower town and a more tourist-friendly zone lined with relaxing cafés and restaurants. Its centrepiece is a cumbersome statue of a rather self-satisfied-looking Pascal Paoli.

Place Gaffori

Place Gaffori, the hub of the old **haute ville**, is dominated by a statue of General Gian'Pietru Gaffori pointing vigorously towards the church. On its base a bas-relief depicts the siege of the Gaffori house by the Genoese, who attacked in 1750 when the general was out of town and his wife Faustina was left holding the fort. Faced with weakening colleagues, she is said to have brandished a burning torch over a barrel of gunpowder, threatening to blow herself and her soldiers to smithereens if they surrendered, a threat that toughened them up until Gaffori came along with reinforcements. The house stands right behind, and you can clearly make out the bullet marks made by the besiegers.

Opposite the house, the **Église de l'Annonciation**, built in 1450 but restored in the seventeenth century, is where Joseph Bonaparte, Napoléon's brother and future king of Spain, was christened. Inside, there's a delicately carved **pulpit** and a wax statue of St Theophilus, patron of the town, on his deathbed. The saint's birthplace – behind the church in place Théophile – is marked by the **Oratoire St-Théophile**, a large arcaded building which commands a magnificent view across the gorges of Tavignano and Restonica. Born in 1676, Blaise de Signori took the name of Theophilus upon entering the Franciscan brotherhood, and went on to study in Rome and Naples, then to found numerous hermitages in Italy. In 1730 he returned to Corsica, where, after a few years' activity in the fight for independence, he died on May 9, 1740. He was canonized in 1930, the only Corsican to achieve sainthood, and on the anniversary of his death a commemorative Mass takes place in the oratory, followed by a procession from the Chapelle Ste-Croix, carrying a huge figure of Christ.

For the best view of the citadel, follow the signs uphill from place Gaffori to the viewing platform, aptly named the **Belvédère**, which faces the medieval tower, suspended high above the town on its pinnacle of rock and dwarfed by the immense crags behind. From here you can also admire the vista of the converging rivers and encircling forest – a summer bar adds to the attraction.

Just above place Gaffori, left of the gateway to the citadel, stands the **Palazzu Naziunale**, a great, solid block of a mansion that's the sole example of Genoese civic architecture in Corte. Having served as the seat of Paoli's government for a while, it became the **Università di Corsica** in 1765. Run by Franciscan monks, the island's first university offered free education to all (Napoléon's father studied here), and the monks taught the contemporary social thought of philosophers such as Rousseau and Montesquieu as well as traditional subjects such as theology, mathematics and law. The university closed in 1769, when the French took over the island after the Treaty of Versailles, not to be resurrected until 1981. Today several modern buildings have been added and it houses the Institut Universitaire d'Études Corses, dedicated to the study of Corsican history and culture.

The Citadelle and Museu di a Corsica

The monumental gateway just behind the Palazzu Naziunale leads from place Poilu into Corte's Genoese Citadelle, whose lower courtyard is dominated by the modern buildings of the **Museu di a Corsica** (June 20–Sept 19 daily 10am–8pm; April–June 19 & Sept 20–Oct daily except Tues 10am–6pm; Nov–March Tues–Sat 10am–6pm; €5.30). This state-of-the-art museum, designed by Turin architect Andréa Bruno, was inaugurated in 1997 to house the collection of ethnographer **Révérend Père Louis Doazan**, a Catholic priest who spent 27 years amassing a vast array of objects relating to the island's traditional transhumant and peasant past. Gifted to the state in 1972, the three thousand pieces he collected remained in storage for nearly a quarter of a century until a suitable site could be found to exhibit them. With its huge tinted windows and sweeping views, the building certainly makes the most of the location, but ultimately upstages the somewhat lacklustre exhibits inside it. On the first floor, old farm implements and peasant dress are the mainstay of the **Louis Doazan Gallery**, while the adjacent **Musée en train de se faire** (Museum in the Making) gallery explores aspects of contemporary Corsican society, including industry, tourism and religious brotherhoods. In addition, a couple of rooms at the head of the main staircase house themed temporary exhibitions of Corsica-related art and photography. If the amount of money lavished on the museum seems out of all proportion to its contents, bear in mind the importance of its symbolic value, at a time when the island as a whole is earnestly seeking to define what constitutes "Corsican culture". This may go some way to explaining the conspicuous absence of references to less palatable facets of the island's identity, such as vendetta and banditry.

The entry ticket to the museum also includes admission to the adjacent **Citadelle**. The only such fortress in the interior of the island, it was founded in the fifteenth century and served as a military base for the Foreign Legion from 1962 until 1984. Reached by a huge staircase of Restonica marble, a medieval tower known as the **Nid d'Aigle** (Eagle's Nest) forms its highest point. The tower is the only original part of a complex built by Vincentello d'Istria in 1420; the barracks (*caserne*) were added during the reign of Louis-Philippe. These were later converted into a prison, in use as recently as World War II, when the Italian occupiers incarcerated Corsican resistance fighters in the tiny cells. Adjacent to these is the **échauguette**, a former watchtower which, at the time of Paoli's government, was inhabited by the hangman. This was a job no Corsican would take – accustomed to killing with guns and knives, they found the practice of hanging someone to death too demeaning and dishonourable. A Sicilian duly volunteered, and in 1766 James Boswell visited the poor reprobate: "a more dirty rueful spectacle I never beheld", he wrote of the wretched specimen he found cowering in the turret, with a "miserable bed and a little bit of fire" as his only comfort.

Eating and drinking

Corte has only a handful of restaurants worthy of note, plus the usual pizzerias and crêperies. As a rule of thumb, avoid anywhere fronted by gaudy food photographs and multilingual menus; their dishes may be cheap, but they offer poor value for money – for a few euros more, you'll eat a lot better in one of the places listed below. Cortenais specialities are stuffed trout, and lasagne with wild-boar sauce, but if you just want a hot snack try the pizza van parked opposite *Café de France* in place du Duc-de-Padoue. The **bars** along cours Paoli are patronized mainly by locals, while tourists hang out in those lining place Paoli.

Cafés and bars

Les Délices du Palais cours Paoli. Frilly little crêperie-cum-salon-de-thé whose bakery sells a selection of delicious Corsican patisserie: try their *colzone* (spinach pasties), or *brocciu* baked in flaky chestnut-flour pastry.

L'Escapade place Paoli. Inexpensive crêpes from €3 to €7, but best of all are their homemade ice creams: 24 flavours, including melt-in-the-mouth watermelon (*pastèque*) and pear (*poire*), served as single scoops or *coupes*.

De la Place place Paoli. On the shady side of the main square, this is the place to hole up for a spot of crowd-watching over a *barquettes de frites* and draught Pietra.

Restaurants

L'Albadu 2.5km southwest of town ☎04 95 46 24 55. Bargain €15 set menu – muscat, *brocciu* fritters, soup, main meat course, cheese, dessert,

coffee and as much wine as you like – with most ingredients straight off the farm. Everyone sits together around long tables, which makes for a lively atmosphere. Advance booking essential.

A Cantina 20m south of place Gaffori, towards the Belvédère. Artisanal charcuterie and cheeses served in an attractive stone cellar, with a tasting counter and shop upstairs. Pricy (set menu €9 consisting of ham and cheese), but unbeatable quality. Open July & Aug only.

U Museu rampe Ribanelle in the *haute ville* at the foot of the citadel, 30m down rue Colonel-Feracci. Congenial and well situated, with lots of choice on its mixed menus. Try the €14 *menu corse*, featuring lasagne in wild-boar sauce, trout, and *tripettes* (imaginatively translated as "trips"). Their hot goat's cheese (*chèvre chaud*) salad, filling enough for two, comes on a groaning bed of richly flavoured potatoes. Great value for money, atmospheric terrace and the house wines are local AOC.

Le Paglia Orba 1 av Xavier-Luciani ☎ 04 95 61
07 89. Quality Corsican cooking at very reasonable
prices, served on a raised terrace overlooking the
street. Most people come for their succulent pizzas
(€6–8), but they also offer plenty of choice à la
carte, particularly for vegetarians (baked aubergine
with chestnuts or stuffed onions), and do some
imaginative salads (such as chicken in Cognac).
Pan-fried veal served with *stozapreti* (nuggets of
brocciu and herbs) is their *plat de résistance*.
Menus from €13.

Au Plat d'Or place Paoli ☎ 04 95 46 27 16. The
classiest option in Corte: Corsican specialities made
from locally produced ingredients, and served
under awnings on the shady side of place Paoli.
Meat and seafood dishes (such as brochettes of
beef with fragrant wild mushrooms or river trout in
Cap Corse liqueur) are their forte, but they also do
pizzas, pastas and homemade desserts. Menu for
€19 (four courses). Closed Sun.

Relais du Lac Pont de Tagone, Vallée de la
Restonica, 10km southwest of Corte ☎ 04 95 46
14 50. A good way out of town, but this is a wonderful spot to round off a day's hiking, with tables
set beside a rushing stream. Top-notch local cuisine of mostly meat and fish grilled on a wood fire,
and served alfresco or inside the wooden cabin.
Menus from €17. Book ahead in summer.

La Restonica *Hotel La Restonica*, Vallée de la
Restonica, 2km southwest of town ☎ 04 95 45 25
25. Warm-toned riverside dining salon attached to
Corte's most stylish mountain auberge. Go for
their €23 menu featuring *specialitités cortenaises*
such as trout stuffed with garlic and *brocciu*. The
best eating option if you're staying in either of the
Colonna hotels.

Listings

Banks All the main banks on cours Paoli have
ATMs that accept Visa and MasterCard; the Société
Générale stands halfway along, and changes euro
traveller's cheques free of charge

Bookshop Maison de la Presse, 22 cours Paoli,
has a good selection of books about Corsica, and
occasional English-language newspapers.

Bus information Corte is the midway point for
Eurocorse Voyages' Ajaccio to Bastia bus, which
runs twice daily except Sun (☎ 04 95 46 01 09),
tickets from *Bar Colonna*, av Xavier-Luciani. You
can get to Bastia on Mon, Wed and Fri with
Autocars Cortenais, 14 cours Paoli (☎ 04 95 46 22
89), which also operates services to Aléria from
outside the train station on Tues, Thurs and Sat.
During the summer, Corte is connected to Porto via
Calacuccia and Évisa by Autocars Beaux Voyages'
service over Col de Verghio ☎ 04 95 65 11 35,
which leave from place Paoli.

Car rental Corse Automobile, Zone Artisanale,
RN200 ☎ 04 95 46 24 54 or 06 08 93 53 58;
Europcar, 9 cours Paoli ☎ 04 95 46 08 02.

Horse riding The Centre Équestre l'Albadu, ancienne route d'Ajaccio, 2.5km southwest of town
(☎ 04 95 46 24 55), offers horse treks at €15 an
hour, €27 for 2hr or €40 per half day (with a chance
to bathe and picnic by the Tavignano). In a complete
day you can ride deep into the mountains (€70). This
centre is among the best of its kind on the
island and the rates are rock-bottom for Corsica.

Hospital av du 9-Septembre ☎ 04 95 46 05 36.

Internet access Cyber Snack, in the *Café du
Cours* on cours Paoli.

Outdoor equipment Omnisports Gabrielli (☎ 04
95 46 09 35), at the north end of cours Paoli (two
doors up from the Société Générale bank), is the
best-stocked outdoor equipment shop on the
island.

Pharmacies Several on cours Paoli.

Police 4 av Xavier-Luciani ☎ 04 95 46 04 81.

Post office Av du Baron-Mariani, off place du
Duc-de-Padoue.

Taxis Michel Salviani ☎ 04 95 46 04 88 or
Thrérèse Feracci ☎ 04 95 61 01 17.

Train information At the SNCF station ☎ 04 95
46 00 97.

Around Corte

The **Gorges du Tavignano**, virtually on the town's doorstep, offer an exhilarating hike from Corte but are accessible only on foot. The less energetic
can simply drive southwest to the **Vallée de la Restonica**. A torrent of jade-
green water punctuated with enormous boulders, the river is followed closely by the road out of Corte, which comes to a stop within striking distance
of the stunning **Lac de Melo**, the **Lac de Capitello** and **Monte Rotondo**
– a sprawling mountain that may not be much to look at from a distance but
is a superb sight close up, with its ring of crags encircling a cluster of blue
glacial lakes.

Vallée du Tavignano

The medieval cobbled path winding up the **Vallée du Tavignano**, Corsica's deepest and most spectacular gorge, offers one of the island's classic walks. You can pick up the trail, a stage of the Mare a Mare Nord long-distance footpath (covered on p.400 and marked in orange paint flashes), from the bottom of rue col-Feracci, below the citadel, and follow it for two days as far as the source of the river at Lac de Nino (see p.336). There's a newly built **refuge**, *A Sega*, situated at the halfway point, from where the orange waymarks peel north up the side of the Tavignano into the Niolo Valley. Yellow paint flashes, meanwhile, continue west towards the watershed and Lac de Nino – a key stage on the GR20 and as idyllic a trekking destination as you could wish for.

From the trailhead in Corte, the old mule track steadily climbs the steep left bank of the river across a bare hillside scarred with the remains of old farming terraces. Massive rocks border the river below, which you can scramble down to in places for a secluded swim. Some 5km into the walk, the gorge proper begins and the scenery becomes wilder, with rock faces surging up on each. Passing through patches of dense maquis interspersed with evergreen oak and chestnut trees, you gradually rejoin the river, crossed at the **Passarelle de Rossolino** footbridge after around two and a half hours. Once on the true right bank, the mountainside grows steeper as the path skirts the **Ravin de Bruscu**, swathed in forest that was severely damaged by fire in 2000, then winds gently above the stream to the refuge, reached after five and a half hours from Corte. From here, you can press on to Lac de Nino, cross the Col de l'Arinella pass (1592m) into the Niolo, return by the same route to Corte (a 4hr hike), or climb into the Vallée de la Restonica via the plateau d'Alzo (see box below). Either way, a worthwhile investment would be IGN topo-map **#4251 OT**, available at the bookshop mentioned in "Listings", p.344.

Vallée de la Restonica

Dividing the barren wastes of the Rotondo massif and the cloud-swept plateau d'Alzo, the **Vallée de la Restonica** is lined with some of the most spectacular glacier-moulded gorges in the Mediterranean – a riot of twisted granite

---

The Lost Arch hike and Alzo eclipse

Connecting the Restonica and Tavignano valleys via the Plateau d'Alzo, one of the best day-hikes in the Corte region begins 10.5km up the Vallée de la Restonica, from a car park known as **parking de Frasseta**, under some chestnut trees on the right (north) side of the road. As this route ends in town and there are no bus services up the valley, you'll have to hitch a ride as far as the trailhead, marked by a signboard. From here, the path climbs northeast through dense forest along a series of switchbacks. Just after the **Funtana Bianca** spring (1450m), it emerges from the tree cover to begin a long ascending traverse to the **Plateau d'Alzo**. Each year on July 26–28, this high pastureland, scattered with old stone *bergeries*, witnesses one of the island's weirder natural phenomena, when the sun disappears behind the red mass of Paglia Orba to the west, only to reappear moments later through the pierced peak of Capu Tafonatu. The Plateau d'Alzo also has its own strange rock archway, the **arche de Padule**, passed by the trail before it begins a long descent to the **refuge de la Sega**, on the floor of the Vallée du Tavignano. For more details of this route, consult topo-map IGN 25, #4251 OT (ref A8/B8).

Allow three hours to reach the refuge from parking de Frasseta, and another four to walk down the valley to Corte (along the route described at the top of the page).

A jagged-topped arc of granite splashed with small blue lakes, **Monte Rotondo** (2622m), Corsica's second-highest mountain, looms southwest of Corte at the head of the Restonica Valley. The peak can be scaled from two directions, but the most common approach is from the north, via the beautiful Lac d'Oriente. Though technically straightforward between July and late September, this route is a long hard slog involving 3360m of ascent and descent, much of it across steep and boulder-choked terrain. Don't consider attempting it unless you're in good shape and properly equipped (see p.367), and check the weather forecast carefully before you set off. Of the many hikers that tread the Rotondo trail during the summer, most only aim to reach the lake, a rewarding return trip (4hr 30min) in itself.

The **trailhead** lies 11km up the Restonica Valley, 700m beyond the Tagone bridge (where the road crosses from the north to the south side of the gorge) – look for the red spray-painted sign on a rock to the right. From here, a wide forestry track strikes steeply up the side of a stream valley, zigzagging through fragrant pine woods to the **bergeries de Timozzo** (1hr 15min), where it levels out briefly before climbing a long ridge. Follow the red-and-yellow splashes of paint rather than the cairns (which mark a less well-defined path that gets lost in maquis), crossing the stream near the head of the valley.

Enfolded by the Rotondo massif, the **Lac d'Oriente** (2hr 30min) is a great place to picnic before pressing on to the summit. From here, the trail, which restarts at the south side of the lake, is marked every 10m or so by cairns; as long as you keep close to these, the ascent across the moraine that follows is safe and enjoyable. However, things get a little trickier towards the top, where patches of snow and ice can be hazardous, particularly during early summer (an ice axe or snow stick is recommended if you're attempting this route before August); keep an eye out, too, for loose rocks, as these can be lethal for anyone ascending below you. The last stretch of the climb is a very steep clamber up a narrow corridor; patches of ice are more common on the left side of this, so pick a route up the right (sunnier) side. From the **ridge** (4hr 15min), drop down slightly to the left and follow the cairns to a cleft that leads up the crow's-nest **summit** (4hr 30min). On a clear day, the views from the top are sublime, taking in all of the island's major peaks, both coasts, the shores of Tuscany and, if you're lucky, the distant Alps. If you have an all-season sleeping bag, it is possible to bivouac in the tiny tin-roofed **Helbronner refuge** just below the summit and enjoy the spectacle at dawn.

Return by the same route, or down the south side of the mountain, via the beautiful **Lac de Bellabone**, to the **Petra Piana refuge**. Note that times given do not take into account rest breaks; allow a total of eight hours for the return trip to the top from the Restonica Valley and back (5hr 15min ascent and 2hr 45min descent), and aim to start walking by 7am, which will get you to the summit well before the clouds blister up at around 2pm.

cliffs carpeted by thick Laricio pine forest. Unfortunately, it is also among the few motorable routes into the wild heart of the Corsican watershed which, along with its proximity to Corte, means the entire fifteen-kilometre stretch from town to the *bergeries* de Grotelle can get hideously congested in high summer, so avoid the area completely between July and early September, or else take it in from the marked forest trail that winds all the way to the *bergeries* along the riverbank.

The **gorges** begin after 6km, just beyond where the route penetrates the **Forêt de la Restonica**, a glorious forest of chestnut, Laricio pine and the tough maritime pine endemic to Corte, recognizable by its conical shape. Not surprisingly, it's a popular place to walk, picnic and bathe – the many pools fed by the cascading torrent of the Restonica River are easily reached by scrambling down the rocky banks.

The **bergeries de Grotelle**, 15km from Corte, mark the end of the road, with an outsize car park that barely accommodates the summer crowds. From here, a well-worn path winds along the valley floor to a pair of beautiful glacial lakes. The first and largest, **Lac de Melo**, is reached after a fairly strenuous hour's hike through the rocks. Particularly steep parts of the path have been fitted with stanchion chains and vertical iron ladders, causing some visitors to freeze with vertigo halfway up. If you're attempting this walk in early spring, you should also expect to encounter deep snow patches in places, especially once you're past Lac de Melo, where a steeper trail over a moraine climbs up to the second lake, **Lac de Capitello** – the more spectacular of the pair. Hemmed in by vertical cliffs, the deep, turquoise blue pool affords fine views of the Rotondo massif on the far side of the valley, and in fine weather you can spend an hour or two exploring the surrounding crags, scoured by rock pipits. Beyond here, the trail climbs higher to meet the GR20, and should be attempted only by experienced and well-equipped mountain walkers.

South of Corte

The main road south of Corte, the N193, slices into the heart of the Corsican mountains, tracked by the railway through Venaco, Vivario, Vizzavona and Bocognano – a rattling ride that's worth taking even if you have your own vehicle. East from **Vivario** a memorable drive takes you southeast over the Col de Sorba to **Ghisoni**, a mountain base dominated by the peaks of Kyrie-Eleison and the craggy Monte Renoso. You have a choice of spectacular exits from Ghisoni: east through the Défilé de l'Inzecca, a short cut down to the eastern plain; or south along the zigzagging route to Col de Verde, offering incredible views of the peaks. South of the pass, the villages of the Haut Taravo Valley, **Zicavo** and **Cozzano**, make ideal bases for trips into the hills, including **Monte Incudine**, the southernmost high summit of the island.

Back on the N193 and the rail line, **Vizzavona**, a scruffy cluster of rail buildings and hikers' hotels, lies just below the highest point of the road before its descent to Ajaccio. A beautiful forest spreads one side of the settlement up the flanks of mighty Monte d'Oro, but for the best views of this giant pyramidal peak you should head down to **Bocognano**, about 7km from the Col de Vizzavona.

Aside from the handful of hikers' refuges and gîtes d'étapes that punctuate the region's footpaths, **accommodation** is very limited in these parts, with the odd hotel at Vezzani, Vivario and Vizzavona.

The Venachese

"My journey over the mountains was very entertaining. I past (sic) some immense ridges and vast woods. I was in great health and spirits, and fully able to enter into the ideas of the brave rude men whom I found in all quarters," wrote James Boswell in 1765 as he made his way south of Corte to his meeting with Pascal Paoli. These days the same journey through the Venachese tends to be conducted at a brisker pace via the high-grade Route Nationale or narrow-gauge railway, but the route is punctuated by a succession of large, well-populated villages from where you can strike into the hills.

Some of the old shepherds' trails in the Venachese have been cleared and way-marked by the Parc Naturel Régional. Six return routes of varying length and difficulty feature in their excellent leaflet *Balades en Corse: Venachese*, which you can pick up at the park office in Corte, and in most tourist offices. For an easy four-hour ramble, try the circular *boucle* from Venaco village to **Pont de Noceta**, 4km south-east as the crow flies, on the Vecchio River, which passes a couple of pleasant bathing spots and old dry-stone grain storage huts known as *aghja*.

Of the more strenuous routes (*boucles sportives*) pegged out by the PNRC in the vicinity, the most rewarding is the five- to six-hour circular itinerary around the Misongno Valley. The trailhead lies a couple of kilometres above **Santo-Pietro-di-Venaco** near the end of a forestry track: look for a signboard pointing to the left off the *piste*. From there a well-waymarked, worn trail cuts steeply southwest up the spur of the mountain to the **Chapelle Sant'Eliseo** (1555m), Corsica's highest pilgrimage place. In common with its namesake above Lac de Creno in the northwest (see p.185), the chapel hosts a Mass in August, which gathers together Venachesi dispersed on the Continent. Sant'Eliseo is traditionally the patron saint of shepherds and, in the past, the region's *pastori* would walk up here to place a cheese on the altar to petition for a fruitful year. Set against the spectacular snow-streaked east face of Monte Cardo (2453m), with a dramatic view across the Tavignano plain, the recently restored shrine should be open but you'd do well to check in the village before setting off. Beyond it, the path skirts the **bergeries de Polvarella** and then arcs gradually around the head of the valley, climbing to another *bergerie* before swinging eastwards to begin the long descent back down to the road. With IGN map **#4251 OT** you'll find it easier to locate the point, just below the **bergeries de Tatarellu**, where a side path peels northeast down a spur to Pinzo Corbino (1047m) – the most direct route back to Santo-Pietro-di-Venaco.

Swathed in chestnut forest, the first one you come to along the main road is **SANTO-PIETRO-DI-VENACO**, 7.5km south of Corte, where there's a good-value **hotel**, *Le Torrent* (☎04 95 47 00 18; June–Oct; ❸), a somewhat dowdy, old-fashioned place tucked beneath a terrace by the river. Also in the village, the welcoming **gîte d'étape** *Chez Antoinette et Charles* (☎04 95 47 07 29, ⓦwww.antoinette-et-charles.fr.st), a night halt on the Mare a Mare Nord (*variant*) footpath, offers beds in four-person dorms (€27 for obligatory half board) or more comfortable en-suite **chambre d'hôte** accommodation at the unbeatable price of €61 (for two sharing). The rooms here are spotless and good value, and the hosts very hospitable.

Both places provide inexpensive bases from which to complete the wonderful round walk to the **Chapelle Sant'Eliseo** (1555m; see box above), a tiny shrine set against the massive east wall of Monte Cardo, from where you can begin a high-level traverse of the valley head via old shepherds' *bergeries* or strike further up the mountain to the more exposed Arête de Cardo – one of Monte Rotonco's spurs. The friendly owner of the gîte d'étape is a qualified mountain guide and will advise you on the various routes in the area.

Venaco

A couple of kilometres south of Santo-Pietro, the road sweeps through **VENACO**, an elegant village emerging from the verdant lower slopes of Monte Padro. You might want to halt here to admire the views – from the terrace of the Baroque church there's a spectacular panorama of the lower Vallée du Tavignano to the east – or enjoy a meal at the *Restaurant de la Place* on the main square (☎04 95 47 01 30), which offers a good-value €15 *menu fixe* featuring spinach pie and red mullet, river trout or sardines stuffed with *brocciu*, rounded off by homemade walnut flan.

Venaco also harbours one of the area's few good **campsites**, the *Camping Peridundellu* – take the D43 towards the Tavignano Valley and you'll see it after 4km on your right (☎04 95 47 09 89; April–Oct). It's very cosy, with room for a couple of dozen tents, and the farmhouse doubles up as a simple restaurant (fixed four-course menu at €14) serving such delights as homemade charcuterie, goat's cheese in flaky pastry and *fiadone*.

Vivario

Gustave Eiffel (of Eiffel tower fame) built the dizzying **Pont de Vecchiu** railway bridge at the foot of Monte Rotondo, 5km south of Venaco. Alongside it, the even more impressive new road bridge, opened in 1999, spans the 222-metre-wide gorge at a height of 137.5m. A series of tortuous switchbacks beyond here heralds your arrival at **VIVARIO**, located at the junction of the routes to the Forêt de Rospa-Sorba and the Col de Verde. Straddling the main highway and surrounded by fire-scarred forest and maquis, the village makes a less appealing place to spend the might than most hereabouts, but if you're following the Mare a Mare Nord you'll find its excellent little **shop**, near the fountain in the centre, a convenient place to stock up on supplies before heading into the pristine country to the west.

The grandiose Manganello Valley, tracked by the Mare a Mare as far as the refuge de l'Onda (see p.384), once supported its own **wild man**, dubbed by folk chroniclers as *un Mowgli corse*. In 1800 a 10-year-old boy went missing here after an argument with his parents, and stayed missing for twenty years until a group of hunters ensnared him by the Vecchiu. The unfortunate soul was carted off to be reunited with his parents but, unable to adapt to his new life, perished after a few months. The only traversable spot across the Gorge du Vecchiu, a three-hour walk west of Vivario, is a three-metre jump still known as the **Saut du Sauvage**, or "Wild Man's Leap". Vivario's other claim to fame is as the birthplace of the infamous **Bartolomeo brothers**, who were abducted by pirates here in the sixteenth century and went on to lead highly eventful lives. Shipwrecked off the coast of Italy, they escaped the clutches of their Saracen captors and swam to safety at Talamona on the Tuscan shore, where they subsequently settled. The elder of the two, later known as Bartolomeo de Talamona, rose to become an admiral in the local navy, and used his position to exact revenge on the pirates who had kidnapped him in his youth, ruthlessly pillaging the Mytilena region of Algeria, home of the dey of Algiers – the Red Beard, or Barbarossa, of pirate legends. It is said that the sultan was so incensed at Bartolomeo's behaviour that he attacked Talamona in 1544, only to find his adversary dead and buried, whereupon he exhumed the Corsican's corpse and burned and scattered what was left by way of retribution. The other brother, Bartolomeo de Vivario, eventually returned home from Talamona and worked for the Genoese for a while, before defecting to Sampiero Corso's side in the Wars of Independence, in the course of which he was mortally wounded.

If you feel like a **short walk** from Vivario, head 1km south of the village to a stony car park on the side of the main road, from where a clear path leads to the **Fort de Pasciolo**, an evocative ruin set high on a rounded hilltop 1km or so west of the N193. Facing a great circle of peaks above the deep gorge of the Vecchiu, the fort was built around 1770 by the French, and later transformed into a prison to incarcerate the rebels of Fiumorbo (see p.298).

Campers are well provided for with two pleasant sites just south of the village. The quieter of the pair, set up primarily for walkers, is the *Camping de Savaggio* (☎04 95 47 22 14; open year round), 3km south along the N193 – look for a sign pointing west off the highway. A small field next to the rail line with around thirty pitches for tents, a café and basic provisions store, it occupies an out-of-the-way spot close to the Mare a Mare Nord trail, and has a 22-bed **refuge** (open all year). A couple of kilometres further south down the highway, just after the point where the main road crosses the railway, another sign indicates the way to *Camping Le Soleil* (☎04 95 47 21 16; May–Oct), an equally congenial site only two minutes' walk from **Tattone** station. The fine views up the valley to Monte d'Oro are only slightly marred by the proximity of a large and rather grim sanitorium just down the road.

Vizzavona and around

Monte d'Oro dominates the route south of Vivario to **VIZZAVONA**, 30km beyond Corte. Shielded by trees, the village, a cluster of mostly tin-roofed forestry huts and old station buildings, is invisible from the main road, so keep your eyes peeled for a couple of lanes dropping down on the right, one of them signposted for the **gare de Vizzavona** – the place where the bandit Bellacoscia famously surrendered to the police at the age of 75 (see p.352). Marking the midway point of the GR20, Vizzavona is always crowded with walkers during summer, and those on a modest budget are well catered for by the handful of gîtes d'étape, hotels and hikers' cafés grouped around the railhead. The station building also houses the best-stocked shop on the GR20, the Épicerie Rosy, which keeps a supply of stove fuel and blue camping gas canisters as well as overpriced food supplies.

Top of the range here is *I Laricci* (☎ & ℱ 04 95 47 21 12; April–Oct; ❹), a recently converted red-and-white alpine-style building with pitched roofs and Moroccan carpets decorating the walls of its dining room. Rooms here are invariably booked up well in advance, but you can nearly always get a bed in their annexe, which houses a handful of six-person dorms (€30 per bed for obligatory half board). More conventional gîte d'étape accommodation is offered at *Resto-Refuge-Bar de la Gare* (☎ & ℱ 04 95 47 22 20; May–Oct), directly opposite the station. When full, the dormitories here are stuffy and cramped; half board (€30) isn't obligatory, which is just as well as the food isn't up to much, either. For a bed, count on €12, with an additional €2 for a hot shower. There's nowhere decent to camp at Vizzavona; no one will stop you putting your tent up in the field behind the station, but the spot lacks sanitation and gets filthy at the height of the trekking season.

La Foce and Cascades des Anglais

If your budget can stretch to it, head 3km further south along the main road to the hamlet of **LA FOCE**, near the col proper, where the venerable old *Monte d'Oro* (☎04 95 47 21 06; ⓦ www.sitec.fr/monte.oro; ❹) occupies a prime spot overlooking the valley. With its period furniture and fittings, *fin-de-siècle* feel and magnificent terrace looking out onto the mountain, this ranks among the most congenial hotels in Corsica. It was originally built in 1880 as a guesthouse for government engineers and has altered little since. Considering the location and charm of the place, the tariffs are also very reasonable, and they provide complimentary transfer to and from Vizzavona if you phone ahead. In addition, the hotel offers gîte d'étape and refuge accommodation in a rear annexe for around €14/€10 per bed.

The fifth-highest peak on Corsica, **Monte d'Oro** (2389m) stands on the edge of the island's interior range and thus affords superb views not only of the other four big mountains – Cinto, Rotondo, Renoso and Incudine – but also of Ajaccio and the southwest coast. The route up it is well frequented, but involves some exposed scrambling towards the top and you should be prepared to cross the odd névé (patches of deep ice or snow), until late June. The exposed position of the peak also means it is particularly vulnerable to sudden and extreme changes in weather, so check the forecast before you set off and make sure you follow the advice on clothing, equipment and mountain safety on p.367.

There are two ways to the summit from Vizzavona. We recommend you ascend the easier one, via the Cascade des Anglais and the main route of the GR20 along the River Agnone, and then follow the "Variant" of the GR20 over the summit and down the east flank of the mountain via the *bergeries* de Pozzatelli – a fine round walk that should take you about eight hours. Take along a copy of the FFRP's topo-guide for the GR20, which clearly maps the route, or IGN Top 25, **#4251 OT** (ref D9/D10).

From Vizzavona, follow the red-and-white-waymarks of the GR20 for thrity minutes until the **Cascade des Anglais**. Once across the ruisseau d'Agnone, the path climbs northeast along the left bank of the stream, zigzagging steeply up pastureland strewn with elms and, later, denuded rocky terrain towards the **Crête de Muratellu** (2020m). Just below the ridge, you leave the waymarked section of the GR20 and follow its variant (cairned and waymarked in yellow) northeast towards **Bocca di u Porcu** (2159m). The final leg to the summit involves some climbing for which you'll need a head for heights but not ropes.

The **descent** to Vizzavona is well cairned. You have to head north and northeast from the summit, past a small grassy plateau known as **Bratu Scampicciolo**, and down the steep zigzags of **La Scala** to the distinctively shaped rock dubbed **La Cafetière**. Shortly after, the route veers due east and drops down the side of a stream gulley, penetrating the treeline just above the **bergeries de Pozzatelli**. The remaining leg keeps to the forest, much of it damaged by fire and clear cutting. Allow at least two and a half hours to reach Vizzavona from the summit – and at least double that for the ascent.

Immediately behind the *Monte d'Oro* stands the tiny **Chapel de Notre-Dame-des-Neiges** ("Our Lady of the Snows"), to which travellers traditionally paid their respects while crossing the pass. The shrine was the centre of a dispute during World War II when it was used by Italian troops billeted in the hotel to stable mules. The protests of the owner, Mme Plaisant, had no effect, but when the Italians' High Chaplain happened to be passing and noticed the act of sacrilege, he had the offending soldiers pull down the chapel and rebuild it from scratch as an act of purification. Masonry for the job came from the ruins of the old French **fort**, whose vestiges can still be seen on a forested ridge 1km southwest – look for the wide path running north into the woods from the picnic tables and car park at the col.

The glorious forest of beech and Laricio pine carpeting the valley below the pass, the **Forêt de Vizzavona**, is among the most popular walking areas in Corsica, thanks to the easy access by main road or train. A lot of people come here to tackle the ascent of Monte d'Oro (see box above), but there are many less demanding trails to follow. One of the most frequented of these is the walk to the **Cascades des Anglais**, which can be reached from Vizzavona via an uncharacteristically gentle section of the GR20 but is more commonly approached from La Foce. Some 200m down the main road from *Hôtel Monte* *d'Oro* (in the direction of Vizzavona/Corte), look for the forest *piste* plunging north through the woods to the river; follow the green waymarks for a little over a quarter of an hour until they merge with the red-and-white ones of the GR20, which passes a stone's throw from the falls, where the River Agnone crashes into emerald-green pools. These are perfect for bathing, but the site is far from a secret. Its popularity dates from the late nineteenth century, from which time it became a favourite summer picnic spot of British aristocrats residing in Ajaccio (whence the falls' name).

Bocognano

From the Col de Vizzavona, the route winds southwards for 6km before reaching the appealing ochre cottages of **BOCOGNANO** (Bucugnanu). Set on a plateau amidst a chestnut forest, the village gives a perfect panorama of Monte d'Oro's pale-grey needles, and is well placed for walks to the **Cascade du Voile de la Mariée**, where the River Gravona crashes from a height of 150m in a series of cascades. The approach to the falls is via the D27, which turns southwest at an inconspicuous junction on the western edge of the village. Follow the winding road to its end, roughly 3km later, from where a path winds up through the forest to the falls.

Bocognano is indissolubly associated with Antoine and Jacques **Bellacoscia**, born here in 1817 and 1832, fathered by a man who earned the family surname – meaning "beautiful thigh" – by also fathering eighteen daughters by three sisters with whom he lived simultaneously. Antoine, the elder son, took to the maquis in 1848, having killed the mayor of the village after an argument over some land. With his brother he went on to commit several more murders in full view of the hapless gendarmes, yet remained at liberty thanks to the support of the local population. In 1871 Antoine and Jacques managed to gain a safe pass into Ajaccio to organize an expedition to fight for the French in the war with Prussia. They returned from the war with their reputations restored, and took up residence in the family home, from where they continued to flaunt the law. In 1888 the police finally succeeded in ousting them from their house, which was converted into a prison. Antoine eventually surrendered when he was 75, at Vizzavona station on June 25, 1892, whereupon he was acquitted and exiled to Marseille in true Corsican tradition. The fate of Jacques is unknown.

Ghisoni and around

Nestling in a huge hollow at the head of the Vallée du Fiumorbo, **GHISONI** is separated from the Venachese by a 1500-metre-high ridge crossed at the **Col de Sorba**. The D69, which wriggles south from the pass to the village, affords tantalizing glimpses of the Renoso massif, and the majority of the people who come here do so to climb the peak (see p.353), or en route between Zicavo and the east coast via the Col de Verde.

Ghisoni's only **hotel** is the unsightly mustard-coloured *Kyrié*, close to the centre of the village (℡04 95 57 60 33, ℻04 95 57 63 15; ❹). It's an unexciting place, but the rooms are clean (the cheaper ones on the top floor enjoy the best views of the valley) and there's a sunny bar-**restaurant** on the ground floor where *cannelloni al brocciu*, stuffed trout, and chestnut-flour and leek fritters are the house specialities, all home-cooked by the *patronne*. Menus range from €14 to €18.

Further down the hill, *A Stazzona* (closed Tuesday) is a smaller, family-run bistro with a rear terrace jutting over a brook, where you can dine on tomato and mozzarella salads, locally made charcuterie, pizzas and the *plat de résistance*, stuffed trout (only €8). There's no need to book a table in season, but should you be here from October through to May reserve before 7pm at the nearby *épicerie*.

The only other place to eat and drink in the village is the dingy *Bar Jacques*, whose streetside *terrasse* sits next to a rusting but nonetheless impressive statue of Neptune, seemingly misplaced this far into the mountains. In fact, the work was originally destined for a coastal *commune* in Cap Corse, but when it came to paying for the thing the council in question declared itself broke and Ghisoni snapped it up instead.

Hugging the sinuous Fium'orbo River, the road running **east from Ghisoni** plunges steeply downhill through the **Défilé des Strette** gorge, giving spectacular views of the two peaks on the far side of the valley: **Kyrie** (1535m) and **Christe Eleison** (1260m). It was at the foot of these mountains that the last group of **Giovanalanis**, devotees of a breakaway Franciscan sect whose rituals were falsely rumoured to include mass orgies, were massacred at the behest of Pope Urban V in 1362. Hounded to this remote spot, they were captured and bound for burning, but just at the point when the wood was to be set alight an old priest took pity on the heretics and administered their last rites. The assembled crowd is then said to have taken up the last line of the prayer – *Kyrie eleison, Christe eleison* – which echoed through the gorge and across the mountains, giving the peaks the names by which they are known to this day. Further east, the main road skirts the Sampolo reservoir before penetrating the spectacular **Défilé de l'Inzecca**, a sheer trench slicing the coastal range (see p.299). The gorge forms a little-frequented short cut from the interior to the fertile eastern plains, and after the shattered rock formations, cuttings and tunnels marking the road, the lush orange groves and vineyards around Ghisonaccia come as something of a shock.

E'Capannelle and Monte Renoso

An endless series of tight switchbacks wind 17km up the flank of the Fiumorbo Valley from Ghisoni to **E'Capannelle** (1586m), a little-used ski resort on the lower slopes of the Renoso massif. As a target for a drive into the mountains, the *station* – a major port of call on the **GR20** – is a dud: the once grassy slopes surrounding it have been badly carved up by a decade of skiers struggling on inadequate snow, while the restricted views of the peaks are marred by decaying chair lifts and *téléphérique* pylons. The one reason you might wish to venture up here is to get yourself into position for an early start up Monte Renoso. Dormitory **accommodation** is offered by the *Gîte d'étape "U Fugone"* (℡04 95 57 01 81, ℻04 95 56 39 34), in the station itself, where half board (€28 per head) is obligatory. Its rooms are fairly well ventilated and kept impeccably clean. The same can't be said of the grim little municipal-run **refuge** just up the hill, which lacks even a dependable water supply (as an inducement, one imagines, to pay for the gîte's facilities). With your own tent, you'd be better off **camping** or bivouacking for free around the stone *bergeries* below the *station* and paying €2.50 for a token to use *U Fugone*'s solar-powered shower block. Ask at the bar – which is also the place to stock up on trekking provisions if you're following the GR from here.

Monte Renoso

E'Capannelle stands at the beginning of the standard route up **Monte Renoso** (2352m), the most southerly of Corsica's 2300-metre-plus summits. With a light pack and an early start, you can reach the top and return by lunchtime, or else press on south along the summit ridge, dropping down the far side via the GR20's superb high-level Variant (waymarked) towards Col de Verde (as outlined on p.389) and then hitch back. Either way, take note of the advice on equipment, clothing and mountain safety in Chapter 8: exposed to coastal weather, this can be a treacherous route at any time of year, even in summer, when electrical storms may descend with little warning.

From the *station*, the waymarks lead you steeply uphill, zigzagging between the chair-lift pylons to gain a ridge at 1725m (in only half a kilometre). Cairns then flag the route across a more gentle grassy hollow, at the end of which you'll crest a bouldery rise at the 2000m mark for your first sight of **Lac de Bastiani** (2092m), a grey expanse of water framed intermittently by snow-drifts. Skirting the northern shores of the lake, the path then steepens considerably as it traverses a scree-covered cwm to reach the summit ridge – a vast, rocky crest, falling away steeply on both sides to reveal magnificent views of southern Corsica to Sardinia. Allow around two and a quarter hours to reach the summit proper from E'Capannelle, and a good hour for the descent afterwards by the same path.

If you carry on south along the waymarked route past the **Punta Orlandino**, you'll reach the **Col de Pruno** (2262m) in another thirty minutes or so. From here the path descends sharply across boulders and alder scrub to the **bergeries des Pozzi**, then strikes east across lush alpine meadows to the Plateau de Gialgone, after which it joins the **GR20**. At this point, you can either follow the GR20 north, hugging the contours of Renoso for another three and a half hours to get back to the E' Capannelle refuge, or take the quicker and easier route east to the D69 where it crosses Col de Verde (see below).

Col de Verde and around

Dividing the Fiumorbo and Taravo valleys, **Col de Verde** (1289m) provides a convenient springboard for walks up into the high country of the watershed, the best of them via the red-and-white waymarks of the GR20, which makes another of its infrequent drops to road level here. Slap on the pass, the privately run *Refuge San Petru di Verdi* (☎04 95 24 46 82; late-May to mid-Oct) has a relaxing, shady little terrace café serving quality snacks and drinks, and a cluster of wood-lined bunkhouses around the back where you can sleep in spotlessly clean dorms (€10 per bed). Campers are welcome to pitch up in the garden for €5 per person, which includes the use of solar-heated showers.

The two most obvious **walks** from the col are both well-marked and well-frequented stretches of the GR20. Starting at the forestry *piste* on the far side of the road from the refuge, the first strikes southeast into the woods, emerging after 45 minutes or so to begin a long, sweeping traverse of the valley head to **Bocca d'Oro** – an ascent of roughly 550m which should take a little under two hours. From there you can press on for another ten minutes to the **refuge de Prati** (1820m), a wonderfully sited hut from which the mountain falls away to the hazy eastern plain and Tyrrhenian Sea.

Alternatively, the GR20 can be followed west from Col de Verde through the **Vallon de Marmano**, site of some immense pine trees, the largest of which towers to 55m and is thought to be the tallest in Europe. Around one and a half hours into the walk, the red-and-white waymarks reach the **Plateau de Gialgone**, where you should turn left off the GR20 and follow the orange waymarks up to the **bergeries des Pozzi**. Beyond here the trail winds up to **I Pozzi**, patches of lush marshy ground scattered with lakes and winding watercourses interconnecting at different levels, eventually striking up the sheer, boulder-covered southern limit of the Renoso massif. Allow roughly two and a half hours for the walk to I

Pozzi, and another hour for the remaining climb to the summit of Monte Renoso. The essential IGM map covering both of the above routes is **#4252 OT**.

Haut Taravo: Zicavo and Cozzano

From its mouth on the Golfe de Valinco, the **Vallée du Taravo** cleaves diagonally inland, narrowing and deepening as it approaches the watershed at Col de Verde. Ringed by jagged, blue–grey granite ridges, the valley's upper reaches, known as the **Haut Taravo**, form a fertile basin of lush chestnut, beech and pine forests fed by meltwater streams tumbling from the mountains. The region's villages, many of them linked by the **Mare a Mare Centre** long-distance footpath (see p.402) are definitive *Corse profonde*, where the ageing human population is far outstripped by the number of semi–wild pigs, and where you're almost guaranteed not to meet another tourist.

The *chef lieu* of the Haut Taravo is **ZICAVO**, a handsome village famed for its charcuterie and, according to local folklore, vampires (*streghe*) and zombies (*acciacciatori*), said to emerge from the forest to feed on the crushed skulls of unwary travellers. The generic term for these mythical horrors is *grammanti*, which probably harks back to the Saracen raids of the fourteenth-century corsair d'Agramante, who plagued the area from his stronghold on the gulf.

Autocars Santoni's daily **bus** service from Ajaccio connects the village with the coast, providing one of the most convenient and dependable means of access to the deep interior of the island. Zicavo has three unexpectedly pleasant **places to stay**, all with satisfying little **restaurants**. The most welcoming of them is the **gîte d'étape** *Le Paradis* (℡04 95 24 41 20; ❷), run by a garrulous former schoolteacher and her family, which offers dorm beds for €10 per person or smart little double rooms from €33. You can also camp here (€5 per head), and eat home-cooked food on a flowery stone terrace. Next door, *Hôtel Le Florida* (℡04 95 24 43 11; ❸) is slightly more upmarket and more secluded than the old-established *Le Tourisme* in the centre of the village (℡04 95 24 40 06; ❷), which has fifteen rooms, the best of the (en-suite and with terraces) occupying the lower storey. In the bar downstairs, the *patronne* serves two menus (€13 and €17) of quality local charcuterie, free-range meat from the mountains and cheeses made up on the nearby Coscione Plateau.

Cozzano

A conical cluster of old granite tower houses ranged around a slender stone campanile, the next village up the valley from Zicavo, **COZZANO**, makes a better base for extended walks in the Haut Taravo, not least because of its excellent **gîte d'étape**, the *Bella Vista* (℡04 95 24 41 59, ✉renucciauberge@aol.com; March–Oct) on the northern outskirts. Advice on the most rewarding itineraries to follow, backed up with loans of maps and unfailingly warm hospitality, is doled out by father and son, Pierre and Baptiste Pantalacci, while Madame takes care of the cooking. The food (€13 for an evening meal or €28 half board) is superb, the wine beguilingly spicy and the hillsides riddled with enough trails to keep you here for at least a couple of days. Beds cost around €10 per person and they've three double rooms at bargain prices (❶).

For more comfort, try the *Auberge A Filetta* (℡04 95 24 45 61, ℻04 95 24 47 05; ❹), down on the other side of the village, where half board (€40 per head or €63 for two sharing) is obligatory. The same family also runs a block of very swish self-contained apartments on the opposite side of the road (❷–❸ depending on the length of stay), with terraces and great views over the valley.

Taking its name from the massive anvil-shaped rock just below its summit, the four-kilometre hump of **Monte Incudine** (2136m), south Corsica's highest mountain, is crenellated by numerous peaks, the highest of which can be climbed from Zicavo via waymarked paths. The route poses no technical difficulties, but you'll need an early start to reach the top and then press on further to the refuge d'Asinao, just below the summit, from where it is possible to reach Bavella or Quenza the following day. With a car, you might consider cutting short the first section of this route by driving as far as the chapelle de San Petru, or hitching a ride to the refuge des Bergeries de Basetta, also on the D428; the *gardien* of the refuge both do the journey daily in summer, which could save you a long slog over the dullest stretch of the walk. Wherever you decide to start, a worthwhile investment is a copy of a GR20 topo-guide (see "Books", p.444) containing the relevant sections of the two maps covering the route.

The classic approach to Monte Incudine begins with a long ascent of the east side of the Vallée du Taravo, via a link section of the GR20 that joins the main path with Zicavo. Follow the yellow waymarks south out of the village along the D69 for around 1km, at which point the path turns left off the road and climbs southwards through dense beech and chestnut forest. Having emerged from the woods and rounded the shoulder of Punta de l'Erta, it then keeps to largely level ground to cross the ruisseau de Tinturaio at the head of a small valley, climbing to join briefly the winding D428. A left turn here will take you 1km north to the **bergeries de Bassetta** (2hr 30min) where old shepherds' huts have been converted to accommodate a **refuge** of eighteen dorm beds plus a handful of more comfortable wooden chalets. The food served in the little café-**restaurant** is top-notch mountain cuisine: €9 for a filling bean and pork stew or €18 for a full three-course meal. Depending on whether you sleep in the dorms or chalets, half board is priced at €7.50 or €30.50.

Rejoining the path where you left it at the sharp bend in the D428, the waymarks continue eastwards to the **Chapelle de San Petru**. From here, a generally easy two hours takes you past the **refuge de Matalza** (neither staff nor water) and across the northern fringes of the atmospheric and beautiful **Plateau de Coscione** (an account of which appears on p.253) to the **junction with the GR20**, at 1450m. A sign points the way west from the intersection to the **Auberge de la Passerelle**, the halfway stage. Throughout the summer, this privately run refuge dishes up hearty Corsican stews and pasta to hungry hikers, and sells energy-rich food, as well as shots of local *anis* to steel you for the stiff ascent ahead.

From the auberge, a thirty-minute climb following the red-and-white waymarks of the GR20 brings you to the ruins of the **refuge de Pedinieddi**, now disused, beyond which the path rises gradually, with fine views over the Plateau de Coscione. This is where the final ninety-minute haul to the summit starts, with an initial steep climb along a stream gully to the **Col de Luana**, followed by a wonderfully exposed, rocky ridge walk to the top (2134m), marked with a large crucifix.

You can either descend by the same route, or else continue southwest to the Bocca Stazzunara pass (2025m), where the GR20 veers east and drops very steeply down the exposed east side of the Vallée d'Ainao to the **refuge d'Asinao** (reached after 1hr 20min from the summit). Most hikers call it a day here, but from an intersection twenty minutes below the refuge, routes lead down the valley to Quenza and Bavella (4hr 30min). The best option of the three paths off the mountain is the "**Variante Alpine**" of the GR20, marked with yellow splashes, which strikes steeply uphill around an hour after the refuge. Crossing the heart of the Bavella needles massif, this ranks among the most challenging, and spectacular, sections of the GR20, and shouldn't be missed if you have a head for heights (certain pitches involve loose scrambles and crossing steep, smooth boulders). Don't, however, attempt this route if the rock is wet. From the refuge d'Asinao to Bavella, allow 4hr 30min for the "Variante Alpine" and around five hours for the standard route.

Travel details

Trains

Corte to: Ajaccio (4 daily; 1hr 30min); Bastia (4 daily; 1hr 10min); Bocognano (4 daily; 1hr); Calvi (2 daily; 2hr 30min); L'Île Rousse (2 daily; 1hr 55min); Ponte Leccia (4 daily; 30min); Venaco (4 daily; 13min); Vivario (4 daily; 20min); Vizzavona (4 daily; 40min).

Venaco to: Ajaccio (4 daily; 1hr 20min); Bastia (4 daily; 1hr 35min); Bocognano (4 daily; 40min); Calvi (2 daily; 3hr 50min); Corte (4 daily; 15min); L'Île Rousse (2 daily; 2hr 20min); Ponte Leccia (4 daily; 45min); Vivario (4 daily; 15min); Vizzavona (4 daily; 30min).

Vivario to: Ajaccio (4 daily; 1hr 5min); Bastia (4 daily; 1hr 50min); Bocognano (4 daily; 30min); Calvi (2 daily; 3hr 5min); Corte (4 daily; 30min); L'Île Rousse (2 daily; 2hr 35min); Ponte Leccia (4 daily; 1hr); Venaco (4 daily; 10min); Vizzavona (4 daily; 15min).

Vizzavona to: Ajaccio (4 daily; 55min); Bastia (4 daily; 2hr); Bocognano (4 daily; 15min); Calvi (2 daily; 4hr); Corte (4 daily; 1hr); L'Île Rousse (2 daily; 2hr 50min); Ponte Leccia (4 daily; 1hr 10min); Venaco (4 daily; 35min); Vivario (4 daily; 15min).

Buses

The tables below summarize which bus companies cover which routes, how often they run and how long journeys take. Start by looking up your intended destination in the first table; then, using the company's acronym (eg AM or EV), go to the second table for more detailed route and frequency information. Precise departure times can be checked in advance either via the bus companies direct, or (if your French isn't up to that) Corte tourist office on ☎ 04 95 46 26 70.

Corte to: Ajaccio (EV; 2hr); Bastia (EV; 1hr 15min); Calacuccia and the Niolo (AM; 1hr 30min); Évisa (AM; 2hr 15min); Porto (AM; 3hr).
Ponte Leccia to: Calvi (ABV; 1hr).

AM: Autocars Mordiconi ☎ 04 95 48 00 04. Corte–Calacuccia–Albertacce–Col de Verghio–Évisa–Porto; July to mid-Sept Mon–Sat 1 daily.
EV: Eurocorse Voyages ☎ 04 95 21 06 30. Ajaccio–Bocognano–La Foce (Col de Vizzavona)–Vivario–Venaco–Santo-Pietro-di-Venaco–Corte–Ponte Leccia–Bastia; Mon–Sat 2 daily.

8

Long-distance
walks

CHAPTER 8

Highlights

* **Monte Corona** – Arguably the most spectacular viewpoint in all Corsica, most easily accessible via Orto di u Piobbu refuge. See p.373

* **Cirque de la Solitude** – Stanchion cables, fixed ladders and chains ease the crossing of this, the most vertical and compelling stretch of the GR20. See p.376

* **Golo Valley** – Deep turquoise pools, Laricio pines and alpine meadows, with Pagia Orba as a backdrop. See p.378

* **Lac de Nino** –Serene glacial lake ringed by turf *pozzines* and jagged, snow-streaked mountains, where wild horses and pigs graze in summer. See p.379

* **Arête a Monda** – A razor-sharp ridge high above the Haut' Taravo Valley, lined with pinnacles, tilting slabs and wind-sculpted buttresses. See p.393

8

Long-distance walks

C orsica is virtually unique in the Mediterranean for offering both superb mountain scenery and a world-class outdoor infrastructure. The thousand kilometres of waymarked trails that crisscross the island, backed up by a network of impeccable refuges and hostels, enable you to explore some truly spectacular wilderness regions without the hassle of having to carry excessive amounts of gear and supplies. Couple this with weather that's dependably warm and sunny from early May until the end of October and you'll appreciate why Corsica ranks among Europe's top trekking destinations.

Since it was first inaugurated in the late 1970s, the single most compelling attraction for serious walkers has been the **GR20**, regarded as among the most rewarding of Europe's *haute routes*. For extreme mountain environments, awesome landscapes and pure physical challenge, it's in a class of its own, traversing the island via a series of notoriously taxing ascents and descents. Of the thousands of people that attempt it each season, less than half manage to complete all sixteen stages. Those that do, however, are invariably as amazed by the scenery they encounter along the way – the colossal pine trees, semi-frozen lakes and massive granite peaks – as by the ingenuity of the path itself, which penetrates terrain normally the exclusive preserve of rock climbers.

Although well deserved, the GR20's reputation tends to eclipse the existence of Corsica's other long-distance paths. But the lower-altitude coast-to-coast routes – known as the **Mare a Mare** and **Tra Mare e Monti** trails – offer some superlative walking in their own right. In addition to gorgeous scenery from start to finish (much of it within sight of the sea) they pass at regular intervals through hill villages, allowing you to experience traditional island life at close quarters. This means you not only get to walk through miles of oak-, chestnut- and pine-forested river valleys, but can also break your days with leisurely lunches or coffee stops on plane-shaded squares.

The **best periods to walk** depend on the route you're aiming to follow. For the GR20, summer – from early June until mid-October – is the only season when you can be sure of avoiding snow on the highest passes. The lower-altitude routes, by contrast, can be hard going from mid-June until mid-September because of the extreme heat along their exposed coastal sections. To

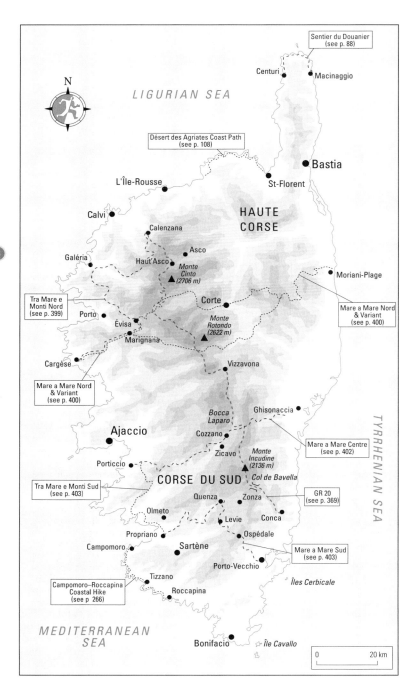

enjoy fully any of the routes that drop to sea level, you should come in the spring or autumn when temperatures are bearable and the flora at its most abundant.

Coastal walks

Lots of walkers come to Corsica expecting the kind of multi-stage coastal paths common in Britain and Ireland, and are disappointed to find most headlands swathed in impenetrable maquis or blocked by rocks. There are, however, some notable exceptions. Exploiting the old Genoese custom officers' footpaths (*sentiers des douaniers*) that formerly encircled the whole island, three waymarked routes have recently been set out along some of Corsica's most unspoilt shorelines.

Winding around the far northern tip of **Cap Corse**, the oldest-established of them is the two-day route between Macinaggio and Port-Centuri, which passes through the Site Naturelle de Capandula, a four-square-kilometre reserve encompassing the deserted islets of Finocchiarola and Giraglia. Other landmarks encountered include the watchtowers of Agnello and Santa Maria, an ancient chapel and a string of sheltered sandy coves. For more on this path, see **p.88**.

Further southwest, a longer three-day itinerary skirts the edge of the **Désert des Agriates**, Corsica's largest coastal wilderness, between St-Florent near Bastia and Plage de Perajola at the mouth of the Ostriconi Valley. Crossing two of the island's most spectacular beaches, the plages de Loto and Saleccia, the first stage of this walk is well frequented in season, but once beyond the midway point you'd be unlucky to encounter another walker. In addition to the beaches, the path also winds past the famous Tour de Mortella, on the Golfe de St-Florent, which took a pounding from Nelson in the eighteenth century. A fuller account of the route appears on **p.108**.

Cleared only over the past two or three years, the *sentier* along the **Sartenais coast** in the far south of the island presents another mouthwatering prospect. Starting at Campomoro, at the far west end of the Golfe de Valinco, you can head southwest to Tizzano via the Tour de Senetosa and a chain of exquisite white-sand coves in around six hours. The second day is shorter, but passes some even larger beaches that remain inaccessible by road, as well as some memorable rock formations. Ending at beautiful Roccapina, with its distinctive Rocher du Lion and views across the straits to Sardinia, this is probably the most varied of the three coastal paths. Plans are afoot to extend it all the way to Bonifacio, which would make a superb four-day itinerary. More details on the Sartenais coast path are featured on **pp.241 and 266**.

Don't be fooled by the absence of serious gradients into underestimating the potential rigours and **dangers** of these coastal walks. **Route finding**, in particular, can be a problem, especially early in the spring before the paths have been properly cleared. Waymarkers do exist but they're far less frequent than those up in the hills and cannot be relied upon without the aid of an IGN **map**. Spiny maquis is another attendant hassle, tearing your clothes, rucksacks and sleeping mats to shreds. Perhaps the biggest risks of all, though, are **dehydration** and **heat stroke**. None of the three paths has much shade and from June until the end of September the sun can be merciless. Nor are there many water sources along the way, which means you have to carry between three and five litres with you, topping up wherever possible. Bear in mind, too, that if you injure yourself you'll probably have a very long walk out to reach help: some sections of the above paths may remain deserted for days on end, even at the height of the trekking season in late spring and the autumn.

More specific tips on how to tackle each coastal route, with information on reaching the trailheads and where to sleep and eat along the way, are to be found in the relevant chapters.

The paths: waymarks and maps

Well conceived and impeccably waymarked, Corsica's long-distance footpaths are a dream to follow. Every ten metres or so a blob of coloured paint or tape on a rock, tree, lamppost or wall reassures you you're on the right track. Up on the GR20, the *balisage* (sometimes called *flèchage*) comprises flashes of red and white; on all other coast-to-coast routes, you'll be following single orange spots.

With the aid of the waymarkers you should easily be able to find your way between stages. For a fuller picture of the route's topography, however, some kind of **map** is essential. The most detailed on the market are the IGN's (Institut Géographique National's) splendid Séries Bleues TOP maps which, in addition to helpful shading to emphasize the contours, pick out footpaths in easy-to-read red. At a scale of 1:25,000 (1cm = 250m), they're beautifully drawn but cost €9 each, which can considerably bump up the overall expense of your trek; a full set for the GR20, for example, will set you back around £36/US$56.

A cheaper alternative would be to invest in the FFRP (Fédération Française de la Randonnée Pédestre) **Topo-guide** for your chosen itinerary. These basically consist of extracts from the relevant IGN Séries Bleues maps, reduced in size and interspersed with helpful route information and background on the region (in French only). You'll find them on sale at most bookshops and newsagents in Corsica, and in your home country at the specialist outlets listed on p.24.

Useful hiking vocabulary

balisé (adj)/**balisage** (m) – waymarked/way-marking
berger (m) – shepherd
belvédère (m) – viewpoint
bifurquer (à gauche/à droite) (vb) – to bear (left/right)
boussole (f) – compass
bergeries (f) – high-altitude shepherds' huts
brêche (f) – pronounced gap in a ridge or seam of rock
bocca* (f) – pass
châtaigneraie (f) – chestnut wood
chemin (muletier) (m) – (mulepackers') path
cascades (pl) – waterfall
cirque – steep-sided amphitheatre of cliffs at valley head
col – pass
courbe (f) – bend
crête (f) – ridge
défilé (m) – gorge, ravine
descente (f) – descent
ébouli (m) – boulder choke
étape (f) – stage (of a hike)
fleuve (m) – river
fontaine (f) – spring
franchir (vb) – to cross
gardien/nne – warden (of refuge)
gîte d'étape (m) – hikers' hostel

hébergement (m) – accommodation
IGN – Institut National Géographique
lacets – zigzags
longer (vb) – to follow (eg a river)
météo (f) – weather forecast
montée (f) – ascent
névé (m) – patch of eternal snow
passerelle suspendue (f) – rope bridge
pente (f) – slope
partage des eaux (m) – watershed
pozzines* (pl) – rivulets in spongy turf
piste (f) – unsurfaced road
PNRC – Parc Naturel Régional Corse (Corsica's National Park Authority)
raide (adj) – steep
randonnée (f)/**randonneur** – hike/hiker
ravitaillement (m) – provisions
refuge (m) – bothy, hikers' shelter
rive (gauche/droite) (f) – (left/right) bank (of a stream or river)
ruisseau (m) – stream
sac à dos (m) – rucksack, backpack
sentier (m) – path
sommet (m) – summit (of a mountain)
torrent (m) – mountain stream
vallée (f) – valley
Variant (m) – alternative route

*Corsican words

Accommodation, eating and drinking

Among the great plus factors of Corsica's trekking routes is the quality of accommodation laid on by the PNRC. Although they frequently struggle to keep up with demand in peak season, the island's refuges and gîtes d'étape provide inexpensive shelter (and often meals) at the end of each stage, enabling you to walk unencumbered by a heavy pack if you choose.

Along the GR20, **refuges** mark the start and finish of virtually every *étape*. Whether simple wooden shepherds' huts or more ambitious glass-and-steel structures, they all offer basic bunk beds, use of a well-equipped kitchen, dining room, deck and shower-toilet block for around €8.5 per night. You can also pitch a tent or bivouac in designated areas around them for €6, which includes the use of an exterior gas-fuelled stove and access to the toilet block (but not to the utensils and interior kitchen).

From June until late September, all of the refuges on the GR20 are staffed by wardens (*gardiens*), most of whom provide expensive supplies (packed to the hut each day by mule) and rustle up simple meals in the evening. Kitted out with radios, they are also the best source of advice on impending weather conditions and can summon a rescue helicopter if required.

At those occasional points on the GR20 where the path dips to road level, and at the end of each waystage on lower-altitude routes, accommodation is offered by **gîtes d'étape**. More comfortable than refuges, these are essentially hostels providing bunk-bed accommodation in communal dormitories (for around €11 per head), along with breakfast and evening meals (around €26 for half board, or *demi-pension*). Standards of cooking and hospitality vary between establishments but most gîtes are very congenial places to rest up after a day on the trail. The only catch is that they tend to get booked well in advance, so if you intend to rely on them be sure to reserve (by telephone or letter) as far ahead as possible and re-confirm a day or two before your expected arrival date.

Food is likely to comprise most of the weight in your backpack, at least along the GR20, where opportunities to re-provision are less frequent than on the island's other long-distance footpaths. Aim to carry at least two or three days' worth of supplies with you; during July and August, refuges stock basic provisions (*revitaillement*), but you can't bank on them in June or September/October. The food is always sold at grossly inflated prices, but paying them buys you the luxury of not having to carry so much heavy food in your rucksack– a godsend given some of the gradients. Where the path descends to road level (as at Haut'Asco, Col de Verghio and Vizzavona), you'll always find a shop or bar selling supplies for hikers but, again, they'll be pricy. Dehydrated and dried food is obviously best: pasta, couscous, rice or "boil-up" powder meals (widely available in Corsican supermarkets, where they're much cheaper than at specialist outdoor shops). The one thing to avoid while hiking strenuous routes is **alcohol**, which gives you a short burst of energy but will demand it back with interest the following day. As anyone who's nursed a hangover after a evening's premature celebrations along the GR20 will tell you, wait until you've finished before popping any corks.

Except along some of the highest, driest stretches of the GR20, finding clean drinking **water** is rarely a problem, which is just as well, as you can expect to get through between three and four litres per day – or four to five on the GR20 in summer. On Corsica's low-altitude routes, a couple of litres should see you through: the paths regularly cross villages, streams and springs where you can top up (note that "*Non Potable*" signs on fountains and springs mean they're not safe to drink). Our route descriptions indicate the location of reliable springs along the paths, as do IGN topo-guides and maps. Even at altitude, however, all torrents, streams and rivers in Corsica should be regarded as being contaminated with animal waste, or dead animals themselves, and treated accordingly; if you do need to drink any, boil or clean it first with water **purification tablets** (chlorine-based ones are fine, and healthier over long periods than iodine).

Equipment

In the light of the potential dangers posed by the volatile weather and tough terrain of the mountains, it is essential to be properly equipped for any hike, whether a short *boucle de journée* (day-walk) or *grande randonnée* (serious trek).

Essential checklist

There are no hard and fast rules about what to pack. The following lists summarize the most useful items for trekking in varied weather conditions during the summer season.

Kit

Adjustable (telescopic) trekking poles Knee-savers on those crunching GR20 descents.

Bivouac bag An ideal weight-saving alternative to a tent, a bivvy bag will provide an additional insulating layer if you're sleeping under the stars; dry nights are the norm through the summer, and you can get by without a tent, bedding down inside refuges (or gîtes) if the weather looks dodgy.

Body wallet

Boots Two- to three-season for the GR20; or two-season/multi-activity shoes on lower-level routes. Choose ones with Vibram soles and ankle support.

Fleece

Gloves

Hats A sunhat and a warm hat.

Head torch

Jacket Lightweight wind- and waterproof, ideally made of breathable fabric such as Gore-Tex.

Penknife

Shorts and long trousers (both loose or made of four-way stretch material).

Sleeping bag Three- to four-season, or comfort down to minus 5 degrees minimum for the GR20; two-season for lower routes.

Sleeping mat If you're camping or biouacking.

Slippers or outdoor "Teva"-style sandals – great for resting your feet at the end of the day.

Soap The bio-degradable liquid kind.

Socks Purpose-made trekking socks that wick out sweat are best.

Stove Multi-fuel burners are best; Bleuet Camping Gas canisters and methylated spirit (known as *alcool à brûler* in French) are the only fuels routinely available in Corsica.

Sunglasses

Thermal T-shirts Made of modern wicking textiles.

Toilet paper

Water bottle or "Platypus-Hoser"-style reservoir.

Water purification tablets

Medical supplies

Antiseptic cream or spray

Deep heat spray or balm

Glasses or contact lenses Bring spare pairs.

Hypodermic needles For piercing blisters.

Insect repellent

Nail scissors or file To prevent in-growing toenails.

Pain killers Anti-inflammatory, Ibroprufen-based.

Plasters

Prescription drugs Bring a supply of any you might need.

Silicon blister pads

Sterilized gauze

Sun cream High-factor.

Zinc tape

Your top priority should be a good pair of **boots**, preferably leather ones with plenty of ankle support. These days, lightweight boots made from synthetic waterproof and breathable fabrics are popular, especially in summer, and although they may be fine for Corsica's low-altitude hikes you should think twice about using them on the GR20, much of which crosses long expanses of broken boulders and granite scree that can be merciless on your ankles. Don't, whatever you do, attempt anything more ambitious than an hour-long amble along level ground in trainers, no matter how comfortable they may feel.

Unless you're planning some hard-core winter adventure sports activity, you won't need to hike with a **tent** in Corsica, although many hikers regard the additional weight as a worthwhile trade-off for a bit of extra privacy. All of the footpaths are well served by gîtes and refuges. It is technically forbidden to **bivouac** within the Parc Naturel (except in the purpose-built *aires de bivouac* outside the GR20 refuges), but in practice no one is likely to stop you as long as you don't light fires and leave rubbish behind. An army-style poncho or large plastic bivvy bag can come in handy for this, and you'll need at least a three-season sleeping bag to bivouac at altitude along the GR20, especially during the first and last months of the trekking season – June and September – when freezing temperatures are not uncommon.

As for **clothing**, expect to have to add and remove layers constantly. During ascents, shorts and vest are usually adequate, even at altitude, while on the way downhill you may need long sleeves and long trousers. A good fleece can also prove invaluable, as can a lightweight coat of some kind, ideally one made of waterproof breathable fabric such as Gore-Tex or Triple Point Ceramic. Anyone attempting the GR20 might also consider shelling out on some kind of under-wear made of wicking fibre such as Polartec, which prevents the build-up of sweat that can cause sudden drops in body temperature when you stop moving; they're not cheap, but over a fortnight on the GR20 you'll easily get your money's worth. In summer, however, you should take along a sunhat and high-factor sun cream – sunstroke, caused by prolonged dehydration and exposure to strong sunlight, is a big problem if it hits you three or four hours from the nearest refuge.

Health and safety

Serious injuries are rare on Corsica's trails, but any foray into the mountains implies an element of risk and you should be equipped accordingly. Its exposed position means that the island is prone to sudden and dramatic changes in **weather**, which can transform a leisurely ramble into a battle with the elements with little warning. This is particularly true of the GR20's high ridge sections, where electric storms are near daily occurrences during hot periods. Just how lethal the interior mountains can be was vividly demonstrated in the mid-1990s when seven people died on the lower flanks of Monte Cinto on a single night, after being overtaken by a freak blizzard in July.

As a base requirement, therefore, carry waterproof clothing and a change of kit in your pack. Ensure, too, that your sleeping bag is stored in a plastic bag to stop it getting wet, and that you have enough warm gear, food and water to survive a night outdoors if you have to. Take into account the terrain ahead and assess how exposed to the elements you'll be should conditions take a sudden turn for the worse. **Forecasts** (in French) can be obtained by telephone on ☏ 08 36 68 02 20, but your best source of advice are the refuge and gîte wardens, who receive meteorological bulletins by radio each day.

Low-impact walking

Corsica's natural environment comes under intense pressure from the hundreds of thousands of visitors who enjoy it each summer. You can, however, **minimize your impact** on the island's wilderness areas by observing a few common-sense dos and don'ts.

Don't pollute water sources: never defecate or use detergents within 25m of a stream of spring; if there's a toilet and wash block within reach, use it.

Don't defecate on or near the paths: if you get taken short, dig a hole somewhere discreet and well away from the path for your faeces, which will attract flies and cause a health hazard if left unburied.

Dispose of your toilet paper hygenically: never leave it in the open to rot.

Don't light fires or leave cooking stoves unattended.

Don't leave litter behind you: refuges and gîtes d'étape all have trash bins which are emptied regularly throughout the summer (by helicopter from the more remote stretches of the GR). Remember that some organic refuse such as orange peel can take weeks or months to degrade.

Don't pick wild flowers, even those that grow in abundance.

In the summer months, the **sun** is more likely to pose a threat than storms. When walking on hot, exposed trails, always wear a hat and drink plenty of fluids. Nothing saps your energy faster than **dehydration**, which can be easily avoided by gulping down as much water as you can before setting off and then keeping topped up at regular intervals throughout the day. Use our route descriptions and maps to gauge how long you'll have to walk before reaching a water source and never run low; remember that when it comes to liquid, "little and often" is the golden rule. Early symptoms of sunstroke include dizziness, headaches, acute fatigue and nausea. The only remedy is to rest up, cool down and drink lots of fluid.

Sunstroke may set you back a day or two at worst, but the most common reason trekkers abandon the trail altogether are **blisters**. Caused by rubbing from ill-fitting or stiff boots, these can also be avoided by making sure your footwear is well worn in before the start of the trek. A good sock combination will also help: take along a thin inner pair and a thicker outer one, both made from wicking textiles that ensure your feet stay dry, and remove them during rest breaks. If blisters do begin to build up, the worst thing you can do is ignore them. At the first hint of rubbing deploy a Compeed-style silicone blister pad and some zinc tape. Should this fail you'll have no option but to burst the blister with a hypodermic syringe or sterilized needle (essential components of any trekker's medical kit). Allow the wound to breathe afterwards and then apply antiseptic cream and a plaster to keep it clean.

In the event of a serious, life-threatening accident, or if you need to be evacuated by helicopter for any reason, contact the local **mountain rescue** service, the Peloton de Gendarmerie de Haute Montagne (PGHM) in Corte on ☏04 95 30 36 32 or 04 95 29 18 18. They can also be reached via the police ☏17 or fire brigade ☏18. Note that from a **mobile phone**, dialling ☏112 will get you through to the emergency services even in areas where your network may not offer coverage. Bear in mind that the gendarmerie, who operate the PGHM, are entitled to charge a large sum for their help, and will almost certainly do so if they feel you have been imprudent in any way – another good reason to arrange dependable **insurance** cover before leaving home (see p.25).

Costs and money

Helicopter evacuation excepted, the cost of trekking in Corsica is surprisingly low, especially for the GR20 where opportunities to spend are few and far between. Resist the temptation of cold beers from the *gardiens'* refrigerators and you should be able to get by on very little indeed. Allowing £8/US$12.50 per day for food and £4/US$6.30 for refuge accommodation, it would be theoretically possible to complete all sixteen stages without spending much more than £150/US$240. In practice, however, most walkers get through double that. Take your time, splash out on hotel beds and restaurant meals, catch taxis to and from the trailhead, and you'll be looking at more like £400–500/US$630–800 for the fortnight.

On lower-level routes, which pass through villages at regular intervals, café, restaurant and hotel bills tend to put greater strain on wallets. But you can economize considerably by sleeping and eating in gîtes d'étape, where a dorm bed costs around £7/US$11 per night, or £16/US$25 for half board (*demi-pension*). Add in the cost of supplies, and a typical five-day trek wouldn't have to set you back more than £130–150/US$200–240. With a budget of £200/US$300 or above, you could afford to stay in comfortable hotels and eat out most days.

Note that once away from the main towns on the coast, banks and ATMs are a comparative rarity (on the GR20 they're non-existent), so be sure to take enough cash on your trek to see you through.

The GR20

Although it has only recently begun to attract the attention of North American and British walkers, the GR20 has long been France's most illustrious *Grande Randonnée*. The trans-Pyrenean GR10 may be longer, and the Tour de Mont Blanc may scale higher mountains, but "*le Grand GR*", as it's colloquially known in Corsica, still tops most French trekkers' hit lists. As the subject of innumerable magazine features, a clutch of specialist guide books and, in 2001, a hit movie, *Les Randonneurs*, its fame has spread far beyond the core of confirmed enthusiasts who tend to tackle paths of comparable scale on the Continent. Some 17,000 people travel to the island each year expressly to walk the route, many of whom have never ventured on foot to such altitudes before. If you're one of them, the landscapes awaiting you over the first few stages alone – not to mention the experience of hauling yourself and your gear up and down a succession of mighty slopes – may come as a revelation. In very few places on the globe do mountain ranges nudging 3000m surge straight from the sea, and none are so well served by marked trails and refuges as this.

Even for experienced mountain walkers, though, the wild granite peaks and high ridges of the Corsican watershed cannot fail to disappoint. All of the island's major summits – névé-encrusted until well into the summer – lie within reach of the path, and there are numerous alpine-style alternative routes, scrambles and multi-pitch climbs to distract the more adventurous.

One sure fire way to improve your chances of finishing, and actually enjoying, the GR20 is to **minimize the weight of your pack**. With two big bottles of water and three days' worth of food to carry on top of your equipment, this can be difficult, but a heavy rucksack can place a critical amount of strain of your knees and feet, and generally make life uncomfortable – especially during ascents and descents. The majority of people who bail out of the route over the first three days do so because of problems related to overweight sacks: blisters; knee or ankle strain; or excessive fatigue.

Before setting off, therefore, weigh your gear carefully (you can do this at any hunting and fishing store on the island). As a rule of thumb, men shouldn't carry over 15kg, and women 10kg. Any more than that and you ought seriously to consider ditching some stuff. Go through your rucksack and remove anything you can live without – even excess toothpaste, antiseptic cream and shampoo. Consider, too, replacing heavy cotton clothes with lightweight purpose-made ones. Aside from being more comfortable, wicking garments can also be washed and dried more quickly, which allows you to make do with a single spare shirt, for example, rather than several.

One thing you shouldn't scrimp on, however, is **water**. Springs are few and far between up on the watershed. Run out and you'll be risking dehydration, which can precipitate severe tiredness and sunstroke. Plan ahead: always keep at least half a litre in reserve and stash a strip of chlorine purification tablets in your kit in case you need to fill up with stream water.

Devised by the alpinist Michel Fabrikant in the early 1970s, the GR boasts some impressive **vital statistics**. Between the starting point at **Calenzana**, near Calvi in the northwest of the island, and **Conca**, near Porto-Vecchio in the southeast, sprawl 170km of relentlessly rugged country. To cross it, you have to negotiate a total of 19,000m of ascent and descent, climbing to a maximum altitude of 2225m (or 2706m if you climb Monte Cinto as a side trip). Some particularly steep and exposed sections – such as the notorious Cirque de la Solitude (see p.376) – involve pitches fixed with ladders, chains and stanchion cables, while early in the season patches of melting snow can impede progress towards the highest passes.

Don't, however, let the GR20's somewhat exaggerated reputation put you off. Strenuous though it undoubtedly is, the route is perfectly manageable for anyone in reasonable shape. No technical expertise is required, and even walkers with a poor head for heights usually manage the trickier pitches with ease.

All the same, the GR20 should always be approached with respect. Fatalities and serious accidents do occur – albeit very rarely – usually because of recklessness in poor conditions. Be aware that the weather at altitude can change dramatically and if it does you need to be prepared, with solid equipment and adequate supplies (see p.366). Above all, **never lose sight of the waymarks** unless you know exactly where you are and what you're doing, and have the necessary navigation skills to find your way back to them again if the rain or mist sweeps in. This applies especially to **solo trekkers**. On the GR20 you're seldom alone for long, but wander only a short distance off the path and you'll find it difficult to call for help in the event of an injury.

How long will it take?

Most walkers take between ten and twelve days to complete the GR20 from start to finish. It's possible to cover the ground more quickly than that (the record, held by a bank clerk from the Niolo Valley, is a superhuman 36hr), but to do so you'd have to double or triple up stages most days, which can alter the whole complexion of the route (especially if you're not very fit).

Also worth bearing in mind are the tempting side trips and alternative routes you can make from the main GR itinerary, notably the ascents of Corsica's highest peaks, which all lie within reach of the path. Such detours can add a few days to your overall time, but they're well worth the extra effort, taking you into terrain that's in every way a notch above what you cross on the red-and-white waymarked route.

In short, try not to rush your trek. Far too many people treat the GR20 like some kind of assault course, to be completed as fast and aggressively as possible. But ultimately it's more important that you walk at whatever pace you feel most comfortable with. As long as the weather is fine make the most of it: stay at altitude for as long as you can and take plenty of rest breaks to enjoy the scenery. It's amazing how many trekkers scramble out of the refuges into the pre-dawn darkness only to arrive at the end of the *étape* by lunchtime, spending the afternoons lazing around the huts instead of amid the very landscape they've travelled so far to experience.

The GR20 is described below in sixteen stages. Within those stages, times given are always from the start of that stage.

Stage one: Calenzana to Ortu di u Piobbu refuge

Stage summary
Walking time: 5hr 30min
Distance: 21km
Total ascent: 1610m
Total descent: 300m
Highest point reached: Refuge d'Ortu di u Piobbu (1570m)
IGN Map reference: #4149 OT & #4250 OT

Taking you from the coastal maquis belt to the rocky heights of the watershed, stage one provides a stark introduction to both the pains and pleasures of the GR20. With virtually no let-up in the gradient and three days' worth of supplies in your pack, you'll probably find yourself taking lots of breathers to gaze at the progressively spectacular views across the Balagne and interior range that unfold as the path progresses. This is one day when advance fitness preparation will definitely pay dividends. In all, the *étape* involves 1550m of altitude gain – more than one and a half times the height of Ben Nevis – much of it over ground exposed to the full glare of the mid-morning sunshine. With a dawn start, the first long climb of the day (to Bocca a u Saltu) can be tackled in cool shadow, but once beyond the pass the only shade comes from wind-blown pines as you enter an archetypal Corsican landscape of green-tinged granite interspersed by alder bushes and shimmering silver birch coppices.

Water is short on this stage. Some seasonal streams may be found in early summer, but don't rely on them. Carry at least three litres.

The official trailhead of the GR20 at **Calenzana** (covered in a separate account on p.138) stands at the top of the village, as indicated by numerous PNRC signboards. Flanked on one side by the tiny **Oratoire Sant'Antoine** and on the

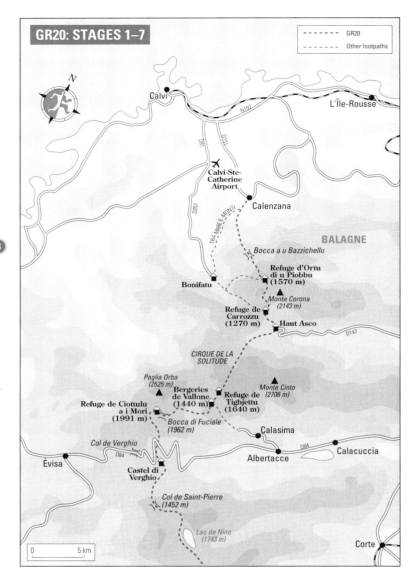

other by a covered spring (the first and last convenient filling point of the *étape*), the path strikes immediately uphill via a sunken cobbled mule track, emerging shortly after to open pasture dotted with solitary pines and chestnut trees. Scratchy maquis closes in as you approach the first ridge of the day, just below which a signboard indicates the **junction** (50min) of the GR20 and orange-waymarked Tra Mare e Monti. Bear left here to begin a gradually ascending traverse to the **promontoire d'Arghioa** (2hr), a rock outcrop where the path cuts decisively into the line of the hill and starts a long, steep ascent culminating at the **Bocca a u Saltu** (1250m; 3hr 15min).

The tone of the route changes abruptly on the far side of the pass as the way-marks plunge into old-growth pine forest. With the bulk of Monte Corona looming above, you then start to climb again into a long, convoluted traverse across a rocky slope that's steep in places. In early summer, clumps of spotted orchid enliven this enjoyable scramble, whose trickiest pitch is made easier by a fixed stanchion cable that you'll be glad of in wet weather.

Having climbed out of the valley to a second pass, the **Bocca a u Bazzichellu** (1486m; 4hr 30min), the GR20 continues uphill in an easterly direction, emerging from the forest to a superb view of the interior mountains. From here on, the going gets a lot easier. Sweeping around the head of the Melaghia Valley, the route then winds at a mostly even gradient to a boulder-choked spur, over which a short climb leads you to the **refuge d'Ortu di u Piobbu** (1570m; 5hr 30min).

Monte Corona

With an early departure from Calenzana, strong walkers can expect to arrive at Ortu di u Piobbu by midday, leaving plenty of daylight left for the enjoyable – if somewhat strenuous – **ascent of Monte Corona**. Given the length, extreme gradients and water shortages of the second *étape* to Carrozzu, the climb, which yields a spectacular panorama of the watershed's big peaks to the south, affords a more sensible way to pass the afternoon than pressing on. You'd have to be very fit, fully acclimatized to the sun and altitude, and travelling light to double up the GR's first two stages.

The round trip to the summit of Monte Corona and back takes around 2hr 30min; leave mid-afternoon as the views from the summit are best towards sun-set time (you'll also stand a better chance of spotting mouflon in the early evening). If you're heading off alone, it's also a good idea to inform the *gardiens*.

Immediately behind the hut, yellow paint blobs mark the path, which zigzags steeply uphill through birch woods to the windy **Bocca Tartagine** (1852m), gateway to the remote Giunssani region (see pp.148–150). From here, look for cairns striking steeply up to the right along a ridgeline cluttered with alder scrub and boulders. Eventually, after a frustratingly slow half hour or so, you'll emerge at open scree, across which the path to the summit is well trodden and easy to follow. Extending as far as the tip of Cap Corse, south to the snow-tinged massif of Monte Cinto and over the entire Balagne coast, the views are magnificent. Descend by the same route; you'll need a head torch.

Stage two: Refuge d'Ortu di u Piobbu to refuge de Carrozzu

Stage summary
Walking time: 6hr 15min
Distance: 13km
Total ascent: 670m
Total descent: 975m
Highest point reached: Ladroncellu traverse (2030m)
IGN Map reference: #4250 OT

Some of the longest, hardest climbs and descents of the entire GR20 occur on stage two. But as recompense you've a correspondingly memorable traverse to look forward to midway through the day, affording one of the route's definitive panoramas. Once again, water sources are virtually non-existent and you'll need to carry plenty of liquid to get you through the last section of the *étape*, a knee-crunching drop down a steep, south-facing slope that's a veritable furnace in sunny weather.

The stage gets underway with a short ascent through the woods and over a rounded spur, on the far side of which the **bergerie de la Mandriaccia** huddles beneath a dense pine canopy. Beyond the old shepherds' hut, a boulder-covered rise heralds the start of a hefty 2hr 30min climb across a mixture of smooth-backed slabs and large boulders. Its steepest section comes after you pass an arrowed turning to a **spring** hidden in the rocks just off the path, with the gradient only easing off as the waymarks approach the **Bocca Piccaia** (1950m; 3hr 15min), a superb little col from where a wild vista extends southwards to Paglia Orba.

A further short climb though the rocks overlooking the pass takes you over the 2000-metre mark for the first time. Skirting the southern flank of Capu Ladroncellu, the ensuing traverse is the day's highpoint in every sense. Most people kick back for an hour or two here to enjoy the amazing views, which encompass a huge chunk of the watershed and rugged northwest coast. Dominating the horizon, the distinctive profile of Paglia Orba marks the route you'll be following over the coming days.

From the level path around the summit of Capu Ladroncellu, an entirely different kind of traverse opens up to the south. After a sheer drop, the red-and-white waymarks guide you up a narrow curving ridgetop to the **Bocca d'Avartoli** pass (1898m; 4hr 15min), where they switch repeatedly from one side of the *crête* to the other to navigate a route through a dramatic sequence of wind-eroded outcrops and pinnacles.

At **Bocca Carrozzu** (1865m; 5hr) – or Bocca Inuminata as it's marked on some maps – you get your first sight of the refuge far below on the valley floor. However, a relentlessly steep, hot and slippery descent across loose scree has to be tackled before you can sun yourself on the hut's deck. On the way down, look out for lammergeiers (see p.436) soaring around the spectacular red crags of the Cirque de Bonifatu, which loom above the hut.

Thanks to its sheltered situation deep in the pine forest, the **refuge de Carrozzu** (1270m; 6hr 15min) used to be one of the most congenial stops on the GR20. But in recent years the hut and its camping-bivouac area have strained to cope with the summer influx. Toilet facilities are particularly inadequate, so brace yourself for some unpleasant mess and queues if you come here in July or August.

Congestion becomes marginally less of a problem beyond Carrozzu, largely because this is the point where most of those for whom the first two days of the GR have been too much drop out: a **liaison path** leads in around 1hr 30min from the refuge to the roadhead at **Bonifatu**, from where you can catch a bus or hitch to Calvi, or head off on the less arduous Tra Mare e Monti route towards Galéria.

Stage three: Refuge de Carrozzu to Haut'Asco

Stage summary
Walking time: 5hr
Distance: 6km
Total ascent: 860m
Total descent: 715m
Highest point reached: Bocca a i Stagni (2010m)
IGN Map reference: #4250 OT

The crux of stage three – and the cause of more dropouts than any other stretch of the GR20 – is the ascent of the Spasimata Valley, which begins just over the rise from Carrozzu. Although no more taxing than anything on the previous two days' terrain, the giant staircase of smooth-backed granite slabs leading to the Lac de la Muvrella comes as a rude shock to tired legs first thing in the morning, and many walkers turn tail while they can still beat an easy retreat to Calvi. Those that prevail, however, can look forward to the route's best views of Monte Cinto's north face, which holds a fair splattering of snow until well into July.

The climb begins as soon as you've crossed the swaying cable bridge ten minutes' or so beyond Carrozzu (one of the GR's classic photo opportunities). Although straightforward enough in dry conditions, it should nevertheless be approached with caution in wet weather, when the stanchion cables attached to some of the more steeply inclined pitches come into their own.

Depending on how early you set off from the refuge, you should emerge from the valley shadow into bright sunshine shortly before arriving at the **Lac de la Muvrella** (2hr 45min), a tiny altitude lake cradled in a hollow just below the pass. The grassy banks around it provide perfect spots from which to admire your morning's work stretched out below, and contemplate the remaining short but steep pull to the col ahead, which early in the season can be complicated by a fair-sized névé. On setting off for the couloir leading to the pass, look out for the famous rock formation to its left, known for obvious reasons as "**The Red Indian's Head**".

Reached after around three hours, the **Bocca di a Muvrella** (1860m) reveals another sweeping vista across the hinterland of Corsica's west coast, but for an uninterrupted view of Monte Cinto you'll have to press on to the second pass of the day, which the GR20 approaches after a short zigzagging drop and a more gentle traversing climb. Once at the **Bocca a i Stagni** (2010m; 3hr 30min) you can either linger to admire the spectacle of the Cinto massif in all its glory, or else get stuck into the abrupt 588-metre descent to the old ski station at **Haut'Asco** – one of the sheerest on the route. Winding over a steeply piled chaos of sharp-edged boulders, this descent is another that should be undertaken with particular care in rainy conditions.

For a full account of Haut'Asco – including reviews of its limited accommodation and eating options and a route description for the **ascent of Monte Cinto** – see p.328.

8

LONG-DISTANCE WALKS | The GR20: Stage three

Stage four: Haut'Asco to refuge de Tighjettu/bergeries de Vallone

Stage summary
Walking time: 5hr/5hr 30min
Distance: 7km/8km
Total ascent: 1000m/1000m
Total descent: 740m/840m
Highest point reached: Bocca Minuta (2218m)
IGN Map reference: #4250 OT

No stretch of the GR20 is approached with quite as much trepidation as the Cirque de la Solitude, the defining feature of stage four. A sheer-sided amphitheatre enclosed by the gloomy west wall of the Cinto massif, it's the passage GR veterans love to talk up, mainly because of the famously long sequence of chains, ladders and cables lining it. The gradients are certainly the steepest of the whole route, but Via Ferrata this certainly isn't and most people end up wondering what all the fuss is about. In any case, bottling out isn't an option: to skip the next couple of stages would require a long and expensive taxi ride or unpredictable hitchhike to Col de Verghio, which would, quite apart from the time spent travelling up the Niolo Valley, also mean missing out on the magnificent Golo River section of stage six.

The cirque aside, stage four is a case of "*plus ça change, plus c'est la même chose*": another long climb to start the day and a boot-jamming descent to wind things up. The initial section of the *étape*, however, begins with a fairly leisurely, but extremely scenic, ascent of the Asco Valley's head, in the course of which you get some spectacular views of the Cirque de Trombolacciu's peaks through the charred pines to the south.

If you're covering this stretch early in the morning, look out for mouflon scouring the crags high above the river as you approach the **ancien refuge d'Altore**, a former GR20 hut that was fire-bombed by "nationalists" back in the 1980s. From the rubble-strewn balcony where the refuge used to stand, an impressive névé usually lines the steep climb up to **Bocca Tumasginesca** (aka Le Col Perdu 2183m; 2hr 15min), which should take around thirty minutes. On fine, clear mornings you can sometimes see the snowcapped Alps floating above the distant horizon from here.

The view north, however, tends to be overshadowed by your first sight of the **Cirque de la Solitude** plummeting from the far side of the pass. Get here early in the day before the queues build up around the chain and ladder pitches and you can expect to complete the sheer two-hundred-metre descent and correspondingly steep climb up the other side of the chasm, in around 1hr 30min. But hold-ups are par for the course unless you're comfortable on steep, exposed rock, in which case bypass some of the climbing aids, many of which are essential only in wet weather (when you'd be foolhardy to wander away from the waymarks without ropes and harnesses).

From **Bocca Minuta** (2218m; 3hr 45min), take one last look at the magnificent view over the cirque before beginning the long descent to Tighjettu. Funnelling you down the side of a broad south-facing moraine, the **Ravin de Stranciacone**, this stretch can be hot going in warm weather, and tough on the knees, with the waymarks dropping sharply down inclined boulders.

Many trekkers are happy enough to call it a day at the **refuge de Tighjettu** (1640m; 5hr), perched on a spur overlooking the valley, but a more congenial place to rest up lies a short way further down the trail. Run by a local family from the Niolo Valley (see p.336), the **bergeries de Vallone** (1440m; 5hr 30min) comprises a cluster of old shepherds' huts recently converted to service walkers. Large canvas tents provide basic dormitory shelter, or you can camp and bivouac. Included in the €3.5 fee is the use of a flush toilet and access to a water tap and spring. Tasty Niolin specialities – from ewe's cheese omelettes to full-blown four-course meals – are also served up on their wooden deck, along with hot and cold drinks, and the views are great.

Stage five: Bergeries de Vallone to Ciottulu a i Mori

Stage summary
Walking time: 3hr
Distance: 6km
Total ascent: 550m
Total descent: 200m
Highest point reached: Refuge Ciottulu a i Mori
IGN Map reference: #4250 OT

Stage five of the GR20 is a comparatively short and easy *étape*, with only one significant ascent – the climb up Bocca di Fuciale to enter the Golo Valley. Most people combine it with the previous stage from Haut'Asco, which makes for a long day but leaves you in a prime position to scale Paglia Orba – Corsica's third-highest mountain – the following morning.

A gentle forest walk gets the *étape* underway as the path winds around the base of Paglia Orba via a series of side ravines. Giant Laricio pines shade most of the route until it bends decisively westwards to begin the assault of **Bocca di Fuciale** (1962m; 2hr 30min), reached after a long clamber across steadily steepening, exposed rock. A broad saddle coated in red scree, the pass itself is bleak, snow-patched and scoured by strong winds, but it is worth hanging around there for a while on the off chance of spotting the herd of mouflon who habitually graze above.

The waymarks then continue uphill to the right of the pass, before dropping down through juniper scrub to the GR20's highest refuge, **Ciottulu a i Mori** (1991m; 3hr). Overlooking the beautiful Golo Valley from a natural balcony on the base of Paglia Orba, the stone-built hut is smaller than most on the route – with only 29 beds inside and little shelter for campers and bivouackers around it – but the location is superb.

Paglia Orba

With its awesome fin-shaped summit, **Paglia Orba** is Corsica's most spectacular massif, even if not its highest. The two-hour ascent from Ciottulu a i Mori presents no technical difficulties in fair, dry weather, but you'll most definitely need a head for heights to enjoy some of the scrambling involved, which exposes you to the full dizzying drop of the north face – one of the

Mediterranean's most challenging rock-climbing locations. Allow **three hours** for the round trip from the *refuge*, and leave early in the morning to catch the best views, which are as amazing as you'd expect for a mountain that peaks only 19km from the sea. Confirmed scramblers might also consider the rewarding side trip to **Capu Tafonatu**, an extraordinary natural arch said to have been created by the Devil in a fury (see p.336), which can be reached by following a well-cairned route from the Col des Maures (see below).

From immediately behind the refuge, a clearly marked path picks its way up the side of the scree-covered ravine to the **Col des Maures** (2335m), a rocky saddle in the ridge separating Paglia Orba from its sister peak, Capu Tafonatu. Turn left and follow the sequence of small cairns to reach the latter, but be warned that the two-hour round trip requires some hairy scrambling across very steep and exposed rock. Even competent climbers should think twice before attempting it if there's even a hint of rain.

The same applies to the next section of the ascent up Paglia Orba, which begins to the right of Col des Maures. Although not especially difficult, it includes a couple of pitches that are a notch trickier than any on the GR20, one of them a narrow ledge passage above a vast cliff. Once atop Paglia Orba's forepeak, though, it's plain sailing through the Combe des Chèvres, a hidden dip encrusted in eternal snow, and thence across the windy ridgetop to the summit proper. Allow 1hr 30min for the ascent, thirty to forty minutes for the descent, and a good hour to take in the stupendous view from the top.

Stage six: Ciottulu a i Mori to Castel di Verghio

Stage summary
Walking time: 2hr 15min
Distance: 8km
Total ascent: 0
Total descent: 580m
Highest point reached: Refuge Ciottulu a i Mori
IGN Map reference: #4250 OT

By the standards of the GR20, stage six is a rest day – a chance to recover from the travails of the previous five *étapes* with regular dips in the Golo River, which flows through a series of deep turquoise pools, waterfalls and stands of magnificent Laricio pines. Presided over by the red bulk of Paglia Orba to the north, the valley rising from it also ranks among the most beautiful in Corsica and in fine weather the grassy banks, old-growth forest and paved Genoan mule track that usher you towards the stage end make a blissful change from the uncompromising terrain now behind you.

From Ciottulu a i Mori there's a choice of routes down the head of the Golo basin: either follow the cow track that plunges steeply downhill from in front of the hut; or else stick to the red-and-white waymarks as they sweep around a grazed spur to the west and then cut downhill to the **bergeries de Tula**. From this junction on the valley floor, a well-worn track then winds south alongside the Golo, which it crosses a couple of times. Lying only a couple of hours' gentle walk from the main road at Col de Verghio, the beautiful natural pools passed on this stretch are popular day-trip destinations, so expect plenty of company from midday onwards.

After the second and last river crossing, the next landmark on the stage is the **bergeries de Radule** (1hr 15min), a cluster of restored dry-stone huts that are these days among the few working dairies on the GR20. Camping is prohibited here, but you're welcome to re-fill your bottles from the spring nearby and, at times when the shepherds are in residence with their flocks, strong goat's and ewe's cheese is available.

The *bergeries* stand more or less at the midway mark of the *étape*, but the remaining half is largely a dull plod through dense pine forest. You'll know when you're nearing the end (2hr 15min) when you start to hear the unfamiliar sound of traffic drifting through the trees.

A full account of **Col de Verghio** and the Niolo Valley appears on p.179.

Stage seven: Castel di Verghio to Manganu

Stage summary
Walking time: 5hr 30min
Distance: 17km
Total ascent: 670m
Total descent: 475m
Highest point reached: Bocca a e Rete (1883m)
IGN Map reference: #4251 OT

Stage seven is essentially a transitionary section of the GR20, connecting the high mountains of the northwest with the Rotondo massif in the deep interior. Your first good sight of the serrated ridges that will dominate the trail ahead comes on reaching Lac de Nino – Corsica's most photographed altitude lake and the undisputed highlight of this *étape*. Many trekkers are tempted to double up such an easy stage, but it's a shame to rush past the lake, which makes as serene a spot to spend an afternoon as you'll encounter on the GR20.

At Castel di Verghio, a PNRC signboard on the right-hand side of the D84, 20m below the ski station's bivouac area, marks the re-start of the red-and-white waymarks, which veer immediately into cool pine forest. Having levelled off, the path then winds at an uncharacteristically even gradient for an hour or so through beech and pine woodland until it reaches the start of the day's main ascent. Compared with the rigours of the preceeding *étapes*, the climb to the **Col de Saint-Pierre** (or Bocca San Pedru in Corsican; 1452m; 1hr 15min) is a gentle one. This whole portion of the route follows paths originally set down for horses and flocks of sheep so it keeps to easy slopes. All the same, the views – of Paglia Orba and the Niolo Valley on one side, and down to the west coast on the other – are wonderful, improving gradually as you progress southeast along the ridgetops towards the **Bocca a e Rete** (1883m).

Once over the pass, Lac de Nino (1743m; 3hr 15min) is revealed for the first time in all its glory. Despite the hordes of walkers, joggers and trout fishermen who pour through here in summer, the eleven-metre-deep lake still exudes an air of sublime tranquillity. Herds of wild ponies and pigs graze its banks, which are sliced by winding water courses known as *pozzi* in Corsican (or *pozzines*

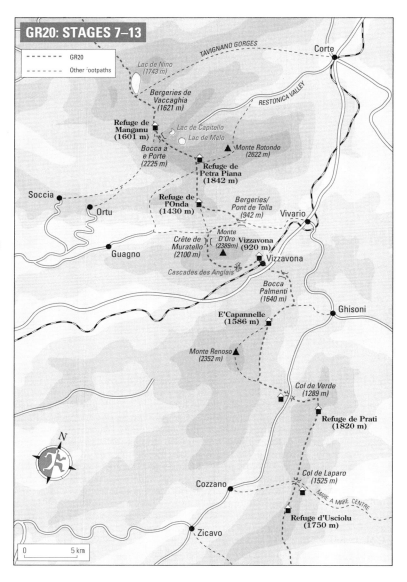

GR20: STAGES 7–13

- - - - - GR20
- - - - - Other footpaths

TAVIGNANO GORGES

Corte

Lac de Nino
(1743 m)

RESTONICA VALLEY

Bergeries de
Vaccaghia
(1621 m)

**Refuge de
Manganu
(1601 m)**

Lac de Capitello
Lac de Melo

Monte Rotondo
(2622 m)

Bocca a
e Porte
(2225 m)

**Refuge de
Petra Piana
(1842 m)**

Soccia

**Refuge de
l'Onda
(1430 m)**

Bergeries/
Pont de Tolla
(942 m)

Vivario

Ortu

Crête de
Muratello
(2100 m)

Monte
D'Oro
(2389m)

**Vizzavona
(920 m)**

Guagno

Vizzavona

Cascades des Anglais

Bocca
Palmenti
(1640 m)

Ghisoni

**E'Capannelle
(1586 m)**

Monte Renoso
(2352 m)

Col de Verde
(1289 m)

**Refuge de Prati
(1820 m)**

N

Col de Laparo
(1525 m)

Cozzano

MARE A MARE CENTRE

**Refuge d'Usciolu
(1750 m)**

Zicavo

0   5 km

in French). Concerns about the fragility of this unique spot, and its delicate turf shores in particular, have led the PNRC to install a *gardien* to ensure the ban on camping and lighting of fires is respected. You can, however, fill up your water bottles at the spring on the lake's southern shore, followed by the GR20 waymarks.

Having crossed the grassland plateau enfolding Lac de Nino, the route strikes gently downhill again along the banks of the Tavignano River, which it leaves soon after to cross a rocky area dotted with gnarled beech trees and alder bushes. One and a half hours after leaving the lake you arrive at the **bergeries de Vaccaghia** (1621m; 3hr 45min), whose stone huts enjoy a spectacular view south over the next stretch of the GR20. This is the point at which the yellow- and orange-waymarked route from the refuge a Sega (described on p.345) intersects the GR20, and some trekkers peel left here to follow the lower route down the Tavignano Valley to Corte.

The shepherds at de Vaccaghia don't encourage campers, but are happy to sell you cheese for the onward leg over the **Pianu di Campotile**, the giant, triangular-shaped plain spread out below. It takes 45 minutes or so to cross the plateau, on the far side of which, at the **Bocca d'Aqua Ciarnente**, the GR20 crosses another yellow-waymarked route: this one drops off the opposite side of the watershed towards Soccia (see p.187), via the Lac de Creno (another beautiful altitude lake; see p.187) in around 2hr 30min – the quickest route to a roadhead between here and Vizzavona.

The **refuge de Manganu** (1601m; 4hr 30min) is another beautifully situated hut, with fine views of the surrounding peaks from its deck and a rushing stream to splash around in if the weather's hot. Basic supplies are sold during the evening, in addition to chilled beers and soft drinks from a solar-powered refrigerator. There's not much space inside, but the *gardien* has erected a dozen or so tents to provide additional shelter.

Stage eight: Refuge de Manganu to refuge de Petra Piana

Stage summary
Walking time: 5hr 45min
Distance: 10km
Total ascent: 980m
Total descent: 740m
Highest point reached: Bocca a e Porte (2225m)
IGN Map reference: #4251 OT

With its panoramic views across the watershed and intense sense of verticality, this *étape* perfectly epitomizes the GR20 and many rate it as the most memorable of the route. After a hefty initial ascent, the waymarks squeeze through a niche in the ridge high above Manganu to enter a spectacular world of bare granite cliffs and pinnacles that tower above the head of the Restonica Valley, famed for its twin lakes, Melo and Capitello. Keeping close to the *partage des eaux*, the route remains above 2000m for most of the day, so check the weather forecast before you set off – some of the exposed ridge sections you'll be crossing are no places to be stuck in during an electric storm. Take plenty of water along, too, as springs are few and far between.

After the gentle slopes of the previous two stages it's back to business as usual, with the route heading uphill from the time it crosses the bridge beside Manganu. A couple of open, flatish areas of *pozzi* provide brief respites, but basically you're climbing for the first 2hr 30min or so up a picturesque valley head lined by slabs, alder scrub and a small lake. Eventually the waymarks reach the foot of a shadowy moraine from which the pass is clearly visible.

At an altitude of 2225m, the **Bocca a e Porte** (or Brêche de Capitello, as it's designated on some maps; 2hr 30min), is the highest point attained by the GR20. Appropriately enough, it also marks one of the route's most dramatic changes in landscape, revealing not only the lakes of the Restonica Valley but also a panoramic sweep of peaks stretching south along the line of the watershed. Care should be taken crossing the two névés immediately below the pass, and throughout the steep section that follows, which requires some simple scrambling.

A messy, steep descent across mostly bare rock brings you after 30min or so to the ridge. Look out for a second *brêche*, flanked by a pair of pinnacles, where yellow waymarks plunge left towards Lac de Capitello (see p.347), the smaller and higher of the two lakes visible below. Winding along the ridge, the GR20, meanwhile, presses on to **Bocca a Soglia** (2052m; 3hr 45min), where a second yellow-waymarked route drops sharply downhill, this time to Lac de Melo (see p.347).

At this point the GR switches suddenly northeast and contours across the mountainside for a while before beginning a steep 210-metre climb to **Bocca Rinosa** (2170m; 4hr 45min), from where you get a magnificent view north across the watershed to Monte Cinto and Paglia Orba. The last pass of the day, **Bocca Muzzella** (2206m), affords another spectacular view south to Monte d'Oro and Monte Renoso, and you may well want to lounge around in the rocks here for a while to steel yourself for the short, sharp descent to follow.

With its back against the sheer south wall of Monte Rotondo and its front opening onto a hypnotic expanse of ridges and peaks, the **refuge de Petra Piana** (1842m; 5hr 45min) is a fine place to soak up the atmosphere of the high watershed. Resisting the temptation to press on southwards, many trekkers linger here for an extra day or two, taking the opportunity to scale Monte Rotondo (Corsica's second-highest mountain), whose summit can be reached in an unforgetable 2hr 45min climb from the hut. The one downside of the site, at least for anyone bivouacking, is its comparative lack of shelter; aside from a few straggly alder bushes and piles of stones there's little to break the chilly wind that blows up the valleys most nights. A small range of basic provisions is available from the *gardienne*, but a better place to stock up on supplies is the bergeries de Tolla, midway through the next stage.

Monte Rotondo

Petra Piana forms the base camp for the southern approach to Monte Rotondo (2622m) – an ascent that's far less daunting than it looks from below. Only 780m – an average GR20 climb – separates the hut from the summit, which can be reached in around 2hr 45min (3h 30min–4hr there and back). Moreover, the route is well cairned, free of technical obstacles and a joy to walk: aside from the astounding 360-degree panorama from the top, you pass a large glacial lake that stays frozen for most of the summer, and get an unsurpassed view over the remaining portion of the GR20. All the same, the ascent should be undertaken with caution. At this altitude, weather can change suddenly and in the wet the boulders of the granite moraine you have to traverse to reach the summit become very slippery. Waterproofs, emergency warm gear, food and water are essential, and if you're going it alone make sure you leave your name with the *gardien/nne* (and inform him/her when you're back safely).

The trail follows the course of the stream flowing past Petra Piana. Having crossed a grassy hollow, you ascend across rough bouldery ground and rock bands to a ridge from where the south face of the mountain and lake are fully revealed for the first time. The cairns then lead around the southeast shore of the **Lake Bellavone**, from where they strike across the huge scree- and boulder-covered cirque below the summit, reaching the ridgetop at a rock pinnacle called "Le Fer de Lance" on IGN maps after around 2hr 15min. Approached via a short chimney, the **Helbronner Shelter** (named after the first person to climb Rotondo) is a tiny hut that's left open year round in case of emergencies. A five-minute scramble, some of it involving one or two exposed but straightforward moves, takes you from there to the summit.

For a full account of the much longer **northern approach** to Monte Rotondo, see p.346.

Stage nine: Refuge de Petra Piana to refuge de l'Onda

A change of tone marks stage nine of the GR20, at least if you take the soft- er, conventional route: a long meandering descent through pine forest along the banks of a rushing torrent, followed by an equally gradual climb to just above the treeline again. Numerous opportunities to swim and lounge in the sun punctuate this stretch, and you can re-provision at the picturesque berg- eries de Tolla midway along.

Alternatively, a more challenging, high-level Variant runs between the two refuges via the ridges. Truer to the spirit of the GR, it takes you along one of the narrowest section of the watershed, offering great views down to both coasts and back across the central range. In terms of time, there's little to choose between the two, with the low route only shaving around 30min off the total walking time. The one thing that might deter you from following the yellow- waymarked Variant is bad weather; the exposed ridgetops are no fun at all in misty or wet conditions.

Petra Piana to Onda via the bergeries de Tolla (the low-level route)

> **Stage summary**
> Walking time: 4hr
> Distance: 11km
> Total ascent: 500m
> Total descent: 910m
> Highest point reached: Refuge de l'Onda (1430m)
> IGN Map reference: #4251 OT

The trailhead for both onward routes stands just west of the refuge, at a junc- tion marked by a PNRC signboard. Follow the **red-and-white waymarks** southeast steeply downhill to the **bergeries de Gialgo** and thence across a succession of streams at a more leisurely gradient. On reaching the confluence of the Rotondo and Manganello torrents, the path, by this point paved and worn by centuries of transhumant traffic, follows the stream bank down through a mixed forest of beech and Laricio pine where you'll encounter plen- ty of tempting pools and smooth rocks to swim from.

A better-than-average choice of food – from staple supplies and local cheese to full-blown cooked meals – is available at the **bergeries de Tolla**, reached after roughly three hours near the end of this long descent. Make the most of the laid-back atmosphere. Spanning the beautiful **confluence** of the Manganello and Grotaccia, the **cable bridge** (942m) ten minutes or so below heralds both a change in direction and gradient.

From the **path junction** of the Mare a Mare Nord Variant and GR20, the red-and-white waymarks lead southwest to begin the ascent to Onda. Gentle to start with, the slope steepens gradually the higher through the woods you climb, emerging from the trees to open mountainside again after around one hour.

Petra Piana to Onda via the high-level route

Stage summary

Walking time: 3hr 30min
Distance: 8km
Total ascent: 390m
Total descent: 800m
Highest point reached: Onda (1430m)
IGN Map reference: #4251 OT

Follow the yellow paint flashes and sign marked "*par les crêtes*" from the bifurcation just beyond Petra Piana refuge to pick up the GR20's high-level Variant to Onda. This is an immensely enjoyable stretch (at least, in fine weather), and far less of a straightforward ridge walk than it might look from the hut. Some simple scrambling is required to navigate around the lumpy outcrops that periodically block the ridgeline. But, once again, clever waymarking makes light of these and most of the time you'll be striding along clear paths with 360-degree views.

Although little of the Variant follows level gradients, there's only one prolonged descent: the final drop to the **Bocca d'Oreccia** (1427m), where the route intersects first the orange-waymarked **Mare a Mare Nord Variant** and, after a short climb, the red-and-white flashes of the main GR20 arriving from the east. If you're intending to stopover at Onda, drop left (west) off the ridge here. Otherwise, follow the main route onwards for the long haul up to the Crête de Muratello.

Refuge de l'Onda

Clinging to a shadowy ledge just below the ridgetop, the **lefuge de l'Onda** (1430m; 4hr/3hr 30min) is far from the most enticing hut on the route, but it does enjoy great views east over the tree tops to Monte Rotondo. Campers and bivouackers are somewhat cooped up in a fenced enclosure below the refuge proper, where a toilet block and spring provide basic amenities. For supplies, ask at the *bergeries* nearby, which stock essentials such as cheese, charcuterie and even fresh fruit during the season.

Confronted with the uninspiring prospect of a sleepy afternoon at Onda, many trekkers elect to press on across Monte d'Oro to Vizzavona. If you're one of them, be warned that this makes for a long, tough day. In addition to the 600-metre haul to the Crête de Muratello, you'll have to contend with the gruelling 1100-metre descent down the Vallée de l'Agnone on the other side. Bear in mind, too, that the most compelling approach to Vizzavona is via the summit of Monte d'Oro – a longer, high-level Variant outlined below – which would require loads of stamina to complete on the back of the *étape* from Petra Piana.

Stage ten: Onda to Vizzavona

Comprising a short, sharp climb followed by a long descent, stage ten can seem a deceptively easy one. But take a closer look at the map and you'll see a disconcerting number of contour lines stacked up between Onda and Vizzavona, and those who've doubled the *étape* will certainly know all about it by the time they arrive at the railway line.

The payoff for the unrelenting gradients are more breathtaking vistas, as the GR20 scales the shoulder of mighty Monte d'Oro, the peak whose imposing profile has dominated the route since leaving Petra Piana. Rather than follow the conventional path down the Vallée de l'Agnone, intrepid trekkers can peel off the main path to pursue the more challenging *haute route* over the summit of the mountain, which winds down to Vizzavona via an even longer, steeper track. Either way, a superb day's walking is guaranteed. A full account of **Vizzavona**, including accommodation and places to eat appears on p.350.

Onda to Vizzavona via the valley

Stage summary
Walking time: 5hr
Distance: 11km
Total ascent: 670m
Total descent: 1100m
Highest point reached: Crête de Muratello (2100m)
IGN Map reference: #4251 OT

Stage ten kicks off in typically uncompromising fashion, with a lung-stretching two-hour ridge ascent to the **Crête de Muratello** (2100m). You'll be heading steeply uphill right from the start and there's no let-up in the gradient until the pass, a rocky doorway from where you get your last dramatic view of northern Corsica. On the far side, the more subdued mountains of the island's southern watershed rise above Vizzavona, still hidden by a fold in the valley.

Don't be lulled into thinking the crux of the day's work is done: the long, arcing descent down the Vallée de l'Agnone takes a good three hours in dry conditions. The first hour, across a messy combination of boulders, steeply tilting slabs and alder scrub, is particularly taxing on the knees. The going gets easier only once you've crossed the river for the first time, where the leafy beech woods begin to yield to the mature pines of the Forêt de Vizzavona proper.

Enclosed by an awesome cirque of crags, this valley has been a popular leisure destination for as long as there has been tourism in Corsica. At roughly the two-hour mark, the **Cascades des Anglais** (see p.351), a sequence of picturesque waterfalls and deep turquoise pools, recalls the era when wealthy British aristocrats used to travel up here to picnic away from the summer heat of Ajaccio. Today, it remains a well-frequented spot, visited in large numbers by day-trippers from the car park on the nearby Route Nationale.

Beyond the falls, the now well-beaten path drops steeply through the woods and then hugs the river as far as a **footbridge**, which you should ignore and head past if you're making for the *Hôtel-Refuge Monte d'Oro* at La Foce (see p.350). To reach the Gare de Vizzavona, cross the bridge and follow the *piste* around to the right. The station lies roughly 45 minutes' walk further down the trail.

Onda to Vizzavona: high-level Variant via Monte d'Oro

Stage summary
Walking time: 7hr
Distance: 12km
Total ascent: 1000m
Total descent: 1500m
Highest point reached: Monte d'Oro (2389m)
IGN Map reference: #4251 OT

Roughly ten minutes into the descent from the **Crête de Muratello**, a line of yellow waymarks strikes left off the main GR20. They form the start of a high-level Variant which, instead of plunging down the head of the valley, traverses the top of it to scale **Monte d'Oro** (2389m). If you've the legs for it and are not perturbed by the prospect of some exposed scrambling, the ascent of Corsica's fifth-highest peak offers a more enjoyable route to Vizzavona than the somewhat monotonous descent of the Vallée de l'Agnone. The one catch is its overall length. Although you've only 300 additional metres to cover between the pass and the summit, the spectacular drop down the far eastern flank of the mountain involves nearly 1500m of altitude change. While perfectly manageable as a single *étape* from Onda, you'd have to be fit to tackle this after trekking all the way from Petra Piana. Note, too, that due to its proximity to the sea, Monte d'Oro gets more than its fair share of high winds, rain storms and generally murky conditions, which can sweep in very suddenly and make progress down the steep summit ridges slow going.

The route (basically a reverse version of the one described on p.351) is fairly well marked with a mixture of paint flashes and cairns. It follows the main western spur up to **Bocca di u Porcu** (2160m) and thence southeast towards the summit, accessed via a steep boulder-choked couloir running off a gully. The last stretch involves a bit of scrambling which, although straightforward enough in dry weather, would be tricky in the wet. Allow 1hr 30min for the climb.

The **descent** drops down the same gully by which you approached the summit, but at the bottom the waymarks and cairns peel left (east). Having crossed a grassy hollow, you then penetrate a dark and windy ravine, known as "La Scala" ("the Staircase"), where there are nearly always large névés. Beyond it, a rock pinnacle called "La Cafetière" flags the start of a zigzagging descent down a stream channel towards the treeline.

The famous Forêt de Vizzavona closes in below the **bergeries de Pozzatelli** (1500m), which you should reach in roughly 1hr 30min from the summit. Following a well-marked path from there, the remaining two hours to Vizzavona cut between the corners of a giant forestry *piste* before turning left to cross the Agnone just below the station.

Stage eleven: Vizzavona to E'Capannelle

Stage summary
Walking time: 4hr 30min
Distance: 16km
Total ascent: 1000m
Total descent: 340m
Highest point reached: Bocca Palmenti (1640m)
IGN Map reference: #4252 OT

With the most rugged portion of the watershed now behind you, the GR20 takes on a more subdued quality beyond Vizzavona. There's plenty of excitement still in store – especially if you opt to follow the more sporting high-level Variants over Monte Renoso and the Aiguilles de Bavella – but for the next couple of stages at least, shady forest, gushing streams and verdant mountain flanks take the place of bare granite.

After a stiff but steady climb out of Vizzavona to the Bocca Palmenti, stage eleven of the GR20 settles into a long traverse through mostly wooded terrain that rarely strays far from contour level. Coverable in an easy 4hr 30min, it is the obvious one to double up if you're keen to push on quickly to Conca, although by doing that you'd be forsaking the chance to scale Monte Renoso – the last big peak of the central range – en route to Col de Verde.

With your back to Vizzavona station, turn right and follow the road uphill, past the shrine dedicated to Notre Dame de la Forêt, where the waymarks head right into the trees (as indicated by a PNRC signboard). They cross the highway shortly after and then continue northeast, following and intermittently cutting across the bends in a broad *piste forestière*. Having quit this for the last time, the GR then swings decisively south, zigzagging up through some majestic old pines towards the treeline. Just before reaching the pass, **Bocca Palmenti** (1640m; 2hr 15min), look out for a dressed spring to the left of the path. Denuded by severe overgrazing, the col can be hot work and you'll be glad of the chance to cool off before pressing on south to the **bergeries d'Alzeta** (1553m).

Beyond the shepherds' huts, the tree cover returns slightly, masking the views down the vertiginous Fiumorbo Valley to the east coast, visible for the first time on the GR20. The path remains shaded most of the way to the **bergeries de Cardu** (1515m; 3hr 15min), where there's another spring and a signboard pointing way down the mountain to the village of **Ghisoni** – a route waymarked in yellow, which drops 865m in around 1hr 30min (for more on Ghisoni, see p.352).

The remaining 1hr 15min to E'Capannelle (1586m; 4hr 30min) continues to contour through pine forest and skirts a third *bergerie* at **Scarpacceghje** (water available), before climbing to follow briefly a surfaced road. Having left it, the waymarks then descend across open maquis to the fringes of the ski station.

E'Capannelle

Presiding over a horribly scarred hillside that's strung with rusting ski lifts and pylons, the former *station de ski* at **E'Capannelle** is perhaps the least appealing stop on the GR20. First impressions are only compounded on arrival at the refuge (to the right of the path), which is in a lamentable state, with no running water or bivouac area and scant facilities inside. The intention of the local municipality which ostensibly runs it seems to be that you should plump for the relative comforts of the nearby **Gîte d'Étape U Fugone** (☎04 95 57 01 81; May–Sept), which offers basic but clean dormitory accommodation at the obligatory half-board rate of €30 per head. Alternatively, pitch your tent (or bivvy bag) in the grassy areas among the nearby *bergeries* and pay to use the gîte's bathroom (€2.50; tokens available on request at the bar).

Even if you're only passing through, it's hard not to be tempted on to *U Fugone's* sunny deck for a reviving pit stop. In addition to the usual range of drinks, meals and hot snacks can be ordered here from a limited menu of mostly local specialities. They also sell a good selection of **trekking supplies** from the bar.

Stage twelve: E'Capannelle to refuge de Prati

A choice of two very different onward routes presents itself at E'Capannelle. Contouring around the northern flank of the Fiumorbo Valley, the conventional itinerary proceeds in very much the same vein as the previous *étape*, at least as far as Col de Verde, where a pleasant café-cum-refuge makes a nice spot to re-fuel ahead of the ensuing 1hr 45min climb up to the refuge de Prati. If, however, you're hankering for a return to more typical GR20 scenery, consider the more dramatic, longer Variant over the top of Monte Renoso, Corsica's fifth-highest mountain and the last summit over 2300m reachable from the path. As the latter option takes a couple of hours longer than the normal route, people who choose it tend to prefer to bed down for the night at Col de Verde rather than press on to Prati. Either way, it's worth bearing in mind the length and overall difficulty of stage thirteen, which is a tough one to combine with its predecessor. Plenty of trekkers do walk all the way from E'Capannelle to the refuge d'Usciolu in a day, but invariably regret it.

E'Capannelle to Col de Verde: the low-level route

Stage summary
Walking time: 5hr
Distance: 19km
Total ascent: 850m
Total descent: 620m
Highest point reached: Refuge de Prati (1820m)
IGN Map reference: #4252 OT

The waymarks follow the line of the old ski lift uphill from E'Capannelle initially, peeling left after the second pylon to crest a spur. After a short descent down the other side, you arrive at the picturesque **bergeries de Traghjete**, whose stone huts huddle beneath the snow-flecked crags of Renoso, visible for the first time above. A short but fairly steep descent from here down the side of a stream gully brings you to the **Pont de Casaccie** on the main D168. The GR20 uses it to cross the stream, and then drifts back into the forest off the right side of the road shortly afterwards.

Once clear of the tarmac, the path locks into a level gradient of around 1500m which it more or less maintains for the next couple of hours, rising and falling periodically to ford the succession of streams that slice through it. At the 2hr 45min mark, the path emerges briefly from the forest to cross a cropped clearing, the **Plateau de Gialgone**, where a PNRC signboard indicates the turning for Monte Renoso (this is where you'd have rejoined the main GR20 if you'd followed the Variant over the mountain).

A gradually steepening descent takes you back into the forest from the plateau and down to cross the Marmano stream via a **footbridge** (1390m), from the far side of which the route swings insistently east. Ten minutes or so further down the trail, look out for a sign nailed to a tree to the left of the path marked "**Le Sapin de Marmano**". Until a bolt of lightning lopped nearly 3m off its top, this mighty fir was allegedly the tallest in Europe at 56m, with a girth of 6.3m.

Having reached the top of a low rise, the Col de la Flasca, the red-and-white waymarks drift down the line of a wooded combe. However, at various points they get muddled with an older routing of the path, which meanders northeast along the ridgetop (where you might be lucky to come across glades of giant yellow gentian flowers). Either way, keep heading downhill and you'll eventually end up on the D69 at **Col de Verde** (Bocca de Verdi in Corsican; 1289m; 4hr 15min).

A welcome opportunity to break for coffee and stock up on supplies for the next leg is provided by the *Refuge San Petru di Verdi* (℡04 95 24 4 82; late-May to mid-Oct), a seasonal café run by a local man and his wife from Leeds, who also operate a smart little refuge. Rates are standard: €10 for a bed, or €4 to pitch a tent; bivouacking is free (but you pay €1.5 for use of the solar-powered hot showers). A modest selection of provisions (including quality local charcuterie and cheese) is on sale at the bar, where you can also order hot meals and snacks.

E'Capannelle to Col de Verde: the high-level Variant

Stage summary

Walking time: 6hr 30min
Distance: 16km
Total ascent: 815m
Total descent: 1110m
Highest point reached: Monte Renoso (2352m)
IGN Map reference: #4252 OT

The high-level Variant from E'Capannelle, via the summit of Monte Renoso, is an altogether more challenging and memorable route than the lower one, although it does add at least half a day's walking to the *étape*. Most people who follow it end up spending the night at Col de Verde, making up time by leapfrogging Prati to reach Usciolu the next day.

Cleaving straight up Renoso's scarp ridge from the *station de ski*, the route, after skirting the Lac de Bastiani, swings south over the summit and then keeps to the massif's watershed ridge before delving steeply downhill to a beautiful hanging valley on the far side. From there it bends east to rejoin the main GR20 at the Plateau de Gialgone, around five hours after leaving E'Capannelle. It's well cairned throughout and easy to follow, but don't underestimate the dangers of the broad, shelving summit stretch in particular, which, like Monte d'Oro, is especially vulnerable to rapid changes in weather because of its proximity to the sea. Mist and cloud can sweep in to obscure the ridge in minutes, in which case you'll need IGN map #4252, a compass and adequate navigation skills and equipment to get you off the mountain in minimal visibility.

Weather permitting, the payoffs are some magnificent views of southern Corsica from one of the island's most highly rated ridge walks, and the chance to explore an exquisite hidden valley carpeted with *pozzi*. In addition, you'll have the satisfaction of knowing you've followed the route originally envisaged by the GR20's mastermind, Michel Fabrikant; the lower-level one was originally intended only as a bad weather alternative.

Col de Verde to refuge de Prati

The remaining portion of stage twelve takes you 550m higher up the watershed to Bocca d'Oro. From the café at the col, head along the *piste* that rises from the far side of the road and keep an eye out for the point five minutes later where the waymarks veer left into the woods. Zigzagging up the side of the stream valley swathed in mixed beech and pine, the path emerges from the treeline after around 30min and then begins to swing east into a sweeping traverse of the valley head. The final push to the pass is quite hard going, but the great views back over Monte Renoso provide regular excuses to stop.

Having reached **Bocca d'Oro** (1840m; 1hr 30min), you'll notice a dramatic change in landscape as the mountainside falls steeply away to the eastern plains and Ligurian Sea. On a clear day, the Tuscan coast is visible on the horizon as you drop gently across closely cropped grass, studded with outcrops of wind-eroded granite, to the hut.

Refuge de Prati (1820m; 1hr 45min) is optimally placed to make the most of the wonderful views. It was completely rebuilt in 2000 after a fire that resulted from a lightning strike and now ranks among the more attractive huts on the route, with beds for 22 people, a well-equipped kitchen and breezy deck. Facing due east, this is a perfect place to watch the sunrise over the sea, but if you're camping or bivouacking outside be warned that the site tends to be a very windy one and that there's very little in the way of shelter. Prati's unusually exposed, remote position, high in the mountains amid open grassland, explains why it was chosen as parachute drop zone during World War II, when Allied aircraft supplied the Corsican Resistance with arms, munitions and supplies – as recalled by a small plaque nearby.

Stage thirteen: Refuge de Prati to refuge d'Usciolu

Stage summary
Walking time: 4hr 45min
Distance: 10km
Total ascent: 760m
Total descent: 830m
Highest point reached: Punta della Capella (2042m)
IGN Map reference: #4253 ET

Few sections of the GR20 convey quite as vividly as does this one the sense of walking along an island watershed. For most of the day you'll be high up on the windy ridge dividing the Taravo Valley from the eastern plain, clambering over exposed outcrops, squeezing through narrow crevices and trying to stay upright on some skiddy inclines. **Water** is predictably scarce: you'll need at least enough to see you through the first 2hr 30min, when the path reaches a spring near the Col de Laparo.

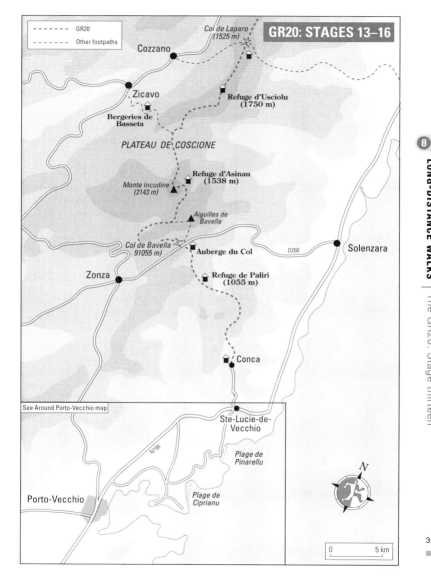

Having passed the memorial plaque to the Corsican Maquis at Prati, the waymarks make for the outcrop to the south and get stuck straight into the convoluted climb to the **Punta della Cappella** (45min), reached after an enjoyable traverse of a small, steep-sided cirque. At 2042m, the *punta* is the penultimate landmark above 2000m crossed by the GR (the last is Monte Incudine); scramble up to the summit itself, just to the right of the path, for the best of the day's views.

From here on, the route snakes insistently southwards, switching to alternate sides of the ridgeline via a series of rocky depressions. One or two passages require some simple handholds, and there are a couple of steep, gravelly zigzags as you drop from the Punta di Campitello (1937m) to the Col de Rapari, an open, grassy balcony offering a fine view over the Taravo Valley.

A much gentler descent from there takes you past some dramatically wind-bent beech trees to the largest gap in the ridge at **Bocca di Laparo** (1525m; 2hr 15min), where the orange waymarks of the **Mare a Mare Centre** cross the GR20. These lead down the side of the valley to **Cozzano** village (covered in a separate account on p.355) in around 2hr 30min, but leave you with a lengthy detour to rejoin the GR20; by dropping off the path, you'd also miss out on the most inspiring stretch of the *étape* between Col de Laparo and Usciolu.

From the col, the waymarks delve once again into the trees via a winding, moss-covered mule track that looks as ancient as the hills. After five minutes, it skirts a privately run **refuge** offering shelter and basic supplies, as well as a welcome source of fresh drinking water. Although their spring is dependable enough, the hut itself was firebombed recently by local "nationalists" so don't rely on it being there.

The trail winds on at contour level for another twenty minutes or so before bending decisively into the line of the mountain for the long, hard ascent back up to the ridge. On windless days, this can be a killer climb, hampered by clouds of flies, but en route you pass a magical little hollow filled with asphodels – the obvious place to break before the final push to the top. Having reached the ridge, however, the waymarks continue to climb in earnest, only levelling off at the **Bocca Punta Bianca**, from where you gain an impressive view north.

After one further, more gentle ascent – to **Bocca Furmicula** (1950m; 4hr) – the rest of the *étape* is plain sailing in fine weather, but beware if storm clouds are threatening as you drop downhill towards the refuge: this stretch is notorious for lightning strikes and at least two GR20 trekkers have been killed here in the past few years.

The **refuge d'Usciolu** (1750m; 4hr 45min) is a model hut in every way, with a magnificent outlook southwards across the Coscione Plateau to Monte Incudine and a *gardien* who brings a great sense of vocation to his work. His little shop (evenings only) stocks a good range of reasonably priced provisions (including fresh bread), packed up by mule from Cozzano every day. You can also order filling bowls of hot vegetable stew (order in advance on arrival; €7) and even send postcards and letters, complete with a special "Refuge d'Usciolu – GR20" postmark. The only catch is the congestion of the camping/bivouacking area, where flat ground and space are at a premium.

Stage fourteen: Refuge d'Usciolu to refuge d'Asinao

Stage summary

Walking time: 6hr 30min
Distance: 17km
Total ascent: 1000m
Total descent: 1230m
Highest point reached: Monte Incudine (2134m)
IGN Map reference: #4253 ET

Three distinctly contrasting landscapes characterize stage fourteen, as the GR20 makes its way across the last of the watershed's major massifs, **Monte Incudine**. The first is a knife-edge ridge known as the Arête a Monda, through whose pinnacles, tilting slabs, boulders and weirdly eroded buttresses the way-marks trace an ingenious course before dropping sharply back to the treeline. Between it and the pale grey mountain wall bounding the southern horizon stretches a broad area of moorland called the Plateau de Coscione, where for centuries shepherds from surrounding valleys have brought their flocks in summer. The GR20 cleaves diagonally across the middle of the depression in a little over an hour, and then bends east to attack the mountain, the last significant obstacle of the route.

The top of Incudine, however, feels frustratingly far off for the first couple of hours of the *étape*. Progress along the arête, reached after a short initial climb from the refuge d'Usciolu, is hampered by the vast outcrops jammed along it. But the waymarking is superb throughout, picking an inspired path that switches repeatedly from one side of the ridge to the other. In the thick mist that frequently shrouds this ridge you'll certainly be glad of them. Periodically obscured by the billowing cloud, glimpses of the Taravo Valley and Plateau de Coscione through gaps in the arête remind you that you're still at 1800m. Only after skirting the **Punta di a Scadatti** (1834m; 1h 30min) to pass through the Brèche di a Petra di Leva does the route begin to yield ground.

At the **Bocca di l'Agnonu** (1570m; 2hr 10min) – shortly after passing a **spring** on your right – the GR20 finally hits a more or less level gradient. A PNRC signboard stands at the pass, pointing the way southwest to **Zicavo**, the largest village in the Taravo Valley, which lies at the end of a two-hour down-hill walk. For trekkers heading south on the GR20, this is the most direct route off the path. An account of **Zicavo**, including reviews of its places to stay and full details of transport connections to Ajaccio, appears on p.355.

Most walkers, however, press on through the atmospheric beech woods and mossy boulders lying beyond the pass to a forested rise from which is revealed a fine view over the **Plateau de Coscione**. The next hour or so takes you across the rolling heath and numerous streams dissecting it to a **junction** (1450m; 3hr 15min), where the liaison path from Zicavo rejoins the GR20 (a more detailed description of this route appears on p.356). Follow the *piste* downhill from there to the Furchinesu stream, crossed via the GR20's final cable bridge.

From here on, it's uphill all the way to the top of Monte Incudine, an easy ascent of around 2hr 15min in total. Once out of the woods lining the Furchinesu, the first landmark you pass is the ruined refuge of **I Pidinieddi**

LONG-DISTANCE WALKS | The GR20: Stage fourteen

(1623m; 4hr), the remains of which lie scattered around a grassy hollow. Ten minutes' walk further uphill, behind a coppice of trees, flows the **spring** that used to serve the hut; take on enough liquid here to get you over the mountain as there are no more water sources beyond this point.

From the spring, the path strikes straight up the mountainside until it reaches the ridgetop at **Bocca di Luana** (1805m), where it veers south-southwest to follow the ridge all the way to the **summit** (2134m; 5hr 30min), marked by a crucifix. In clear weather the views, which encompass all of Corsica's southern tip and even the coast of distant Sardinia, are magnificent, not least of all because of the Aiguilles de Bavella, which you see looming above the watershed for the first time here.

The descent from Monte Incudine follows a gentle incline at first until the waymarks reach a niche in the ridge, where they switch suddenly eastwards into a drop of what looks like an alarming gradient. This descent down a messy mixture of sharp-edged boulders, slabs, grit and scrub, takes around 1hr 15min in dry weather; in the rain you should negotiate it with extreme caution.

Visible an hour or so before you reach it, the **refuge d'Asinau** (1538m; 6hr 15min) sits at the foot of Monte Incudine, surrounded by odorous alder scrub at the head of an overgrazed valley. It's a wild spot soaked in high mountain atmosphere – the last such hut on the GR – but once again sheltered, flat camping and bivouac space is at a premium; if you aim to sleep outside, get here fairly early in the day. Some basic provisions (including cold Pietra beers) are sold by the *gardienne*; the next source of supplies is the Col de Bavella.

Stage fifteen: Refuge d'Asinau to refuge de Paliri

Stage summary
Walking time: 6hr
Distance: 18km
Total ascent: 710m
Total descent: 860m
Highest point reached: Foce Dinosa (1206m)
IGN Map reference: #4253 ET

Moving on from Asinau, you can either trudge the long, flat, slow route along the side of the valley and around the spur to the Col de Bavella, or else bite the bullet and opt for the so-called "Variant Alpin", a much steeper alternative that takes you through the heart of the Aiguilles before dropping down the other side to the pass via a dramatic couloir. Don't let the name intimidate you – it's actually less nerve-wracking than several passages you'll already have covered. That said, the initial approach to the needles is steep, and one of the pitches involves clambering up another fixed chain.

Aside from the great views over Incudine, the chief incentive to choose the latter route is that it's simply far more fun than the conventional one, which is in essence a dull plod as far as the col, where the two paths merge. From here on, the GR waymarks follow an ancient transhumant corridor – much of it with original paving stones and buttressed corners intact – through the magnificent red cliffs and pine forest of Bavella, a landscape emblematic of the island's mountains since Edward Lear sketched it to such dramatic effect at the end of the nineteenth century.

Refuge d'Asinau to the Col de Bavella via the low-level route

After crossing a level stretch through the boulder field beside the refuge d'Asinau, the red-and-white waymarks descend at a gradually steepening gradient down the line of the hillside to a path junction, where a liaison route to the village of Quenza (see p.252) peels off the GR20. Shortly below it, you ford the Asinau to begin a short climb up the opposite side of the valley through silver-birch forest. At the 1382m mark (only 70m higher than the river), the path hits a level that it keeps to for most of the remaining route to the mouth of the valley.

The first and only real landmark of note along the way is the **junction with the Variant Alpin**, reached after 45min. Beyond it the path undulates across a succession of shallow clearings and side valleys, gradually descending as it rounds the spur of the mountain.

Having crossed the Caracuttu stream and dropped to 1005m, you then turn northeast and dig into the thirty-minute climb to the pass up the flank of the Ceca la Volpe ravine. As you do so, keep a close eye on the waymarks or you could end up drifting down sheep tracks at contour level to the stream, leaving you a stiff scramble to regain the path. With the imposing Aiguilles looming over the main road, the statue of Notre Dame de la Neige at the **Col de Bavella** hoves into view after 3hr 15min from the Variant Alpin junction. A full account of the village just below the col, including accommodation reviews and transport details, appears on p.256.

Refuge d'Asinau to Col de Bavella via the Variant Alpin

Designated by yellow paint flashes, the "Variant Alpin" zigzags steeply uphill from its bifurcation with the main path, 45min into stage fifteen, through a long coppice of birch trees. Once you're clear of the woods the gradient eases a little as the route bends into a long southerly traverse across boulders and juniper scrub, with towers VII, VI and V of the Aiguilles rearing vertically above. Having skirted the base of tower IV (Punta di u Pargulu), the waymarks then regain the watershed at **Bocca di u Pargulu** (1662m), a spectacular pass from which you get a marvellous view back across the Asinau Valley to Monte Incudine.

From there, the Variant drops steadily south past the east side of towers III and II. You'll need hand holes at several points, most notably a large tilted slab crossed with the help of a ten-metre **fixed chain**. Beyond it, a succession of steep pine- and boulder-covered slopes lead to a second pass below tower I, **Bocca di u Truvunu**, from where a sustained scramble down a narrow couloir funnels you to the Col de Bavella. Allow at least 3hr for this Variant section.

Col de Bavella to refuge de Paliri

The final leg of the *étape* takes around 1hr 45min of mostly unstrenuous walking to cross the Crête de Punta Tafonata, the jagged ridge dividing the gorge north of the col from the wilderness area to its east. A spring stands at the trailhead, next to the *Auberge du Col*, from where you follow a winding *piste* for ten or fifteen minutes until it meets a path junction, marked by a PNRC signboard. Bear left here (a right turn would take you to the Trou de la Bombe, a walk described on p.256) and follow the red-and-white waymarks as they drop downhill to cross a stream and, shortly afterwards, join another *piste*.

Before beginning the last short climb of the *étape*, you might feel like a swim, in which case head upstream from the bridge where the *piste* crosses a small river; hidden among the trees are some waterfalls with a couple of deep pools.

The 200-metre ascent to the **Foce Finosa** (1206; 1hr) is rewarded with a panoramic view over the wild country crossed by the GR on its last stage to Conca. Numerous large boulders provide vantage points over the valley during the descent, which brings you to the **refuge de Paliri** (1055m) after 45min.

Eager to polish off the final *étape* before nightfall, many trekkers hurry through Paliri. But the GR20's last hut, which stands slap in the centre of a spectacular forest wilderness, makes an ideal base from which to explore one of Corsica's most dramatic and distinctive landscapes. On all sides vast red cliffs soar above the pines, some pierced by weird holes from which you might see climbers dangling on ropes a thousand or more feet off the ground. Despite the proximity of the busy road, barely any day-trippers make it out here so savour the isolation and grandiose scenery while you can; the coast and its crowds lie only half-a-day's walk away.

Stage sixteen: Refuge de Paliri to Conca

Stage summary
Walking time: 5hr 15min
Distance: 12km
Total ascent: 520m
Total descent: 1360m
Highest point reached: Refuge de Paliri (1213m)
IGN Map reference: #4253 ET/#4254 ET

The final stage of the GR20 continues southeastwards along the old transhumant route formerly used by shepherds from the coast around Conca to herd their sheep to the high summer pastures of Incudine and Coscione. The consequent heavy grazing has over the centuries had a devastating impact on this rocky hinterland: greenery is scarce and signs of human settlement virtually non-existent. The ghostly ambiance is underlined by the ghoulish rock formations flanking much of the path, and by the ranks of charred trees lining the lower reaches of the valleys – the result of a huge bush fire that swept through here in 1985.

As the peaks of Bavella recede into the haze behind you, the forest gradually peters out to be replaced by Corsica's famous maquis, which reasserts itself here for the first time since the climb out of Calenzana, at the very start of the walk. The return of the **heat**, too, will take you back to the rigours of that initial ascent. With bodies well adjusted to the cooler climes of the interior, many trekkers succumb to sunstroke and severe dehydration during the latter stages of this *étape*; so carry plenty of liquid (at least double what you've been carrying in the mountains) as there's only one spring along the route and it's easy to miss.

A leisurely descent through well-shaded forest gets the stage underway, as the waymarks drift down the floor of the valley below Paliri. From stream level, a

△ Climbing Monte Cinto

short ascent brings you to a gap in a prominent rocky spur affording uninter-rupted views over the Punta d'Anima Damnata (1091m), the conical hill immediately northwest that's become a climbing hot spot. Once through the niche, you then start to contour around the rim of the valley head, with Monte Bracciutu dominating the landscape to the north.

After an hour, the path bends decisively south around a spur, which it crosses at the Foce di u Barcciu (907m). This point marks the start of the GR20's last significant ascent, which starts gently enough but steepens considerably towards the top, with the mule path cutting in zigzags to the pass, **Bocca di u Sordu** (1040m; 1hr 45min). From the far side, a fine view unfolds of Conca's desert-ed hinterland, bounded by the blue Golfe de Porto-Vecchio in the distance.

The next stretch takes you across a small, sun-bleached plateau scattered with extraordinary rock formations, from the edge of which the waymarks drop sharply downhill to the ruined bergeries at **Capeddu** (850m; 2hr 15min), where you'll find the only dependable spring of the *étape* (look for the path leading north off the GR20 and follow it for 100m; the spring is on its left) and a permitted camping/bivouacking area. The descent continues in earnest from there, dropping 250m or so in less than 30min through fire-blackened forest to ford the Punta Pinzuta stream, which the path first climbs above and then re-crosses shortly after.

Having crossed the stream a second time, you have to pull up a short, steep ascent to reach another pass, beyond which the route enters a long, sweeping traverse of a valley at contour level. This section through the maquis can be particularly hot work in the afternoon, when the sun will be directly ahead of you. But by now, a narrow, door-sized gap in the shadowy ridge ahead will be clearly visible. The final pass of the GR20, **Bocca d'Usciolu** (587m; 4hr 15min) provides an appropriately distinctive landmark at which to pause to contemplate your achievement: 170km distance covered, with some 19,000m of ascent and descent, over some of the roughest terrain in Europe.

Below you, spread out in the shadow of Punta d'Ortu, lies the village of Conca (252m; 5hr 15min), reached after an easy forty-minute descent through dense maquis. Close to the road, a dressed spring marks the official end of the walk and the termination of the trusty red-and-white waymarks. To find the gîte d'étape, just keep plodding downhill along the lanes – the locals will wave you in the right direction. For an account of **Conca**, see p.288.

The Mare a Mare and Tra Mare e Monti Trails

For all its undeniable attractions, the GR20 affords a very unrepresentative pic-ture of the island. To get a taste of the real *Corse profonde* – its sleepy granite vil-lages, chestnut orchards, ancient mule paths and river valleys – you have to drop off the GR onto the network of lower-altitude trails. **Waymarked in orange**, the Mare a Mare ("Coast to Coast") and Tra Mare e Monti ("Between the Mountains and the Sea") paths may not present such a physical challenge as the *haute route*, but – as their names imply – they're no less compelling and many people find them a lot more enjoyable. Aside from the more subdued nature of the terrain (much of which is dominated by the sea), Corsica's cross-country routes are serviced by a network of well set up little gîtes d'étape where you can end a day's trekking with a carefully cooked meal and bottle of wine, sleep on a mattress and carb up the following morning with a full French breakfast.

Supplies are available in village shops most days, and you can expect a lot more contact with local people than you get up in the high mountains. One of the principal motivations for establishing these routes in the first place was to provide a source of income for the depopulated villages along them, and it's fair to say you receive a much warmer and more genuine welcome while walking in the Corsican interior than is par for the course on the coast.

The outlines featured below will give you a rough idea of what to expect on each of the routes, along with essential practical information to help you get to the trailheads, book accommodation and find supplies. Whichever itinerary you choose to follow, take along the relevant IGN **maps**, the FFRP's topoguide, *Corse: entre mer et montagne*, or Trailblazer's *Trekking in Corsica* (see "Books", p.444). The latter two publications include all the maps you'll need, along with stage timings and a wealth of background information on the areas crossed.

The Tra Mare e Monti Nord

The **Tra Mare e Monti Nord** is the oldest and most famous trail in Corsica after the GR20, zigzagging down the northwest coast from Calenzana to Cargèse via Galéria, Porto and Évisa. It's also one of the few waymarked routes on the island that rarely strays far from the sea, so the views are superb from start to finish. Chief among the highlights is the beautiful Scandola nature reserve, with its outlandish red cliffs, Girolata, a superbly isolated fishing village otherwise accessible only by boat, and the astounding views over the Grande Barrière and Golfe de Porto to be had from Capu di Curzu on stage five. Elsewhere, you get to walk through old-growth Laricio pine forests, cross time-worn Genoese footbridges, and swim in some of the loveliest natural river pools in Corsica.

One factor you should certainly bear in mind when contemplating this route is the **heat**, which renders it all but off-limits between mid-June and October. Early spring, when the coastal flora is at its most colourful, is the best time to trek along the west coast.

Tra Mare e Monti practicalities

The Tra Mare e Monti is broken into ten stages of between 3hr 30min and 6hr 30min, which take between seven and ten days to walk. Gîtes punctuate every *étape*, although there are comparatively few places to re-provision; you'll probably find yourself making a detour to Porto to shop. ATMs are also thin on the ground; once clear of Cargèse, Porto and Galéria are the only places to stock up on cash.

For details on how to travel to and from the trailheads by public transport, see the relevant accounts on p.181 (for Cargèse) and p.140 (for Calenzana). SAIB (☎04 95 22 41 99 or 04 95 21 02 07) is the bus company covering the west coast, with services between Ajaccio and Ota via Cargèse running twice daily in July and August, with 1–2 services daily Monday to Saturday during the rest of the year. You can also get to Marignana and Évisa from Ajaccio with Autocars Ceccaldi (℡04 95 21 38 06) whose minibuses operate year round (daily Mon–Sat).

Tra Mare e Monti gîtes d'étape

With the exception of Cargèse (which has a clutch of small hotels; see p.182) every stage of the Tra Mare e Monti is covered by a gîte d'étape. However, demand for beds frequently outstrips supply, especially between May and mid-June and during September, when you shouldn't expect to find a free space unless you've pre-booked. Alternative accommodation is available only at Calenzana, Galéria, Évisa and Cargèse; elsewhere you might have to be prepared to bivouac or camp.

Calenzana *Gîte d'étape municipal* ℡04 95 62 77 13. Large, impersonal place with four-bed dorms. Usually crammed, because it also serves the GR20. Limited camping space. May–Sept. See also p.140.

Bonifatu *Auberge de la Forêt* ℡04 95 65 09 98. Well-run gîte with particularly good restaurant but unappealing camp ground to the rear. April–Sept.

Tuarelli *L'Alzelli* ℡04 95 62 01 75. Gorgeous location beside a deep stream where you can swim. Their terrace is also pleasant, and the food good. April–Oct.

Galéria *Chez M. Rossi* ℡04 95 62 00 46. Friendly place 1km southwest of the beach and village centre, with large garden for tents. April–Oct. See also p.152.

Girolata *Le Cabane du Berger* ℡04 95 20 16 98. The nicest of the pair in this village, with wooden cabins set under eucalyptus trees behind the beach. Their (optional) half board isn't up to much, though. The same applies to *Le Cormorant* ℡04 95 20 15 55, overlooking the jetty, where half board is obligatory.

Curzu *Chez M. et Mme Sagny* ℡04 95 27 31 70. Modern three-storey building on the southwest side of the village, next to the main road. Provisions available. March–Oct.

Serriera *U me Mulinu* ℡04 95 26 10 67. The shabbiest gîte on the route, fifteen minutes' walk out of the village centre. March–Oct.

Ota *Chez Félix* ℡04 95 26 12 92. Occupying a prime spot with fine views over the valley from its sociable terrace. Open all year. *Chez Marie* (*le Bar des Chasseurs*) ℡04 95 26 11 37. Pleasant enough, and a good fallback if *Chez Félix* is full. April–Oct.

Marignana *Ustaria di a Rota* ℡04 95 26 21 21. Arguably the most convivial stop on the route, if not in all Corsica. In addition to a quality Corsican restaurant, they've a well-stocked bar and even a small concert hall. April–Oct.

Revinda *E'Case* ℡04 95 26 48 19. A prime spot high above the west coast, with the character of a mountain hut more than a gîte. Meals available. April–Oct.

The Mare a Mare Nord

Scenic diversity is the hallmark of the **Mare a Mare Nord**, which begins at Moriani-Plage on the east coast and winds west through the heart of the mountains to Cargèse. After a prolonged initial climb from sea level to enter the Bozio region, the path passes through a succession of hill villages to Corte, and then presses up the old Genoan mule track along Tavignano gorge to reach the Niolo Valley via the Col de l'Arinella. With the dramatic Monte Cinto and Paglia Orba massifs looming to the north, the trail then crosses the Col de Verghio into the Spelunca gorge, dropping through Évisa and Marignana (where it joins the Tra Mare e Monti) to follow deserted ridgetops and forested valleys back down to the sea.

No two days of the route are alike and following it gives a vivid taste of the Corsican interior. But for an even more intense feeling of wilderness, the Mare a Mare Nord's Variant, which peels off the main path after three stages and bypasses Corte in favour of the isolated forest area further south, is the one to go for. Crossing the watershed at Onda, where it intersects the GR20, the Variant presents more of a challenge as it passes through comparatively few villages. Accommodation and re-provisioning opportunities are few and far between, but the payoff is a feeling of remoteness you rarely experience on more frequented routes.

The **downside** of the Mare a Mare Nord as a whole is the couple of relatively dull stages towards the start of the walk. With a little more time, however, it is possible to avoid these by combining the principal route and its Variant to create a giant **circular itinerary**, starting in Cargèse and progressing east to Corte, where you can jump on a train to Vivario and pick up the onward section back to Marignana. **Another variation** would be to follow the GR20 from A Sega in the Tavignano Valley and walk to Col de Verghio via the beautiful Lac de Nino instead of the Niolo.

Mare a Mare Nord practicalities

Both **trailheads** are readily accessible by public transport (see p.181 for Cargèse and p.318 for Moriani), and you can jump on or off the main path at regular intervals during the summer, when the Niolo Valley is served by bus (see p.357). The Variant section, however, crosses a total backwater where you'll have to hitch if you decide to leave the path. Finding food can also be a problem on the Variant: from June until Sept, supplies are sold (at inflated prices) at the *bergeries* below the refuge d'Onda, but beyond there the only place you can buy provisions before Marignana is the village shop at Pastricciola (open Tues, Thurs & Sat only).

Pressure on gîte beds isn't too bad on this route, at least until you reach Marignana, from where the hostels serve two different walks and are thus correspondingly popular.

Mare a Mare Nord principal gîtes d'étapes

I Penti Santa-Reparata-di-Moriani, *Luna Piena* ☎ 04 95 38 59 48. Privately run twenty-bed gîte, with great views of the eastern plain.

Pianello ☎ 04 95 39 60 74. Municipal gîte with eighteen bunk beds, in the first Bozio village of the route.

Sermano ☎ 04 95 48 67 97. Matchless views of the interior range, dominated by Monte Rotondo and Corte in the foreground, from this cosy gîte with only sixteen places.

Corte *U Tavignano* ☎ 04 95 46 16 85. Secluded in woods behind the citadel. See also p.341.

Calacuccia *Le Couvent* ☎ 04 95 48 02 73. Double rooms as well as dorms, and fully equipped kitchen (but no meals), 1km west of Calacuccia in the hamlet of Sidossi. See also p.335.

Albertacce ☎ 04 95 48 05 60 or 04 95 48 08 05. Basic hostel on the roadside, with small dorms but good self-catering kitchen. See also p.335.

Évisa *Sarl u Poggiu* ☎ 04 95 26 21 28. Very comfortable place, just below the village centre, offering better-than-average food. See also p.176.

Marignana (see Tra Mare e Monti above).

Revinda (see Tra Mare e Monti above).

Cargèse See p.182.

Mare a Mare Nord Variant gîtes d'étape

Poggio-de-Venaco ☎ 04 95 47 02 29 or 04 95 47 03 45. Close to Corte, with 24 beds.

Santo-Pietro-di-Venaco ☎ 04 95 47 07 29. Not the most inspiring of locations, but large and well equipped.

Vivario See p.349.

Onda See p.384.

Pastricciola ☎ 04 95 28 91 88 or 04 95 28 91 60, or leave a message on ☎ 04 95 28 96 34. 1km from the centre of village, and a bit institu-tional, but friendly, and there's a washing machine.

Guagno ☎ 04 95 28 33 47. Municipal gîte with two fourteen-bed dorms and lower-than-average rates, but no meals.

Soccia See p.187.

Letzia ☎ 04 95 26 63 24. Fully equipped self-catering chalets in woods next to a riding centre, run by the local mairie, at bargain rates. Reserve ahead; ask to speak to Carole Paoli.

The Mare a Mare Centre

The **Mare a Mare Centre** footpath cleaves diagonally across the middle of Corsica, between Ghisonaccia on the eastern plain and Porticcio at the southern tip of the Golfe d'Ajaccio. Accessible to all from late April to November, it sees relatively few hikers, though the route is as varied and scenic as any on the island, with some particularly memorable stretches along remote ridges overlooking the sea.

The trailhead is 2.5km south of Ghisonaccia on the N198, near a bridge called Pont de l'Abatescu, which you can reach on any of the buses running between Bastia and Porto-Vecchio. From here the path cuts across fruit orchards and vineyards, nurtured by the River Fium'orbo, from which this region takes its name, to begin a gradual ascent of the coastal range.

Once over the Col de Laparo (1525m), where the route crosses the GR20, you enter the backwater region of Haut Taravo, named after the river that drains into the Golfe de Valinco near Propriano. From there the path heads west via remote Cozzano and Tasso villages to Guitera-les-Bains, where it climbs out of the Taravo Valley and over thickly forested spurs into Frasseto. Exposed ridges characterize the remaining few stages of the trail as it strikes north from Quasquara to scale the rocky Punta d'Urghiavari, before bending southwest to cross the main Ajaccio–Bonifacio road at the Col St-Georges. From here, another sharp ascent takes you onto a high ridge, and the path gives little ground until its junction with the Tra Mare e Monti trail near the isolated village of Bisinao, where it swings northwest towards Porticcio.

The most obvious **variation** for the Mare a Mare Centre would be to combine it with a few *étapes* of the GR20, which it intersects at Col de Laparo. Following the route from west to east, instead of the conventional east-west direction, you can build on your altitude gain (and improved fitness) by swinging north along the GR20 to the refuge de Prati (see p.388), and press on from there towards Col de Verde. Weather permitting, the superb high-level Variant over Monte Renoso (described on p.353) would provide the ideal culmination of this extremely varied route.

Mare a Mare Centre practicalities

The Mare a Mare Centre has grown in popularity over the past three or four years, but it's still one of the quietest waymarked paths on the island. That said, you'd do well to reserve your gîte beds in advance as there is little by way of alternative accommodation in most villages. Although divided into seven stages (of between 3hr and 6hr 30min), the itinerary may be completed in six days by combining the first two *étapes*, making a longer-than-average first day from Ghisonaccia to Catastaghju (7hr).

There are **grocery stores** at Cozzano (stage two) and Sampolo (early in stage three), but none after that. This is one route on which you'll save yourself a lot of effort by eating in the gîtes d'étape, which all serve filling hot meals each evening (with advance warning). **Buses** connect Cozzano with Ajaccio (daily Mon–Sat with Autocars Santoni ☎04 95 22 64 44 or 04 95 24 51 56), and you can travel to and from the Col St-Georges on any of the services running between the capital and Propriano/Porto-Vecchio in the south (see pp.291–292).

Mare a Mare Centre gîtes d'étape

Ghisonaccia See p.297.

Serra-di-Fiumorbu ☎04 95 56 75 48 or 06 81 04 69 49. A stone building on the village outskirts with 25 beds.

Catastaghju ☎04 95 56 70 14 or 04 95 56 10 89. Dorm accommodation for 24 in a converted hydroelectricity station.

Cozzano *Bella Vista* ☎04 95 24 41 59. One of the friendliest, best-run gîtes in Corsica, in a gorgeous village: 26 beds, camping space and a couple of doubles, as well as top-notch cooking. See also p.355.

Tasso ☎04 95 24 52 01. Four- to six-person dorms offering 22 beds. Well set up for self-caterers, but they also offer half board.

Guitera-les -Bains ☎04 95 24 44 40 or 04 95 24 42 54. Small dorms, camping space and a very pleasant terrace.

Quasquara ☎04 95 53 61 21. Dorm space for 33 and a well-equipped kitchen.

Col St-Georges ☎04 95 25 70 06. A very swish gîte, but marred by its location on the side of a main road.

Porticcio See p.214.

The Tra Mare e Monti Sud

The recently inaugurated **Tra Mare e Monti Sud** hiking trail runs from Porticcio to Propriano, divided into five relatively easy stages of between 3hr 45min and 6hr. The scenery along the route, which winds southwest along the ridge dividing the Golfe d'Ajaccio from the Golfe de Valinco, is nowhere near as dramatic as on the Tra Mare e Monti Nord trail (see p.400), but the gentle, maquis-covered hills and rocky coastline make it an enjoyable hike that will particularly appeal to less experienced walkers. It also takes you within striking distance of beaches at Capo di Muro (covered on p.215), the prehistoric site at Filitosa (see p.232), and the picturesque resort of Porto-Pollo (see p.227). The only real drawback is that, unlike most of the long-distance footpaths in Corsica, this one does not have gîtes d'étape at each stage, which means you have to shell out on hotels or campsites for at least three of the four or five nights.

To create an excellent ten-day walk across the south of Corsica, you could combine this route with the Mare a Mare Sud (see below), which begins at its terminus, in the hamlet of Burgo near Propriano.

Tra Mare e Monti Sud practicalities

The trail's only two **gîtes d'étape** are at Bisinao (☎04 95 24 21 66) and Burgo (☎04 95 76 15 05). Both are heavily booked during the summer, when you should reserve at least a couple of weeks in advance to ensure a bed. For reviews of hotels and campsites in Porticcio, Côti-Chiavari, Porto-Pollo, Olmeto and Propriano, see the relevant accounts.

The Mare a Mare Sud

The **Mare a Mare Sud**, which meanders between the gulfs of Valinco and Porto-Vecchio in southern Corsica in four to five days, is a relatively gentle route that takes you through the prettiest corners of southern Corsica. Encompassing the deep-blue inlets of the coast and the pale-grey peaks of the Alta Rocca region, its landscapes are unremittingly beautiful and unspoilt. This is a particularly good option for forest lovers: long stretches of the path wind through tracts of ancient oak and pine forest, regularly crossing streams and rivers where you can swim and sunbathe miles from any road. Several prehistoric sites – including the wonderful Cucurzzu remains at Levie – and a well-preserved Pisan chapel also lie within a stone's throw of the route.

Mare a Mare Sud practicalities

Divided into five stages of between four and six hours, the Mare a Mare Sud can be attempted at any time of year, even high summer, thanks to the amount of tree cover along the route. Its **trailheads** are both some way inland. As neither is served by public transport you'll have to brace yourself for a long walk or else catch a taxi. From Porto-Vecchio, the start of the path at **Alzu di Gallina** takes between 1hr 30min to 2hr to reach on foot. Striking uphill through maquis and then monotonous pine forest, the first *étape* is a bit dull and many people elect to skip it by hitching or catching a bus to Ospédale (see below) and continuing from there. If you begin the walk at Propriano, you'll have a 2hr 30min hike along the road to reach the start of the path at **Burgo**: follow the N196 for 30min until you reach a Total petrol station, and turn right along the D257, following the road for 7km until you see the gîte on your left. The trailhead lies a little further up the road on the opposite side.

Buses connect many of the villages on the path with Propriano and Porto-Vecchio, allowing you to join and leave the route at several points. Autocar Ricci's service (year round Mon–Sat; ℡04 95 76 25 59) stops at Sainte-Lucie and Levie; for Quenza, pick up Balési Évasion's minibus (July & Aug Mon–Sat; Sept–June Mon & Fri only).

Mare a Mare Sud gîtes d'étape

The Mare a Mare Sud's modest length, coupled with the proximity of its trail-heads to some of Corsica's finest beaches, ensure it receives a steady stream of walkers from May onwards. Beds in the gîtes are thus at a premium, so book well ahead and expect to have to pay for half board, which is obligatory in most of them. The only hotel along the route is at Quenza (see p.252), but there is a pleasant *chambre d'hôte* in Sainte-Lucie (see p.245) and plenty of shops, restaurants and cafés elsewhere.

Burgo *U Fracintu* ℡ 04 95 76 15 05, ℻ 04 95 76 14 31. Sixty beds in two-, four- and six-person dorms in a large gîte overlooking the valley. Half board €26–35 depending on size of dorm.

Sainte-Lucie-de-Tallano *U Fragnonu* ℡ 04 95 78 82 56, ℻ 04 95 78 82 67. An old stone house on the edge of the village. See also p.245.

Serra-di-Scapomena ℡ 04 95 78 64 90, ℻ 04 95 78 72 43. Four-bed dorms and a superb east-facing balcony. April–Oct.

Quenza *Corse Odyssée* ℡ 04 95 78 64 05, ℻ 04 95 78 61 91. Tucked away a kilometre or so north-

east of the village; follow the signs up the road beyond the *Auberge Sol e Monti*. See also p.252.

Levie *Bienvenue à l'Alta Rocca* ℡ 04 95 78 46 41. Not the most inspiring gîte on the route (it's run by the local municipality), but it's on the edge of the area's liveliest village. See also p.247.

Cartalavonu *Le Refuge* ℡ 04 95 70 00 39. Situated high in the massif d'Ospédale in a converted summer *bergerie*. Half board is optional, because the only place to eat for miles is the wardens' own Corsican speciality restaurant (see p.286).

Contexts

Contexts

The historical framework 407–419

The Corsican troubles: an overview 420–431

Corsican wildlife 432–438

Books 439–445

The historical framework

Invasion and resistance are recurring themes throughout Corsica's history. This has always been an island of particular strategic and commercial appeal, with its sheltered harbours and protective mountains, set on the western Mediterranean trade routes within easy reach of several colonizing powers. Greeks, Carthaginians and Romans came in successive waves, landing on the eastern coast, driving native Corsicans into the high interior and battling against new predators in their turn. The Romans were ousted by Vandals, and for the following thirteen centuries the island was attacked, abandoned, settled and sold as nation-states and empires squabbled over Europe's territories, and generations of islanders fought against foreign rule and against each other. In the light of this turbulent past, it seems inevitable that Corsica's early history, unexplored until the twentieth century, should have its own pattern of invasion and occupation.

Beginnings

For thousands of years, the relics of Corsica's **Stone Age** were simply accepted as an inexplicable aspect of the island's landscape. In 1840 Prosper Mérimée, then Inspector of Historic Monuments, described the simple **menhirs** (from the Celtic *maen hir* – "long stone") of the southwest and tabulated various primitive stone monuments elsewhere in Corsica, but the origins and functions of these stone slabs and figures remained unknown until 1954, when French archeologist Roger Grosjean set about excavating and recording the megalithic sites. Only when his excavations started in earnest did a picture emerge of a complex prehistoric society that developed its religious and cultural framework over several millennia.

The first settlers

It's now believed that Corsica's **original inhabitants** arrived from northern Italy in the **seventh millennium BC**, long before the monument-building era. Making their shelters in caves and under cliffs, they survived by hunting, gathering and fishing. A thousand years later came new settlers with new skills, building villages, planting crops and herding cattle. The practice of **transhumant pastoralism** – driving sheep to graze on the uplands in summer, then down to coastal pastures in the winter – may have been started in this era, and is still followed by Corsican shepherds to this day. In the **fourth millennium**, the creators of the island's **megalithic** buildings migrated into the Mediterranean area from Asia Minor and the Aegean. There are numerous interpretations of the stone monuments and tombs that were erected during the next 2000 years, but the most widely held opinion is that they were connected with the veneration of ancestors and the spirits of the dead, and perhaps centred on an Earth Deity or Mother.

At first the dead were buried in underground tombs or **cists**, and were represented, commemorated or maybe guarded by single menhirs placed nearby.

Clusters of these tombs and menhirs have been found in the southwestern Sartenais region and near Porto-Vecchio. Cist burial later gave way to the custom of setting stone sarcophagi or **dolmens** (table stones) above ground and covering them with earth; around a hundred of these, measuring about 2m by 2.5m, have been discovered (now exposed after the erosion of the soil), one of the best examples being at **Fontanaccia**. At a later stage the menhirs acquired human forms and features: some were given swords or daggers, some were carved with rudimentary shoulder blades or ribs, and no two statues were the same. The function of these eerie warrior figures, most of which were found at **Filitosa** (see pp.232–234), can only be imagined. Suggestions range from representations of dead spirits to trophies of war, each one marking a defeated invader.

The Torréens

The culture embodied by these carved menhirs reached its peak towards 1500 BC, when new aggressors – portrayed, perhaps, by the stone warriors – landed in the south and made their first base near Porto-Vecchio. Naming this civilization the **Torréens**, after the dry-wall **torri** (towers) they raised in various parts of the island, Roger Grosjean posited that they were the same people as the seagoing Shardana who are known to have attacked Egypt in the late second millennium BC, and that the bronze weapons with which they subdued the islanders were the weapons depicted on the sword-bearing menhirs of Filitosa.

Their towers, each one built around a central cavity with smaller chambers to the sides, were found to contain remnants of fires, and may have been used to cremate the dead or even sacrifice the living. Fragments of the earlier, Neolithic structures, perhaps destroyed as the Torréens advanced along the island, were incorporated in their walls. Grosjean has traced the invaders' progression to the west, as they drove the megalithic natives further into the interior and finally to the north, where the natives were left to pursue their own beliefs and practices in peace. Stone menhirs were still being created in northern Corsica as the Iron Age got under way, centuries after the Torréen invasion, while in the south of the island – according to Grosjean – rivalry between Torréen settlements precipitated another migration, this time south to the island of Sardinia.

Greeks, Romans and Saracens

In 565 BC, Corsica's first major colony was founded at Alalia (Aléria) by Greek refugees from **Phocaea**. For a few decades these settlers made a successful living, planting vines and olive trees and enjoying a brisk trade in metals and cereals, but within thirty years they were fighting off an invading fleet of **Carthaginians** and **Etruscans**. By 535 BC, devastated by their losses in battle, the Greeks had abandoned Alalia to the Etruscans, who in turn were briefly succeeded by Carthaginian settlers in the third century BC.

By now Corsica had attracted the attention of the **Romans**, who sent in troops under the command of Lucius Cornelius Scipio in 259 BC. The indigenous islanders, enslaved or driven into the mountains by each successive invading power, joined forces with the Carthaginians and their leader Hanno to resist Roman occupation. Although the east coast was soon conquered and settled, it took another forty years before Corsica (together with Sardinia) could be brought within Roman administration, and another century of rebellion passed before the island's interior was overpowered.

For more than 500 years Corsica remained a province of the Roman Empire. A string of ports was established along the south coast – subsequently flattened by invasion and malaria – and a settlement built at **Mariana**, to the south of present-day Bastia, though Aléria remained the largest settlement. From the third century AD onwards, **Christianity** was introduced to the island and bishoprics were established at Mariana, Aléria, the Nebbio, Sagone and Ajaccio.

This comparatively stable period in Corsican history came to an end as the Roman Empire disintegrated and the **Vandals** started to harass the coast. By 460 AD the Vandals were established on the island, only to be defeated by Belisarius and his Byzantine forces in 534, but absorption into the Byzantine empire did little to protect Corsica from the Ostrogoths and later from the **Lombards**, who managed to annex Corsica in 725 – by which time the coastal settlements were suffering frequent raids by the Saracens (or Moors). In 754 Pépin the Short, King of the Franks, agreed to hand Corsica over to the **papacy** once it was free of the Lombards; when the Lombards were driven out twenty years later, Pépin's son, Charlemagne, honoured the promise.

Within thirty years of its transfer to papal sovereignty, parts of Corsica were being overrun by the **Saracens**. These invaders retained their grip for another two centuries, despite the brief triumph of **Ugo della Colonna**, reputedly a Roman aristocrat sent to "liberate" the island by Pope Stephen IV, but more likely a semi-legendary figure based on Count Boniface of Lucca, who gained a foothold on the island in 825, building the fortress of Bonifacio on its southern tip.

Whatever the facts may be, Ugo della Colonna became a useful point of reference for the local Corsican families, who began to assert their authority as the Moors retreated under pressure from an allied force of Pisans and Genoese at the start of the eleventh century. During the Saracens' rule, the native islanders had been confined to the interior, where they had developed a system of administration based on mountain communities, with elected leaders who took every opportunity to make their status hereditary. This period saw the rise of such mighty clans as the **della Rocca** and **Istria** families, the dominant dynasties among the feudal lords known as the **Cinarchesi**, most of whom claimed descent from Ugo della Colonna. As their feuds and rivalries intensified, some swore allegiance to the pope, who in 1077 placed Corsica under Pisan protection; others turned for support to the Genoese, who claimed their own right to the island.

The Pisan period

In 1133, Pope Innocent II split Corsica's bishoprics between Pisa and Genoa, an action that did nothing to stem the enmity of the two republics. For two centuries, while Corsica remained **officially governed by Pisa**, the Genoese stayed on the offensive, capturing Bonifacio in 1187 and Calvi in 1268. Nevertheless, the Pisans were able to impose a framework of government built around the local parish or **piève**. A massive programme of church-building got under way, each church providing the focus for its *piève*, which in turn linked several village communities.

In the meantime, the Corsican nobles continued to flex their muscles. **Sinucello della Rocca**, a vassal of Pisa who held lands in the southwest, took advantage of the running dispute with Genoa and made his own bid for power, taking arms against other Corsican nobles and switching his loyalties between Pisa and Genoa as necessary. He eventually gained control of almost the whole island, drawing up a constitution and earning the name **Giudice** (Judge) for his sense of justice, but his success had made him few friends, and the rival *signori* soon turned against him. When Genoa defeated the Pisan fleet at **Meloria in 1284** and finally took control of the island, della Rocca retreated to his original base in the southwest and was eventually betrayed by his own illegitimate son. Captured by the Genoese, he died in prison in 1306.

The Genoese period

Despite **Genoa**'s decisive victory at Meloria, the republic's struggle to control Corsica was by no means over. In 1297, the island, along with Sardinia, was handed by Pope Boniface VIII to the **kingdom of Aragon**, setting off yet another territorial war – one that was to rumble on for two hundred years more. While Genoa held fast against Aragonese attempts to realize their claim to Corsica, the *signori* continued to fight it out among themselves. A people's revolt led by **Sambocuccio d'Alando** drove out the battling nobles of the northeast, and led to a political split between two areas of the island. In the northeast, the area known as *Diqua dai Monti* ("this side of the mountains"), the ancestral lands were taken over by village communities to form the **terra di commune**, officially protected by the Genoese, who founded and fortified Bastia in 1380. The southwest – *Dila dai Monti* – remained the **terra dei signori**, ruled in effect by the Cinarchesi, who looked to the more distant power of Aragon for support.

Generations of *signori* kept up a relentless effort to bring the whole island under their rule. Backed by Aragon, **Arrigo della Rocca** gained considerable successes against the Genoese in 1376, and then his nephew, **Vincentello d'Istria**, gained control of most of the island as viceroy of the king of Aragon from 1420 until 1434, when he was captured by Genoese forces and publicly beheaded. In 1453, in a bid to overcome such ambitious nobility, Genoa put Corsica into the hands of the **Bank of Saint George**, a powerful financial corporation with its own army. For ten years the bank imposed a tough military government, building a series of coastal watchtowers, restoring battered fortifications and containing the fractious warlords.

Sampiero Corso

Events in Europe brought this era to an end: **Henry II of France**, at war with Charles V, struck a blow against the Hapsburg emperor's Genoese allies by sending a fleet to capture Corsica. Leading the invasion was mercenary **Sampiero Corso**, who took possession of the entire island except Calvi and Bastia. French rule lasted all of two years, before Corsica was passed back to Genoa under the Treaty of Cateau Cambresis in 1559. Corso, however, was rather less inclined to relinquish his supremacy, and led a successful uprising against the Genoese in 1564, again securing control of most of the island. He was finally defeated by a vicious Corsican custom – the **vendetta** – according to which any act of violence or dishonour had to be avenged by the victim's relations. Corso was murdered in 1567 by the brothers of his wife Vannina d'Orso, whom he had strangled in the belief that she had betrayed him to his Genoese enemies. His killers were heftily rewarded by the Genoese.

Genoese consolidation

In the late **sixteenth century** the Corsican population was reeling from years of war, pirate attacks, famine and malaria. The Genoese republic, now governing the island directly, was finally able to impose an administration of sorts. A governor was installed in Bastia to oversee the network of provinces and parishes, leaving local government to the Corsican communities and their assemblies (*consulta*). Attempts were even made to clamp down on the vendetta, but with no success – hundreds of murders were committed each year in the name of honour.

Nevertheless, in comparison with the previous pattern of civil war and invasion, the 170 years of direct Genoese rule were relatively peaceful. Corsicans enjoyed a certain degree of freedom to run their own affairs, and the rural economy developed and prospered – factors that were eventually to undermine the Genoese supremacy. Influential families, beneficiaries of the boom in agricultural trade, formed an articulate and ambitious new class. Excluded from the top ranks of government and resentful of Genoa's trade monopolies and high taxes, they provided the leadership for a Corsican society growing in political maturity and aspirations. Circumstances came to a head in the early eighteenth century, when discontent exploded into armed rebellion.

The Wars of Independence

The hated Genoese taxes were the trigger for **revolt in 1729** when, having suffered a series of failed harvests, one village near Corte refused to pay. Its defiance developed into a full-scale uprising and the reinforcements sent in to suppress it were soon overpowered. Rebellion spread quickly across the island and was formalized in **1731**, when a popular assembly declared **national independence**, adopting a constitution and forming a parliament with a representative from each village. The Genoese, besieged in their coastal fortresses, turned for help to Emperor Charles VI, who responded with six battalions, which helped recapture St-Florent and Algajola from the insurgents. Under pressure from the emperor's troops, the Corsicans agreed to a settlement in 1732, winning several concessions from the Genoese, including access to public office.

The fighting resumed as soon as the emperor's soldiers had withdrawn, but the rebels made little progress, being short of resources and blockaded by a Genoese fleet. Salvation arrived in 1736 in the bizarre form of **Théodore von Neuhof**, a Westphalian adventurer brought up in the French royal court, who had spotted in Corsica's chaos an opportunity for glory. Having persuaded Tunisian financiers to back his venture, von Neuhof sailed into Aléria with ample supplies of money, arms and ammunition. The rebels had little choice but to accept his offer of support and they crowned him **king of Corsica**, though his authority was severely restricted by a new constitution, an executive council and an elected legislature. King Théodore's reign lasted eight months, by which time a lack of military success and depleted funds had provoked the hostility of many Corsicans; in November 1736 their monarch left the island, promising to find new allies.

Still the Corsicans and Genoese were in stalemate, each side unable to raise enough funds or forces to influence events decisively – until, in 1738, Genoa appealed to Louis XV of France and received several regiments commanded by the Comte de Boisseux. The following year, after the deployment of a further detachment of French troops, a thousand Corsicans were forced to flee the island. Among the refugees was **Giacinto Paoli**, one of the first leaders of the revolt, who went into exile in Naples with his teenage son Pascal.

The French pulled out of Corsica in 1741, but before long the major European powers were fighting over the island again, hoping for a strategic advantage in the War of the Austrian Succession. A British fleet carrying Austrian and Sardinian troops joined forces with the Corsican patriots, who elected **Gian'Pietru Gaffori** their commander. The 1748 Treaty of Aix-la-Chapelle marked an end to British involvement in the struggle, but the Corsicans continued their campaign, drawing up a new constitution in 1752. Gaffori led a determined drive against the Genoese, eventually capturing their stronghold at Corte, despite the fact that his son had been abducted and held hostage within the city walls. His heroic reputation among the Corsicans was matched by that of his wife, who prevented her household from surrendering to enemy troops by threatening to light a barrel-load of gunpowder and blow them and herself to smithereens.

Paoli's independent Corsica

The rebels lost their dynamic commander in 1753, when Gaffori was assassinated, and in 1754 **Pascal Paoli**, son of the exiled Corsican leader, was called back to Corsica to take over leadership of the rebellion.

Paoli returned with a keen sense of constitutional theory and a thorough political education. Having been elected leader of the nation in 1755, he introduced a constitution according to which every man over 25 had a vote and every parish could send representatives to the Public Assembly, which in turn elected an executive council of state. Paoli himself was in charge of military and foreign matters, but all other policies required the Assembly's agreement. Rapid steps were taken to boost the islanders' flagging morale and pitiful resources: schools were built and a university was founded in Corte; a mint and a printing press were established; mines and an arms factory were put into production. The death penalty was rigorously enforced for vendetta killings, which finally began to decline. Under Paoli's command the Corsican patriots and their enlightened system of government found admirers among the liberals and radicals of Europe. Jean-Jacques Rousseau toyed with the idea of moving to the island and writing its history; James Boswell came to meet Paoli and sang his praises in his journal of the visit, published in 1768 (see p.437).

In the meantime, events were overtaking the Corsicans. French forces occupied five coastal towns in 1764, and in **1768** the **Genoese ceded their rights** to the island, selling their claim to France under the Treaty of Versailles. An invading force landed within a month of the treaty being signed, taking possession of Cap Corse. Paoli's men – and women – kept up the pressure, hiding out in the maquis and launching guerrilla attacks on the French, but when a new detachment of troops was sent in there was little hope for the Corsicans, who suffered a terrible defeat at the **Battle of Ponte-Nuovo** in May 1769. Pascal Paoli was obliged to flee to England.

French rule to the twentieth century

Though sporadic resistance continued even after Paoli's departure, Corsica was brought fairly painlessly within the monarchy as a Pays d'État, with its own biennial gathering of churchmen, nobles and commoners. As part of its programme of assimilation, the French offered Corsica's noble families scholarships to its prestigious military schools. Among the successful applicants was the son of Paoli's ex-secretary – **Napoléon Bonaparte**.

During the next twenty years of rule by the French monarchy, the drive for independence gradually subsided and, when the revolutionaries ousted Louis XVI in 1789, Corsica urged the Assembly to make the island a fully integrated part of the French State. The royal ban imposed on political exiles was lifted, and Paoli returned to be elected president of the Corsican Conseil-Général. His authority was at first accepted by the Paris Convention, but soon Paoli fell out of favour after a Paris-instigated campaign to conquer Sardinia ended in failure. When it became known that Paoli was to be arrested, the Corsican Assembly came to his defence, naming him **Father of the Nation**. Paoli's supporters turned on the French and pro-French on the island; the Bonaparte family, who had long since transferred their loyalty to France, left their Ajaccio home to the looters and were hastened to Toulon by Napoléon, by then serving in the French army.

The Anglo-Corsican interlude

Aware of the superior strength of French forces, Paoli called on his old English allies for help, and in 1794 **Sir Gilbert Elliot** arrived with reinforcements who quickly captured St-Florent, Bastia and Calvi (where Nelson lost the use of one of his eyes). In return for this intervention, Britain demanded a stake in the island's government, and in June **1794** an **Anglo-Corsican kingdom** was proclaimed.

To the bitter disappointment of Paoli and his supporters, Sir Gilbert was made viceroy of the new kingdom, with the power to dissolve parliament, nominate councillors and appoint the highest officers of state. When the Corsican members of parliament responded by electing Paoli their president, Sir Gilbert threatened to pull out his troops, and they were forced to back down. A series of riots followed, and a nervous Sir Gilbert persuaded the king to exile Paoli once again – this time for good. But the damage was already done: Paoli loyalists joined the French in their attacks on British soldiers, and in September 1796 Sir Gilbert and his troops sailed away, leaving the island to be retaken by France.

The Napoleonic era and its aftermath

Apart from a brief stay in Ajaccio in 1799, **Napoléon** paid scant attention to his homeland during his period of power. A number of uprisings on the island during the 1790s were put down with brutal force, and opposition to Napoleonic rule led to widespread revolt by an alliance of Royalists, Paolists and British supporters in 1799. This, too, was stamped out and its leaders executed. In 1801 the constitution was suspended and Général Morand arrived to administer a harsh military rule. His reign of terror lasted until 1811, when the almost equally unpopular Général César Berthier took his place. In the same year the island was made a single *département* of France (it had been divided into two in 1796), with its capital in Ajaccio. Resistance to the French continued, and in 1814 the citizens of Bastia appealed to Britain to intervene on their behalf. A detachment of British troops was sent, but in April of that year Napoléon abdicated and the soldiers were recalled.

After 1815 and the **restoration of the French monarchy**, the governing state made some attempts to develop the island's economy, opening mines and foundries, setting up a railway, introducing an education act, and building roads and schools. But most of their schemes had little success, and Corsica remained a marginal and largely neglected part of the country. For Corsicans, the real opportunities lay in France, and young islanders began to turn away from the old villages, seeking their careers and education on the mainland. The romance and drama that visitors such as Edward Lear and Prosper Mérimée discovered in mid-nineteenth-century Corsica veiled a grim picture of poverty, malaria and violence – vendetta, though on the decline, was still claiming up to 160 victims a year (see p.244). In the last half of the century, **emigration** surged so dramatically that within sixty years the population had been halved.

The twentieth century

In 1909, as a result of a commission set up by Georges Clemenceau, French minister of the interior, the French government promised more investment and development for Corsica. This plan, however, was shelved with the outbreak of **World War I**, which itself reduced Corsica's population still further, taking over 20,000 lives (a higher per capita casualty rate than any other part of Europe).

During the 1920s and 1930s Mussolini set his sights on Corsica, and while the Nazis were busy invading France, 85,000 Italian troops descended on the island. They were later joined by a force of 10,000 Germans (who dug into the far south to defend the Straits of Bonifacio) – an occupying force of around one to every two islanders. With the Italian surrender in 1943, Kesselring's Ninth Panzer Division and the remaining German troops on the island were evacuated from the east coast, while the Corsican Resistance and Free French troops attacked them from the hills. By mid-September, Corsica had become the first *département* of Metropolitan France to be liberated. Allied troops and air forces moved in, and from 1946 kick-started the postwar economy of the island by clearing the east coast of malarial mosquitoes.

In the postwar years, Corsica was earmarked by the French government as a target for development, and in 1957 two State-sponsored organizations were set up to exploit its potential: **SOMIVAC** – the Société pour la Mise en Valeur Agricole de la Corse – introduced modern agricultural techniques; **SETCO** – the Société pour l'Équipement Touristique de la Corse – provided funds to build a tourist industry. Both organizations met with considerable distrust, seen as threats to an ancient way of life that had evolved and survived during centuries of hostile occupation. Nevertheless, the development gathered pace and, after 1962, when Algeria gained its independence, the situation was complicated by a massive influx of pieds-noirs refugees from the ex-French colony. Over 15,000 settlers poured into Corsica during the next twenty years, many of them buying up the newly developed land and hotels, adding to Corsican fears of losing control of their resources. Summer **tourists** began to arrive in steadily rising numbers, topping the half-million mark in the early 1970s (and now heading for two million annually).

Calls for autonomy

It was against this background of insecurity and mounting frustration with the ineffectiveness of Paris's half-hearted economic policies that demands for greater administrative power were increasingly voiced from the 1960s. Led by the **Simeoni brothers**, Max and Edmond, a party of nationalist students known as L'Action Régionaliste Corse (**ARC**) started to call for decentralized government, for restrictions on the east coast tourist developments, for a Corsican university (Paoli's had been closed by the French), and for compulsory schooling in Corsican language and history.

A number of more radical **autonomist movements**, varying in tactics and demands, entered the political scene, and from the mid-1970s these won substantial support for their manifesto of a national assembly and demand for investment in controlled development and protection of the land. Meanwhile, following the **Aléria siege** of 1975, when two policemen died in a shoot-out with armed separatists (see p.301), a group of activists operating as the **FLNC** (Fronte di Liberazione Naziunale di a Corsica) embarked on a programme of bombing campaigns, targeting the tourist villages and foreign-owned properties that they believed were destroying Corsica's land and culture.

In the early 1980s the autonomists profited from a change of policy in France favouring increased decentralization. A Corsican university was re-established in 1981, providing a channel for the ambitions and political ideas of the younger generation. In the following year, Corsica became the first of the French regions to be granted a National Assembly, with limited powers over policy, administration and finance. Nonetheless, benefiting from close links with the IRA, a more ruthless and efficient FLNC intensified its paramilitary activities. Dozens of explosions heralded the election of 1984, as allegations of fraud and corruption were levelled against the politicians.

In 1987, **Charles Pasqua**, the (then) minister of the interior, mounted a clampdown on the FLNC. At the same time, nationalist political parties continued to poll around seventeen percent of the vote in elections, though a crisis was brewing that would inflict considerably more damage to the nationalist movement than any of Pasqua's heavy-handed tactics. Following a period of deepening political divisions, in 1990 the movement split into two opposing factions: **Cuncolta** and their armed wing, the FLNC Canal-Historique; and the **MPA**, whose paramilitary group dubbed itself the FLNC Canal-Habituel.

Soon an all-out blood feud erupted between the two, which claimed hundreds of lives and sent the murder rate spiralling to thirty per year. Visitor numbers dropped back to their lowest levels in a decade, while the French government seemed content to watch from the wings as the paramilitaries destroyed each other far more effectively than the security forces had been able to do.

Public opinion on the island had by now started to swing decisively against the FLNC and its various splinter groups, with the overwhelming majority of Corsicans opposed to independence from France. What little support for the armed struggle remained evaporated almost completely in February 1998 after the government's most senior representative in Corsica, **Préfet Claude Érignac**, was gunned down while leaving the opera with his wife. Three days after the atrocity, the island's trade unions and most of its political parties staged a fifteen-minute silence calling for an end to the violence.

Since the time of the ancient Greeks, Corsica has been regarded as strategically vital for control of the Mediterranean's seaways, and **World War II** was no exception. Claiming the island had to be secured to protect his North African colonies, Mussolini – who had long regarded Corsicans as Italians in all but name – dispatched a "Liberation Force" of 85,000 troops in the autumn of 1942. By that time, however, the Allies had already invaded North Africa and were mustering for an attack on southern Europe. Neither Mussolini nor Hitler knew where this was to begin, but Corsica, within easy reach of both the French and Italian coasts, was an obvious *point d'appui*. In fact, Churchill and Roosevelt had already settled upon Sicily as the landing site, and in order to throw the Axis off the scent had ordered that resistance activities in Corsica be stepped up as a diversionary tactic.

As the submarine, *Le Casabianca*, surfaced for the first time off the island's coast in December 1942, its crew and captain, **Jean L'Herminier**, can have had little inkling that their top-secret operation was in essence the start of wide-scale strategic deception. Backed by the American secret service, the "**Pearl Harbour**" mission (see p.174) was the first of a dozen or so similar landings in which agents, arms, munitions and money (provided mainly by the British and Americans) were ferried from Algiers to supply the nascent Corsican Resistance. Further consignments were flown in by the RAF as the partisan networks, marshalled by emissaries sent by rival Free French generals **de Gaulle** and **Giraud**, became better established. As well as putting in place a force that might later tie down occupying troops and armoured divisions, the hope of Allied Command was to fool the Germans into re-deploying resources away from the real invasion site in Sicily.

Other, smaller-scale feints were devised by Churchill's secret service. The most famous of them (the subject of the postwar best-seller, *The Man Who Never Was* by Ewen Montagu) was the beaching near Huelva in Spain of a corpse in naval uniform carrying faked dispatches which confirmed Eisenhower's army was set to attack southern Europe through the French Riviera. Among the many repercussions of this splendid *ruse de guerre* was that Hitler did exactly as Churchill had intended by ordering the reinforcement of Sardinia and Corsica in 1943.

When it became clear, in July of that year, that Eisenhower's invasion of Sicily was after all the Allies' main thrust, the Führer changed tack, removing his forces from Sardinia to fortify Corsica, from where they could more easily be removed to the Italian mainland ahead of the Allies' advance. This gave the British and Americans a golden opportunity to destroy Marshal Kesselring's Ninth Panzer Division as it lumbered unprotected by air support along the exposed, flat shoreline of Corsica's east coast. The Allied air force, however, had its hands full already, and the job of forestalling what soon become a full-scale retreat fell to the Corsican Resistance, beefed up by a French colonial force from North Africa.

By the summer of 1943, some 12,000 partisans had been placed under arms on the island, organized into regional cells by the left-wing **Front National**. Known as the **Maquis** after the dense scrub in which most hid out, the Resistance bided its time in the bush while waiting for the green light from Algiers. This eventually came with the capitulation of Mussolini's successor, Marshal Badoglio, in September 1943, just as the Germans were retreating up the east coast from Sardinia.

The surrender placed the Italians in an awkward position. Reviled by the islanders but no longer allied to the Germans, many Italian troops regarded Corsican retribution as less of a risk than Nazi justice and mutinied or fled to the mountains to join the Maquis. In the event, their mistrust proved well placed. Following a fierce fire fight outside Bastia, Hitler personally ordered the execution of the captured Italian officers, but Kesselring's general, **Von Senger und Etterlin**, ignored the Führer's instructions, sending the prisoners directly to Leghorn (Livorno) instead where no such orders existed.

By mid-September, the German evacuation had reached its peak, with 3000 troops per day being airlifted or shipped off the east coast. Meanwhile, the Maquis and Free French army (dispatched by Général Giraud from Algiers and now numbering some 6600 men) had fought their way northeast through the interior from Ajaccio and were closing in from the hills behind Bastia. Strafed by the Allied air forces, and torpedoed by British submarines in the Tyrrhenian Sea, the retreating German army was effectively surrounded by October 2. By the time Von Senger und Etterlin stepped onto his launch to leave that night, approximately 27,000 German troops and up to 100 tanks had been removed to safety, for the relatively cheap price of a handful of ships (and one million litres of top Corsican wine, which rampaging German troops poured down the drains before they left).

Corsica was officially liberated on **September 16, 1943**, but was not yet out of trouble. Due to crossed wires in Allied Command, American bombers mounted a devastating broad-daylight raid on October 4 – as most of Bastia was partying in the streets. Hundreds were killed, and the Vieux Port, in particular, took a dreadful pounding. This fatal error soured celebrations on the island, and did little to calm the nerves of de Gaulle, who was already in a fury. Credit for the Liberation had gone to his arch rival, **Général Giraud**, who had dispatched the Free French troops without consulting the Committee of National Liberation, or CFLN (the de facto government in exile) in Algiers. Much to his right-wing adversary's chagrin, Giraud had also allowed the communist-dominated Front National to take control of communications and local government on the island, setting a potentially undesirable (from de Gaulle's point of view) precedent for the future recapture of French territories. ("He has stolen my Corsica!" de Gaulle is famously said to have cried.)

Backed by Roosevelt, Giraud was much more popular than de Gaulle – according to one eminent British historian, not least because "he grew a very large moustache and laughed at other people's jokes, whereas de Gaulle wasn't much of a success at either". Ultimately, however, charm proved powerless in the face of the future French president's wiliness, and within six months an outmanoeuvred Giraud was sacked from the CFLN and consigned to political obscurity.

De Gaulle's anger at the way Corsica had been liberated may go some way to explaining why this episode in the history of World War II rarely occupies the place it deserves in the history books. But the liberation provided an important platform for the ensuing invasion of southern France. Corsica became the Allies' key maritime and secret service base in 1944, and a vital staging post for craft bound for Italy. An additional, often forgotten, fact is that the liberation of the island could not have been achieved without the help of several thousand Arab and West African soldiers, hundreds of whom died in battle alongside Corsican partisans. A memorial on the **Col de Teghime** honours their bravery in the face of a considerably larger and better-equipped German army.

More on the submarine Le Casabianca's daring missions of 1942–1943 appears in a separate box on p.197. Chapter 1 also includes a feature on Corsica's most famous World War II casualty, the novelist **Antoine de Saint-Exupéry** (see p.76), who disappeared on a reconnaissance flight out of Bastia airport in 1944. The same piece also locates the Allied and Axis **war graves** on the slopes southwest of Bastia, near where some of the fiercest fighting took place.

The dramatic swing of support away from the separatists in the wake of the Érignac murder, however, was to be short-lived. Érignac's successor, **Préfet Bernard Bonnet**, a hardliner dispatched by Prime Minister Lionel Jospin to impose law and order on the island, soon became embroiled in scandal after it was discovered he had ordered the destruction by undercover gendarmes of an illegal beach shack near Ajaccio. The **Affaire de la Paillote**, as the scandal was dubbed by the press, threatened for a while to implicate even the Elysée Palace when Bonnet accused Jospin of using him as a fall guy for his moribund Corsica policies.

The Matignon Accords

It is impossible to say how much of the mud stuck to Jospin, but L'Affaire de la Paillote certainly did little to enhance the prime minister's hitherto squeaky-clean image in the eyes of French voters. More certain is that anti-French feeling intensified on the island in the wake of the Bonnet revelations and that to seize back the initiative, the Jospin administration had to come up with something visionary.

The deadlock seemed at last to be broken with the so-called **Matignon Accords**, a portfolio of radical proposals offering major new devolutionary concessions to the nationalists in exchange for peace. These included the transfer to an elected assembly on the island of responsibility for culture, education and regional development and, following a change to the French Constitution earmarked for 2004, greater legislative and regulatory powers.

Gaullist opposition to the package was predictably bullish: Jospin's plain-speaking, staunchly Republican interior minister, **Jean-Pierre Chevènement**, resigned over the bill, which he and his right-wing Jacobin cronies condemned as "a victory for blackmail by a violent minority of Corsicans . . . a cowardly abdication of state responsibility (and) . . . a bomb beneath the French Republic". His warnings that Jospin's line on Corsica would inevitably lead to calls for greater devolution by other French minorities seemed to come true in August 2001 when delegations of Bretons, Savoyards, Catalans and Basques convened with local nationalists in Corte.

In Corsica itself, however, the eighteen-month Matignon talks were hailed as a major step forward. Nationalist violence subsided, a ceasefire held and the separatists finally got together to discuss the fine print with government representatives. In May 2001, the French parliament gave the green light to the package, followed by a vote of approval by the Corsican regional assembly.

The success of the Matignon Accords, however, depended entirely upon the strength and resolve of Jospin's government, and both started to waver badly the following year. During the run-up to the 2002 elections, moderate nationalists began to withdraw their support, complaining that the text of the accords didn't go far enough. Then the upper house of parliament in Paris watered it down further, removing some of the proposed powers. Finally, France's Supreme Court declared the whole process unconstitutional.

With the victory of Jacques Chirac and the resounding defeat of Jospin in the presidential election of June 2002, Matignon looked doomed. Violence once again erupted ahead of the first visit to the island of Chirac's tough homeland security tsar, Nicolas Sarkozy. This was followed at the peak of the tourist season in August by a *nuit bleue* (nocturnal press conference) called by the a coalition of paramilitary groups to announce the end of their ceasefire; more bombs and rocket attacks ensued.

A more detailed account of the recent armed conflict with the French state is featured in "The Corsican Troubles" on pp.420–431.

The nail in the coffin for Matignon came soon after when the newly inaugurated prime minister **Jean–Pierre Raffarin** visited Corsica. He used the opportunity to declare that his government would not honour promises made by the previous administration and proposed instead a pan-French plan for limited devolution to all regions. Even the most moderate of moderate nationalists were furious. Leader of Corsica Nazione, Jean-Guy Talamoni, summed up the widespread resentment when he insisted that the island would not consent to being "lumped in with some uniform and general decentralization programme".

Corsica today

One of the principal debates surrounding the Matignon Accords was the potential **environmental impact of devolution**. Corsica welcomes nearly two million visitors annually, yet the level of development, even on the coast, remains relatively restrained. The paramilitaries' predilection for blowing up foreign-owned villas and holiday complexes generally takes the credit for this. But the truth is that French environmental law has kept the concrete at bay. As well as forbidding any permanent construction within 100m of the shoreline, the stringent **lois littoral et montagne** obliges developers to obtain State approval for any project inside an area designated as environmentally fragile or of outstanding natural beauty. All 360 of Corsica's *communes* fall into such categories.

However, in discussions leading up to the Matignon reforms, environmentalists repeatedly raised the spectre of what might happen if the island's newly elected representatives, endowed with powers to circumvent the *lois littoral et montagne*, were unable to resist pressure from developers. One of their prime responsibilities, after all, would be the regeneration of the island's economy. Corsican landowners are understandably licking their lips at the prospect of devolution: many have already been courted by investors, along with local politicians and developers, all of whom stand to make fortunes if the current building restrictions are ever relaxed.

Such concerns reflect not only the fragility of the island's natural environment, but also the chronically depressed state of its **economy**. Tourism and related industries currently account for between ten and twelve percent of GDP, while agriculture earns a paltry one to two percent. Unemployment may be nonexistent for three months over the summer, but in winter rises to nearly ten percent – which doesn't take into account the huge numbers of islanders who migrate to the Continent to work off season. Another revealing statistic is that over thirty percent of all those employed in Corsica work for local councils. Industry generates only seven percent of GDP, with barely one percent of companies boasting a workforce of more than fifty people. In short, Corsica produces very little and would be economically unviable were it not for tourism and the vast subsidies from both the French State and EU.

If the island were ever to gain the legislative and regulatory powers its politicians and nationalist paramilitary groups demand, its elected representatives would be under great pressure to deliver tangible results. Couple this with the potentially huge sums of venture capital waiting in the wings and you'll see why even some confirmed nationalists regard the future of Corsica with some trepidation.

CONTEXTS | The historical framework

The Corsican troubles: an overview

To the outsider, Corsica may seem peaceful enough. But you don't have to look too hard to find signs of the 25-year conflict being waged between local nationalist extremists and the French State. On the outskirts of larger villages high walls and electric fences surround fortified gendarmeries; bullet marks mar the façades of many post offices, banks and government buildings; black graffiti defaces most road signs; and the rubble of bombed-out holiday villas dots coastal landscapes from Cap Corse to the Bouches de Bonifacio.

Spawning more than five hundred bombings, arson and machine-gun attacks annually, the conflict, which in recent years has descended into factional infighting among the islanders themselves, has left few families unscathed. Since 1986, the murder rate in Corsica has run at an average of between thirty and forty per year – for a population of 270,000.

The chances of your getting caught up in any violence while on holiday are virtually nil, but the Corsican troubles remain a defining feature of island life, as integral to local society as the sectarian war of Northern Ireland or the Mafia's presence in Sicily, with which *le problème corse*, as the troubles are euphemistically dubbed on the mainland, shares many similarities.

The roots of nationalism

Although Corsica has always maintained its own culturally distinct way of life, the conviction that the islanders' unique language and customs should form the basis of an individual nation is a relatively new phenomenon. Not until the Wars of Independence and rise of **Pascal Paoli** (see p.316) in the mid-eighteenth century did nationalism gather any momentum, inspired by wide-spread outrage at the atrocities perpetrated by the French in the wake of the Genoese withdrawal in 1768. Before this time, any seeds of nationalist consciousness that may have taken root were stifled by instability or foreign oppression. Since the time of the Romans, Corsica has witnessed 19 changes of overlords, 37 popular revolts and 7 spells of outright anarchy.

The other force that has traditionally mitigated against the emergence of a unified Corsican nation has been **clannism**. In common with many Mediterranean societies, the island has always been riven by internal divisions: between families, hamlets, villages, valleys, and between coastal peoples and shepherds in the mountains. All too often, these differences were perpetuated by **vendettas** resulting from some kind of perceived slight to an individual or family's honour (see p.244). The prevalence of such feuds, which were commonplace until the end of the nineteenth century, ensured that mutual mistrust, suspicion and the readiness to resort to violence became firmly ingrained in the Corsican psyche.

Economic decline

The **revival** of Corsican nationalism in the twentieth century emerged essentially as a response to the island's steady economic decline under French rule. Whereas the Genoese had instigated a coherent and productive agricultural policy (whence the vast chestnut forests of Castagniccia and olive groves of the Balagne), the only distinguishing feature of their French successors' approach to the island's economic woes was **neglect**. With its agricultural produce no longer in demand, Corsica's crops literally withered on the vine.

Emigration, to the cities of the mainland and French colonies in Africa and the Americas, left whole regions perilously underpopulated by the start of the twentieth century. The world wars took their toll, too. Per capita, Corsica lost more of its menfolk on the battlefields of Europe than any other *département* in France. Experience of the wider world also encouraged those who survived to emigrate after demobilization. Between 1937 and 1956, census figures show the island's population dropped to a little under 76,000, while during the 1960s port records registered 10,000 more annual departures than arrivals.

The effect of such widespread emigration on the Corsican economy was devastating. Not only were there now fewer hands to work what little land remained under cultivation, but the drop in population also meant a much smaller labour pool, discouraging potential investors. By the mid-1960s, the island was officially the poorest *département* in France, importing six times what it exported, yet with a cost of living thirty percent higher than the average on the mainland.

The response of the French government to such poverty, however, continued to lack vision, while makeshift decisions issued by Paris throughout this era compounded Corsica's economic problems. Eager to put it on a par with the rest of the country, **de Gaulle** whittled away at the island's special fiscal exemptions, which had been in place since 1811, imposing duties on public transport and gambling, as well as tobacco and alcohol. As a result, the cost of transporting goods to Corsica increased, further worsening the balance of payments and contributing to inflation. To Corsicans, it seemed as if France was actively penalizing the island for being an island. To rub salt into the wound, neighbouring Sardinia, which also had become depopulated and poor, began to thrive from the 1950s on, thanks to massive investment and dispensations from the Italian government, which had put its economy on a level playing field with that of the mainland.

The rise of the FLNC

The adoption of violence by Corsican nationalists arose out of a widespread sense of frustration and powerlessness in the face of continued French indifference. Peaceful protests had consistently failed to galvanize Paris. Strikes called by an increasingly militant workforce in the early 1960s proved little more than a shot in the foot: when dockers downed tools in 1961, the resulting disruption provoked two major Italian shipping firms to remove their operations from the island altogether.

The mounting dissatisfaction may have rumbled on without erupting for another decade, had it not been for a string of controversies that struck in quick succession during the early 1960s. The first was the arrival, in 1962, of 15,000 pieds-noirs. The influx of newcomers provoked alarm among Corsican traditionalists that the island was being used as a "dumping ground" at the cost of indigenous culture and was losing control of its resources. Fears of exploitation were whipped up further the following year, when the government announced it wanted to export cheap **electricity** generated in Corsica to Sardinia. Considering Paris's long-term economic neglect, the plans were regarded as adding insult to injury.

The gravest insult to Corsican pride around this time, however, came direct from de Gaulle himself. When world opinion made it impolitic to stage **nuclear tests** in the French-occupied Sahara, de Gaulle and his team of military advisers chose **Argentella**, southwest of Calvi, as a potential atom bomb testing site. News of the plans was greeted with public outrage in Corsica. An island-wide general strike and referendum showed unanimous opposition to the proposals, and 30,000 demonstrators took to the streets of Ajaccio and Bastia (the largest crowds to gather on the island since Liberation Day in 1943). De Gaulle, however, refused to back down.

At this point, local "vigilance committees", monitoring government surveyors on the northwest coast, lost patience with peaceful protest and took the law into their own hands. Armed patrols located a couple of engineers, and nearly killed them (even though, as it turned out, the men had nothing to do with the nuclear tests). The remaining government technicians were immediately recalled to Paris and the Argentella project was shelved.

Aside from being a rare example of how – at a time when anti-nuclear protesters were in prison in both the US and UK – a small population was able to reverse the nuclear policy of a national government, the Argentella episode marked a watershed in the island's history: it was effectively the first time since the Wars of Independence that Corsicans had taken up arms against the French State.

ARC and the Aléria siege

The impetus Corsica needed finally to launch a nationalist political party came with the return from the mainland of radicalized students after the university-led revolution in Paris of **May 1968**. In its infancy, the nationalist political scene was dominated by two groups: right-wing conservatives from established bourgeois families, and a smaller contingent of young Maoist and Trotskyists. The latter emerged as the dominant force in the **ARC** (L'Action Régionaliste Corse), founded in 1967. Regaled by the stirring, newly revived **polyphony** singing of groups such as Canta U Populu Corsu, its conferences resounded with the rallying cry "*I Francesi fora!*" ("French out!").

Direct conflict with the French government, however, didn't come until 1975, when the radical armed wing of the ARC, led by the **Simeoni brothers**, occupied a wine cellar near **Aléria** on the east coast to voice their anger at Paris's lack of action over a wine-adulteration scandal. A 1250-strong force of armed police was dispatched by Giscard d'Estaing to break the siege, and during the shoot-out that followed two policemen were killed.

In the wake of Aléria, on the anniversary of the Battle of Ponte-Nuovu (when Pascal Paoli's army was routed by the French) a clandestine nocturnal press conference – or *nuit bleue* – was held by balaclava-wearing nationalist gunmen to announce the formation of the Fronte di Liberazione Naziunale di a Corsica, or **FLNC**. The stated aim of the (then) poorly equipped, poorly trained paramilitary group was total freedom from French dominion.

The early years of armed struggle: 1976–82

The first two years of **armed struggle** were relatively restrained, with attacks directed against strategic government targets, such as Ajaccio airport, where an Air France Boeing 707 became an early casualty of the conflict. But after 1978 the tone became more militant. A right-wing anti-separatist group, **SAC** (Service d'Action Civique), believed to have been covertly funded by the government, was attempting to infiltrate and sabotage the FLNC, who responded by setting up a unit called **Secteur V**, charged with mounting bomb attacks on the mainland.

Proof that Paris and the SAC were in cahoots came in 1980 with the capture of three active French secret service agents in **Bastelica** (see p.218). The men were taken at gunpoint to the *Hôtel Fesch* in Ajaccio, and held until the building was stormed six days later. No one was killed, but the nationalists involved were seized and sent to swell the growing ranks of Corsican prisoners in mainland France.

The debacle infuriated the FLNC rank and file, and plunged the island into its worst spell of nationalist violence to date. This period also saw the spread of **racketeering** as the FLNC's principal means of raising funds. Protection money was increasingly demanded of hotels, restaurants and other tourist-oriented businesses across the island, while hold-ups and armed robberies proliferated.

By the beginning of the 1980s, however, it was clear that small-time villains had started to cash in on the troubles by running rackets behind a veneer of FLNC "respectability". In order to differentiate the *pur et dur* (pure and hard) from the *truands et petits voyous* (crooks and little yobs), the leadership imposed what it called **impôt révolutionnaire** (revolutionary tax). "Contributors" were notified when their payments were due in the magazine *Ribombu*, mouthpiece of the FLNC's newly formed political wing, **A Cuncolta di i Cumitati Naziunalisti**, or Cuncolta.

With the election of François Mitterrand and his socialist government in 1981, hopes were high that some kind of solution to *le problème corse* might at last be attainable. Corsica was granted its own **Assemblée Régionale** the following year (months ahead of any other region in France), and behind-the-scenes talks were held with the FLNC. Despite this, nationalist attacks continued to spiral, with 800 in 1982 alone.

The Pasqua crackdown

The situation seemed to have reached a stalemate by 1985, when Jacques Chirac's Gaullist home affairs minister, **Charles Pasqua**, instigated a crackdown on nationalist activities under the slogan "*Terroriser les terroristes!*" ("Terrorize the terrorists!"). Journalists who didn't tow the government line were purged, overtly nationalist music groups such as I Muvrini were banned and "Wanted" posters stuck everywhere. Suspected FLNC activists were rounded up and tension rose to a new high.

Meanwhile, in a bid for greater respectability, the FLNC declared a **war on drugs**. "*A droga fora!*" replaced anti-French invective as the graffiti writers' preferred slogan, and brutal summary justice awaited anyone identified as a dealer. But the campaign looked to be running out of control when two Tunisian immigrants accused of trafficking were gunned down in January 1986, provoking outrage both on the island and in mainland France.

From this point on, the **bombing of holiday villas** became the FLNC's prime propaganda ploy. Justified by the nationalists' claims that Corsica needed to be protected from foreign "influences" in general and modern architecture in particular, the nationalists' destruction of second homes on the island was, and continues to be, a vote winner. No islanders like to see ugly new buildings appearing along the coast, least of all ones occupied only for a couple of months each year, so when the FLNC reduce them to rubble they are regarded by many Corsicans, even those who may not otherwise support nationalist terrorism, as providing a much-needed service. Of course, house bombing also provides a potent lever with which to extract "revolutionary tax" from holiday-home owners.

Break-up of the FLNC

The late 1980s saw a marked softening of the French government's line on Corsica. With the backing of Mitterrand and his new socialist prime minister, Michel Rocard, home affairs minister **Pierre Joxe** visited the island nineteen times during his tenure. For the first time, recognition of *un peuple corse* (a Corsican people) and special status for the region, such as that enjoyed by former colonies L'Île de la Réunion and Martinique, were mooted.

The FLNC, however, procrastinated about how to respond to the new initiative, paralysed by mounting divisions between its hard- and soft-liners. Joxe began to lose patience as the disputes over his proposals intensified. Eventually, the strain exploded with the departure of one of the Front's key military leaders, **Pierrot Poggioli**, to form a rival nationalist party, L'Accolta Naziunale Corsa, or **ANC**. One of the most-respected old guard of the early FLNC era, Poggioli condemned the "Mafia-ization" of the separatist movement, and the corrosive effects of "revolutionary tax".

Intelligence reports, meanwhile, hinted at a massive **build-up of arms** in Corsica, but with the nationalists in apparent disarray, an all-out internecine feud rather than an intensification of violence against the State seemed the more likely outcome.

The Ribombu incident

The catalyst for the **break-up of the FLNC**, and the ensuing war between its respective factions, came at the end of 1990. Bastiais hardliners, marshalled by one of Cuncolta's leaders, **Charles Pieri**, tried forcibly to take over the movement's paper and main mouthpiece, **Ribombu**. When its editor realized what was happening, he telephoned the head of Secteur V in Ajaccio, charismatic Aléria veteran **Alain Orsoni**, who immediately travelled north to intervene. The two factions traded insults, but it was Pieri and his men who were left humiliated after Orsoni accused them of betraying FLNC activists while in police custody. The gauntlet had been thrown down.

Ripples from the "*Ribombu* incident" rocked the movement to its grass roots. Within a few months, the FLNC had split into three groups, each with its own political wing: Led by Alain Orsoni, the **MPA** (Mouvement Pour l'Autodétermination) lined up alongside **FLNC–Canal Habituel**, while **Cuncolta** aligned itself with the **FLNC–Canal Historique** The rogue element in the equation was Pierrot Poggioli's ANC and its small *bras armé* (armed faction), **Resistenza**, who initially sided with the Canal-Historique but would later switch to Orsoni's camp.

The lines were now drawn for a bloody vendetta-like feud. Murders multiplied across the island as activists were picked off in tit-for-tat killings and reprisals, known as *règlements de compte* (settling of scores). Each faction's business interests were also targeted in a protracted bombing campaign.

One of the major flash points in the conflict occurred in May 1995, when the 35-year-old leader of Cuncolta, former primary schoolteacher **François Santoni**, and his friend, Gallo, ran into an ambush while motorcycling on the outskirts of Ajaccio. Gallo was killed in the encounter, but Santoni escaped. The next day, FLNC-Canal Historique vowed to track down all seven members of the hit squad involved, suspected to be from the MPA/FLNC-Canal Habituel. Consequently, the summer of 1995 was the bloodiest in living memory. Fifteen key figures, and dozens of minor activists in the nationalist movement, would be murdered, while those that survived were forced into hiding.

1996: Tralonca and the Bastia bombing

President Chirac and Prime Minister Juppé's public response to the relentless violence in Corsica was to initiate another law-and-order crackdown, declaring that it was "unacceptable for there to be one set of laws for Corsica and another for mainland France". Meanwhile, their junior ministers – as it later transpired – pursued secret negotiations with the terrorist groups, striking deals to secure an uneasy peace.

The most tangible result of these covert talks was the now famous *nuit bleue* at **Tralonca**, near Corte, when, on a freezing January night in 1996, six hundred FLNC-Canal Historique commandos gave a press conference to announce a temporary **ceasefire**. Armed to the teeth with Kalashnikovs, Israeli sub-machine guns, grenades, new flame throwers and AK47s stolen from the UN in Bosnia, the balaclava army presented a chilling photo opportunity for invited journalists. The promised truce, however, didn't last long.

Six months later it was broken in the most dramatic fashion, with the explosion of a **car bomb in Bastia**. The intended target was **Charles Pieri**, Cuncolta's national secretary. Timed to detonate in broad daylight as he was leaving the headquarters of his security firm in the Vieux Port, the device killed one Cuncolta member, Pierre-Louis Lorenzi, and injured fourteen innocent passers-by. Pieri himself sustained extensive injuries, but survived.

This was the first occasion in the history of Corsica's recent troubles that a large bomb had exploded during the day in a busy public place. The prime suspects were Orsoni's MPA/FLNC-Canal Habituel, but they moved swiftly to deny responsibility, raising suspicions that the attack had been an act of "outside provocation". One prominent MPA activist said it was "inconceivable" that such indiscriminate violence could have been perpetrated by Corsican paramilitaries. The finger of blame thus shifted towards the government, or some kind of anti-separatist group.

Contrary to expectations, the Bastia bombing did not spark off a spate of reprisal killings. The possibility that the attack may have been the work of *agents provocateurs* rather than merely another *règlement de compte* seemed to jolt the paramilitaries into realizing the extent to which their factional infighting was playing into the hands of their enemies. For a while, it seemed as if the attack on Pieri might shock the warring wings of the FLNC into another ceasefire.

Apart from costing the paramilitaries dozens of their best men, six years of intense internecine war had left the political process in disarray. No one seemed to know any longer who was negotiating with whom, or why, or what the ultimate aims of the armed struggle were.

Part of the problem lay in the fact that many of the sources of conflict back in the early 1970s no longer existed. Since the inauguration of the FLNC, the government had shown itself willing to address the island's problems: two general amnesties had been called, Corsican had been recognized as an official language and the university at Corte resurrected.

Vast sums had also been poured into developing the island, to reduce unemployment and promote a sustainable economy. Corsica today boasts four international airports, eight maritime ports, high-specification trunk roads and ample, inexpensive air and sea links with the mainland, bankrolled by vast handouts from both the EU and national government. Around 500 million euros of direct subsidies and a further 1.32 billion euros of local government funding come to Corsica each year, making it the most heavily subsidized region of Europe. Corsicans are also exempt from social security contributions, and the island as a whole enjoys preferential tax status.

The majority of islanders benefit directly from this special treatment, and from State employment (one third of the total workforce is employed by the government or government-funded local councils), as well as welfare handouts of various kinds. It's hardly surprising, therefore, that public support for independence has gradually diminished over the past two decades. These days only the hardest of hardliners in the movement favour complete secession.

The new pragmatism is most vividly reflected in the agendas of Corsica's myriad nationalist parties, who have consistently polled between 15 and 25 percent of the vote in regional elections. The most moderate among them is the UPC – direct successor to the original autonomist party, the ARC. While the dust was still settling after the Bastia bomb, its annual convention in Aléria set out a list of **key demands** from the French government. These ranged from greater tax-raising and legislative powers for the *assemblée régionale*, to a lower rate of VAT on the island, mandatory teaching of language in schools, a special Corsican *carte d'identité* and recognition of *le peuple corse* as a "national minority".

Juppé's revenge

In late 1996, during a period when France's new right-wing Gaullist government was constantly reaffirming its refusal to negotiate with terrorists, an unexpected twist came about when the prime minister himself, Alain Juppé, became embroiled in a scandal after the Cuncolta leader, François Santoni, claimed he had had secret talks with the government.

The most sensational of Santoni's accusations centered on the *nuit bleue* at Tralonca, which, he claimed, had been staged with the full connivance of the government. The prime minister had allegedly wanted a big turnout to ensure that the FLNC's rank and file would not later be able to disassociate themselves from the ensuing ceasefire. Juppé vociferously denied the charges, but the mud stuck.

Santoni's revelations had apparently been prompted by the prime minister's orders that participants of the Tralonca *nuit bleue* should be arrested – regarded by the FLNC as a flagrant betrayal of the covert agreement. Soon after, the city hall in Bordeaux, where Juppé is mayor, was bombed, and death threats issued to the French premier. But the FLNC clearly underestimated the prime minister's stomach for a fight. The personal attacks merely seemed to steel Juppé's resolve to defeat the terrorists.

Within a couple of months, he ordered a massive **crackdown** on lawlessness and corruption in Corsica, during which police raids netted all but one of Cuncolta's leaders, including Santoni, who was charged with extortion offences after the owner of the **Sperone golf course**, near Bonifacio, had gone to the police about protection threats he'd received (a story described in more detail on p.277). To everyone's amazement, the response from the paramilitaries was muted. The rate of attacks on mainland France dropped, and no general strike was called on the island itself, where there seemed to be a tangible shift in public mood away from the nationalist cause.

The Érignac murder

The general election in June 1997 of a socialist government under **Lionel Jospin** coincided with the announcement by FLNC-Canal Historique of yet another **ceasefire**, this time allegedly to encourage concessions from the new administration. When these failed to materialize, however, the truce was called off and bombings resumed.

Manifeste pour la Vie

Among the few local voices courageous enough to speak out against nationalist violence has been that of "**Manifeste pour la Vie**" ("Demonstrate for Life"), a women's movement launched in Ajaccio in January 1996. One of its founder members was Laetitia Sozzi, whose husband, Robert, a former paramilitary, was shot after denouncing links between the FLNC and corruption in the building industry. At the core of the movement is its rejection of what it calls "the establishment of a system based on terror".

Manifeste's demonstrations consistently attract crowds of thousands – an impressive statistic, given that any woman who marches behind the banner of "*Non à la loi des armes*" ("No to the rule of the gun") knows that by doing so she is opening herself to intimidation from the paramilitaries. Anonymous phone calls, letters and death threats have been directed against Manifeste activists, while Cuncolta's newspaper, *Ribombu*, has several times indulged in vitriolic attacks, subsequently condemned by *La Ligue des Droits de l'Homme* (League of Human Rights) as "shameful and archaically misogynistic". In recent years, the local headquarters of a pro-*Manifeste* trade union was also sprayed with bullets; another found a bomb outside its Ajaccio office. Such intimidation, however, did not prevent women activists from gathering over 5000 signatures in a petition condemning paramilitary activity – an unprecedented achievement on an island where speaking out against violence is regarded as taboo.

Thus it was initially the FLNC-Canal Historique who were to be held responsible for the brutal murder of the French government's most senior representative in Corsica, **Claude Érignac**, gunned down in front of his wife while leaving a classical music concert in Ajaccio on February 6, 1998. The FLNC-Canal Historique, however, surprised everyone by condemning the attack. That no one admitted responsibility for the highest-profile assassination in the island's history was widely regarded as symptomatic of the indiscipline and confusion that had overtaken the separatist struggle.

After a fifteen-month investigation, police arrested seven men but announced that their prime suspect for the murder was a goatherd from Cargèse called **Yvan Colonna**, an activist from one of Corsica's more militant breakaway terrorist groups. Now regarded as France's most wanted criminal, Colonna evaded capture and remains at large, hiding out in safe houses on the island, where he is protected by sympathizers and Corsica's implacable *loi de silence*.

L'Affaire de la Paillote

The hunt for Érignac's murderer was a top priority for the man sent by Lionel Jospin to replace him. Heralded as an "iron fist" to clean up the island, 53-year-old **Préfet Bernard Bonnet** was a less sympathetic, less diplomatic character than his predecessor who, in his first year as governor, mounted a heavy-handed crackdown on violence, corruption and organized crime: dozens of prominent figures were detained; banks and local development funds investigated for fraud; and several buildings belonging to or built by known mobsters bulldozed.

Such tactics were expected to upset powerful players on the island. So little heed was paid on the continent to rumours claiming Bonnet – and more specifically the much loathed GPS, an élite squad of paramilitary police which he'd insisted on deploying when he took up office – had stoked the flames of division within the nationalist movement by mounting undercover operations. Such rumours would soon come home to roost in dramatic fashion.

On the night of April 19, 1999, three men wearing black balaclavas landed an inflatable Zodiac on **Cala d'Orzu** beach, on the south side of the Golfe d'Ajaccio (see p.215). They carried with them incendiary devices and jerrycans of fuel, which they used to blow up a shack-restaurant (*paillote*) called *Chez Francis*, leaving behind them a note accusing its owner, Yves Feraud, of being a "cop grass". On an island inured to such attacks, the photos of the resulting destruction might normally have made it onto page three of *Corse-Matin* and then been forgotten. Within days, however, police investigating the crime scene made an extraordinary revelation: articles found amid the débris on the beach (a blood-soaked jacket, an army commando knife and government-issue two-way radios) suggested this was no Mafia or militant separatist attack, but some kind of bungled police operation.

Reaction on the island quickly turned from extreme amusement to indignation and outrage. Nationalists had long claimed the State had been waging a "dirty tricks" campaign and suspicion soon circled on Bonnet and his henchmen. Soon after the fire-bombing, three GPS agents were arrested. Next to be picked up, to the amazement of the national media, was their boss, **Col Henri Mazares** (Corsica's chief of police), who was promptly charged with arson.

More incriminating revelations followed as the bonfire of "**l'affaire de la paillote**", spread upwards. Mazares eventually admitted his complicity in the attack on *Chez Francis*, but he also insisted he was acting under orders and could prove it. When Bonnet himself was then called in for questioning and held, the nationalist press had a field day: "Bonnets by day - balaclavas by night!" ran one Cuncolta headline.

The préfet denied any involvement to begin with, mounting a brief hunger strike in his VIP Paris prison cell. But as more and more evidence came to light he changed his tune and instead accused the prime minister of masterminding his "judicial and media lynching" as a cover-up for the government's flawed Corsica policies.

Jospin responded by sacking Bonnet, whose arrest he described as "a heavy blow to the State, the Republic, the government and to Corsica". The scandal, however, continued to rear its head throughout the following year as the trials of the various agents and police officials implicated rumbled on. In the end, the disgraced préfet was given a three-year prison sentence. Jospin's credibility, and that of his interior minister, took a huge knock and may well have played a significant part in the socialist government's resounding defeat in the elections of 2002. On the island itself, thousands took to the streets calling for greater autonomy. Having dipped in the late-1990s with the upsurge in FLNC violence and murder of Préfet Érignac, public support for the nationalists' cause was once again on the rise.

The Matignon Accords

To regain some of the ground lost by Bonnet's bungle, Jospin tried a more softly-softly approach over the following eighteen months. Offered as a trade-off for peace, his package of far-reaching devolutionary measures – known as the **Matignon Accords** (discussed in more detail in on p.418) – were well received by most nationalists and seemed the best hope for decades of breaking the political deadlock. Even hard-line separatists met with State officials to discuss the portfolio, while the French parliament gave its blessing in a ground-breaking vote.

While these political discussions were being held, the FLNC feud had entered a new and seemingly conclusive phase. At the centre of the power struggle was **François Santoni** – now released from prison after the Sperone golf course scandal – and former Cuncolta national secretary **Charles Pieri** (the activist injured in the Bastia Vieux Port car bombing). The political rivalry between the two men took on a sexual dimension after Pieri became involved with Santoni's former girlfriend, Marie-Hélène Mattei, a nationalist lawyer who'd also served time over the Sperone extortion.

The gloves came off after Pieri took over as head of Cuncolta from his arch adversary. Santoni's revenge was a whistle-blowing book about the FLNC and its corruption by organized crime. Co-authored with fellow dissident nationalist, Jean-Michel Rossi, *Pour solde de tout compte* took the form of an extended interview with journalist Guy Benhamou in which the two spilled the beans on the inner workings of the paramilitary groups – the personal feuds, corruption, covert negotiations with the French State and overall lack of ideological direction. By naming names and generally discrediting the FLNC, Rossi and Santoni were breaking the island's age-old, sacred *loi de silence* – the punishment for which they had themselves, by their own admission, meted out in the past.

It was therefore no surprise when, in August 2000, news broke that Rossi and his bodyguard had died in a hail of bullets over their morning coffee outside the Bar Piscine on the main square in L'Île Rousse. Pieri could not be connected with the murder, but soon after was imprisoned for "criminal association" and possession of illegal firearms.

Santoni, who by then had formed his own breakaway political group and armed wing (Armata Corsa) must have realized he was living on borrowed time. His revelations, both in *Pour solde de tout compte* and subsequent interviews in the press, were calculated to create the maximum embarrassment among his enemies. An attempted assassination had nearly succeeded in 1995, and others were bound to follow. "Those who killed Jean-Michel Rossi would like to finish the job with me," he told reporters in the spring of 2001. "I will make headlines soon."

And so indeed he did, on August 17 of that year, when gunmen descended on a wedding he was attending in the south Corsican village of Monaccia-d'Aullène and shot him dead. In Paris, those opposed to Jospin's Matignon Accords seized the incident as a stick with which to beat the prime minister's Corsica policies. His former interior minister, Jean-Pierre Chevènement, who'd resigned over the proposals, claimed the murder "(emphasized) the illusions on which the Matignon process rests. By giving the priority to a violent minority, which continues its blackmail through terror, the Government has shut itself in a frightening head-to-head encounter with them. The process itself engenders violence."

Pegged to the waning popularity of Jospin and his socialist government, the Matignon talks gradually ground to a halt after key parts of the initiative were watered down. With his resounding defeat at the polls in June 2002, and the inauguration of a more staunchly Republican cabinet opposed to any special treatment for Corsica, any significant breakthrough seemed unlikely. After one of the longest collective ceasefires in the history of the island's armed conflict, car bombs and rocket attacks once again boomed through the streets of Ajaccio at the height of the tourist season, after a coalition of balaclava-wearing paramilitaries announced in a *nuit bleue* an end to their truce, promising more violence on the Continent.

Prospects for peace

At the time of writing, in late 2002, the prospects of Corsica's paramilitaries renouncing the armed struggle seem as distant as they have at any point in the past 25 years. Few would deny that the State, while lavishing funds and tax exemptions on the island, has failed to devise an effective and lasting economic strategy. But this does not explain why so many initiatives by a string of successive administrations have failed, nor why violence continues to be the island's predominant response to its political differences with the motherland.

To understand the real roots of *le problème corse* you have to look to Corsica's traditional culture. As Nicolas Giudici, one of the most-respected commentators on the troubles, has pointed out, "Corsica is an ancient Mediterranean society, convinced of the legitimacy of its ways of doing things – which means factions, clans, infighting and vendettas."

Compounding the persistence of clannism in Corsica is the fact that nowadays the potential pickings of patronage and corruption are richer than ever before. Since 1994, more than 800 million euros has poured in from the EU, to augment the 500 million euros of state subsidies the island receives each year and the 1.32 billion euros of funding for its bloated bureaucracy. "The vast proportion of (this money)" admitted a government report in 2002, has been "misappropriated", both by corrupt mayors and paramilitary movements. The internecine war being waged between the various feuding families and groups is in essence a struggle to control the flow of cash.

Another, more nefarious, element in the whole equation is **organized crime**. The Corsican **Mafia**, which dominates the underworlds of Marseille and Paris, has traditionally limited its activities to the mainland. But in recent years, the mob, or *milieu* as it's known in French, has moved in on the extortion rackets being run by the paramilitaries at home. In the process, the dividing line between nationalist and Mafia violence has become blurred – a process vividly described by Rossi and Santoni in *Pour solde de tout compte*.

After 25 years, the nationalist movement seems less dominated by political ideology and visions of a better future than by the macho, violent culture of the island's past. Adherence to the old ways, however, is not going to be relinquished overnight on an island where clan rivalries and mistrust of government are firmly rooted, nor where anyone who openly opposes the paramilitaries effectively risks their life.

Corsican wildlife

The Parc Naturel Régional de la Corse, established in 1972, now embraces about a third of Corsica, largely down the mountain spine but reaching the sea in the northwest. Managing important sites such as Scandola, the Restonica Valley, the Finocchiarola isles in the north and the Îles Lavezzi in the south, the park authorities ensure the survival of the mouflon and other endangered species, and increase the accessibility of the wildlife of Corsica, through the publication of excellent books and booklets and through the maintenance of footpaths. The ruggedness of Corsica's heartland naturally restricts intensive exploitation, but even in areas where human intervention has occurred the island's terrain is extraordinarily rich. The lush chestnut woodland of the Castagniccia, for example, is the result of plantation, and the tangled, headily scented maquis which clothes more than half of Corsica might seem a natural cover, but is in fact what comes in after fire or on abandoned grazing land.

The habitat zones

Corsica's landscape has three well-defined **habitat zones**, the lowest of which is the Mediterranean zone, which runs from the sea to an altitude of 1000m. Corsica is noted for its clean seas and varied marine life. At places along the coast you'll find pristine sand dunes, lagoons and estuaries, all three of which are now hard to find elsewhere in the Mediterranean. Trees sometimes grow right at the edge of the beach: the highly resinous **Aleppo pine** prefers rocky ground at this level, while the **stone pine** (or umbrella pine) is often seen growing singly but sometimes in groves – some of the best specimens are at Palombaggia beach near Porto-Vecchio. Stands of tall Australian **eucalyptus** can also be found in many places, planted in the late eighteenth century to rid localities such as Porto, in the northwest, of malaria.

However, the typical indicator of the Mediterranean climate is the **olive tree**. Solitary specimens can be found everywhere in Corsica's Mediterranean zone (the oldest giant is near the deserted convent below Oletta at the foot of Cap Corse), while the largest groves are in the Balagne and near Propriano. At these lower altitudes erect "funeral" cypresses are often planted alongside family tombs. Three species of oak also identify this zone – the **cork oak** (its trunk dusky red when newly stripped), the evergreen **holm oak** (which has spiny leaves on sucker shoots and is found in both shrub and tree forms) and the **kermes oak** (rarely tree-sized, and with holly-like leaves).

Introduced shrubs and trees that thrive in this Mediterranean climate include **orange** and **lemon** in groves and gardens, red or purple **bougainvillea** in gardens, **palms** in town squares, pink and white **oleanders** and the gigantic cactus-like **Mexican agave** on roadsides.

Another characteristic of the Mediterranean zone is that the **maquis** springs up after fire or when fields or open grazings are abandoned. Its most easily recognized plants are the shrubs of the **cistus** family, carrying pink or white flowers with crumpled petals, which are shed at the end of each day. Some cistus have highly scented gummy stems and leaves – the Montpellier cistus, which likes acid granite soils and has masses of small white flowers, is perhaps the most fragrant of all.

Cistus bushes often indicate open, newish maquis, which in time will grow into an all-but-impenetrable scrub, with yellow-flowered **brooms** (some of which are wickedly thorny), the taller **strawberry tree** (the red strawberry-like fruits are edible but pappy), the pungent **mastic** and **myrtle**, **rosemary** and white-flowered **tree heather**, which grows 2m tall or more. In the "tall" maquis, cork, holm oaks and other trees come in, and as their crowns broaden they begin to shade out the shrubs below them, until eventually woodland or forest results.

Towards the top of the Mediterranean zone these trees might be joined by **maritime pine**, which unusually keeps large cones of different ages on its branches, and it retains those branches even when they are starkly dead – the Restonica Valley has many examples. **Sweet chestnut** also makes an appearance (it is most widespread between 500m and 800m), as does bracken. Groves of ancient chestnuts can be found near most of the hill villages, where the production of chestnut flour used to play an important part in the economy. Nowadays the chestnuts are given over to pigs (and pâtisseries), and many of the trees display dead, antler-like branches as a result of attacks of mildew and parasites.

At around 1000m, the **mountain zone** succeeds, as oaks and chestnuts give way to forests of the native, tall-trunked **Laricio** (or Corsican) **pine**, perhaps mixed with **beeches** and **firs**. The Aïtone, Valdo-Niello, Bonifato and Tartagine are among the most magnificent of these forests, featuring centuries-old Laricio pines reaching up to 40m that are the tallest conifers in Europe.

Above 2000m stretches the **alpine zone** – open and largely rocky, perhaps with scatters of ground-hugging bushy alders, and often with a wonderful variety of flowers.

Wild flowers

Many Corsican plants are distinctive of the island – of the 2000 species of **wild flowers** found here, eight percent are native to Corsica or shared only by Corsica and Sardinia. Which species you'll see will depend on the soil, the bedrock, the altitude and, of course, the time of year. Spring is glorious, with wild flowers everywhere, and many species celebrate a "second spring" after the summer drought: **cyclamens** and **autumn crocus** appear with the autumn rains, for example, and the handsome **bush spurges** of Cap Corse are in vivid green leaf in winter and spring, but reduced to bare twigs in summer.

Flowers of the Mediterranean zone

On the seashore in summer, the dramatic **yellow-horned poppy** is worth looking for, with its very long curved seed pods. Colourful **sea stocks** and **sea lavender** grow on shingle and on rocks, where carpets of **stonecrop** – with fleshy red leaves and heads of small blue flowers – also make a handsome showing. The **sea holly**, one of the most beautiful of all wild plants with its grey-green spiny leaves and blue flower heads, sometimes forms low mats a couple of metres across – you'll see it on the open sands at Cargèse, for example. Here and at the back of other sandy beaches you can also find the white **sea daffodil** flowering in August, and almost anywhere you might come across carpets of **Hottentot fig**, with its brilliant lilac or yellow-orange flowers.

In spring, various wild flowers brighten the clearings among the colourful **maquis** shrubs. If the maquis is invading old grazing land, or if the open patch is overgrazed and impoverished, there will probably be **asphodel** growing; its delicate white flowers are withered husks by summer, although the tall spikes remain. Many of Corsica's fifty or so species of **wild orchid** flower in the maquis: one of the most handsome is the pink **butterfly orchid**, and there are always a good number of the unmistakable hooded **serapias** group, which are purple or dark red. French **lavender** is common, its small, almost black flowers carried below striking purple sails, and in some areas wild **gladiolus** can be seen along the roads or even as a weed in the ploughed fields – it has smaller flowers than the garden hybrids but is easily recognizable.

The verges and rocky cuttings of roads and lanes through the maquis and between the fields are home to **wild pinks** (some of the mountain pinks are endemic to the island), **ferns**, **honeysuckle** and **eglantine** (a wild white rose looking rather like cistus). Wild **asparagus** is often found growing around the olive groves, while in spring **tassel hyacinths** and white **Florentine iris**, the original fleur-de-lis, flower on open soil (the iris is also popular in gardens).

Flowers of the mountain and alpine zones

In the chestnut woods and amongst the pines of the mountain zone grow the handsome green tufts of the **Corsican hellebore**, a poisonous species endemic to Corsica and Sardinia. **Foxgloves** may be found here, and in spring scatters of **cyclamen** mix with **violets** along the stream-sides, together with hosts of delicate white or lilac **anemones** in some areas. **Autumn crocus** and **squill** also flower here and elsewhere towards the end of the year. Wherever you find beech trees at this height, you might look for wild red **peony**.

Although the mountain zone is harsh, there can be a surprising variety of flowers when the snow melts, many of them endemic – indeed, half of those you see might grow only in Corsica and Sardinia, such as a Corsican alpine groundwort and a blue mountain columbine. And many common enough in the Alps are not found here, suggesting that these two islands separated from mainland Europe at a far-distant time in the past.

Birds

As a result of the closed breeding of its resident island populations, Corsica's **birds** often display certain differences from those of mainland Europe. Songbirds such as the blackbird have a song that's distinct from that of related European species, and the birds' normal habitats are in many instances extended in some way. In Corsica the blackbird ranges from coastal maquis to the high mountains, while the explosive "chetti" call of the small brown **Cetti's warbler** is heard not only in the reed beds around the coastal lagoons but also in the maquis up to 500m. The most-renowned Corsican example is the elusive **Corsican nuthatch** of the Aïtone and other high pine forests. The **treecreeper** is another, while there are also forms of **great spotted wood-**

pecker and **wren** shared with Sardinia. Corsica is the place to add the **Dartford warbler** to your list – it is a localized and rare resident in the south of Britain; here it is common in the coastal maquis but as a darker, smaller sub-species.

Because of its position, Corsica is probably visited by the majority of trans-Mediterranean **migrants**, many of which make landfalls on the headlands or lagoons. The **spring** and **autumn** list includes common and curlew sandpiper (the latter is the commonest migrant wader here), reed bunting, marsh and Montague's harriers, pied flycatcher, grey heron, black kite and tree pipit. Of the birds that come to **winter** on the island, the sparrow-like dunnock is one of the commonest in the maquis, and amongst the other regulars are snipe, cormorant, common starling, gannet, pochard, tufted duck, teal, black-necked grebe, redwing and song thrush. Others such as the wood pigeon are resident, but numbers swell in winter, when incomers fly in to gorge on the plentiful crops of acorns.

Seabirds and wetland species

In general most **coastal birdlife** is centred on remote headlands and islands. Scandola, for example, has osprey, peregrine, rock dove and blue rock thrush (which also nest on bare slopes inland to 1800m). Shearwaters nest in some places, but you'll see fewer **gulls** than you might expect. Herring gulls nest at Scandola and Capo Rossu and other remote sites, and you may spot the Mediterranean gull (black-headed in summer) and the slim-winged Audouin's gull, which nest on several offshore islands. Shags, too, nest on rocky shores and are often seen flying low over the sea.

Despite widespread drainage for vineyards, fruit and other crops, the string of lagoons off the east coast remain one of the most extensive wetland units of the whole Mediterranean, attracting great crested and little **grebes**, pochard and mallard, and the water rail with its incredible pig-like cry. Reed, moustached, Cetti's and other **warblers** call from the reed beds, while marsh harrier and hobby hunt across them. In winter, Biguglia and the other lagoons are an important station for ducks, grey heron, wintering kingfisher and others.

Maquis species

The **maquis** in its various forms offers ideal nesting for **warblers** and birds such as red-backed shrike, pipits, buntings and even the highly colourful bee-eater. The **linnet** picks out more open areas, as does the **stonechat** and the red-legged **partridge** (the grey has been introduced for shooting in some places). These birds all follow the maquis as it spreads up the valleys and slopes inland, but where it grows tall and is invaded by holm oak and other trees (as seen in the Fango Valley, for example) the scrub warblers such as Dartford and Sardinian leave, while the blackcap and subalpine remain. Being evergreen, the maquis maintains its insect larder in winter, when many of its resident birds are joined by migrant cousins.

Kestrel and buzzards (widespread but nowhere very common) patrol above the maquis, as does red kite, which prefers the lower scrubby maquis to the taller growth. At night the clear bell-like notes of the **Scops owl** and the call of the nightjar echo across the maquis, mingling with the constant croaking of frogs.

The chestnut groves are comparatively empty of birdlife, but look for the endemic **treecreeper** here, and also the **mistle thrush** and the **wryneck**, the last now rare almost everywhere.

Mountain species

In the **mountain** and alpine levels, grey wagtail and dipper forage in the spray of the torrents, where the crag martin is often seen as well. The pine forests have **goldcrest**, **coal tit** and the endemic **nuthatch** – this last, found from the Tartagine in the north to Ospédale in the south, is smaller than its mainland cousins and is more often heard than seen. Sparrowhawk and goshawk have a presence in these pine woods, as does the crossbill.

A feature of some parts of the **high mountains** are *pozzines* – small table-lands of peaty turf cut by meandering streams. Here **lark** and **wheatear** are often seen, with even blackbird and chaffinch if there are scrubby alders for cover. The blue rock thrush, though nesting on the coast at Scandola and else-where, can be met as high as 1500m. The central mountains are the domain of the yellow-beaked **alpine chough** and the rare **lammergeier** and **golden eagle**. Bonelli's eagle is reported from the Asco Valley, but it is not known if it nests.

Garden species

Gardens attract many birds, such as blackbird, warblers, hooded crow and tur-tle dove – the latter are widely shot when they fly in in spring, but there are always some to be heard in summer. (The collared dove is a recent colonist and still uncommon.) Gardens also attract the spotted flycatcher – the Corsican form scarcely lives up to its name, with few if any speckles, but it is quickly recognized by its lively fly-catching sorties, usually returning to the same post. In the Nebbio and a few other spots, the **hoopoe** (with its dramatic crest) is also seen in gardens at dawn. The towns attract **house martin** and **swifts** – both the familiar Eurasian swift and the similar pallid swift.

Mammals

Woodmouse, shrew, rabbit, brown hare, weasel and hedgehog are as familiar in Corsica as elsewhere in Europe, but there are no squirrels. Squirrel-like nests in shrubs or low trees may be those of the black rat, while a sighting of a small brownish animal with squirrel-like bushy tail would be the **fat dor-mouse**, though it is shy and nocturnal. The slimmer **garden**, (or **oak**) **dor-mouse**, with white underside to body and tail, is also resident. Both these animals may search houses for a hibernation den in autumn, and you often hear them scratching around in the attic. Bats are common everywhere: in the gorge of the Bonifato forest behind Calvi, for example, they swarm out at sunset.

The fox is seen, and there are reports of a wild cat in remote parts of the island such as the Aïtone Forest – it may turn out to be a tribe of striped feral cat, domestic stock now living wild. There are similar indecisive reports of pine marten in these forested areas.

Around five hundred **mouflon** – a wild sheep, the males sporting massive curved horns – are found in two main areas: at Asco and at Bavella. They might be the relic of an original wild population that began to be domesticated in Neolithic times, or they may be the descendants of escapees from those first domestic flocks.

Forests

Aïtone – magnificent specimens of Laricio pine; in the remoter reaches (towards Monte Cinto), wild boar, eagle and mouflon. See p.178.

Bavella – impressive though fire-damaged hunting reserve; chance of sightings of mouflon and eagle. See p.255.

Bonifato – classic "chaos" of rocks and forest, pines and maquis. See pp.151–152.

Castagniccia – chestnut woods. See p.307–317.

Ospédale – pines and other trees. See p.285.

Tartagine – bat caves and magnificent pines. See p.115.

Valdo-Niolo – the largest of the island's forests, with fine examples of Laricio pine. See p.336.

Vizzavona – some of the finest pines and beech. See p.351.

Other wildlife zones

Asco Valley – possible sightings of mouflon, eagle, lammergeier; Corsican nuthatches can also be sighted amid the Laricio and maritime pine forest at the head of the valley. See p.325.

Biguglia and the east coast lagoons – birdlife. See p.77.

Bonifacio – limestone cliffs with rare flowers. See pp.270–276.

Calanches de Piana – flowers and coastal birds. See p.171.

Cap Corse – remote maquis, good for birds (maybe eagles attracted by remoteness); nature reserve on Finocchiarola isles. See pp.78–96.

Désert des Agriates – a largish area of thin maquis growing on rocky, impoverished terrain; good for flowers and nesting birds. See p.110.

Fango Valley – good walking through mix of maquis and forest habitats. See p.154.

Îles Sanguinaires – distinctive island vegetation. See p.212.

Îles Lavezzi – nature reserve off Bonifacio. See p.278.

Niolo – alpine choughs and other mountain birds. See pp.330–338.

Restonica – Corsican and maritime pine. See p.345.

Scandola – supreme nature reserve of international importance; classic lava-column geology; osprey and other birds; marine life. See p.170.

The **sanglier** (wild boar) is found throughout the maquis and in the lower mountains, and has something of a cult status in Corsica. Many villages organize weekly hunts over the winter, culling an estimated 10,000 each year from an average population of 30,000. Even though the males are smaller than their continental cousins, the Corsican boar can still reach 80kg, and is a formidable animal, being armed with tusks for rooting and grubbing – you'll come across the disturbed ground during walks in the maquis. It is a Corsican habit to let domestic **pigs** roam free in the chestnut and beech woods on the mountain flanks, so there is certainly interbreeding between boar and pig, yet about forty percent of the wild-boar stock remains untainted.

The native **red deer** – the smallest of all red deer – became extinct only a few decades ago, but some Sardinian stock can be seen in a paddock near Quenza in the south, from where they are released into the surrounding forest.

Offshore, the common and striped **dolphins** and the common **porpoise** patrol, if no longer as regularly or in the numbers that were once seen. The endangered monk seal of the Mediterranean was last seen in Corsican waters in 1982. The **fin whale**, however, is often seen with young off Cap Corse in springtime.

Reptiles and insects

Corsica's hot rocky landscape suits reptiles, and **lizards** are always seen scuttling across walls and rocks. The **Tyrrhenian wall lizard** is a sometimes abundant species found only in Corsica and Sardinia, and the mountain lizard is also endemic, but their variable colouring makes identification of lizard species difficult. Their cousins, the plump but flattened **geckos**, are most often noticed high on room walls and ceilings, which they patrol after sunset, dealing with mosquitoes and other irritations.

There are no poisonous snakes on the island. The **grass snake** is seen in damp places, while the **whip snake** – a slender snake often with a barred pattern – is found on sunny hillsides and other dry habitats. It will attempt to bite if annoyed – its French name is *coléreuse*, "quick-tempered one".

Hermann's tortoise is a fairly common sight in some areas, and a centre for tortoise breeding and release has recently been created near Ajaccio. The European pond **terrapin** might be seen in secluded pools and other still waters that have overgrown banks.

Endemic to the island is the **brook salamander**, olive-grey and brown and with a clear yellow stripe down its spine, found near running water up to 2000m. The rather larger **fire salamander**, with dramatic black and yellow skin, might also be seen.

Most piercingly vocal are the **edible frog** and the **common tree frog**, which has enormous vocal sacs for its small size. The **green toad**, with spotted green and white skin and shrill warbling call, is also reasonably common.

The frog chorus takes over from the summer daytime chorus of the **cicadas**, especially loud in the vicinity of their favourite umbrella pines. The cicadas are just one of a host of grasshoppers, bushcrickets, beetles, bees and **butterflies** that make Corsica so fascinating for anyone with any interest in natural history. Some butterflies will be familiar from northern Europe, such as the migrant painted lady and the red admiral. Of the Mediterranean species, one of the most handsome is the large and strong **two-tailed pasha**, which feeds on the strawberry tree of the maquis. **Hummingbird hawk moths** of various kinds are commonly seen in gardens, hovering in front of the flowers.

Damselflies and mayflies are a common sight dancing over the streams, and the dramatic and fierce **hawker dragonflies** – a birdwatcher's insect if ever there was one – may spend the day hunting across the maquis, far from water.

Geoffrey Young

Books

Very few books about Corsica have been written in English, and the great majority of them are out of print, so you'll have to resort to secondhand book-shops or libraries if you want to get stuck into most of the titles listed below. Those currently out-of-print are marked "o/p" in the reviews that follow. For the benefit of fluent French readers, we've also included a handful of French titles, which you can buy in any good bookshop in Corsica and mainland France or order via the Internet at ⓦwww.fnac.fr. In the UK, virtually any French book in print may be ordered from The European Bookshop, 5 Warwick St, London W1R 5RA ⓣ020/7734 5259, ⓦwww.eurobooks.co.uk. Best among the bibliographies of writing about the island is the World Bibliographical Series' *Corsica*, compiled by Grace L. Hudson, which you should be able to get hold of through any academic library. Titles marked ⋆ are particularly recommended.

Travel

James Boswell *An Account of Corsica: the Journal of a Tour to that Island and Memoirs of Pascal Paoli* (In Print Publishing, UK). Typically robust account of the author's eventful trip to the island in 1765 to seek out Pascal Paoli in his hideout at Sollacaro. The meat of the book lies in its expansive description of the encounter with the charismatic rebel leader, but the travelogue leading up to it proves more entertaining. After the journal's publication, Boswell became famous as an advocate of Corsican independence. Recently re-issued in a handsome hardback facsimile edition.

Thomasina M.A.E. Campbell *Notes on the Island of Corsica* (Hatchard, London, UK; o/p). This quirky 1868 travelogue, by an indomitable Scottish lady who was a friend of Edward Lear, begins with the caveat: "To the genuine British grumbler (who ought never to leave England unless accompanied by his own cook and a cow, and frequently not even then) Ajaccio says 'Remain At Home!'". It proceeds in rambling fashion, with greater attention to the minutiae of travel and flowers than history and culture, but includes some entertaining episodes.

⋆ **Dorothy Carrington** *Granite Island* (Penguin). Published originally in French, *L'Île de Granite* is a portrait of Corsica woven around Lady Rose's first visit of 1947 (when she "re-discovered" the Filitosa menhirs), with experiences, meetings and historical asides drawn from later decades adding depth. Although something of a historical document itself these days, it remains by far the most erudite and rounded account of the island ever written, in any language.

Sir Gilbert Elliot *Life and letters of Sir Gilbert Elliot first Earl of Minto from 1751 to 1806* (Longmans, London, UK; o/p). Sir Gilbert became viceroy of the island during the Anglo-Corsican interlude and this book, compiled by his great-niece, collates his most memorable correspondance from the period, framed by a contextual essay and short biography. As interesting for its insights into the historical personalities of the era (including Paoli), as its vivid evocations of the mountains and forest.

Gustave Flaubert *Voyage dans les Pyrénées et en Corse* (Flammarion, France). Flaubert's parents promised him a trip to Corsica if he passed his baccalaureate, and this book is an account of the trip the young novelist-to-be subsequently made in the summer of 1840. Full of freshness, sensuality and descriptions of the island's landscape and people, it follows the 19-year-old's progress across the Pyrenees to the Mediterranean, with a poignant interlude describing his secret love affair with a beautiful Peruvian woman in Marseille.

Richard T.N.B.C. Grenville *The private diary of Richard, Duke of Buckingham and Chandos* (Hurst & Blackett, London, UK; o/p). Regarded as the first modern-style

Une Lady Corse

"Almost colourless, its outlines uncertain, it swam in the early morning mist, a creation half-materialized, an ectoplasm of the sea in trance." **Dorothy Carrington**'s first sight of Corsica in 1948, as recounted in *Granite Island*, has about it the air of a prophetic vision; and so indeed it must have seemed twenty years after the fact, when she settled down in a gloomy basement in Ajaccio to sieve through two decades of discoveries, encounters and wonderment. Distilled into three-hundred pages of unfailingly elegant prose, the book she eventually published in 1971 – a heady mix of travelogue, historical tract and ethnography – provides a compelling portrait of an island poised on the brink of massive change, as its traditional ways were about to be subsumed by modernity. For the first time since Boswell's *Journal*, it brought Corsica to the attention of an international public, and reminded Corsicans themselves of the richness of their cultural heritage – a service for which the islanders, even those who may never have set eyes on the book, remain grateful. Decorated Chevalier de l'Order des Arts et des Lettres and granted an honorary doctorate by the University of Corte, Dorothy Carrington is still a household name in her adopted home, where she lived and wrote for nearly fifty years.

The future author of *Granite Island* was born Frederica Dorothy Violet Carrington at Perrott's Brook in Gloucestershire in 1910, into a landed family. Her father, a hero of the Boer war, was a friend and comrade of Cecil Rhodes, her mother a glamorous Edwardian hostess with a passion for liberal politics, music, painting and the ballets of Diaghilev. Both parents, however, died prematurely, and the young Dorothy found herself packed off to wealthy relatives in rural Gloucestershire. But she was never one for the sedentary hunting and shooting life and escaped as soon as she could to study English at Oxford. It was there she first met the dashing but impoverished Austrian Franz Von Walschutz, with whom she eloped first to Paris, and later to Rhodesia (Zimbabwe).

The thrill of life on an African farm having subsided, Dorothy left Von Walschutz and returned to London's prewar arts scene, mixing with an international bohemian intelligentsia. It was while organizing an exhibition in 1942 that she first met the surrealist painter, **Francis Rose**. The son of a wildly beautiful Franco-Spanish arts impresario, Laetitia Rouy, Rose had grown up in Paris knowing Sarah Bernhardt, Jean Cocteau and Isadora Duncan, and had designed sets and costumes for Diaghilev while still in his 20s. It was said to have been in praise of a retrospective show of his work that his eventual patron, Gertrude Stein, made her famous remark, "A Rose is a Rose is a Rose".

Francis and Dorothy fell in love to a background of the London underworld. Though both from aristocratic families, neither had a penny to rub together during "that bitter, gritty spring", as she would later describe it, living on a diet of dandelion leaves picked amid the wreckage of the blitz. Undeterred by their poverty, Rose proposed on the tube in 1943, and they celebrated their engagement at a down-at-heel

tourist to visit the island (in 1828–1829), the Duke of Bucks arrived in Ajaccio by yacht and conducted a tour with his eye more on Corsica's landscape, village life and banditry than its lofty historical figures, which makes this a much more original read than most of its predecessors.

★ Edward Lear *Journal of a Landscape Painter* (Century, UK; o/p). After Boswell, the book that first brought images of Corsica to a mass readership in England. Lear visited the island in the 1860s, and produced a work remembered less for its lacklustre prose than beautifully atmospheric engravings, prominently featured by Dorothy Carrington in *Granite Island*. A collector's item these days, but available through many libraries and well worth tracking down.

Alan Ross *Time Was Away – A Journey Through Corsica* (Collins

café in the docks. The waiter that night was a Corsican, **Jean Cesari**, who on subsequent visits impressed and befriended the couple with his ability to conjure French baguettes from war-time rations, and with his stories of his romantic homeland – of its grandiose landscapes, chestnut gathering in the snowy mountains, mysterious "dream-hunters" and romantic *bandits d'honneur*. Cesari also talked of the enigmatic standing-stones scattered under the olive trees on his cousin's farm, many of them carved with faces and weapons. Fresh from editing an anthology of travel writing (*The Traveller's Eye*, published in 1947) and eager for her own real adventures, Dorothy was hooked.

So it was, at the end of 1947, that Lord and Lady Rose set off – titled, but with virtually no money – in search of the Cesaris' menhirs. They carried with them little more than two suitcases crammed with sugar and coffee, then unavailable on the island. In the wake of World War II, Corsica was a land that had altered little in a century or more. At first the Roses revelled in its simple pleasures and Mediterranean exoticism, marvelling at the wonderful mountains, Genoese citadels, turquoise water, and the singer-poets who wandered from house to house improvising verses in Corsican. With food straight from cottage gardens and orchards, they ate better than they had for years; in an interview forty years later, Dorothy fondly recalled how, if they needed salt, they'd "scrape some of the rocks with a teaspoon".

But Francis, hankering for the sophistication of London and Paris society, soon grew weary of life in Corsican peasant villages and left his wife to her new passion. In truth, he was gay and the marriage, which had never been an entirely happy one, was effectively over. Having retired to Britain Lord Rose became a poverty-stricken, camp recluse in Surrey, where he is said – in homage to the *fin-de-siècle* Parisian surrealists he so admired – to have attended church dressed in a Mexican sombrero, leading a cat on a gold chain.

Dorothy, meanwhile, felt re-born. In Corsica she had at last found her life's work, a field equal to her appetite for hidden history and travel. The menhirs talked of by Jean Cesari did indeed turn out to be every bit as extraordinary as she'd hoped, and it was she who first recognized their significance, persuading Roger Grosjean – the man generally credited with the "discovery" of **Filitosa** (see p.232) – to begin archeological digs (a fact still not mentioned by the site's guides). Later, she unearthed in forgotten archives a copy of Pascal Paoli's original Constitution of Independence, and showed the world how it had been a model not only for its French equivalent but also the Constitution of the United States of America.

Dorothy Carrington lived the rest of her long life in Ajaccio, producing a succession of erudite volumes on Corsica (notably on Napoleon and the island's disappearing occult traditions). She died seven months after her ninetieth birthday, surrounded by her books and a handful of Francis Rose's paintings, working on the same antiquated typewriter with which she had written *Granite Island*.

Harvill, UK; o/p). Dour, essentially impressionistic account of a visit to Corsica in 1947, while the island was still "sunk in a post-malarial torpor". In later years, the author admitted to being "over-influenced by the travel books of Graham Green and detached camera-eye style of Christopher Isherwood", but his account makes an interesting snapshot, even if it doesn't stand much comparison with Dorothy Carrington's book, researched the same year. Illustrated with bold woodcuts by artist John Minton.

Geoffrey Wagner *Elegy for Corsica* (Cassell/Southern Illinois UP; o/p). A highly readable miscellany drawn from an American's extended sabbaticals on the island in the 1960s. Portraits of local people (from Calenzana pimps to Niolo shepherds) are threaded together with historical anecdote, descriptions of festivals, contemporary issues and a host of literary snippets to give a slice of island life at this formative point in Corsica's history.

History and society

 Dorothy Carrington *The Dream Hunters of Corsica* (Phoenix). Based primarily on first-hand interviews conducted between 1947 and 1995, this popular, accessible compendium of folklore expands with characteristic elegance on *Granite Island*'s coverage of matters occult, notably *mazzeri* – "dream-hunters" who can foresee death – and the evil eye.

Dorothy Carrington *Napoleon and his Parents on the Threshold of History* (Viking/Nal-Duhon; o/p). Lucid study of Napoléon's early years in his native country, from the Battle of Ponte-Nuovo until the death of his father in 1785, derived from the archives of Prince Napoléon and other previously unconsulted private collections. The most thorough work on this period, illustrated with fac-similes of little-known documents.

Philippe-Jean Catinchi *Polyphonies Corses* (Cité de la Musique/Acte Sud, France). Concise, richly illustrated history of Corsican song, from timeless shepherds' *paghjella* to Tino Rossi and I Muvrini. Most of the tracks on the accompanying CD are very much in the field recording mode, but still represent the broadest cross-section of traditional Corsican music so far compiled on a single disc, and the explanatory notes are more copious than usual.

Maurice Choury *Tous Bandits d'Honneur!* (La Marge Éditions, France). Popular history of Corsica's struggle against the Axis forces, June 1942 to October 1943, focusing mainly on the socialist Front National's contribution to the Resistance. Choury was one of the leaders of the Maquis and offers a vivid insight into the compelling, often tragic events leading up to island's liberation.

Vincent Cronin *Napoleon* (Fontana/HarperCollins). Enthusiastic and accessible biography, recently republished in paperback, which attempts to explain the life of France's great emperor in personal as well as military terms. Arguably the best route into this crowded field.

Desmond Gregory *The ungovernable rock: a history of the Anglo-Corsican Kingdom and its role in Britain's Mediterranean strategy during the revolutionary war* (Associated University Press, Toronto; o/p). The definitive account of Britain's short and ultimately fruitless rule of Corsica, which involved historical figures such as Nelson, Sir John Moore, Admiral Hood and Sir Gilbert Elliot.

Capitaine Jean L'Herminier
Casabianca (France Empire, France).
The submarine *Casabianca*'s derring-
do adventures in 1942–43, as recalled
by its redoubtable commander. If
you can handle the obscure nautical
vocabulary, this makes an engrossing
read and brings into sharp relief the
nuts and bolts – and sheer perilous-
ness – of the Resistance struggle
during World War II.

Moray McLaren *Corsica Boswell:
Paoli, Johnson and Freedom* (Secker &
Warburg, London; o/p). Fellow Scot
McLaren follows in the footsteps of
Boswell, giving as he does so a readable account of the island's history and
condition in the 1960s. He then pur-
sues the story back to Britain, through
Boswell's fund-raising campaign for
the patriots to Dr Johnson's famous
meeting with Paoli, and the rebel
leader's eventual exile in London. An
ambitious work that was the first in
English to unravel the legacy of James
Boswell's visit and subsequent espousal
of the partisans' cause.

Carola Oman *Nelson* (The Reprint
Society, UK; o/p). The definitive
biography of Britain's most illustrious admiral, whose misadventures in
Corsica nearly cost him his life.
Published in 1947, but written in a
nautical style reminiscent of Nelson's
own era.

Aylmer Vallance *The Summer King*
(Thames & Hudson; o/p). Popular,
illustrated biography of Theodor von
Neuhoff, self-styled "King of
Corsica", which attempts to separate
the wheat of fact from the chaff of
fiction put about by the man himself
during his chequered lifetime. Also
worth tracking down if the subject
grabs you is Valerie Pirie's *His
Majesty of Corsica* (Collins, UK; o/p),
written a couple of decades previously in 1939.

★ **Jean-Michel Rossi and
François Santoni** *Pour solde de
tout compte* (J'ai Lu/Editions Denoel,
France). Nationalist paramilitaries of
various persuasions had published

memoirs before, but none were so
candid and confessional as this best-
seller of 2000, which blew the lid off
the murky world of the FLNC.
Allegedly written as an act of
revenge on a long-time adversary
within the movement, it details how
the island's various armed groups
became progressively corrupted by
Mafia money over the 1990s.
Further revelations about clandestine
talks with government ministers
proved equally explosive. The ideal
next step if you're inspired to harden
your grip on the issues outlined in
the essay on "The Corsican
Troubles" on p.420.

Paul Silvani *Et la Corse fut Libérée*
(La Marge Éditions, France). Written
as recently as 1993, this prize-winning history of the liberation quickly
established itself as the classic version, drawing on recently released
records, contemporary documents
and firsthand accounts to reconsti-
tute the dramatic events of 1942–43.

Peter Adam Thrasher *Pascal Paoli:
an enlightened hero 1725–1807*
(Constable, London; o/p). The best
English-language biography of the
great man, covering events from his
birth in Castagniccia in 1725 to his
death at the age of 82 in London.
Some of Thrasher's conclusions have
been contested by later historians,
but as an introduction to this revolutionary French thinker, whose
achievements ultimately had a bearing on both the French and
American constitutions, it's hard to
beat.

Patrick Whinney *Corsican
Command* (Patrick Stephens, UK).
Wittily written memoirs of clandestine operations in Corsica between
1943 and 1944, when the Allies were
running naval missions to the Italian
coast (often using captured Italian
boats and their crews). Of particular
interest is the author's description of
Bastia in the wake of the German
withdrawal, illustrated with photos
that capture the feel of the times.

Literature

Gabriel Xavier Culioli *La Terre des Seigneurs* (Lieu Commun, France). Phenomenally successful novel following the evolution of a family through a century of Corsican history. Full of fascinating background on island politics, village life and the impact of emigration and the world wars on traditional society. The present edition republishes the (lengthy) introductory essays from previous ones – vivid historical testaments themselves, as a member of Culioli's family was imprisoned in the 1990s for terrorist offences.

Alphonse Daudet *Letters from my Windmill* (Penguin). Inspired by a visit to the island in the winter of 1862, Daudet's most famous anthology of short stories includes his tale of a lonely Corsican lighthouse keeper on the Îles Sanguinaires, near Ajaccio, and a chilling account of the sinking of the *Sémillante*, in which 773 troops and sailors en route to the Crimean War were drowned – the Mediterranean's worst ever maritime disaster.

Gustave Flaubert *Memoires d'un Fou* (Flammarion, France). Flaubert romanticizes the *bandits*, the maquis, the mountains and the sea in letters to his sister.

Guy de Maupassant *Un Bandit Corse et Autres Contes* (Marzocchi, France). Maupassant, France's most illustrious short-story author, spent two months in Corsica in 1880, and the lively tales in this anthology were all inspired by his visit. The *Bandit Corse* has become a classic, and is said to have been avidly read by the *bandits* themselves after its publication.

Prosper Mérimée *Colomba* (Hachette, France). Short novel loosely based on a real-life blood feud that divided the village of Fozzano in the 1830s. A son returns to Corsica and is expected to avenge the death of his father. Though far from historically accurate, the story vividly evokes the violent spirit of the times and was a roaring success for Mérimée, inspiring a mini tourist invasion in Fozzano.

Walking and climbing

David Abram *Trekking in Corsica* (Trailblazer, UK). Trailblazer's guide to the island's long-distance footpaths covers the GR20, Mare a Mare Nord & Sud and Mare e Monti Nord routes, as well as the Campomoro–Roccapina coast path. Even allowing for our inevitable bias (it's written by the same author as this Rough Guide) this is the most comprehensive book of its kind in English (if not in any language), with 320 pages of lively route descriptions and background features, plus 67 hand-drawn trekking maps listing stage times and other points of interest. You also get

a handy full-colour field guide to common Corsican flora.

Robin G. Collomb *Corsica Mountains* (West Col, UK). Covers all the routes up principal mountain peaks (and many obscurer ones), with information on different approaches and ascents, backed up with line diagrams, though the information on the island's footpaths is patchy and more than a decade out of date.

Féderation Française de la Randonnée Pédesetre/Parc Naturel Régional de Corse (FFRP, France) *Corse: entre mer et montagne* and *Corse: a travers la mon-*

tagne corse. This pair of colour topoguides, co-published by France's national trekking authority and the PNRC, splices together excerpts of the relevant IGN maps for the island's main trails with bare-bones route descriptions and other practical info. Accurate and lightweight, they've been the benchmark guides for years, although neither is currently available in English. You can order them at ⓦwww.ign.fr.

Flora and fauna field guides

Bertel Brun *Birds of Britain and Europe* (Hamlyn). The classic tome on the subject, showing most of the species you're likely to come across.
Burton, Arnold & Ovenden *Field Guide to the Reptiles and Amphibians of Britain & Europe* (HarperCollins). The indispensable companion for those wishing to differentiate Tyrrhenian from Bedriaga's wall lizards, and many more besides.
Davies & Gibbons *Wild Flowers of Southern Europe* (The Cowood Press, UK). Some 200 pages shorter than Grey-Wilson & Blamey's guide, but nicely designed, concise and photographic, with coverage of pretty much every flower you can expect to encounter.

★ **Grey-Wilson & Blamey** *Mediterranean Wild Flowers* (HarperCollins). The definitive guide, though at 560 pages it's a bit heavy to lug around on walks, and doesn't come cheap.
Higgins & Riley *Butterflies of Britain and Europe* (HarperCollins). Essential reading for keen butterfly spotters.
Jacquie Grozier *Birdwatching Guide to France South of the Loire* (Arlequin Press, UK). Includes a site guide to the island's ornithological hot spots.
Thibault & Bonaccorsi *Birds of Corsica* (BOU, UK). Written by Corsica's most eminent ornithologists, this essentially academic study lists all 323 species present on the island and places them in the wider context of the Mediterranean.

You can't travel far in Corsica without coming across the island's ubiquitous national symbol, the **Moor's head**. Depicting the profile of a young black male with a white scarf, or *bandeau*, tied behind his head, this enigmatic image crops up everywhere, from car stickers to key rings, postcards to football pennants. Yet its origins are obscure, shrouded in a mixture of myth and historical fact.

The first concrete associations of the Moor's head with Corsica date from the early seventeenth century, when it featured on German maps of the island. This inspired Théodore von Neuhof to use the image on the single silver coin he had minted to mark his short reign as king of Corsica. Not until November 24, 1762, however, was it declared the official symbol of Corsican Independence, at the instigation of Pascal Paoli.

The choice of the Moor's head seems somewhat strange, given the fact the symbol was known to have originally come from Spain and was at one time synonymous with the threat of colonial rule. It first came to the region on the battle standards of the Crown of Aragon, who ruled neighbouring Sardinia following the expulsion of the Saracens during the Crusades. Indeed, the white *bandeau*, which on Aragon standards was drawn covering the eyes rather than the forehead, is believed to symbolize the defeat of the Muslims and their forced conversion to Christianity, while the four heads featured on the dragonese arms refer to the legend of the four Muslim chiefdoms killed in the **Reconquista** of Spain.

The association of the Moor's head emblem with the defeat of the Saracens during the Middle Ages finds echoes in an old Corsican legend. In the story, a young woman named Diana from Aléria, on the east coast, was abducted by Moorish pirates and taken to Grenada. However, her fiancé, Paoli, managed to free her and, after crossing the Sierra Nevada, returned safely to Corsica. The king of Grenada, Mohammed Abdul Allah, was furious at being outwitted by a peasant and instructed his top general, Mansour ben Ismail, to recapture the fugitives dead or alive. After landing at Piana on the west coast, the Moors are then said to have raped and pillaged their way across the mountains to Aléria, where they were engaged, and eventually defeated by, a courageous Corsican army. In the course of the battle, Paoli avenged Diana's abduction by slaying Mansour and parading his disembodied head at the end of a stick around the entire island – whence the now famous image.

In more recent times, the Moor's head has been appropriated by the nationalist movement as the unofficial emblem of the Corsican Independence struggle. Wherever you find a French *tricolore*, you're almost certain to see a black-and-white Moor's head flag flying provocatively nearby.

Language

Language

The Corsican language 449

Corsican words and phrases 449

French pronunciation 451

Learning materials 452

French words and phrases 452

A food glossary 456

Language

Top of the nationalist agenda since the 1970s has been the revival of the Corsican language, which has survived despite repression by successive ruling powers. Travelling around the island's more rural areas, you'll regularly hear its distinctive rhythms and intonations – spoken by young as well as old. An estimated seventy percent of locals claim to be fluent speakers, but few use the language in their day-to-day lives and the trend is definitely a downward one. As a visitor, you can expect to get by well enough with French; English tends to be spoken only in the coastal resorts, and even then not all that well.

The Corsican language

Corsican, originally a Latin-based language with resemblances to Romanian, developed an Italianate vocabulary and syntax during Pisan and Genoese occupation. Arabic and French influences have added to the complexity of the tongue, which was predominantly an oral one until around two hundred years ago – hence the confusing variety of spellings for place names, which endure despite periodic attempts at standardization. The commonest variants come about through the transposition of *ll* and *dd* – as in *casteddu* and *castellu*. Buildings and monuments are often labelled in different languages (San Pietro/San Pietru), and on maps you'll find mountain passes, rivers and regions marked in a mixture of Italian, French and Corsican – the *u* ending (pronounced as in English "zoo") is a frequent indicator of Corsican usage. Deep in the country, many old people are still easier with Corsican than French, so a few phrases will be met with surprise and pleasure. Pronunciation is generally as for Italian, but look out for two tricky clusters of consonants – *chj/chi* and *ghj/chi*, pronounced "ty" or "dy".

Corsican words and phrases

Basics

yes – **iè**	this – **quellu/quella**
no – **nò**	that – **quessu/quessa**
OK – **và bé**	now – **ora**
please – **fate u piacè**	later – **dopu**
thank you – **a' ringraziavvi**	open – **apertu**
where – **induve**	closed – **chiusu**
when – **quandu**	with – **cù**
what – **chi**	without – **senza**
how much – **quantu**	good – **bonu**
here – **custi**	bad – **male**
there – **custà**	big – **grande/maio**

small – **piccola/chjucu**
cheap – **bonu mercatu**
expensive – **cara**
hot – **caldu**
cold – **fredda**
more – **piu**
less – **menu**
nothing – **nulla/nunda/nudda**
today – **oghje**
tomorrow – **dumane**
day – **ghjurnu**
week – **simana**
month – **meze**

yesterday – **ieri**
day before – **avant'ierisera**
night – **a notte**
car – **a vittura**
girl – **zitella**
boy – **zitellu**
it's good – **he bonu**
something – **qualcosa**
I want – **vogliu**
next week – **simana'dopu**
next month – **meze'dopu**
morning – **a mane**
evening – **a sera**

Greetings and responses

hello – **bonghjornu**
goodbye – **a'vedeci**
good evening – **bona sera**
goodnight – **bona notte**
sorry – **me dispiace**
excuse me – **scusame**
How are you? – **comu sì?**

I (don't) understand – **(nò) capiscu**
Do you speak English? – **parla inglese?**
My name is . . . – **me chjamanu . . .**
What's your name? – **cumu a chjamanu?**
I am English – **sò Inglese**
Let's go – **andemu**

Questions and requests

Do you have? – **avetene?**
Give me (one like that) – **datemi**
That's enough – **basta**
What would you like to drink? – **chi vulete beie?**
I'd like a lemonade/coffee – **a me una limnata/caffè**
How much? – **quantu costanu?**
Is there . . .? – **c'he . . .?**
  a room – **una camera**
  with two beds – **cù duie letti**

with shower/bath – **cùillad uscia/bag narola**
It's for one person/ two people – **ci ne vole una/duie persona**
How long are you staying? – **quantu ci avete da stà?**
For one night/one week – **pé una notte/una semana**
It's fine – **và bé**
It's too expensive – **he troppu caru**

Directions

Where is . . ? – **induv'é . . .?**
It's near – **he vicinu**
It's far – **he lontana**
left – **sinistra**
right – **dritta**
straight on – **sempredrittu**

How long will it take to get to Ponte Leccia? – **quantu ci vole à ghjunghje à u Ponte à a Leccia?**
What's the time ? – **chi ora he?**
It's three o'clock – **sò trè ore**

Months and seasons

January – **ghjennaghju**
February – **febbraghju**
March – **marzu**

April – **aprile**
May – **maghjiu**
June – **ghjiugnu**

July - ghjugliu		December - dicembre	
August - aostu		winter - imbernu/ingnernu	
September - sittembre		spring - veranu	
October - ottobre		summer - estate	
November - novembre		autumn - auturnu	

Numbers and days

1 - unu (una)		21 - vintunu	
2 - dui (duie)		22 - vintidui	
3 - trè		30 - trenta	
4 - quattru		40 - quaranta	
5 - cinque		50 - cinquanta	
6 - sei		60 - sessanta	
7 - sette		70 - settanta	
8 - ottu		80 - ottanta	
9 - nove		90 - novanta	
10 - dece		100 - centu	
11 - ondeci		101 - cent'e unu	
12 - dodeci		102 - cent'e dui	
13 - tredeci		Monday - luni	
14 - quattordeci		Tuesday - marti	
15 - quindeci		Wednesday - mercuri	
16 - sedeci		Thursday - ghjovi	
17 - dicessette		Friday - venneri	
18 - diciottu		Saturday - sabatu	
19 - dicennove		Sunday - dumenica	
20 - vinti			

Words of the countryside

bird - acellu		plateau - pianu	
mountain - montane		cliff - scuglialu	
mountain pass - bocca/foce		bridge - ponte	
mountain peak/summit - capu/cima/monte/punta		river - fiume	
		tree - arburu	
forest/wood - furesta/valdu		beach - a marina	
lake - lavu		village - u paese	

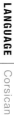

LANGUAGE | Corsican

French pronunciation

One easy rule to remember is that **consonants** at the ends of words are usually silent. *Pas plus tard* (not later) is thus pronounced "pa-plu-tarr". But when the following word begins with a vowel, you run the two together: *pas après* (not after) becomes "pazaprey". **Vowels** are the hardest sounds to get right. Roughly:

a as in hat	I as in machine
e as in get	o as in hot
é between get and gate	o, au as in over
è between get and gut	ou as in food
eu like the u in hurt	u as in a pursed-lip version of use

451

More awkward are the **combinations** *in/im*, *en/em*, *an/am*, *on/om*, *un/um* at the ends of words, or followed by consonants other than *n* or *m*. Again, roughly:

in/im like the an in anxious

an/am, en/em like the don in Doncaster when said with a nasal accent

on/om like the don in Doncaster said by someone with a heavy cold

un/um like the u in understand

Consonants are much as in English, except that: *ch* is always "sh", *c* is "s", *h* is silent, *th* is the same as "t", *ll* is like the *y* in "yes", *w* is "v", and *r* is growled (or rolled).

Learning materials

Rough Guide French Phrasebook (Rough Guides). Mini dictionary-style phrasebook with both English–French and French–English sections, along with cultural tips for tricky situations and a menu reader.

French Experience (BBC Books). Crammed with authentic, modern materials and learning prac-tices, the BBC's latest French self-tutor, accompanied by audiocassettes, CDs and a TV series (on video), makes the competition look dowdy and dated. A particularly upbeat volume

2 includes sections on French from around the Francophone world. Easily the best choice for beginners and intermediate learners.

Collins French Dictionary (Collins). The best two-in-one reference tool for learners, with over 80,000 entries, 120,000 translations and a user-friendly grammar section.

Mini French Dictionary (Harrap/Prentice Hall). French–English and English–French, plus a brief grammar and pronunciation guide.

Basic words and phrases

French nouns are divided into masculine and feminine. This causes difficulties with adjectives, whose endings have to change to suit the gender of the nouns they qualify. If you know some grammar, you will know what to do. If not, stick to the masculine form, which is the simplest – it's what we have done in this glossary.

For specific hiking vocabulary, see p.364.

today - **aujourd'hui**

yesterday - **hier**

tomorrow - **demain**

in the morning - **le matin**

in the afternoon - **l'après-midi**

in the evening - **le soir**

now - **maintenant**

later - **plus tard**

at one o'clock - **à une heure**

at three o'clock - **à trois heures**

at half past ten - **à dix heures et demie**

at midday - **à midi**

man - **un homme**

woman - **une femme**

here - **ici**

there - **là**

this one - **ceci**

that one - **celà**

open - **ouvert**

closed - **fermé**

big - **grand**

small - **petit**

more - **plus**

less - **moins**

a little - **un peu**

a lot - **beaucoup**

cheap - **bon marché**

expensive - **cher**

good - **bon**

bad - **mauvais**

hot - **chaud**

cold - **froid**

with - **avec**

without - **sans**

Numbers

1 – un	21 – vingt-et-un
2 – deux	22 – vingt-deux
3 – trois	30 – trente
4 – quatre	40 – quarante
5 – cinq	50 – cinquante
6 – six	60 – soixante
7 – sept	70 – soixante-dix
8 – huit	75 – soixante-quinze
9 – neuf	80 – quatre-vingts
10 – dix	90 – quatre-vingt-dix
11 – onze	95 – quatre-vingt-quinze
12 – douze	100 – cent
13 – treize	101 – cent-et-un
14 – quatorze	200 – deux cents
15 – quinze	300 – trois cents
16 – seize	500 – cinq cents
17 – dix-sept	1000 – mille
18 – dix-huit	2000 – deux milles
19 – dix-neuf	5000 – cinq milles
20 – vingt	1,000,000 – un million

Days and dates

January – janvier	Tuesday – mardi
February – février	Wednesday – mercredi
March – mars	Thursday – jeudi
April – avril	Friday – vendredi
May – mai	Saturday – samedi
June – juin	August 1 – le premier août
July – juillet	March 2 – le deux mars
August – août	July 14 – le quatorze juillet
September – septembre	November 23 – le vingt-trois novembre
October – octobre	1997 – dix-neuf-cent quatre-vingt-dix-sept
November – novembre	2000 – deux mille
December – décembre	2001 – deux mille un
Sunday – dimanche	2010 – deux mille dix
Monday – lundi	

Talking to people

When addressing people you should always use *Monsieur* for a man, *Madame* for a woman, *Mademoiselle* for a girl. Plain *bonjour* by itself is not enough. This isn't as formal as it seems, and it has its uses when you've forgotten someone's name or want to attract someone's attention.

excuse me – pardon	my name is … – Je m'appelle …
do you speak English? – vous parlez anglais?	I'm English – Je suis anglais(e)
	Irish – irlandais(e)
how do you say it in French? – comment ça se dit en français?	Scottish – écossais(e)
	Welsh – gallois(e)
what's your name? – comment vous appelez-vous?	American – américain(e)
	Australian – australien(ne)

453

Canadian - canadien(ne)
a New Zealander - néo-zélandais(e)
yes - oui
no - non
I understand - je comprends
I don't understand - je ne comprends pas
can you speak slower please? - s'il vous
   plaît, parlez moins vite
OK/agreed - d'accord
please - s'il vous plaît
thank you - merci
hello - bonjour
goodbye - au revoir
good morning/afternoon - bonjour

good evening - bonsoir
good night - bonne nuit
how are you? - comment allez-vous?/ça
   va?
fine, thanks - très bien, merci
I don't know - Je ne sais pas
let's go - allons-y
see you tomorrow - à demain
see you soon - à bientôt
sorry - pardon, Madame/je m'excuse
leave me alone! (aggressive) - fichez-moi la
   paix!
please help me - aidez-moi, s'il vous plaît
help! - au secours!

Finding the way

bus - autobus/bus/car
bus station - gare routière
bus stop - arrêt
car - voiture
train - train
taxi - taxi
ferry - ferry
boat - bâteau
plane - avion
train station - gare (SNCF)
platform - quai
what time does it leave? - il part à quelle
   heure?
hitchhiking - autostop
on foot - à pied
where are you going? - vous allez où?
I'm going to .... - je vais à ....
I want to get off at .... - je voudrais descen-
   dre à ....
the road to .... - la route pour....
near - près/pas loin
far - loin
left - à gauche

right - à droite
what time does it arrive? - il arrive à quelle
   heure?
a ticket to .... - un billet pour....
single ticket - aller simple
return ticket - aller retour
validate your ticket - compostez votre billet
valid for - valable pour
ticket office - vente de billets
how many kilometres? - combien de kilo-
   mètres?
how many hours? - combien d'heures?
straight on - tout droit
on the other side of - à l'autre côté de
on the corner of - à l'angle de
next to - à côté de
behind - derrière
in front of - devant
before - avant
after - après
under - sous
to cross - traverser
bridge - pont

Questions and requests

The simplest way of asking a question is to start with *s'il vous plaît* (please), then name the thing you want in an interrogative tone of voice. Similarly with requests. For example:

where is there a bakery? - s'il vous plaît, la
   boulangerie?
which way is it to the Genoan watchtower? - s'il
   vous plaît, la route pour la tour génoise?
we'd like a room for two - s'il vous plaît, une
   chambre pour deux?

can I have a kilo of oranges? - s'il vous plaît,
   un kilo d'oranges?
where? - où?
how? - comment?
how many/how much? - combien?
when? - quand?

why? – pourquoi?
at what time? – à quelle heure?

what is/which is? – quel est?

Accommodation

room for one/two people – chambre pour une/deux personne(s)
double bed – lit double
room with a shower – chambre avec douche
room with a bath – chambre avec salle de bains
for one/two/three nights – pour une/deux/trois nuit(s)
can I see it? – je peux la voir?
room on the courtyard – chambre sur la cour
room over the street – chambre sur la rue
first floor – premier étage
second floor – deuxième étage
with a view – avec vue
key – clef
to iron – repasser
do laundry – faire la lessive

sheets – draps
blankets – couvertures
quiet – calme
noisy – bruyant
hot water – eau chaude
cold water – eau froide
is breakfast included? – est-ce que le petit déjeuner est compris?
I would like breakfast – je voudrais prendre le petit déjeuner
I don't want breakfast – je ne veux pas de petit déjeuner
can we camp here? – on peut camper ici?
campsite – camping/terrain de camping
tent – tente
tent space – emplacement
youth hostel – auberge de jeunesse

Driving

service station – garage
service – service
to park the car – garer la voiture
car park – un parking
no parking – défense de stationner/station-nement interdit
petrol station – poste d'essence
fuel – essence
(to) fill it up – faire le plein
oil – huile
air line – ligne à air

to put air in the tyres – gonfler les pneus
battery – batterie
the battery is dead – la batterie est morte
plugs – bougies
to break down – tomber en panne
gas can – bidon
insurance – assurance
green card – carte verte
traffic lights – feux
red light – feu rouge
green light – feu vert

Cycling

to adjust – ajuster
axle – l'axe
ball bearing – le roulement à billes
battery – la pile
bent – tordu
bicycle – le vélo
bottom bracket – le logement du pédalier
brake cable – le cable
brakes – les freins
broken – cassé
bulb – l'ampoule
chain – la chaîne
frame – le cadre

gears – les vitesses
grease – la graisse
handlebars – le guidon
inner tube – la chambre à l'air
loose – dévissé
to lower – baisser
mudguard – le garde-boue
pannier – le panier
pedal – la pédale
pump – la pompe
rack – la porte-bagages
to raise – relever
to repair – réparer
saddle – la selle

455

spanner – la clef
to straighten – redresser

stuck – coincé
tight – serré

doctor – médecin
I don't feel well – je ne me sens pas bien
medicines – médicaments
prescription – ordonnance
I feel sick – je suis malade
I have a headache – j'ai mal à la tête

stomach ache – mal à l'estomac
period – règles
pain – douleur
it hurts – ça fait mal
chemist – pharmacie
hospital – hôpital

Other needs

bakery – boulangerie
food shop – alimentation
supermarket – supermarché
to eat – manger
to drink – boire
camping gas – camping gaz
tobacconist – tabac
stamps – timbres

bank – banque
money – argent
toilets – toilettes
police – police
telephone – téléphone
cinema – cinéma
theatre – théâtre
to reserve/book – réserver

A food glossary

Basic terms

Always call the waiter or waitress Monsieur or Madame (Madamoiselle if a young woman), never Garçon, no matter what you were taught in school.

pain – bread
beurre – butter
oeufs – eggs
lait – milk
huile – oil
poivre – pepper
sel – salt
sucre – sugar
vinaigre – vinegar
bouteille – bottle
verre – glass
fourchette – fork
couteau – knife

cuillère – spoon
table – table
la carte – menu
l'addition – the bill
chauffé – heated
cuit – cooked
cru – raw
fumé – smoked
salé – salted/spicy
sucré – sweet
emballé – wrapped
à emporter - takeaway

Snacks

un sandwich/une baguette – a sandwich
jambon – with ham
fromage – with cheese
saucisson – with sausage
à l'ail – with garlic
au poivre – with pepper

pâté (de campagne) – with pâté (country-style)
croque-monsieur – grilled cheese and ham sandwich
croque-madame – grilled cheese and bacon, sausage, chicken or an egg

oeufs - eggs
   au plat - fried
   à la coque - boiled
   durs - hard-boiled
   brouillés - scrambled
omelette - omelette
   nature - plain
   aux fines herbes - with herbs
   au fromage - with cheese
salade de - salad of
   tomates - tomatoes
   betteraves - beets

concombres - cucumber
carottes râpées - grated carrots
épis de maïs - corn on the cob
crêpe - pancake
   au sucre - with sugar
   au citron - with lemon
   au miel - with honey
   à la confiture - with jam
   aux œufs - with eggs
   à la crème de marrons - with chestnut
      purée

Soups (soupes) and starters (hors d'oeuvres)

bisque - shellfish soup
bouillabaisse - Marseillais fish soup
bouillon - broth or stock
bourride - thick fish soup
consommé - clear soup
pistou - parmesan, basil and garlic paste
   added to soup
potage - thick vegetable soup

rouille - red pepper, garlic and saffron mayonnaise served with fish soup
velouté - thick soup, usually fish or poultry
assiette anglaise - plate of cold meats
crudités - raw vegetables with dressings
hors d'œuvres variés - combination of the
   above, plus smoked or marinated fish

Fish (poisson), seafood (fruits de mer) and shellfish (crustaces or coquillages)

anchois - anchovies
anguilles - eels
barbue - brill
bigourneau - periwinkle
brème - bream
cabillaud - cod
calmar - squid
carrelet - plaice
claire - type of oyster
colin - hake
congre - conger eel
coques - cockles
coquilles St-Jacques - scallops
crabe - crab
crevettes grises - shrimp
crevettes roses - prawns
daurade - sea bream
éperlan - smelt or whitebait
escargots - snails
flétan - halibut
friture - assorted fried fish
gambas - king prawns
hareng - herring
homard - lobster

huîtres - oysters
langouste - spiny lobster
langoustines - saltwater crayfish (scampi)
limande - lemon sole
lotte - burbot
lotte de mer - monkfish
loup de mer - sea bass
louvine, loubine - similar to sea bass
maquereau - mackerel
merlan - whiting
moules (marinière) - mussels (with shallots
   in white wine sauce)
oursin - sea urchin
palourdes - clams
praires - small clams
raie - skate
rouget - red mullet
saumon - salmon
sole - sole
thon - tuna
truite - trout
turbot - turbot

Fish cooking terms

aïoli – garlic mayonnaise served with salt cod and other fish
béarnaise – sauce of egg yolks, white wine, shallots and vinegar
beignets – fritters
darne – fillet or steak
la douzaine – a dozen
frit – fried
friture – deep-fried small fish
fumé – smoked
fumet – fish stock
gigot de mer – large fish baked whole
grillé – grilled
hollandaise – butter and vinegar sauce
à la meunière – in a butter, lemon and parsley sauce
mousse, mousseline – mousse
quenelles – light dumplings

Meat (viande) and poultry (volaille)

agneau (de présalé) – lamb (grazed on salt marshes)
andouille, andouillette – tripe sausage
bœuf – beef
bifteck – steak
boudin blanc – sausage of white meats
boudin noir – black pudding
caille – quail
canard – duck
caneton – duckling
contrefilet – sirloin roast
coquelet – cockerel
dinde, dindon – turkey
entrecôte – ribsteak
faux filet – sirloin steak
foie – liver
foie gras – fattened (duck/goose) liver
gigot (d'agneau) – leg (of lamb)
grillade – grilled meat
hâchis – chopped meat or mince hamburger
langue – tongue
lapin, lapereau – rabbit, young rabbit
lard, lardons – bacon, diced bacon
lièvre – hare
merguez – spicy, red sausage
mouton – mutton
museau de veau – calf's muzzle
oie – goose
os – bone
porc – pork
poulet – chicken
poussin – baby chicken
ris – sweetbreads
rognons – kidneys
rognons blancs – testicles
sanglier – wild boar
steak – steak
tête de veau – calf's head (in jelly)
tournedos – thick slices of fillet
tripes – tripe
veau – veal
venaison – venison

Meat and poultry dishes

bœuf bourguignon – beef stew with Burgundy, onions and mushrooms
canard à l'orange – roast duck with an orange-and-wine sauce
cassoulet – casserole of beans and meat
coq au vin – chicken cooked until it falls off the bone with wine, onions and mushrooms
steak au poivre (vert/rouge) – steak in a black (green/red) peppercorn sauce
steak tartare – raw chopped beef, topped with a raw egg yolk

Meat cooking terms

blanquette, daube, estouffade, hocheôt, navarin, ragoût – all are types of stew
aile – wing
carré – best end of neck, chop or cutlet
civit – game stew
confit – meat preserve
côte – chop, cutlet or rib
cou – neck
cuisse – thigh or leg
épaule – shoulder

médaillon – round piece
pavé – thick slice
en croûte – in pastry
farci – stuffed
au feu de bois – cooked over wood
au four – fire-baked
garni – with vegetables
gésier – gizzard

grillé – grilled
magret de canard – duck breast
marmite – casserole
mijoté – stewed
museau – muzzle
rôti – roast
sauté – lightly cooked in butter

For steaks:

bleu – almost raw
saignant – rare
à point – medium
bien cuit – well done
très bien cuit – very well cooked
brochette – kebab
beurre blanc – sauce of white wine and
  shallots, with butter
chasseur – white wine, mushrooms and
  shallots

diable – strong mustard seasoning
forestière – with bacon and mushroom
fricassée – rich, creamy sauce
mornay – cheese sauce
pays d'Auge – cream and cider
piquante – gherkins or capers, vinegar and
  shallots
provençale – tomatoes, garlic, olive oil and
  herbs

Fruit (fruit) and nuts (noix)

L

abricot – apricot
amandes – almonds
ananas – pineapple
banane – banana
brugnon, nectarine – nectarine
cacahouète – peanut
cassis – blackcurrants
cérises – cherries
citron – lemon
citron vert – lime
figues – figs
fraises (de bois) – strawberries (wild)
framboises – raspberries
fruit de la passion – passion fruit
groseilles – redcurrants and gooseberries

mangue – mango
marrons – chestnuts
melon – melon
myrtilles – bilberries
noisette – hazelnut
noix – nuts
orange – orange
pamplemousse – grapefruit
pêche (blanche) – (white) peach
pistache – pistachio
poire – pear
pomme – apple
prune – plum
pruneau – prune
raisins – grapes

Terms:

beignets – fritters
compôte de... – stewed...
coulis – sauce

flambé – set aflame in alcohol
frappé – iced

Vegetables (légumes), herbs (herbes) and spices (épices)

ail – garlic
algue – seaweed
anis – aniseed
artichaut – artichoke
asperges – asparagus
avocat – avocado

basilic – basil
betterave – beetroot
carotte – carrot
céleri – celery
champignons, cèpes, chanterelles – mushrooms of various kinds

chou (rouge) – (red) cabbage
choufleur – cauliflower
ciboulettes – chives
concombre – cucumber
cornichon – gherkin
échalotes – shallots
endive – chicory
épinards – spinach
estragon – tarragon
fenouil – fennel
flageolet – white beans
gingembre – ginger
haricots – beans
 verts – string (French)
 rouges – kidney
 beurres – butter
laurier – bay leaf
lentilles – lentils
maïs – corn
menthe – mint
moutarde – mustard

oignon – onion
pâte – pasta, pastry
persil – parsley
petits pois – peas
pignons – pine nuts
piment – pimento
pois chiche – chick peas
pois mange-tout – snow peas
poireau – leek
poivron (vert, rouge) – sweet pepper (green, red)
pommes (de terre) – potatoes
primeurs – spring vegetables
radis – radishes
riz – rice
safran – saffron
salade verte – green salad
sarrasin – buckwheat
tomate – tomato
truffes – truffles

Terms:

beignet – fritter
farci – stuffed
gratiné – browned with cheese or butter
jardinière – with mixed diced vegetables
à la parisienne – sautéed in butter (potatoes);
 with white wine sauce and shallots

parmentier – with potatoes
sauté – lightly fried in butter
à la vapeur – steamed
**Je suis végétarien(ne). Il y a quelques
 plats sans viande?** – I'm a vegetarian. Are
 there any non-meat dishes?

Desserts (desserts or entremets) and pastries (pâtisserie)

bombe – moulded ice-cream dessert
brioche – sweet, high-yeast breakfast roll
charlotte – custard and fruit in lining of
 almond fingers
crème Chantilly – vanilla-flavoured and
 sweetened whipped cream
crème fraîche – sour cream
crème pâtissière – thick, eggy pastry-filling
crêpes suzettes – thin pancakes with orange
 juice and liqueur
fromage blanc – cream cheese
glace – ice cream
ile flottante/œufs à la neige – soft
 meringues floating on custard

macarons – macaroons
madeleine – small sponge cake
marrons Mont Blanc – chestnut purée and
 cream on a rum-sponge cake
mousse au chocolat – chocolate mousse
palmiers – caramelized puff pastries
parfait – frozen mousse, sometimes ice cream
petit Suisse – smooth mixture of cream and
 curds
petits fours – bite-sized cakes/pastries
poires belle Hélène – pears and ice cream in
 chocolate sauce
yaourt, yogourt – yoghurt

Terms:

barquette – small boat-shaped flan
bavarois – refers to the mould; could be a
 mousse or custard
coupe – serving of ice cream

crêpes – pancakes
galettes – buckwheat pancakes
Gênoise – rich sponge cake
sablé – shortbread biscuit

savarin – filled, ring-shaped cake
tarte – tart

tartelette sarrasin – small tart

Corsican starters and charcuterie

cannelloni al brocciu – pasta stuffed with brocciu and mint with tomato sauce
omelette al brocciu – omelette filled with *brocciu*
suppa di pesce/soupe de poisson – fish soup served with toast and garlic

suppa Corsa/soupe Corse – vegetable soup with beans
coppa – smoked pork shoulder
figatellu – pork liver sausage
lonzu – smoked pork fillet
prisuttu – cured ham

Corsican main dishes

aziminu – rich, heavily spiced, garlicky fish stew
bianchetti – little fish fried in batter
cabrettu a l'istrettu – strongly spiced kid stew
formaghju di porcu – pork brawn seasoned with onion, garlic, pepper and maquis herbs
fritelle di gaju frescu – fritters made with chestnut flour and brocciu
lasagne di cignale – wild boar lasagne
pivarunata – peppery beef and potato stew with pimentos

stifatu – a roll of stuffed meats – goat, lamb and sometimes blackbird – served with grated cheese
tianu d'agnellu – lamb stew
tianu di cingale/ sanglier en daube – wild boar stew with potatoes
tianu di fave – pork and bean stew
tianu di pisi – onion, carrot, pea and tomato stew
tripette – tripe in tomato sauce

Corsican cheese and puddings

brocciu – soft white cheese made with curds
canistrelli – soft shortbread-type biscuits made with white wine and honey
fiadone – tart filled with brocciu

fritelli/ beignets – small doughnuts, sometimes made with chestnut flour
fromage Corse – uniquely flavoured indigenous hard cheese

Index

and small print

Index

Map entries are in colour

A

A Cupulatta 210
A Filetta 127, 333
Abbartello 231
accommodation 34–37
Aiguilles de Bavella 257
airlines
  in Australia & New Zealand 18
  in UK & Ireland 14
  in USA & Canada 16
AJACCIO 193–209
  accommodation 198
  airport 195, 208
  banks 207
  bars and cafés 206
  Bibliothèque Municipale ... 204
  bus services 209
  bus station 195
  campsites 198
  car rental 207
  casino 206
  Cathedral 202
  Chapelle Impériale 204
  cinemas 207
  Citadelle 202
  discos 206
  ferry dock 195
  ferry services 208
  history 194
  hospital 208
  Hôtel de Ville 120
  hotels 198
  Internet access 208
  Maison Bonaparte 202
  market 203
  motorbike rental 208
  Musée A Bandera 199
  Musée Capitellu 202
  Musée Fesch 204
  Place de Gaulle 199
  Place Foch 200
  police 208
  post office 208
  restaurants 204–207
  St-Érasme 202
  Salon Napoléonien 200
  taxis 208
  tourist office 197
  train services 209
  train station 195
Ajaccio region 194
Ajaccio 196
Alando 306
Albertacce 335
Aléria 299–304
Aléria 303
Aléria siege 301, 422

Algajola 131
Alo Bisuje 265
Alta Rocca 242–257
Altiani 305
Ambiegna 190
amianthus 95
Anse d'Eccica 241
Anse de Portigliolo 215
Antisanti 305
Aregno 143
Asco 327
ATMs 28
Aullène 250
Authentica 40
Avapessa 146

B

Baie de San Ciprianu 288
Baie de Stagnolu 288
Baie de Tamarone 88
The Balagne 113–156
The Balagne 114
bandits 268, 246, 263
banks 29
Barcaggio 90
Barghiana 155
bars 40
Bastelica 218
Bastelicaccia 217
BASTIA 61–75
  accommodation 66
  airport 66, 75
  arrival 66
  banks 74
  bars and cafés 72
  beaches 71
  bike rental 74
  buses 66, 75
  campsites 67
  car rental 74
  cinemas 73
  Église St-Jean-Baptiste 69
  ferry dock 66
  ferry services 75
  festivals 73
  history 63
  hospital 74
  hotels 66
  Internet access 74
  L'Arinella 71
  Maison Mattei 68
  market 69
  Musée d'Éthnographie 70
  nightclubs 73
  Nouveau Port 66

  Oratoire de l'Immaculée
    Conception 68
  Palais des Gouverneurs 70
  Place St-Nicolas 68
  post office 74
  restaurants 71–73
  taxis 74
  Terra Nova (Citadelle) 70
  Terra Vecchia 68
  theatre 73
  tourist office 66
  train station 66
  train services 75
  Vieux Port 69
Bastia and northern
  Corsica 62
Bastia 65
Bavella 256
Belgodère 148
Bettolacce 90
bicycles 32
birds 434
Bocognano 352
Bonaparte, Napoléon
  .... 87, 146, 193, 194, 195,
  200, 201, 202, 204, 209,
  210, 214, 313, 413–414
Bonifacio 270–276
Bonifacio 272–273
Around Bonifacio 277
books on Corsica .. 439–445
Boswell, James 91, 92,
  94, 227, 234, 235, 281,
  316, 343, 347, 412, 439
The Bozio 305
buses from Britain 21
buses, in Corsica 33
Bussaglia 166
Bustanico 307

C

Cala d'Arana 241
Cala di l'Avena 266
Cala di Conca 241
Cala d'Orzu 215, 428
Cala di Tivella 241
Cala Francese 89
Cala Genovese 89
Cala Longa 241
Cala Piscona 231
Cala Rossa 288
Calacuccia 333
The Calanches 163, 171

Calasima 336
Calcatoggio...................188
Calenzana 138, 370
Calvi......................117–127
Calvi 119
Calzola 235
Camera 91
Campana 314
camping 36
Campo dell'Oro
  airport 195, 208
Campomoro...................240
Canari 94
Canelle 91
Cani................................291
Canta U Populu
  Corsu 263
canyoning 49
Cap Corse 78–96
Cap Corse.......................79
Capicciolo 231
Capo di Muro................215
Capo d'Orto...................173
Capo Pertusato..............278
Capo Rosso 174
Capu Tondu 152
car rental 30
Carabelli, Colomba 236
Carbini 249
Carcheto 312
Cargèse.................180–183
Carrington, Dorothy 126,
  189, 207, 232, 236, 247,
  249, 258, 290, 317, 439,
  440–441, 442
Carta-Lavonu 286
Casa di u Lurcu 102
Le Casabianca.....109, 174,
  183, 184, 197, 416
Casaglione 190
Casamaccioli 337
Cascade de
  Sant'Alberto 220
Cascade du Voile de la
  Marée 352
Cascades des
  Anglais 351
Cascades de
  Radule................336, 337
The Casinca 244, 317
Casinca and
  Castagniccia 308
Cassano.........................142
Casta..............................108
Castagniccia........307–317
Casteddu d'Araggiu......289
Castellare di-Casinca....317
Castello 84
Castello di a Rocca 236

Castello di San
  Colombano 90
Cateri 142
Cauria 265
Cauro 220
Ceccia 290
Centuri-Port 91
Cervione.......................310
chambres d'hôtes...........35
Chapelle de Notre-Dame-
  de-la-Serra 127
Chapelle Sant'Eliseo.....348
Chapelle St-Jean-Baptiste,
  Ste-Lucie....................247
Chera 291
chestnuts 312
Chez Tao's 125, 126
children, travelling with ...54
Cima a e Folicce.............94
The Cinarca 188–190
Cinarca, Guidice della ..189
Cirque de Bonifato........151
climate................................x
climbing 48
Col d'Arcarotta..............311
Col de l'Arinella.............334
Col de Bavella...............395
Col de la Croix 168
Col de Larone 257
Col de Mercuju 217
Col de la Palmarella.....168
Col de Prato.................315
Col de San Stefano 105
Col de Serra....................91
Col de Sevi 186
Col de St-Eustache 251
Col de Teghime.............104
Col de la Vaccia 251
Col de Verde .354, 388–390
Col de Verghio 179
Columbus,
  Christopher 118, 124
Conca 288, 370, 398
consulates in Marseille ...52
Corbara.........................145
Central Corsica 324
Eastern Corsica.............296
Corsican
  language.............449–451
Corsican
  nuthatch 328, 434
Corso,
  Sampiero ..218, 219, 220,
  408
Corte......................338–344
Corte 339
costs 27
Côti-Chiavari.................216
Couvent de Corbara 144

Couvent d'Orezza 316
Couvent St-François-di-
  Niolu...........................333
Couvent de San
  Damiano.....................263
Couvent de Santa
  Catalina 85
Cozzano................355, 392
credit cards.....................28
crime 51
currency 27
cycling............................32

D

debit cards......................28
Défilé de
  l'Inzecca............299, 353
Défilé de Lancône.........105
**Désert des
  Agriates** 107–110
Désert des Agriates coast
  path...............108, 137, 363
Disabled travellers 52
diving 50
Dolmen de
  Fontanaccia 264, 265
Dolmen de Monte
  Recincu 102
drinks 40
driving 30

E

E'Capannelle..353, 387–390
Eaux d'Orezza...............313
Église de la Trinité et San
  Giovanni, Aregno 143
Église St-Jean-Baptiste, La
  Porta 315
electricity.........................55
Elliot, Sir Gilbert.....64, 316,
  414, 439
email 43
emergency phone
  numbers.......................52
employment....................56
Erbajolo.........................306
Erbalunga........................83
Érignac,
  Claude 195, 415, 428
Ermitage de la Trinité 277
Étang de Biguglia 77
Étang de Diane 303
Évisa 176
exchange rates 27

F

Favalello 306
Felce 311
Feliceto 147
ferme-auberges 35
ferries
  from France...................20–21
  from Italy 20–21
  from UK & Ireland 19
  to France ..134, 208, 240, 285
  to Italy 285
  to Sardinia........................276
festivals 45–47
Figari 269
Figari airport 271, 285
Filitosa..........232–234, 408
Filitosa............................233
Filosorma 150–155
Fiumorbo......................298
flights
  booking online 11
  from Australia &
    New Zealand 17
  from UK & Ireland 12
  from USA & Canada 15
FLNC (Fronte di
  Liberazione Nazionale di
  a Corsica)...415, 421–431
flowers 433
Fontaine de Salario.......210
food...........37–40, 456–461
Foreign Legion......118, 122
Fôret d'Aïtone 178
Forêt de la Restonica ...346
Forêt de Valdo-Niolo....336
Fozzano 243
Franceschini, Davia 145
French embassies and
  consulates....................22
French words and
  phrases 450–456

G

Gaffori, Gian'Pietru
  ....338, 341, 412
Galéria...........................151
gay & lesbian issues 54
Genoan towers 103
Ghisonaccia 297
Ghisoni.................352, 387
Girolata
  ...152, 163, 168–170, 184
gites d'étape...........36, 365
Giunssani 148–150
Golfe d'Ajaccio 211–217
Golfe de Porto 161–175

Golfe de Sagone..180–185
Golfe de Santa Manza ..279
Golfe de Valinco ..227–242
Golfe de Valinco............228
Gorges du
  Prunelli 217–220
GR20 ....36, 49, 140, 149,
  152, 179, 288, 323, 328,
  329, 350, 351, 353, 354,
  356, 361, 369–398
GR20 stages 13–16 391
GR20 stages 1–7 372
GR20 stages 7–13 380
Granite Island
  ....126, 189, 232, 236
Granitola 337
Guagno-les-Bains.........186

H

Haut Taravo...................355
Haut'Asco 328, 375
Haute-Balagne
  coast 129–138
Haute-Balagne coast....130
health 26
hiking...............48, 364–369
history of Corsica..407–419
horse riding.....................49
hotels 35
house rental 36

I

Îles Lavezzi 276, 278
Îles Sanguinaires...........212
insurance 25
Internet access 44

L

L'Île Rousse 132–136
L'Île Rousse 133
L'Incinosa.....................186
La Canonica...................78
La Foce 350
La Marana.......................76
La Porta 315
Lac de Capitello............347
Lac de Creno 187
Lac de Melo 347
Lac de Nino 336
Lac d'Oriente 346
Lama 137
language 447–461

hiking..........................364
Lavasina..........................81
Lear, Edward..193, 225, 325,
  414, 441
Les Millelli 209
Levie 247
Long distance walks 362
Loreto-di-Casinca 318
Lumio 129
Luri 93

M

Macinaggio 87
Mafia 431
mail services 42
mammals 436
Manso 155
maps 23, 364
maquis ....viii, 435
Mare a Mare Centre.....186,
  187, 188, 298, 355, 392,
  402–403
Mare a Mare Nord........176,
  180, 305, 306, 307, 333,
  334, 335, 345, 384,
  400–401
Mare a Mare Sud 243,
  247, 249, 251, 253, 254,
  286, 403–404
Mariana 76, 409
Marignana 177
Marine de Sisco.............85
Martello towers 103
Massif de l'Ospédale 285
Matignon Accords..418, 429
Mausoleo 150
mazzeri.........................290
Mérimée, Prosper 225,
  236, 242, 243, 244, 245,
  249, 257, 414, 444
Mezzo Mare 212
micheline 34, 66, 75
Miomo............................67
mobile phones 43
Moltifao 326
money 27
Monte Cinto ..329, 334, 375
Monte Corona...............373
Monte Incudine......356, 393
Monte d'Oro 351, 386
Monte Piano Maggiore .306
Monte Renoso 353, 389
Monte Rotondo...346, 382
Monte San Petrone.......314
Monte Sant'Eliseo.........187
Monte Stello 81, 84

Montemaggiore.............142
Monticello 146
Moor's head..........315, 446
Moriani Plage................309
Morosaglia 315
Morsiglia 92
motorcycles 32
Moulin Mattei..................91
mountain biking 49
Murato 106
Muro.............................146
Musée d'Archéologie
    Jérôme Carcopino 302

N

Nebbio 96–110
Nebbio 97
Nelson,
    Horatio 64, 102, 120
newspapers 44
Niolo 330–338
Nonza.............................95
The Northwest...............160

O

Oletta 105
Olivo...............................90
Olmeto 236
Olmeto-Plage................231
Olmi-Capella 150
online resources..............23
opening hours.................45
Orto...............................188
Ospédale.......................285
Ota 175

P

package holidays......13, 16
Paglia Orba...179, 337, 377
Palaggiu 265
Palge de Tenutella 231
Paoli, Pascal...64, 87, 120,
    132, 135, 146, 186, 195,
    227, 234, 235, 244, 306,
    308, 309, 313, 315, 316,
    317, 338, 412, 413, 420,
    446
Partinello 18
Patrimonio....................104
Penta-di-Casinca..........318
Petreto-Bicchisano 250
photographic film..........56

Piana 172
Pianotolli-Caldarello......269
Pianu di Levie 248
Piazza.............................93
Piazzole........................313
Piedicorte-di-Gaggio 305
Piedicroce 312
Pietracorbara 85
Pietrapola.....................298
Pieve (Cap Corse)..........94
Piève (Nebbio)...............106
Pigna............................143
Pino...............................93
Pioggiola 149
pirates 103
Plage d'Agosta 214
Plage de l'Arinella 279
Plage d'Arone 174
Plage d'Asciaghju 287
Plage de Balistra...........280
Plage de Baracci 232
Plage de Calalonga 279
Plage de Campitellu 232
Plage de Caneti 279
Plage de Capu
    Laurosu 239
Plage de Caspio 168
Plage de la Catena 279
Plage de Chevano 269
Plage de Chiuni 183
Plage de Cupabia 229
Plage d'Erbaju 268
Plage de Gratelle 168
Plage de Guignu 110
Plage des Îles.................89
Plage du Liamone.........188
Plage de Loto 101, 109
Plage de Lozari 137
Plage de Maora 279
Plage de Menasina 183
Plage de Padulone 303
Plage de
    Palombaggia..............286
Plage de Pero 183
Plage du Phare 239
Plage de Pianterella......279
Plage de Piranellu.........288
Plage de Portigliolo.......239
Plage de Puraja 239
Plage de Roccapina 268
Plage de Ruppione........215
Plage de Saleccia 109
Plage de Santa
    Manza 279
Plage de Sperone 279
Plage de Stagnone 185
Plage de Taravo 231
Plage de Tralicetu 264

Plage de Verghia...........215
Plage de la Viva 213
Plateau de Coscione
    ....253, 356
Poli, Théodore 179, 246
police 51
polyphonic singing...x, 127,
    144, 206, 263, 330–331
Ponte Leccia.................326
population..........................vi
Poretta airport.....66, 75, 76
Port de Chiavari............215
Porticcio........................213
Porticciolo 86
Porto....................161–166
Porto 162
Porto-Pollo....................227
Porto-Vecchio......281–285
Porto-Vecchio 281
Around Porto-Vecchio...287
postal services................42
Pozzo 84
Propriano 237–240
Propriano......................238
Prunelli-di-Fiumorbo 299
Pruno-Casette 314
public holidays................45
Punta di Pozzo di
    Borgo 210
Punta Muvrella..............329

Q

Quenza.................252, 395

R

Rade de Santa Maria......89
radio...............................44
rainfall...............................x
Rapale...........................106
refuges 36, 365
Renno 186
Réserve Naturelle de
    Scandola....163, 170, 184
restaurants 38
Revinda.........................183
Ribombu incident 424
Roccapina.....................268
Rogliano..........................89
Rondinara 280
Rossi, Tino 211
route de Bavella.............255
route de la Corniche 81
route des
    Sanguinaires.......211–213

Sagone...........................184
Saint-Exupéry,
    Antoine de....................76
Ste-Lucie-de-Tallano 245
San Cesariu 142
San Michele de Murato..105
San-Giovanni-di-Moriani
   309
San-Martino-di-Lota 81
San-Nicolao 309
San-Tommaso-di-
    Pastoreccia 317
Sant'Antonino 142
Santa Giulia 286
Santa Julia 96
Santa-Lucia-di-Mercurio
   307
Santa Maria Assunta 101
Santa Maria Sicché 220
Santa-Maria-di-Valle-di-
    Rostino.......................317
Santa di u Niolu 337
Santo-Pietro-di-Tenda ..106
Santo-Pietro-di-Venaco 348
Santa Reparata di
    Balagna......................146
Santa-Reparata-di-Moriani
   309
Santa Restituta, church of
   141
Santa Severa 86
Santoni, François
    ....267, 425, 429–430
Sari d'Orcino.................189
The Sartenais 257–269
Sartenais coast path
    ....241, 266, 363
Sartène.................258–264
Sartène 261
Scamaroni, Fred 230
Seneca 93
Sentier de Guy le Facteur
   169
Sentier du Douanier
    ....88, 91, 101, 363
Sentier des Douaniers ..230
Sermano 307
Serra-di-Fiumorbo 298
Serra di Scapomena.....251
Sisco 85
Site Naturel de
    Capandula....................88
snakes...........................438
Soccia 187
Solenzara.......................297

Sollacaro 234
Sorbollano.....................251
The South......................226
Speloncato.....................147
Spelunca gorge.............175
St-Florent......................97
St-Florent 98
Stazzona 313
Ste-Catherine airport 118
Stopione 86

Tappa 291
telephone codes 43
telephones 42
television 44
temperatures x
time differences 56
Tiuccia 184
Tizzano..................241, 266
Tolla.......................192, 217
Tollare.............................90
Tomino 86
Torre 289
tortoise sanctuary 210
Tour de Capannelle.......229
Tour de Capitello...........214
Tour di Capo di Muro....216
Tour Franceschi 90
Tour d l'Isolella...............214
Tour de Mortella....101, 102
Tour de l'Omigna 183
Tour d'Orchinu 183
Tour de l'Osse.................86
Tour de Santa Maria 89
Tour de Sénèque 93
Tour de Senetosa..........241
tour operators
    in Australia & New Zealand 19
    in UK 15
    in USA & Canada................17
tourist offices, French
    government..................23
Tra Mare e Monti...167, 170,
    176, 361
Tra Mare e Monti Nord..140,
    152, 153, 154, 155,
    399–400
Tra Mare e Monti Sud
    ....229, 231, 403
trains
    from the UK...................18–19
    in Corsica..........................34
Tralonca 307, 425
transport 30
traveller's cheques..........28

U Catenacciu 260

Val d'Ese 218
Valle d'Orezza 313
Vallée de l'Asco.....325–329
Vallée du Fango 154
Vallée da la Restonica ..345
Vallée du Tavignano
    ....304–307, 345
Vallica...........................150
The Venachese......347–350
Venaco 348
vendetta.......225, 236, 243,
    244–245, 258, 262, 410,
    420
Venzolasca....................318
Vescovato 318
Via Ferrata....................327
Vico 185
Vignale 90
visas...............................22
Vivario 349
Vizzavona
    ....350, 385, 386, 387
von Neuhof,
    Théodore....244, 310, 411

watchtowers 103
wildlife 432–438
wine 41
    Clos d'Alzeto 189
    Clos Nicrosi 87
    Domaine d'Alzipratu 141
    Domaine Fiumicicoli 264
    Domaine Pietri 93
    Domaine Renucci 147
    Domaine de Toraccia........288
    Sartène 258
wiring money 29
working in Corsica..........56
World War I 414
World War II 416–417

Zerubia..........................251
Zicavo 355, 393
Zilia 141
Zonza 254

Twenty years of Rough Guides

In the summer of 1981, Mark Ellingham, Rough Guides' founder, knocked out the first guide on a typewriter, with a group of friends. Mark had been travelling in Greece after university, and couldn't find a guidebook that really answered his needs.There were heavyweight cultural guides on the one hand – good on museums and classical sites but not on beaches and tavernas – and on the other hand student manuals that were so caught up with how to save money that they lost sight of the country's significance beyond its role as a place for a cool vacation. None of the guides began to address Greece as a country, with its natural and human environment, its politics and its contemporary life.

Having no urgent reason to return home, Mark decided to write his own guide. It was a guide to Greece that tried to combine some erudition and insight with a thoroughly practical approach to travellers' needs. Scrupulously researched listings of places to stay, eat and drink were matched by careful attention to detail on everything from Homer to Greek music, from classical sites to national parks and from nude beaches to monasteries. Back in London, Mark and his friends got their Rough Guide accepted by a farsighted commissioning editor at the publisher Routledge and it came out in 1982.

The Rough Guide to Greece was a student scheme that became a publishing phenomenon. The immediate success of the book – shortlisted for the Thomas Cook award – spawned a series that rapidly covered dozens of countries. The Rough Guides found a ready market among backpackers and budget travellers, but soon acquired a much broader readership that included older and less impecunious visitors. Readers relished the guides' wit and inquisitiveness as much as the enthusiastic, critical approach that acknowledges everyone wants value for money – but not at any price.

Rough Guides soon began supplementing the "rougher" information – the hostel and low-budget listings – with the kind of detail that independent-minded travellers on any budget might expect. These days, the guides – distributed worldwide by the Penguin Group – include recommendations spanning the range from shoestring to luxury, and cover more than 200 destinations around the globe. Our growing team of authors, many of whom come to Rough Guides initially as outstandingly good letter-writers telling us about their travels, are spread all over the world, particularly in Europe, the USA and Australia. As well as the travel guides, Rough Guides publishes a series of dictionary phrasebooks covering two dozen major languages, an acclaimed series of music guides running the gamut from Classical to World Music, a series of music CDs in association with World Music Network, and a range of reference books on topics as diverse as the Internet, pregnancy and unexplained phenomena. Visit **www.roughguides.com** to see what's cooking.

Rough Guide credits

Text editor: Jo Mead
Series editor: Mark Ellingham
Editorial: Martin Dunford, Jonathan Buckley, Kate Berens, Ann-Marie Shaw, Helena Smith, Olivia Swift, Ruth Blackmore, Geoff Howard, Claire Saunders, Gavin Thomas, Alexander Mark Rogers, Polly Thomas, Joe Staines, Richard Lim, Duncan Clark, Peter Buckley, Lucy Ratcliffe, Clifton Wilkinson, Alison Murchie, Matthew Teller, Andrew Dickson, Fran Sandham, Sally Schafer (UK); Andrew Rosenberg, Yuki Takagaki, Richard Koss, Hunter Slaton (US)
Production: Susanne Hillen, Andy Hilliard, Link Hall, Helen Prior, Julia Bovis, Michelle Draycott, Katie Pringle, Zoë Nobes, Rachel Holmes, Andy Turner, Dan May

Cartography: Maxine Repath, Melissa Baker, Ed Wright, Katie Lloyd-Jones
Cover art direction: Louise Boulton
Picture research: Sharon Martins, Mark Thomas
Online: Kelly Martinez, Anja Mutic-Blessing, Jennifer Gold, Audra Epstein, Suzanne Welles, Cree Lawson (US)
Finance: John Fisher, Gary Singh, Edward Downey, Mark Hall, Tim Bill
Marketing & Publicity: Richard Trillo, Niki Smith, David Wearn, Chloë Roberts, Demelza Dallow, Claire Southern (UK); Simon Carloss, David Wechsler, Megan Kennedy (US)
Administration: Julie Sanderson, Karoline Densley

Publishing information

This fourth edition published February 2003 by **Rough Guides Ltd**,
80 Strand, London WC2R ORL
Penguin Putnam, Inc., 375 Hudson Street, NY 10014, USA
Distributed by the Penguin Group
Penguin Books Ltd,
80 Strand, London WC2R ORL
Penguin Putnam, Inc.,
375 Hudson Street, NY 10014, USA
Penguin Books Australia Ltd,
487 Maroondah Highway, PO Box 257, Ringwood, Victoria 3134, Australia
Penguin Books Canada Ltd,
10 Alcorn Avenue, Toronto, Ontario, Canada M4V 1E4
Penguin Books (NZ) Ltd,
182–190 Wairau Road, Auckland 10, New Zealand
Typeset in Bembo and Helvetica to an original design by Henry Iles.

Printed in Italy by LegoPrint S.p.A.

496pp, includes index
A catalogue record for this book is available from the British Library.

ISBN 1-84353-047-3

Help us update

We've gone to a lot of effort to ensure that this edition of **The Rough Guide to Corsica** is accurate and up to date. However, things change – places get "discovered", opening hours are notoriously fickle, restaurants and rooms raise prices or lower standards. If you feel we've got it wrong or left something out, we'd like to know, and if you can remember the address, the price, the time, the phone number, so much the better.

We'll credit all contributions, and send a copy of the next edition (or any other Rough Guide if you prefer) for the best letters. Everyone who writes to us and isn't already a subscriber will receive a copy of our full-colour thrice-yearly newsletter. Please mark letters: "**Rough Guide Corsica Update**" and send to: Rough Guides, 80 Strand, London WC2R ORL, or Rough Guides, 4th Floor, 345 Hudson St, New York, NY 10014. Or send an email to **mail@roughguides.com**

Have your questions answered and tell others about your trip at **www.roughguides.atinfopop.com**

Acknowledgements

Continued thanks to friends old and new for hospitality, advice and support during the research trips for this book: Phillipe Gabrielli, Serge Battesti, Paul and Mattieu Ceccaldi, the Pantalacci family in Cozzano, the *Hôtel Aiglon* in Zonza, and staff of Voyages Ilena in London.

At Rough Guides, thank you to: editor Jo Mead for doing such a fine job at short notice, for leaving my long boxes un-chopped and for revamping the index; Katie Lloyd-Jones for her splendid map revisions; Link Hall for layout; Sharon Martins and Louise Boulton for picture research; and Carole Mansur for proofreading.

On the home front, thank you once again to VSJM for holding the fort while I was away, and for coping with holes in the shed roof and other jobs neglected as this book sprawled into the autumn of 2002.

Readers' letters

Many thanks to all those readers who took the trouble to write in with feedback on the last edition, in particular:
James & Katie Bannister, Philip Barbour, Robin Boyle, Hilary Burland, John Crammer, Wendy Dunn, B R Edwards, Gary Elflett, Christopher Fitzgerald, Marci Foracieppi, David J Fowler, Sally Gray, M J Groves, Claude Guerlain & Scott Karpuk, Khurshid A G Hanif, John Hartley, Glen Haven, Sarah Jackson, Nicholas Jacobs, Jane Kaye, Anne Langley, Ian McCrerie & Ann Marsh, Anna McGowan, Philippa McLatchie, Menno Nobel, Helen Orme, Karine Pellaumail, Diana Perkin, Ken Pirie, Margaret Robshaw, John Rogers, D W Small, Angela Stephenson, Peter Symon, Terry Walton, Victoria Ward, Anne Weston, Gillian Wightwick.

SMALL PRINT

Photo Credits